AF668014

THE GITA

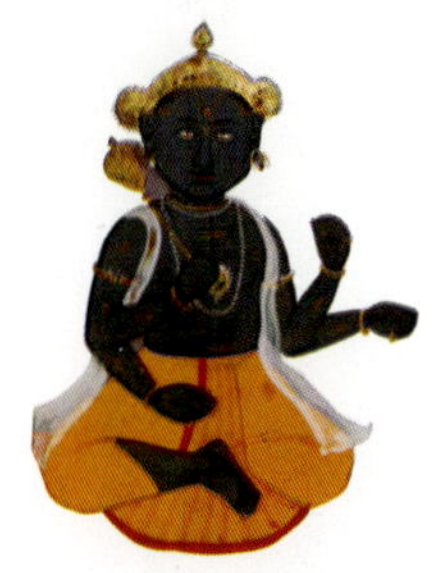

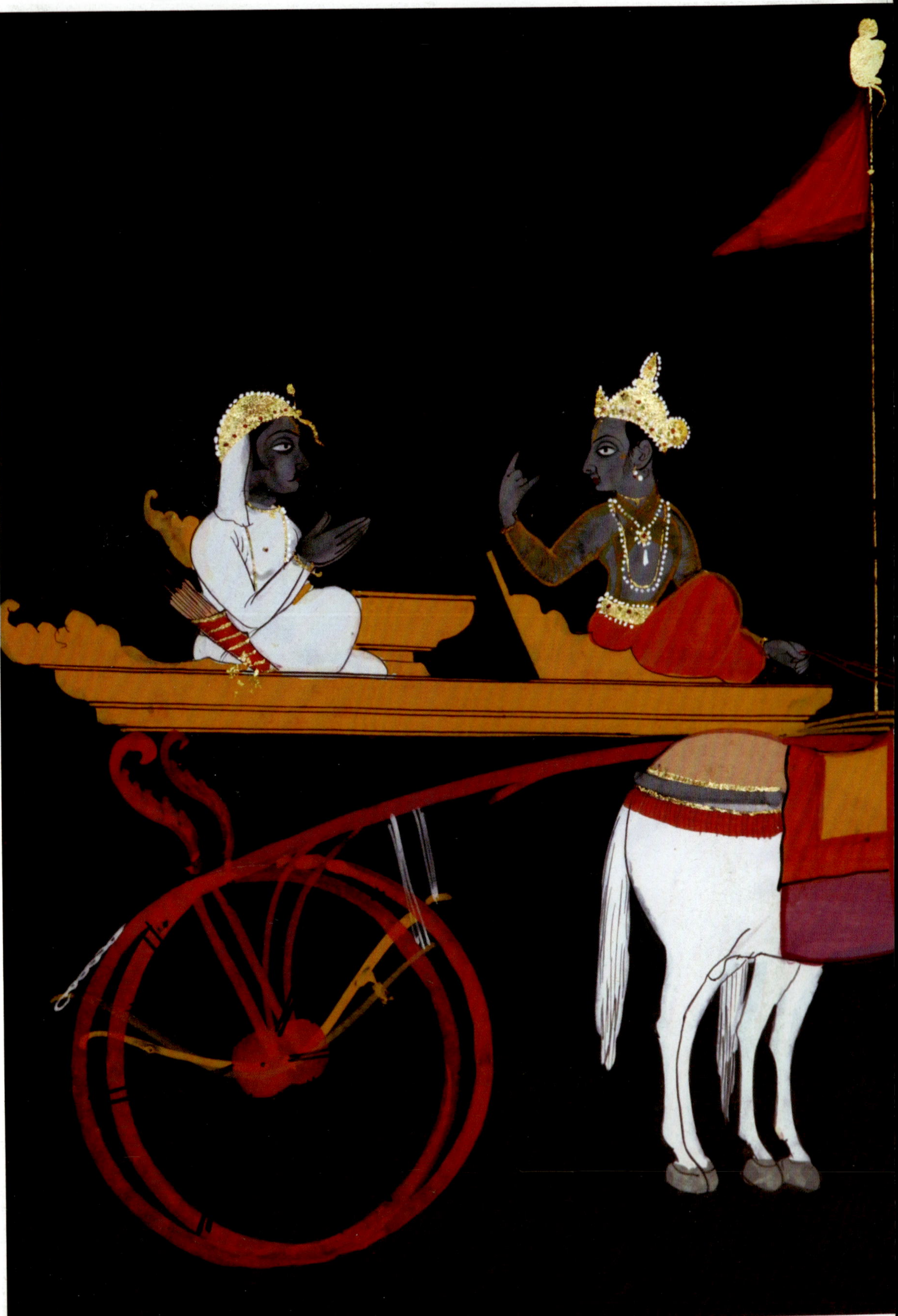

THE GITA

Mewari Miniature Painting (1680-1698) by Allah Baksh

ALOK BHALLA
CHANDRA PRAKASH DEVAL

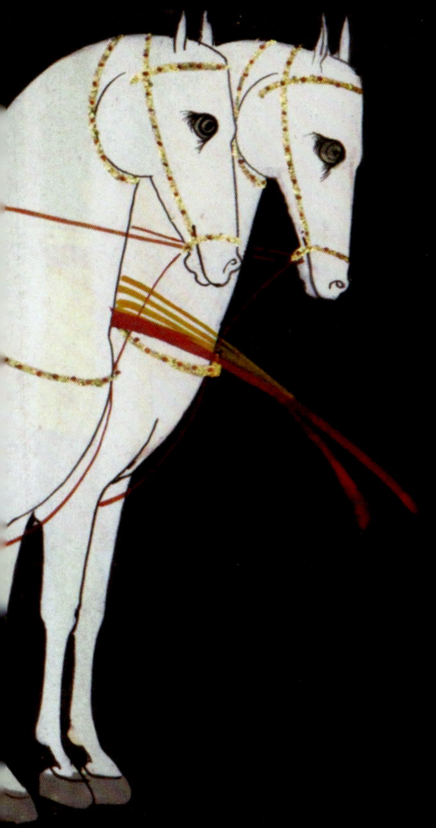

NIYOGI
BOOKS

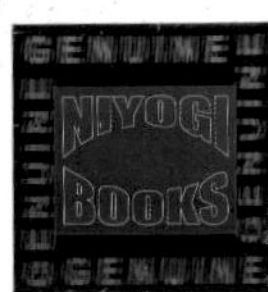

Published by

NIYOGI BOOKS

Block D, Building No. 77,
Okhla Industrial Area, Phase-I,
New Delhi-110 020, INDIA
Tel: 91-11-26816301, 26818960
Email: niyogibooks@gmail.com
Website: www.niyogibooksindia.com

English text and commentaries © Alok Bhalla
Hindi translations © Chandra Prakash Deval
Mewari paintings © Udaipur Government Museum

Hindi Editor: Vandana Gupta
Design: Shashi Bhushan Prasad
Photographs: Ashok Dilwali

ISBN: 978-93-86906-93-9
Publication: 2019

All rights are reserved. No part of this publication may be reproduced or transmitted in any form or by any means, electronic or mechanical, including photocopying, recording or by any information storage and retrieval system without prior written permission and consent of the Publisher.

Printed at: Niyogi Offset Pvt. Ltd., New Delhi, India

CONTENTS

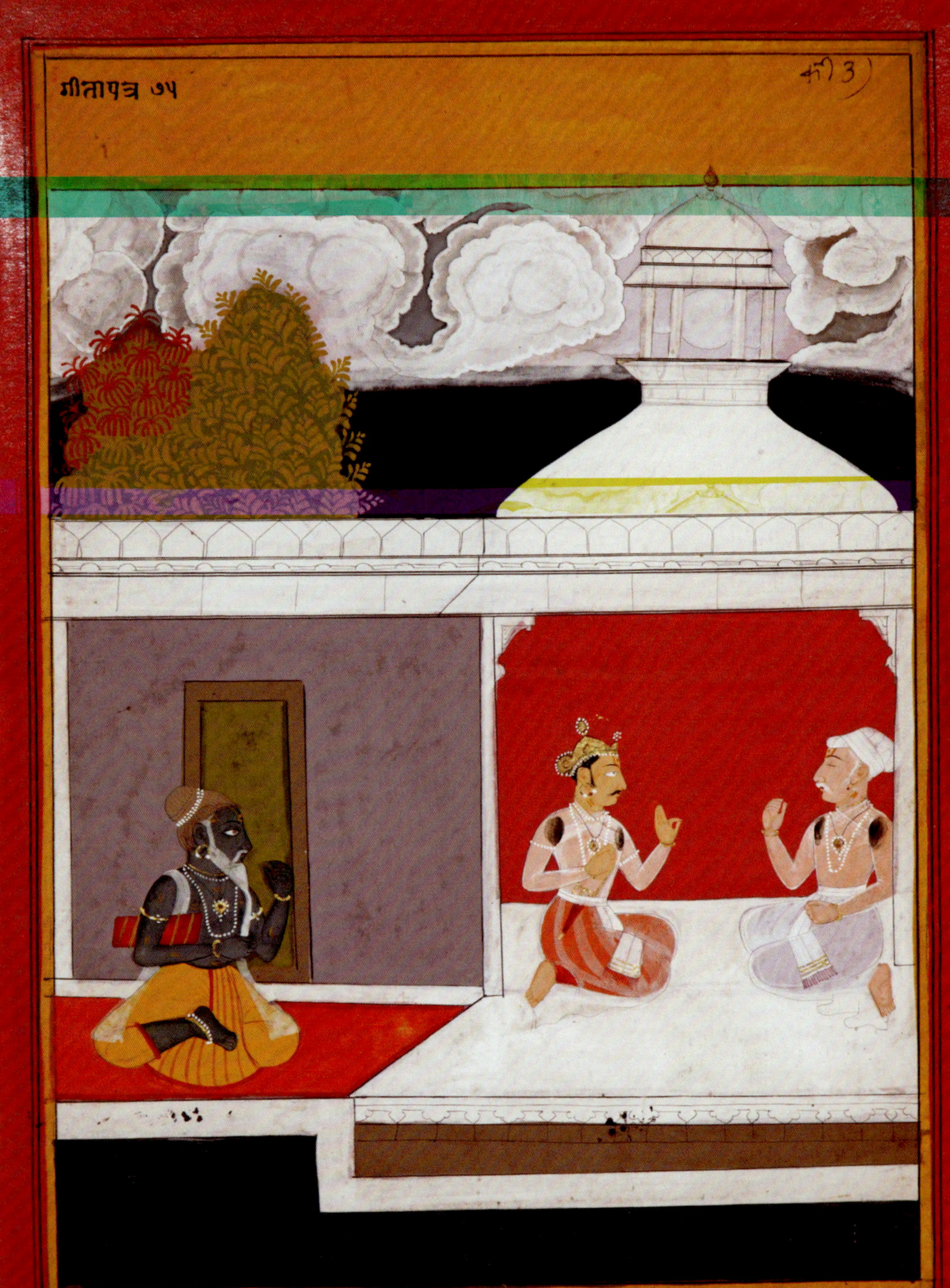
गीतापत्र ७५

ACKNOWLEDGEMENTS

It has taken me more than two years to write the commentary in this book on the miniature paintings of the *Gita* from Mewar by Allah Baksh. Chandra Prakash Deval, an authority on Rajasthan's cultural history, has translated the colloquial Mewari version of the *Gita* accompanying every painting into Hindi. It would not have been possible to write this book without his expertise.

We would like to acknowledge that we heard about the existence of these paintings from Mubarak Ali, the Curator of the Government Museum in the City Palace of Udaipur. We are grateful to the exceptional courtesy extended to us by him and his staff. It is difficult to describe our excitement and delight when he agreed to let us look through the museum's collection of more than 4,000 scintillating paintings about the *Mahabharata* and gave us permission to write about the folio. What, however, took us completely by surprise were the 550 odd illustrations of the *Gita*.

The well-known photographer, Ashok Dilwali, who shared our enthusiasm, took more than 4,000 high resolution images of these paintings and must be thanked. The conditions under which he worked were basic, but he did so without complaining.

We are grateful to Bikash Niyogi whose commitment to the project from the outset was evident when he decided to accompany us to Udaipur. We hope that the publication of these paintings will make them accessible to both scholars and the general public.

Deval would like thank the S. H. Raza Foundation for offering him a fellowship and Rakesh Soni for help with the Hindi text.

I am grateful to many scholars, students and friends who were kind enough to discuss these paintings with me. Each conversation helped me clarify my argument about the artist's intentions and his craft, and sharpen my translations of the verses of *Gita* into simple English prose. Sections of my commentary were written at Gandhi's Sabarmati Ashram in Ahmedabad. Tridip Suhrud, the Ashram's former Director, changed my thinking about the *Gita* when he gave me a copy of Mahadev Desai's, *The Gospel of Selfless Action*, a work of rare brilliance. I was invited to talk about these paintings by the Philosophy Department, St. Stephen's College, Delhi; the

Psychology Department, Ambedkar University, Delhi; and the Lalbhai Dalpathbhai Museum, Ahmedabad.

Nirmalkanti Bhattacharjee, the Editorial Director at Niyogi Books, gently urged me to edit my first draft and make it more succinct. Venkat Rao has been a 'constant gardener' with me in the field of Indian art for many years; Bharani Kollipara offered useful comments. I also want to thank Vijay Tankha, Ratan Parimoo, Ashwin Sanghi and Namita Gokhale for their help.

Deval and I are grateful to our families and friends for being with us in faith and love, while we were working on this project.

Finally, I should add that, while Deval was always ready to clarify sections of the *Gita*, I take full responsibility for my reading of the paintings about Krishna's celestial song.

Alok Bhalla

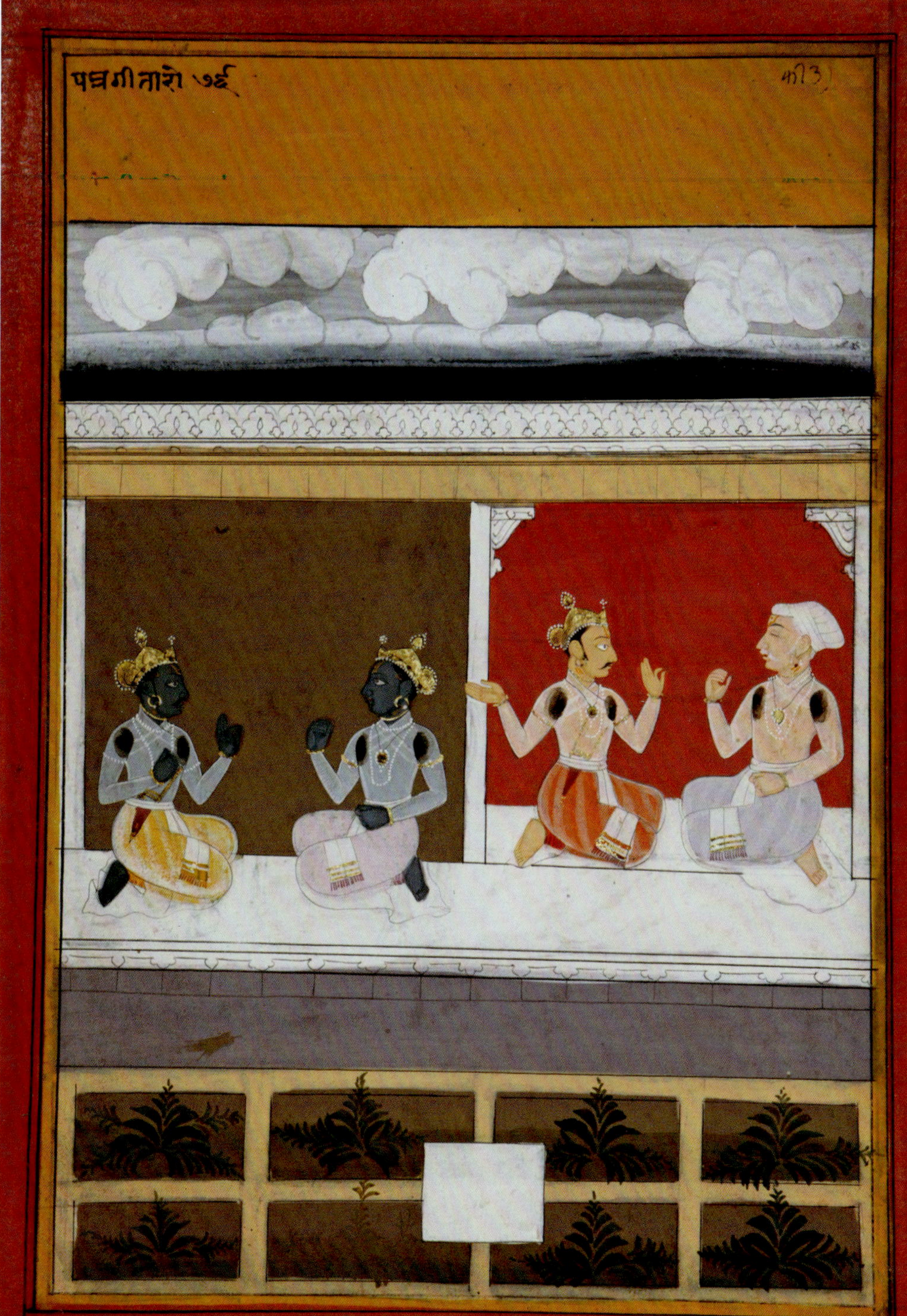

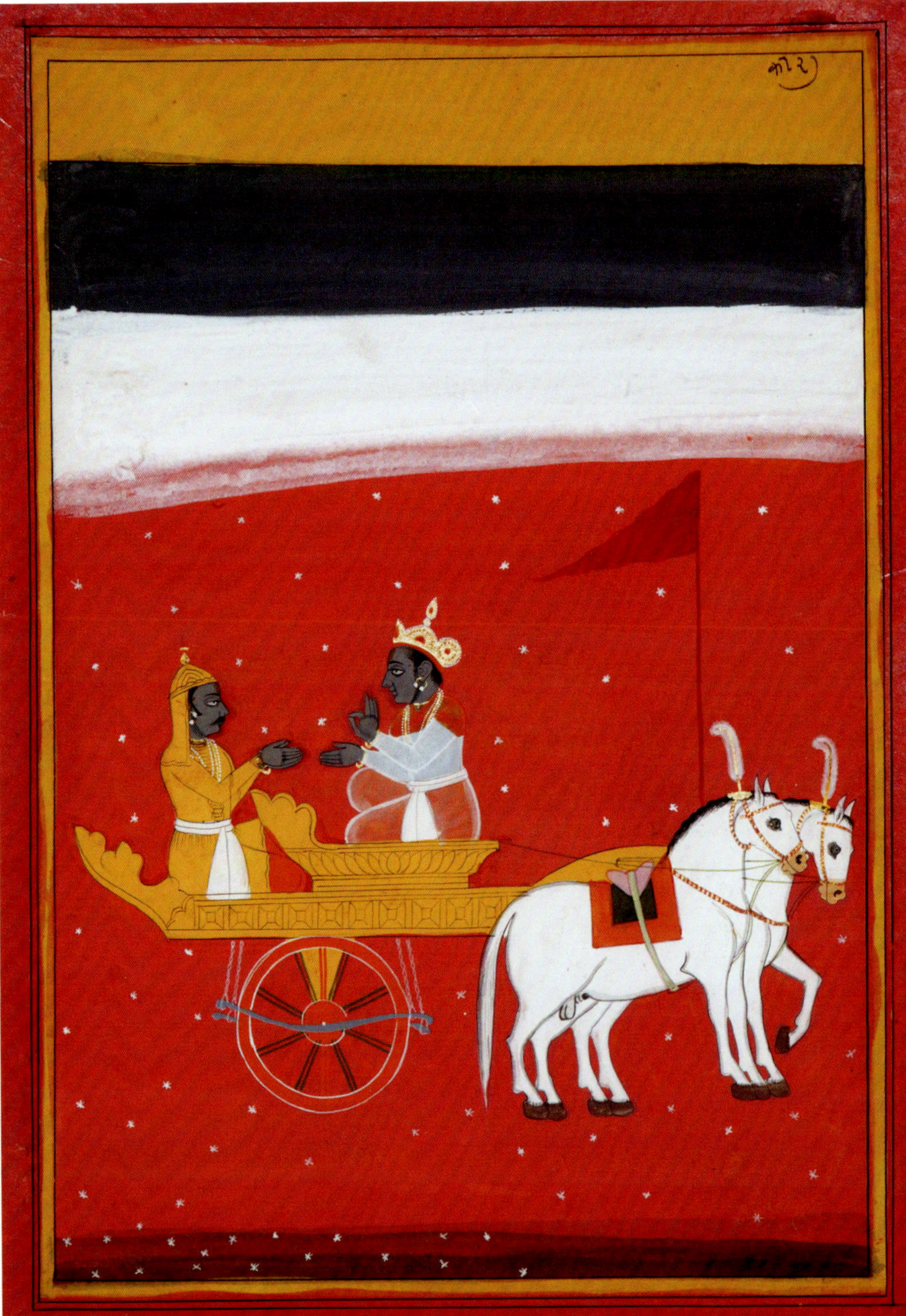

INTRODUCTION

Painting is the best of all arts, conducive to dharma and emancipation....

The Vishnudharmottara[1]

The miniature paintings of the *Gita*, published here for the first time, are from the late 17th century Mewar. These paintings, created under the patronage of Maharana Jai Singh of Mewar, are part of the collections of three different museums in Rajasthan: The Government Museum in the City Palace, Udaipur; the Udaipur Sangrahalay, Ahar; and the City Palace Museum, Jaipur. The paintings belong to the Mewar School of Painting and should not be subsumed under the broader classification of Rajput Paintings.

The courts of the Rajasthani rulers were distinctive centres of cultural sophistication and were proud of their individual political lineage.[2] The inner form—the style, colouration, design, idiom, sensibility, images or philosophic thought—of these miniature paintings from Mewar is recognisably different from those painted in Bikaner, Kishangarh, Bundi or Jodhpur. Each school has its own uniquely illustrated version of Hindu epics, bardic songs, heroic tales and vernacular romances. There are, however, two important aspects that Rajasthani miniature paintings from the 16th century onwards have in common. They use visual and literary production to assert the moral and political legitimacy of their kingdoms. This self-fashioning was important since they were being culturally and politically challenged by the powerful Mughal rulers who took pride in their discernment as connoisseurs of art.[3] From the time of Akbar (1542–1605), Mughal emperors had consciously commissioned translations and paintings of the cultural and religious texts of India to establish their own authority over the subcontinent's complex and diverse traditions. Illustrated versions of Sanskrit epics and myths, local legends and songs gave them a frame to define their ambitions, understand the social and moral

1 *A Treatise of Indian Painting and Image-Making*, translated by Stella Kramrisch (1928; rpt. Calcutta: University of Calcutta Press, 1993), p. 62.

2 Pramod Chandra, *On the Study of Indian Art* (Cambridge; Mass.: Harvard University Press, 1983), p. 107.

3 B. N. Goswami, *Oxford Readings in Indian Art* (New Delhi: Oxford University Press, 2018), pp. 277–79.

presuppositions of the people as well as envision a future for their kingdoms.[4] Akbar, for example, commissioned two illuminated manuscripts of the *Ramayana* in 1588 and 1594 (the latter for his mother, Hamida Banu Begum), and Jahangir used the genius of his court painters like Nadirul'asri Mansur, Bishan Das and Abu'l-Hasan to illustrate numerous Indian texts for his personal library. In response, in the 1640s, Maharana Jagat Singh of Udaipur gave two great painters of Udaipur—Sahibdin and Manohar—the task of creating a unique version of the epic on a grand scale. Each of them painted different sections of the *Ramayana* and put together a folio of more than 400 drawings. Maharana Jagat Singh also invited them to produce an illustrated version of the *Bhagavata Purana*. Sahibdin artistically transformed "the story of Rama's suffering, heroism and devotion to duty...into a sophisticated expression of Rajput ideals and society."[5] The rulers of Mewar, who preceded and followed Maharana Jagat Singh, cultivated painting as part of their project of resistance to the Mughal rule. Thus, during his days of refuge in Chawand, a small village in the Aravalli hills, Maharana Pratap Singh (1572–1597) gave Nasiruddin (Nasar Deen) the responsibility of painting the *Ragamala* poems in his own personal style.[6] It is possible that the father of Allah Baksh, the painter of this *Gita* folio, was Pyare Khan who belonged to the lineage of Nasiruddin.

The difference between the paintings from Rajasthan and the Mughal court is well defined by Ananda Coomaraswamy. Mughal art, he says, was refined, aristocratic and worldly. It was more interested in either commemorating the pomp and pageantry of courtly life or drawing portraits of emperors for posterity. In contrast, Rajasthani paintings, mainly inspired by popular Vaishnavism, were celebrations of the generosity of the divine which transfigures a common and ordinary world into a thing of beauty.[7] Emperors and palaces were alien and far removed from the everyday life-experiences of the painters from various regions of Rajasthan. Simpler in line and form, their images are sensitive and austere.

What gives these *Gita* paintings by Allah Baksh their significance is that they have no precedent in the history of Indian miniature art. Different art traditions of the country have, of course, painted romantic or dramatic images of Krishna as a lover or

---

4 Audrey Truschke, *Culture of Encounters: Sanskrit at the Mughal Court* (Gurgaon: Penguin, 2016), pp. 244–47.

5 J.P. Losty, *The Ramayana: Love and Valour in India's Great Epic* (New Delhi: Niyogi Books, 2008), p. 18.

6 Losty, pp. 6–9.

7 Ananda K. Coomaraswamy *Rajput Painting* (London: Oxford University Press, 1916), pp. 6–8; 14–15.

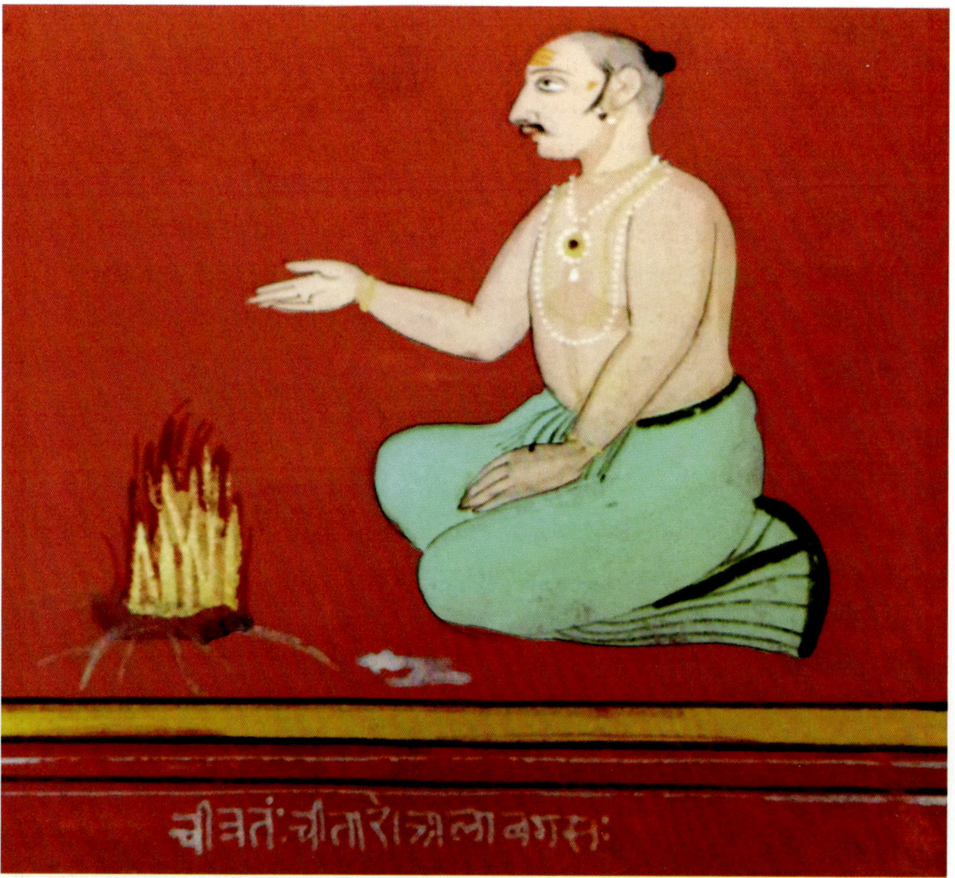

Fig. 1: The script under the painting for *Bhishma Parva*: 52, identifies the artist of the entire *Mahabharat* folio commissioned by Maharana Jai Singh as follows: '*Chitrakar* Allah Baksh.'

Fig. 2: This is the colophon for verse 72 of Chapter 2 of the *Gita* folio, which says that the paintings were commissioned by Maharana Jai Singh between 1680 and 1698 and that the Mewari text was written by Bhatt Kishandas.

a charioteer. These *Gita* paintings are, however, exceptional because the great religious poem has never been illustrated in its entirety, shloka by abstract shloka. There is no other miniature artist who has engaged with the song's metaphysical argument with such calm intelligence and imaginative empathy. The radiant beauty of the paintings suggests that for the painter, the *Gita* is a magnificent conversation between man and god about the pity and the sorrow of war; about how one can become more human-hearted; how one can ensure that our actions are life-creating and not merely self-directed. Their special emphasis is on the need to find a compassionate way of being on the earth, rather than on the call to arms for the sake of a kingdom. Allah Baksh's works of visionary thoughtfulness deserve an honoured place in the history of Indian miniature art and in the great library of Indian scriptures and their interpretations. Unfortunately, very little attention has been paid to them.

As the *Gita* has 700 or 701 verses (the textual tradition is divided over number of verses in Chapter 13), we can assume that there must have been an equal number of paintings—one for every verse. Unfortunately, we have only found about 500 paintings and do not know the whereabouts of the rest. We have, for example, located only one painting each for Chapters 1 and 17. All the paintings are fairly large in size: 37x24 centimetres. The *Gita* folio is only a fraction of the 4,000-odd *Mahabharata* paintings by Allah Baksh in the collections of the three museums in Rajasthan.

The paintings in the *Gita* folio do not mention the name of the painter. We did, however, trace one painting from the Bhisham Parva: 52 of the *Mahabharata* narrative which is signed. An inconspicuous and hesitant note in the lower margin of the painting states that the '*chitrakar*' or painter is Allah Baksh (see figure 1). We are astonished by the humility of the man and by his confidence in the idea that it is not the business of an artist to reveal himself. His greater task, instead, is to guide the reader of Krishna's discourse and the viewer of the paintings to listen to the *Gita* in wonder—to listen to a song about the divine origins of the universe; to think in awe about what it means to be alive; and to ask, in sorrow, why the beauty of the inward soul that Krishna reveals is tarnished so often. The signature, however, only deepens the shadow of anonymity which surrounds the name Allah Baksh. It is possible that he belongs to the family of Nasiruddin of Chawand. We can surmise nothing more about his lineage and guess even less.

The colophon of each painting is yellow-ochre in colour and carries a Mewari translation of the verse being illustrated. The text is written in black ink. The folio was commissioned by Maharana Jai Singh of Mewar and was painted between 1680 and 1698, as the notes appended to the paintings for verse 72 of Chapter 2 and for verse

43 of Chapter 3 tell us. The notes also inform us that the Mewari text was written by Bhatt Kishandas. The Mewari translation of the *Gita* makes no attempt to capture the sonority of Sanskrit poetry. Instead, it is written in simple, colloquial Mewari prose that renders the erudite arguments of the *Gita* accessible to any reader and speaker of Mewari. Krishna no longer speaks in classical Sanskrit shlokas to the scholar or the philosopher, but to ordinary men or women who care to listen, read and think.

It is important to add that one of the defining characteristics of this Mewari version of the *Gita* is that whenever Arjuna speaks to Krishna, he first calls out: 'Hey, Krishna.' His voice is intimate, friendly and devoid of fear; it is not a sublime address to the grandeur of the divine. It assumes, instead, an easy access of man to god and expects nothing but a conversation about how one should live in a world of violence—what is worthy, what is worthwhile. The quiet confidence of 'Hey, Krishna' is momentous, because one can imagine Arjuna saying to god a complex series of things:

> *I recognise your presence; I turn to you to help me think, so, draw upon the wisdom of ages to guide me; I shall follow what you tell me, but only if what you say respects my intellect and sounds right to my own heart. Therefore, Hey, Krishna, let your answer be offered as reverence to my mind so that I can honour the greatness of your own being and be in consonance with the finest of dharmic ideals. Anything less than that, offered as an anodyne for my present difficulty, would be a betrayal of my faith in the nobility of your imagination and of my friendship with the divine in you.*

'Hey, Krishna' does not, therefore, sound like rapture; instead, it simply assumes Krishna's mortal and earthly guise and makes him part of a dialogue about why and how we become participants in violence even as we long for peace. Krishna's reply is equally generous and friendly towards a sincere man asking for guidance and illumination. Krishna invariably begins his response, not by admonishing Arjuna for his doubts and ambiguities, but by reaffirming his friendship, his commitment and moral attentiveness to a man's anxieties. 'Hey, Arjuna, listen,' he says, as he calls Arjuna back from the abyss of despondency and urges him to think again about the need for ethical action. God in his wisdom knows how patiently the mind must be cultivated.

The accompanying paintings respond to the diction of the prose translation with their own rich-toned serenity. Their colours are clear, luminous and calm; their lines are restrained and precise; their images are meditative, unostentatious and drawn from daily lives lived in confidence; they are free from heroic posturing, spiritual pride and armed might. Together, they persuade one to pause and listen to the *Gita* again, not as a sermon which forbids discussion and debate, but as a guide to a thoughtful soul-seeking knowledge about how to live with others in peace. The paintings, like Krishna's words, grow in the mind's eye and acquire a moral significance.

The paintings illustrating the entire *Mahabharata* folio, from the *Adi Parva* onwards, are horizontal, indicating that the epic tells a story which relentlessly follows the lives and fate of a people from their mythic beginning to their cataclysmic end. The *Gita* paintings, however, are vertical or upright. There are some possible reasons for this significant decision. One is that the *Gita* is a dramatic pause in the narrative and a visionary breakthrough in the *Mahabharata*'s story of time, change and suffering. Before the war begins, Arjuna requests his charioteer, Krishna, to drive him into the no-man's land between the two armies. Instead of seeing enemies at war, he sees friends and families, teachers and brothers preparing to kill each other for land, kingdom and glory. He is not only filled with anguish, but more importantly, he is also "*overcome with great compassion*"[8] and his "*heart melts with pity*."[9] The emphasis of Allah Baksh's visual interpretation of the *Gita* is on ahimsa or non-violence, and *anarsamasya* or the ability to feel the pain of others; the ability to discriminate between what the self desires and what it should renounce in the interest of others. Arjuna's capacity to be horrified by war is a sign of his moral strength, not of his lack of courage.

In terms of narrative time, the moment of the *Gita* is brief. The *Gita* is preached in the *Bhishma Parva* of the *Mahabharata* during the short pause between the first hint of dawn in the horizon when the armies gather across from each other and sunrise which signals that the war can begin. It is like a visionary flash when, quite suddenly, the divine breaks into time, or when the debris of time and life fall away, and one thinks only of those deeds that are "eternally humane."[10] The soldiers on either side only notice

8 Italics added. Most translations and interpretations of Chapter 1, verse 28 focus on Arjuna's anguished heart. Mahatma Gandhi's translation, however, is radically different. He underlies the idea that Arjuna is overwhelmed by compassion. Mahadev Desai, *The Gospel of Selfless Action Or the Gita According to Gandhi* (Ahmedabad: Navjivan, 1946), p. 140. Hereafter, referred to as Desai in the text.

9 This is the translation of verse 28 offered by Shri Purohit Swami. It is different from Mahatma Gandhi's but adds to the emotional resonance to Arjuna's anguish. *The Geeta: The Gospel of the Lord Shri Krishna* (London: Faber and Faber, 1965), p. 17. Hereafter, referred to as Swami in the text.

10 The phrase is from Northrop Frye's *Fearful Symmetry: A Study of William Blake* (Boston: Beacon Press, 1947), p. 248.

a spectacular instant. Arjuna, moved by pity, lays down his arms. Krishna drops the reins of the horses, and turns to reason with and bless him. Allah Baksh banishes the soldiers to the periphery. They are rarely visible in his paintings. His focus of attention is only the 'chariot of learning' on which Krishna and Arjuna sit discussing the ethics of war. The space around the chariot is miraculously filled with familiar images of the sky, earth, water, fire, trees, flowers, fakirs, lovers, music, birds, temples, idols, books, gods and goddesses; an ordinary world, which a moment ago was threatened by extinction, is now saved by the painter's imagination and the poet's verse; by allegories of peace, not threnodies of war.

The other reason for the verticality of these paintings may be that while the *Gita* is an integral part of the *Mahabharata*, it is not a linear narrative whose argument moves logically towards a conclusion. It is, instead, a dialogue.[11] As in any philosophic dialogue, what Krishna says can always be interrupted either by enigmas that puzzle the mind or by the need for repetitions and clarifications. The form of a discourse assumes that all the participants in the conversation have the moral freedom not to accept an argument or refuse to act till reason, in its integrity and honesty, is satisfied. A dialogue does not demand one's surrender to any authority—transcendental or secular. This does not mean that what is said is either insignificant or unworthy. What it implies, instead, is that the concerns being explored are of extraordinary importance for the fate of earth; that the destiny of all living beings is dependent on what is disclosed and understood. *Each verse should be read as a unique moment of revelation. No verse in itself is the answer.* Every verse is distinct, and no single idea can be isolated as the *essence* of the *Gita*.

A slow reading of each painting reveals that Allah Baksh has meditated deeply on the *Gita*. He feels no scholarly or priestly compulsion to place special emphasis on a morally declarative verse which gives an unambiguous answer to Arjuna's questions: 'How should we live? Why should I, or anyone else, fight to seek revenge, save honour, overcome fear, feel envy, or crave for a kingdom or wealth? Are we not, each of us, in our fragility and transience, so linked to each other that injury to one is injury to the entire *shristi* (the universe)?' Instead, the folio offers a different and more exciting interpretation. If there is an emotion or ethic which resonates through Allah Baksh's painting of the *Gita*, it is the search for compassion or mercy in all relationships between man, nature and god. This transforms the *Gita* into a dialogic journey; or,

11 Barbara Stoler Miller, in contrast, says that the *Gita* has a strong narrative drive. See 'Introduction' in *The Bhagavad-Gita: Krishna's Counsel in Time of War* (New York: Bantam, 1986), p. 17.

rather, a pilgrimage with a visionary guide who is always willing to give attentive replies to questions that trouble the soul; thereby, becoming an example of the most humane of Socratic ideas that to know the self, one must seek to conduct an unending discussion, *not a dispute*, in which nothing is enough and nothing is too much.[12] The poet of *Katha Upanishad* says:

> Know thou the soul (*atman*, self) as riding in a chariot,
> The body as the chariot.
> Know thou the intellect (*buddhi*) as the chariot-driver.
> And the mind as the reins. (III.3.3)

That is why image of Krishna and Arjuna on the chariot pulled by white horses is repeated in all the paintings in this folio. The chariot may, of course, be read symbolically as the composite image of the body, soul, reason and divine inspiration.

As Allah Baksh seeks a visual form for each verse, he pauses with meditative deliberateness on each verse without an anxious reaching for a final, conclusive answer. As we move from one painting to the next, it seems as if he is enacting a ceremony of words and images in search of wisdom. Is Allah Baksh unconvinced that war is inevitable? Does he feel, as Yudhishthira does in *Sabha Parva*, that Krishna and Arjuna on the chariot have been yoked together by destiny and are invincible in battle?[13] Their reappearance from painting to painting suggests that. Does Allah Baksh think that to read the *Gita* is to realise that its music of peace emerges from 'old time' and shall continue to be heard uninterrupted to 'new eternity'?[14] Unlike many commentators of the *Gita*, Allah Baksh is not ambiguous about the text. The *Gita*, he believes, asserts that a life of ahimsa is the inalienable *adhikaar* (right) of god and all living and non-living beings. That is why the visual space surrounding the chariot is free from the bluster and noise of war, the melodramas of heroic victory and defeat. There are, instead, an infinite variety of images of ordinary things and beings around the chariot. They create a serenity in which one can recognise the long and visionary

12 Plato, "Protagoras," *Collected Dialogues*, edited by Edith Hamilton and Huntington Cairns (Princeton: Princeton University Press, 1961), p. 336.

13 *The Mahabharata*, vol. 1. Translated by Kisari Mohan Ganguli (1896; rpt. New Delhi: Munshiram Manoharlal, 2008), p. 492.

14 This is a variation of what Henry David Thoreau felt when he read the *Gita*. Paul Friedrich, *The* Gita *within Walden* (New York: State University of New York Press, 2008), p. 25 and p. 66.

history of the survival of gods, earth and human beings. Of course, at the end of the dialogue of the *Gita*, the artist resolves, as Arjuna does, the mystery of who we are and how we should act by asserting that life has its beginning and end in the presence of Krishna.

This folio is the work of faith and not of scepticism. It is by an artist who longs, not for triumph, but for peace, for *shanti*, which Anandavardhana says is the final *bhava* (emotion) of the *Mahabharata*.[15] Perhaps, the dharma of Allah Baksh's paintings is best expressed by the following lines from Ashvaghosa's *Buddhacharitra*:

> For to kill some helpless being to obtain results
> Does not benefit a good and compassionate man,
> Even if that rite yields everlasting results;
> How much less when the results are ephemeral?[16]

The philosophic urge of the *Gita* is to postpone war for as long as possible; the tragedy of the *Gita* is that it is helpless to avert it; the greatness of the *Gita* is that human beings continue to meditate upon the dialogue, between god and man, about what is good and how it can be sustained.

---

15 For Anandavardhana, *shanti* or peace is the predominant emotion of the *Mahabharata*. See Alf Hiltebeitel, *Nonviolence in the Mahabharata* (London: Routledge, 2016), pp. 142–44.

16 *The Life of the Buddha*. Translated by Patrick Olivelle (New York: New York University Press, 2009), p. 323.

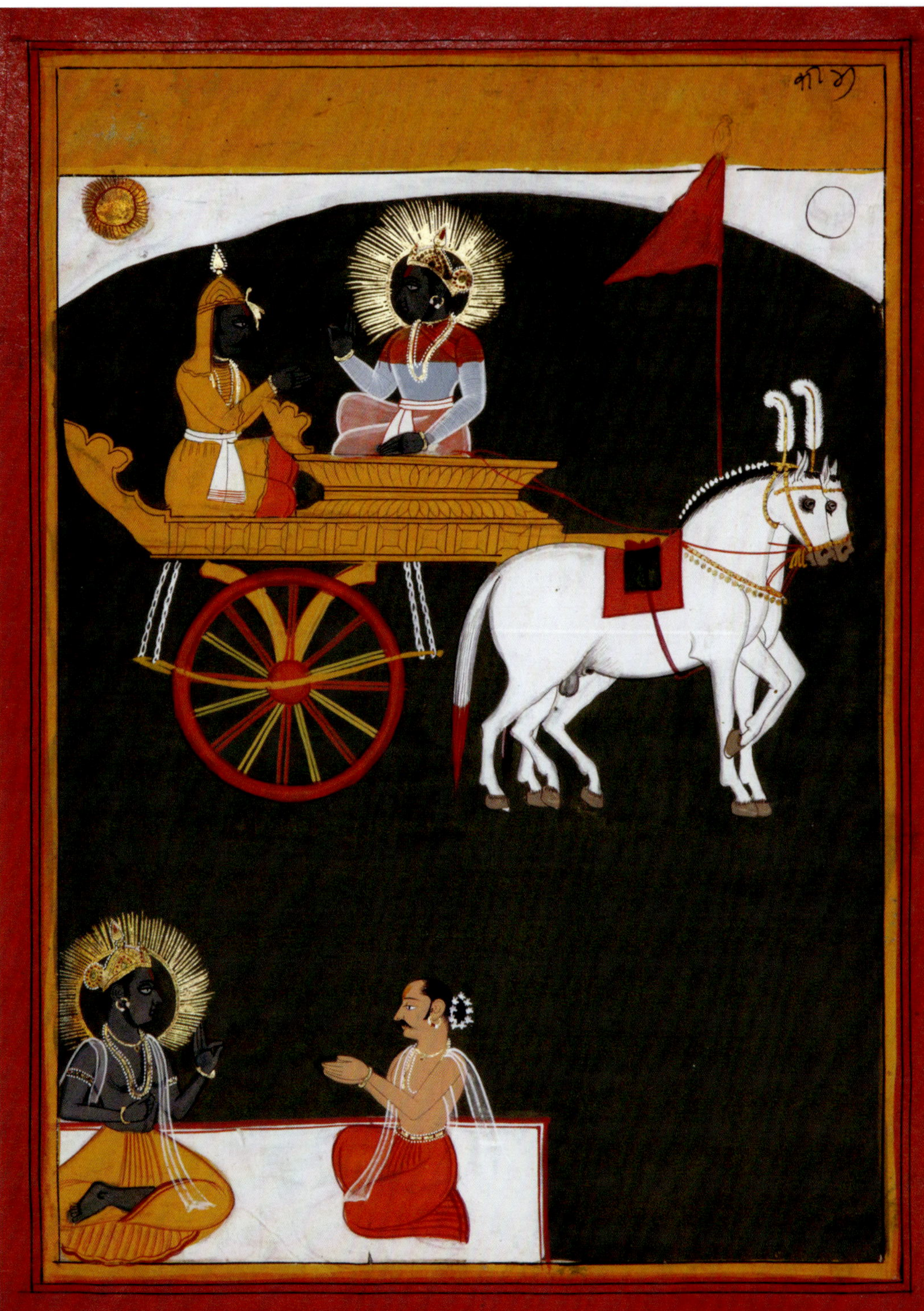

CHAPTER 1

The *Gita* is part of the *Bhishma Parva* of the *Mahabharata*. A long conversation between Arjuna and Krishna at Kurukshetra, the *Gita* opens with Sanjaya describing the tumult on the battlefield to the blind Kaurava king, Dhritarashtra. There are soldiers, chariots, flags, horses and elephants everywhere. The air is filled with the triumphant sounds of kettledrums, trumpets, conches and slogans which "violently shake heaven and earth with their echoes" (Swami 19). Sanjaya identifies the bravest of warriors on both sides of this fratricidal war between the Pandavas and their kinsmen, the Kauravas, by name. The act of naming is important because it acknowledges the fighters as unique individual human beings who are irreplaceable.

The first chapter of the *Gita* has forty-seven verses. They must all have been illustrated by Allah Baksh. We have, unfortunately, found only one painting illuminating verse 14. It depicts a dramatic moment. Arjuna and Krishna's chariot, pulled by white horses, enters the battlefield. The chariot has a colourful canopy mounted on a frame. The horses, painted with great self-assurance and skill, are calm. In keeping with the passionate energy and the tension of war, the background colour is a fiery red of great intensity. Like Sanjaya, Allah Baksh focuses his attention exclusively on Krishna and Arjuna. Both announce their presence by blowing their white conch shells. Nothing is allowed to distract the eye from these two noble figures who are the main personae of the great dialogue the *Gita* records. At first, it seems as if they are indistinguishable from each other. Yet, when one looks carefully, one begins to notice subtle differences in appearance. Arjuna is more warrior-like. He carries a long sword and a black shield. His body is firm and erect. He has a well-trimmed moustache which curls up. His saffron-

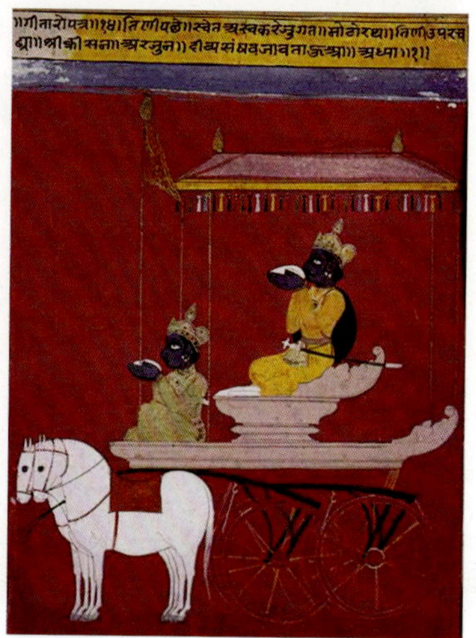

|14| इसके पश्चात श्वेत घोड़ों से युक्त विशाल रथ में बैठे हुए कृष्ण और अर्जुन ने भी दिव्य शंख बजाए।

|14| Seated in the big chariot pulled by white horses, Sri Krishna and Arjuna blew their divine conch shells.

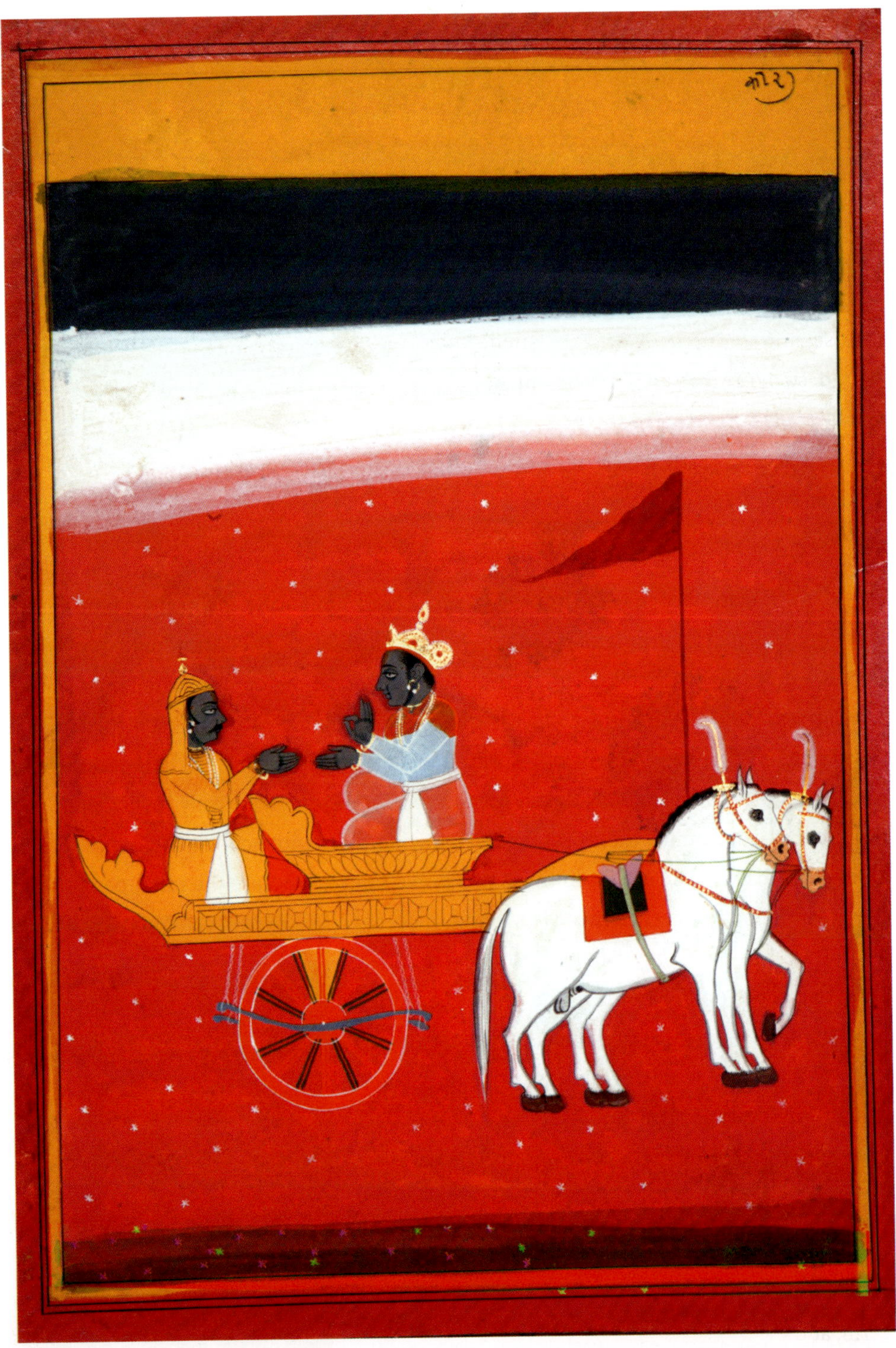

yellow *jama* glows like the sun and radiates the confidence of a man of power. He sits at the centre of a slightly raised lotus-shaped seat. Krishna's face, in contrast, is gentler. He is dressed in a softer silver-coloured robe and is unarmed. The chariot shall, henceforth, be a constant presence in every painting illustrating the *Gita*.

Just before sunrise, when Arjuna's chariot draws up in the empty space between the two armies, a hush falls over the entire field. Arjuna recognises his kinsmen, teachers and friends in the Kaurava army. He is "overcome with great compassion" (Gandhi's translation, Desai 28). Pity or compassion for all those who will die in the war is at the centre of the *Gita* discourse. Perhaps, the most important lesson of the *Gita* is that those who define heroic achievement only in terms of valour in battle inevitably end up destroying families, cities and kingdoms. Arjuna understands that if the war is inescapable, he must ensure that its rage does not destroy his humanity.

In anguish, Arjuna puts down his bow and arrow, sits on the chariot's floor and turns to Krishna:

> My limbs fail me and my throat is parched, my body trembles and my hair stands on end...Ah, my Lord! I crave not for victory, nor for kingdom, nor for any pleasure...I would not kill...even for the three worlds: why then for this poor earth? ...We are worthier of a nobler feat than to slaughter... (Swami 32–37).

This is a tense moment in the *Gita*. Arjuna can no longer find in himself the intellectual, moral and imaginative clarity to affirm that what he is about to do has sanctity. Krishna takes upon himself the task to be his friend, teacher and spiritual guide through a tragic world where the choice to act is as capable of leading to disaster as is the decision to walk away and become an ascetic in the forest.

The slow, deep-sounding cadence of pity in Arjuna's words—so full of genuine sorrow for the fate that awaits the earth and a profound desire not to cause it harm—defines the ethic of Allah Baksh's paintings of the *Gita*. It is sad that we have not been able to find the other paintings for this chapter. Judging from the works that follow, we can be sure that in the missing pages of Allah Baksh's folio the images of Krishna on the chariot revealing the mysteries of life to Arjuna must have promised that the memory of the sacred will never be erased; that, even as the world slides into the dark ages, the poet's plea for mercy shall be heard.

The tragedy of the *Mahabharata* is that this voice becomes dimmer as time goes by till, at the very end, Vyasa wonders in despair if anyone can still hear the voice of ahimsa.

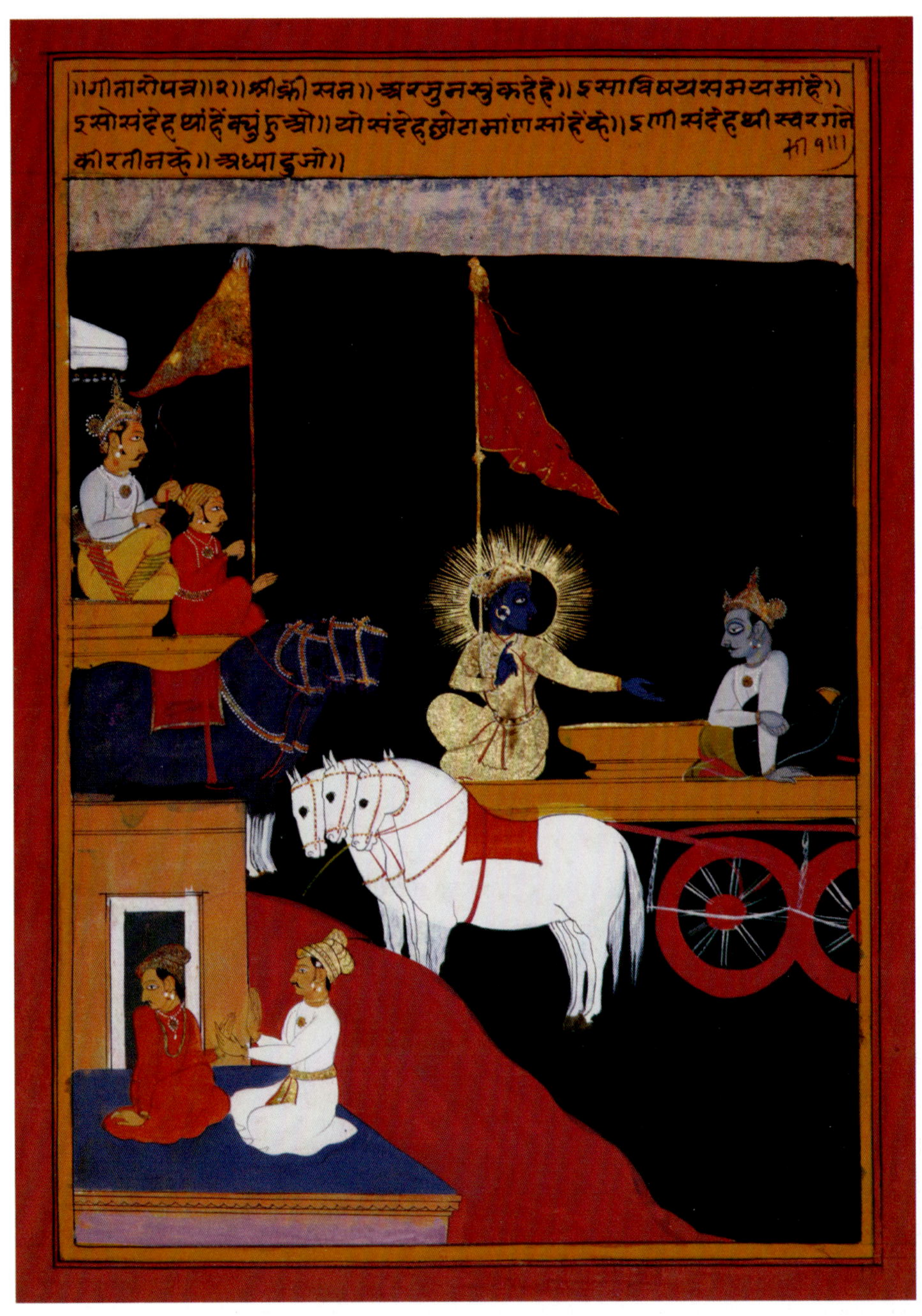

|2| श्री कृष्ण बोले- हे अर्जुन! तुझे इस असमय में यह मोह किस हेतु से हुआ? क्योंकि न तो यह श्रेष्ठ पुरुषों द्वारा आचरित है, न स्वर्ग को देने वाला है और न कीर्ति को लाने वाला ही है।

|2| Sri Krishna says to Arjuna: Why are you dejected at this moment of crisis? Only the weak are dejected. Despondency neither leads to heaven nor brings fame.

CHAPTER 2

Sanjaya has been granted the visionary power to describe what happens on the battlefield to Dhritarashtra. It is Sanjaya who tells the king that Arjuna, heart-broken and overwhelmed by grief, has cast aside his bow and collapsed on the chariot's floor.

Chapter 2 opens with Krishna consoling Arjuna and beginning his great discourse on how human beings must act in the face of adversity and seek deliverance from the suffering of time and change.

We react simultaneously to the text, images and colours in the painting for verse 2. The written words in the ochre band are simple and direct; the drawings are precise and sharp; the colours are clear without any melodramatic excess and are often charged with meaning. We are invited to read and contemplate the quiet ceremony of words and colours, language and lines, gods, brave warriors and ordinary men that Allah Baksh places before us. The physical and sensuous presence of nature (sky, clouds, earth, monkey, horses, elephants) and objects designed by human intelligence (chariot, building, reins, saddles, flags, armour) do not permit us to instinctively evoke the infinite or the divine. The painting slows us down to think—think about our biological existence in the physical world and our rational existence in society, before wondering about our moral relation with the divine.

The chariot stands against a background that is unrelentingly black, suggesting the depth of Arjuna's existential turmoil and his hesitation to initiate action which could lead to annihilation. In contrast, the elegance of the white horses yoked to the chariot helps us identify where the good resides. The painting has three centres which attract equal attention. Arjuna is the image of despondency: his weapons set aside, head bowed, face haunted and eyes filled with tears. Krishna's face glows with golden light. His eyes blaze with anger; his gestures suggest both chastisement and instruction. Dejection and self-pity, he tells Arjuna firmly with his right index figure raised, never help brave men win the earth or gain heaven; when the enemy is morally blind and spiritually obdurate, compassion is misplaced for it neither leads to right action nor restores a just society.

Separated by a red strip of the battlefield, and facing Arjuna, is Duryodhana. He is armed, erect and confident. Untroubled by moral ambiguities, armoured with a sense of certainty, he is eager for battle. Krishna knows that war is inevitable; it is neither the caprice of gods nor the fatality of history; Arjuna, a man of noble courage, must fight to restore the earth.

In the corner, far from the battlefield, is an ordinary, peaceful scene drawn with clarity and detail. Two figures sit on a blue platform outside a room with yellow walls and a white doorframe. Ornately dressed, they are not warriors. One figure is an image of despair, while the other is urging him back to the world of light and change. They are mirror images of Arjuna and Krishna in everyday life. It is as if Krishna's counsel is being repeated in daily life where people must be chastened, consoled and counselled to heal their secret wounds and consider rationally what the turmoil of daily existence demands. If we look up at the text and think about what we have read, seen and heard, we notice an infinite blue sky separated from the passion (*tamas*) of the battlefield.

The emotion (*bhava*) of the painting for verse 3 is similar. Painted against an angry red background, Krishna berates Arjuna for being un-Aryan; a weak betrayer of his martial and manly traditions. The Kaurava army, he tells Arjuna, is not stronger. It is only numerically larger and has brute strength on its side as the painting emphasises. The raised trunk of the elephant is aggressive; its sharp tusks are dangerous. The Kauravas dwarf Krishna's chariot and the soldier beside it. The skill with which the Kauravas are painted is admirable; but our eyes always shift to Krishna and Arjuna in the chariot because they possess the radiance of justice.

In a moment of ironic wit, Allah Baksh places the small image of Hanuman, sitting defiantly atop the pennant on Arjuna's chariot, across from the huge elephant.[1] Equally inspired is the way he sanctifies the chariot-space with the lustre of Krishna's presence—his self-confident yogic posture, his eyes sparkling with passionate argument. Together, Krishna and Hanuman form the central axis of the painting.

Stung by Krishna's taunt, Arjuna picks up his bow, something he rarely does again in the paintings. His shoulders are no longer slumped although his face looks ghostly. He has not overcome remorse; his conscience still continues to whisper that it may be better to forego a kingdom than to kill. Surely, he does not doubt his valour. But to fight well, to fight legitimately for a just cause, he needs more than Krishna's rhetorical attack on his agility as a warrior.[2] While Krishna's speech is harsh, the painter hears a slight

---

1 Irony does not mean lack of earnestness. It makes the familiar seem strange, and so deepens our understanding. Jonathan Lear, *A Case for Irony* (Cambridge, Massachusetts: Harvard University Press, 2011), pp. 15–36.

2 Simone Weil, on Arjuna in *The Notebooks of Simone Weil*, translated by Arthur Wills (London: Routledge, 2004), p. 97.

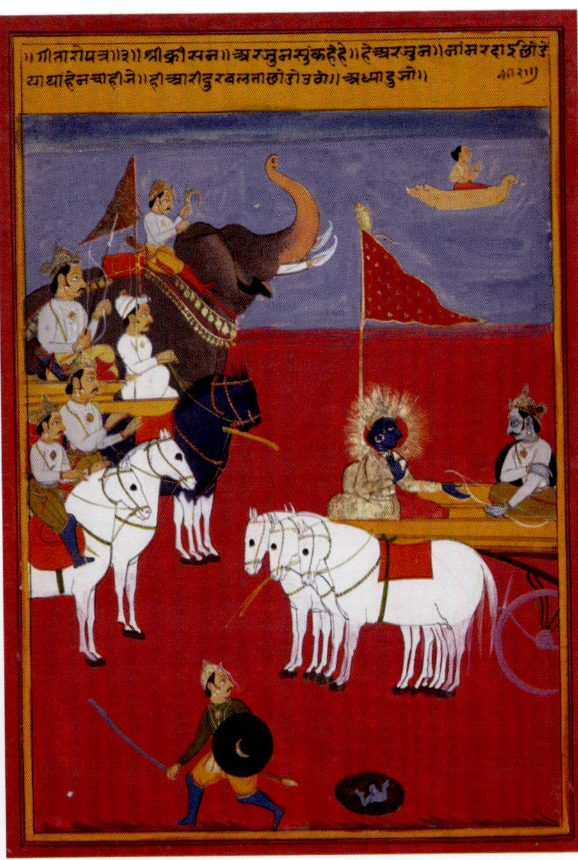

|3| इसलिए हे अर्जुन! नपुंसकता को मत प्राप्त हो, तुझमें यह उचित नहीं जान पड़ता। हृदय की तुच्छ दुर्बलता को त्याग कर युद्ध के लिए खड़ा हो जा।

|3| Hey Arjuna! Do not yield to unmanliness; it does not become you. Cast off this ignoble weakness of the heart; get up and fight.

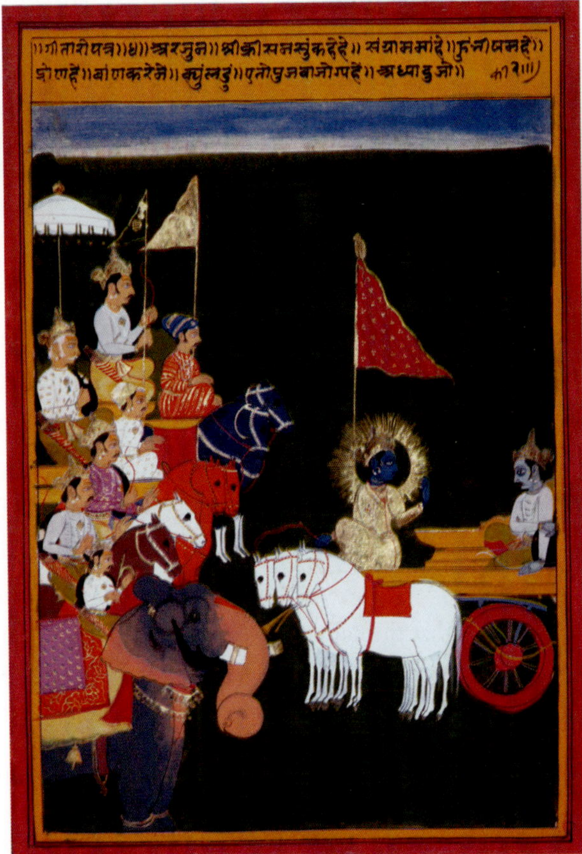

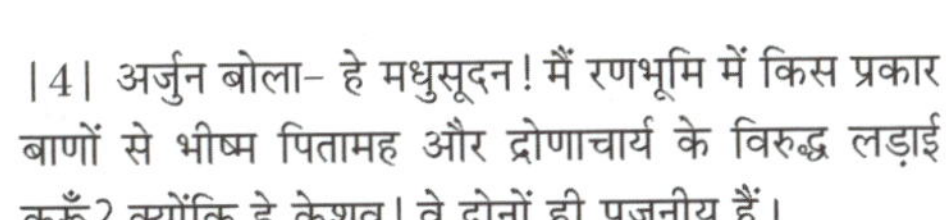

|4| अर्जुन बोला- हे मधुसूदन! मैं रणभूमि में किस प्रकार बाणों से भीष्म पितामह और द्रोणाचार्य के विरुद्ध लड़ाई करूँ? क्योंकि हे केशव! वे दोनों ही पूजनीय हैं।

|4| Arjuna replies: Hey Madhusudan! In this battlefield, how can I shoot arrows at Bhishma Pitamah and Dronacharya? Both are worthy of reverence.

shift in tone and shows it by making a subtle change in Krishna's gesture. The left hand is still extended as in a difficult argument, but the right is held up in benediction.

Arjuna still seems to lack moral confidence. But, in the painting, reassurance is offered by a visionary image in the blue sky. If Arjuna were to look past his selfhood, he would see a sage flying in a saffron bird-shaped boat. The bird-boat is not an arbitrary, whimsical image but an imaginative interpretation of the verse. In mythic iconography, a bird-messenger helps gods conduct a conversation with earth-dwellers. In Buddhist imagery, a bird-boat signals that an *arhat* is 'in the stream' heading towards salvation. Sometimes bird-messengers are signs of blessing; sometimes omens of disaster.[3] The bird image here challenges our assumptions about this verse.

Arjuna agonises over the fact that the forces arrayed against him consist of his relatives and teachers. Appropriately, the colours in the painting for verse 4 are darker; the blue sky is remoter and the Kaurava army more belligerent. Allah Baksh recognises this moment as Arjuna's descent into the dark night of the soul. Arjuna struggles with the idea that the earth's history is tarnished by injustice and bloody contests where both the victors and the defeated are victims. The painting dramatically explores the ethical contradictions Arjuna cannot resolve. The anguish the colour black evokes returns to dominate the painting and determine our emotional response. Psychologically, Arjuna is in that liminal state where his duty as a warrior who must restore order and his abiding love for his antagonists are equally valid. The intensity of his inner turmoil is brilliantly visualised.

In the painting, his bow is not in Arjuna's hand. As he looks past Krishna, he sees Dronacharya, who taught him statecraft and war, the aged Bhisma, his moral preceptor under the white parasol, and Dhritarashtra's sons. They are noble and worthy of respect. The warriors facing him are not enemies, but his distinguished relatives. He feels compassion and more than compassion, love. His question is crucial. It is not a sign of unmanliness or faintheartedness, as Krishna implies, but of a genuinely troubled conscience. Why should we add to the world's sorrows for transitory gain? Why is it more worthy to fight and risk being morally contaminated than to sacrifice what the self desires or public approval demands? Radhakrishnan, surprisingly, asserts that Arjuna 'is not a seeker of knowledge'[4] as he only wants to know how to act. Allah

3 In Chapter 1 of the *Gita*, Arjuna speaks about seeing "evil omens" (verse 31). S. Radhakrishnan, says: "Arjuna's attention to omens indicates his mental weakness and instability." *The Bhagavadgita* (New Delhi: HarperCollins, 2014), p. 101.

4 Radhakrishnan, *The Bhagavadgita*, p. 113.

Baksh understands that for Arjuna, the Kauravas are, above anything else, 'fellows in mortality, in life on earth.'[5] In the painting, he continues to show Arjuna arguing with Krishna. The Kauravas, on the other hand, are indifferent to the death of others; they do not need words or morality for victory, but determined action. Can moral arguments, one wonders, stop men intent on evil? Yet, the ordeal of hesitation and indecision must be endured before deciding that war is the only moral choice.[6] Would it matter, Arjuna wonders, if he wins or loses? Would life be worth living after so much killing?

Verse 6 expresses the idea that Arjuna would rather lose his life than kill the sons of Dhritarashtra. Allah Baksh reverses the direction of the chariots to capture this poignant moment. Arjuna is morally alone; the incandescent vermillion background and the warring soldiers below the chariot underline the idea that his questions about the fate of his moral self are not separate from justice. The Kauravas are not the enemy in the abstract. His moment of self-doubt should not be dismissed as 'ignorance' or 'weakness.'[7] This war radically challenges the basic ethical assumption that the *Mahabharata* has been at pains to teach thus far: a good king, a good society, a good man are all obliged to be responsible for the life of someone else. Dhritarashtra is blind to this basic ethic, even as he listens to the *Gita* being retold to him by Sanjaya. Duryodhana is too obtuse to have moral reservations. Arjuna must examine his soul to see if he has not been corrupted; endure the ordeal of doubt if his resolve is to be morally and spiritually worthy. He alone will have to decide. Indeed, what is profound about this dramatic encounter is that Krishna has to convince Arjuna through reason and intense argument that the decision to fight is in conformity with moral law, with dharma. Arjuna is not required to accept what Krishna says reverentially. That would not only be inane superstition and pedantry, but also idolatry which violates the uniqueness of each self. A conversation between god and man, a questioning dialogue between the man of wisdom and his disciple, is not alien to the Indian tradition and would never invite the charge of heresy. The *Rig Veda* states: 'Save us, today, Mitra and Varuna,/ From those foes who do not ask questions.../ And do not rejoice in conversation.'[8]

5 Stanley Cavell, in *Philosophy and Animal Life*, edited by Stanley Cavell et.al. (New York: Columbia University Press, 2008), p. 16.

6 Jacques Derrida, quoted by Cavell, *Philosophy and Animal Life*, p. 102.

7 Radhakrishnan, p. 113.

8 Arindham Chakrabarti, 'Just Words: An Ethics of Conversation in the Mahabharata', in *Mahabharata Now: Narration, Aesthetics, Ethics,* edited by Arindham Chakrabarti and Sibaji Bandyopadhyay (New Delhi: Routledge, 2014), p. 245.

Indeed, the finest teaching of the *Gita* is that one acts well if one thinks well; and, thinking well demands the courage to even question god till one is satisfied by the answers he is obliged to give.[9] Deeply moved by Arjuna's scepticism and Krishna's replies, Simone Weil intriguingly remarks that although Arjuna knows he will have to fight, he pauses to take a measure of the world from all points of view. Had he not heard the *Gita*, he would still have fought, but would have fought badly.[10] War must wait till reason finally understands that violence is the only option for justice.

In verse 7, Arjuna pleads with Krishna to teach him how to resolve his moral confusion. In the painting, Arjuna has turned away from the abyss of despondency, as well as the menacing presence and noise of the Kaurava army. By placing the chariot near the left frame of the painting, near the Kaurava army, the artist astutely suggests that Arjuna is still at the edge of ethical fear, the pain of carnage and, perhaps, the ultimate futility of victory or defeat. He has not yet surrendered to Krishna. Allah Baksh, however, recognises Krishna as the avatar of Vishnu and places him on an elevated lotus-shaped seat—the lotus being a sign of victory over the demon of chaos and despondency.[11] The lotus seat, in turn, rests on an inverted lotus. Together they form an intersecting cone signifying time past, present and future, or the inseparable relation of time and eternity. The lotus seat is, like the chariot, an incandescent yellow. Krishna himself sits in the posture of a yogic seer with his right palm raised in a gesture of quiet benediction instead of anger and chastisement.

Further, the chariot's wheel has sixteen spokes. According to the Upanishads, sixteen is the number of elements required for the creation of the world: five elements (earth, water, light, air and ether), five organs of action, five organs of the intellect, and the mind.[12] The chariot itself stands in a space lit by a serene blue-green light, suffusing the painting with silence. One feels something momentous is about to be said, something that needs the attention of Arjuna's entire being.

The figures at the bottom left are mirror images of Krishna and Arjuna. They are not on the battlefield but on a white marble platform. Krishna is sitting on a bright

9 Michel De Montaigne's essay, 'On Pedantry,' in *The Complete Works*, translated by Donald M. Frame (New York: Everyman's Library, 1948), pp. 19–27.

10 Weil, *Notebooks*, p. 97.

11 Heinrich Zimmer, *Myths and Symbols in Indian Art and Civilization*, edited by Joseph Campbell (New York: Harper and Row, 1962), p. 17.

12 See Kapila Vatsyayan, 'Indian Arts: Their Ideational Background and Principles of Form,' in *Paroksha: Coomaraswamy Centenary Seminar Papers*, edited by Gulam Mohammad Sheikh, K.G. Subramanyan and Kapila Vatsyayan (New Delhi: Lalit Kala Akademi, 1984), pp. 51–59.

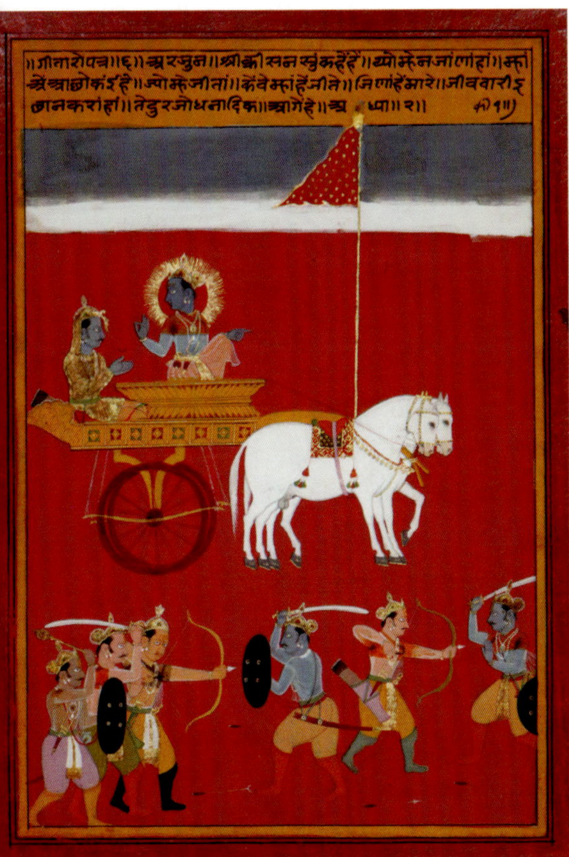

|6| अर्जुन आगे श्री कृष्ण से कहने लगा कि हम यह भी नहीं जानते कि हमारे लिए युद्ध करना और न करना- इन दोनों में से कौन-सा श्रेष्ठ है अथवा यह भी नहीं जानते कि उन्हें हम जीतेंगे या हमको वे जीतेंगे। और जिनको मार कर हम जीना भी नहीं चाहते, वे ही हमारे आत्मीय धृतराष्ट्र के पुत्र हमारे मुकाबले में खड़े हैं।

|6| Arjuna says to Sri Krishna: I do not know if we should fight or not. Which is better? I do not know if we shall win or they shall defeat us. Will I care to live after killing the sons of our honoured kinsman, Dhritarashtra, who are ranged against us?

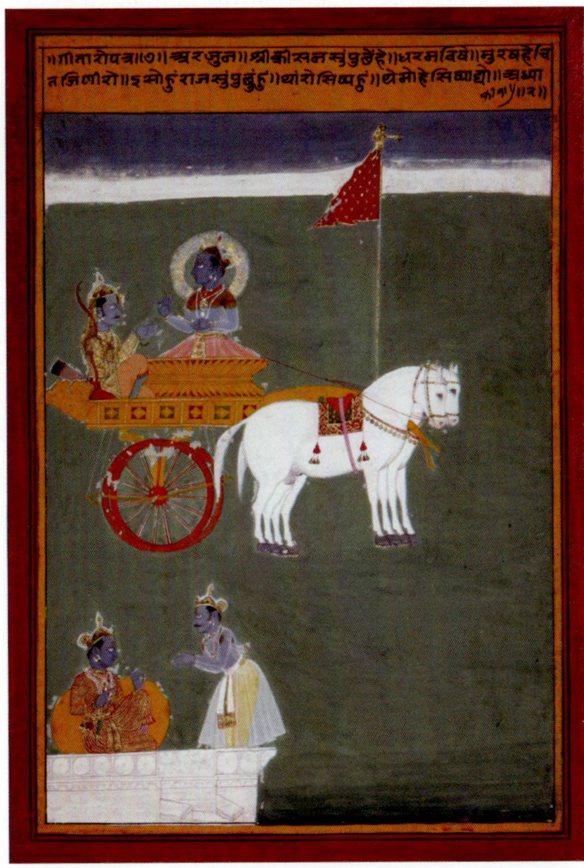

|7| अर्जुन श्री कृष्ण से कहने लगा कि कायर स्वभाववाला मैं धर्म के विषय में जानने को उत्सुक हुआ। मैं आपसे पूछता हूँ कि जो साधन निश्चित कल्याणकारी हो, वह मेरे लिए कहिए क्योंकि मैं आपका शिष्य हूँ। आप की शरण में आया हूँ, मुझे शिक्षा दीजिए।

|7| Arjuna says to Sri Krishna: I am guilty of self-pity and confused about what my dharma is. Because I am your disciple, I beseech you to tell me what is good for my well-being. I have sought refuge in you, teach me.

yellow seat. Arjuna stands before him with folded hands. Krishna is beautifully dressed in a pale red robe laced with gold, while Arjuna wears a saffron *jama*. Both are unarmed. Is the painter suggesting to his royal patrons that the questions about the dharma of rulers should also be asked about the conduct of all kings and courtiers? That the well-being of a kingdom lies neither in asserting the self-will of kings nor in the unquestioning obedience of the courtiers? That a critically alert populace is necessary for the maintenance of a good social order? Is there an oblique reminder of the fact that Dhritarashtra, who remains unmoved by Arjuna's sorrow and pity, is also listening to the *Gita*?

As Arjuna's questioning continues, there is a return to the mood of sorrow. In the painting for verse 8, Arjuna's body droops in despondency. Krishna regards him sternly, and chastises him. The anguish, however, is moderated by the other figures and colours. There are two handsome men in a deep pink semi-circle in the lower half of the painting. A confident ruler sits leaning against a golden yellow bolster, placed on an ornate golden platform under a glowing white tasselled parasol. A courtier, who is opulently dressed in a sky-blue garment, kneels before him. We are asked, once again, to think about the ideal relation between the ruler and the ruled. These questions will continue to be the subject of debate throughout the *Mahabharata*.

Making an imaginative leap, the painter guides our attention to the top left corner where a yogi sits quietly on a wooden platform with a white parasol above his head. He occupies a space on the same axis as the other figures, but belongs to the realm of the sky and the gods. Is he like the learned sages who travel in bird-boats, an enlightened man on his way to nirvana, free from the burden that perplexes Arjuna? How different he is from Arjuna's teachers who are arrayed against him on the battlefield! Should we ask what the ideal relation between a teacher and his pupils ought to be?

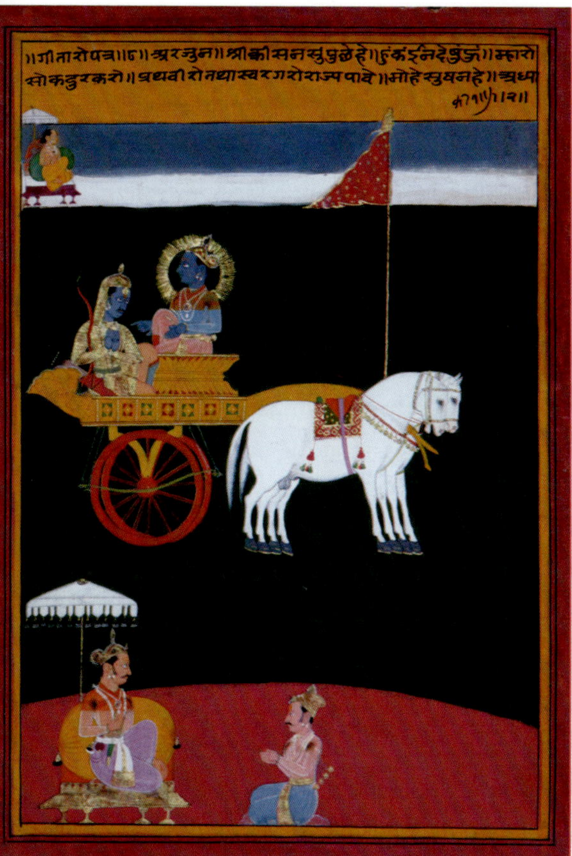

|8| अर्जुन श्री कृष्ण से पूछ रहा है कि हे केशव! मुझे कुछ नहीं सूझता। मेरा शोक दूर कीजिए। पृथ्वी और स्वर्ग का राज्य भी मिल जाए, तो मुझे सुख (चैन) नहीं।

|8| Arjuna says to Sri Krishna: Hey Keshav! I am confused and do not know what to do! Even if I win the kingdoms of earth and heaven, I will not be at peace.

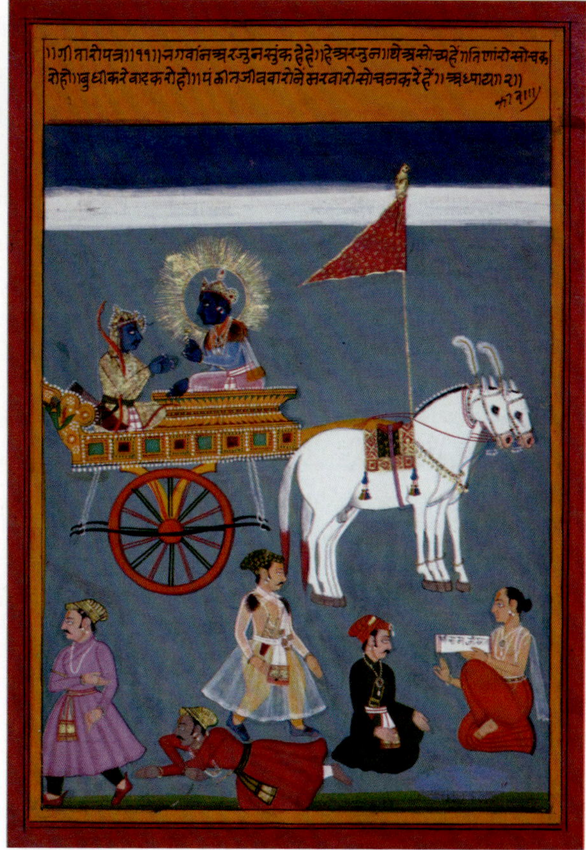

|11| श्री कृष्ण तब अर्जुन से बोले कि हे अर्जुन! तू न शोक करने योग्य मनुष्यों के लिए शोक करता है परन्तु जिनके प्राण चले गए हैं, उनके लिए और जिनके प्राण नहीं गए हैं उनके लिए भी पंडितजन शोक नहीं करते।

|11| Then Sri Krishna says to Arjuna: You grieve for those who are worthy of grief, but the wise do not grieve for those who are dead or for those who are living.

Empathetic to Arjuna's lament, verse 11 meditates on the emotion: grief. It is worthy to grieve for those who are wise and good, Krishna says. Yet, it is also folly to grieve since the world is a passing show; forms of life appear and vanish in an endless cycle. In the painting, Arjuna, his hands folded, listens with attention. He knows that the world is transitory. He wants to avoid the sin of inflicting harm; hence, his grief. In Chapter 1, he had thrice asked about the 'sin' of killing his kinsmen.[13] In the *Drona Parva*, Yudhishthira hears a terrifying story about how Mrityuni (Death) is assured by Brahma that she commits no sin when someone dies. However, Arjuna continues to ask how he can evade the sin of transforming the earth into a charnel house? As colours carry emotional information, the painting's visual structure adds to Arjuna's pathos with an enticing wash of colours. A narrow strip of green earth at the bottom, where human beings enact life's daily routine, quietly shades into the vast grey-blue space where the eye meets the white band of the horizon, before moving up to a blue sky. The effect is not of grief, but of beauty, peace and harmony.

There is a dramatic tableau in the lower half of the painting. On the right, far from the armies, a brahmin sits reading the *Ramayana*. Four well-dressed men first approach him and then turn away. Are we invited to meditate on the number four which often structures the meaning of life and time in the *Mahabharata*? Do the men represent the four-fold cycle of life, its four stages and yugas? War disrupts this temporal process; violates life's cycle. That is why Arjuna hesitates.

For the first time in verse 12, Krishna reveals his divine kinship with Arjuna. Both have existed since primordial time and shall do so till eternity. The brick-red background wash is unevenly applied. But the chariot is more ornate and the horses are like marble statues with elaborate filigreed designs on the saddle, halter and bridle. The painting's lower half is enigmatic. Four figures sit on a white space marked as sacred, by an ochre outline. The two blue-bodied men on the right are surely Krishna and Arjuna. Krishna is given a slightly elevated position. Perhaps, what is suggested is that the conversation between the two, friend and guide, god and man, is both ancient and will continue even after the war, given that the anguish of ethical choice is not unique. Are the figures on the left, towards whom Arjuna gestures in recognition, Dhritarashtra and Sanjaya? Or, do they represent teachers and students who hear the *Gita* from age to age, yet remain ignorant and belligerent?

---

13 D. Dennis Hudson, 'Arjuna's Sin: *The Bhagavad-Gita* in its Epic Context,' in *Krishna's Mandala: Bhagvata Religion and Beyond* (New Delhi: Oxford University Press, 2010), pp. 154–72.

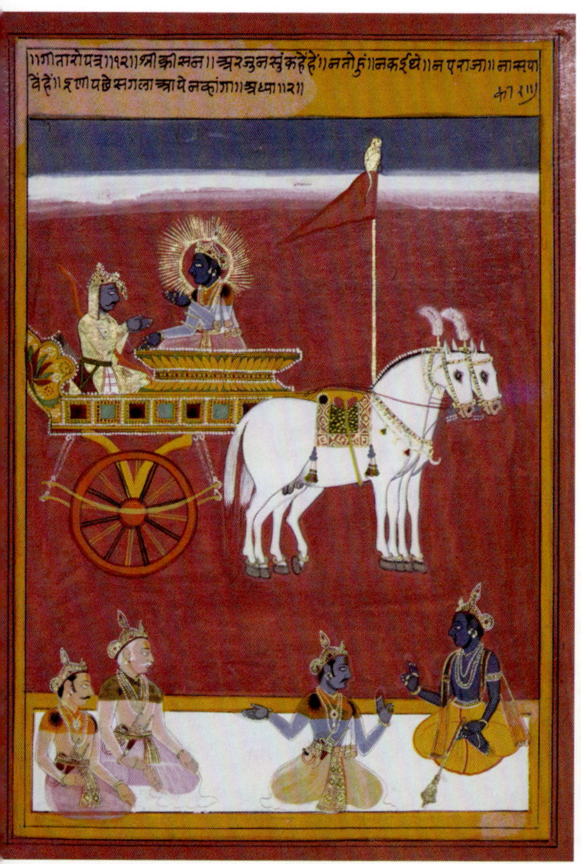

|12| श्री कृष्ण अर्जुन से कह रहे हैं कि हे अर्जुन! ऐसा नहीं है कि मैं किसी काल में नहीं था या तू नहीं था अथवा ये राजा लोग नहीं थे और न ऐसा ही है कि इसके आगे हम सब नहीं होंगे।

|12| Sri Krishna says to Arjuna: Hey Arjuna! There was never a time when I did not exist; when you and those princes did not exist; nor shall we cease to exist in the future.

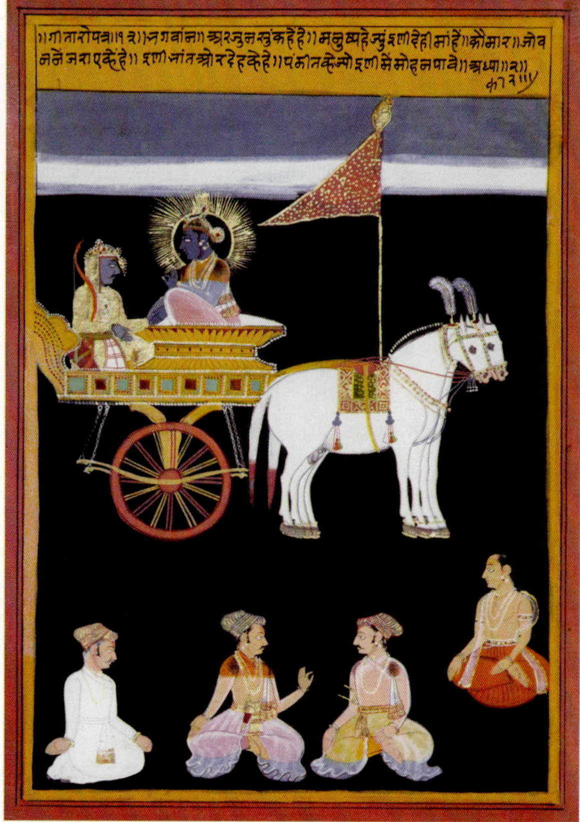

|13| श्री कृष्ण अर्जुन से कहने लगे कि हे अर्जुन! जैसे मनुष्य की इस देह में बचपन, जवानी और बुढ़ापा होता है, वैसे ही उसे अन्य शरीर की प्राप्ति होती है। बुद्धिमान इस देह के मोह में नहीं पड़ते।

|13| Sri Krishna says to Arjuna: Hey Arjuna! Just as this human body changes from childhood to youth and old age, it also changes into other bodies. The wise are not attached to this body.

The white platform, in keeping with the conventions of Indian miniature art, does not create the illusion of depth and perspective. It is never the intention of conceptual art to imitate nature or give realistic information. Instead, it is concerned with visualising, through 'clear and simple' designs, impressive in their 'solemn consistency', an abstract idea or a sacred moment.[14]

In verse 13, Krishna's purpose is two-fold. Trying to shake Arjuna out of his self-absorbed brooding, Krishna tells him that each individual matures, changes and is finally erased, and urges him to imagine that each body is instinct with the same divine spirit. If he has this two-fold perception, he will cease to be enamoured of his particular physical form, but try to cultivate his primal or divine self.

As listening to the *Gita* must have been a ceremonious part of the Mewar court, in this beautiful work, Allah Baksh creates a ceremony of colour and line, physical beauty and gesture. The three figures of different ages at the bottom of painting are so placed in relation to Krishna so as to form a triangle. None of the four is looking towards Krishna. Do they represent different levels of awareness leading to knowledge and wisdom? On the right, at a slightly elevated level, a learned man sits in calm contemplation. Is he a disinterested observer of the lifecycle? He gazes into the surrounding darkness and remains unmoved. Does he not look at Krishna because he knows that the divine is everywhere? On the opposite end, both pictorially and psychologically, there is a lonely man dressed in white who is oblivious to the animated conversations around him. Is he a distinct, self-absorbed being aware only of his separate ego identity? Or, is he a replica of Arjuna in daily-life who has begun to question his place in the scheme of things? There are two colourfully dressed men in earnest conversation at the centre. The gesture of one is a mirror image of Krishna's. He seems to be instructing the other. Both are respectfully aware of their individual existence in the presence of the other. Their two-fold awareness is the first step out of the melancholy that Krishna has been urging Arjuna to overcome.

The painting for verse 14 is gorgeously imagined. It gives a visual shape to Krishna's assertion that everything in the created world participates in an eternally recurring cycle of birth and death, joy and sorrow, summer and winter; but to take this repetitiveness as the ultimate truth is to confuse reality and illusion, slavery and freedom, heaven and hell. This earthly cycle exits. It has a form and a shape. The paradox is that while there is emptiness at its core, it is out of this emptiness that form takes its shape. To understand and accept this eternal emergence, extinction and re-emergence of life in time on earth,

14 E.H. Gombrich, *The Sense of Order: A Study in the Psychology of Decorative Art* (London: Phaidon, 1979).

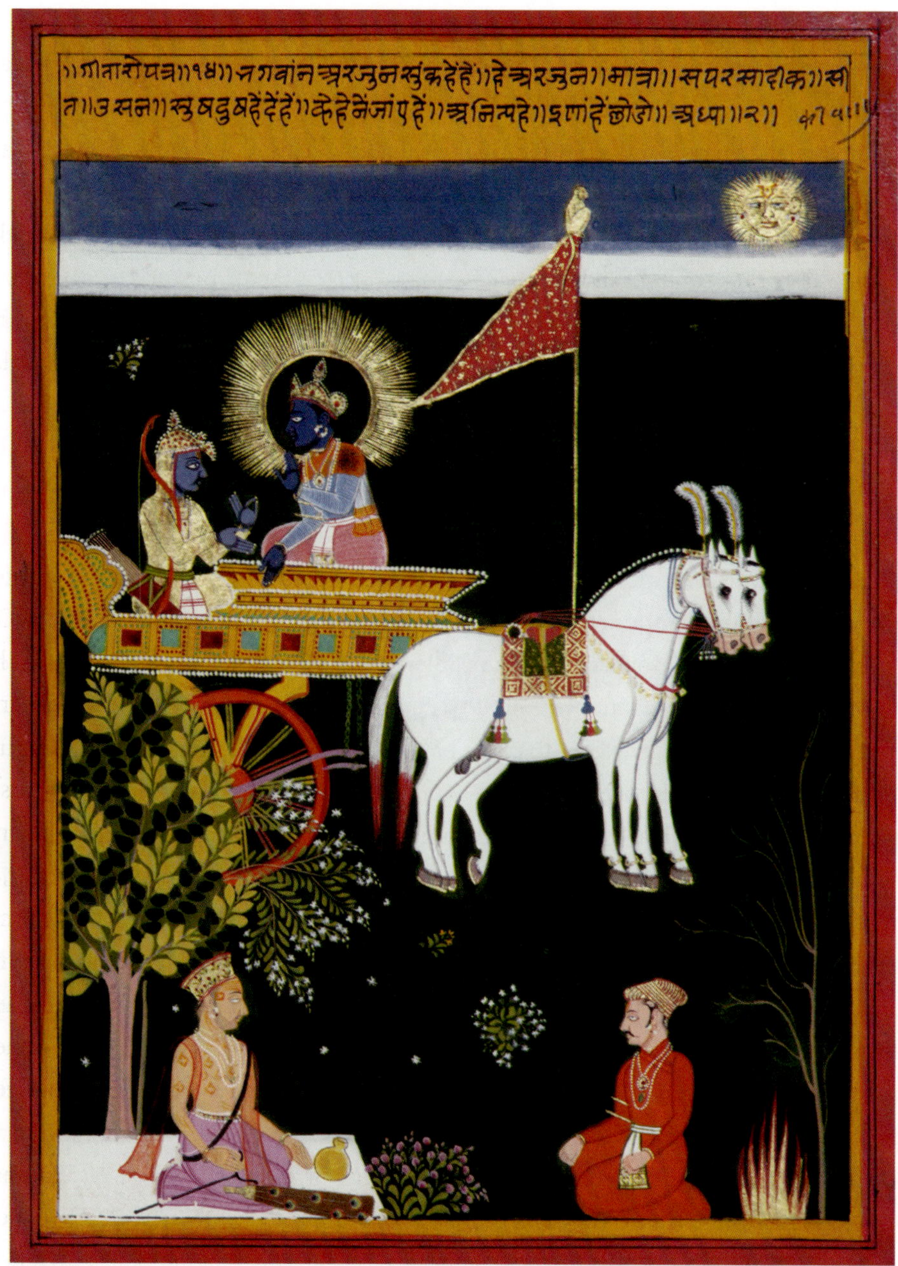

|14| श्री कृष्ण अर्जुन से कहने लगे कि हे अर्जुन! सर्दी-गरमी और सुख-दुख को देने वाले इन्द्रिय और विषयों के संयोग तो अनित्य हैं, वे आते हैं और जाते हैं। इसलिए इन्हें जाने दे। सहन करना सीख।

|14| Sri Krishna says to Arjuna: Hey Arjuna! Like other experiences, summer-winter and joy-sorrow are illusions; they are transient; they come and go. Let them be. Learn to endure.

one needs wisdom and imagination. Only then can one be part of this whirligig without lamentation or ecstasy; watch its *lila* (play) with poise and dignity; act in the world according to the demands of dharma.

On the left, there is a decorative tree with yellow leaves, surrounded by bushes. White flowers are scattered on the ground. Is it the tree of virtue mentioned at the beginning of the *Adi Parva* (I, 65–66)—the archetype of the tree of life in all myths of origin? The flowers light up the space. A sage, with a fan of peacock feathers, sits under the tree and teaches the prince kneeling before him. The tree, the flowers and the human figures are surely not only signs of spring, but also of an ideal social order without conflict. But as one looks up, one remembers the war; and the fact that all ideal springs and summers are transitory, all gardens wither. Above the chariot, in the blue sky, in the far horizon in the east, the golden sun is harsh and remote. As the eye circles back to the earth past a vast dark space, it sees a dry tree on the right. A fire burns near it. Both are symbolic of winter and death as part of the lifecycle. Can it also be the tree of wrath mentioned in the *Adi Parva* growing besides the tree of virtue—like the tree of bitter knowledge in the Bible?[15] The sage sits between a green tree, which is spring's delight, and a withered tree, symbolic of winter, age and decay. The eye has nowhere else to go except to circle back to the flowering tree and so repeat the natural cycle. In the painting there is no sign, no guide to the gate of imagination. If the *Mahabharata* is read as a book of lamentations, then the *Gita* is a moral guide out of 'the grievousness of the condition of being human.'[16] The discourse on the chariot glows with visionary possibility.

For the wise man, Krishna continues in verse 15, joy and suffering are the same; he remains detached, always. That is what moksha means: the final release from the wheel of time. The painting is richly coloured and imagined. It suggests a parallel between two kinds of *dharmakshetras* or the fields of ethical action. The first is that of a warrior, the second of the renunciant. The painter meditates on both because they are repeatedly offered as injunctions in the *Mahabharata*: 'Do the work' and 'renounce all work' (*Shanti Parva*, 19:1). That is why the framed space has no worldly markers—neither palaces nor homes. Ironically, in the epic no warrior attains *moksha*; and every sage who goes to the forest to find the truth is waylaid by desire and is thwarted.

15 See Bhattacharya, 'Significance of the Early *Parvans*: Modes of Narration, Birth Stories and Seeds of Conflict,' in *Mahabharata Now*, p. 41.

16 Stanley Cavell, *In Quest of the Ordinary: Lines of Scepticism and Romanticism* (Chicago: University of Chicago Press, 1988), p. 172.

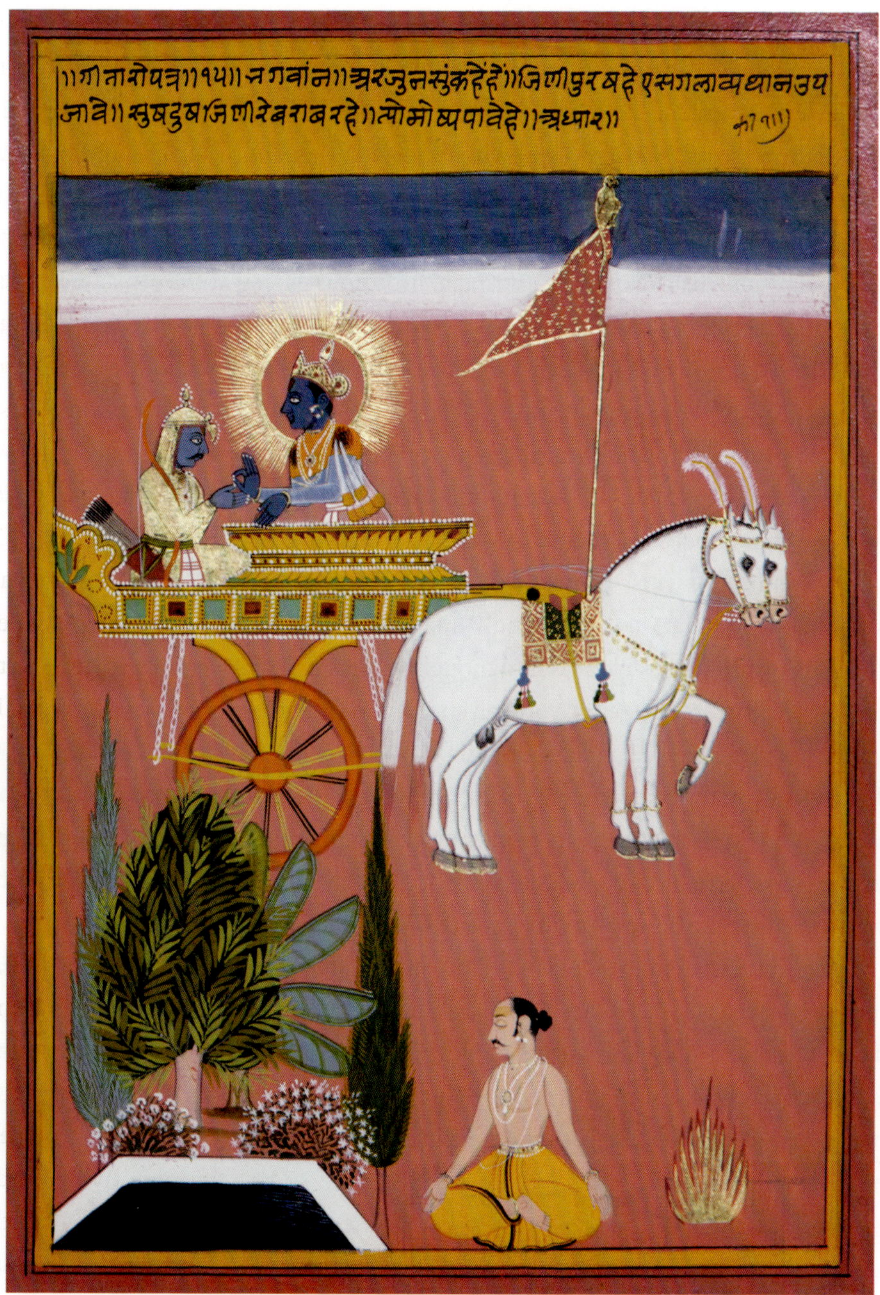

|15| श्री कृष्ण अर्जुन से कहते हैं कि हे अर्जुन! दुख और सुख को जो समान समझता है, उस (धीर) पुरुष को ये (इन्द्रिय और विषयों के संयोग) व्याकुल नहीं करते। वह मोक्ष पाता है।

|15| Sri Krishna says to Arjuna: Hey Arjuna! The brave man, for whom joy and suffering are the same, is never despondent. He attains moksha.

Just as Arjuna continues to wonder if he can be sufficiently disengaged from his family, we wonder if ascetic monasticism, which the figure in the lower half of the painting represents, can be genuinely authentic in the midst of natural beauty and opulence. The ascetic sits between a ritual fire that demands sacrifice and a pool of blue water surrounded by trees, white flowers and fruit. The fire and the green grove are not realistic, but are the work of an artist who is in love with their forms. The ascetic has turned his back on the sacrificial fire and is gazing at the sensuous garden. Had Arjuna chosen the path of asceticism, would he still not be self-deluded? Should the ascetic cut down trees of such loveliness, uproot the flowers and leave the fruit untouched to rot? Would that not be a grievous violation of dharma too? This is immediately followed by another thought which Krishna has been enunciating with such eloquence. If both the warrior and the ascetic live in a world which is perishable, how do we choose between them?

The painting for verse 16, concerned with esoteric ideas about existence, non-existence and annihilation is profoundly imagined. Allah Baksh has the incomparable gift of transforming abstract ideas into thoughtful visual images. The irony is that in the midst of war there are images of a golden sun, a beautiful tree whose green leaves never fall, a fan-like banana tree and a clear blue sky—conventional signs of perfection and endless fertility in the phenomenal realm. They persuade us to ask: is this earthly realm not real? Will Arjuna not be responsible for its annihilation? Can a wise man agree to its erasure? Existence is temporal, but is it not through such a world that earth-dwellers apprehend either the boundaries of eternity or the edge of nothingness?

A richly attired man in a golden turban and a red robe is placed deliberately below Arjuna on the chariot. Is his life-history an alternative to the war that confronts Arjuna and the internal conflict that torments him? The man sits calmly gazing at the tree of beauty growing before him. What can he possibly learn by doing so? Is this the tree of poetic knowledge Vyasa talks about in *Adi Parva*? Should one recall those countless poets and seers, who have sat under trees to tell stories, waiting for some saving vision?

Framed by the tree and the partially visible fan of the banana leaves are two men reading from a palm-leaf book with the words '*Sri Ram Ji*' on the title page. The *Ramayana* is a constant moral touchstone, an ideal point of reference, throughout this *Gita* folio. Both Rama and Krishna are incarnations of Vishnu. Like Arjuna, Rama is a good man who is compelled to fight. There is also an analogy made between the predicaments of Rama and Arjuna. The two brahmin readers of the *Ramayana* have all the visual markers (posture, knotted hair, saffron and ochre-coloured lower garments, and a

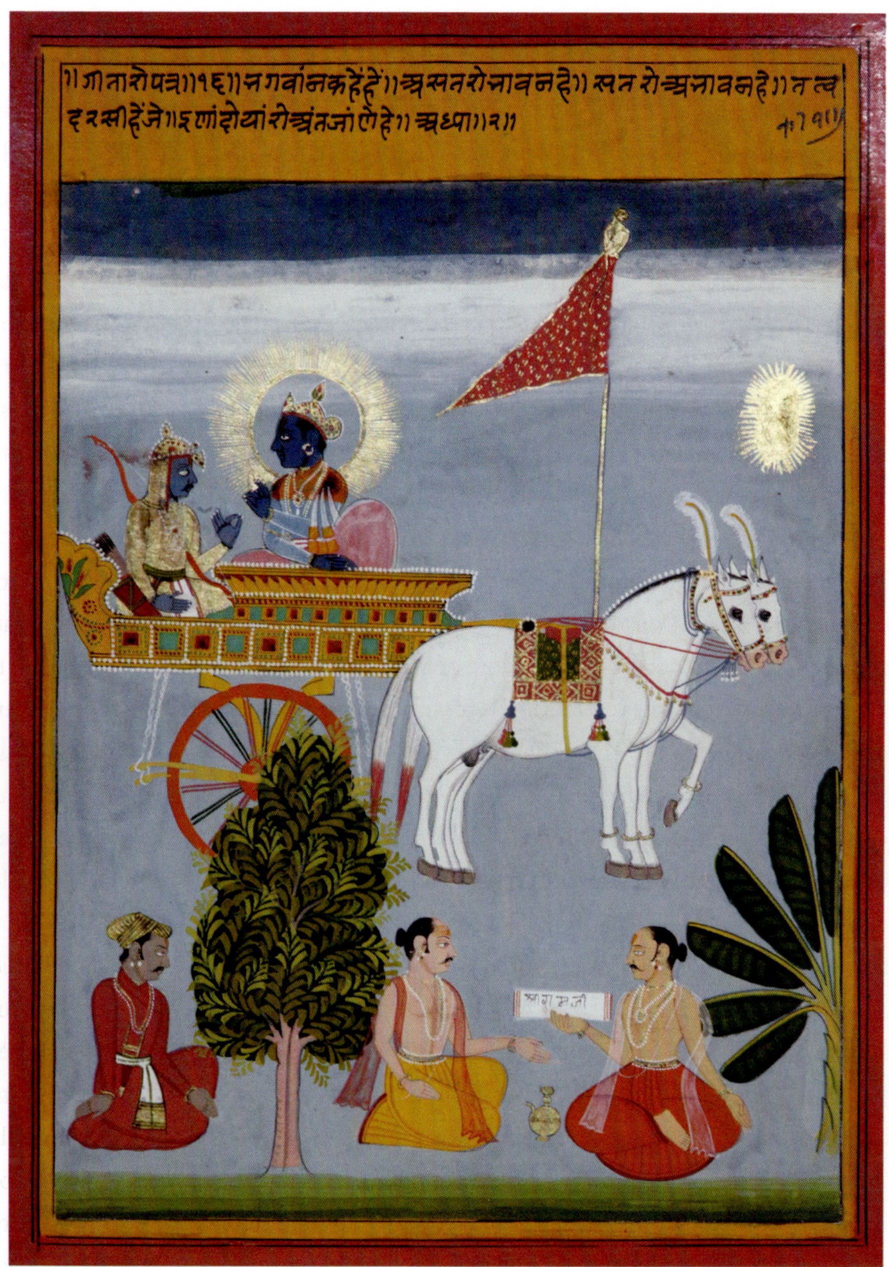

|16| श्री कृष्ण अर्जुन से कहने लगे कि हे अर्जुन! असत् वस्तु की तो सत्ता नहीं है और सत् का अभाव नहीं है पर तत्वदर्शी इन दोनों तत्वों को देख लेता है और दोनों का अंत जानता है।

|16| Sri Krishna says to Arjuna: Hey Arjuna! That which does not exist, shall never be; that which exists, shall never be annihilated. The wise man understands the truth of both and draws his conclusions.

ritual water jug) of men who have the cultural authority to interpret the scriptures. One should, however, remember that the dialogic form of the *Gita* urges its readers not to accept moral commandments without critical questioning, though the *Gita* also insists that scriptural knowledge is not essential to experience the divine. The two readers of the scriptures in the painting do not look up and beyond their textual concerns. Had they done so, they would have had an unmediated vision of Krishna.

Though its subject is sombre, the lines of beauty and natural gracefulness do not disappear from the painting for verse 18. Krishna says that, since the body is perishable, the Eternal is indifferent to its survival or extinction. Arjuna wonders: if the Eternal manifests itself in the multiplicity of the universe, would the violation of a single creature not also be a violation of the Supreme? He continues to listen in reverential silence. In the painting, he appears a little dazed; fearful of what lies ahead. Krishna's argument, that all manifest beings are perishable, does not resolve the moral issue for it can also be used to abstain from the fight. If war is only endless killing with no clear moral purpose, is it not the duty of a dharmic man to be the advocate of all living beings under any circumstance? Does the killing of a sparrow not desecrate the eternal?

The lower section of the painting is a witty response to sectarian debates around Krishna's verses. They are the subject not of moral action but of dry interpretative argument between two groups of people in ordinary life. Two brahmins are engaged in an earnest discussion about the meaning of the *Ramayana*, while the wealthy courtiers seem to be engaged in a passionate dispute about court politics. An armed man, with a shield, is shown seated on a slightly elevated ground. Interestingly, unlike the *Gita*, the *Mahabharata* pays scant attention to the thousands of soldiers who will be slaughtered.

Is it sufficient to say that one can go to war because the Atma, the divine portion of all living beings, neither kills nor can be killed? Will such an argument cleanse the conscience of those who inflict the wound? It is an old question; an old argument. How is killing justified? Who justifies it? From whom does the authority to go to war derive its sanctity? How does one know the divine will or recognise the higher good which calls for such an enormous carnage? Verse 19 is only one intervention in the debate. Allah Baksh's painting is strangely static, yet slightly bemused and puzzled. Two richly dressed men are animatedly talking in the pink space below the chariot. Two others, lying on bare earth, are either asleep or dead. The feeling of indifference they evoke is in keeping with Krishna's undifferentiating reflection on matters of life and violent death. Those who are born and those who die, he says, emerge from the same source and return to it. Is Arjuna, however, not asserting his unique selfhood by continuously questioning

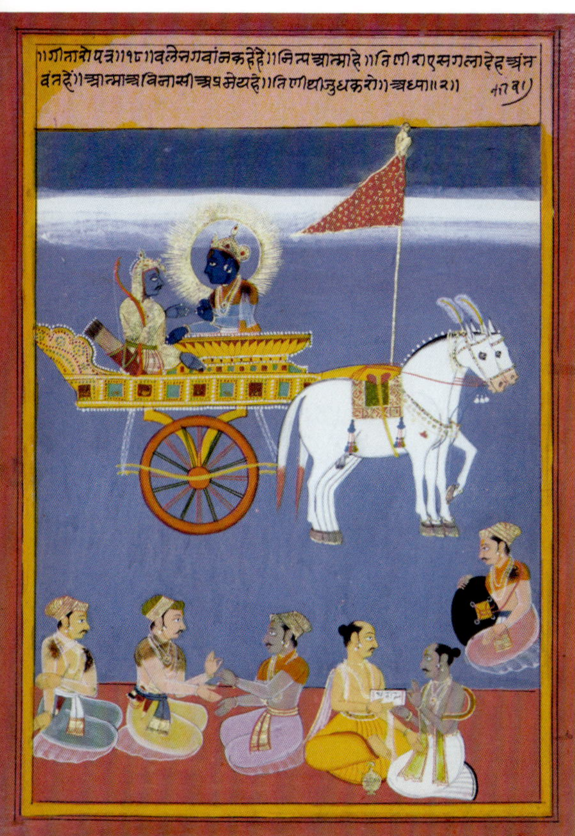

|18| श्री कृष्ण आगे कहने लगे कि आत्मा नित्य है और उसके द्वारा धारण की गई सभी देहें नश्वर हैं। आत्मा अविनाशी अप्रमेय है। इसको जान कर हे अर्जुन! इसलिए तू युद्ध कर।

|18| The Atma is eternal and the material bodies it inhabits are all finite. The Atma is imperishable, indestructible. Understand this, hey Arjuna! Then fight!

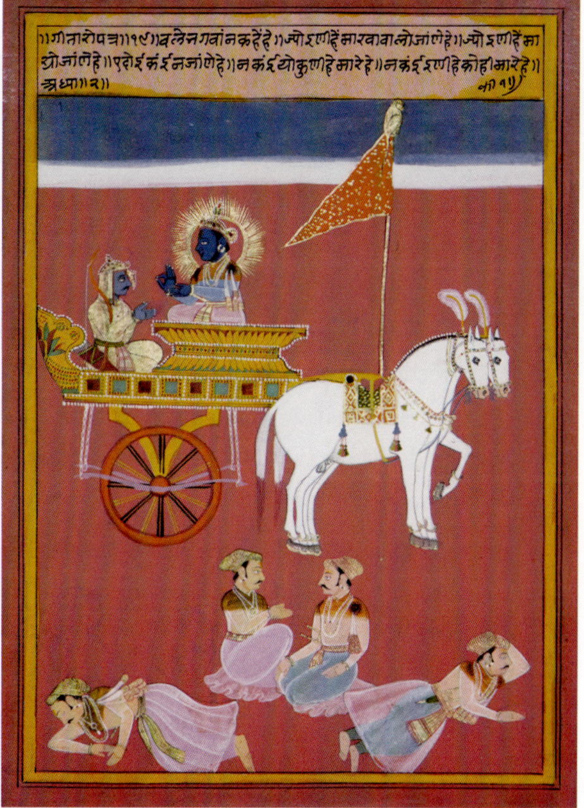

|19| श्री कृष्ण आगे कहने लगे कि हे अर्जुन! जो इस (आत्मा) को मारने वाला जानता है तथा जो इसे मरा जानता है। वे दोनों ही नहीं जानते हैं कि वह (आत्मा) न किसी को मारता है और न (किसी के द्वारा) मारा जाता है।

|19| Sri Krishna further says: Hey Arjuna! He who thinks that the Atma can kill, and he who thinks it can be killed, does not understand that the Atma can neither kill nor be killed by anyone.

Krishna? Is he not saying: 'I am—I am Arjuna—as opposed to and separate from the other whom I may have to kill?' Is he not insisting on his radical difference as a living and moral being? He is not Duryodhana's double even though both will return to the same Being from which they have emerged. The killing of Duryodhana or the death of Arjuna cannot be a matter of indifference, nor can one's own violent death in a vicious world. Some have argued that while the *Gita* is an integral part of the *Mahabharata*, it is not an authoritative guide to action.[17] In any case, Krishna often ignores his own teaching about the indifference of the divine to earthly life and death, and does what he must for victory.

In sympathy with Arjuna's questions, the paintings suggest that Krishna's argument about the indifference of the Eternal can be used equally for action and non-action, self-assertion and surrender, war and renunciation. Thus, Arjuna can withdraw without going through the intellectual adventure of *finding*, and hence *founding*, in his own self a moral basis for action.

The silence of the painting for verse 20 refocuses attention on Arjuna as an intent listener. A hint of mist hangs over the sunlit earth where the war is to be fought. Arjuna hears Krishna say: the eternal sun, remote and indifferent, is the measure of passing time; it consumes days and nights, seasons and yugas. His scepticism about the idea that there is no difference between killing and being killed is part of his education to become a dharma warrior; his doubt is not, as some assert, only a diversion; a momentary swerve away from Yudhishthira whose education is really the subject of the epic.[18] However, Arjuna's education, too, is crucial to the *Mahabharata*'s ethical concerns. So, even as Krishna asserts that nothing is created and nothing is killed, Arjuna is acutely conscious of his existence. He cannot cast a cold eye on what he knows of moral law, freedom, reason and kinships.

The chariot stands on dark-green earth where momentous decisions have to be made. There is a change in the gestures and postures of Krishna and Arjuna. Krishna is no longer an angry chastiser; the tone of what he says is calmer, more philosophical. Arjuna looks more meditative, alert and watchful. Perhaps, he is wondering how metaphysical abstractions can explain the real and frightening world in which he is now located. At this moment, he is not aspiring to be the bravest soldier. He wonders how the Atma inhabits another being and whether reason can justify its annihilation.

---

17 Bimal K. Matilal, quoted by Alf Hiltebeitel, *Dharma: Its Early History in Law, Religion and Narrative* (Oxford: Oxford University Press), p. 22.

18 Hiltebeitel, *Rethinking the Mahabharata*, p. 47.

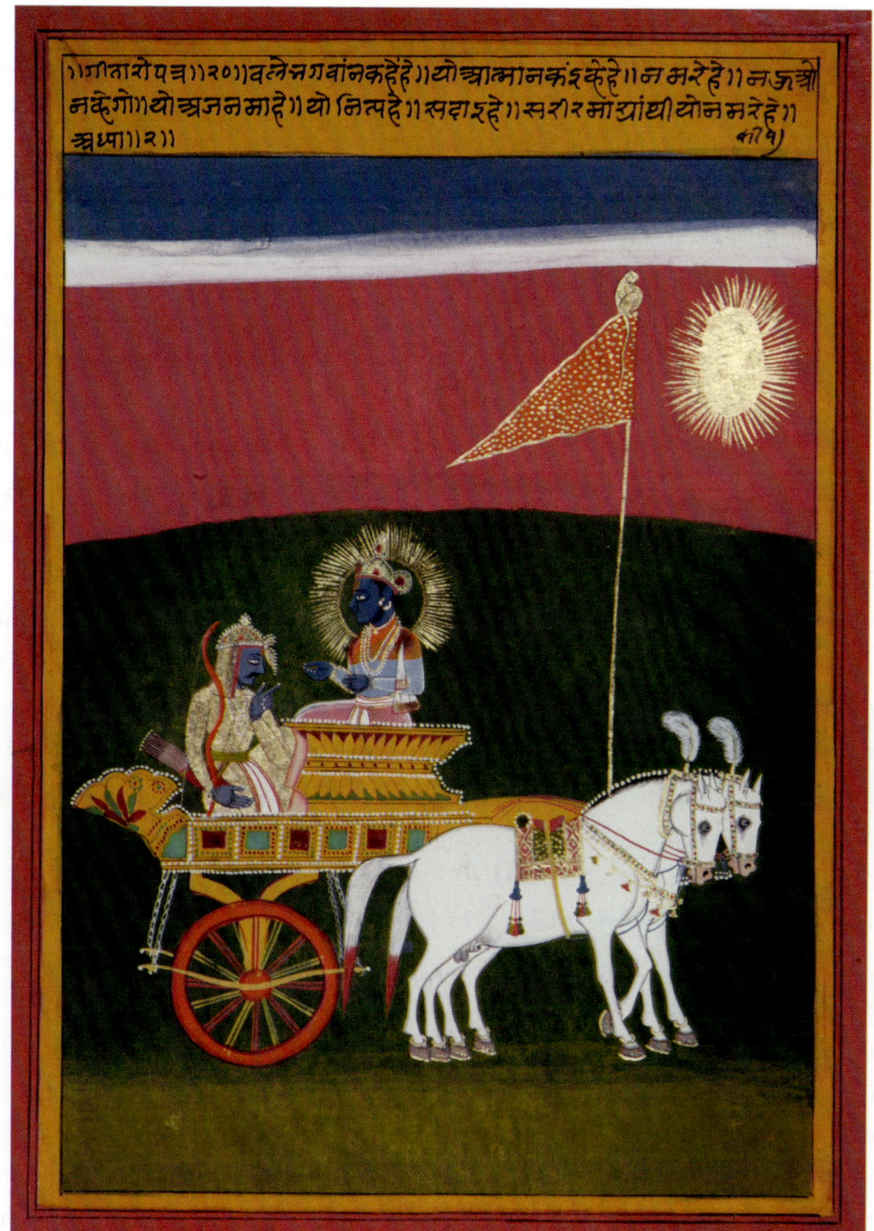

|20| श्री कृष्ण अर्जुन से आगे कहने लगे कि यह (आत्मा) न तो कुछ होता (जन्मता) है और न ही मरता है। एक बार वह जन्म कर फिर से होने वाला नहीं है, क्योंकि वह अजन्मा है, वह नित्य है, सदा रहने वाला है, शरीर के मारे जाने पर भी यह नहीं मरता है।

|20| Sri Krishna further says: The Atma is neither born nor does it die. It is uncreated and, hence, it is never reborn; it is everlasting, eternal; when the body dies, it does not die.

What is fascinating is that while the painter acknowledges the *Gita* as the discourse of Krishna, he confers on Arjuna's thinking self an equal grandeur. He suggests that, like the *Ramacharitra* or the *Buddhacharitra*, the *Gita* is an imaginative dharma-biography of Arjun—an *Arjunacharitra*.[19] It is a record of a valiant man searching for moral perfection in a world where it is seemingly impossible; of an honourable man who is not prepared to do anything 'to which the soul is called, to which the soul is not equal.'[20] While Yudhishthira is the son of Dharma, at this moment it is Arjuna who must save the idea of the good from despair; he must become, like Rama, a parable for righteousness. Rarely does the critical tradition acknowledge that Arjuna is aspiring to be a good man and, therefore, a good warrior.

The painting for verse 21, however, deepens the analogy between Arjuna and Rama even as it continues to grapple with the question: can no living being escape violence either as a slayer or as the slain? If not, will sin inevitably cling to the good and evil alike?

The idyllic scene in the painting leads one further into the enigmas of ethical discourse. A learned anchorite sits beside a pool of water sparkling with pink and white lotus flowers surrounded by green leaves. The flowers are the footprints of those who have walked by with the softest footfall; if one can track their journey, one can be a map-maker of the earth's moral ecology. A pair of beautifully coloured ducks paddle in the water. Two red-headed cranes stand quietly waiting to ensnare fish; rippling circles of water complete cycles of life from eternity to now. A man is calmly reading the *Ramayana*. The blue water seems enchanted in clear sunlight. It abides as a deep source for the land's renewal, just as the *Ramayana*'s dharma-song is the ancient resource of culture. Myth and time meet here, as does the acknowledgement of beauty. But the scene has other resonances too. It recalls the story of chance, cruelty and sorrow that is the impulse behind Valmiki's *Ramayana*. One morning, Valmiki watches the love-play of a pair of *kraunch* birds as he sits beside a river. Suddenly, a hunter shoots the male; the female wails. Shocked and moved by pity, the poet curses the hunter. The first couplet or *shloka* in the *Ramayana* is a song of *soka* (pain). A complex answer to Arjuna's questions is implicit in this story: sorrow is the measure of time and life; one cannot but feel compassion for those who suffer and feel remorse for having caused pain; yet, one should know that life shall be healed and beauty renewed.

---

19 See. Hiltebeitel, *Dharma*, for a discussion of dharma biographies.

20 Stanley Cavell, *Conditions Handsome and Unhandsome: The Constitution of Emersonian Perfectionism* (Chicago: University of Chicago Press, 1990), p. 18.

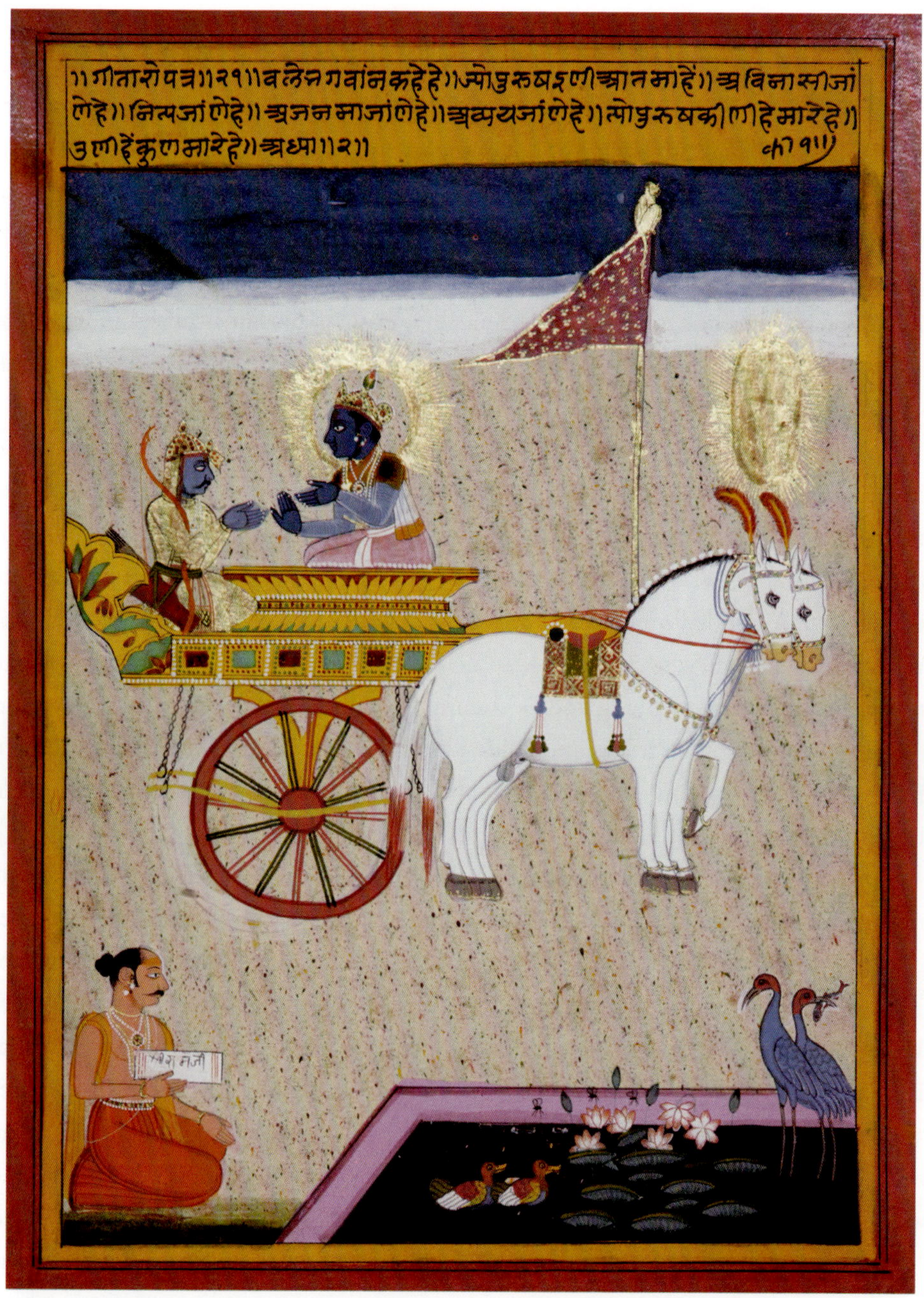

|21| श्री कृष्ण आगे कहने लगे कि हे अर्जुन! जो पुरुष इस आत्मा को अविनाशी जानता है, नित्य जानता है, अजन्मा जानता है, अव्यय जानता है वह कैसे किसी को मारता है और उसे कौन मार सकता है ?

|21| Sri Krishna continues: Hey Arjuna! Can the one who knows that the Atma is indestructible, eternal, uncreated and unchanging, ever kill or be killed?

Krishna adds in verses 22–23 that the Eternal Atma assumes an earthly form, discards it and then reappears in another shape. One could, therefore, say that the body has both a material shape and is phantasmal. Our moral education should prepare us to accept that it fades away and is reborn without despair.

The painting for verse 23 is mysterious and lyrical. The white horses, painted with mastery over line, detail and colour, are restless. Arjuna and Krishna are incandescent against the dark background; golden light radiates from their innermost selves. Krishna's right hand reaches out to Arjuna in friendship, even as his left is raised in a gesture of teaching and blessing. The Atma or Being, Krishna tells Arjuna, is transcendent; beyond the pain or sorrow of time.

What is fascinating is the collage of ordinary things which perish and yet reveal the numinous; which distinctly belong to the earth, society and time, but are part of the indestructible, transcendental Being. Violent death makes its appearance in this primal landscape—a sword, a bow, arrows in a quiver and a shield with gilded flowers lie in a heap. A slender wind-blown banana tree stands next to the images of war. The tree is beautiful, frail, yet tenacious. Like all natural things, it perishes and grows again in the eternal theatre of Being and Becoming. Watching this procession of images is a white cow with golden horns and golden bells. She is symbolic of Krishna's gentler, life-sustaining aspect, but she is also a protector of an 'ethical order' and a witness to its dissolution.[21]

The small upward-leaping flame is on the same vertical line as Hanuman, thereby creating a water–earth–sky axis and reinforcing the idea that a spiritual breeze fuses everything into an indestructible unity. We realise that the *numen* is not utterly separate from the sun we see, the wind we feel, the sword that wounds and the fire that burns the body to ash; it is beyond the sectarian and the particular; it is gentle and peaceful like the cow, wrathful like war. We also realise that the divine is impersonal, invisible, remote and indifferent. Krishna will tell Arjuna, once again: do what is right; be neither attached to the final result nor proud of having done a good deed. One is relieved to see how the colours of the morning, white and blue, break through the overwhelming darkness and dispel the despondency that the bleak images of violence and fire create. It is this complex interplay between innocence and violence, fertility and death, which makes the painting fascinating.

21 Zimmer, *Myths and Symbols in Indian Art and Civilization*, p. 14.

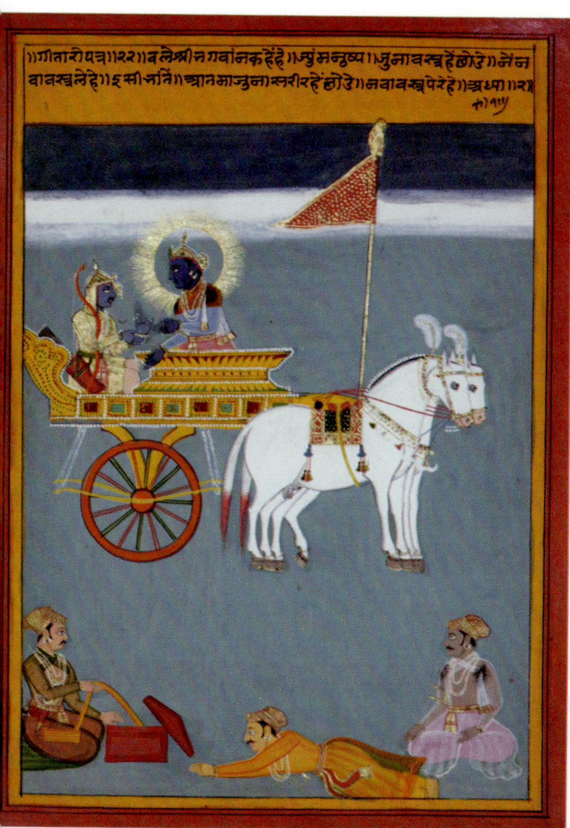

|22| श्री कृष्ण आगे कहने लगे कि जैसे मनुष्य पुराने वस्त्रों को छोड़कर दूसरे नए वस्त्र धारण करता है। इसी तरह आत्मा पुराने शरीर को छोड़कर नया शरीर धारण करती है।

|22| Sri Krishna continues: Just as one discards one's old clothes and puts on new clothes, so the Atma leaves the old body and wears a new body.

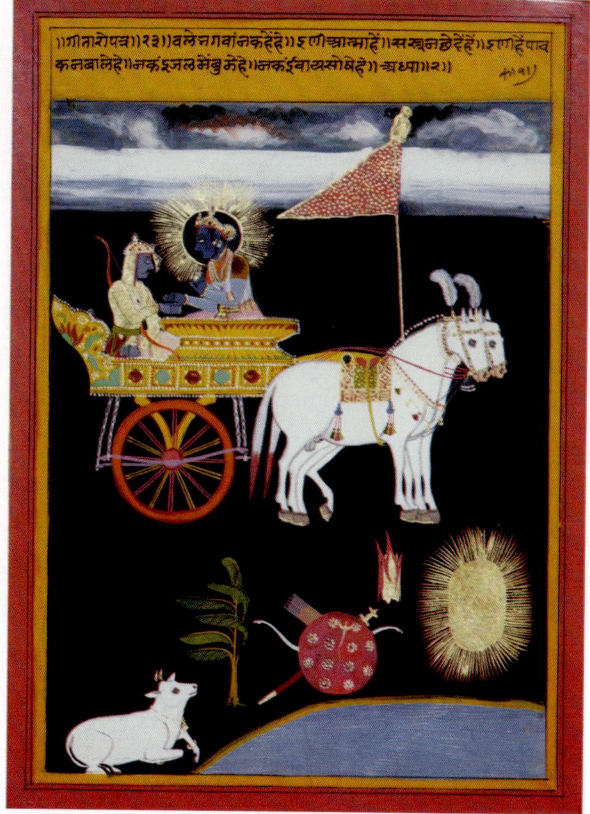

|23| श्री कष्ण अर्जुन से आगे कहने लगे कि इस आत्मा को कोई शस्त्र नहीं काट सकता, न इसे कोई आग जला सकती है, न इसको जल गला सकता है और न वायु इसे सुखा सकती है।

|23| Sri Krishna further says: No weapon can hurt this Atma; fire cannot burn it, water cannot dissolve it and wind cannot dry it.

Verse 24 continues to refine the notion that the Atma is immutable and omnipresent. The images in the painting are austere and abstract, ambiguous and frightening. Five golden suns glow on a red earth. Are they the five Pandavas, sons of celestial gods, who come down to earth? Or, should we read them as fires burning on a blood-soaked earth? Traditionally, the sun is associated both with origins and eternal recurrence. The *Mahabharata* chronicles how *satya yuga* (age of truth) declines into darkness and untruth. The first man, made of red earth, a sign of imagination and energy, belonged to a golden age. The red earth in the *Mahabharata* war is closer to hell where only fragments of slaughtered bodies shall be found. Reinforcing the idea of terror to come, a golden sword, embossed with diamonds, lies near the suns. A small fire burns at the base of the painting. The sword, tempered by fire, may signify steadfastness and courage, sacrifice and power. The dread inspiring scene is softened by a pool of blue water. It is as calm as the sky above. Gazing into its still surface, the self can become conscious of its place in the world of transient nature and eternal Being.

Verse 25 is a moment of transition in the philosophic tone of the chapter. With it, the first part of Krishna's exhortation is over. Arjuna's faith in words which define his ethical world has been shaken. Krishna has re-burnished those words to help him act with conviction—words like Atma, time, justice, virtue, self and death. Arjuna now has a moment to meditate on Krishna's definitions and acknowledge their truth. The artist invites us to think back on the images we have seen thus far, and asks if our understanding of the phenomenal and human world has changed. The painting offers no visual clues; there are no images of blood and fecundity, fire and clouds. A man sits with yogic poise, meditating upon a vast, brown, dry landscape where nothing moves or grows; earth on which battles can be fought. Motionless, impassive, he desires nothing, denies nothing, and so understands, paradoxically, both the emptiness of Being and its plenitude as barren fields can be ploughed and made fertile again.

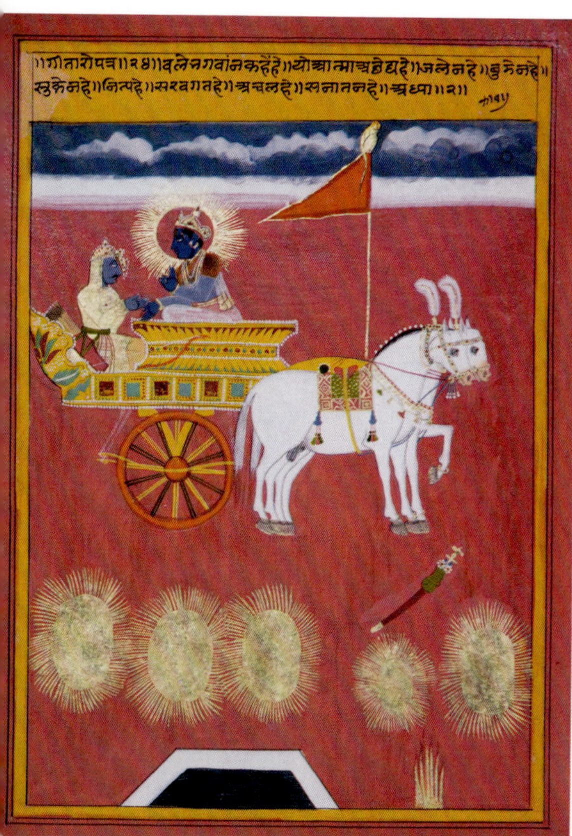

|24| श्री कृष्ण आगे कहने लगे कि यह आत्मा अभेद्य है। यह जलती नहीं, गलती नहीं, सूखती नहीं। आत्मा नित्य है। सर्वव्यापी है। अचल है और सनातन है।

|24| Sri Krishna continues: The Atma is incomprehensible; it cannot burn, dissolve, or die. It is omnipresent. It is immutable and eternal.

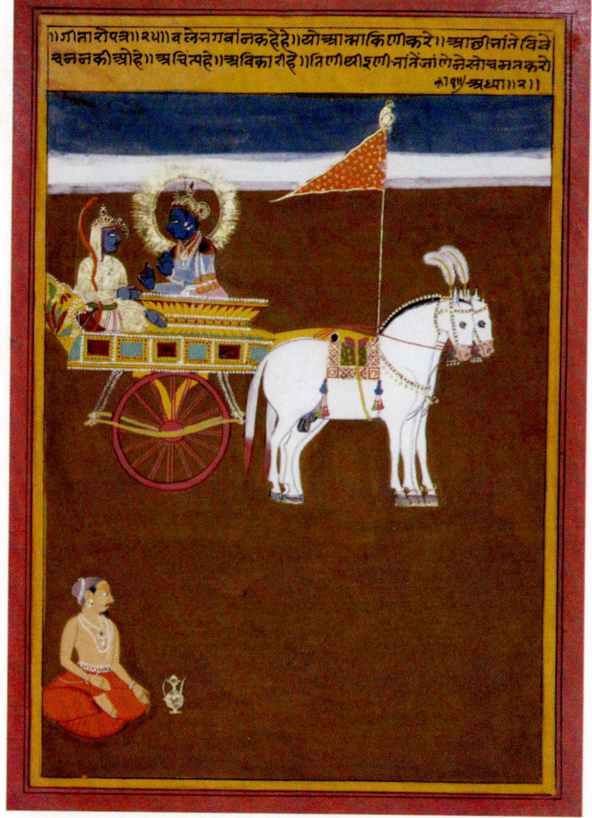

|25| श्री कृष्ण आगे कहने लगे कि हे अर्जुन! यह आत्मा अव्यक्त है, अचिंत्य है और यह विकाररहित कही गई है। इसको इस तरह से जानकर तू शोक मत कर।

|25| Sri Krishna further says: Hey Arjuna! They say that the Atma is invisible, unthinkable and immovable. Know it as such, and do not grieve.

The visual space in the painting for verse 26 is deliberately fragmented. It has no axis and no spatial regularity. Its colours lack harmony. Death, Krishna says, is the phantasmal aspect of the body. One should not mourn for that which does not exist. Making a sweeping gesture, Krishna seems to tell Arjuna: 'Look, down there, where death is! Is the dead man we see only a simulacrum? Death is both a casting away and a throwing out; an old rag for which it is pointless to weep.'

A white pavilion intrudes into the painting's frame. Its inner space is dark as if impervious to the discussion outside. The two figures on the white bed are cocooned in a red cloth. A golden yellow cushion encircles their heads like a nimbus. Self-enclosed and inward gazing, they are caught within the blindness of their own unknowing. They are the opposite of Arjuna, the seeker and suffering voyager, who wants to understand if the blood-tide about to drown his world has any meaning. Provocatively, in the corner of the pavilion, a spectral face sparkles within a halo of golden light. Is it a haunting memory of a dead past, a hallucination? Its presence excites no curiosity in the two sleepers. There can be no hope for those who, unlike Arjuna, are not moved by life's strangeness.

Faced with the knowledge of dissolution, Krishna in verse 27 urges poised acceptance. In the painting, the forefinger and thumb of his right hand are joined to form a circle, and three fingers spread behind in protective harmony. It is a gesture of completion and of nothingness, of perfection and of void. It signifies both the *bindu* (dot)—the essential emptiness into which life and death dissolve, and the *bija* (seed)—out of which all life is resurrected from the earth. Indeed, it is a multivalent gesture of a 'many-centredness of self', 'awakened self-knowledge' and 'generosity.'[22] In Indian classical dance, it is the sign of a peacock dancing in peace; unselfconsciously and gracefully; its tail-feathers spread like falling rain scattering beauty around. Krishna, in folklore, with a peacock's feather in his hair, is a dancer, an artist and a great yogi.

However, the pictorial space is disorienting and disconcerting. It is fragmented by two asymmetric, haphazardly placed buildings with white columns and roofs. Architecturally, the buildings are modelled after two conflicting cultural sources—Mewar and Moghul. Their colours cause dissonance. In one enclosure, a mother and child are wrapped in their own unseeing selfhood; cut off from a world of questions and doubts, passion and suffering. The other building is also closed in upon itself. A man is teaching a boy who seems distracted. The teacher is imitating Krishna's gesture of a

22 Ramchandra Gandhi, *Svaraj: A Journey with Tyeb Mehta's 'Shatiniketan Triptych'* (New Delhi: Vadehra Art Gallery, 2002), pp. 41–49.

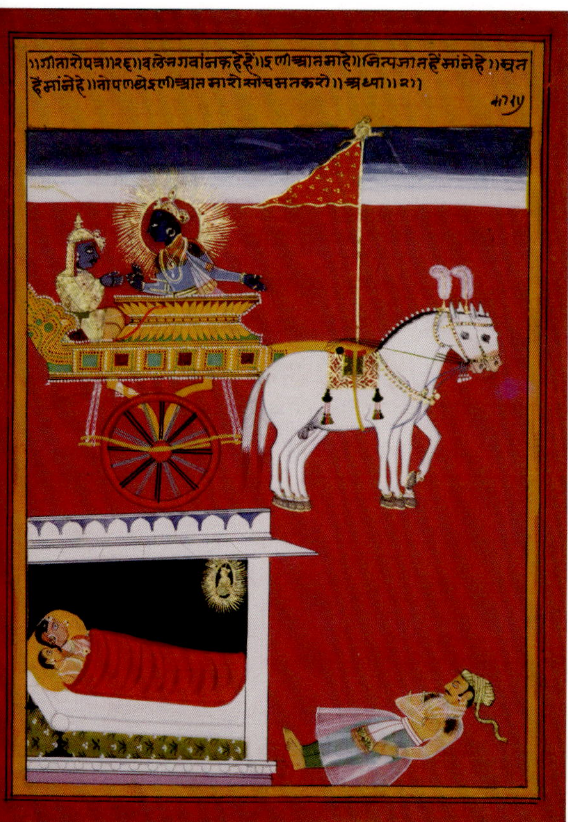

|26| श्री कृष्ण आगे कहने लगे कि हे अर्जुन! यदि तू इस आत्मा को हमेशा जन्मने वाली मानता है और सदा मरने वाली मानता है। तब भी तुझे इस आत्मा की फिक्र नहीं करनी चाहिए।

|26| Sri Krishna continues: Hey Arjuna! You may think that this the Atma is born again and again; and dies again and again. Even then you should not grieve for it.

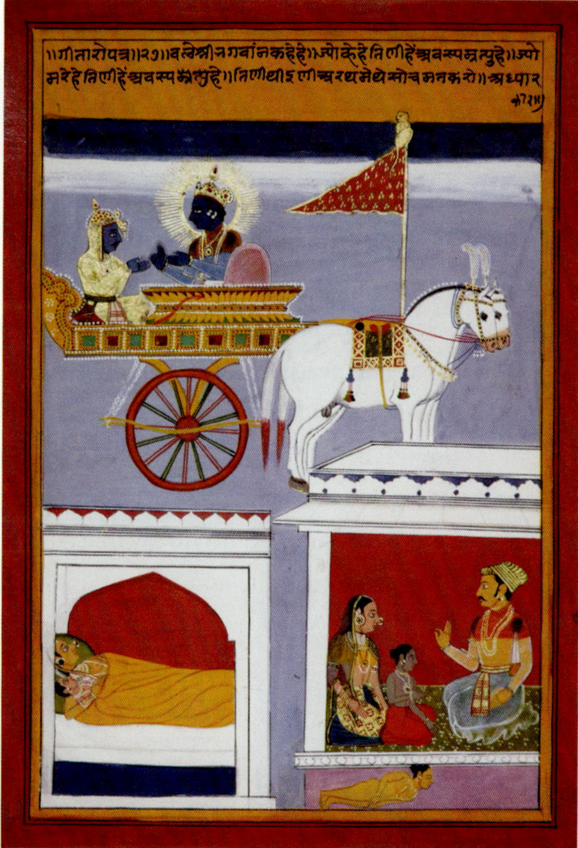

|27| श्री कृष्ण आगे कहते हैं कि प्रत्येक जन्मने वाले का मरना निश्चित है और प्रत्येक मरने वाले का जन्म निश्चित है। इस बिना उपाय वाले विषय में शोक करना उचित नहीं है।

|27| Sri Krishna further says: Everything that is born shall certainly die; and everything that dies, shall certainly be born again. It is not right to grieve for the inevitable.

peacock dancing. But unlike Krishna, he is not a fluid weaver of words who can hold a child's attention. He looks more like a stern teacher who demands unquestioning obedience. How can a law-giver be the singing master of the soul? Hanuman watching the open sky is a reminder that knowledge making is an endless play of ideas. Human beings, before they can be makers of structures, must have the freedom to play with sounds, colours or words. The boy only sees bounded walls—or binding knowledge. But, who is the naked man burrowing under the ground of the house of instruction? Is he is the negation of the ornately dressed teacher above; a subversive force against repressive orthodoxy?

The idea that a mysterious life-force animates everything informs the charming and enigmatic painting which follows for verse 28. Arjuna now sits with his hand raised in *mayur mudra* indicating that he has understood what Krishna means: man is sacred and empty, eternal and deathward bound. A hermit preaches to a group of animals. These images from fables may seem like an intrusion. They have drifted in, quite legitimately, from the wisdom tales in the *Mahabharata* where animals debate with human beings about the ethics of violence and non-violence, faith and betrayal. Indeed, the epic begins with a snake sacrifice and ends with a horse sacrifice. Animals protest the grievous violations. Allah Baksh, perhaps, knew the *Hitopadesha*, the *Panchatantra* and the *Jatakas*. Folk imagination, generally non-sectarian, is receptive to other voices and untroubled when the uncanny breaks through orthodoxy to suggest other ways of thinking about life.

The anchorite, with flowing white hair, sits cross-legged on tiger skin directly below Arjuna. A diaphanous cloth is draped around his shoulder. Is this a scene of ashramite peace from some remembered past? Or, is it a dream of the peace to come, however unattainable it may seem, after an annihilatory war? If Arjuna is a questioner, the teacher is ready to pass on what he has learnt. In the tradition of great seers, his sermon to the animals breaks through our narrow and limited notion of a human-centric, species-identity, to say that Atma inhabits all living creatures. The scene is a fine interpretation of the non-violent implications of Krishna's sermon.

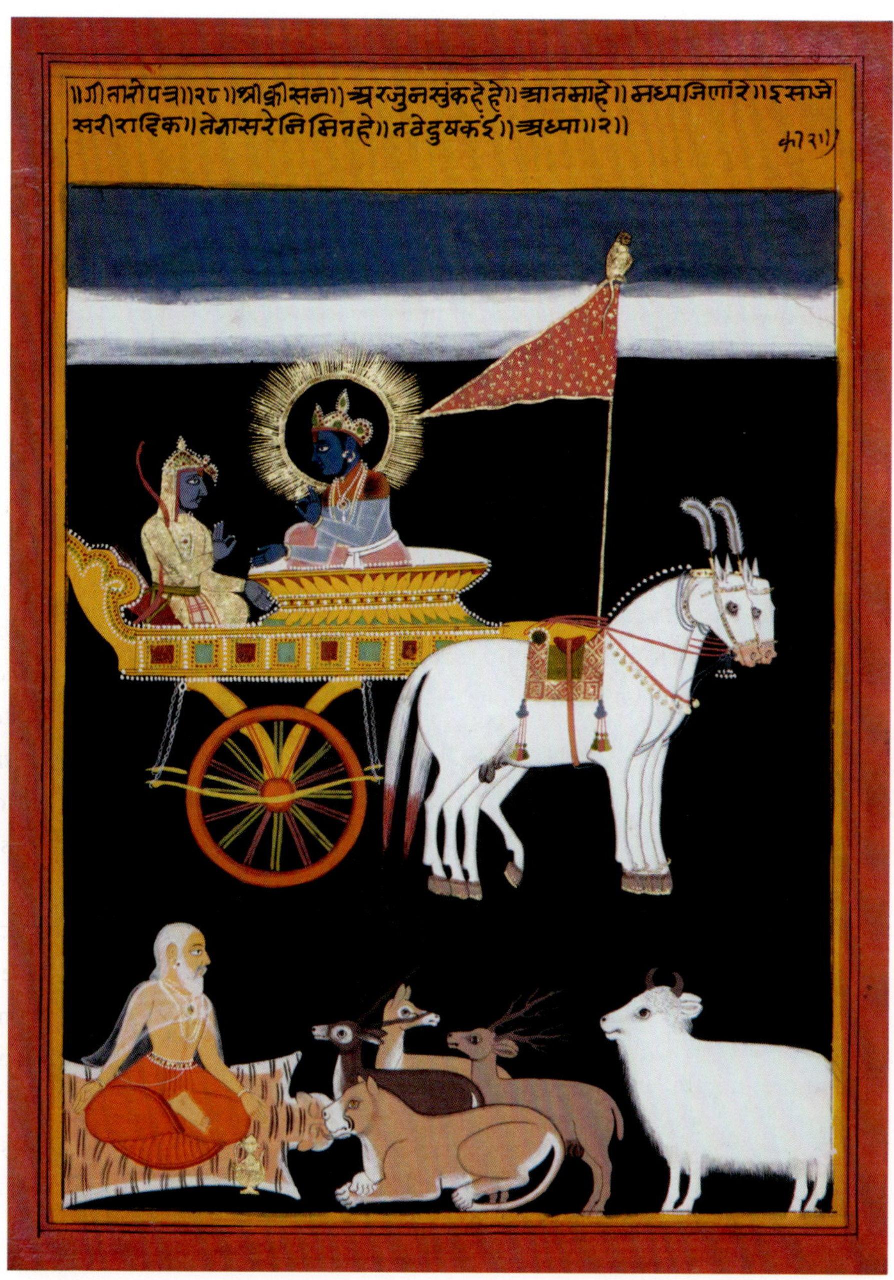

|28| श्री कृष्ण अर्जुन से कहते हैं कि समस्त प्राणी जन्म से पहले अप्रकट थे और मृत्यु के बाद भी अप्रकट हो जाएँगे। केवल मध्य में ही प्रकट होते हैं इसलिए इसमें अप्रकट का क्या शोक करना?

|28| Sri Krishna says to Arjuna: All beings are invisible before birth and shall be invisible after death. They are visible only in the intervening period. So why grieve for those who are invisible?

In verse 29 Krishna clarifies that since the Atma is not external to the self, to look for it with one's senses is to be distracted by the inessential, the superfluous and the transient. That is also why Arjuna should neither grieve over the death of the physical body nor choose to live like an ascetic in search of inner peace. All a good man can hope to do in atrocious times is to act ethically in defence of justice, pity and love. If that requires war, so be it. In the painting for verse 29, while Arjuna and Krishna form a coherent visual unit, the three seekers of the sacred lack unity and a centre. One man worships the sun; the other reads the *Ramayana* and the third listens to the sacred word. For them, the Atma is either visible as an idol, revealed by an oracle, or available in the other holy texts. Searching for the Atma outside the self makes them prisoners of sectarian creeds. Painted against a soft blue-green colour, Allah Baksh's critique of the three worshippers is gentle.

The ink-black background of the painting for verse 33 suggests that Arjuna is still lost in uncertainty. Krishna links war with honour and not with dharma; to lose honour, he says, is sin. The *Jnaneshwari* adds with an uncharacteristic harshness: If Arjuna shuns this war, his reputation will be disfigured like a corpse thrown on wasteland whose flesh and bones have been torn by vultures.[23] In the painting, Arjuna's hands are folded in supplication. He is more honourable, more morally attractive than the soldiers confronting each other. They have the glamour of martial pride, but they lack the human dignity which Arjuna's anguish bestows on him. The symbolism of the blood-red disc in the space between the warriors is not clear. Does it signify the courage and honour of a warrior?

---

23 *Jnaneshwari,* volume 1, translated by V. G. Pradhan (London: George Allen and Unwin, 1967), p. 64. Hereafter, referred to as *Jnaneshwari* in the text.

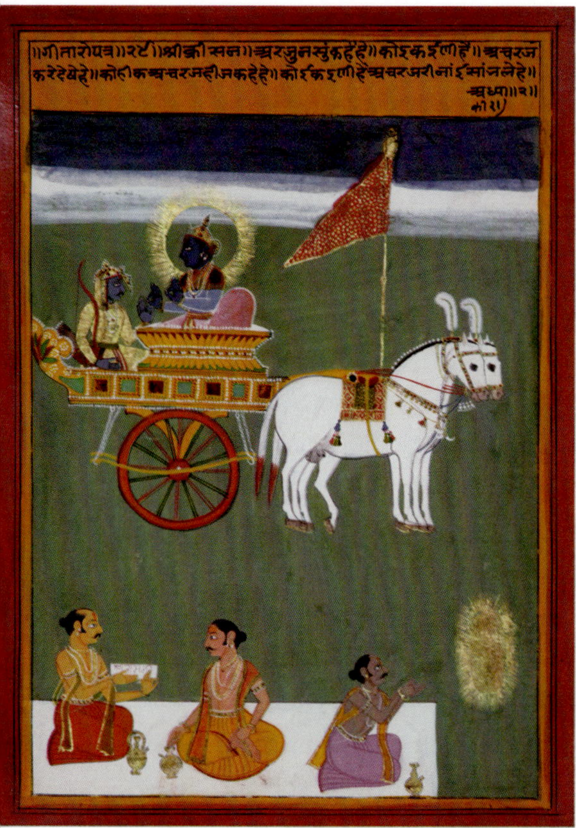

|29| श्री कृष्ण अर्जुन से कह रहे हैं कि कोई प्राणी इस आत्मा को आश्चर्य की भाँति देखता है तो कोई इसे आश्चर्य की तरह ही कहता है और कोई इसे आश्चर्य की तरह सुनता है।

|29| Sri Krishna says to Arjuna: There are some who look upon the Atma in wonder, some who speak about it in wonder and some who hear about it in wonder.

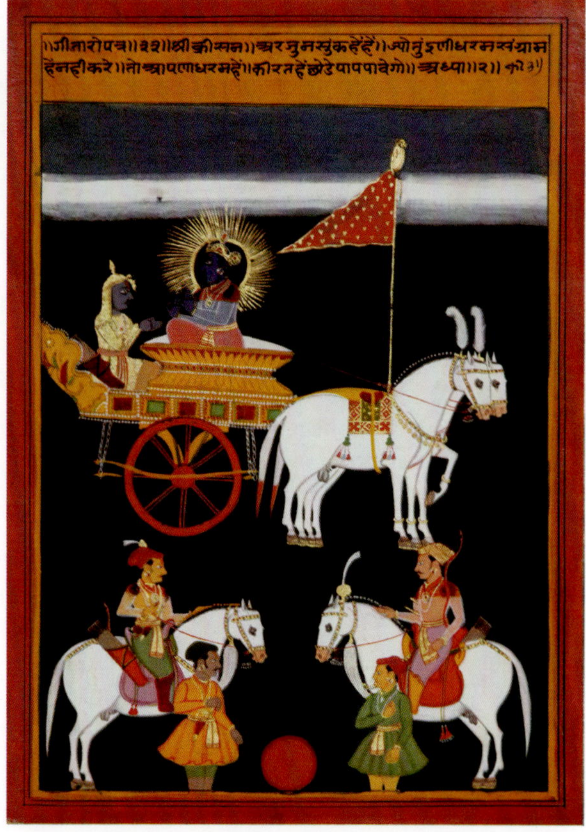

|33| श्री कृष्ण आगे कह रहे हैं कि हे अर्जुन! यदि तू यह धर्म युद्ध नहीं करेगा तो अपना धर्म और अपनी कीर्ति खोकर पाप का भागी बनेगा।

|33| Sri Krishna further says: Hey Arjuna! If you do not fight this righteous war, you will lose your dharma and honour; you will carry the burden of sin.

Indeed, disgrace is the subject of verses 34 to 36. Krishna continues to tell Arjuna that if he chooses not to fight, he would be condemned as a coward. Arjuna looks startled when he hears the word 'disgrace.' One wonders, if Krishna has really forgotten that Arjuna is the very archetype of courage? Further, has the thrust of the *Gita*, thus far, not been that men should be detached and act according to their own conscience, unconcerned with praise or blame? The accompanying paintings show men who are evidently debating the issues raised.

The three debaters in the painting for verse 36 do not seem to deride Arjuna for his ethical doubts about how he should act. The *mayur mudra* of the two men indicates that they are engaged in calm conversation. They show no sign of anger or conspiratorial excitement. Living far from the field of war, their world is not fraught with strife. The 'pitch' of the painting, which is simple, precise and eloquent, is radically different from the interpretation of someone like Sri Aurobindo whose commentary is ungenerous and confrontational. Aurobindo shows no empathy for the compassion that has moved Arjuna to risk his reputation and kingdom. For him, the *Mahabharata* is an allegory of life defined by a perpetual clash of interests. To be faint-hearted and perplexed in a violent world, he thinks, is both folly and sin.[24] His attack is also on the 'heresy' of Buddhism, Christianity and the preachers of ahimsa.[25] Their ideals, he says, seek to overthrow Kshatriya dharma and replace it with the 'dangerous' and impractical doctrine of 'quiescence' and 'self-abnegation.'[26] Unlike Aurobindo, the painter does not forget that the *Gita* is part of a narrative where war becomes necessary *after the failure of all non-violent negotiations.* His paintings suggest that ordinary life on earth is not bloody in tooth and claw; a peaceful dialogue can resolve life's difficulties.

---

24 Sanjay Palshikar, *Evil and the Philosophy of Retribution: Modern Commentaries on the Bhagavad Gita* (New Delhi: Routledge, 2014), p. 92.

25 Sri Aurobindo, *On the Mahabharata* (Pondicherry: Sri Aurobindo Ashram, 1991), p. 68.

26 Sri Aurobindo, pp. 68–75.

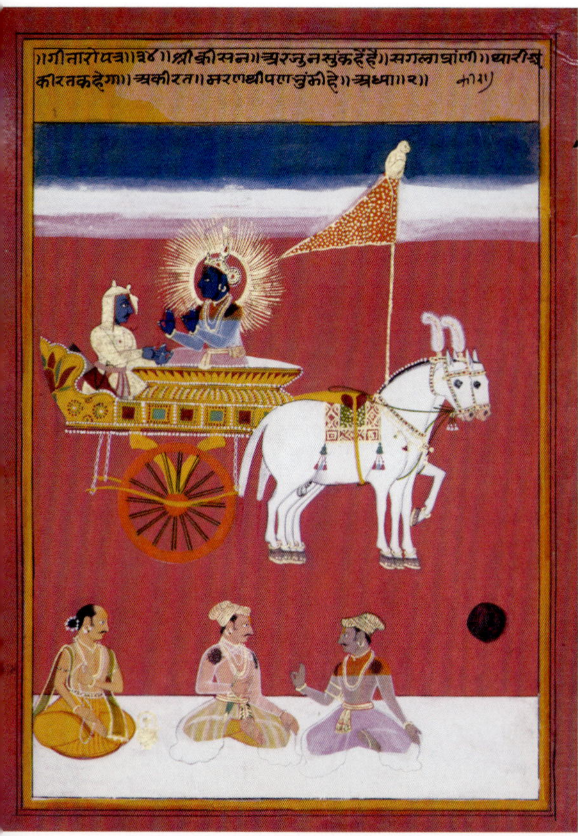

|34| श्री कृष्ण आगे कहने लगे कि हे अर्जुन! तब सारे लोग हमेशा तेरी अपकीर्ति को कहेंगे। सम्माननीय व्यक्ति के लिए अपकीर्ति मृत्यु से भी बढ़ कर होती है।

|34| Sri Krishna further says: Hey Arjuna! Everyone will talk about your disgrace. For an honourable man disgrace is worse than death.

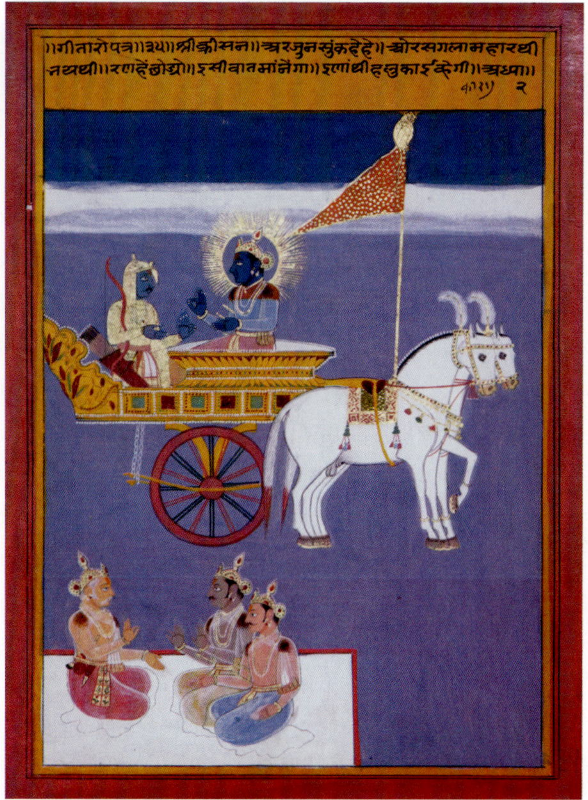

|35| श्री कृष्ण अर्जुन से आगे कहने लगे कि सारे महारथी समझेंगे कि तू डर के कारण युद्ध से हट गया है। जो लोग तेरा आदर करते थे वे भी तुझको तुच्छ समझेंगे।

|35| Sri Krishna further says to Arjuna: All the great warriors will think that you refused to fight because you are a coward. Those who honour you will scorn you.

Arjuna has everything to gain, says Krishna, if he follows his Kshatriya dharma and confronts evil: if he dies, he goes to heaven, and if he wins, he gains an earthly kingdom (verse 37). He should, therefore, stand up and fight. In the painting, the temptation of heaven is indicated by the return of the yellow bird-shaped boat with a blue-bodied holy man in an ochre robe. He is a peaceful witness to the threat of war. Vertically below, a regal figure with a bejewelled crown sits on a golden throne. He carries no emblems of violent power. He is ink-blue in colour, wears large golden earrings, and has vermillion marks on his forehead. Are the heavenly boatman and the peaceful king images of the two alternatives, a place in heaven and an earthly kingdom? The artist has not yet abandoned the third alternative which haunts Arjuna: renunciation of earthly concerns which may also lead to heaven. Sitting on bare earth, and opposite the king, is a poised and elegant yogi. He is also blue-bodied. The distance between Krishna and the two men is almost the same, thereby giving them equal visual importance. This is fascinating since critical commentary often excludes the possibility of renunciation. The artist, however, imagines yet another fate for Arjuna. A sky-blue soldier, in golden armour, lies dead on the ground. His bow has fallen, his pearl necklace is scattered. Soldiers walk past him without pity or remorse. Indeed, one soldier moves threateningly towards the king. The logic of war is always indiscriminate and inconclusive. Are we being persuaded to ask: is the soldier's death, however valiant, not utterly futile? What is the worth of heaven or the throne to the one whose life is so carelessly and ruthlessly thrown away? Does the *Mahabharata* not ask these questions? Has the Buddhist or Jain rejection of violence intruded into this visual commentary?

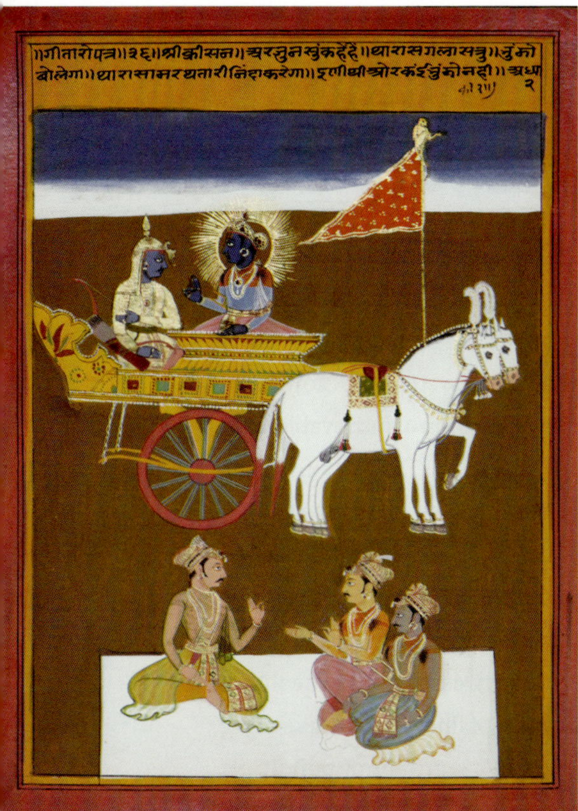

|36| श्री कृष्ण अर्जुन से कह रहे हैं कि तब तेरे सारे शत्रु तेरे सामर्थ्य की निंदा करते हुए कटु वचन कहेंगे। इससे अधिक दुखदायी और क्या होगा?

|36| Sri Krishna says to Arjuna: Your enemies will call you a coward and mock you. What can be more painful than that?

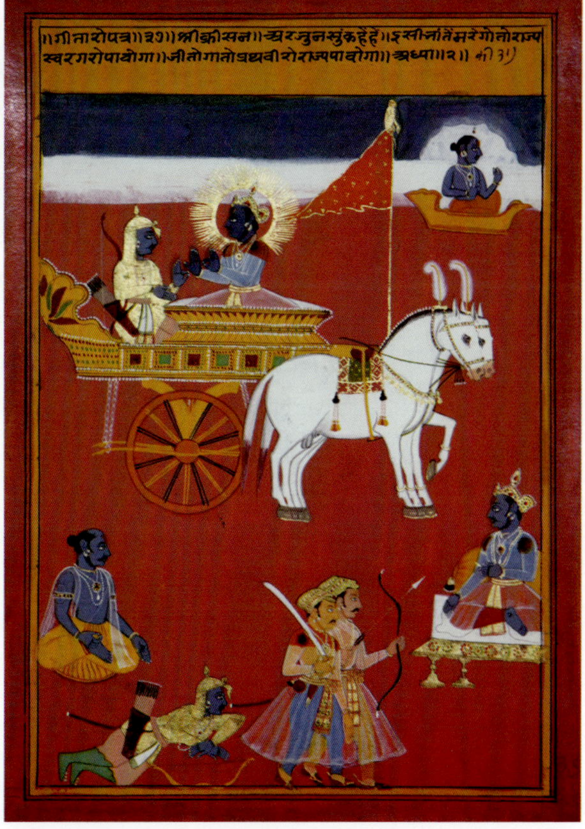

|37| श्री कृष्ण आगे कह रहे हैं, हे अर्जुन! यदि तू युद्ध में मारा गया तो स्वर्ग का राज्य पाएगा और युद्ध में विजय प्राप्त हुई तो धरती का राज्य भोगेगा। (इसलिए हे कुंती पुत्र! युद्ध के लिए निश्चय करके खड़ा हो जा)।

|37| Sri Krishna says: Hey Arjuna! If you are killed in battle, you will attain the kingdom of heaven and if you win the war you will enjoy the kingdom of earth. That is why: Hey Kunti's son! Stand up and fight.

In verses 39–44, Krishna again takes upon himself the role of a philosophic teacher. One should assume that Arjuna is intellectually well-trained. Krishna only wants him to recall what he already knows. In its simplest form, the philosophic system of knowledge, called samkhya, divides the world into *purusha* (immovable Self; consciousness) and *prakriti* (not-Self, matter). The two combine in infinite and subtle ways. *Prakriti* has three innate properties or *gunas*: *tamas* (darkness, ignorance, inertia), *rajas* (energy, activity, attachment, change) and *sattva* (truth, good, harmony, compassion, joy). Krishna will elaborate upon them later. Intelligence (*buddhi*) helps a seeker of wisdom to discriminate between the three qualities, transcend the duality, and achieve the calm of liberation by affirming the divine. In the paintings for verses 39 to 43, groups of pundits sit reciting the scriptures. In the painting for verse 43, a pool of water glows with lotus flowers. The scene is decorative and charming. A man is taking a ritual bath; a stream of water pours out from his cupped hands. A woman with pearl earrings and golden bracelets watches the morning's peace. This daily activity, however, has no symbolic value; no indication of an intellectual quest. It is, as Krishna says, merely a passing show and empty of merit. A life of quiet acceptance is not enough to overcome the world's suffering (Desai 157). Arjuna, in contrast, must repair a damaged world; be a karma yogi; act ethically and so transform the world's *tamasic* state into a *sattvic* one.

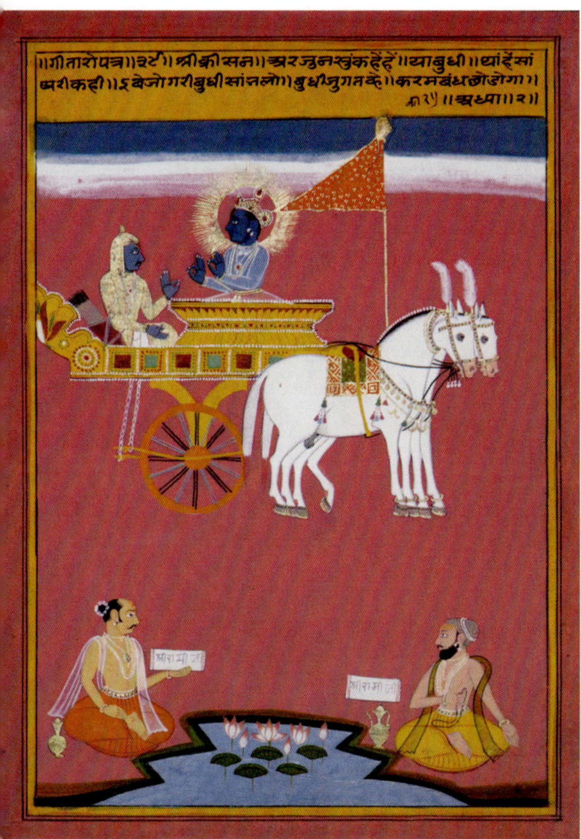

|39| श्री कृष्ण अर्जुन से कहने लगे कि यह मैंने तुझको सांख्य का ज्ञान बताया है। अब तू योग के विषय में सुन। इस बुद्धि से युक्त होकर तू कर्मबंधनों को दूर फेंक देगा।

|39| Sri Krishna says to Arjuna: I have given you the wisdom of samkhya. Now let me tell you about yoga. Once you understand it, you shall cast aside your bondage to karma.

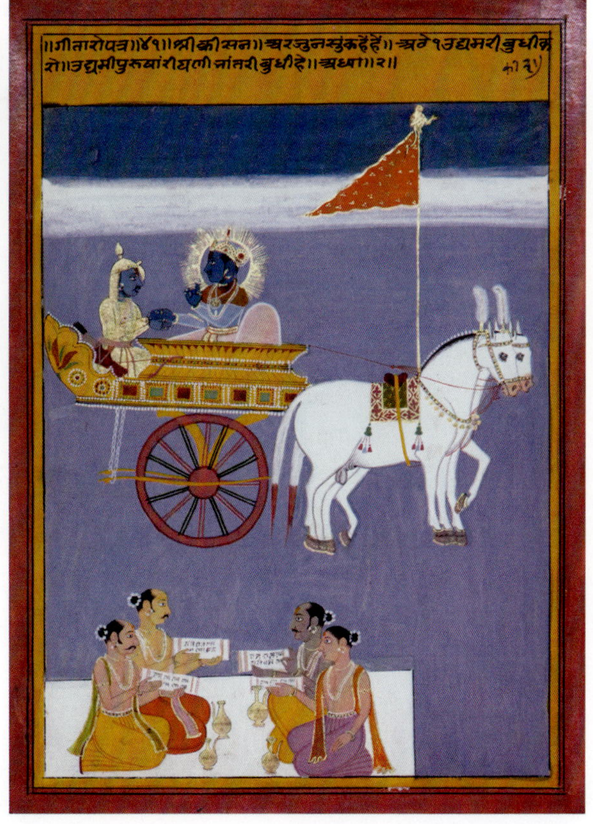

|41| श्री कृष्ण कहने लगे हे अर्जुन! इस कर्मयोग में निश्चयात्मिका बुद्धि एक ही होती है किन्तु अस्थिर चित्त वालों की बुद्धियाँ अनेक शाखाओं में बिखरी हुई होती हैं।

|41| Sri Krishna says: Arjuna! In karma yoga, the intellect is focused on one thing; but the irresolute mind strays down many paths.

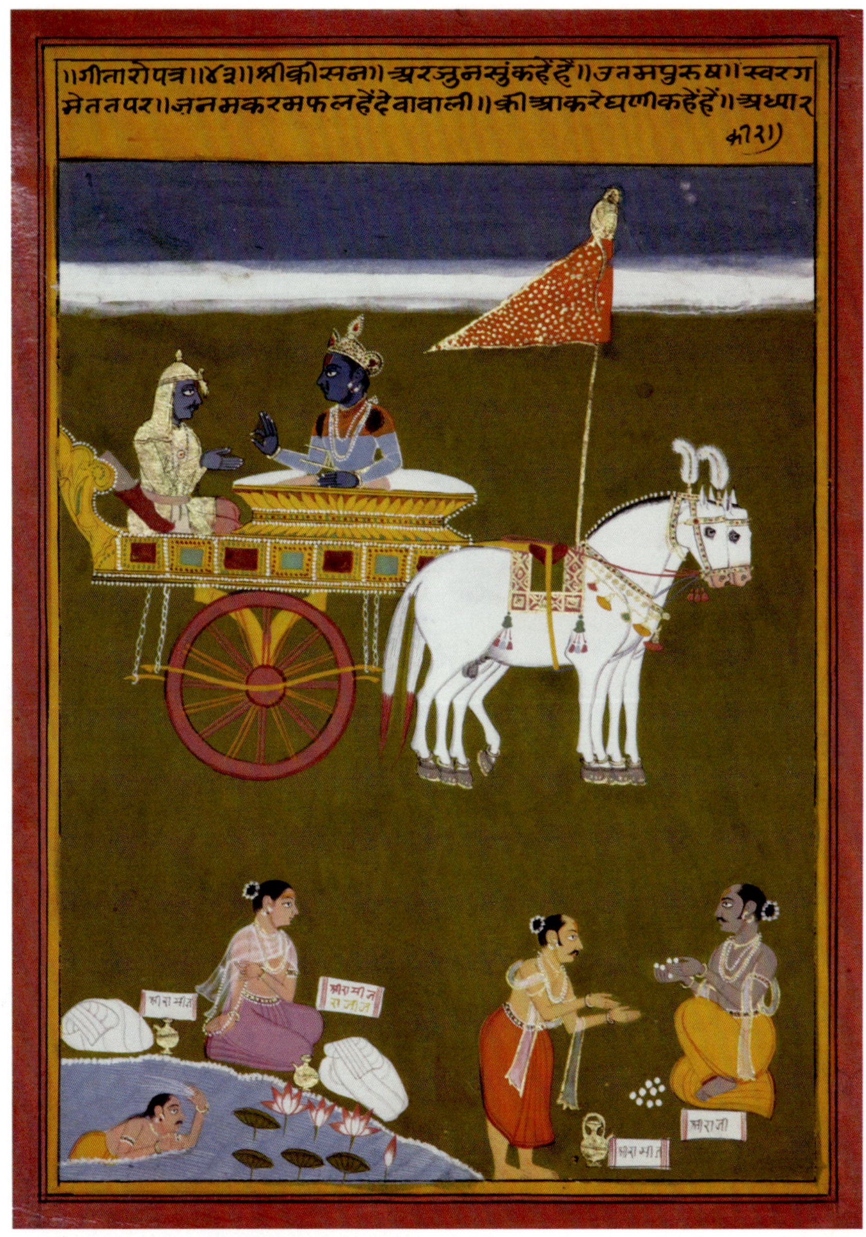

|43| श्री कृष्ण अर्जुन से आगे कहने लगे कि भोगों में तत्पर व्यक्ति जिस वाणी का प्रयोग करते हैं वह स्वर्ग को ही परम प्राप्य मानती है। जन्म रूप कर्मफल को देने वाली होती है, भोग और ऐश्वर्य के लिए बहुत-सी क्रियाओं का बखान करने वाली होती है।

|43| Sri Krishna further says to Arjuna that those who satisfy only their personal desire create their own private heaven. They perform complex rites to gain power and fulfil their selfish ambitions. Such people cannot escape the cycle of rebirth.

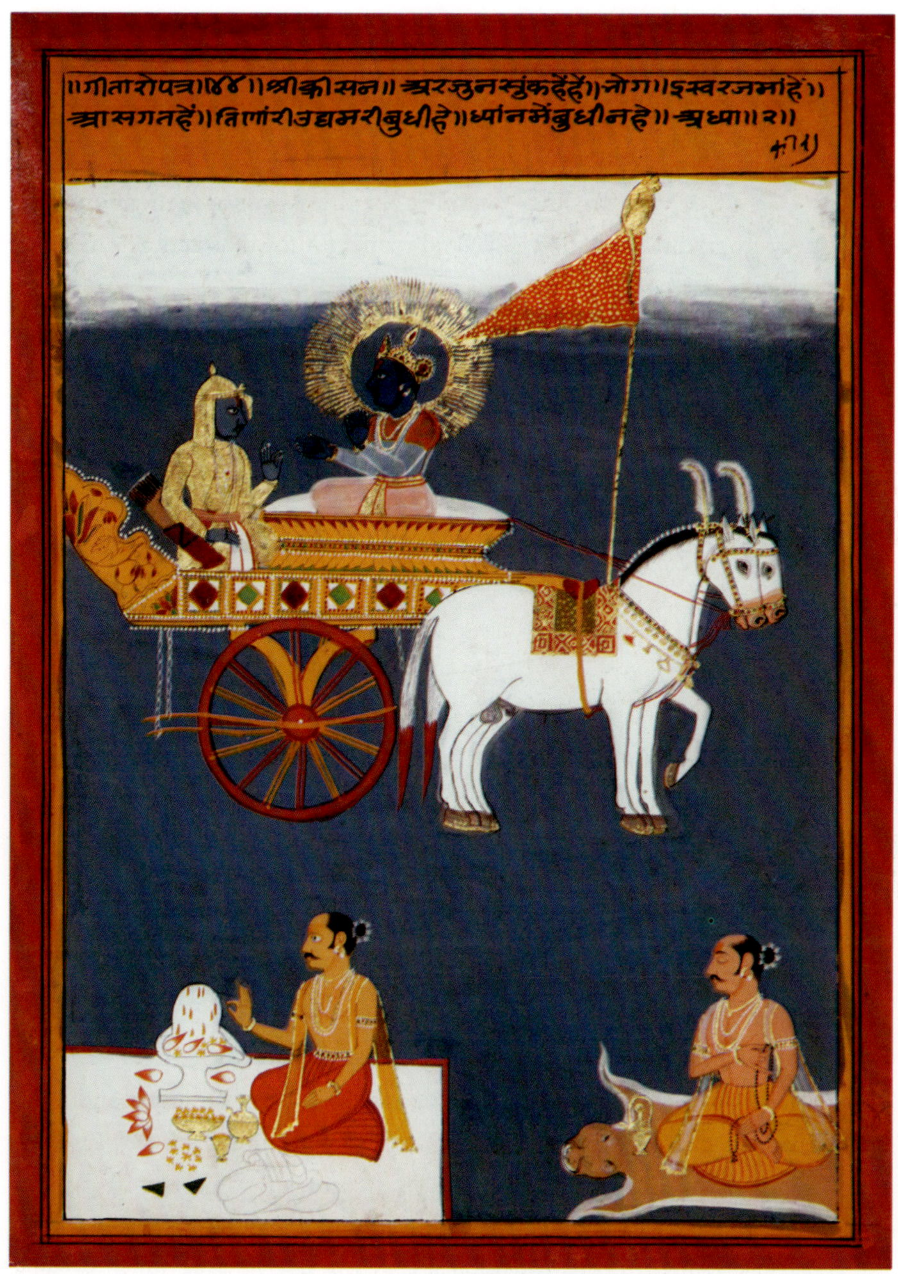

|44| श्री कृष्ण कहने लगे कि हे अर्जुन! भोग और ऐश्वर्य में आसक्त तथा इस वाणी से जिनका चित्त हर लिया गया है, उनमें समाधि के लिए निश्चयात्मिका बुद्धि नहीं होती है।

|44| Sri Krishna says: Hey Arjuna! Those who are seduced by pleasure and power, and those who are satisfied by the words of the Vedas, do not have the intelligence for yogic concentration.

In verse 46, Krishna continues to draw Arjuna's attention away from inherited knowledge and redirect it towards action. The *Jnaneshwari*'s comment on these verses is pertinent:

> Though in the Vedas much is said, and various distinctions are suggested, still we should accept that which is for our own good.
>
> As when the sun is risen, all paths become visible, yet, tell me, is it possible to travel by all of them?...
>
> So do wise men examine the meaning of the Vedas and accept only what they desire and what has to do with the Eternal. (1:61)

The meaning of the Vedas, Krishna tells Arjuna, is so fluid, like water in a pond, that a clever theologian can draw any meaning. The visual translation of the verse is literal. A priest sits in front of four palm-leaf manuscripts of the *Ramayana*. His mind is as full of the scriptures as the pond is overflowing with water. He can draw from them any interpretation to serve his immediate purpose. He speaks with a show of piety to a humble seeker sitting before him with folded hands. There is a fine contrast between the two: the priest is opulently dressed while the man's clothes are simple and unadorned. The distance between them, determined by power, wealth and class is unbridgeable. It is radically different from the intimacy between Krishna and Arjuna. In contrast, Krishna teaches Arjuna to trust his inner voice. The self, he says, must be its own watchman.

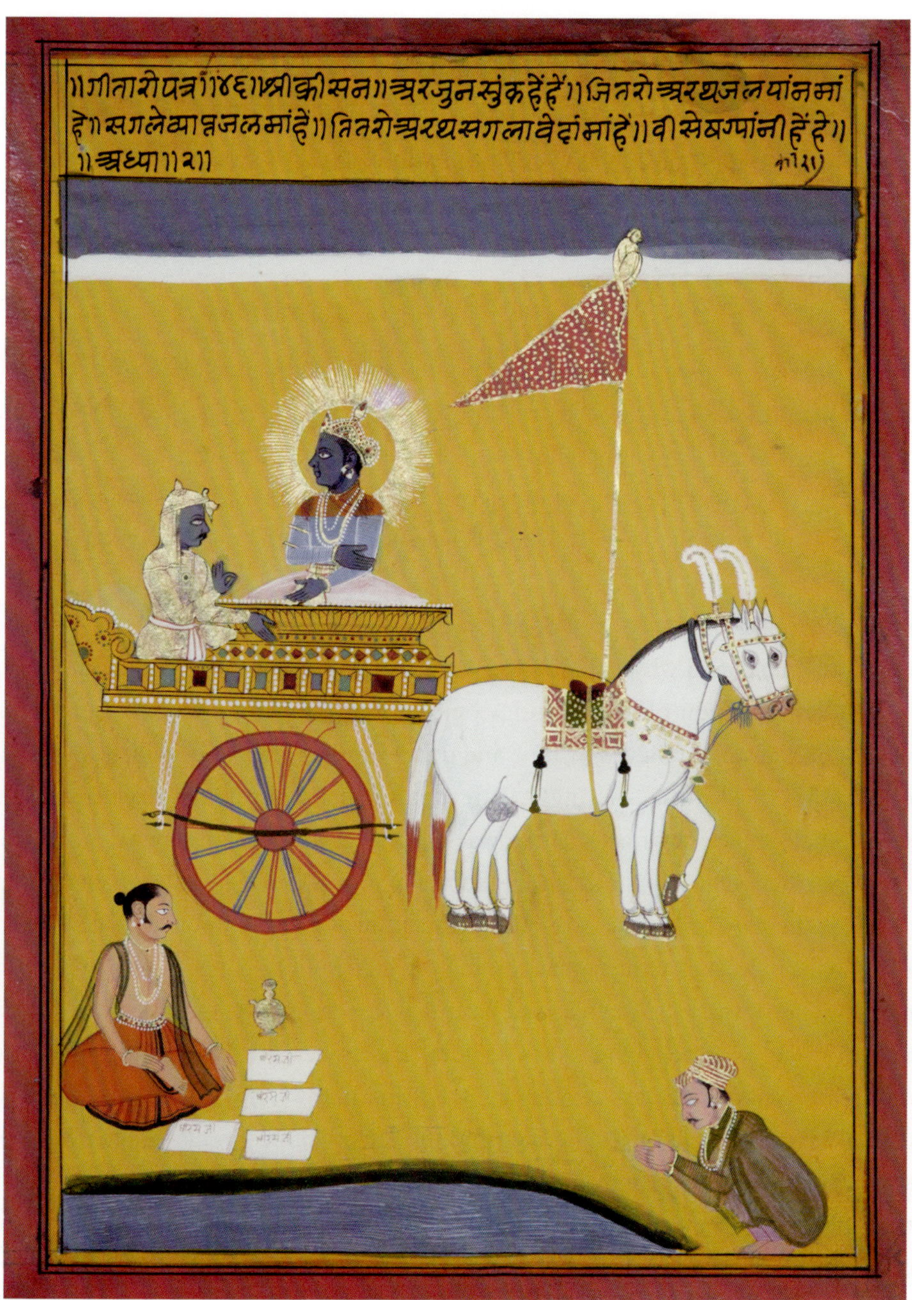

|46| श्री कृष्ण अर्जुन से कहने लगे कि जैसे जब चारों ओर जल ही जल हो तब एक जलाशय का कोई महत्व नहीं रह जाता है, वैसे ही ब्रह्मज्ञानी का वेदों में प्रयोजन नहीं रह जाता है।

|46| Sri Krishna says: Just as there is no use of a pond if water flows out of it from all sides, the wise have no need for the Vedas.

Verse 47 is central to the *Gita*. Krishna tells Arjuna that dharma (ethical action) is unconcerned about its final outcome. Human beings have a right to action, but not to its fruit (*phala*). Otherwise what we do is guided by a 'selfish purpose' (Desai 159). Mahatma Gandhi explains this concept with a morally charged passage from Tolstoy's *What I Believe*:

> The belief in a remuneration of work...rests on the assumption that we have a claim to something; but man has no rights and can have none. He is ever in debt for the welfare given him and therefore can make no demands on any one...This is the necessary condition of both service and *the true welfare of his life* (Desai 158–59).

Those who long only for the fruit of action either fail to act or act badly. It is, however, difficult to understand why Arjuna should fight if it is not to regain a kingdom.

The sophistication of the painting complements the verse's importance. At first, the dark background, relieved by blue and ochre bands, seems to dominate. Soon one notices how crowded the painting is with rituals which Krishna has rejected because they are not disinterested acts. Three priests, dressed in gold, perform a traditional Vedic fire-ritual. One supplicant feeds the fire in a stone brazier with clarified butter, while the other two make sacrificial offerings of grain and seeds. Golden vessels near the fire catch the reflection of the red flames. Indeed, gold (and its sacred equivalents, ochre and vermillion) weaves a fine filigreed harmony through all the figures and objects in the dark space. It is a delight to notice its inflections in nearly every image—borders of white scarves, hoofs, saddles, armour, bells, Krishna's crown and halo, flag, fire, vessels, etc. Gold visually emphasises the fact that the sacred shines in all things if only we learn to see carefully. The unblemished whiteness and innocence of the cow echoes the beauty, the stillness and the calm unselfishness of the horses. How much of their grace and goodwill do the animals in these paintings offer to human beings! They fulfil their life's tasks without asking for rewards. The painting's uncanny wit and intelligence is enhanced by the presence of a blue-bodied anchorite meditating in an ochre-coloured rock-cave in the sky. He sits next to Hanuman in the visual space.

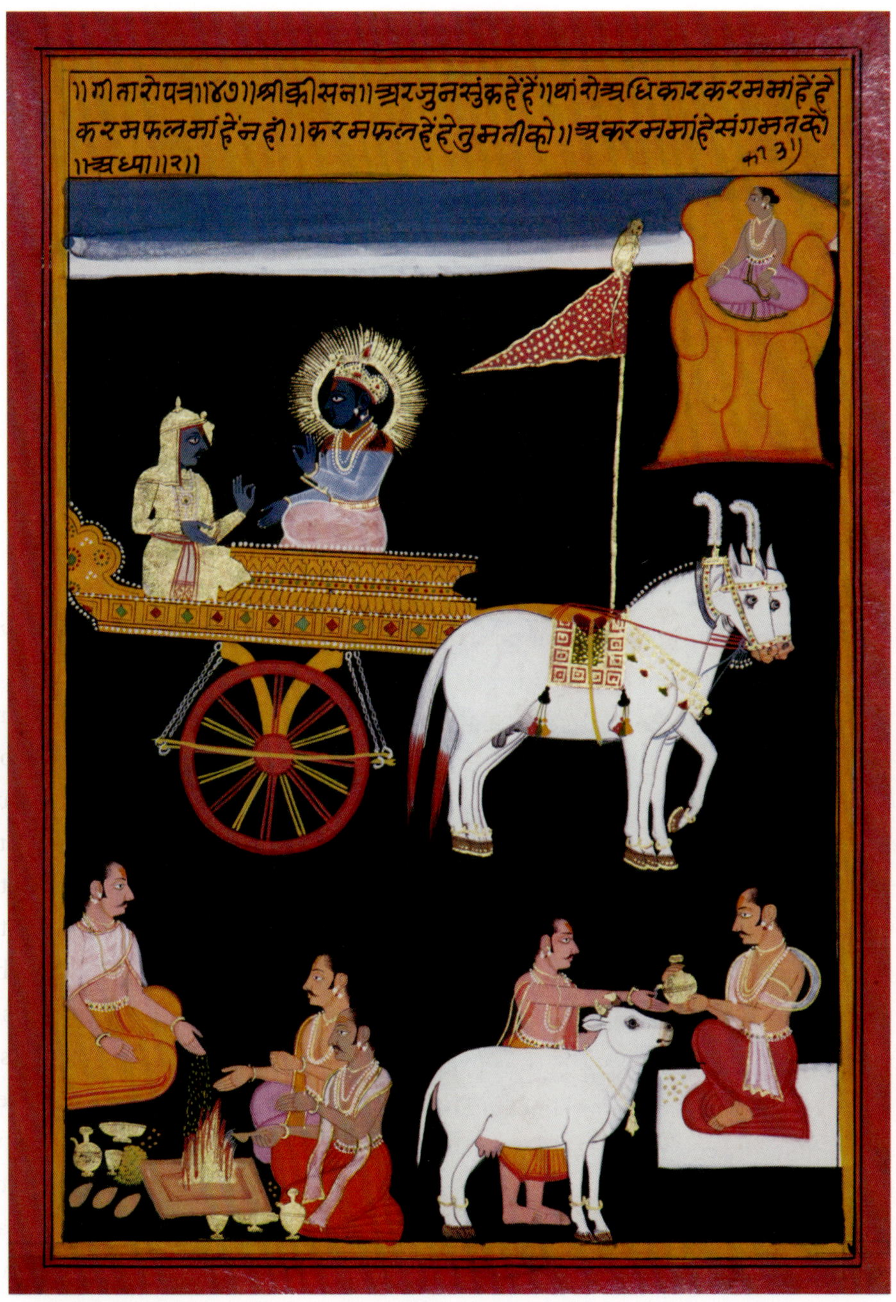

|47| श्री कृष्ण आगे कहने लगे कि हे अर्जुन! तेरा कर्म करने का ही अधिकार है उसके फल का नहीं, अतः तू कर्मों के फल का हेतु मत बन तथा न तेरी कर्म करने में भी आसक्ति ही हो।

|47| Sri Krishna says: Hey Arjuna! You have the right to act, but not to the fruit of action; if you consider only the fruit of action, you will not be able to act.

The bright pink background of the painting for verse 49 is a relief from the darkness of the earlier work. The text is about acting with equanimity in the service of dharma. It is as if a dead, desert space has been touched by a sudden burst of spring; as if the earth has found its reason for being. The sun shines on a cluster of flowering trees. A few branches reach ecstatically towards Krishna and eternity. The banana tree is heavy with fruit. The garden is the opposite of the battlefield. There is, however, an emaciated anchorite with gnarled bones who sits on a tiger skin in the middle of the green bower. Oblivious to the garden's beauty, is he the principle of inaction that weakens the earth's vital energies and turns gardens into desert wastes and good societies into lawless tyrannies? The wise, says Krishna, refuse to sit still. They cannot predict the consequences of action. They act because, as Spinoza says, 'right conduct and serving God [is] happiness itself and the greatest liberty.'[27] Arjuna's hesitation is like the interval between two breaths; like the subtle pulse between stillness and the next moment when time begins to move again; between the decision to act and the action itself. It is a dangerous moment between the hesitation of the spirit and its energetic freedom; an ambiguous moment when the soul faces a future of salvation or of ruin.

27 Quoted by Desai, p. 160.

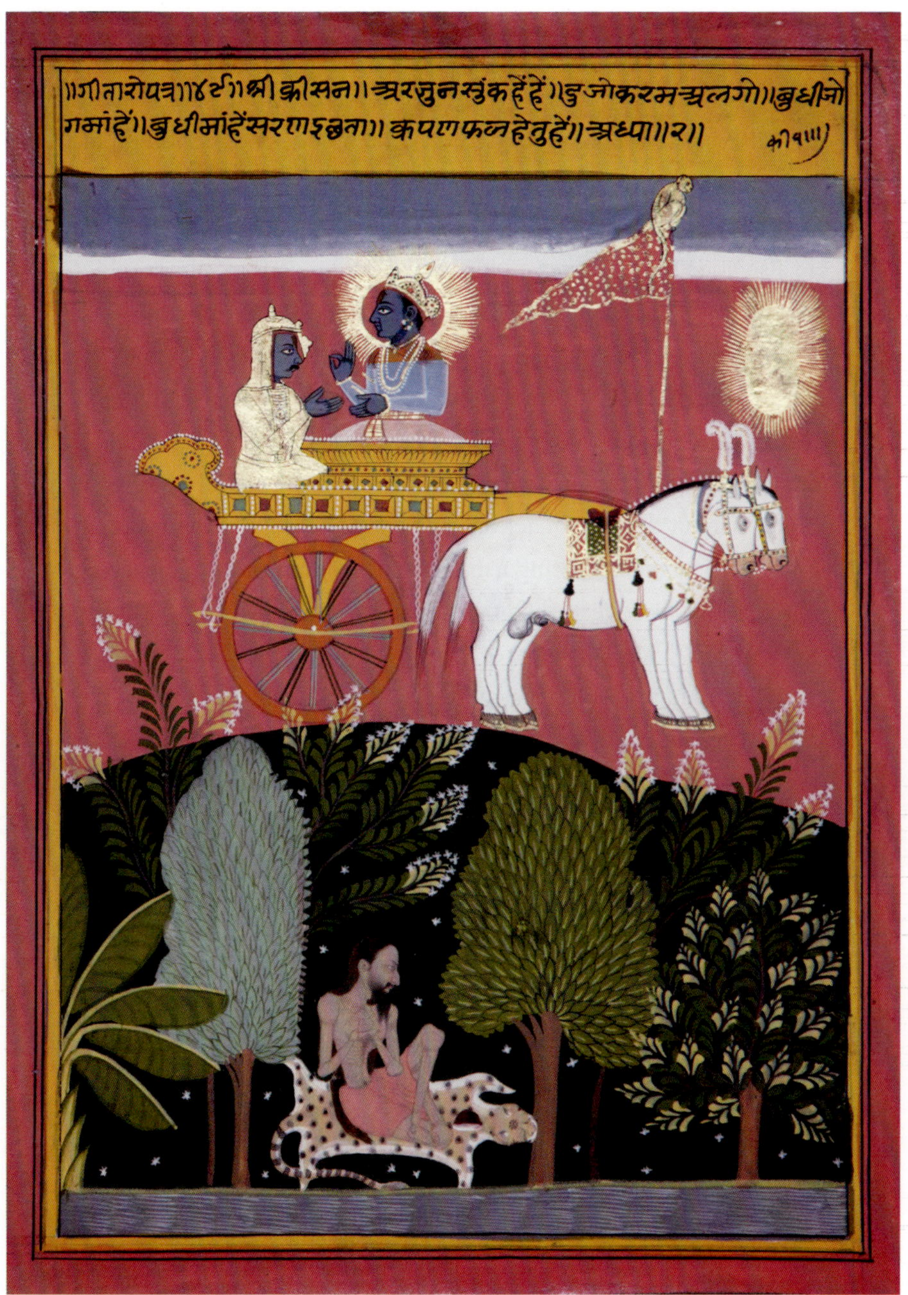

|49| श्री कृष्ण अर्जुन से कहने लगे कि इस समत्व रूप बुद्धियोग से सकाम कर्म अत्यंत निम्न श्रेणी का है। इसलिए हे अर्जुन! तू समबुद्धि में ही रक्षा का उपाय ढूँढ़ क्योंकि फल का हेतु बनने वाले अत्यंत दीन होते हैं।

|49| Sri Krishna says: Highest wisdom lies in acting with equanimity. That is why, hey Arjuna, find a reason for action. Those who act for rewards are extremely weak.

In the next few verses (51–53), Krishna continues to say that, since the world is a place of delusions, the wise are neither proud of their clan nor long for the fruit of their actions. Both attributes are dangerous for the self and confuse the temporal with the eternal. He also adds that a seeker of wisdom should regard all philosophic learning with the same detachment. Arjuna must look within his own self to find a justification for action. Krishna can only show him the consequences of wrong action performed for the wrong reason, but he cannot lead him to victory or salvation. It is now that Arjuna, after a period of quiet listening, asks in verse 54: what kind of man inquires about dharma in action? How does he walk, sit and speak? What physical marks distinguish a man of wisdom whose mind is so poised as not to be disturbed by changing fortunes? In the painting for verse 54, Allah Baksh traces the physical and spiritual biography of such a man, and splits his concerns about knowledge and action into two groups. On the left, a priest gives scriptural instruction to a well-dressed young man. On the right, there are three richly attired noblemen with daggers tucked into their waistbands. Two are arguing, perhaps about the ethics of violence. One is shown walking away. With a dramatic gesture, he seems to reject what the others are saying. Is his vision of moral action radically different? Does he want to renounce the social world, become a homeless wanderer, a sanyasi, whose mind and heart are no longer burdened by his time and place? Arjuna's question about how to distinguish a dharmic man remains seemingly unanswered. What is ironic and fascinating is that Arjuna does not notice that Krishna, in his earthly incarnation, is precisely such a man. And, of course, as the *Gita* progresses, Arjuna himself shall become the dharma warrior who has suffered much and thought deeply about the relation between earthly desire and ethical action, intent only on the 'Pure Good which is God.'[28]

28 Meister Eckhart (1260–1328), quoted by Gandhi in Desai, p. 162.

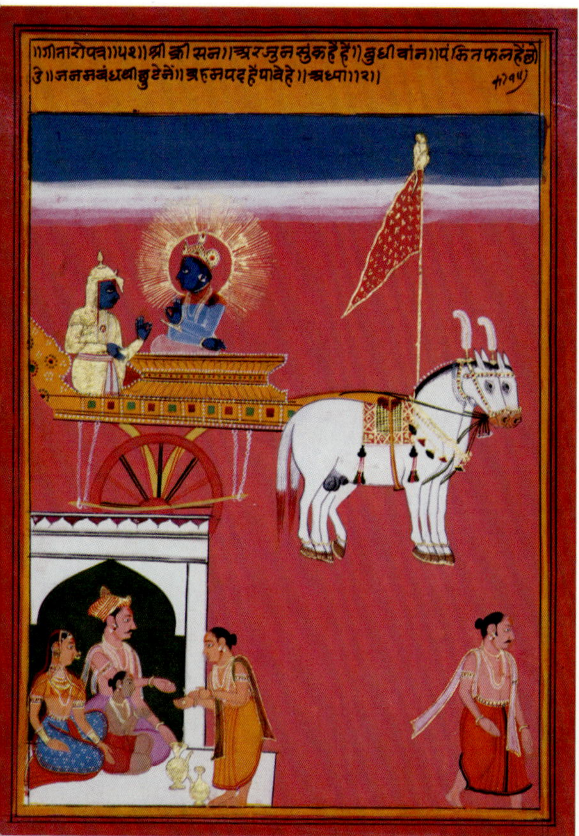

|51| श्री कृष्ण अर्जुन से कहने लगे कि ज्ञानीजन कर्मफलों को त्याग कर, जन्म बंधन के दुखों से परे होकर परम पद को प्राप्त होते हैं।

|51| Sri Krishna says: Arjuna by renouncing the fruits of action and breaking the bonds of birth, the wise achieve salvation.

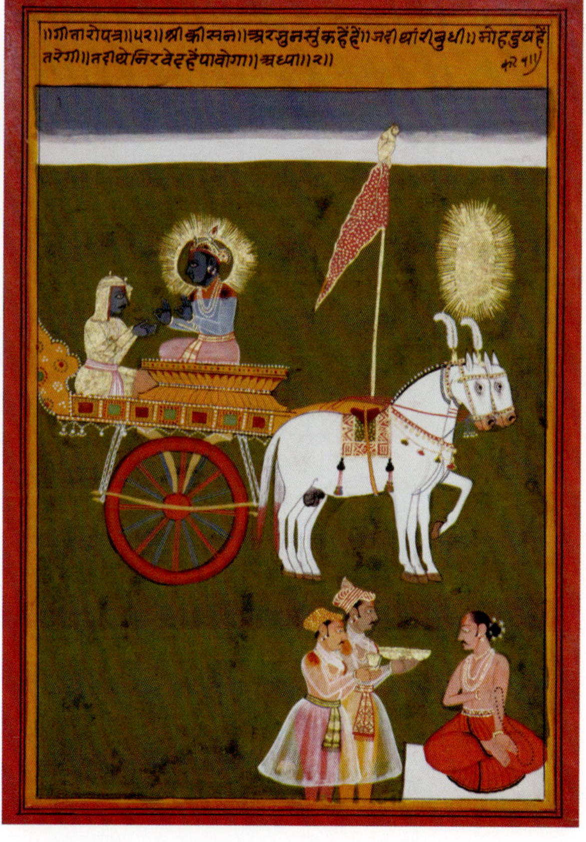

|52| श्री कृष्ण आगे कहने लगे कि हे अर्जुन! जब तेरी बुद्धि मोहरूपी दलदल को पार कर जाएगी तब तू सुने हुए या सुनने में आने वाले सभी भोगों से विरक्त हो जाएगा।

|52| Sri Krishna further says: Hey Arjuna! When your mind leaves behind the swamps of disillusion, then you will be indifferent to all that you have heard or will hear.

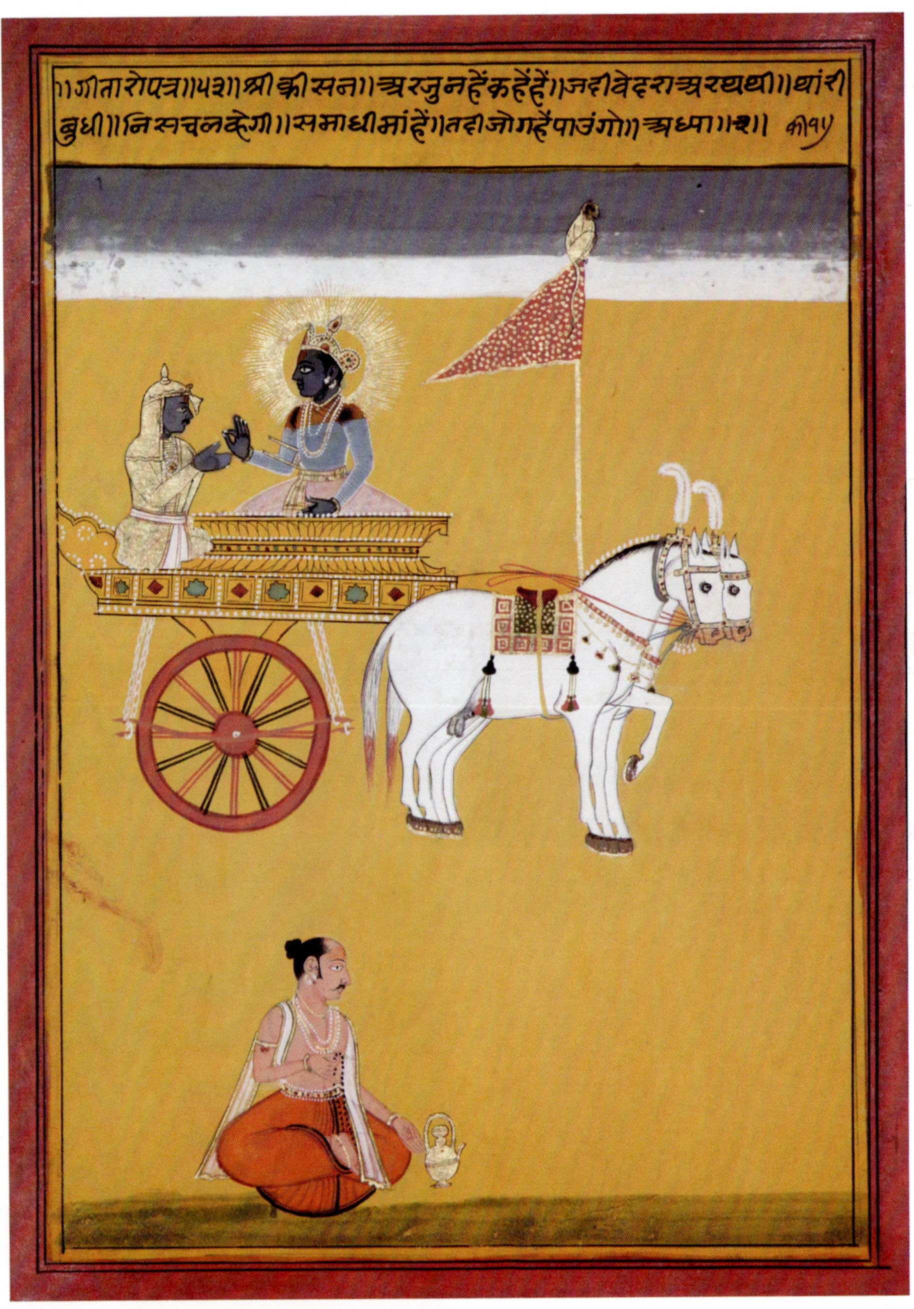

|53| श्री कृष्ण अर्जुन से कहने लगे कि अनेक श्रुतियों के सुनने से विचलित हुई तेरी बुद्धि जब समाधि में अचल हो स्थिर हो जाएगी, तब तू योग की अवस्था को प्राप्त होगा।

|53| Sri Krishna says to Arjuna: When your mind is not bewildered by the multiplicity of scriptures and can meditate calmly, then you will achieve wisdom.

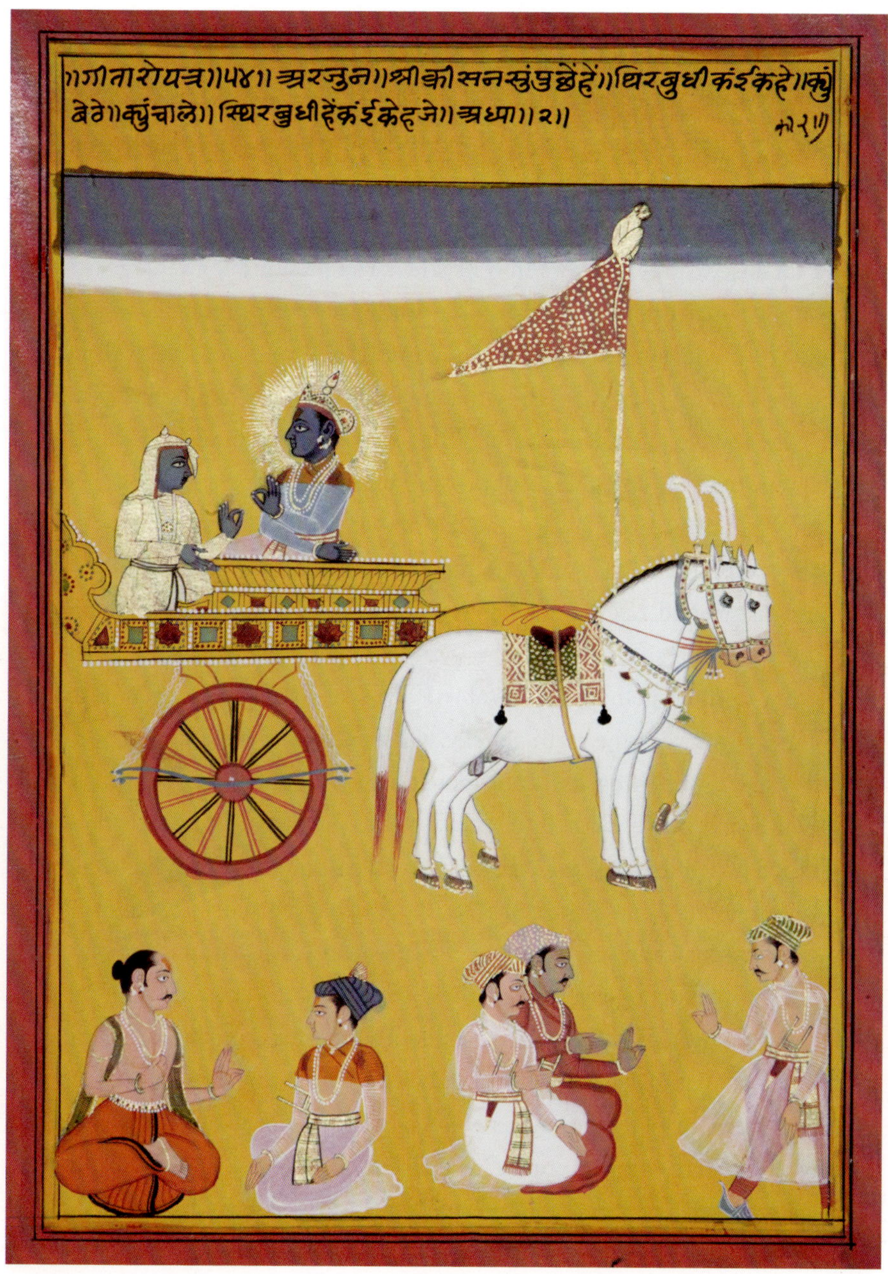

|54| यह सुनकर अर्जुन तब श्री कृष्ण से पूछने लगा कि हे केशव! समाधि में स्थित, स्थिर बुद्धि पुरुष के क्या लक्षण होते हैं? वह स्थिर बुद्धि कैसे बोलता है? कैसे बैठता है और कैसे चलता है?

|54| After he heard this, Arjuna asks Sri Krishna: Hey Keshav! What does the man who is deep in meditation and whose mind is still look like? How does he speak? How does he sit and act?

The sentiments expressed in the verses 56–58 are simple enough: a wise man remains unperturbed both by joy and sorrow, success and failure. Krishna has often said this. However, this time he employs a distinctively new image. A wise man, he says, is like a tortoise who withdraws into its shell. The painting for verse 58 is of particular interest. The green ground is strewn with small white flowers. One can see a tortoise floating on the water of a lake. The verse says that a tortoise is a symbol of the self, immersed in *samsara*. There are two pairs of beautiful birds—red-headed cranes and white egrets. One can imagine a subtle fragrance in the air rising with the same gentle breeze that stirs the flag above Arjuna's chariot. There is a correspondence between the red wheel of the chariot, the clothes of Krishna and Arjuna, the fringe of the saddles and the garment of the wise man sitting beside the lake. Each has been touched by the same spirit. Together they complete an ideal space where there is a concord between the earth, the sky, water and wind. Meditating upon the scene, watching its small movements—birds feeding, tortoise swimming, horses patiently waiting—one begins to feel at peace. The mood of gentle calm makes one forget, at least momentarily, that war is imminent. What more can a 'goodly' earth offer to its inhabitants?

Paradoxically, the painting reveals beauty and simultaneously denies it value; asserts its reality and yet seeks to erase it. As if to suggest how awkward such an aesthetic and ethical position is for a painter, Allah Baksh shows the yogi contorting his body strangely so as to turn away from the scene's loveliness. The problem is that no matter where the yogi turns, his eyes are met by the sparkle of the water, the delicacy of the flowers and the lushness of the green fields. Should one also ask: can one have the experience of seeing and being seen by the divine (*darshan*) if one withdraws one's gaze from the objects of desire?[29]

29 See Diana L. Eck, *Darsan: Seeing the Divine Image in India* (Pennsylvania: Anima Books, 1985).

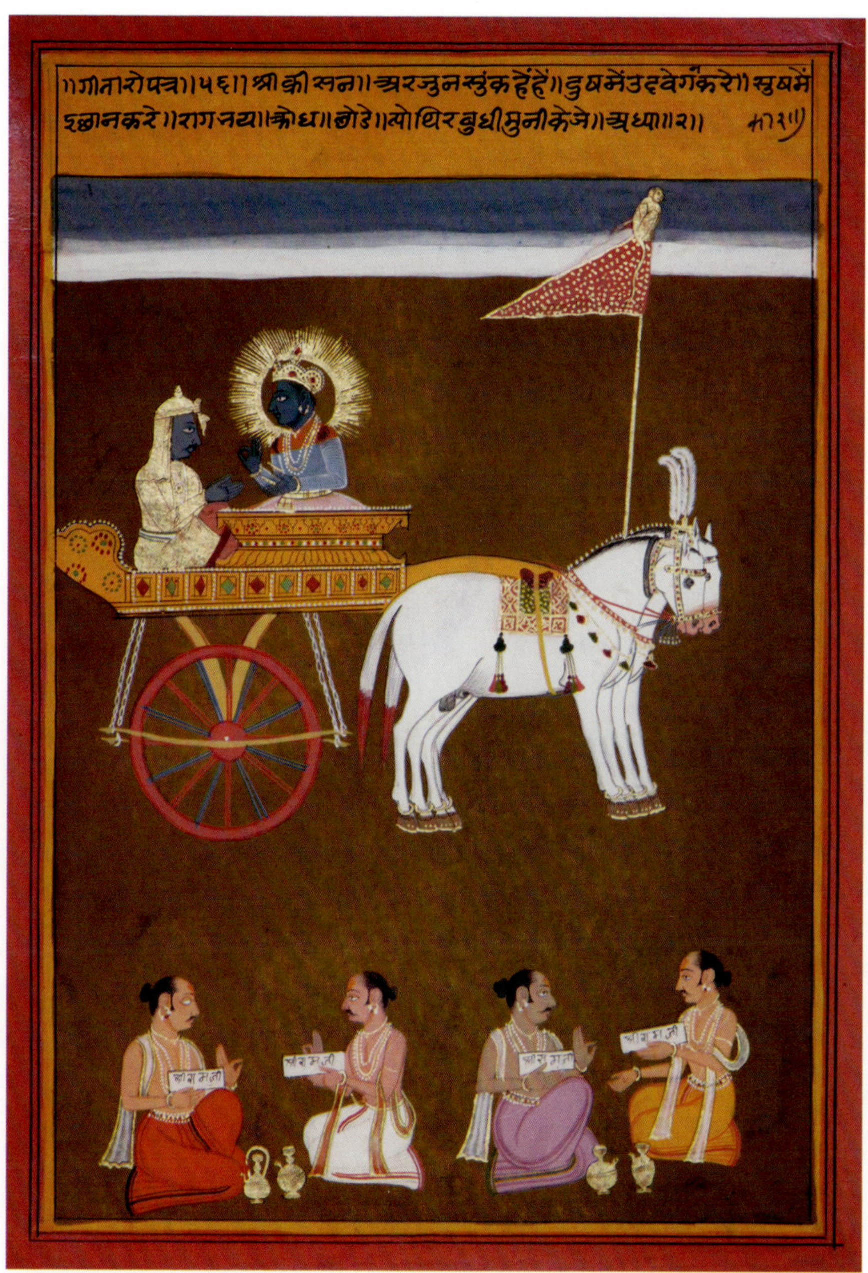

|56| श्री कृष्ण अर्जुन से कहने लगे कि हे अर्जुन! दुखों के आने पर जिसका मन विचलित नहीं होता और सुखों में जिसकी लालसा नहीं है और जो राग, भय व क्रोध से मुक्त हो जाता है, ऐसा पुरुष स्थिर बुद्धि कहलाता है।

|56| Sri Krishna says: Hey Arjuna! A wise man, whose mind is steady, unperturbed by sorrow and not tempted by pleasure, is free from passion, fear or anger.

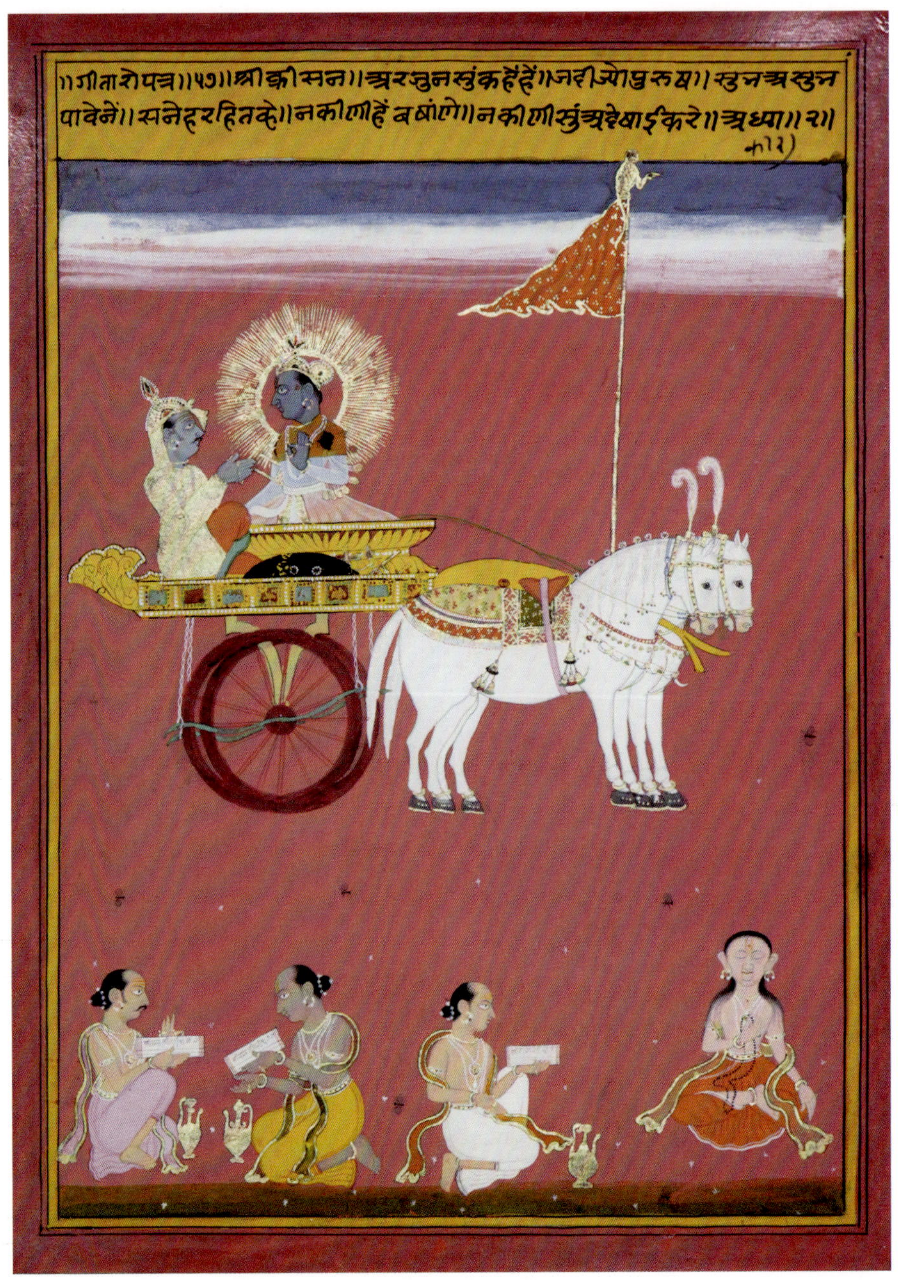

|57| श्री कृष्ण आगे कहने लगे कि हे अर्जुन! जो पुरुष सर्वत्र स्नेह रहित है तथा शुभ या अशुभ फल मिलने पर न तो प्रसन्न होता है और न ही दुखी होता है वह स्थिर बुद्धि कहलाता है।

|57| Sri Krishna says: Hey Arjuna! A wise man whose mind is steady has no personal attachments; he is neither happy nor unhappy if the fruit of his action is good or bad.

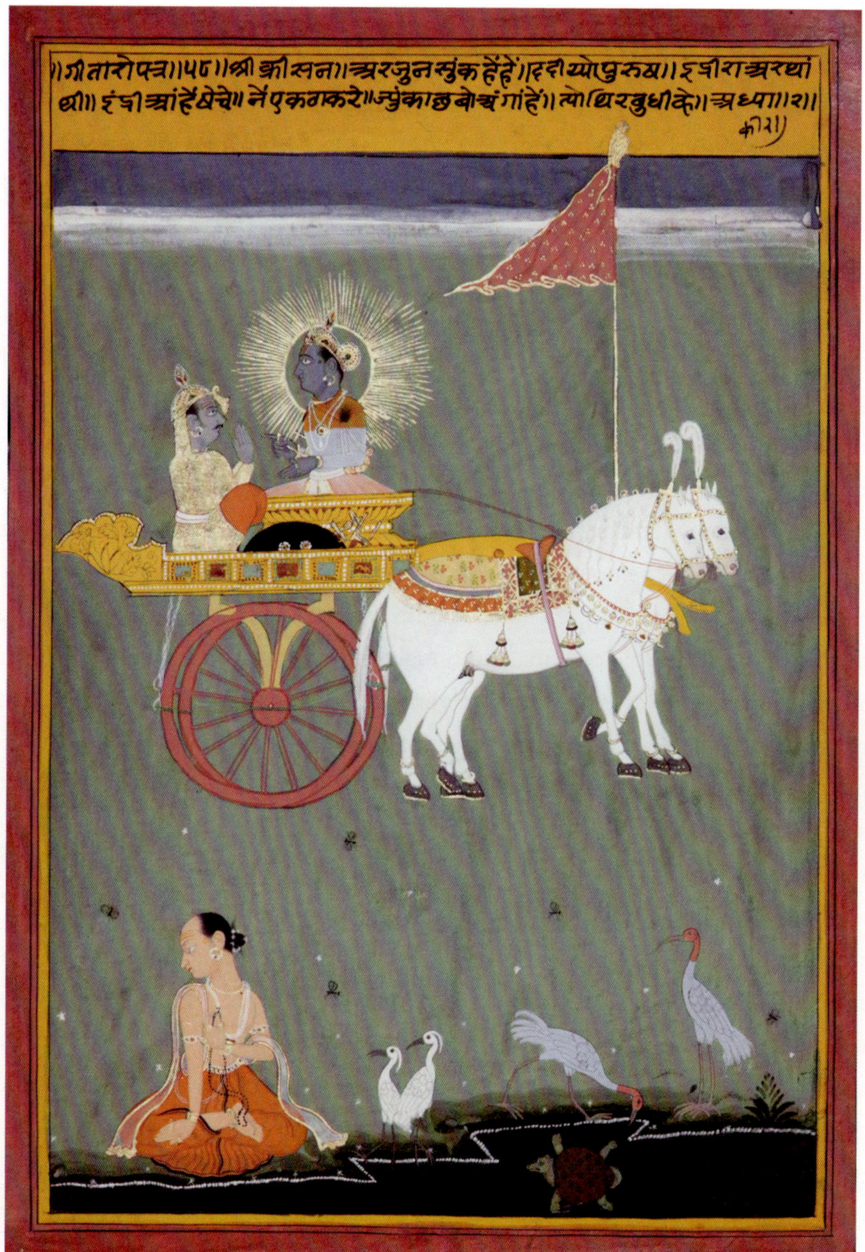

|58| श्री कृष्ण कहने लगे कि हे अर्जुन! जैसे कछुआ अपने अंगों को समेट लेता है वैसे ही यदि पुरुष इन्द्रियों के विषयों से इन्द्रियों को सभी ओर से खींच ले तब उसकी बुद्धि स्थिर है यह जानना चाहिए।

|58| Sri Krishna says: Hey Arjuna! You should know that a wise man whose mind is steady withdraws his senses from all objects of desire like a tortoise withdraws his limbs into his shell.

After the beauty of the previous paintings, the visuals for verse 59 are incandescent. There is an upsurge of colours, flowers and fountains. Inspired, Allah Baksh seems to have effortlessly reached that moment of visionary understanding whereby he can imagine clear forms to express the formless, use sharply drawn lines to show what cannot be revealed, and use colours for complex emotions that cannot be articulated. This is not surprising as India's visual cultures of the sacred have always accepted that the divine can be apprehended through music and song, word and image.

This painting plays with Krishna's primary idea that god is both the absolute 'Other' of the human and utterly familiar. Even more profoundly, its images are symbolic of the notion that the *numen* and the earthly, eternity and time, are interfused. That is why the burnished sun in the garden has the same ineffability as the golden halo around Krishna's head. Is there an unselfconscious echo of the prayer to the sun in the *Isa Upanishad*: 'spread forth your rays and gather up your radiant light that I may behold you of loveliest form?'[30] The sun is not remote. Its light is entangled in the green trees, spread over the open yellow field on which the chariot stands, scattered across the flowers sparkling with red, white and purple colours, and braided in the spray of the water fountains. It shines with equal clarity over the anchorite and the courtier. The garden and the sun are then, at first, to be read as archetypal images of eternal plenitude. One is enchanted. But then one recalls the verse which admonishes those who find delight in the beauty of the sensuous world. One wonders how the anchorite can withdraw his gaze. Does he turn away and forget the garden, only to see it again, recreate it again, be enchanted again, and then struggle to erase it again from his realm of feeling and senses? The difficulty, the verse emphasises, is that the very attempt to deny desire is also the moment when desire is reasserted. What the anchorite has to ask is: in what sense is the garden-world 'other' than himself? This dialogue with desire can end only when he physically ceases to be. The painting, like the verse, is a meditation on the dilemma of our human condition. He faces east where the sun rises and the journey of the day is perpetually renewed.

Standing across from the anchorite is a courtly figure. He is the very embodiment of a man lost in the sensual world and has no wish to escape its enchantment. The colour of his robe is scarlet like the pennant above Arjuna's chariot with similar designs in gold. His shoes are blue; the folds of his turban are elegantly embroidered. And, to complete the picture of an elegant young man who is totally 'lost' in a delightful dream, he is shown gazing upon a delicate white flower on a long green stem. He, more than the anchorite, belongs in the garden.

30 Verse 16 in S. Radhakrishnan, *The Principal Upanishads* (London: George Allen and Unwin, 1953), p. 577.

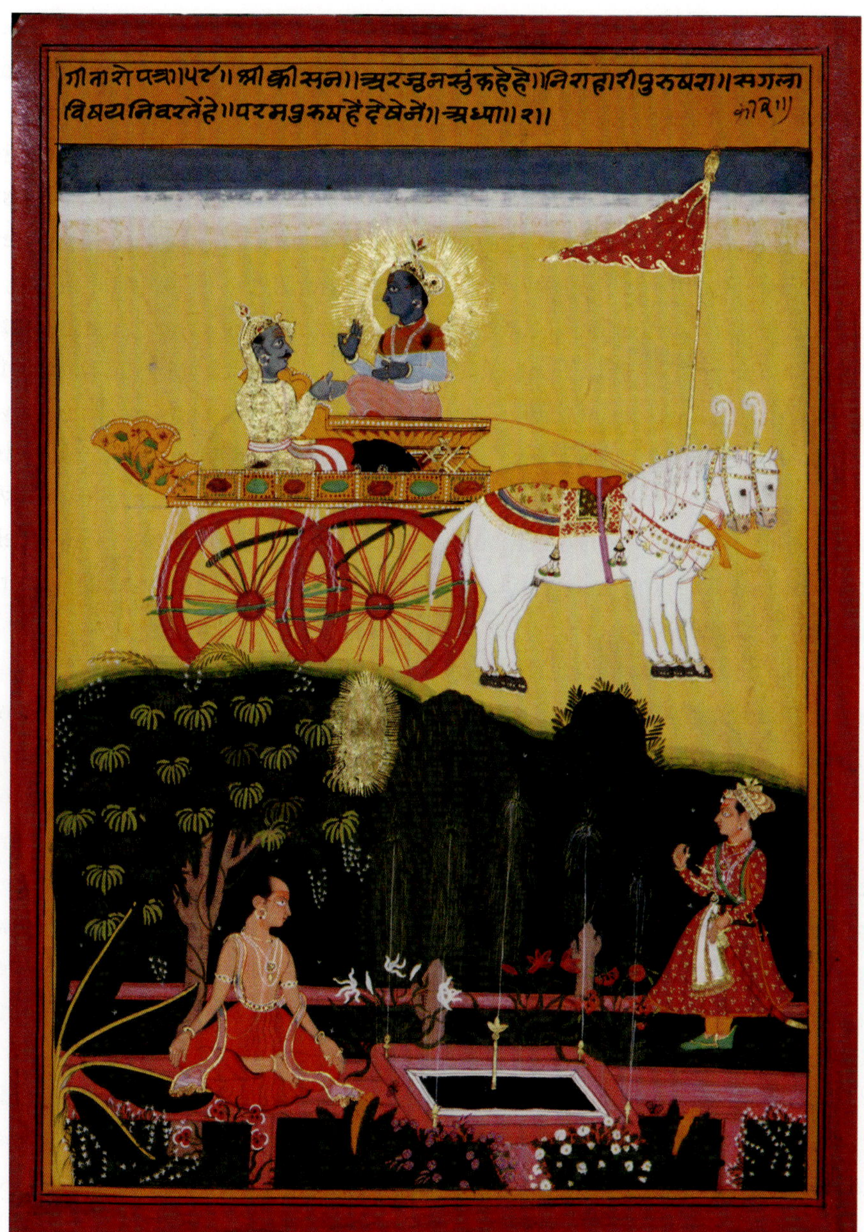

|59| श्री कृष्ण अर्जुन को कहने लगे कि विषयों को ग्रहण न करने वाले पुरुष के विषय तो छूट जाते हैं लेकिन उनमें आसक्ति बनी रहती है पर स्थिर बुद्धि पुरुष की आसक्ति परमात्मा का साक्षात्कार करने से छूट जाती है।

|59| Sri Krishna says: The ascetic who refrains from seeking the pleasure of the senses still desires; but a wise man who concentrates steadily on the Divine is free from desire.

In the painting for verse 60, it is strange to see Arjuna turn away from Krishna. Arjuna's hands are folded; his face is distraught and puzzled. Krishna's gesture urges calm thoughtfulness. At the heart of the verse, in seeming contradiction to the previous one, is the sense that both nature and the divine are always the 'other' of the human; that there is an unbridgeable gap between them. The more the mind tries to understand itself in relation to nature and god, the more it fails to understand; and the more it tries to disassociate itself from the natural or temporal world, the more it gets embroiled in them. Does Arjuna wonder if each inflection of thought is a trap? And that desire is a snare in the path of liberation? Does he not desire the defeat of the Kauravas, or long for peace? Should he not agree with the moral sceptics who accept passion as an intimate part of the psyche, and regard with honest irony commonplace pieties about sublimation or the repression of physical demands, social needs and ambitions? Krishna will, of course, clarify each of these aspects later. But, for the moment, does Arjuna not wonder if it is impossible for human reason to grasp anything more than what the senses offer?

The yogi, in a space separated by a green line, offers a fine counter-point to Arjuna's anxiety. Poised and composed, he sits cross-legged beside a gently meandering stream. His body is fair and his head is half-tonsured. His left hand rests on his knee while the fingers of his right hand keep ritual time on a string of beads. The surroundings are peaceful and lovely. Butterflies hover over the stream, ducks swim calmly in the blue water, red-headed cranes stand patiently, pink lotus flowers light up the place with their splendour, and green ferns grow near the riverbank. The images are well-chosen. They are emblems of sensuous nature at perfect ease with itself. Is the artist's delight in their vibrant colours not a testimony to his own bemused understanding of philosophic asceticism?

The yogi gazes steadily, without surprise, at a dense green tree which is radiant with the presence of the god of love and desire. Kama, dressed in gold and yellow, is dazzling. His body is blue like the sky above and the water below; blue like Krishna and Arjuna. The *Vishnudharmottara* states, Kama 'should be rendered on the earth by reason of his beauty.'[31] He can shape the fate of human beings, and is unpredictable. He carries a bow with a lotus-tipped arrow and his eyes twinkle with mischief. Is he the analogue of Krishna in popular visual and textual lore, the thief of love, the ecstatic dancer, the music maker and the spirit of earthly joy?

31 *Vishnudharmottara*, p. 96.

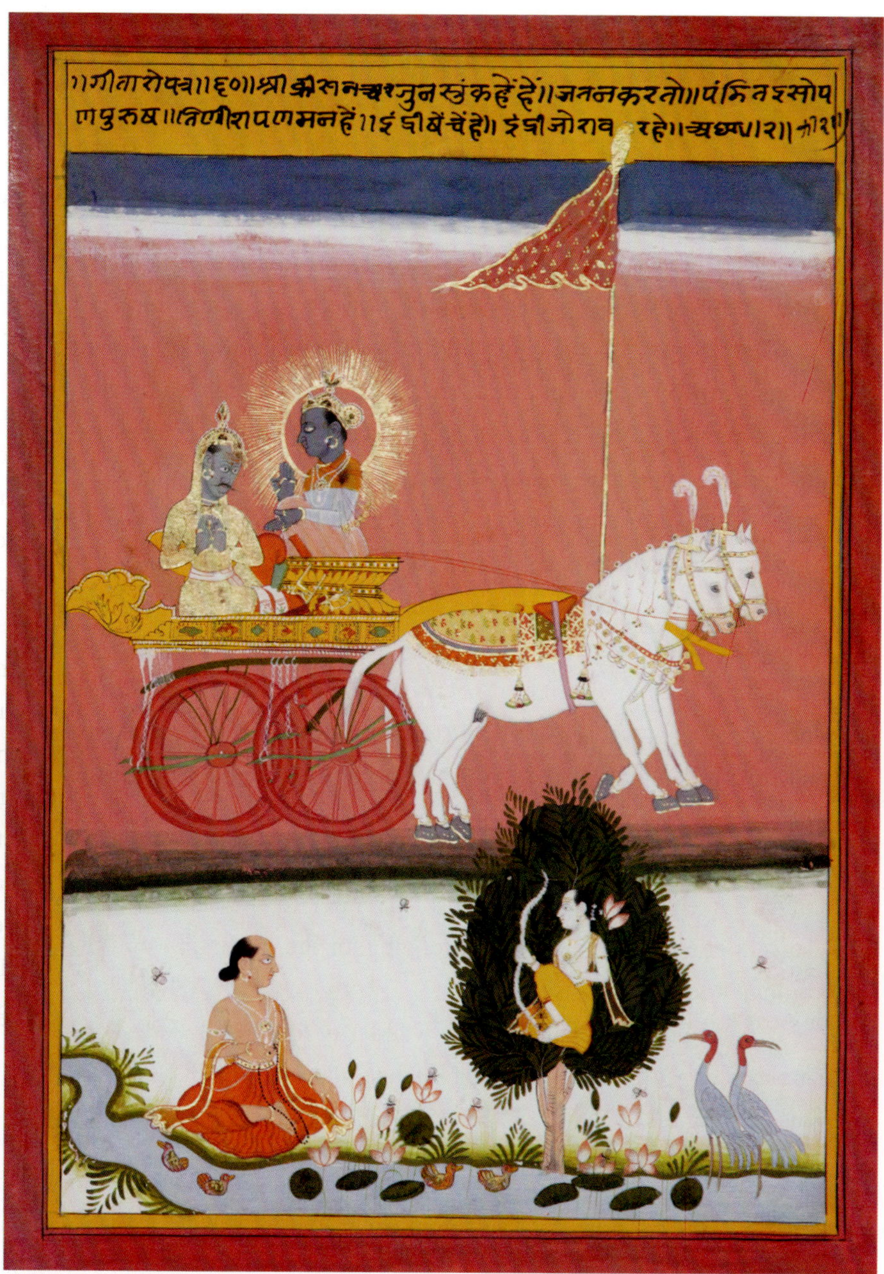

|60| श्री कृष्ण कहने लगे कि हे अर्जुन! निरंतर प्रयास करते रहने पर भी चंचल इन्द्रियाँ बुद्धिमान पुरुष के मन को बलात् हर लेती हैं। इन्द्रियाँ बलवान हैं।

|60| Sri Krishna says: Hey Arjuna! Even after arduous effort, the heart of the wise man can be overpowered by sensual desires. The desires of the senses are powerful.

The painting for verse 61 is attractive but culturally and morally difficult to read. It is a playful meditation on Kama in everyday life. The intense and erotically charged gaze between the young man, with a narrow waist, jasmine flowers in his knotted hair and gentle eyes, on the right, and the gorgeously dressed, elegant woman, with a large gold nose-ring sitting before him on a green field strewn with white flowers, seems like an amused comment on the phrase, 'meditate steadfastly on me' (Swami 25) in the verse, rather than on the moral warning to restrain desires. Why should so natural an attraction between a handsome man, however priestly, and a beautiful woman, invite a stern interdiction when the days are peaceful? Is it not possible for even the most scripturally self-conscious man or woman to be swept away by the erotic and feel no cause for moral censure? Must one evade the erotic, move past all earthly temptations and concentrate on the divine? Should the dissolution into the divine not be the final stage of the lifecycle, its completion? In the *Mahabharata*, there are stories when even the most fiercely determined ascetics surrender to the sensual; their surrender ensures that stories of longing for the earth, time and the human body never cease.

As if to suggest that once the wonder of love slowly fades, one looks back with either nostalgia or rage, the artist paints an aging man sitting on the left edge. He is placed behind the woman and a gentle cow with gold-tipped horns and golden bells. His body sags. He stares at the couple with anger and envy; his arms are tensely crossed. The painting, however, like the *Gita* at this stage, does not resolve the dialogue between passion and asceticism, desire and sacrifice, man and god, time and eternity.

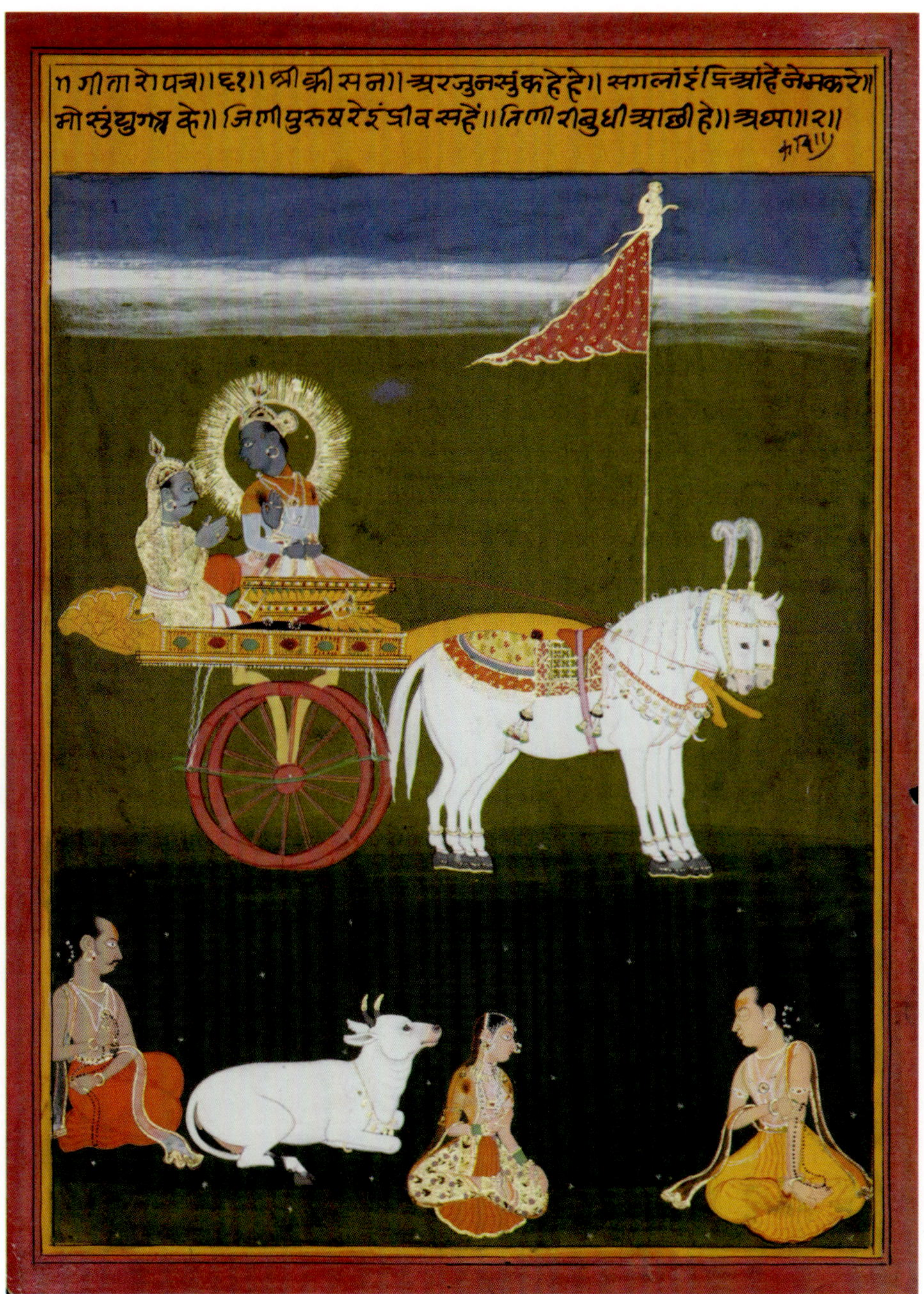

|61| श्री कृष्ण आगे कहने लगे कि हे अर्जुन! इसलिए सभी इन्द्रियों को वश में कर के मुझ से युक्त होकर, मेरे परायण होकर ध्यान में बैठ, क्योंकि जिसकी इन्द्रियाँ वश में है उसी की बुद्धि स्थिर मानी गई है।

|61| Sri Krishna further says: Hey Arjuna, restrain all your desires; sit and concentrate on me, because only the one who can control desire has a steady mind.

The images in these paintings do not narrate a life-story. Instead, they offer us a sense of how life is often lived, just as the scenes of teaching and debate on the chariot give instructions about how life ought to be lived. The painting for verse 62 shows an ordinary family which, in its unknowingness and inattentiveness, fails to see a vision of glory in the tree across from which they sit in their austere house. On one level, the scene is charming. The father points at the heart of his child and the mother looks on lovingly. The family has a sanctified place in the Hindu lifecycle. Even Krishna recognises in the verse that desire must be gratified. But the family is only a stage of life, a passing phase between the physical time of the child and the imaginative time of the divine. The self, as Krishna also teaches, must not linger there for too long; over time desire fades and the frustrated self reacts to the change with longing or anger.

The family in the scene is far from any spiritual understanding. They neither look up towards where Krishna is, nor across to where a tree of beauty grows, offering a *darshan* of Kama and the benediction of love. Just as the tree knows that desire flows through the sap of its being, the wise understand that the divine does not reside in some remote time or space, but in the human body. In the *Isa Upanishad*, the enlightened mind says: 'He who is yonder person...I am he!'[32]

Unlike the family, the tree is unbounded, free, full of vitality and upward trusting; it glows with the presence of a divine being sitting in its lush green leaves. For Allah Baksh, the tree is not merely a place where the holy has chosen to descend for a moment only to vanish again; it is, rather, what incarnation itself means if we see the world not with our physical but our visionary eyes; engage in a dialogue with its living presence. Krishna's appeal to Arjuna, not to think of the fate of the sensual world alone, is reminiscent of the fervent prayer with which the *Isa Upanishad* ends:

> This body then ends in ashes!...
> O Purpose, remember!
> The deed remember!
> O Purpose, remember!
> The deed remember![33]

---

32 *The Thirteen Principal Upanishads*, translated by Robert Earnest Hume (London: Oxford University Press, 1877), p. 365.

33 *The Thirteen Principal Upanishads*, translated by Hume, p. 365.

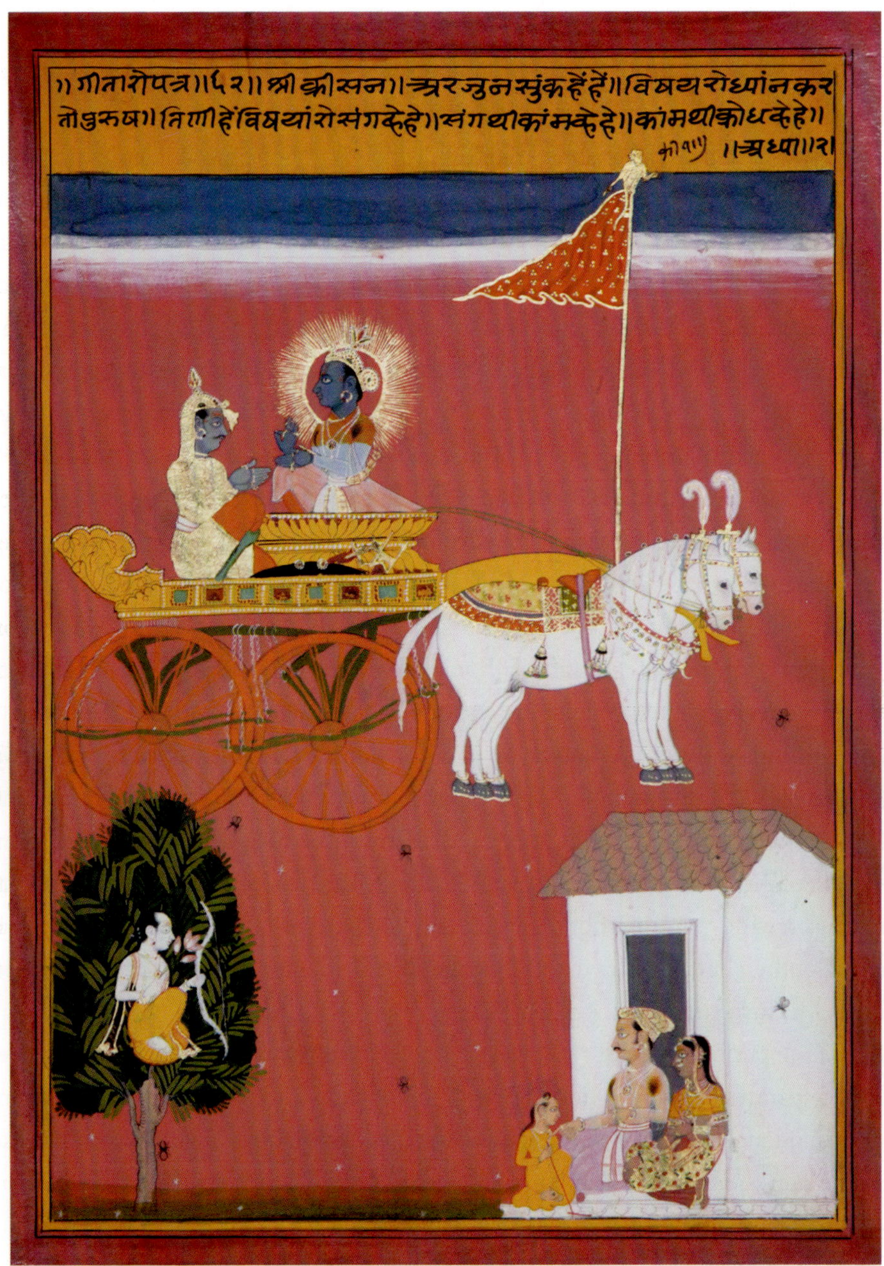

|62| श्री कृष्ण आगे कहने लगे कि हे अर्जुन! विषयों का चिंतन करने से विषयों के प्रति आसक्ति उत्पन्न हो जाती है। आसक्ति से उसकी कामना पैदा होती है और कामना पूरी न होने पर क्रोध उत्पन्न होता है।

|62| Sri Krishna further says: Hey Arjuna! If one thinks about sensuous objects, one is attracted to them. If one is attracted to them, one desires them. And if desire is not satisfied, one becomes angry.

In the psychologically astute verse 63, Krishna explains that anger is a sign of the perversion of reason and the frustration of desire. The background of this painting is appropriately black. The emotion it evokes is melancholy; a state of one who can find no moral purpose in life. For Krishna, memory, which is not anchored in an ethical ideal, is not redemptive. Without a sense of the self's rightful place in the world, memory is only a series of disconnected fragments. But, even if the self recalls an ideal state from which it has fallen (war is a brutal sign of that fall), it can still remain embittered or bewildered. Further, the recollection of a lost ideal paralyses the self in its spiritual solitude if it cannot use the knowledge to make its way to a redemptive future. Similarly, mere longing for change without action is folly. If nostalgia and fantasy are mirror opposites of each other and equally hopeless, is it possible to read the two ornately-dressed learned men sitting across from each other at the lower half of the painting as parodies of those who can reason and dream but cannot act? Between them is a dark figure, crouched in a foetal position inside a red sphere analogue both of the womb and the wheel; birth and time.

The bluish-green background of the next painting for verse 64 is gentler on the eye. Every object has hints of gold: the water jugs, the fringes of clothes, the flames, the saddles and the hoofs of the horses, Arjuna's armour, Krishna's necklaces and crown, the triangular flag and Hanuman. Allah Baksh shows us how the senses can be charmed while the mind remains calm and composed. The mind can acknowledge the beauty and the wealth of the world and not be hypnotised by it. The two learned men have migrated from the previous painting but in a radically altered verbal context. They sit across from each other, but the intervening images transform our reactions to them. A priest is feeding a ritual fire whose golden flames, tinged with red, reach restlessly towards Krishna. The performance of rites may not transform the self, but it may galvanise it out of the paralysis of doubt into action. The fire ritual refines the senses, disciplines the mind and makes the self think again about the relation between the physical senses, the mind and the metaphysical. Of course, there is a danger that the rites performed mechanically and repetitively can make reason inattentive and imagination dull, till the fire is reduced to ash. The other priest, who is calm and controlled, is transfixed by the sun which has come down to earth and shines right beside him. In his transcendental aspirations, he must not forget that earthly fires are necessary for lighting hearths and homes; without them he would cease to be.

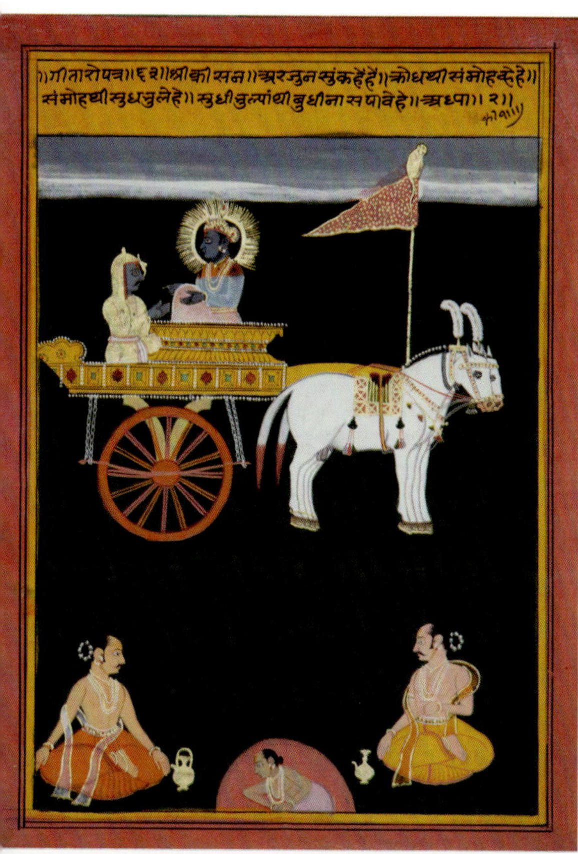

|63| श्री कृष्ण आगे कहने लगे कि हे अर्जुन! फिर क्रोध से मूढ़ता उत्पन्न होती है, मूढ़ता से स्मृतिभ्रम होता है। स्मृतिभ्रम से बुद्धि का नाश होता है, फिर बुद्धि का नाश होने पर व्यक्ति अपनी स्थिति से गिर जाता है।

|63| Sri Krishna further says: Hey Arjuna! Anger leads to folly, and folly to loss of memory. Loss of memory results in the ruin of reason, and one falls from one's rightful place.

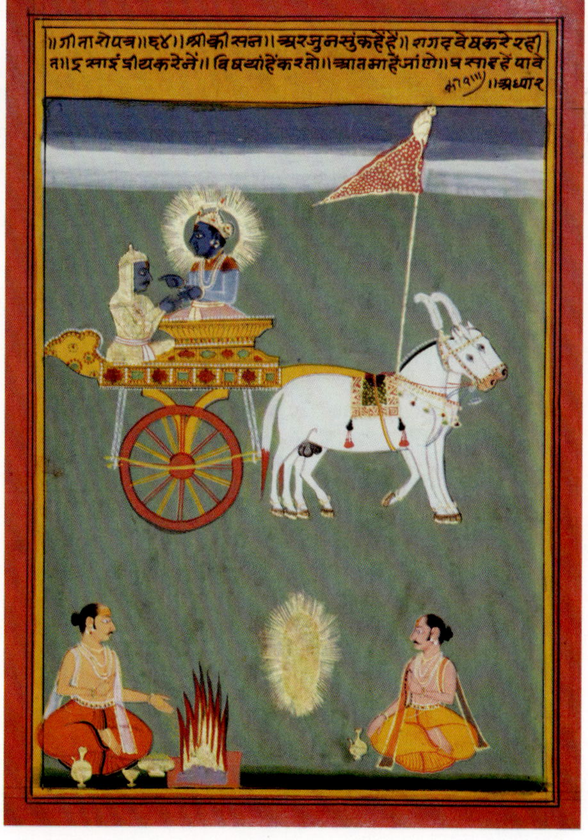

|64| श्री कृष्ण आगे कहने लगे कि हे अर्जुन! जो संयमी पुरुष होता है वह राग-द्वेष से मुक्त अपनी इन्द्रियों को वश में कर के विषयों में विचरण करता हुआ भी प्रसन्न रहता है।

|64| Sri Krishna further says: Hey Arjuna! The one whose mind is steady, who controls his desires and is free from attraction or aversion, can think about sensuous things and be at peace.

The austere simplicity of verse 65 is matched by the minimalism of the painting. The pinkish-red colour suffuses its space with the same sense of *shanta rasa* (peace) as morning sunlight does when the world is at peace. No breeze rustles the banner, the horses are still, and Arjuna listens to Krishna with increasing reverence. What is being presented is a wiser way of managing differences and desires instead of force. The dramatic scene below reminds the self that it is only a wayfarer on earth; that its longings and ambitions are real, of course, but are also only transitory; that no single desire and its fulfilment defines the self and completes it; that since every moment in life's journey is unconditioned and unconditional, any plan one makes can be disrupted by chance intrusions of the graceful or the monstrous. There are two unheroic men, placed deliberately at the very edge of the painting. One of them, stepping out into undefined space, may have decided that having fulfilled the dharma of domestic life, he must cast away all its comforts, abandon its worldly goods and seek release from time's bondage. He is dark, barefoot and carries a small bundle under his arm. The other sits with the yogic poise of a man who is well past temptations and longings. Neither of them shows any sign of ambition, greed, lust or jealousy which twist and torment the psyche.

Till the end of the chapter, Krishna continues to tell Arjuna that it is his destiny to be a hero. He will face ignominy if he refuses. However, he must not fight vengefully. Krishna is, of course, not a preacher of moral restraint. He is urging Arjuna to be like his cosmic father, Indra, a crafter of an ethical civilisation, whose violence is 'controlled' in the interest of a 'social and cosmic equilibrium.'[34] Arjuna continues to hesitate to act till his radical doubts about the ethics of action are resolved.

34 Georges Dumezil, *The Destiny of the Warrior*, translated by Alf Hiltebeitel (Chicago: University of Chicago Press, 1969), p. 116.

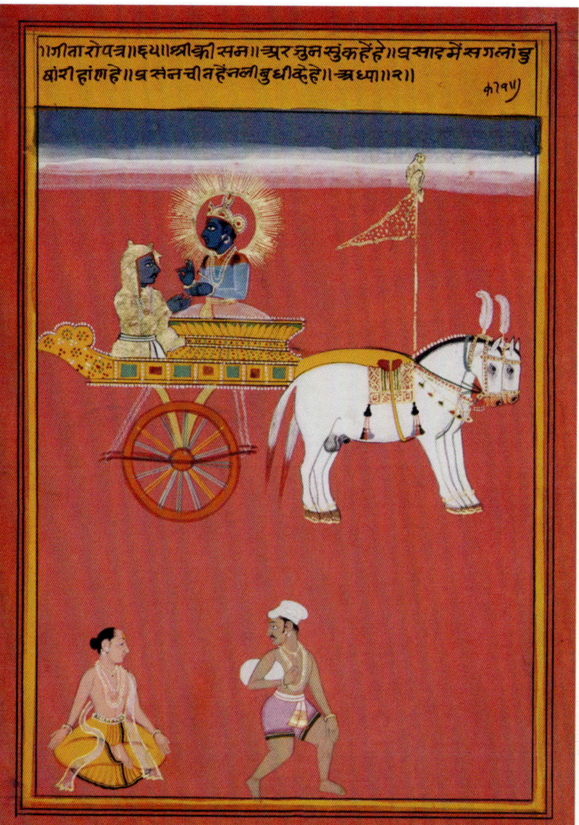

|65| श्री कृष्ण अर्जुन से कहने लगे कि प्रसन्नता से सभी दुखों का नाश होता है और प्रसन्नचित्त वाले की बुद्धि भी शीघ्र ही भली प्रकार स्थिर हो जाती है।

|65| Sri Krishna tells Arjuna that all sorrows end when the self is at peace; and the self soon attains wisdom when the heart and mind are at peace.

|72| श्री कृष्ण आगे कहने लगे कि हे अर्जुन! यही ब्रह्म को प्राप्त हुए मनुष्य की स्थिति है जिसे प्राप्त कर पुरुष मोह में नहीं फँसता। अंतकाल में भी वह ब्रह्मत्व में स्थित होकर निर्वाण पाता है।

|72| Sri Krishna further says: Hey Arjuna! A person who has attained the state of Brahman is never entrapped by desire. At the end of time, the person who is one with Brahman achieves the peace of nirvana. This text has been written for Maharana Sri Jai Singh Ji by Bhatt Kishandas. Sri, Sri, Sri.

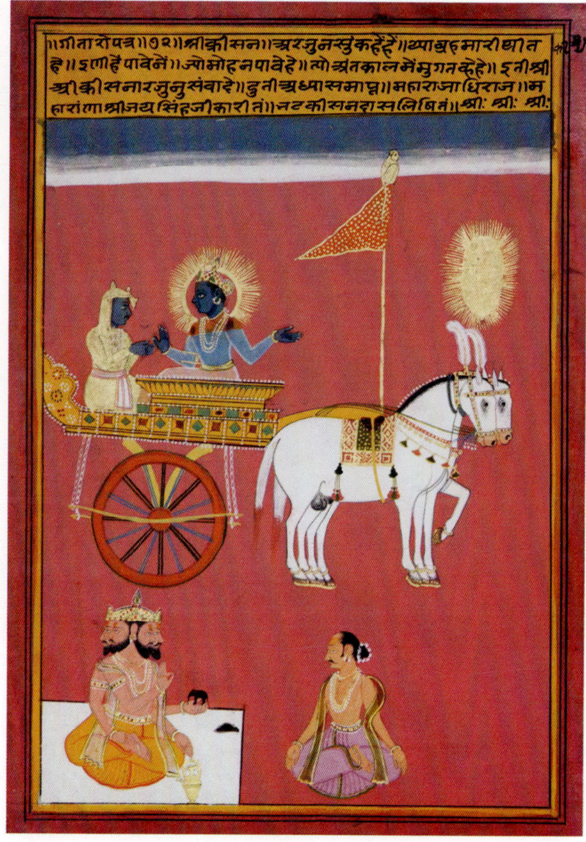

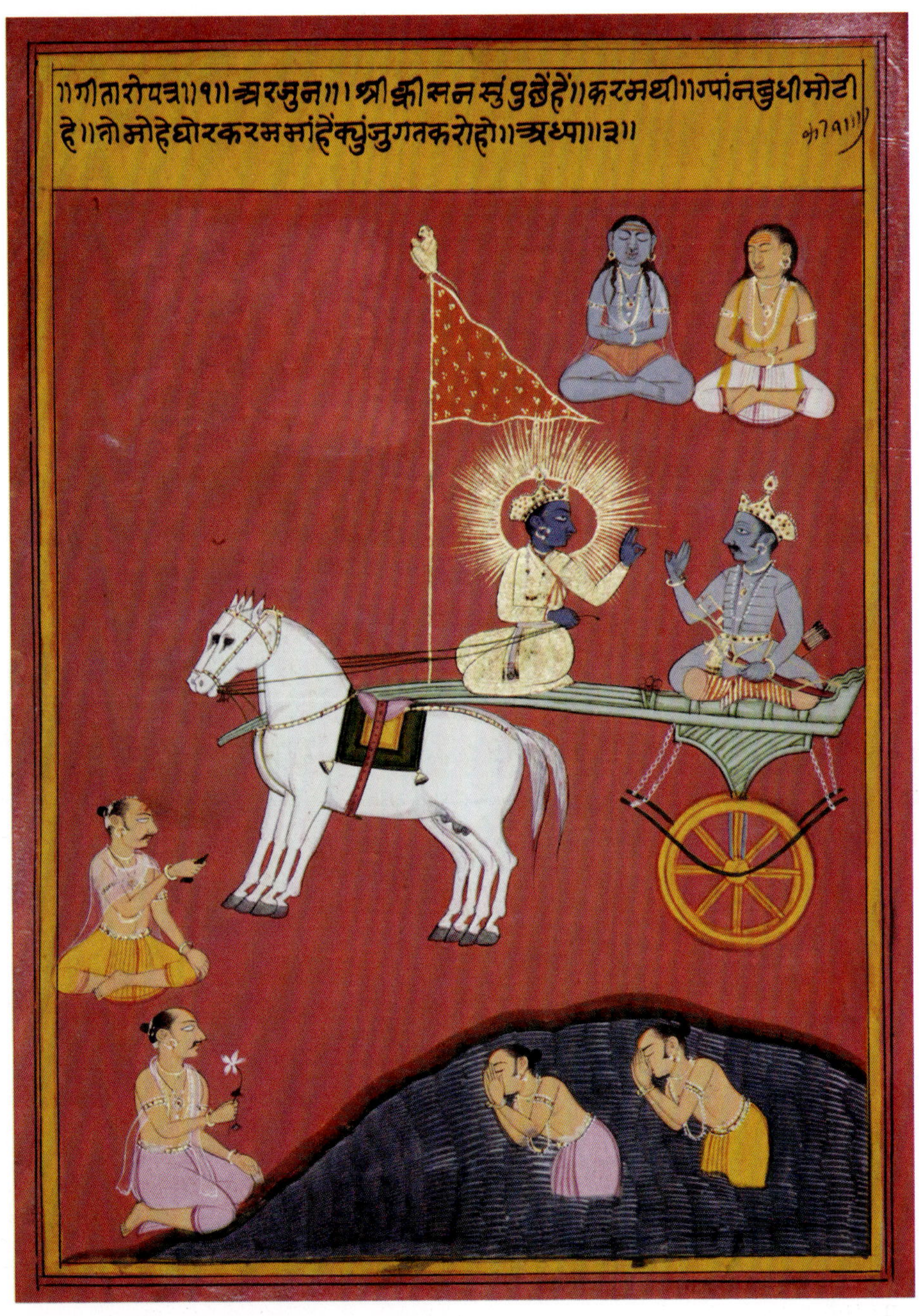

|1| अर्जुन श्री कृष्ण से पूछने लगा कि हे केशव! यदि आपको कर्म से ज्ञान बड़ा लगता है तब फिर आप मुझे भयंकर कर्म में क्यों लगाते हैं?

|1| Arjuna asks Sri Krishna: Hey Keshava! If you think that knowledge is greater than action, then why do you want me to take part in this terrible war?

CHAPTER 3

Exegetes often assume that Krishna's discourse in Chapter 2 is unambiguous. According to them, Krishna tells Arjuna that there is no reason for him to vacillate. Arjuna ought to understand what kind action is demanded of a dharmic soul in times of crisis. The simplicity of the Mewari summary of verse 1, however, suggests that the writer empathises with Arjuna's perplexity. So does the artist. Arjuna's vacillation is not a sign of cowardice or ignorance. His reasoning mind wants to know if violent action is necessary and just. He continues to urge Krishna, like a seeker of knowledge, to help him critically re-examine what tradition says about action, asceticism, power, ahimsa and the survival of his identity. He does so not in the spirit of arrogance but of humility.

Arjuna's request for clarification disrupts the flow of Krishna's discourse. His question is disorienting. The painter responds to Arjuna's dramatic intervention by reversing the chariot's direction. It makes us visually aware of Arjuna's sorrow and tears. Is there a moral law which permits the killing of relatives and friends? Startled, Krishna turns to look back at him. Arjuna's query is not only about acting selflessly. It is more fundamental. Is *himsa* (violence) evil under all circumstances? The dialogue that follows is unprecedented. There are very few religious texts in which a man refuses to obey divine authority untill he is intellectually and morally convinced of its rightness. For example, Jacob and Job in the Bible accept Jehovah's commandments unconditionally, though what they are ordered to do provokes fear and trembling.

The four visual sites in the painting for verse 1 seem like comments upon the dialogue. Each shows a mode of non-violent living, unconcerned with the fearful demands of the divine and the fruit of action. If the painting is read vertically, then Krishna has a place of moral authority. It can, however, also be read non-hierarchically. Two priestly figures in the foreground perform the *surya namaskar* (prayer to the rising sun) standing in a pool of clear blue water. The scene is gentle. The morning ceremony re-establishes the daily covenant between human beings and nature. A man sits calmly at the edge of the pool, holding a white flower. Like the sun-worshippers, he is a witness to the earth's beauty. All the figures are unarmed, peaceful and ordinary men who would instinctively respond to what the 11th century Sanskrit poet, Yogesvar, means when he writes: "my heart belongs to the meadow by the bend of the river."[1] At the third site, an ecstatic worshipper in a yellow dhoti plays the cymbals and sings. He is blissfully unaware of his surroundings. He is seated closer to Krishna. In the top right corner, two worshippers of Shiva and Vishnu meditate serenely with their eyes closed.

In verse 2, Arjuna continues to ask for clarity. In the painting, the chariot stands against a deep green background. Its tone is rich and resonant enough for other colours—white, pink, blue, gold, red or purple—to sparkle. Krishna and Arjuna are not armed. Both wear bejewelled golden crowns. Arjuna's sky-blue clothes, embellished with gold, reinforce his relation to the dark-skinned Krishna. Krishna is adorned with hieratic gold, emphasising his sacredness. He is untroubled by Arjuna's questions. He holds the reins of the horses firmly in his right hand and urges calm with his left. Hanuman sitting on top of the chariot's pennant which flutters well above the blue horizon seems to be a curious reader of Arjuna's question.

The six ascetics on the earth below are sharply drawn. Their distinctive appearance makes it clear that they belong to different religious sects—each seeking wisdom and salvation in their own way. Or, is each of them equally deluded? Does Allah Baksh treat them with irony? Can one detect a slight smile as he paints them, suggesting that their disputes may not provide the clarity Arjuna seeks? They are Shaivites, Vaishnavites and devotees of Rama and Krishna. One has long matted hair; the other has tied his hair in a small knot; the third is well-groomed and ash-smeared; the fourth has dread-locks; and the fifth, wearing an ochre-dyed cloth, has a gentle face and kind eyes. Together they acknowledge the rich variety that marks India's religious sects which thrive beside each other without fear of violence.

In verse 3, Krishna replies that he has already made a distinction between knowledge (the path of samkhya) and action (or karma yoga). Both lead to the Truth if the seeker is guided by wisdom. The painting of the chariot and the white horses is elegant, poised and balanced. It is Allah Baksh's fine response to Krishna's precisely phrased answer. Krishna's distinction between action and knowledge underlies much of the moral and political thought in the *Gita*. In its most elementary aspect, the path of knowledge is an exploration of the inner landscape of the self which may, at times, look like a labyrinth where a wilderness of desires or fantasies of revenge lead the self to a dead end. Only a disciplined yogi, totally detached from fears and temptations, can calmly negotiate a mental and emotional path where nothing touches the soul.

1 *Bright as an Autumn Moon: Fifty Poems from the Sanskrit*, translated by Andrew Schelling, *Manoa*, 25:2 (2013), p, 65.

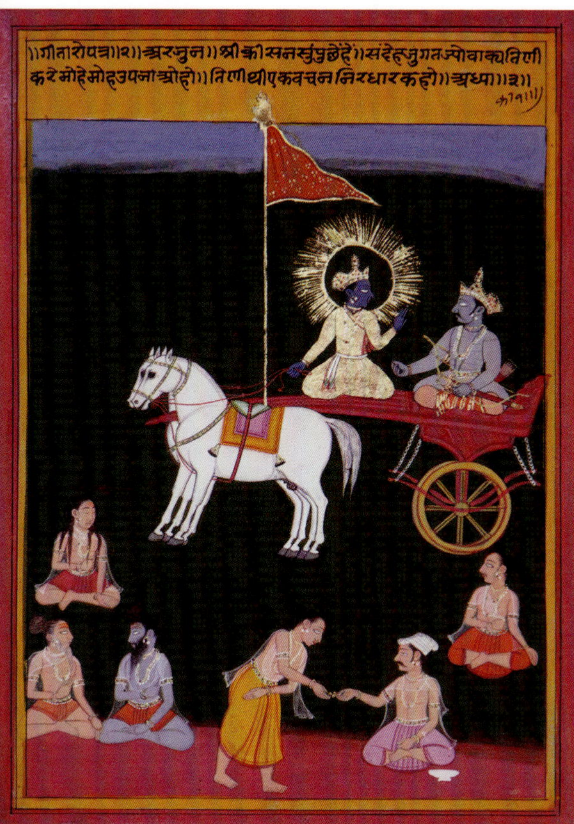

|2| अर्जुन श्री कृष्ण से आगे पूछने लगा कि हे कृष्ण! आप संदेहयुक्त मिली-जुली वाणी से मुझे भ्रम में डाल रहे हैं। आप से निवेदन है कि जिससे मेरा कल्याण हो वह बात मुझे मात्र एक वचन में कहिए।

|2| Arjuna further says to Sri Krishna: Hey Krishna! Your words are ambiguous and contradictory. I am confused. May I request you to tell me unambiguously what I should do for my welfare.

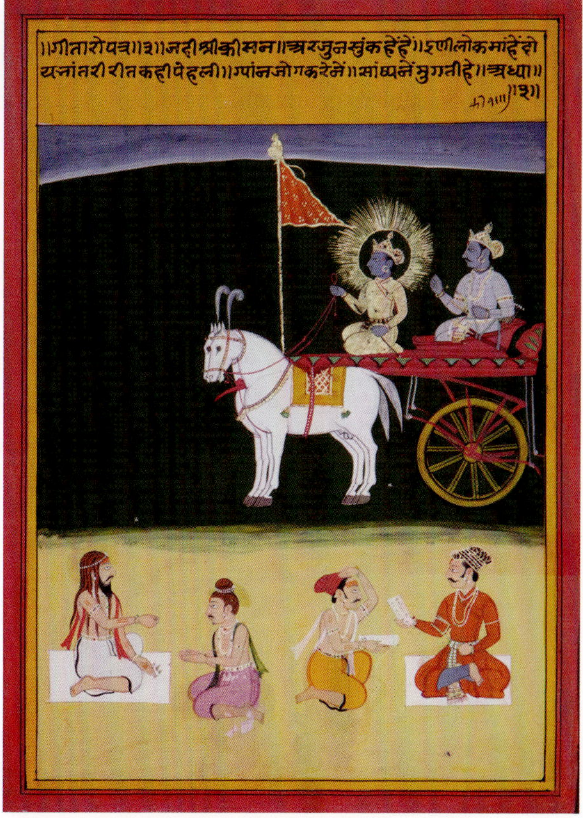

|3| यह सुन कर श्री कृष्ण अर्जुन को कहने लगे कि हे अर्जुन! मैंने बहुत पहले इस लोक में दो प्रकार की निष्ठा की बात कही थी। इसमें सांख्य की निष्ठा ज्ञानयोग से और योगियों की निष्ठा कर्मयोग से होती है।

|3| Upon hearing this, Sri Krishna says to Arjuna: Hey Arjuna! I have already told you that in this world there are two paths to wisdom: one is through knowledge (wisdom of the sankhyas), the other through action (karma yoga).

The Buddha's tranquillity, as he faces Maya's hobgoblins of illusions, is an archetype for all who seek nirvana through knowledge.

The other path to wisdom is that of right action consistent with dharma. Krishna does not dismiss the real world as an illusion. His emphasis is on the self as an active, but detached, participant in the social and political realms. A disciplined self is neither tempted away from the good nor distracted from his duty by the sensual, since sorrow and joy are ephemeral. Allah Baksh's painting continues with carefully observed types of mendicants and knowledge-seekers. There is no central icon. The questioners are located in an empty space conveying a sense of incompletion.

In the painting for verse 4, the chariot stands near a gently sloping hill lit by the mellow morning light. Arjuna and Krishna are too engrossed in their discussion about the ethics of action to notice the beauty of the land. Their earnest discussion is signalled by their gestures. Krishna's eagerness to urge the horses forward is apparent from his pull on the reins and their tense backward thrust. The red colour guides us to explore the other figures in the painting. The man on the left has a red turban with a gold band and is shown wearing a translucent cloth over a pinkish *jama*. He is sitting cross-legged and staring blankly into space. A dagger is tucked into his waistband. He seems like a man who, though capable of action, remains indecisive and, therefore, far from any possibility of attaining knowledge.

At the other end, a bare-bodied renunciant, with an impressive white beard, sits outside a brown thatched hut. His emaciated body is framed by a red door. His matted hair is tied in a knot on the top of his head. His appearance, however, is conventional—a common sight across India's landscape. Does he carry intimations of a mind which has sought and arrived at a vision of holiness or justice? Or, is he at peace with the trees, the sunlight and his dwelling? Is his calm presence not a counter to the horrors Arjuna anticipates? Weary of wars, should one not regard his withdrawal from life's difficulties with empathy? Is he not one of those who can live alone, be attentive and self-controlled?

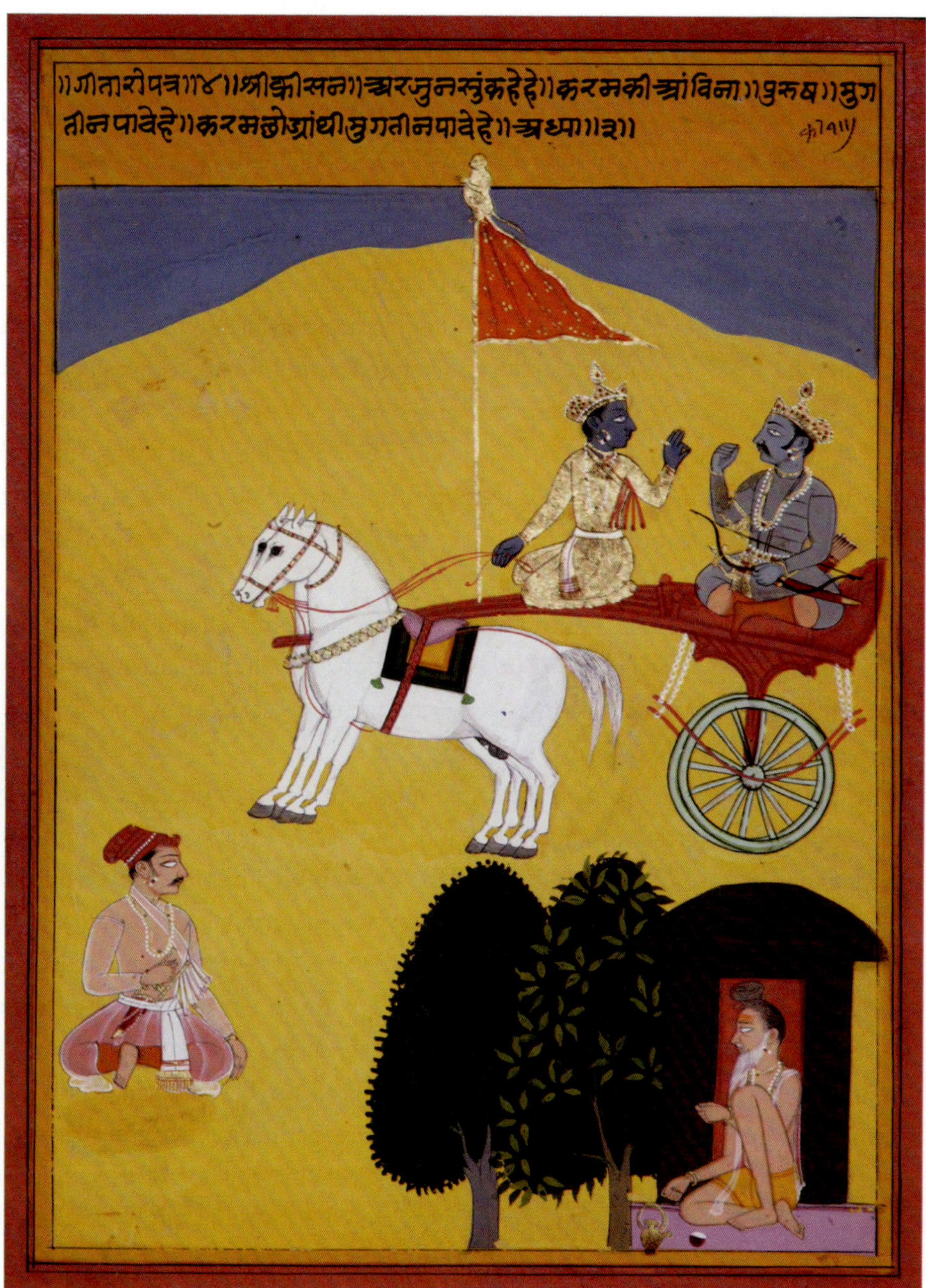

|4| श्री कृष्ण अर्जुन को आगे बताने लगे कि कर्म किए बिना पुरुष कर्मों से मुक्ति नहीं पा सकता और न ही कर्म छोड़ने से मुक्ति पा सकता है।

|4| Sri Krishna says to Arjuna: A human being can neither attain liberation without action nor obtain it by renouncing action.

As Krishna continues with his discourse on the impossibility of life without action in verse 5, Allah Baksh finds visual images to think about the same problem. Seven men are engaged in different activities. Some are silhouetted against a pink background, some sit on green earth depending entirely upon the delighted freedom of the artist. The colours of their clothes, which are not coded either by work, sect, class or rank, add to the glow that emanates from the work. The artist paints, as *Vishnudharmottara* says, "according to his own intellect."[2] The artifice is attractive.

The figures can be read in any order. There is no fixed hierarchical axis around which they are arranged. Unlike Christian metaphysics, no Indian scriptural tradition thinks of an immutable and ideal world arranged along a hierarchical chain of Being, with god in heaven, human beings and hell below. Nor does Indian metaphysics think of a particular direction or spatial side as more auspicious or ethically good. European painting imagines that the higher the place, the closer it is to god. It also thinks of the right hand of god as the hand of grace.[3] For an Indian painter, the divine can be manifest at any place, and all ethical lives and judgements are conditional. Thus, the sage at the end of *Shvetashvatara Upanishad* says: "God faces all the quarters of heaven" (2:16), and wittily adds that a wise man who is untouched by sorrow can "roll up space/ As it were a piece of leather" (6:20).[4]

The human figures are painted with attention to their postures and gestures. They seem familiar and mortal, not archetypal and allegorical. Their corporeal form and features show an unresolved conflict between action and withdrawal, inner turmoil and social temptations—which are, as the verse says, inevitable and unavoidable. In the right corner, a seller of small goods sits with the tools of his trade: a pair of scales, two black pitchers and five wicker baskets which are drawn with such precision that each thin strand of reed is braided and cross-hatched. At the opposite end, a rich man of martial bearing gives alms to a brahmin in a saffron dhoti and an ochre cloth thrown across his shoulders. We have seen these figures earlier, but never in such close interaction. They are part of the active social and moral imagination of our world. In between them sits the cross-legged figure of a yogi with his eyes shut, as oblivious of the swirl of daily life around him as the others are of his presence. Looking at this peaceful scene, one cannot but think with pity about the war to come.

---

2 Kramrisch, *Vishnudharmottara*, p. 6.

3 Kenneth Clark, *The Art of Humanism* (London: John Murray, 1983), p. 90.

4 *Thirteen Principal Upanishads*, translated by Griffith, p. 399 and p. 411.

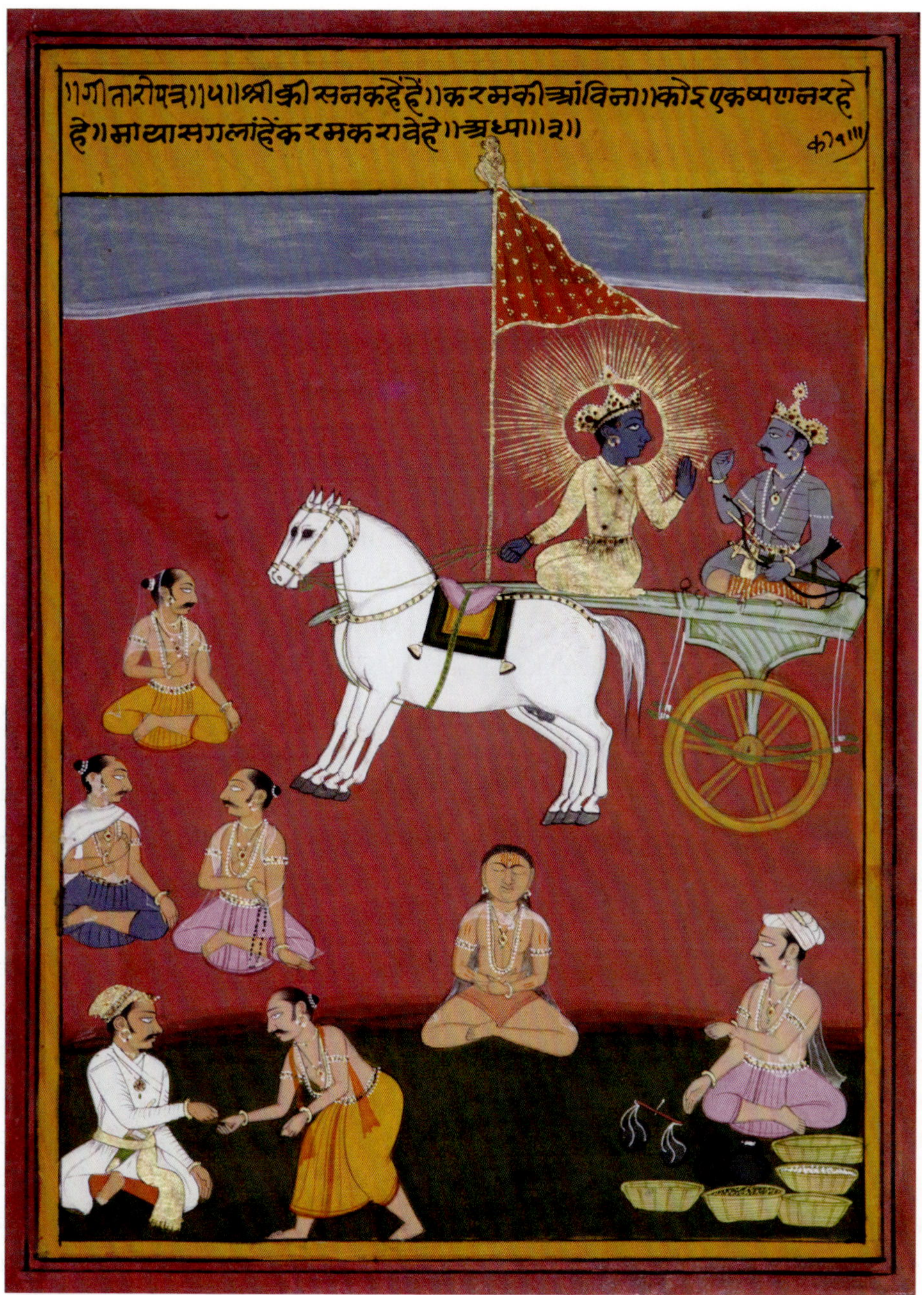

|5| श्री कृष्ण कहने लगे कि क्षण भर के लिए भी कोई कर्म किए बिना नहीं रह सकता क्योंकि सभी को प्रकृति प्रदत्त गुणों के कारण लाचार होकर कर्म करना ही पड़ता है।

|5| Sri Krishna says no one can live even for brief moment without action; helpless before the forces of nature, we are compelled to act.

Verse 6 is about those who withdraw from the world, yet desire it. Krishna calls them hypocrites, despite having earlier said that renunciation was one path to wisdom. Indeed, it is because of this ambiguity that Arjuna asks for clarification. Allah Baksh's painting is gentler and less censorious than Krishna's reply. Its tone and images offer two different messages. Neither of which has priority. What we see or hear, it suggests, depends on who we are. Thus, a religious viewer may only hear the *Gita* as a hymn to moral virtue and see Krishna's golden halo as a sign of his divine right to preach. He would praise the painting as an example of, what Coomaraswamy calls, "visual theology."[5] Allah Baksh, however, is more interesting than a pious illustrator. He is like the great debaters in the *Mahabharata*, who refuse to surrender to authority—divine or scholarly—till their inner voice is convinced of the truth of what is being said. He paints in order to explore, not resolve, his moral doubts about action, power and renunciation.

The painting makes us notice how sceptical the verse is about renunciation as a virtue, by using two contrasting images. The first is of a natural world which is so graceful and beautiful that it fills us with desire. One is charmed by the quiet stillness of the surrounding trees silhouetted against a deep blue sky or lost in the shadows of a green hill. Their formal decorativeness attracts our attention instead of persuading us to turn away. Looked at closely, they reveal the intricacy, variety and subtlety of their leaf-forms. Their internal order is pleasing; their structural symmetry and the gentle modulation of their green tones are impressive. Thus, one pale-green tree has a pattern of five-leaves within a circle. Each of the leaf-circlets is carefully arranged and radiates away from tree-trunk and branches. The leaves of the other tree, darker in tone and half-hidden, are a series of fine cross-hatched lines arranged to create an inner harmony of their own. Maybe, one could interpret the trees allegorically. Such a reading has the sanction of the Upanishadic singers and the Bhakti poets. The sage of the *Shvetashvatara Upanishad* (3:9) exclaims that trees of beauty are "established in heaven"[6] and Tulsidas imagines that trees in a grove are an "assembly of saints."[7]

The sadhu sitting under the tree makes one uncomfortable. If we look at him without mystification, he is a bit comical. Slightly out of proportion, he is like a figure made of soft dough. His ears are too big; the two long braids streaming down beside garlands of pearls are incongruous. His loincloth is uneasily conspicuous; his forehead

5 Quoted by D. Venkat Rao, *Cultures of Memory in South Asia: Orality, Literacy and the Problem of Inheritance* (Heidelberg: Springer, 2014), p. 165.

6 *Thirteen Principal Upanishads*, translated by Griffith, p. 400.

7 *The Epic of Ram*, volume I, translated by Philip Lutgendorf (Cambridge, Massachusetts: Harvard University Press, 2016), p. 87.

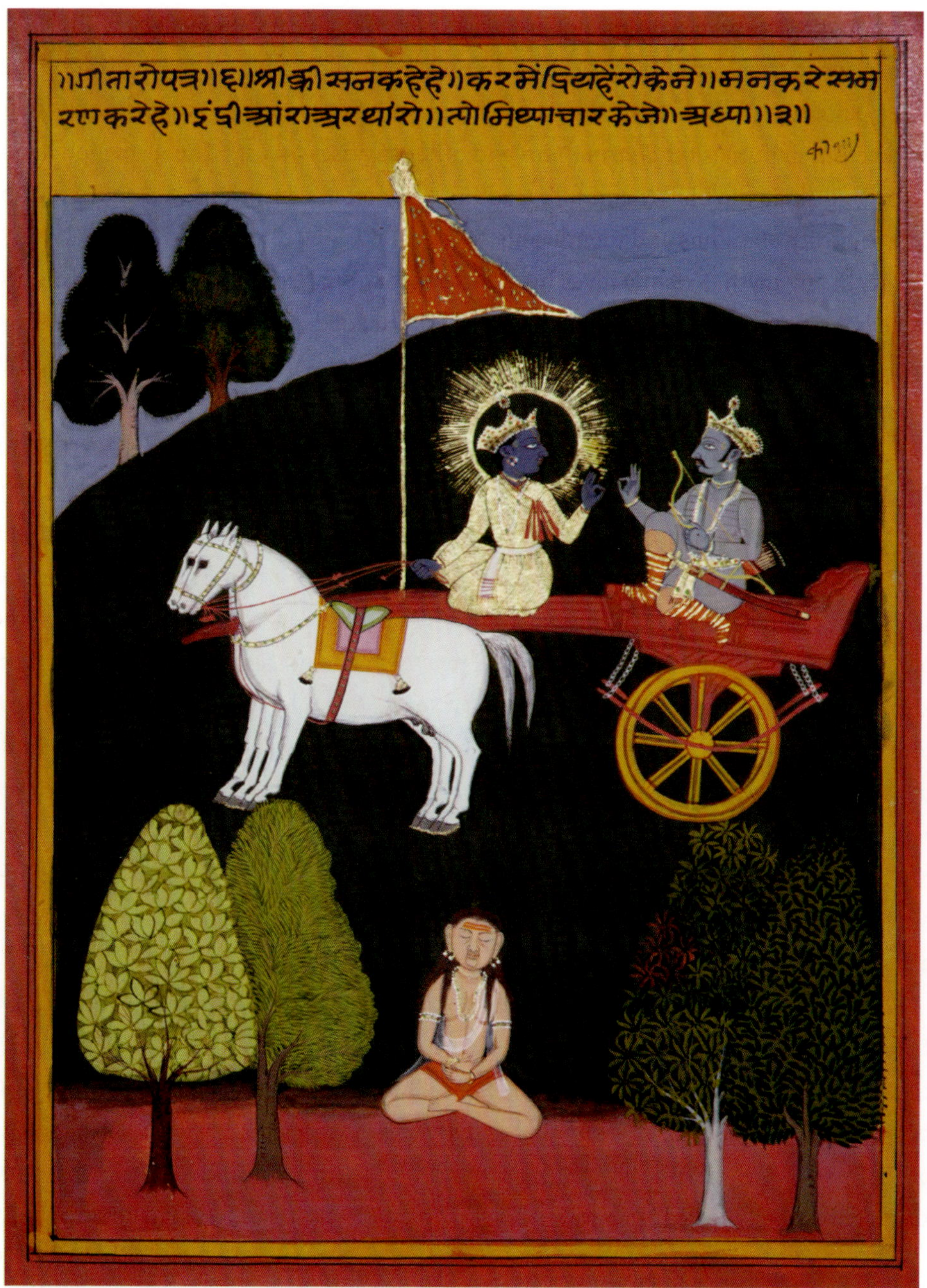

|6| श्री कृष्ण अर्जुन से कहने लगे कि जो प्राणी बाहर से तो कर्मेन्द्रियों को नियंत्रित कर लेता है परन्तु मन से उनका चिंतन करता है, ऐसा मूढ़ मनुष्य पाखंडी कहा जाता है।

|6| Sri Krishna says to Arjuna: A person who has withdrawn from action in the external world, but who still desires it in his heart, is deluded and called a hypocrite.

is awkwardly smeared with orange paste as if to offer a visual equivalent of the word 'hypocrite' in the verse. The caricature seems to be deliberate because there are many other paintings of anchorites that follow the laws of *pramana* or proportion so well-worked out in the *Vishnudharmottara* and other treatises on art.[8] The distortion is not surprising since the bhakti and folk traditions are often censorious and suspicious of the religiosity of sadhus and mendicants.

As in any myth, Krishna gives his ethical theory of action transcendental sanctity. He tells Arjuna that the creation of the world is an act of divine sacrifice. Human beings must imitate that selfless sacrifice for their own salvation. Verse 10 speaks of Prajapati as the Lord of Creation, but the writer of the Mewari text identifies Brahma as the world's maker. There is a precedent for this substitution in the *Mundaka Upanishad*: "Brahma arose as the first of the gods—/The maker of all, the protector of the world (1.1.1)."[9] In the painting accompanying this verse, Brahma, with four heads and four arms, sits in the top left corner in untroubled quietude. His unhurried and unanxious creative confidence is in harmony with the surrounding colours. Separating the earth from the blue sky and the rising sun is a rippling line which has no beginning and no end. In keeping with the significance of Brahma's presence, this line has an imperceptible flow that creates a sense of unending, dynamic creation. We recognise, as Zimmer reminds us, that "Brahma is...the positive aspect of the life-process of the universe, and is never represented as destroying what he has produced."[10] He is the only Indian deity who rarely carries a weapon; he is pure creativity and pure spirituality, unlike Shiva, Vishnu and Indra who represent the benign and the terrible, the creative and the destructive aspects of nature.

Brahma's clothes are carefully pleated and tightly tucked around his thick waist. His beard, in accordance with iconographic convention, is white, indicating that he is the original creator. His body is neither lean like Krishna's nor muscular like Shiva's, but still conveys a sense of perpetual activity.[11] He carries a rosary in one hand. As is traditional, a water-pot lies on the ground beside him. Legend says that "the first seed of creation is sowed" in a water-bowl.[12] To emphasis his peaceful nature, his body

8 Kramrisch, *Vishnudharmottara*, p. 14 and pp. 47–48.

9 *Thirteen Principal Upanishads*, translated by Hume, p. 366.

10 Zimmer, *Myths and Symbols in Indian Art and Civilization*, p. 124.

11 Zimmer, pp. 130–31.

12 Zimmer, p. 133.

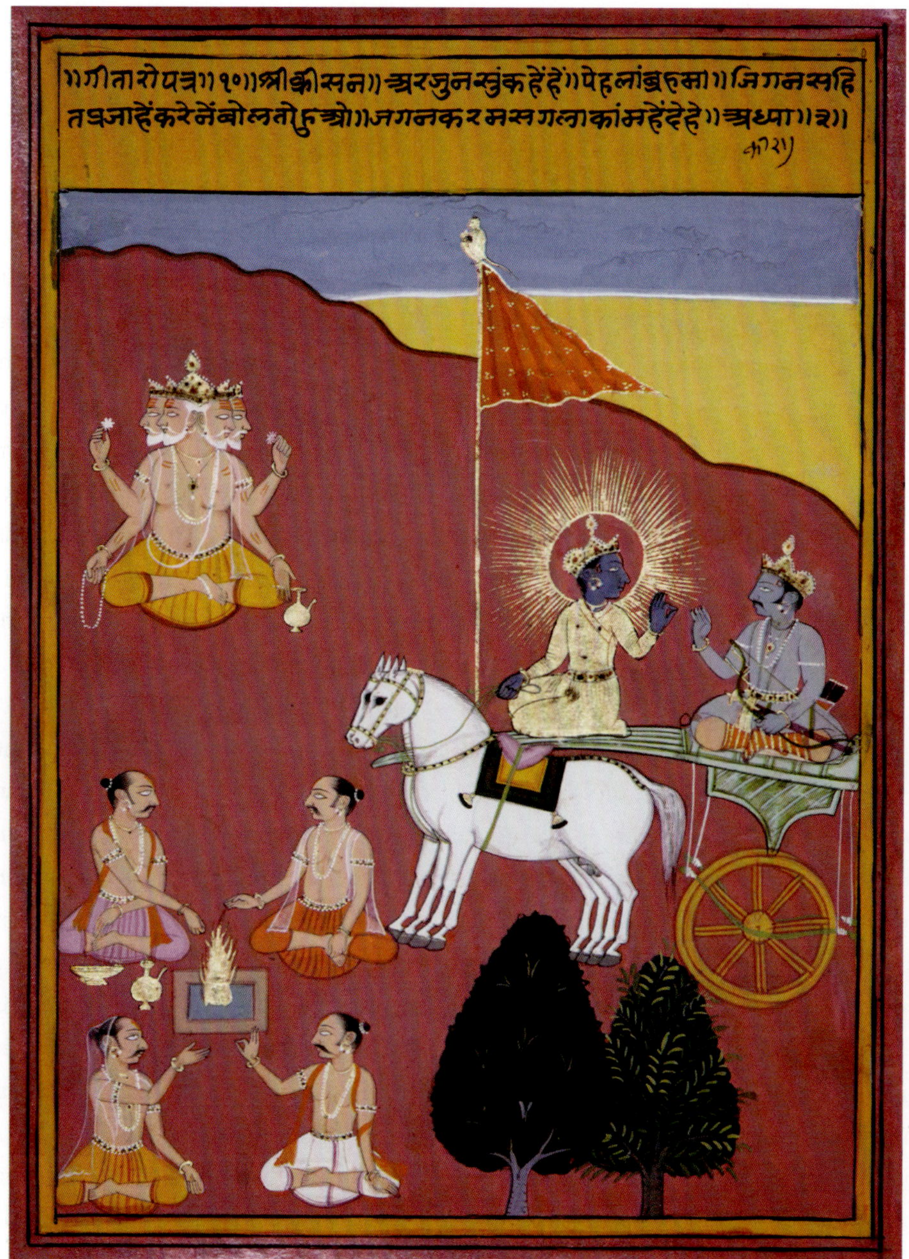

|10| श्री कृष्ण आगे कहने लगे कि सृष्टि के आरंभ में ब्रह्मा ने यज्ञ के साथ प्रजाओं को रच कर कहा कि यज्ञ से तुम वृद्धि प्राप्त करो और यह यज्ञ तुम्हारी सारी कामनाओं को पूरा करने वाला हो।

|10| Sri Krishna further says that in the beginning, when the world was created, Brahma said to all created beings, procreate through sacrifice; such a sacrifice shall fulfil all your desires.

is covered with necklaces of pearls and diamonds, his arms and chest are marked with decorative lines of vermillion, and his head is crowned with a golden peacock feather. Surprisingly, the only traditional emblem he is not carrying is a book (he is said to have written the four Vedas). Four priests sit around a sacrificial ritual fire below Brahma. They seem to be engaged in an ethical or religious argument. Their gestures are delightfully captured. The two groups of disputants are mirror images of each other adding to our sense that scriptural arguments are often futile exercises in narcissism. Would it not be more worthy to look up at the lyrically flowing lines and colours around them and participate in the unending glow of creation which Brahma represents? The two green trees below the chariot are emblems of Brahma who asks for no sacrifice or surrender, but invites everyone to be participants in the world's abundance.

Having established the idea that a good deed performed for its own sake is anchored in the Supreme in verse 11, Krishna urges Arjuna to recognise two ideas about the self. The self, he says, is unique unto itself and, therefore, its own questioner. And, it is an aspect of the Divine. A sovereign, disinterested self can choose to act justly and consciously sacrifice the fruit of action. If Arjuna can do that, he shall inspire awe even in the gods.

The painting accompanying this verse, about worshippers and grace-givers, hints at the presence of the gods, their incarnations and the small ceremonies which sustain daily life. In the corner, there is a white temple with a dome. Its outer walls have no decorative designs. In the sanctum, against a red background, there is a four-armed idol of a Devi. She is richly adorned with a golden crown, necklaces, bracelets and nose rings. Her ornaments, as in most ancient Indian art, are a sign of her sacred and mystical power.[13] Her benign and generous qualities (*saguna*) are reaffirmed by the presence of Ganesha sitting outside the temple's threshold. There is a sense of pleasure in the making of the Ganesha image. His head is red, a colour radiating with the imaginative energy of the earth, his lower garment is saffron, the colour of sacrality, and his body is paunchy, signifying the prosperity of peacetime. In one left hand, he holds a water-pot symbolising his close connection with fertility. Interestingly, in his other left hand, he holds the tusk he has broken off to inscribe the *Mahabharata* as dictated by Vyasa. Of course, as a deity who removes all obstacles and controls the self, he carries a symbolic goad or axe in his right hand. Both the god and the goddess here are the non-violent nourishers and sustainers of the earth's abundance. We are asked to remember this

---

13 Anand K. Coomaraswamy, 'Ornament,' *The Art Bulletin*, 21: 3 (1939), pp. 377–78 and p. 381.

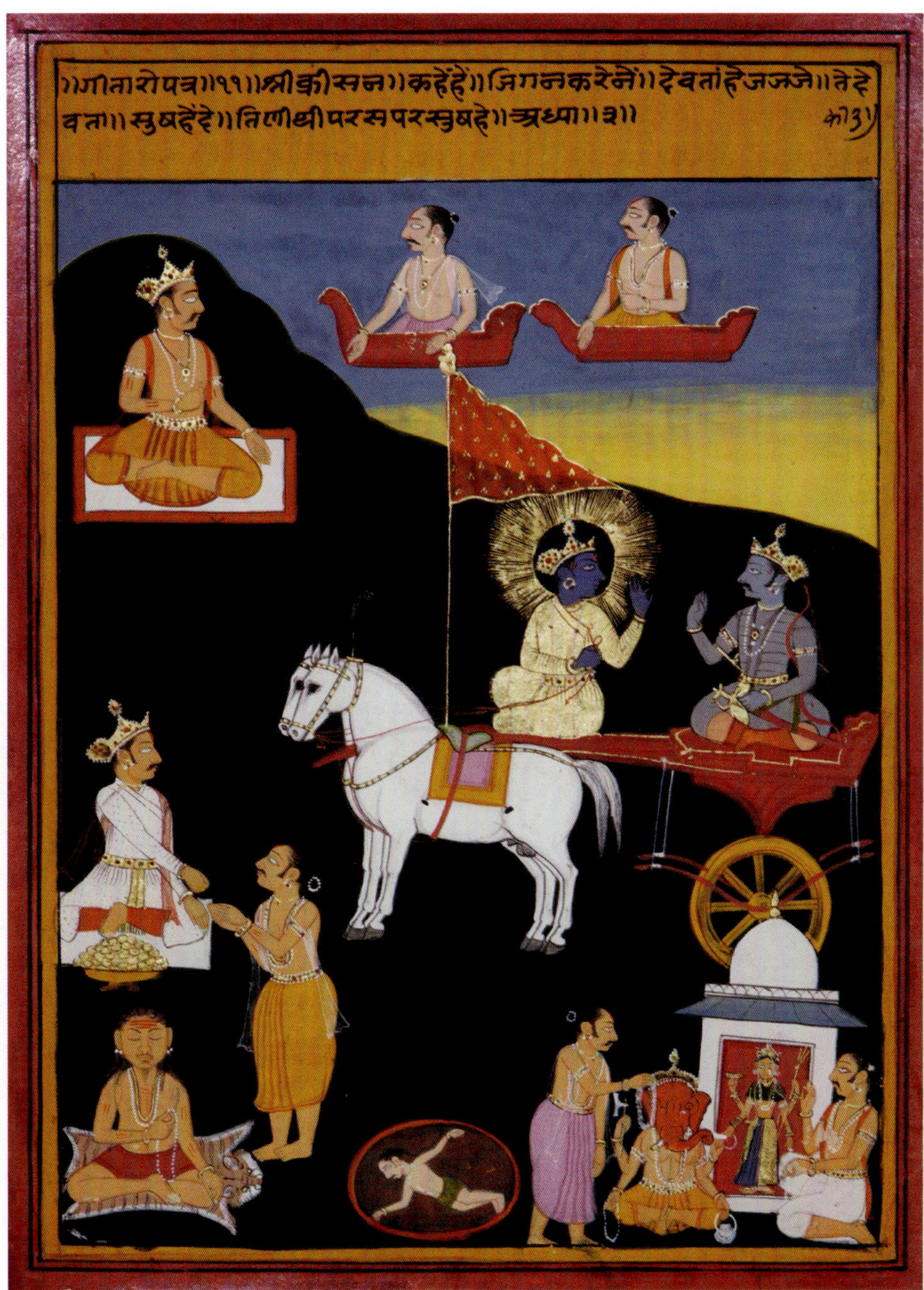

|11| श्री कृष्ण अर्जुन को बताने लगे कि यज्ञ से तुम देवताओं को पोषित करो और वे देवता तुम्हें पोषित करेंगे। इस तरह परस्पर एक-दूसरे को पोषित करते हुए तुम कल्याण को प्राप्त होओ।

|11| Sri Krishna says to Arjuna, your sacrifice shall please the Gods who will then nourish you. Thus, supporting each other, you shall achieve the bliss of liberation.

as we look up from the temple to the chariot and think about the action Arjuna must perform when his kingdom is in crisis.

Apart from this vignette of daily worship, the other four sites in the painting are equally attractive. A Shaivite ascetic sits in deep meditation in the lower right corner. A little above, a handsome prince looks up towards the figure of Krishna, as he gives gold coins to a poor mendicant. In the top left corner, a regal figure watches two sages in red sky-boats. His golden crown with a peacock feather, stately posture and calm demeanour suggest that he may be Indra, the god of the sky, clouds and rain, who offers, as the verse says, "nourishment" (Swami 29) to those who remember him in their sacrifice.

In the painting for verse 12, a spiritually charged blue light spreads its grace over everything. Impatient, Krishna has turned his back to Arjuna whose gesture captures his surprise and bewilderment. In marked contrast, four men sit around a ritual fire discussing matters of scripture and action without anxiety or impatience. The circle formed by men, fire, food and water is like a timeless image of a well-reasoning intellectual community where discussion can happen without the fear of violence. The horses and the elephant too appear to be part of an unthreatening, natural compact between human beings, the earth and the gods. "Nature will give you all the enjoyment you may desire" (Swami 29). Is this what gives the first part of the verse its confidence? The gesture of the divine figure on the top left subtly mirrors Arjuna's emotions, though the emotions he radiates are different. While Arjuna is perplexed, the man seems calm and untroubled. Is the painter dreaming of a possible and different world where choices are not as stark as those presented by Krishna?

Krishna's moral judgement against those who work only for selfish gain continues with the clarity of a prophetic poet who knows from experience how fickle human beings generally are; how quickly they discard ideals for power, wealth or comfort (verse 13). He has the Kauravas in mind for they have the privilege of tradition and knowledge. We, as readers, know that even Dharma's son, Yudhishthira, can falter. To restore wisdom to the human world, Arjuna will have to re-enact the myth of the heroic sacrifice of the self.

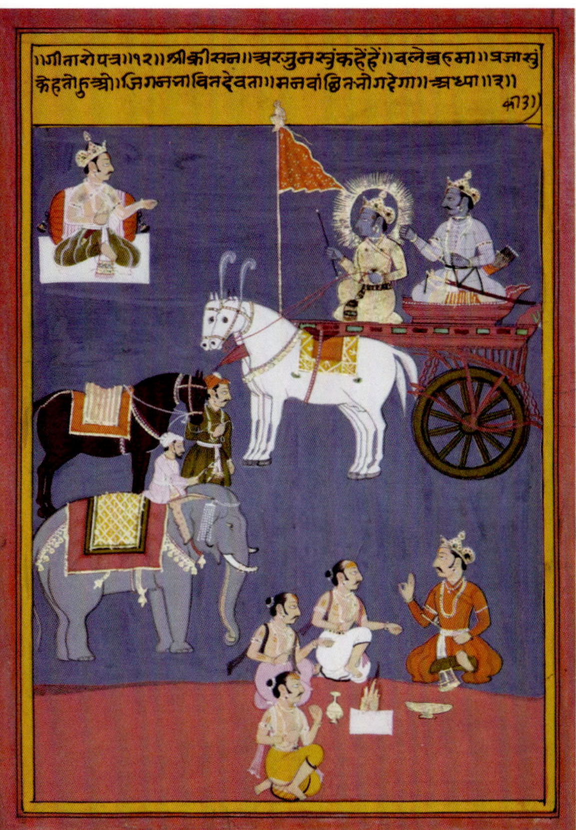

|12| श्री कृष्ण आगे कहने लगे कि हे अर्जुन! यज्ञ से पोषित हो देवता तुम लोगों को इच्छित भोग प्रदान करते रहेंगे पर उन्हें अर्पण किए बिना जो मनुष्य उनके दिए पदार्थों को भोगता है, वह चोर है।

|12| Sri Krishna continues: Hey Arjuna! Nourished by your sacrifices the gods will fulfil all your desires, but the one who enjoys their gifts without offering any sacrifice is a thief.

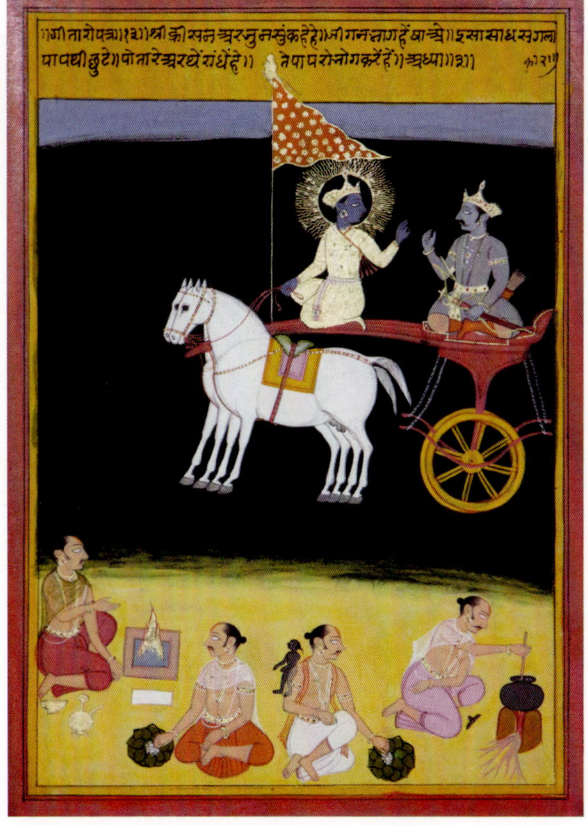

|13| श्री कृष्ण अर्जुन से कहने लगे कि जो मनुष्य यज्ञ से बचा अन्न खाते हैं, वे सब पापों से मुक्त हो जाते हैं और जो पापी केवल अपने लिए ही पकाते हैं वे तो पाप को ही खाते हैं।

|13| Sri Krishna says to Arjuna: Those human beings who eat food that remains after sacrifice attain freedom from all sins, but those selfish ones who cook only to feed themselves feed only on sin.

Allah Baksh understands that a vein of sadness runs through the verse. This painting is among the few bleak ones in the folio. It carries premonitions of an adharmic world where those who do not have a right to wealth snatch it from its legitimate beneficiaries. They are, Krishna says, thieves. The background colour is ominous. Black, mixed with green, gives it an uncanny depth, opening an abyss. There are black spots on the earthen pot, the hearth and the leaf-plates. Half-hidden behind one of the men in the middle is a grotesque, dark, bare-bodied dwarf, with braided hair. He emerges from nowhere like a menacing shadow or an evil emanation. In Indian miniatures, as Kramrisch points out, it is rare to find a human figure which is not completely delineated and fully visible; rarely is it smudged by shadows of other people or objects.[14] Here the sneaking figure points to the sinister triviality of a man who grabs whatever the earth provides for his own selfish use. There are two other morally distinct men who sit before a fire at the other end. The man, who tends the ritual fire, sits erect and confidently. His hand is extended in a generous welcome to anyone who would care to share his food and the knowledge he has to offer. The other has turned his back to us. He is bent over the food he is cooking; his left arm is taut with anxiety.

Verse 14 and the accompanying painting continue with the meditation on the word 'sacrifice' and enlarge its possible meanings. The poet says that all living beings and non-living things—gods, human beings, fields and rain—make some sacrifice to enable the universe to survive and continuously replenish itself. The painter offers an enticing reminder that just as war obliterates the cycle of seasons it hardens the heart and narrows the vision of human beings. Dark clouds promise spring rain, lightning flashes across the sky, the fields are green with new saplings, a farmer cultivates his land, the air is fresh and birds take flight in the morning light. Colour and form enrich the mind; a spirit of peace and harmony defines the relation between men and the earth. The two priests in the left corner complete the natural cycle that the verse celebrates: rain, earth, fire, food, sacrifice and peaceful coexistence as a possible and sustainable vision of life on earth.

14 Stella Kramrisch, *Exploring India's Sacred Art: Selected Writings*, edited by Barbara Stoler Miller (New Delhi: Indira Gandhi National Centre for the Arts, 1994), pp. 124–26.

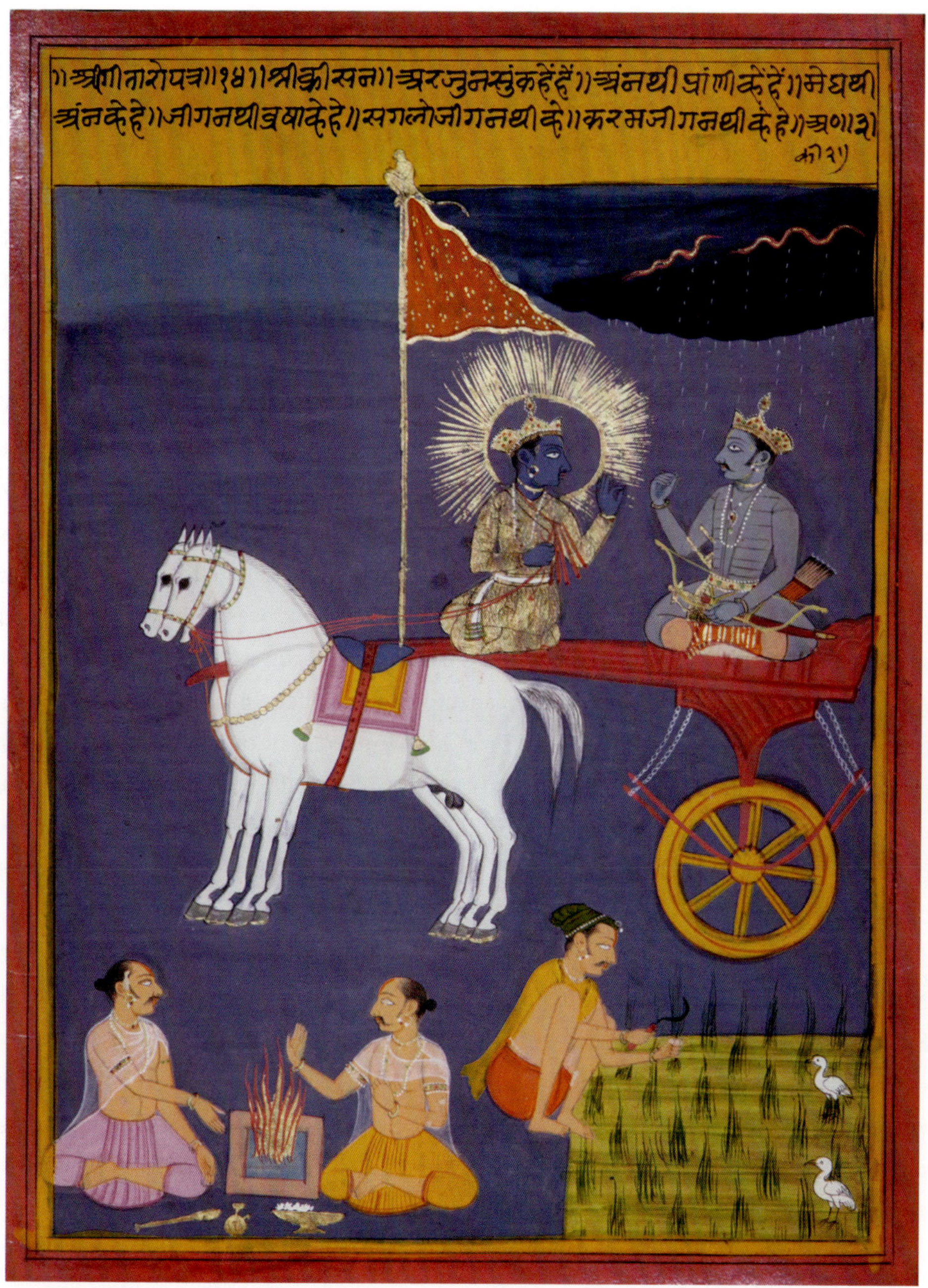

|14| श्री कृष्ण आगे बताने लगे कि प्राणी अन्न से उत्पन्न होते हैं, अन्न वृष्टि से उत्पन्न होता है, वृष्टि यज्ञ से होती है और यज्ञ कर्म से उत्पन्न होता है।

|14| Sri Krishna further says to Arjuna: All living beings depend on food, all food comes from rain, sacrifice is essential for rain, and action is a form of sacrifice.

Knowing that sacrifice has its source in the Vedas is not enough. It is the understanding of the word which must guide action; give a shape to our identity; show us what, why or how to do something; and, what would happen if it is done or not done. In the painting for verse 15, two learned men converse in the top left corner of the painting. They are either sitting on a sunlit earth or with the gods in the sky. Two other pundits perform different rites on the earth below. One is tending to a ritual fire. The other, his back to the fire, is eating a sparse meal off a leaf plate. Instead of wearing his golden armour, Arjuna is dressed in blue. Krishna sits facing Arjuna urging him to set his hesitation aside.

We realise how important the long pause of the *Gita*, before the war begins, is for Arjuna's ethical self. Before he acts, he must examine every shade and corner of his soul to cast out hatred; sacrifice the very idea of vengeance; give up the desire for victory. Only then shall he become a dharma warrior; understand the meaning of justice and mercy. How difficult that is, how nearly impossible, is the epic's ethical concern. The painting is important not only because it pleases the eye, but because it persuades us to see that Arjuna's questioning is a kind of vigilance over his own desires and ambitions. And, of course, it awakens our own introspective intelligence. In empathy with Arjuna, the painter says: We do not need moral sermons; we need to be taught the more difficult art of thinking authentically about moral acts ourselves without seeking the approval of others, however sagacious. The task of learning is "not to furnish us with sight but to direct [our] sight."[15] This is precisely what Krishna teaches. That is why he never belittles Arjuna, but engages with him and his doubts.

In verse 16, Krishna specifically calls upon Arjuna to give up what the body desires. Not to do so is vanity and evil (*Jnaneshwari* 1:90). Sacrifice of the sensuous world, Krishna says, may be required to ensure the earth's survival in evil times. This is, of course, the refrain of all orthodox interpretations of religious texts. The painting for verse 16, however, suggests that in times of peace a grateful acknowledgement of the physical may also be necessary for the recovery of all our ideal dreams. In one corner, a young couple exchange a garland of flowers as they gaze into each other's eyes. The woman is adorned with a large gold nose-ring, bracelets, ear-rings, anklets, necklaces and clothes with golden threadwork. The man is handsome, with a bold moustache and clean cut sideburns. The painting is charming and sensually inviting. Two priests conduct a sacred ritual for the well-being of all. In the sky above, a seer rows by in his

15 Montaigne, Michel de, *The Complete Works*, translated by Donald M. Frame (New York: Everyman Library, 1948), p. 126.

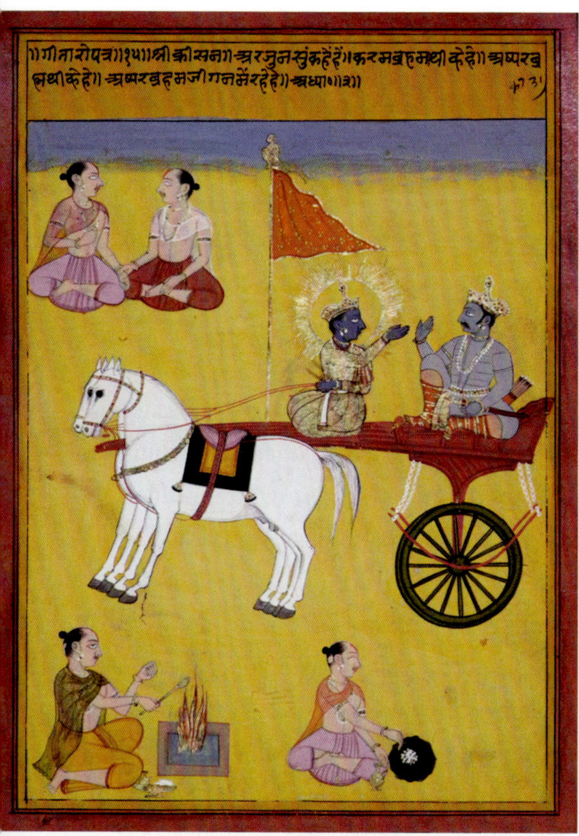

|15| श्री कृष्ण अर्जुन से कह रहे हैं- हे अर्जुन! कर्म तो वेद से उत्पन्न हुए हैं और वेद अक्षर (अविनाशी) ब्रह्म से उत्पन्न हैं और सर्वव्यापक ब्रह्म यज्ञ में रहता है।

|15| Sri Krishna says to Arjuna: Listen Arjuna! The source of action is the Vedas, and in the Vedas the source of action is the immortal Brahma. And Brahma is omnipresent in sacrifice.

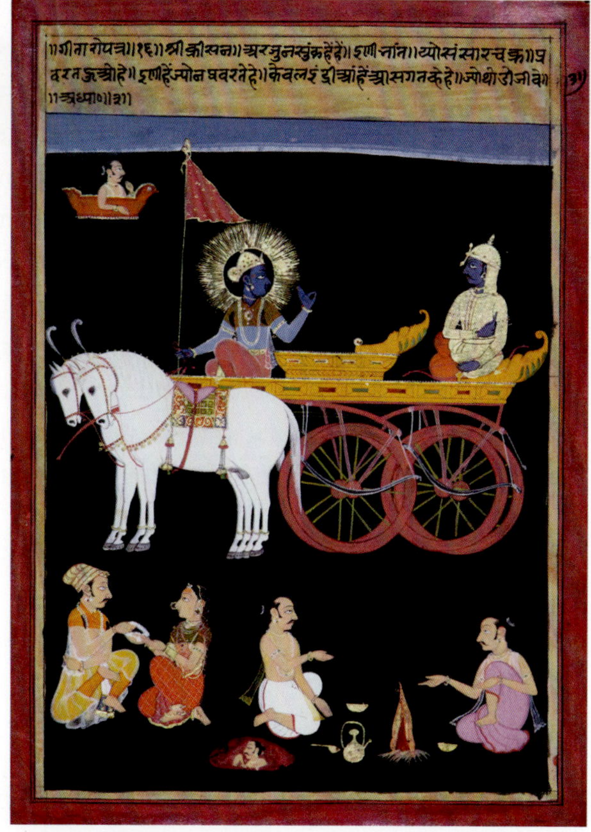

|16| श्री कृष्ण आगे कहने लगे कि हे अर्जुन! जो मनुष्य इस परिवर्तनशील सृष्टि चक्र के अनुकूल व्यवहार नहीं करता, वह इन्द्रियों में आसक्त प्राणी व्यर्थ ही जीता है।

|16| Sri Krishna further says: Hey Arjuna! Any man, who does not follow the law that turns the wheel of change and only fulfils his own sensual desires, lives in vain.

bird-boat looking down with a benevolent eye. As the verse indicates, there is a cyclical relation between heaven and earth; the ethics of one and the generosity of the other sustain the universe. In the lowest half, an enigmatic figure is either sinking into a pit of fire or emerging from it. Is he the vain man who "leads a sinful life" (Swami 29) and cannot escape the wheel of time?

In a surprising move away from his insistence upon action as the way to salvation, in verses 17 and 18, Krishna speaks about the one who has gained sovereign control over his body and mind. In the top left corner of the painting for verse 18, there is a sparkling silver sun with a golden divine figure of Vishnu shimmering in its core. Is the visionary sun the very image of the self-illuminated, self-sufficient, self-generated Atma who doesn't need to perform any action to keep the wheel of dharma turning? Sitting next to the sun, close to the horizon, is another divine figure whose body is blue like Krishna's. He is gazing out at us as if persuading us to concentrate on our own innermost being. There are three typical scenes near the edge of a green field. On the right is an ordinary domestic tableau. A well-dressed man is sitting across from his elegantly attired wife who has just served him food on a leaf plate. Judging from their simple and casual gestures and their postures, they seem to be talking about nothing in particular. Together, they present a happy conjugal scene which is, in the artist's worldview, a perfectly acceptable shape dharma can take in any lifecycle. At the opposite end, a religious ritual is being performed to appease the gods and seek their blessing. This, too, is part of the common routine of an ordinary day when the world is not at war and people are engaged in their daily tasks. In between the two is the figure of a woman who is shown meditating. Detached from the daily world, she attracts attention because, given the times, she is not an expected sight. Her presence says something about the independence of the artist who is willing to give a *yogin* a central place in his work. In the *Mahabharata*, there are women like Sulbha whose intellect is sharp and whose learning puts the most reputed teachers in a quandary.

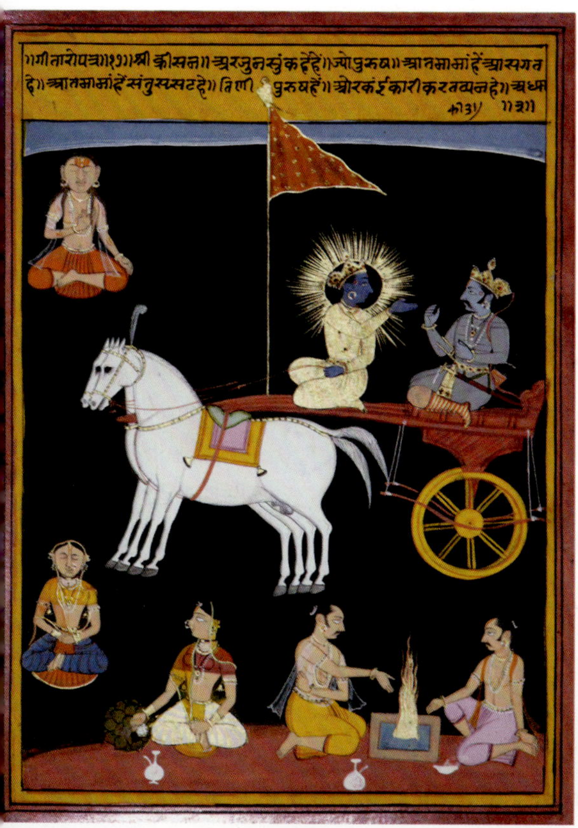

|17| श्री कृष्ण अर्जुन से कह रहे हैं कि जो पुरुष आत्मा में आसक्त है, आत्मा में ही संतुष्ट है, उसके करने को कोई कार्य नहीं है।

|17| Sri Krishna says to Arjuna: The one who concentrates on his Atma and is content within his own self needs to perform no action.

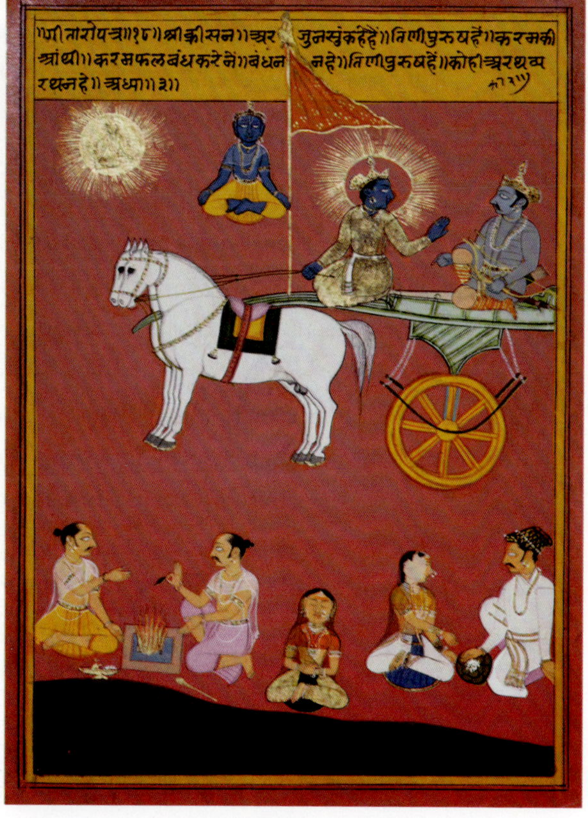

|18| श्री कृष्ण आगे कहने लगे कि हे अर्जुन! ऐसे पुरुष का इस संसार में न तो कर्म करने का कोई प्रयोजन रहता है और न ही कर्म न करने का। यही नहीं, सभी प्राणियों से उसका थोड़ा-सा स्वार्थ का सम्बन्ध भी नहीं रहता।

|18| Sri Krishna further adds: Hey Arjuna! Such a person does not have any reason either to act or not to act in this world. Indeed, his welfare does not in the least depend on earthly creatures.

In the next few verses (19, 20, 21 and 22), Krishna tells Arjuna that he should imitate great men who perform their duty without attachment. This is Krishna's core message. All ritual societies assume that beneficent action in time is an imitation or repetition of what the gods once performed at the beginning.[16] Indeed human deeds acquire meaning or value not because they are independent of the divine, but because they commemorate what the gods did or urged one to do. As the *Taittiriya Brahmana* says, "Thus the gods did; thus men do."[17] Krishna says that he does not have to act in the world since he is not dependent upon it, but has decided to participate in its activities because human survival may depend upon it. The painting for verse 22 is in response to the repetition of the words 'action' and 'work.'

In the painting for verse 22, four uniquely painted sadhus on the green field below, perform different rites of meditation. There is a grotesque figure on the far right. His black hair is matted, beard is white, and his body is smeared with blue-ash. His forehead is marked with two horizontal vermillion lines suggesting that he is a Shaivite. Both his arms are amputated. He sits cross-legged with his eyes shut. No figure like him has appeared in the folio before. Does his presence remind us that, while the *Gita* insists upon the idea that tragic suffering is a result of karmic deviations from dharma, many a time suffering is also inexplicable? One is moved by the feeling of simple devotional acceptance in the yogi's face of what fate has chosen to send his way. The *Gita* is important for the painter because it makes him understand both the complexity and the tragic inexplicability of human life.

There are two other men on the same lower plane of the painting, who are practising *pranayama*, while the fourth blue-bodied figure is lost in meditation. They are oblivious of each other and do not represent Krishna's ideal of a karma yogi. Of course, their withdrawal from the world of action has scriptural sanction as Krishna has already accepted. Allah Baksh is not critical of their ascetic renunciation; he merely records it. Krishna and Arjuna, in contrast, are engaged in a lively exchange; their eyes are alert and their gestures are animated. On the top left, a worshipper sits before the idol of Krishna placed on a raised platform. The priest holds a white conch shell and a golden bell with a long handle as he recites his prayers. The saffron background adds to a feeling of quiet worshipfulness, even as the dialogue between Krishna and Arjuna adds intellectual depth to the work.

---

16 See Mircea Eliade, *Cosmos and History: The Myth of the Eternal Return*, translated by Willard R. Trask (New York: Harper and Row, 1959).

17 Eliade, *Cosmos and History*, pp. 3–25.

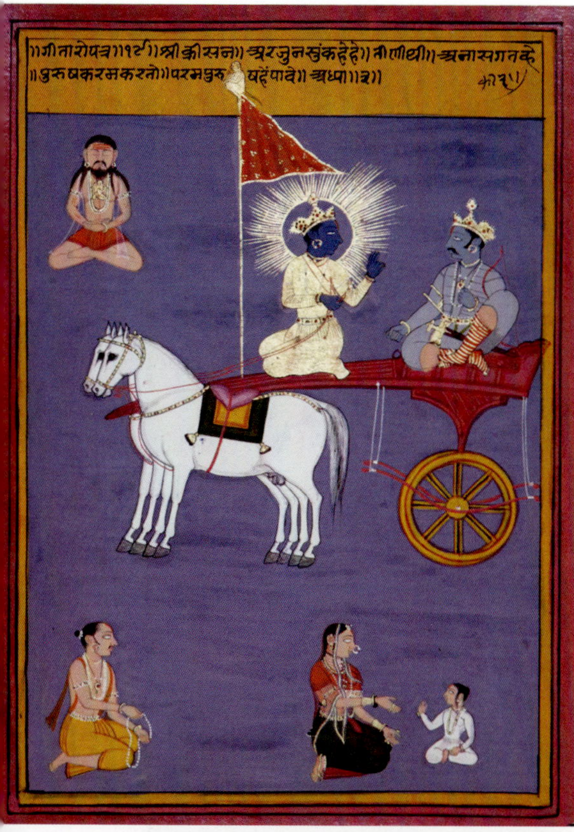

|19| श्री कृष्ण अर्जुन से कह रहे हैं कि इसलिए अनासक्त होकर कर्म को करता रह क्योंकि अनासक्त होकर लगातार कर्म करने से ही परम-पुरुष को प्राप्त होगा।

|19| Sri Krishna says to Arjuna: Act without attachment, because only the one who continues to do his duty without attachment attains the Supreme.

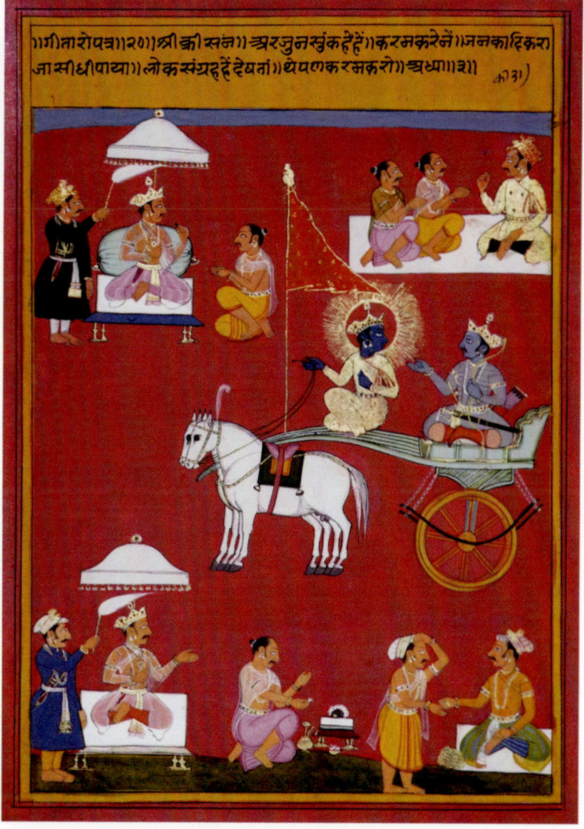

|20| श्री कृष्ण अर्जुन से आगे कहने लगे कि हे अर्जुन! जनक आदि भी कर्म (निष्काम) द्वारा ही सिद्धि को प्राप्त हुए थे, इसलिए लोकसंग्रह के लिए भी तुझको कर्म करना चाहिए।

|20| Sri Krishna further says to Arjuna: Hey Arjuna! Janaka and others attained perfection through action; that is why, for the sake of public good, you should act.

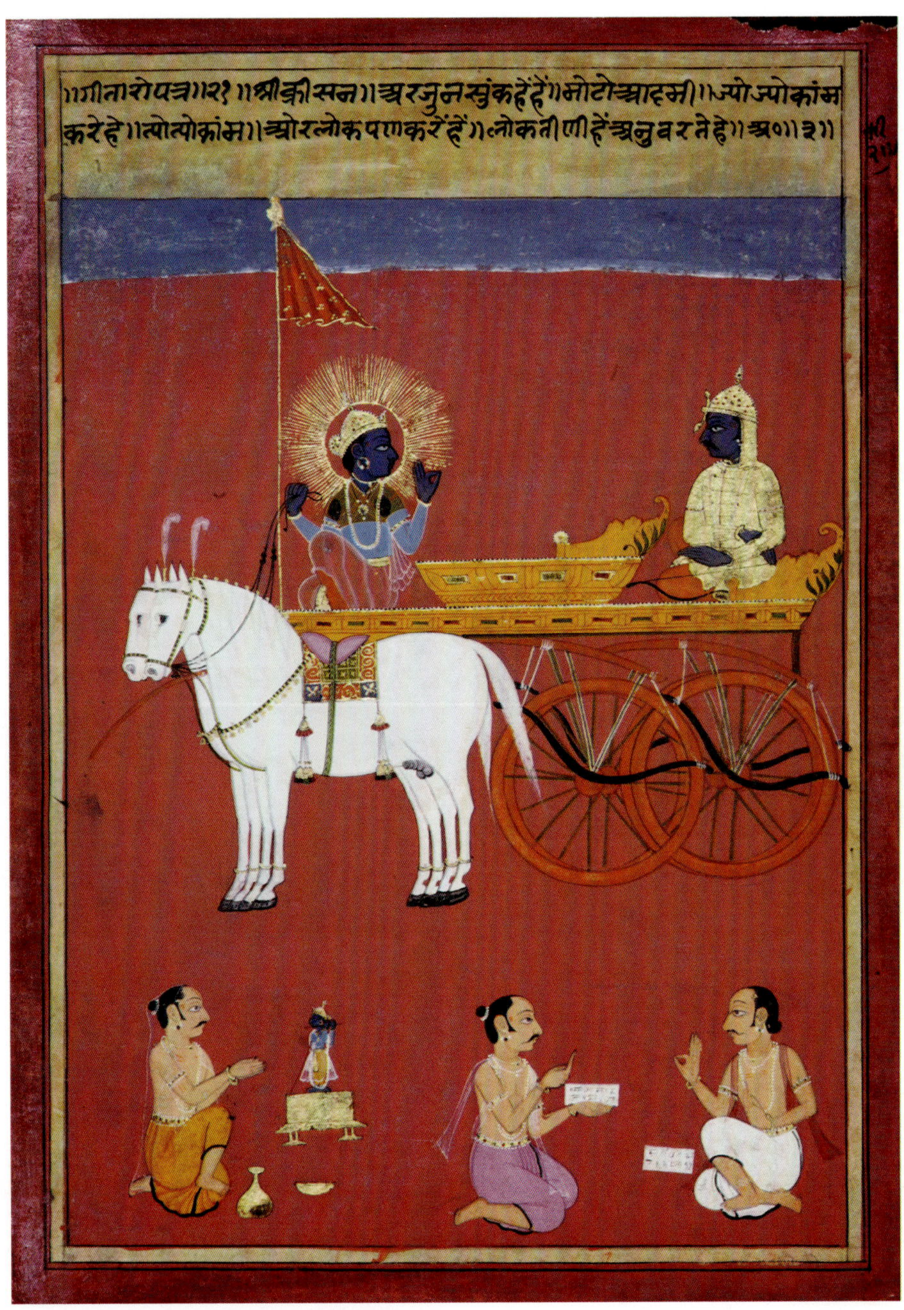

|21| श्री कृष्ण अर्जुन से कह रहे हैं कि बड़ा आदमी जो-जो काम करता है, वही काम, दूसरे प्राणी भी करते हैं। लोक उसका अनुसरण करते हैं।

|21| Sri Krishna tells Arjuna: People imitate the acts of a great man.

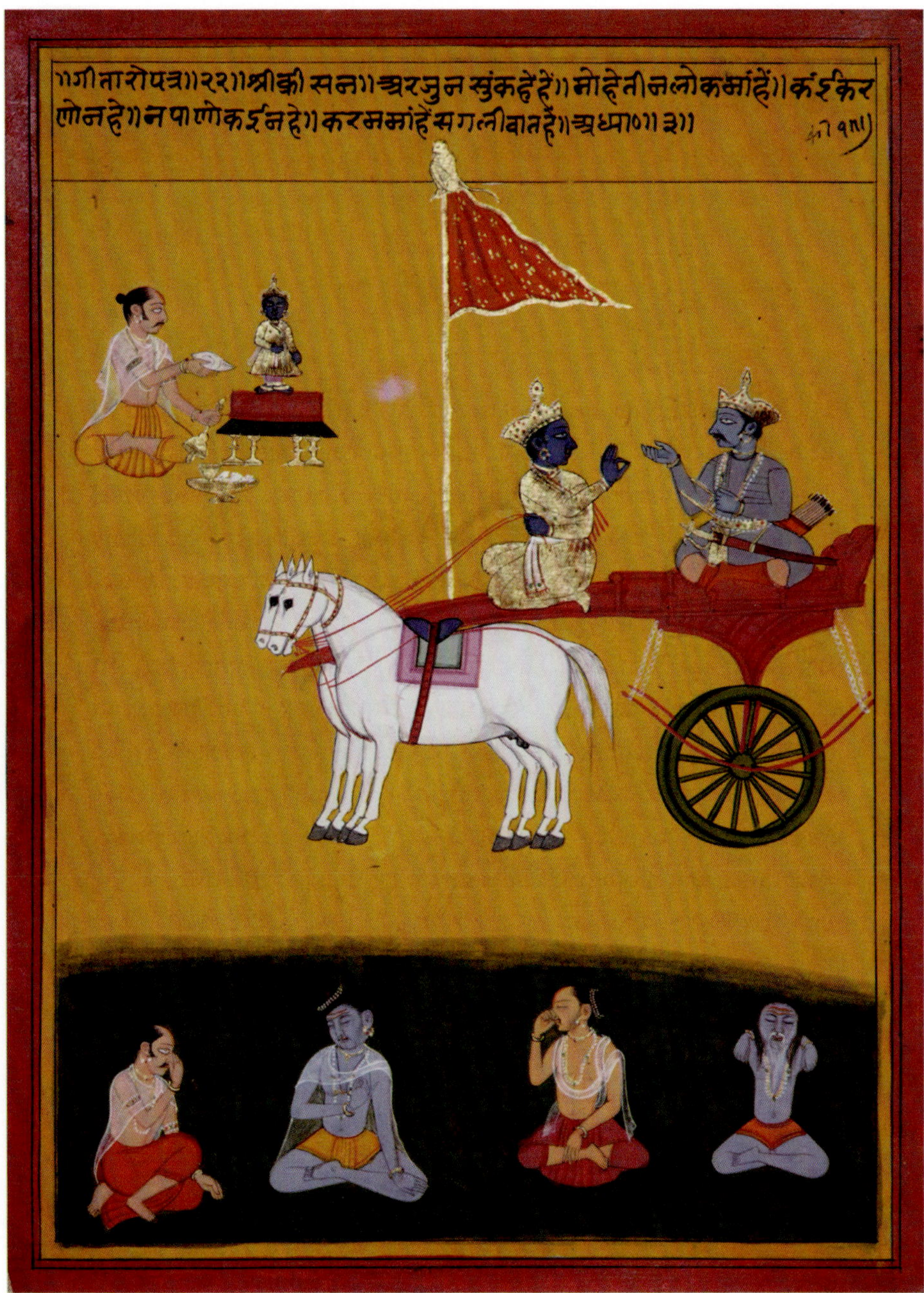

|22| श्री कृष्ण अर्जुन से कह रहे हैं कि हे अर्जुन! तीनों लोकों में न तो मेरा कोई कर्तव्य है और न ऐसी कोई वस्तु है जिसे मुझे पाना है, तब भी मैं कर्म में संलग्न रहता हूँ।

|22| Sri Krishna says to Arjuna: Hey Arjuna! I do not have to act in the three worlds; there is nothing I must achieve; even then I am absorbed in action.

In verse 23, Krishna tells Arjuna that he is divine. He adds that if he had chosen not to intervene, the world would have ceased to be. The illustration is conceptually interesting. Krishna is yet to reveal his majestic form (Vishwarupa) to Arjuna. But Krishna suddenly appears in his divine form next to a lake with lotus flowers. One of the lotus flowers has blossomed dramatically from the life-sustaining waters like a radiant sun. The shore is not special. It is unmarked, flat and ochre in colour. The divine can be incarnated at any place and time and make them holy. Across this incarnation of Krishna, a man sits with his eyes closed meditating on truth, self and eternity. He looks swarthy, his body has yogic poise, his hair is neatly bunched in a top-knot, and his moustache is carefully trimmed and twirled. The irony is that he is so intent on cultivating his inner self that he fails to notice Krishna's presence beside him on earth. Krishna, in the verse, is urging Arjuna not to withdraw from action, but to confront evil. Arjuna sits with his head bowed, his arms folded across his chest, his bow on his knees—the very image of despondency and indecision.

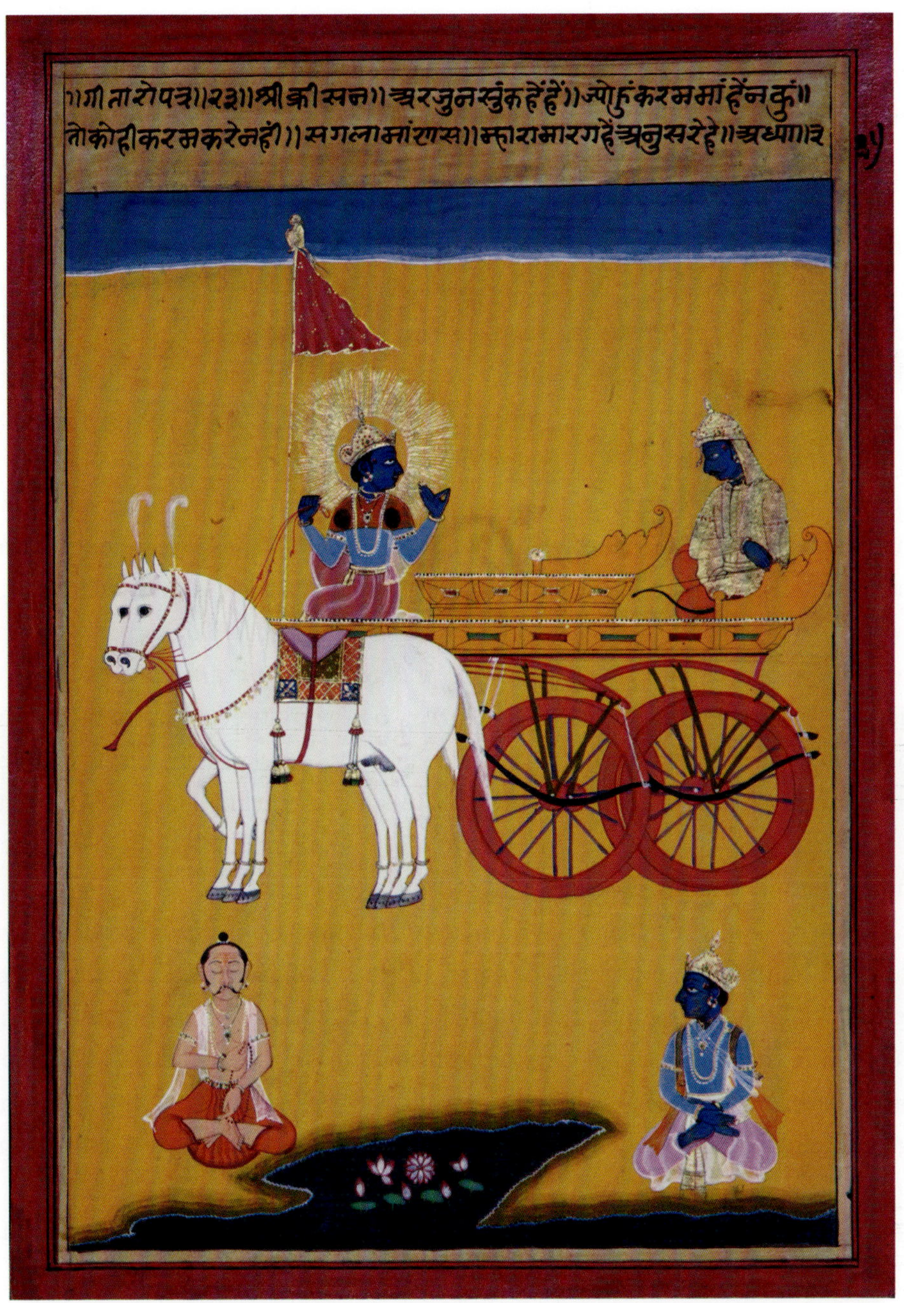

|23| श्री कृष्ण अर्जुन से आगे कहने लगे कि यदि मैं कर्मों को न करूँ तो कोई कर्म नहीं करेगा क्योंकि सभी प्राणी मेरे ही मार्ग का अनुसरण करते हैं।

|23| Sri Krishna further says to Arjuna: If I were not to act, no one will because all living beings follow my path.

Krishna continues to nudge Arjuna towards war in verse 24. In the painting, there are two images of Krishna. Apart from the incandescent one on the chariot, the other image is closer to Krishna as imagined in folk literature. Bare-chested and blue, he is placed at the top left corner. His posture is yogic and calm; his entire being seems gently filigreed with golden light. His crown is inlaid with diamonds. He sits on a stool with golden legs, and rests against a purple bolster with golden tassels. The confidence that Krishna can appear in his earthly *roop* (form; also beauty) as a kind prince is heightened by the purity of the white garment draped across his body with formal elegance. The story that this visionary scene depicts has drifted into the painter's meditation, not from the *Mahabharata* but the *Bhagavata Purana*. The poor brahmin sitting before Krishna on a lower and humbler seat is Krishna's childhood friend, Sudama. The painter treats him with honour. He wears an ochre garment, ornaments and flowers. Krishna has extended his left hand to hold Sudama's foot and wash it with water from a golden jar. In the story, Krishna feeds Sudama and they talk the night away. Sudama has come to ask Krishna for help, but forgets to do so. The story is an anecdotal history of the resilient faith of the poor (*daridranarayana*) who have neither theology nor wealth, neither arms nor power, but who hopes that somewhere and somehow, someone will listen and extend sympathy. The scene is radically different from the tense scene on the chariot. It produces a *bhava* (feeling) of friendly warmth; of the divine speaking with compassion to a simple man who does not doubt. It is another form of dharma in action.

A figure, similar to Sudama, sits unnoticed and unacknowledged before a Shaivite yogi. The contrast between the bountiful giving of Krishna and the austere and harsh neglect of the saddhu is startling and illuminating. The verse says that without Krishna's guidance and active participation in the ordinary and daily life, not only would beauty, mercy, friendship and love vanish, but everyone will wander aimlessly without defence against suffering. One understands with greater sympathy now why Krishna urges Arjuna to fight—fight on behalf of men like Sudama. The two young, charming, wide-eyed couples on either side of the anchorite remind us that Krishna, in texts like Jayadev's *Gita Govinda* (12th century), is also a figure of joyous sensuality.

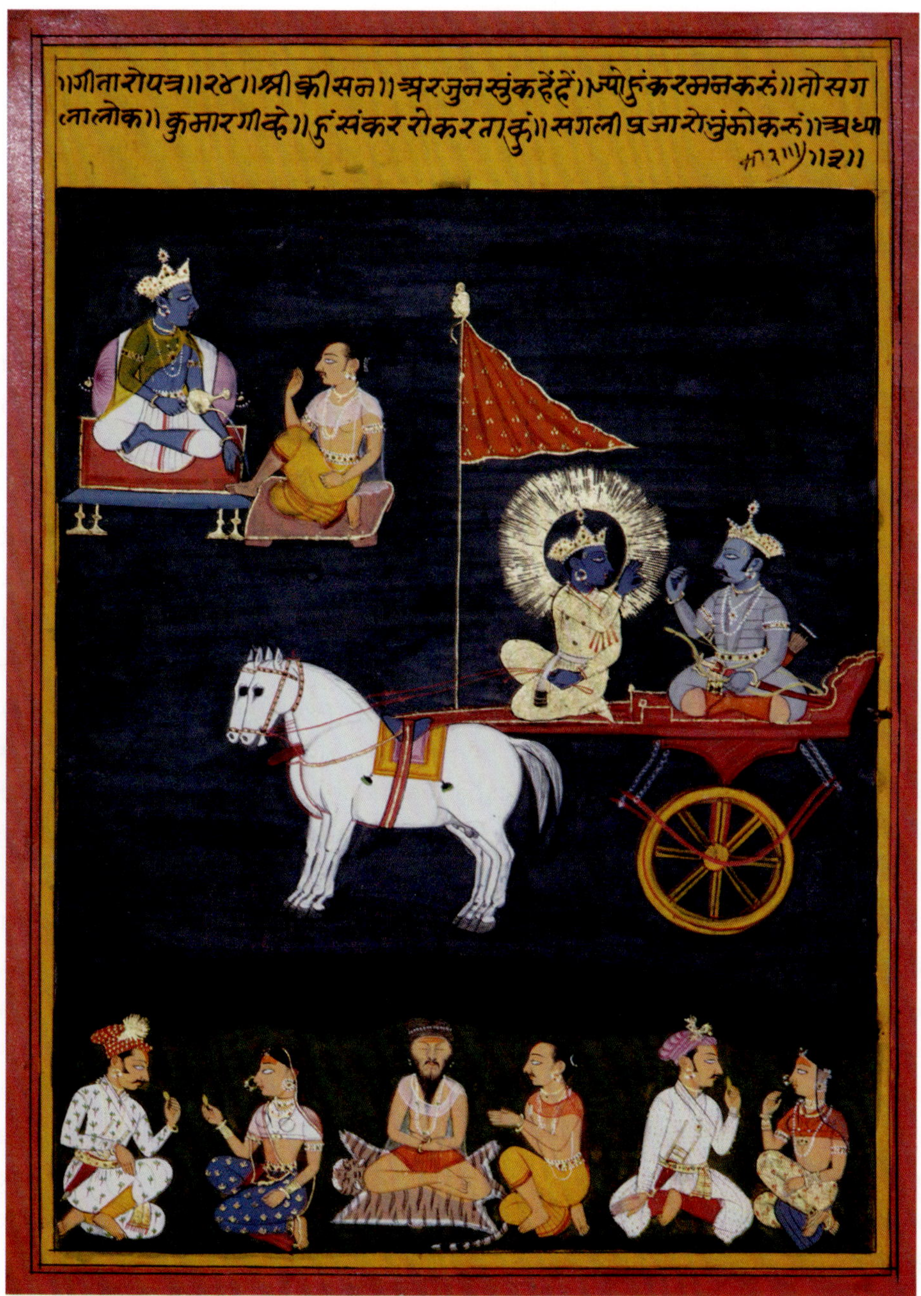

|24| श्री कृष्ण आगे कहने लगे कि हे अर्जुन! यदि मैं कर्म न करूँ तो सारे मनुष्य कुमार्गी हो जाएँगे और मैं संकरता को पैदा करने वाला और प्रजा का नाश करने वाला बन जाऊँगा।

|24| Sri Krishna further says: Hey Arjuna! If I do not act human beings will lose their way, there will be chaos and I shall be responsible for the destruction of society.

In verse 25, Krishna says that a wise man should imitate the selfless sacrifice of his own divinity for the world's salvation. The scenes painted against a solid brown earth are self-conscious and intelligent. They show moments when the eternal intersects with the transient. That is why the different scenes from daily life, placed around Krishna's chariot, are radiant with the divine, and each human figure is drawn with lyrical eloquence. The colours are harmonious, the clothes simple and the ritual gestures precise. There is a sense of vitality in the lives depicted; of small purposeful actions performed with devoted attention. The figures in the painting are not questors after holy knowledge or concerned about the meaning of existence, but they seek, in their own way, to make their presence on earth meaningful. This feeling of being 'present' is evident in the little ritual being enacted in the top left corner. A young woman, unselfconscious of her beauty, stands before the door of her small white home. It is a charming, geometric dream-house; naive in its design and structure. The woman's clothes, in contrast, are sparkling. Red and green, they glitter with spangled light like her bangles and anklets, her nose-ring and necklaces. Another woman sits before a handsome man dressed in a long white *jama* and a saffron-coloured turban. Since their gestures imitate the gestures of Krishna and Arjuna, one can safely assume that they are engaged in a serious but gentle conversation. One must note the woman's confidence. Even though the *Gita* is exclusively masculine and concerned with aggressive intervention in the world's evils, there are countless women in the *Mahabharata* who are intellectual and moral interrogators and advocates of non-violent selflessness.

There is another ordinary structure in the painting. It is grey, elaborate and uninhabited suggesting that while a house can be built with skill, a home is "a sort of man-made dream produced for those who are awake";[18] awake to responsibilities and sorrows of a life no matter how ordinary. The two green trees behind the house are like shadowy, ghostly presences. They add to its desolation. A strange semi-clad anchorite rolls down a green mound in front of the house. His eyes are shut; he is oblivious to the social world around him. Extreme self-inflicted pain on the body is a sign of *tamas*; not of enlightened seeking. Would Krishna regard it as action performed in the interest of the self alone, an act of blind ignorance?

In the space outside the house, a priest is conducting a fire ritual. Although, he is gracefully drawn and painted, he appears self-absorbed and unconcerned with social well-being. There are the two other groups of discussants. Each comprises a brahmin

18 Plato quoted by E.H. Gombrich, *Art and Illusion: A Study in the Psychology of Pictorial Representation* (London: Phaidon Press, 1960), p. 7.

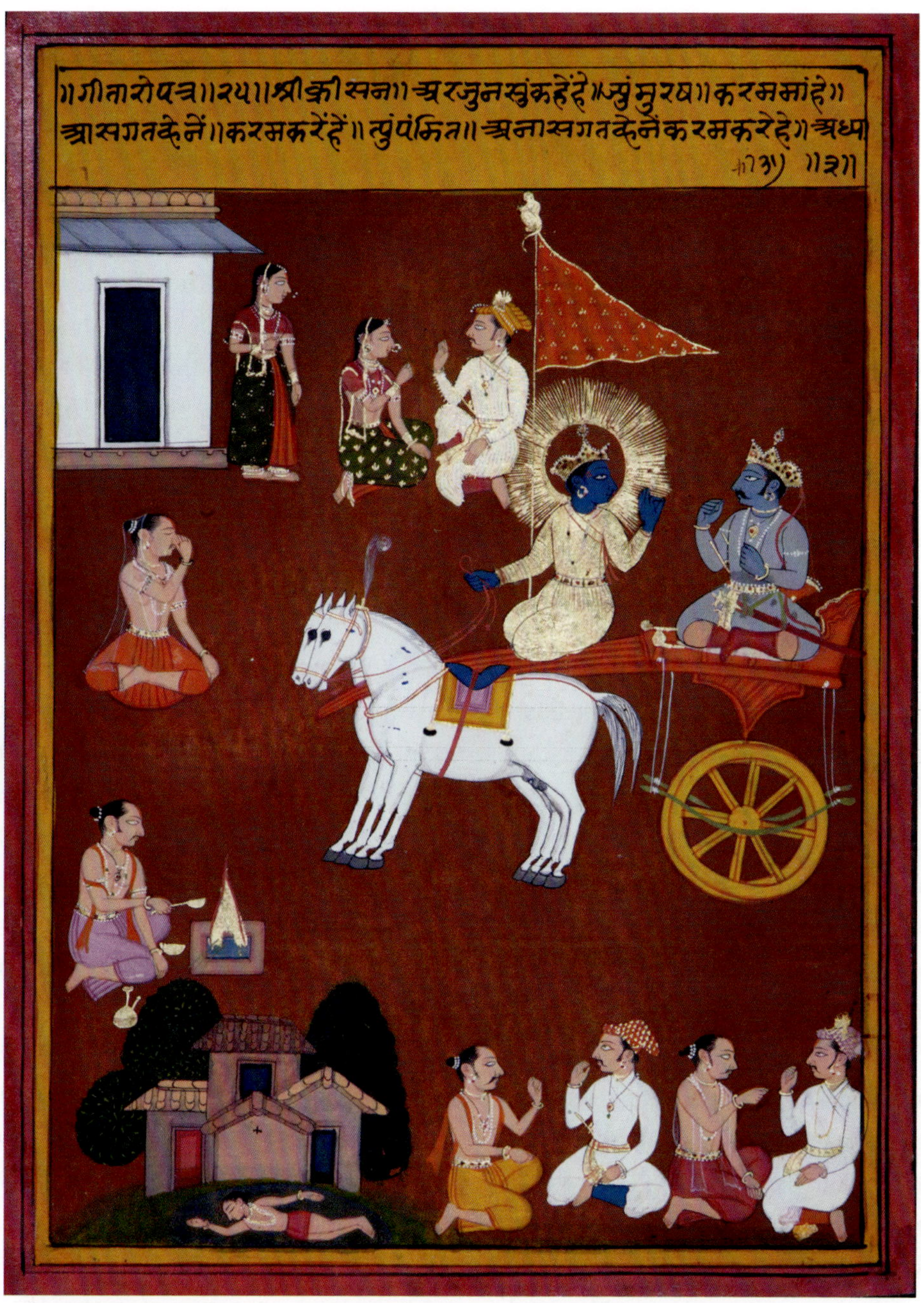

|25| श्री कृष्ण आगे कहने लगे कि हे अर्जुन! जिस तरह अज्ञानी कर्म में आसक्त होकर कर्म करता है, उसी तरह पंडित (विद्वान) को चाहिए कि वह अनासक्त होकर लोक-संग्रह का कर्म करे।

|25| Sri Krishna further says: Hey Arjuna! Just as the ignorant act out of self-interest, the wise act without self-interest for the benefit of the entire social order.

and a noble man dressed in white. They mirror Krishna–Arjuna visually placed above them. Krishna had earlier told Arjuna that an imitation of the selfless sacrifice by gods and heroes can lead to wisdom and salvation. Yet, the sensuous care with which the men are painted suggests that the artist does not judge them as harshly as the practitioners of asceticism; he honours them as earnest seekers.

In verse 28, Krishna distinguishes between action and the quality of action, its intent and achievement. The artist's response is highly abstract. He asks us to think about two sets of complex images: about domestic life and renunciation. At first, they are seemingly distinctive fragments with no obvious thematic link. However, if we start from the lower right and circle up to Vishnu in the sky, with Krishna as a point of moral reference at the centre, then we can see that the painting offers a complete lifecycle. The images recreate life's journey from childhood to familial responsibilities and then to ascetic meditation; an ideal rite of passage to salvation. The reading combines two related Hindu ideas: that each individual is caught up in an inexorable round of birth, death and rebirth; and that each seeks release from this earth-bound life of suffering, ignorance and *maya* by aspiring to become one with *paramatma* or the Supreme.

Each figure on the lower reddish-pink earth makes a distinctive attempt to act selflessly and follow a particular path towards the divine. Allah Baksh, however, paints them with a touch of gentle irony. Each seeks enlightenment, but has not become the detached karma yogi free from any bondage to the wheel of time. Even if they intuitively understand the relation between action, its reason and its consequences, only the next turn of the spiral will take them to a higher karmic level. The bare-bodied man, with a beard and a tight-fitting brown cap, is similar to popular iconic images of bhakti singers like Tulsidas or Surdas. But, he is only a dramatic imitation of the saint poets. This is suggested by the way he extends his right hand as if he has just released the notes of his song for the world's enlightenment. He is self-conscious, not self-lost. He desires appreciation and approval, unlike Mirabai who danced as she sang of Krishna's love for her and her alone. The second figure is a Shiva worshipper. He is calm; his posture is balanced. But, one wonders, given the context of Krishna and Vishnu, whether the worship of Shiva will help him escape the web of desire or if like Ashwatthama he will only gain a conditional boon. The third group is more interesting and unique. Husband, wife and child form a triangle of devotion; they have still not been touched by life's small frailties, its unexpected sorrows. The husband eats food off a leaf-plate while his wife and son wait upon him. The sudden movement of the husband, indicated by the swirl of white tassels on his dress and the awkward gesture of his right arm, give the

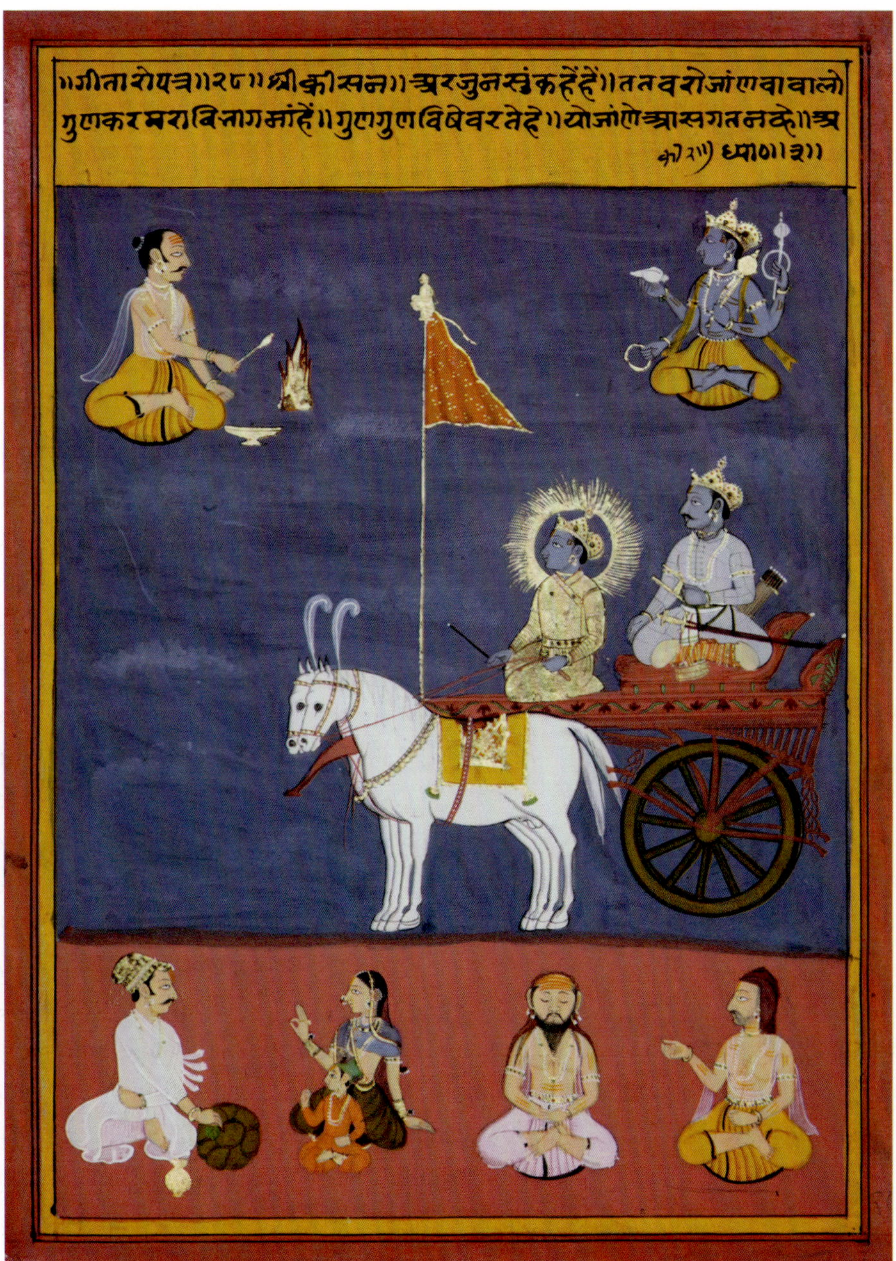

|28| श्री कृष्ण अर्जुन से कह रहे हैं जो तत्व का जानने वाला गुण विभाग और कर्म विभाग को जान कर कि सम्पूर्ण गुण ही गुणों में बरत रहे हैं। यह जान कर वह उनमें आसक्त नहीं होता।

|28| Sri Krishna says to Arjuna: The one who knows the ultimate truth understands the relation between the quality of action and action itself. He is, therefore, detached from both.

painting its dramatic quality. Far above the earth, floating in the sky and facing both Hanuman and Vishnu, is a brahmin who is feeding a ritual fire. Painted with lyrical conviction, has he been granted a vision, a darshan of the divine? Or, is he yet another self-concerned seeker when compared to Savitri in the *Mahabharata* who debates Death, not for her own salvation, but for others; or to Madhavi, who sacrifices her most treasured selfhood to save someone else. The human stories in the painting suggest that abstractions like passion, piety and affection alone are not enough to make one worthy of paradise—especially when rituals are conducted by those who desire salvation.

At the top, floating in the sky, is the iconic figure of Vishnu. His presence, like that of Krishna, is an assurance that there is no limit to mercy and life will not cease to be. It is worth pausing over the figure of Vishnu. He is, of course, blue and handsome. As part of the triumvirate, which includes Brahma and Shiva, he is the gentle mediator between the creative exuberance of one and the destructive power of the other. Here Vishnu's image differs from his usual representations. In his right hand, he carries a conch-shell and not a golden disc. In his left hand, he holds a blue lotus bud instead of a brass mace. If the conch is the symbol of that universal music which rises from the depths of the ocean and fills the sky like Vishnu himself, the lotus is the emblem of the beauty-making imagination of all living creatures. The mace lies, unthreateningly on his left shoulder, while the whirling disc is closer to the earth. Vishnu is, thereby, presented as a gentle, compassionate deity of unearthly grace who has not been called upon to intervene aggressively in a world threatened by evil. Does his presence here represent a peaceful and imaginative path to the making of a good society?

In verse 29, Krishna continues to warn that the world's sensuous qualities can distract those seeking liberation. The human figures in the illustration are painted with sinuous lines and harmonious colours. Their dramatic placement indicates the difference between the profitless learning of those who are engaged in or enchanted by the world's business and the effort needed for enlightenment. There are two groups of people discussing the scriptures, perhaps. Both seem unaware of Krishna's warning about the aesthetic delight and joy life seemingly offers. The carefully cut robes in co-ordinated colours of the group sitting before a teacher suggests that they are men of social consequence. They are wide-eyed and credulous, polite but ignorant. Teaching such men who are unquestioning, Krishna says, is like throwing a stone into a pool of water and setting off ripples whose consequences are unpredictable. The other two figures have appeared often in this folio. They are earnest readers of the scriptures. Their reading is only mechanical and will lock them into the cycle of birth and death.

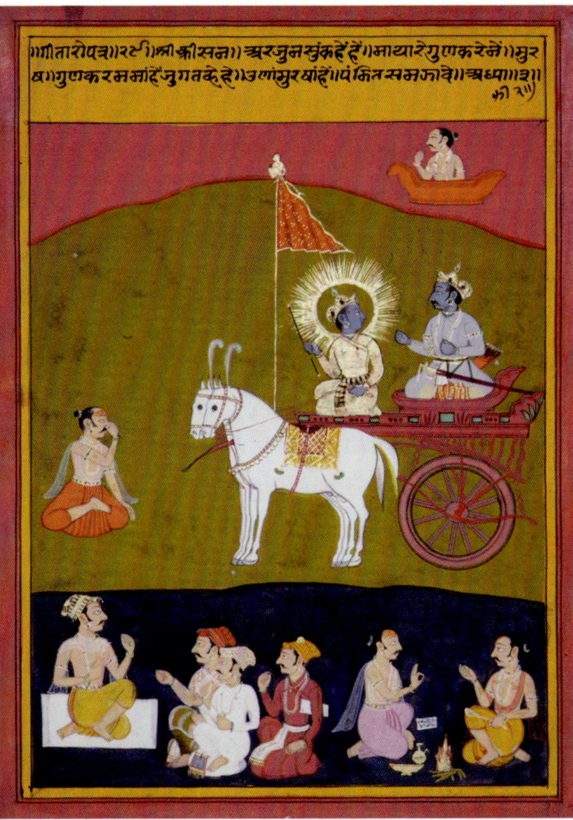

|29| श्री कृष्ण आगे कहने लगे कि हे अर्जुन! प्रकृति के गुणों से मोहित मनुष्य उन गुणों से उत्पन्न कर्मों में आसक्त रहते हैं। अत: जानने वाले ज्ञानी ऐसे मंदबुद्धि मनुष्यों को विचलित न करें।

|29| Sri Krishna further says: Hey Arjuna! Those who are enchanted by the qualities of nature desire what those qualities offer. Let the wise not mislead the ignorant.

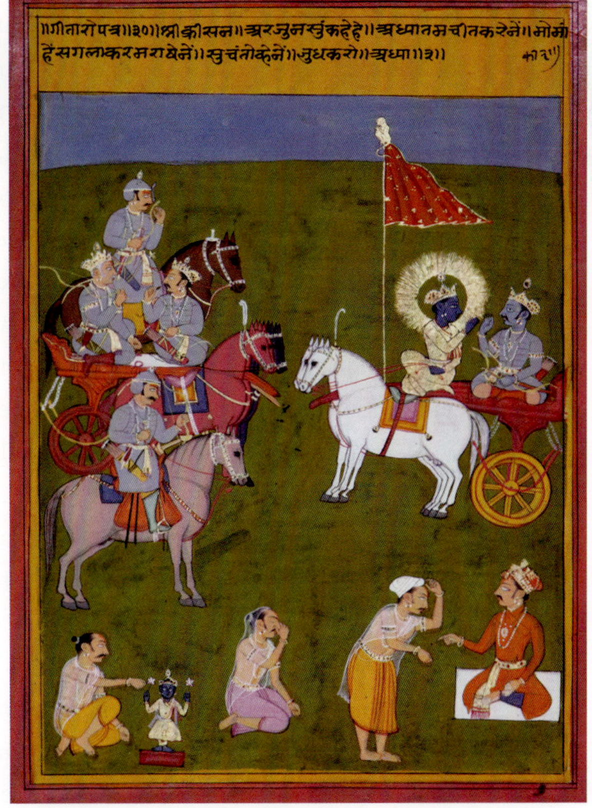

|30| श्री कृष्ण अर्जुन से कह रहे हैं कि अपने चित्त को आत्मा में स्थिर करके सारे कर्मों को मुझे समर्पित कर आशा रहित, ममता रहित और संताप रहित होकर युद्ध कर।

|30| Sri Krishna says to Arjuna: With a calm mind fixed on your self, surrender your hopes, affections and sorrows to me, and fight.

The yogi on the left, a little above the sinuous blue line, is practicing *pranayama*. One wonders if his placement before the horses of the chariot is part of the ironic, but not contemptuous, wit which sometimes characterises these paintings. Are we being told that the practice of yoga for physical well-being alone is useless and that its spiritual results are zero? Maybe, we are being invited to witness the different modes of teaching and learning from the vantage point of the learned boatman in the sky and to choose our path more self-consciously and less ignorantly.

The idea that Allah Baksh is a man of subtle irony is evident in the painting for verse 30 about surrendering everything to Krishna. Read dramatically, the sequence in the lower half is a secular narrative of hope, affection and surrender that is radically different from the sacred one Krishna demands. The man in yellow on the left is appeasing an idol of Krishna for personal gain. Is he the same man standing before a royal prince seeking alms or a favour? But god is not a distributor of charities like a feudal lord. He demands, as religious seekers know, the complete surrender of selfhood, the sacrifice of all desires. Nor does he ask for anything in return; the gods do not make a shopkeeper's bargain.

Since Krishna, once again, asks Arjuna to fight, images of the Kaurava forces reappear. They are led by the aged Bhishma sitting on a chariot pulled by pink and purple horses. The Kaurava side of the painting suggests that its soldiers are spread into the far horizon. Arjuna, on the other hand, has Krishna on his side.

The opposition between faith and scepticism continues to preoccupy verse 32. The Mewari translation is a little more vehement than the original. We are startled by the unexpected appearance of the Devi against a pale yellow sky. Her red and black clothes and her emblems—a trident and a bowl—indicate her dual character. As the mother who holds a bowl brimming with food (*paroma-anna*), she is the benign force that sustains the world; she is the generous dream of life. In a hymn by Shankaracharya, the Devi says: "Whoever eats food, eats food by me." The trident indicates her other sterner aspect. Only the careless ignore it. She incarnates time's implacable thrust towards annihilation. In the painting, her face is calm and enigmatic. Puzzled that she holds both the vessel of abundance and the instrument of death, Shankaracharya asks:

> Who art thou, O Fairest One! Auspicious One!
> You whose hands hold both: delight and pain?

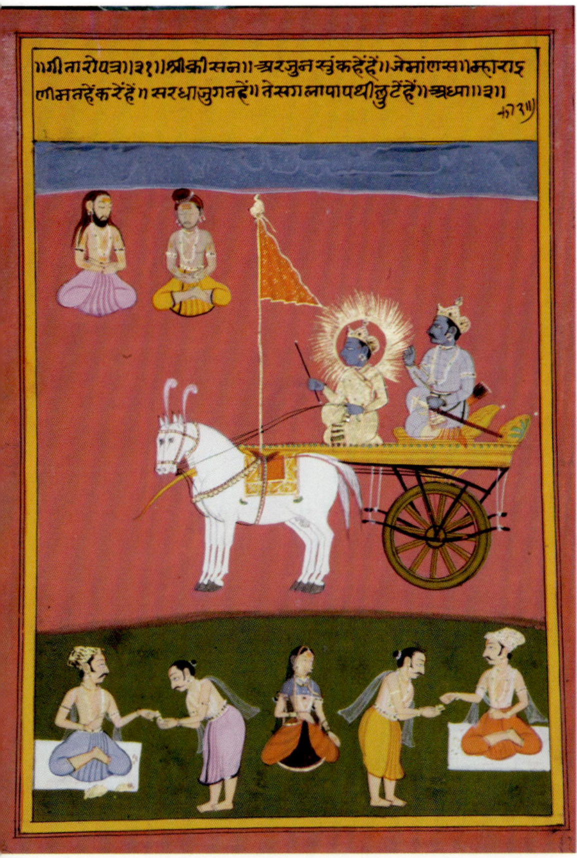

|31| श्री कृष्ण आगे कहने लगे कि हे अर्जुन! जो मनुष्य दोषदृष्टि रहित श्रद्धायुक्त होकर मेरे इस मत का नित्य पालन करता है वह सभी कर्म बंधनों से अर्थात पापों से छूट जाता है।

|31| Sri Krishna further says: Hey Arjuna: Those who follow my precepts without scepticism and with conviction are freed from any sinful consequences of action.

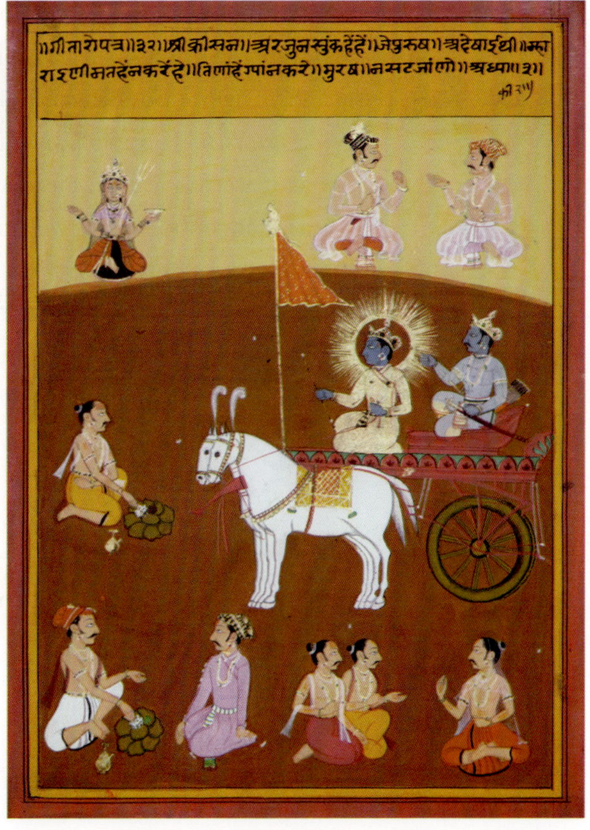

|32| श्री कृष्ण अर्जुन से कह रहे हैं परन्तु जो मेरे इस मत में दोषदृष्टि रखकर नित्य पालन नहीं करता ऐसे विवेकशून्य और सारे ज्ञानों से भ्रमित व्यक्ति को नष्ट हुआ जानो।

|32| Sri Krishna says to Arjuna: Those who are sceptical and do not follow my teaching are unintelligent and ignorant. They shall be destroyed.

> Both: the shade of death and the elixir of immortality,
> Are thy grace, O Mother![19]

A wise man knows that life is shadowed by the dread of death, yet he acts unconcerned with its final outcome. In the battlefield, Arjuna must become such a man.

Verses 33–35 say that daily life is a strange mix of feelings and ideas which entangle human beings; their response is determined by the state of their own awareness. As if to illustrate this idea, Allah Baksh paints figures that have attained different levels of understanding: bare-chested, lonely wanderers, yogis practising *pranayama*, worldly men gossiping and eating. But since we have seen them before, our concentration is on Krishna. He is resplendent (verse 34). We gaze upon him with the same rapt attention as Arjuna. It is as if we too are overhearing Krishna as he tries to convince Arjuna that contraries are woven into the fabric of life. Knowledge should not paralyse him. He should remain detached from the final outcome of his actions because dharma lies in doing what is right. Like an honest questor, Arjuna must discover his own dharma. The *Gita*, like the *Mahabharata*, always upholds the autonomy of the self.

19 Zimmer, *Myths and Symbols in Indian Art and Civilization*, pp. 207–12.

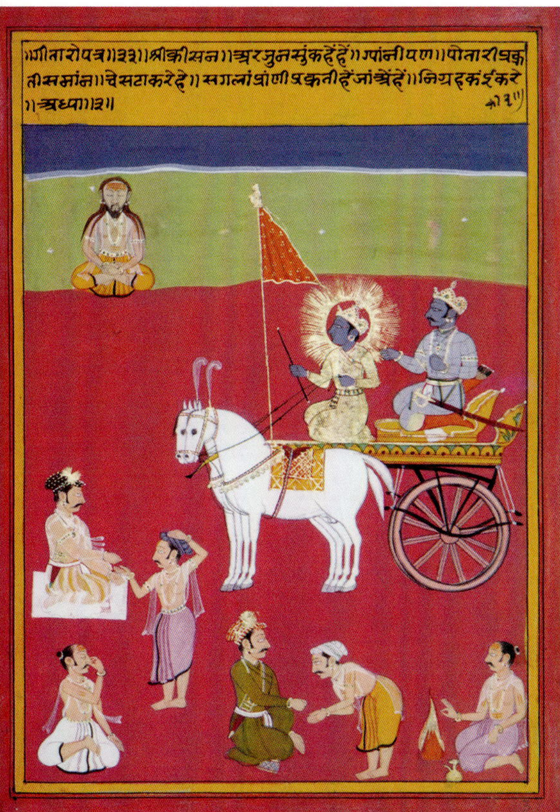

|33| श्री कृष्ण आगे कहने लगे, हे अर्जुन! सारे प्राणी अपने स्वभाव के वशीभूत होकर कर्म करते हैं और ज्ञानी पुरुष भी अपने स्वभाव के अनुसार चेष्टा करता है, फिर इसमें कोई हठ क्या करेगा?

|33| Sri Krishna says to Arjuna: Hey Arjuna! All living beings act according to their character; even the wise act according to their nature. What then is the use of stopping them?

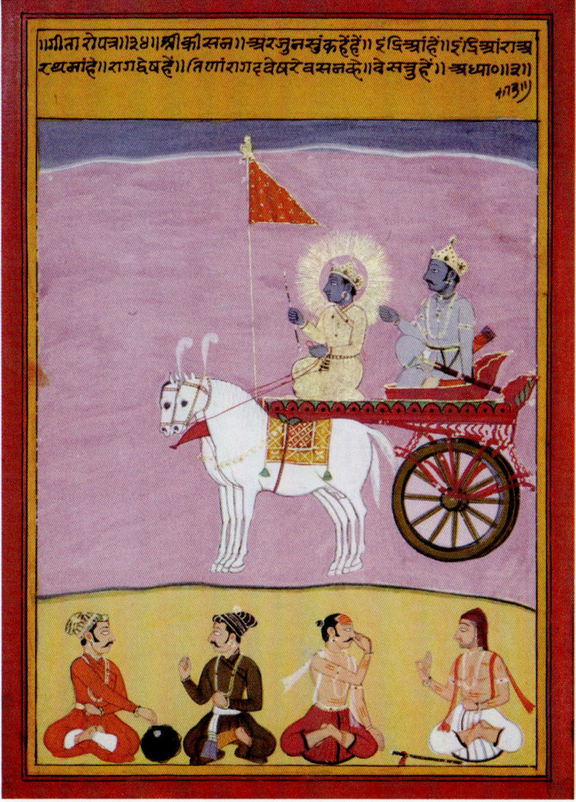

|34| श्री कृष्ण अर्जुन से कह रहे हैं कि प्रत्येक इन्द्रिय के विषय में राग और द्वेष समाए हुए हैं। मनुष्य को राग और द्वेष के वशीभूत नहीं होना चाहिए क्योंकि ये दोनों उसके शत्रु हैं।

|34| Sri Krishna says to Arjuna, love and hate are mingled in every object of sense. A human being should not fall into their trap because they are his enemies.

In the painting for verse 35, a woman stands before her pale brown hut which has been pushed so far out of the frame as to be inconspicuous. She is barefoot and simply dressed. Her gesture of 'giving' is self-assured. She is neither heroic nor stately, but is the image of a life lived graciously. Her dharma is earth-bound: sympathy for the stranger and alms for those who ask. She looks gentle, generous and hospitable as she offers a few coins to a mendicant who is blue-bodied like Krishna. In popular lore, Krishna is a trickster god who disguises himself to test people. The best known example is of him approaching Karna disguised as a brahmin to beg for his sacred armour and amulets to save Arjuna. The woman is not wealthy, but as she stands on a purple platform there is a fine sense of visual equality between the divine mendicant and her. A visionary miracle is in the making: the divine and the human see themselves in each other. She does not regard him as god; she does not have to since she acknowledges him as man. Beyond battlefields, she is not a contestant for power, she is only a representative of the good; her gesture is a hieroglyph of hope. In the renaissance paintings of Christian Europe, there is an inviolable hierarchy, "defined by the laws of a sublime geometry," between the sacred and the profane, the planes of heaven and of earth.[20] In Indian religious art, gods and mortals freely wander across a universe which has no framing borders.[21] That is, perhaps, why the brahmin, sitting a little away from the woman and the mendicant, raises his right hand in blessing.

There is an unusually dramatic scene in the upper half of the painting. The Kaurava army suddenly makes its appearance. The aged man with a white beard is Bhishma. His face is slightly puffed; he is not as muscular as the younger soldiers. Duryodhana sits under a white canopy. Karna, holding the black reins of a black horse, is marked by the emblem of a white elephant against a pinkish pennant. The man on the brown horse, carrying a green flag with the emblem of a fire-altar, is Kripacharya. The scene bristles with tension, especially when read against the human warmth of the scene below it. What is offered for our moral consideration are two alternative modes of living, two alternative moralities, two acts of dharma in a world which is complex and labyrinthine like the human heart. How does one choose? Under what circumstances is that choice to be made?

---

20 Emile Male, *The Gothic Image: Religious Art in France of the Thirteenth Century*, translated by Dora Nussy (New York: Harper and Row, 1958), p. 13.

21 See Lawrence Binyon, *The Spirit of Man in Asian Art* (New York: Dover, 1965), p. 42.

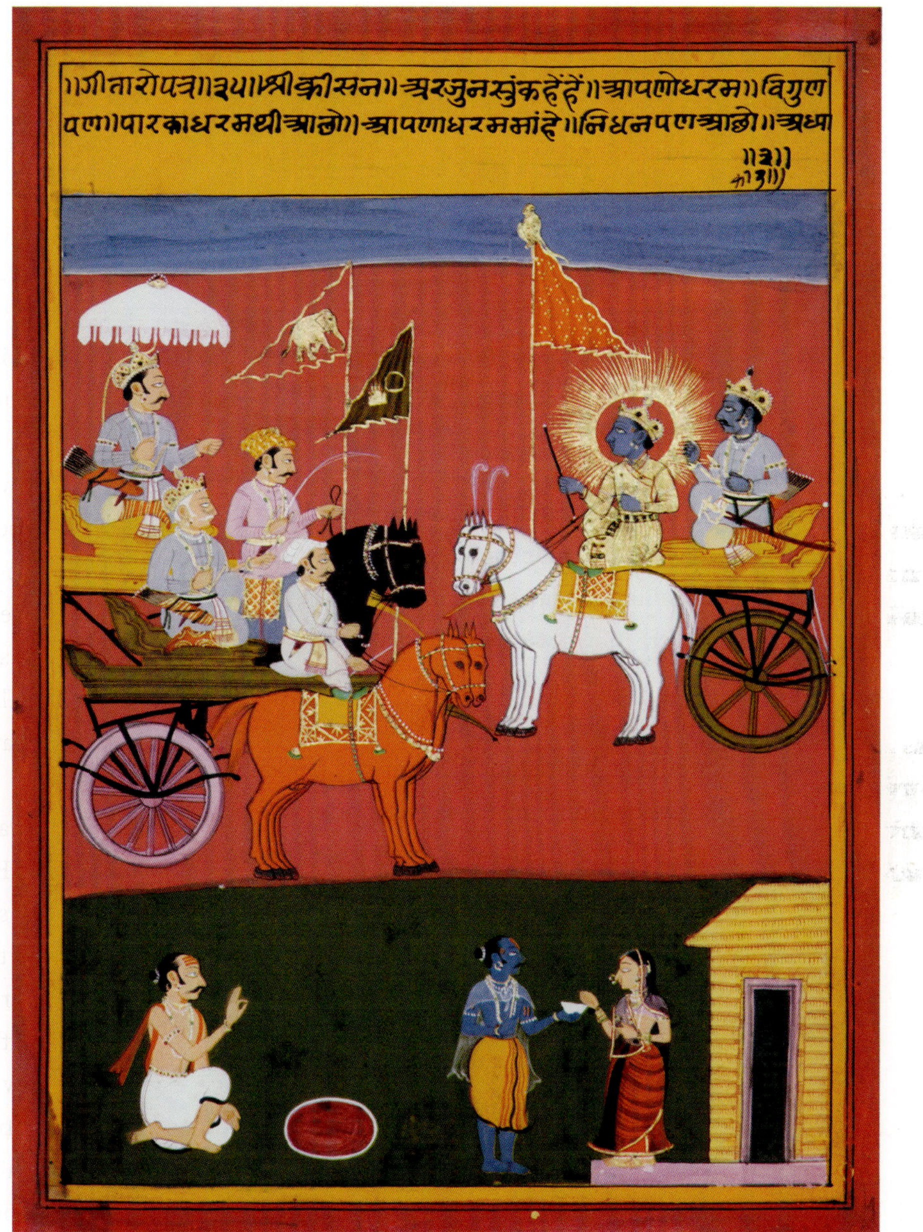

|35| श्री कृष्ण आगे कहने लगे कि हे अर्जुन! अपना धर्म लाख गुणरहित हो पर दूसरे के धर्म से सदा श्रेष्ठ होता है, इसलिए अपने धर्म में मरना भी कल्याणकारी होता है जबकि दूसरे का धर्म भयकारी होता है।

|35| Sri Krishna says to Arjuna: Hey Arjuna! One's own dharma may have a thousand defects, but it is always better than the dharma of someone else. Death, while performing one's own dharma, brings salvation, but seems fearful if one is fulfilling someone else's dharma.

Verse 37 is a meditation on the idea that *tamas* is sin—obsessive passion—for the benefit of the self alone. The social scene offers an ironic glimpse of commonplace moral and social norms. Kama, the god of love, has his back to the ritual of fire and sacrifice. He holds an arrow tipped with a lotus-bud. His eyes are full of mischief at the scene of feudal obligation and favour being enacted before him. The figures he gazes upon are drawn with fine precision and splendid colouration. The aristocratic couple are handsome, sensual, richly attired and have the look of people used to the homage offered by the man bowing before them. Above them is another princely person, wearing a white and a gold speckled turban. He is sitting on an elevated platform, painted in royal red, and is giving money to a poor cowherd. If we recall that the legendary character Krishna is also a cowherd, we can read the irony. None of the people on the yellow earth are aware of the divine chariot near them in a clear blue sky where a discourse about the sorrows of earthly desires is being conducted—a discourse which they will hear from their temple priest, perhaps, only to quickly forget it so as to pursue worldly success or pleasure.

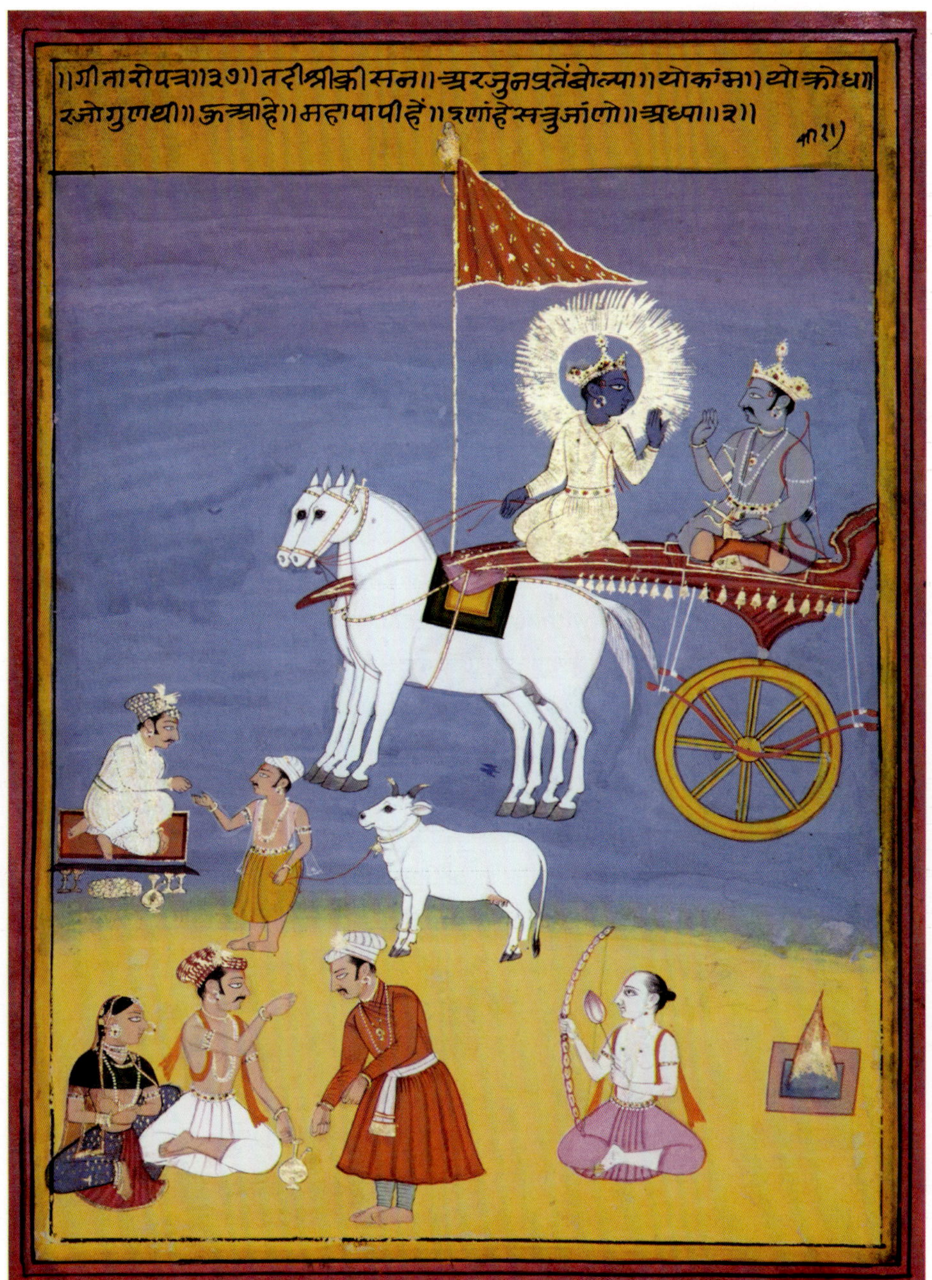

|37| श्री कृष्ण अर्जुन से कहने लगे, यह काम ही क्रोध है जो रजोगुण से उत्पन्न हुआ है, यह सब कुछ खा जाने वाला बड़ा पापी है। इसे अपना शत्रु समझ।

|37| Sri Krishna says: Desire is born of passion; it is a sin which devours everything. Regard it as your enemy.

In a set of metaphors, Krishna tells Arjuna that passion obscures wisdom just as smoke hides fire, dust covers a mirror or a child lies enclosed in the womb (verse 38). Allah Baksh's illustrations are created out of the contrary images in the verse. Fire has archetypal associations with knowledge, imagination and the transformation of nature into culture; mirrors with the presentation of the self in everyday life and with identity; children with unselfconscious innocence and the common hope of leaving a sign of one's presence in historical time. Each image makes one aware of time and change, vanity and desire. Krishna has repeatedly warned Arjuna against them. They make, he tells him, a prison-house of enchantment and so darken the essential wisdom about man's place in the mortal world. Krishna's metaphors also suggest that to regard the visible, the desirable or the innocent as the essence of life is a mistake. Rational knowledge soon smothers the mind in the smoke of scepticism and doubt; self-images, without the guidance of the ideal, distort and falsify decisions; desire is subject to time's decay. If we read the visual images from lower right and swerve up to the left, each of the figures on the yellow earth are discrete examples of stages in life's journey. They are so clearly separated as to offer no natural and organic flow from one to the next. The couple on the right is handsome. They are perhaps talking about domestic or marital affairs as befitting a stage in the lifecycle. The next visual space belongs to a brahmin. His back is turned to the couple as if to indicate his disenchantment with his social and worldly past. The third state is that of death. A dead woman lies rigidly on the bare earth. Her arms are outstretched, nerveless and stiff. An empty pitcher of water lies next to her as a sign of death. The body of a man also lies next to her. His hair is dishevelled and there are ritual marks on his forehead. A fire, at the edge of the land, burns above the dead figures. Here it has no relation to imagination or culture, but to the end of all human journeys in ash and oblivion. It should be noticed that all the figures are entombed within a yellow curve of the earth. Only the flames leap past its material limit before they too turn into smoke. Krishna and Arjuna stand in an utterly different time and space whose limitless vibrancy is indicated by the scarlet colour of the space that surrounds them.

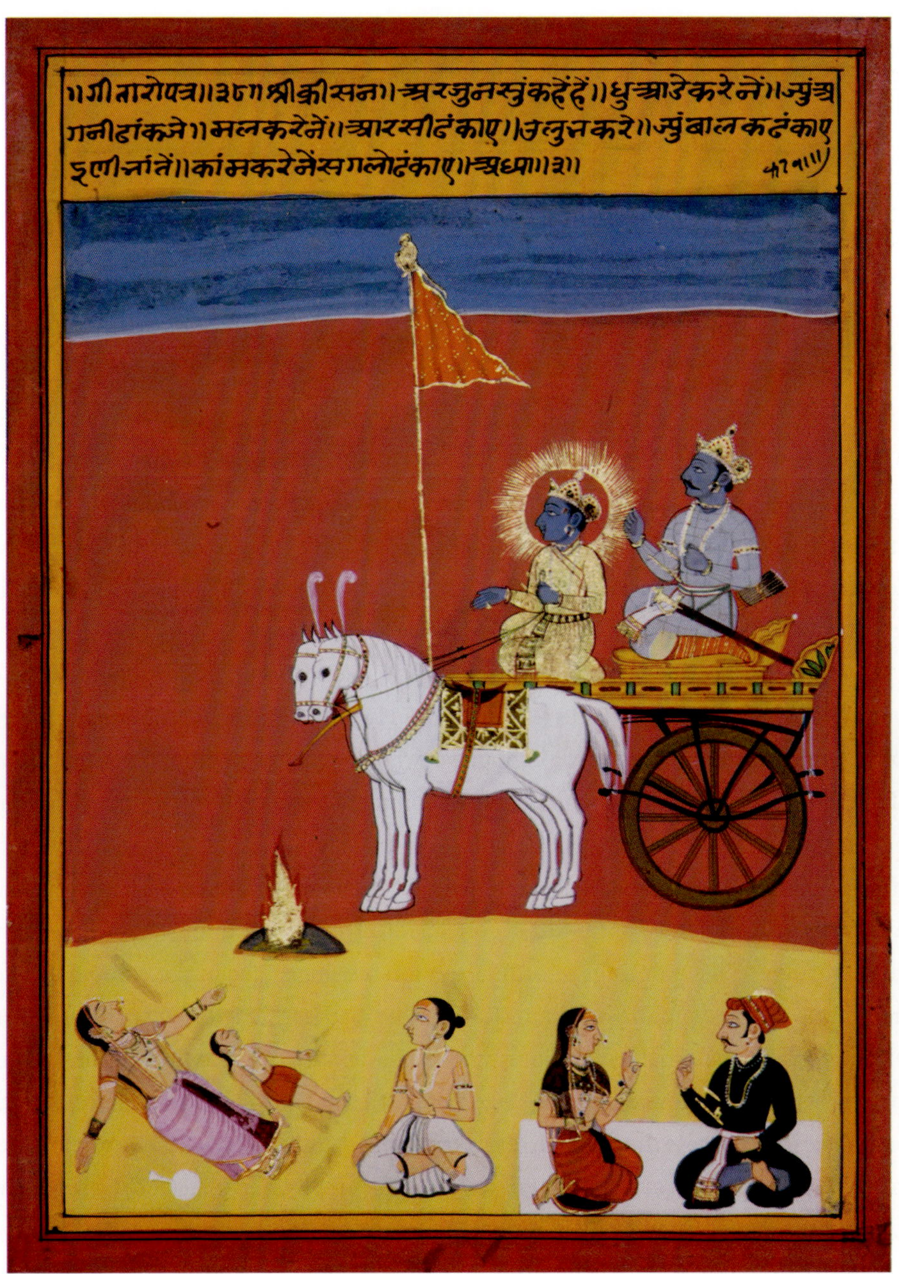

|38| श्री कृष्ण आगे कहने लगे कि हे अर्जुन! जैसे अग्नि धुएँ से, दर्पण धूल से और गर्भ अपनी झिल्ली (जेर) से ढका रहता है, वैसे ही यह ज्ञान उस काम से ढका रहता है।

|38| Sri Krishna says to Arjuna: Hey Arjuna! Just as fire is hidden by smoke, a mirror is covered by dust and a child is enclosed in a womb, so is wisdom obscured by desire.

Krishna's rejection of desire as a motivating force continues in verse 39. It is, he says, the enemy of all that is good. Radhakrishnan invokes Spinoza to gloss this verse:

> For the things which men, to judge by their actions, deem the highest good are Riches, Fame and Sensual pleasure. Of these the last is followed by satiety and repentance, the other two are never satiated; the more we have the more we want; while the love of fame compels us to order our lives by the opinion of others.

Each of these are impermanent and end in conflict, while the love of the eternal leads to joy which is unmingled with sadness.[22] Radhakrishnan uses these comments to support his assertion that the *Gita* demands the abnegation of the body, its passions and its needs; it also urges man's surrender to god's will as the surest road to salvation. However, the verse like Spinoza's comment is tentative and ambiguous. That is why the verse is not a cliché which creates a comfortable spiritual buzz.

Spinoza acknowledges the seductive power of desire and the impossibility of evading it. He does not advocate renunciation. He only urges wise self-consciousness about wealth, honour and erotic longing; an awareness of their complex role in human affairs. He is not a dogmatist who demands complete renunciation; nor does Krishna, at least not in this verse. Instead, Krishna acknowledges that desire is like fire in the soul; it can only be extinguished when the body ceases to be. That is why the verse has the same sense of sadness as Spinoza's conclusion. The painter intuits that sadness, but he also brings to his paintings of ordinary human beings a feeling of compassion for the ethical demands made on them. Kama, who had earlier glowed with intelligent mischief, is here a small, dispirited figure. His arrow, tipped with a lotus flower, appears broken and limp. Rarely has a god of eroticism been so despondent, so utterly lost! As he looks across the field, he sees a half-naked, ash-covered ascetic with matted hair. The ascetic's eyes are closed. He seems determined to so grievously chastise his body that the gods above will recognise his merit and grant him immortality. As if to suggest how unnatural such severe penance is, how lacking in vital reason, the tree under which he sits is mechanically and geometrically drawn. Kama exposes the hubris of those who think that they can gain heaven by self-abnegation alone. In the *Mahabharata*, the gods send down dancing apsaras whose tricks of seduction distract the most austere of saints.

22 Radhakrishnan, *The Bhagavadgita*, pp. 170–71.

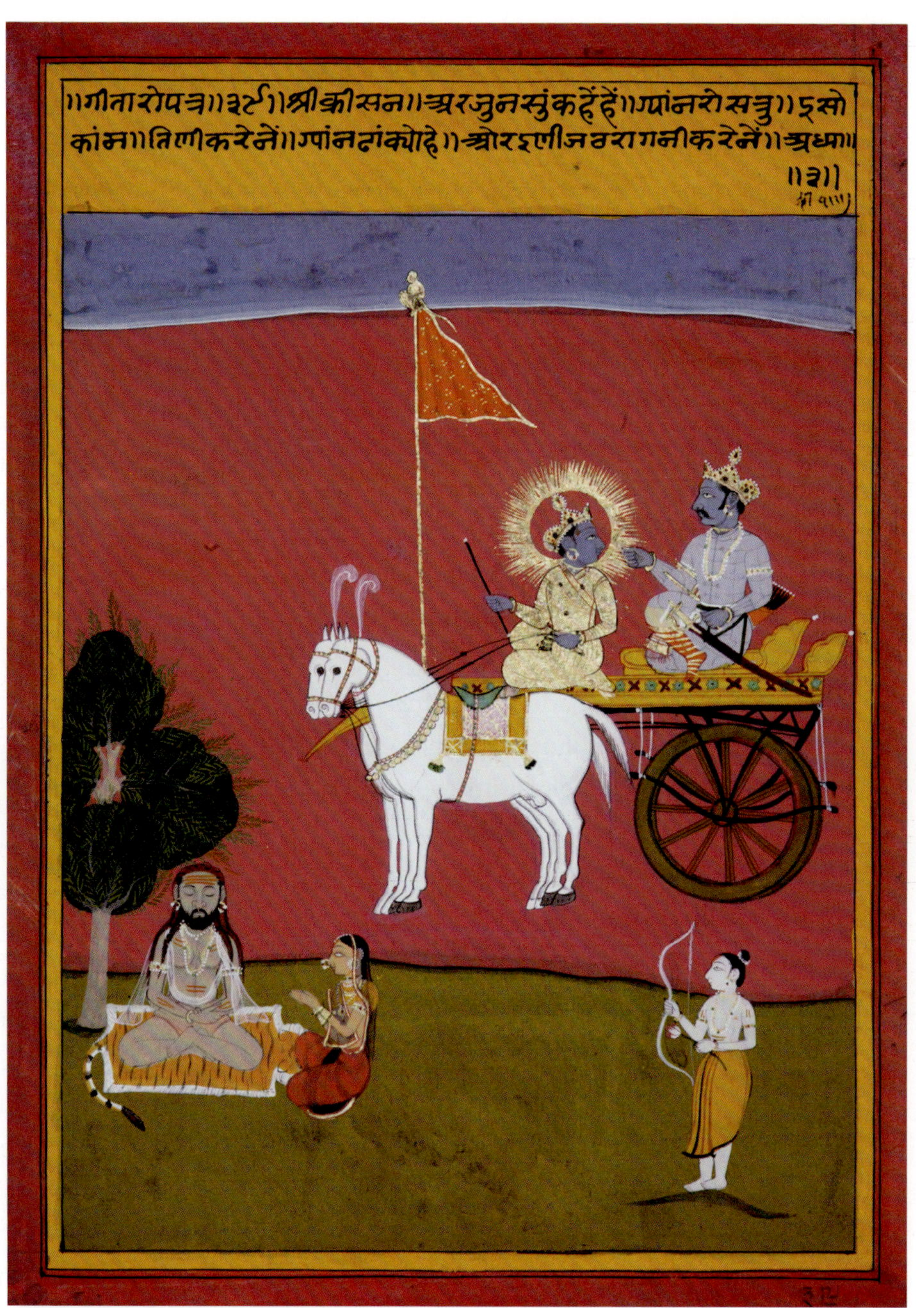

|39| श्री कृष्ण अर्जुन से कह रहे हैं कि कभी न शांत होने वाली अग्नि के समान यह काम ज्ञानियों के ज्ञान को ढक देता है। यही काम उनका नित्य बैरी है।

|39| Sri Krishna says to Arjuna: Desire, which is unappeasable like fire, obscures the wisdom of the wisest of men. Desire is their constant enemy.

In verse 41, Krishna suddenly abandons the rules of discourse which require a patient unfolding of complex moral thought, and issues an injunction to Arjuna: give up all desires. Does the painter see it as a sign of Krishna's irritation at not having persuaded Arjuna to fight? Is that why Krishna dramatically turns his back on Arjuna who is left with both his hands clenched in frustration and dissatisfaction? There is an additional sheen of gold to Krishna's figure, and the pale blue figure of Arjuna almost fades into the deeper blue background. Looking at the two together, one is reminded of Bimal Matilal's assertion that Krishna is never presented as omnipotent, but only as one who does what he can. Nor is the *Gita*, he adds, cited as an authoritative guide to moral action in the *Mahabharata*. It is, instead, an example of the idea that whenever there is a complex moral problem "a higher type of critical thinking comes into play."[23] Krishna himself indicates that there are times when justice and virtue can only be served by violating a moral rule.

The scene below the chariot, painted against a pinkish-red background, is strange. On the left, Krishna sits in the posture of a teacher. His gestures indicate that he is giving moral instruction to a group of three men and two women. The woman closest to Krishna kneels reverentially. But the gestures of the other four indicate both puzzlement and a questioning regard. Are they wondering what sinful desires are and under what circumstances moral law can be violated—similar, perhaps, to the doubts of Arjuna? Two of the beautifully imagined figures, who look the most perplexed, are the human and godly forms of the Sun and the Moon. They are placed at the centre. The figure of the Moon God is a gentle silver-blue, while the Sun God is golden, radiant and self-possessed. Both reveal that the human form itself is divine. Does their confident and reassuring presence not give us delight; is the desire to be in their light a sin? Of course, there are desires like Dhritarashtra's which result in injustice; or of the Kauravas for Draupadi which arise from lust. Since Dhritarashtra too is a listener (we tend to forget this while considering the debates in the *Gita*), is he too not being asked to consider the questions being raised?

23 See Alf Hitelbeitel, *Dharma: Its Early History in Law, Religion and Narrative* (Oxford: Oxford University Press, 2011), p. 21.

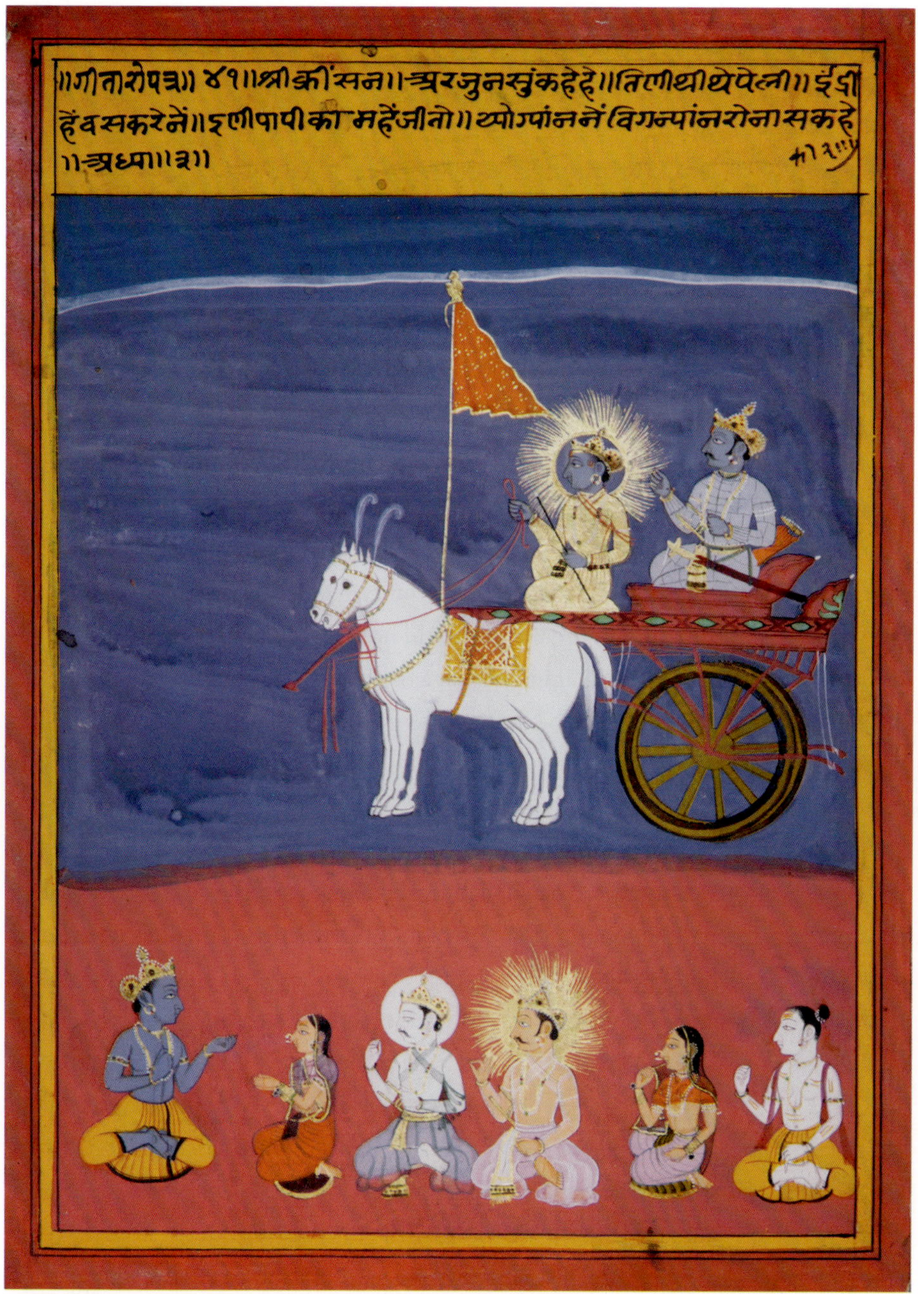

|41| श्री कृष्ण आगे कहने लगे कि हे अर्जुन! तू पहले इन्द्रियों को वश में करके फिर ज्ञान का नाश करने वाले इस पापी काम को मार डाल।

|41| Sri Kriṣhna says: Hey Arjuna! First, control your senses, and then kill all sinful desires which destroy wisdom.

If we read verse 42 literally, we may say, as Radhakrishnan does, that Krishna is proposing a hierarchy of beings and consciousness.[24] But does the painter agree? Is Hanuman, sitting atop the flag on the chariot, inferior in knowledge to the human beings placed visually under the green mound in the painting? Or, can we assume that because the white goat is lower in consciousness it can be sacrificed by man? The assumption, that there is a gradation of beings and of consciousness, is contrary to the profound assertion in Indian scriptural and moral literature that everything is holy, and all aspects of living and being are interdependent. If, however, we regard each as separate, then our understanding will remain partial and will not lead to enlightenment. Thus, the man sacrificing the goat for his own selfish gain will only add to the slaughter about to take place in Kurukshetra. The brahmin who has turned away from the woman and shut his eyes will make the world less sensual but also more crass by transforming sexual desire into something sinful. The moralist does not make society better, only duller; while the one, who condemns the senses as inferior, does not make the world holier, only uglier. The physical, the sensual, the mental and the imaginative have their own ways of knowing, and each adds to the totality of what is to be desired, is virtuous and is to be known. Krishna knows that. But, at the moment, he is trying to persuade Arjuna to surrender his reasoning self to him and fight.

Verse 43 does not extend the argument of the previous one, and so the painter repeats visual images. The challenge of dealing with the senses and desires continues. How can one long for the darshan of the divine if one does not regard sight and its reliability as the greatest value? Surely, one needs to see the goddess in the sky *with* one's eyes, just as one should learn to see *through one's visionary* eyes if one is to acknowledge that the sun is also a celestial being. In any case, Krishna's admonition to abandon desire and surrender the self continues to trouble Arjuna. In the painting, one can feel the silence between the two as Krishna turns his back on Arjuna once again. Arjuna is still left to wonder why he should seek either revenge or power, both of which draw the opprobrium of the wisest. Thus, Sulbha in the *Shanti Parva*, chastising Janaka, says that power, however attained and maintained, is "as insubstantial as burning flames fed by straw or the bubbles of froth seen on the surface of water."[25]

24 Radhakrishnan, *The Bhagavadgita*, p. 172.

25 Chakrabarti, 'Just Words,' *Mahabharata Now*, p. 370.

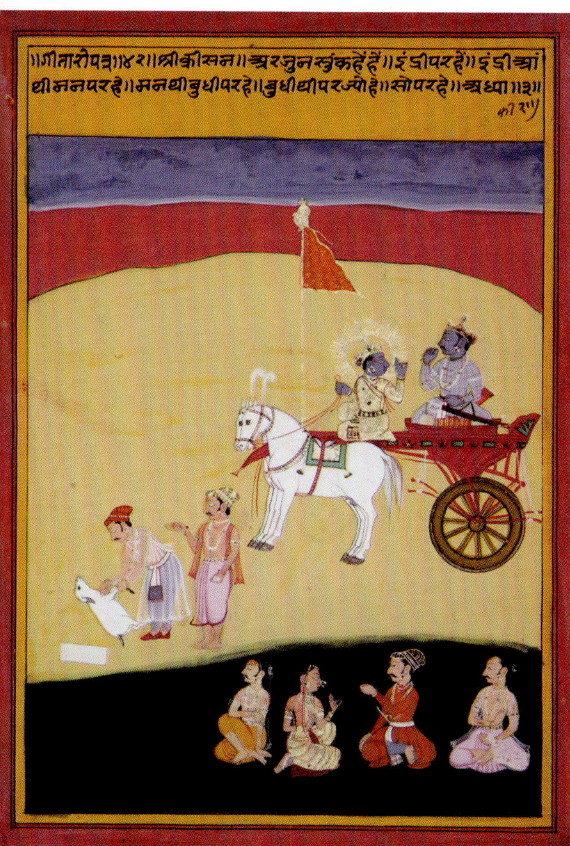

|42| श्री कृष्ण अर्जुन से कह रहे हैं कि स्थूल शरीर से इन्द्रियाँ बलवान, सूक्ष्म और परे हैं। मन इन्द्रियों से परे है और बुद्धि मन से भी परे है किन्तु बुद्धि से भी परे आत्मा है, ऐसा जानो।

|42| Sri Krishna says to Arjuna: You should know that the senses are stronger than the physical body. The mind is stronger than the sense and the intellect is stronger than the mind. But the Atma is even greater than reason.

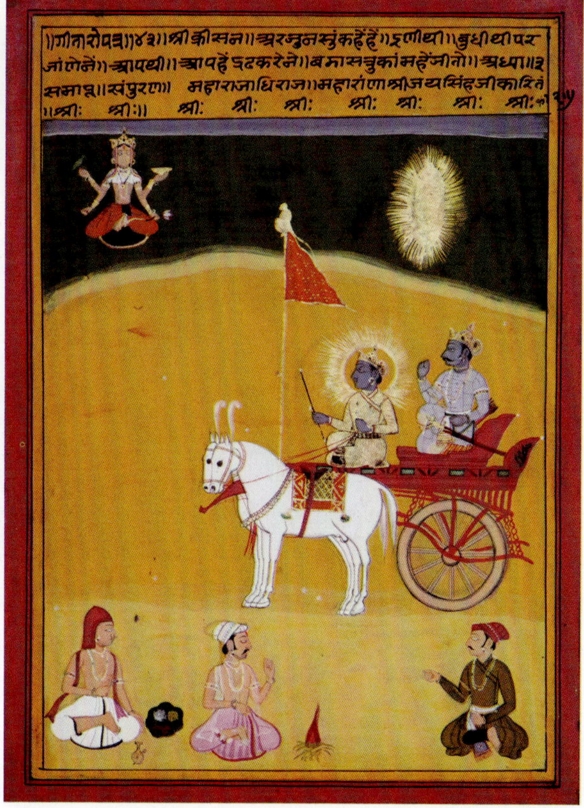

|43| श्री कृष्ण आगे कहने लगे कि इस प्रकार बुद्धि से परे, आत्मा को जानकर और बुद्धि से मन को नियंत्रित करके, हे अर्जुन! तू काम रूप बड़े शत्रु को मार डाल।

|43| Sri Krishna also says to Arjuna: Hey Arjuna knowing that the Atma is greater than the intellect, control your intellect and kill desire, your greatest enemy! This text has been written for Maharaj Maharana Sri Jai Singh. Sri, Sri, Sri, Sri, Sri, Sri, Sri, Sri, Sri.

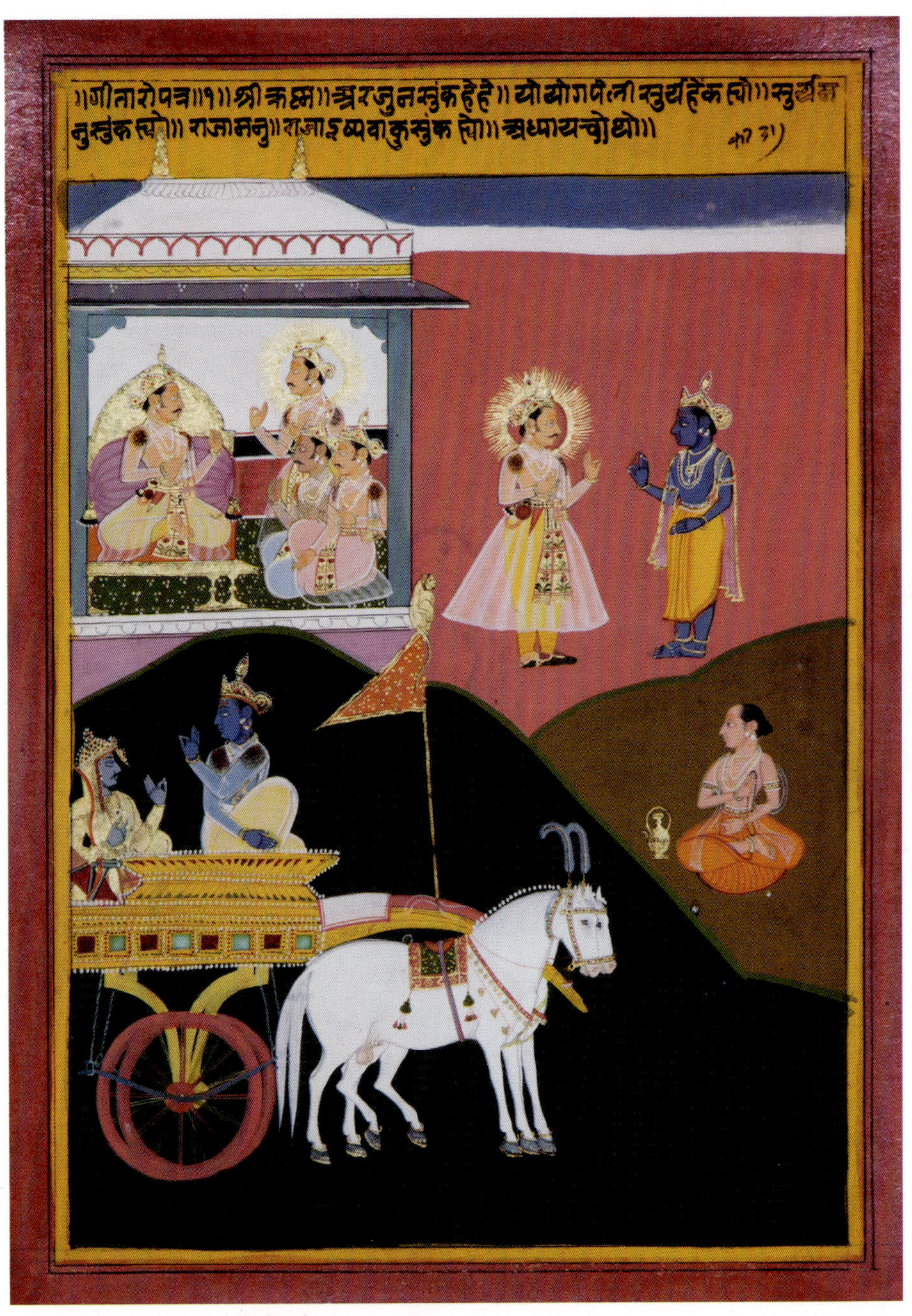

|1| श्री कृष्ण कह रहे हैं कि हे अर्जुन! मैंने सबसे पहले इस योग के ज्ञान को सूर्य से कहा था। सूर्य ने मनु को और आगे मनु ने इक्ष्वाकु को कहा।

|1| Sri Krishna says: Hey Arjuna! I first gave this knowledge of yoga to the Sun. The Sun taught it to Manu and Manu passed it on to Ikshvaku.

CHAPTER 4

In verse 1 Krishna gives Arjuna a minimalist but mythic account of the long descent of Being (Brahman). At the beginning, heaven was a borderless and infinitely expanding realm. Later, Being manifested itself in many shapes in the mortal, finite earth. *Kaal* or Eternal Time was also once without measure. It was first transformed into natural or earthly time of seasonal cycles. It then fell further into historical time of conflict, suffering and death leading to the present moment of war at the edge of annihilation. Like the *Adi Parva*, this narrative alerts us to the idea that the *Gita*'s primary concern of is with the fate of Being in time or the process of becoming.

Initially, Krishna's story seems pessimistic. But, it is soon clear that he recalls the myth for two reasons: to ensure that the memory of earth's connection with Being is not lost; and, to assert that it is always possible to recover or renew it through courage and persistence. Krishna wants to give Arjuna the knowledge (*jnana*) of the beginning of the universe and become conscious of the fact (*prajnana*) that it was '*good*.'[1] The war, he tells Arjuna, is not over a piece of land. It is about restoring dharma itself because the earth's fate depends on it. Arjuna must help to recover the primal unity between the earth and Brahman.

Krishna narrates a four-fold tale about the origin of the universe (verse 2). He is the creator who reveals the mystery of Being to Viwaswana, the founder of the Sun-dynasty, who then gives it to the primal man, Manu the Lawgiver, who finally passes it on to the king of the Ikshvaku clan to which he himself belongs (as does Rama). That knowledge is now threatened with erasure in the present conflict. The story offers no hope of evading this cycle of creation, historical decay and violent destruction. The brief fable contains the basic narrative structure of the *Mahabharata*'s original unity, fragmentation, and the struggle to regain the lost union with the divine. If the *Gita* is a song affirming the divinity of creation, the *Mahabharata* is a lament of its continuous betrayal.

Krishna's mythic narrative about the sacred origin of the universe and its tragic decline follows an archetypal pattern. It began with the golden, spiritual age of the gods, an age of truth (*satya*). After some time, there was a sudden shift to an ethical age of the Sun God when good men in conversation with the gods walked on a fecund

1 The word 'good' rings through Chapter 1 of 'Genesis' in the Old Testament to describe creation.

earth (Manu is both a man of knowledge and an inscriber of laws). In the third phase, human beings had to labour on land and use reason to discover poetry, art, stories and ethics. Soon, individual needs and desires began to impose upon and enclose nature; appropriate it for private ends resulting in the present dark age of conflict. This, Krishna tells Arjuna, is the "supreme secret" knowledge which he wants to reveal, following the "ancient path" of inspired teachers (Swami 33).

The painting illustrating verse 1 finds an admirable way of visualising Krishna's four-fold myth of promise and loss, originary light and encircling darkness, enlightened goodness and moral obtuseness. The pictorial space is unevenly divided into four parts. The colours assigned to each part arouse contradictory moral feelings which remain unresolved. The four sections illustrate divine creation, the birth of the first man (Manu), the making of an ideal society (Ikshvaku), and finally the emergence of the individual self-conscious of its mortality.[2]

The two pink and green spaces on the right are open, bright and peaceful. In the pink space (closer to the rising sun), Krishna is confidentially teaching the Sun God. The scene is dramatic. It shows that the created world is identical to the divine; the earthly and the divine are in perpetual conversation with each other. The *mayur mudras* of Krishna's right hand and the Sun God's left hand imitate each other suggesting that truth, beauty and dharma were once part of the glory of heaven and earth, god and nature.

The green and brown world of nature is inhabited by Manu. He is, Krishna says, the first man of knowledge. Manu is painted as a man of yogic discipline, simplicity and faith. It is his task to lay down both a method of knowing, and what is to be known for human beings to lead a good life in harmony with nature and the gods, a life of dharma. What he knows is what the Sun God teaches him; what he knows surrounds him like sunlight; since what he knows is dharma, he repeats it each day. At this stage, the relation between Krishna, the Sun God and Manu is suffused with the spirit of radical egalitarianism; man, nature and the divine are the same. Manu's name resonates with the cognates in Sanskrit: *man* 'to think' and *manavta* 'humanity.' In the painting, Manu has no ornaments, signs of divinity or heroism. He is unarmed. Since he is prior to social history, the artist gives him a distinct space closer to the rising sun from where he can watch what happens as time becomes more and more entangled in human ambitions and man loses sight of his origins. The green and brown space is sharply demarcated from the eternal pink space.

2 See Northrop Frye, *Anatomy of Criticism: Four Essays* (New York: Atheneum, 1969), pp. 131-145.

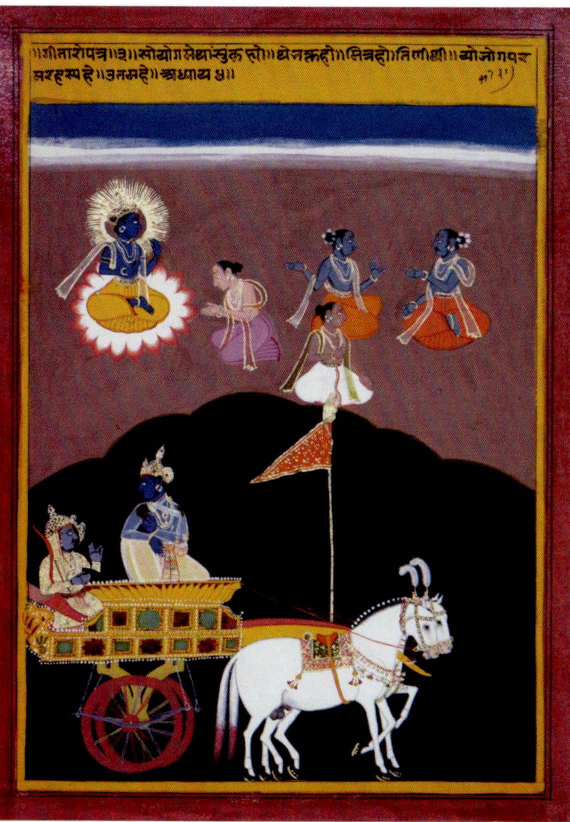

|3| श्री कृष्ण कह रहे हैं कि हे अर्जुन! क्योंकि तू मेरा भक्त और सखा है, इसलिए आज मैंने परम रहस्य वाले इस पुरातन योग का ज्ञान तुझको बताया है।

|3| Sri Krishna further says: Hey Arjuna! Because you are my devotee and my friend, today I have revealed to you the secret of this ancient yoga.

|4| अर्जुन ने पूछा कि हे कृष्ण! मैं यह कैसे मानूँ कि आपने योग का ज्ञान कल्प पूर्व सूर्य को कराया क्योंकि आपका जन्म तो अभी हाल का है और सूर्य तो बहुत पहले था।

|4| Arjuna asks: Hey Sri Krishna! How can I believe that you revealed the knowledge of yoga to the Sun? You were born only recently while the Sun has always existed.

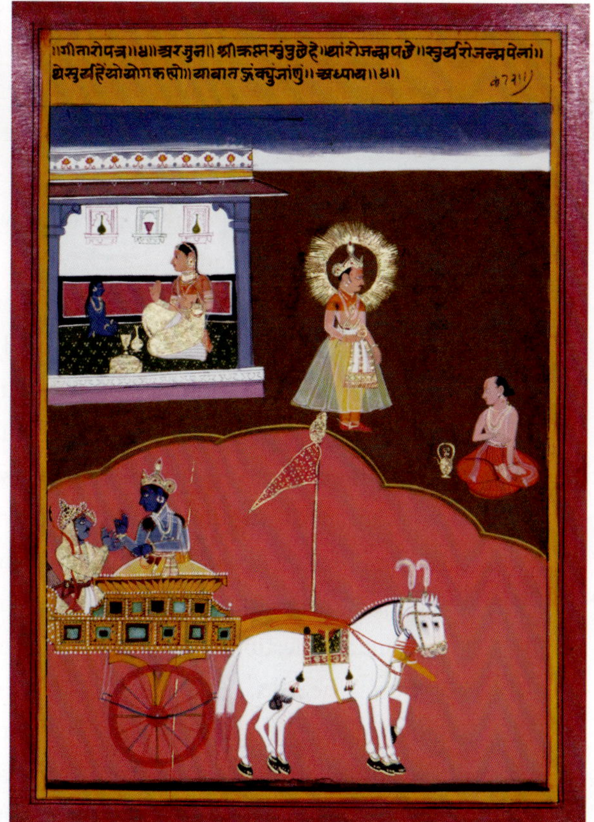

The two images on the left are placed within narrow enclosures. While they carry some of the glow—the memory—of the previous images, they neither promise security nor harmony. The blue palace, with its sumptuous carpet and golden throne, is precariously balanced on the top of a dark hill and is barely stable. It probably depicts the court of the Ikshvaku, or of the Yadavas, who are the mythic descendants of the Sun God. The palace is, of course, the displaced city of man in historical time. Its artistic beauty represents the achievements of human knowledge: structures of art and codes of law. However, it also encloses within its walls political intrigues, selfishness and irrational cruelties which so obsess human beings that they lose sight of their original, imaginative potential. The four princely discussants in the palace no longer have intuitive access to the original wisdom that ought to govern action. They are cut off from the sun by palace walls.

Krishna's chariot stands below the palace in a dark field. Is this a visualisation of what Krishna says: that the ancient knowledge has been forgotten and must be recovered again? The colours used to demarcate the different sites that arouse emotions correspond to the spiritual or moral state of the actors in the four-fold story. It is interesting that part of the chariot breaks out of the framing borders of the painting. This suggests that something escapes our structures of intelligibility; lies outside our rational comprehension. Knowledge of the impending war challenges and undermines the spiritual and moral harmony of *satya yuga*. Dharma is no longer as immediately and unquestioningly coherent as it once was when Krishna could talk to the Sun God and the Sun God to Manu.

The emphasis in the Mewari version of verse 4 is on Arjuna's sceptical response to Krishna's claim that he had, in primordial time, taught both the Sun God and Manu. Was not Krishna born only recently, Arjuna asks, whereas the Sun has existed since eternity? Arjuna knows Krishna only as a friend and companion since Krishna has yet to reveal his divinity. Radhakrishnan draws an analogy between Krishna's declaration that he is eternal with the Bodhisattava, who is born to teach age after age, and Jesus, who says, "Before Abraham was, I am" (John vii, 58). In Buddhist art, the central image of the Buddha is surrounded by repetitive images of his previous incarnations.

Arjuna's question about Krishna's divinity raises an important ethical issue: You are mortal, he asks, how can you also be eternal? Krishna is Arjuna's friend; yet, he neither knows nor comprehends him. Arjuna, too, is not transparent to Krishna. Why else would Krishna work so hard to reveal the mystery of creation and the ethics of action to Arjuna? Present action can imitate the sacred ideal only if one believes it existed. Krishna's declaration of his 'eternity' lays claim to his transcendental and unquestionable moral authority.

In this painting, muted in colour, Allah Baksh responds to this moral dilemma by returning to the four-fold myth of creation. The space is once again divided into four parts. The Sun God stands atop an undulating pink hill like a central point around which all things revolve. His clothes glow in the clear and golden light of dawn. The yoga he is teaching the bare-chested ascetic sitting on a green hill is what he has been taught by the Divine. His student is like Arjuna, a questioner and a pilgrim of knowledge.

At the top left, in an ornate palace with blue arches, a mother gently teaches her child. Her clothes catch the sun's golden light. The child is dark like Krishna. Both are, however, cut-off from the open field of vision where the gods are. The scene dramatises how the knowledge-traditions of a society are transmitted in an increasingly secularised world. What the mother knows in historical time is not intuitively acquired; it is not a vision of the Eternal. In one corner, Arjuna and Krishna are engaged in an animated discussion about the mysteries of the sacred and how they have been forgotten in a time of lamentation and conflict.

The painting for verse 5 is an example of Allah Baksh's free-ranging imagination. It is brilliantly choreographed to show that Krishna and Arjuna have been born and reborn many times. They appear together at five different sites. Though, in each birth, only Krishna, who is omniscient, remembers the past. This reinforces what Krishna says, that when there is adharma and life is threatened, he appears to ensure that it will not be completely erased. The painting first places Krishna and Arjuna closer to the sun and the east. Seated on a marble platform surrounded by green earth, they are visually indistinguishable. Sitting face-to-face, their hands reach out to each other like comrades. They are discussing the gods and what ethical conduct is. In *satya yuga*, Krishna says, when the memory of sacred origins was not lost, all human acts re-established the original coherence of the world. Now, in sadder times, human beings must recognise that they live in a world that is irrevocably sliding into *kali yuga*; into a difficult time of moral ambiguities and suffering. They will have to act to set it right again, but only if they understand what the ideal is and how to achieve it. The present suffering is a necessary rite of passage that a seeker of wisdom must endure; the journey out of mortal time to liberation is a difficult road. Arjuna has no memory of previous births. The present time of war is the only reality he knows. Therefore, Krishna who has knowledge of the past, present and future, must guide Arjuna through his present predicament. Mythic poetry offers many examples of the wise leading despairing souls through purgatorial times to paradise.

Krishna and Arjuna, sitting directly below their paradisal abode, continue their discussion through time. The black rocks on which they sit are symbolic of the hard mortal ground on which they must establish their moral kingdom. Arjuna's gesture is more contentious, while Krishna seems to be urging patience and peace. In the two scenes below, both Krishna and Arjuna are armed. Their chariot seems to be journeying back into the visible frame from some distant place. Krishna is not yet Arjuna's charioteer suggesting a time prior to the Kurukshetra war. He is not facing Arjuna, but is depicted turning back awkwardly to debate a point. The yellow sand-coloured space which surrounds them does not identify any particular moment in time. The metaphor of sand suggests how moral values shift from generation to generation. In the adjoining space, in perhaps another time, they appear as riders passing through a valley of dark-blue rocks. The sequence, perhaps, indicates a difficult moment when the vision of heavenly freedom and intuitive morality is blocked. In mythic tales, images of rocks indicate the hardening of imaginative powers and the closing-in of the egoistic self upon its own fantasies and fears without any external reason or sanction.

The eye follows the two riders in the lower left corner out of the frame. It then watches them re-enter on the top left, sitting on their familiar chariot with white horses. The repetition makes it clear that the two heroes are on the battlefield. Arjuna is a warrior in golden armour and Krishna is sitting in his mustard-coloured lotus shaped seat as the charioteer. At the end of this visual journey, we are back where we started from, but like Arjuna, we have become more aware, more conscious of history and time. What Arjuna has specifically learnt is not just the story of past time and the role he and Krishna may have played in it; not just the genealogy of his clan, but how and why their past together can be used with courage and imagination to meet the contemporary crisis; and why he must confront the terror of war. He has not yet overcome fear nor has he resolved his doubts, but he now knows that he has in Krishna a wise counsellor.[3]

3 See Frye, *Words with Power*, p. 26.

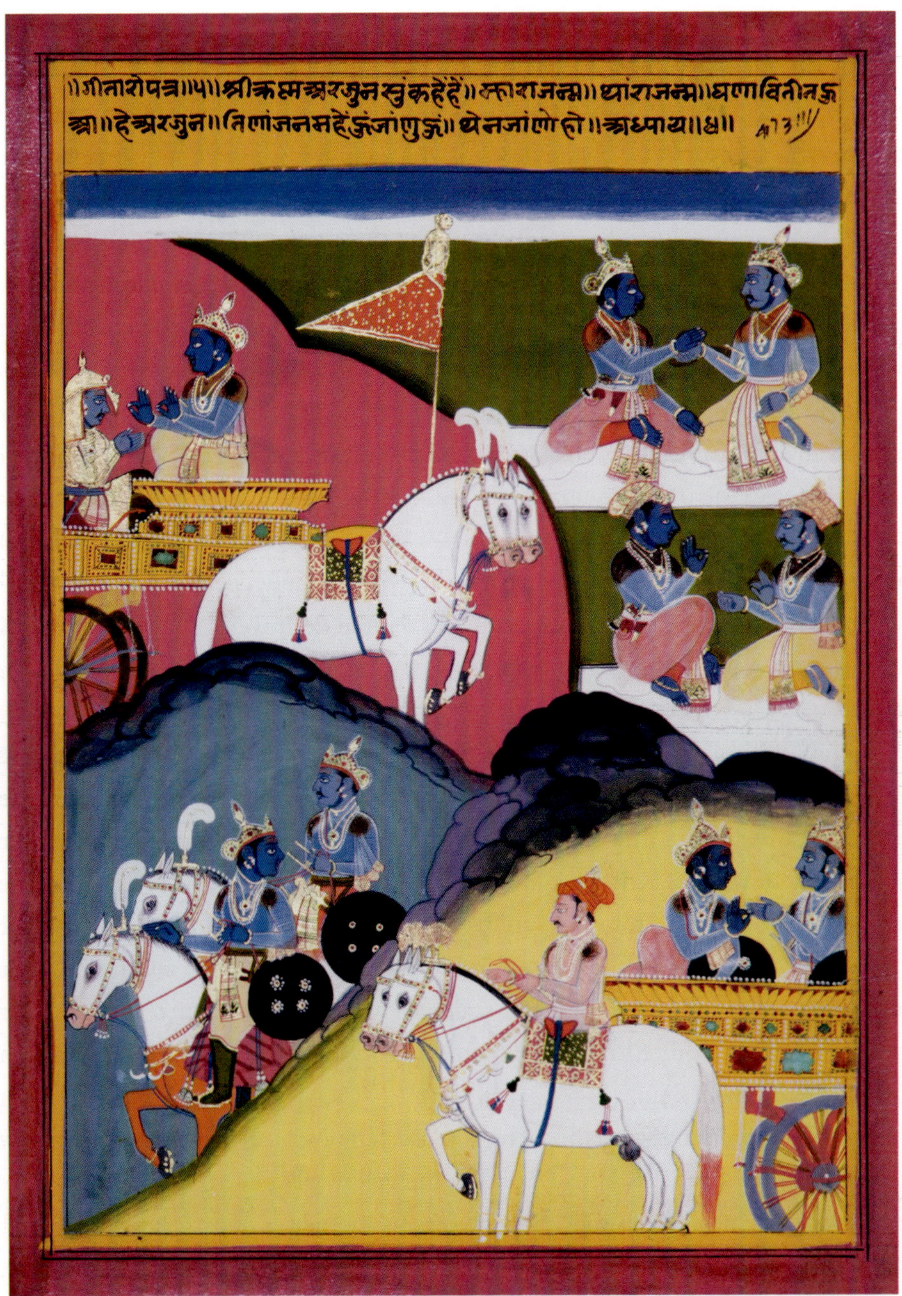

|5| श्री कृष्ण कहने लगे कि हे अर्जुन! मेरे और तुम्हारे बहुत सारे जन्म हो चुके हैं। मैं उन सबको जानता हूँ, पर तुम नहीं जानते।

|5| Sri Krishna says: Hey Arjuna! You and I have been born many times. I know each of my births, but you do not.

The next few shlokas continue to discuss Krishna's divinity and his incarnations in the world. Allah Baksh's paintings explore the relation between holiness, beauty and peace. As if to emphasise Krishna's effulgence, he places a bright golden sun at the top eastern corner for verse 6. The dazzling sun signifies two seemingly contradictory ideas. One: Krishna is pure transcendence; the absolute Brahman. Two: as incarnate man, he is untarnished goodness. Like sunlight, the clarity of his goodness is at times obscured either by forgetfulness or by distorting emotions. The *Gita*'s intention is to slowly, layer by layer, remove the misperceptions about Krishna so as to enable man to rememorialise the original sense of wonder that defined the relation between the earth and the divine. Indeed, Krishna explicitly tells Arjuna that, from yuga to yuga, he has assumed an earthly form to protect the original good from adharma. The paintings for verses 6-8 make the threat to an ethical life from war and corruption explicit. Allah Baksh's ahimsic interpretation of these verses is in tune with Gandhi's unambiguous rejection of the idea that they are urging war. Krishna only declares that, since he is the creator of the universe, he is also its preserver and destroyer. While he may choose to punish the wicked, that right belongs only to "an all-knowing God or an *avatara*" (Desai 194).

In the remarkable painting for verse 6, three human incarnations of Krishna sit in a circle below the sun. Each faces away from the sun and looks to the earth. Their gestures promise peace. The lotus flowers they carry as emblems signify beauty and sacrality. The images of Krishna diminish in size and lose some of their radiance as they move further away from the sun. Golden halos sparkle around the heads of the two Krishnas nearest to the sun. The third Krishna, without a halo and farthest from the sun, is smaller and more human in scale. All four images present a divine Krishna who has yet to make his entry into human time, but is moving further away from his original oneness with Being.

The radical break between the sacred and the temporal is represented by the fourth Krishna, born as a dark child to Devaki in the yellow pillared room. The building is far from the bright sun. Krishna, lying next to his mother, is now the archetype of the human condition; helpless, dependent and under the threat of imminent death from an evil king, Kansa. As a human being, he is the image of our temporality; as a divine being, Krishna is a reminder that life can always be lived virtuously and well.

There is a dark chasm in the lower half of the painting, where the chariot of Krishna and Arjuna stands. Sunlight does not seep through darkness to lighten the burden of Arjuna's sorrow which Krishna understands, for he has confronted the same anguish

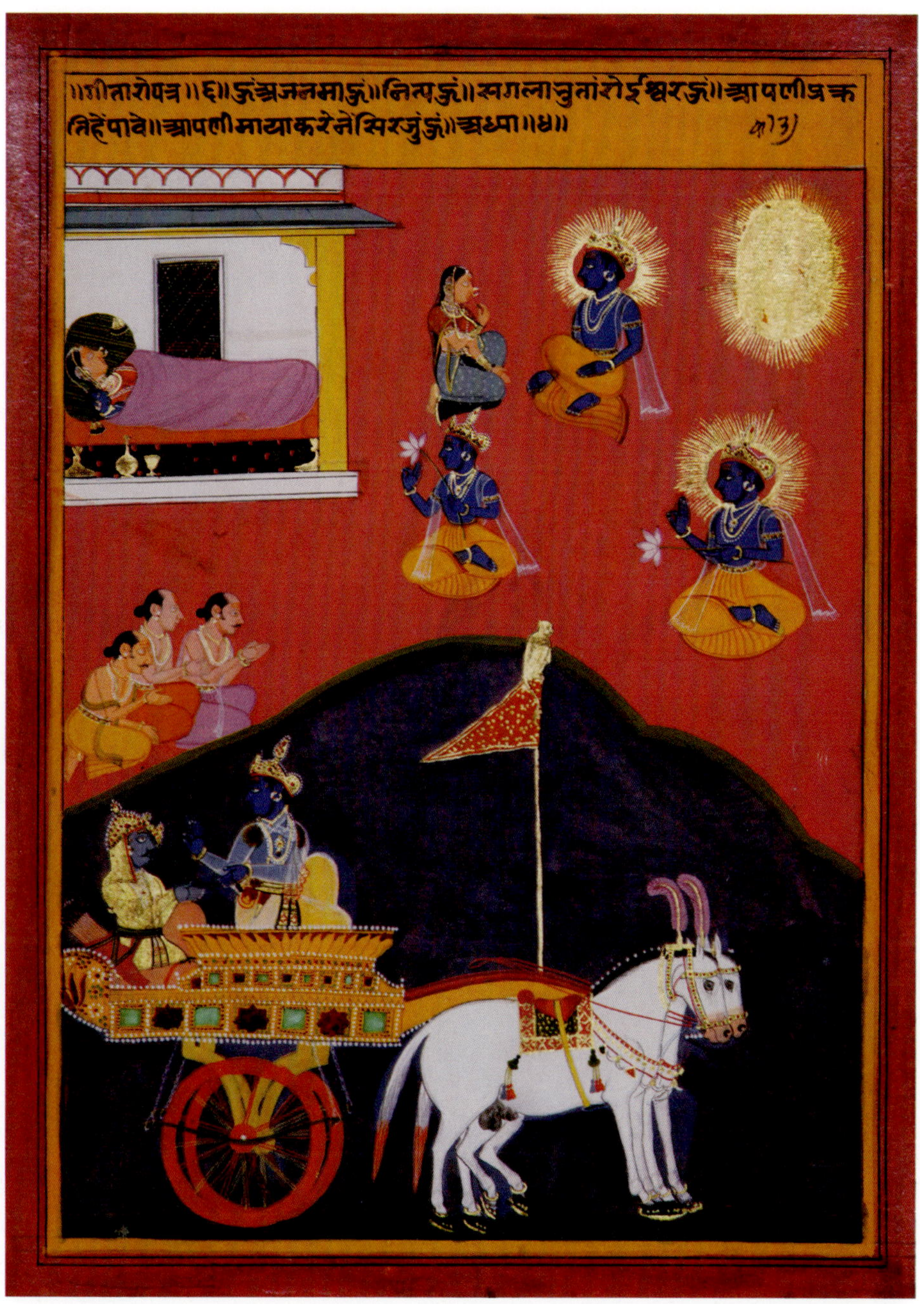

|6| श्री कृष्ण आगे बोले, हे अर्जुन! मैं अजन्मा, अविनाशी और सभी प्राणियों का ईश्वर होते हुए भी अपनी प्रकृति को वश में कर अपनी योग माया से प्रकट होता हूँ।

|6| Sri Krishna further says: Hey Arjuna! Though I am unborn, imperishable and the lord of all living beings, yet I manifest myself through my yogic power.

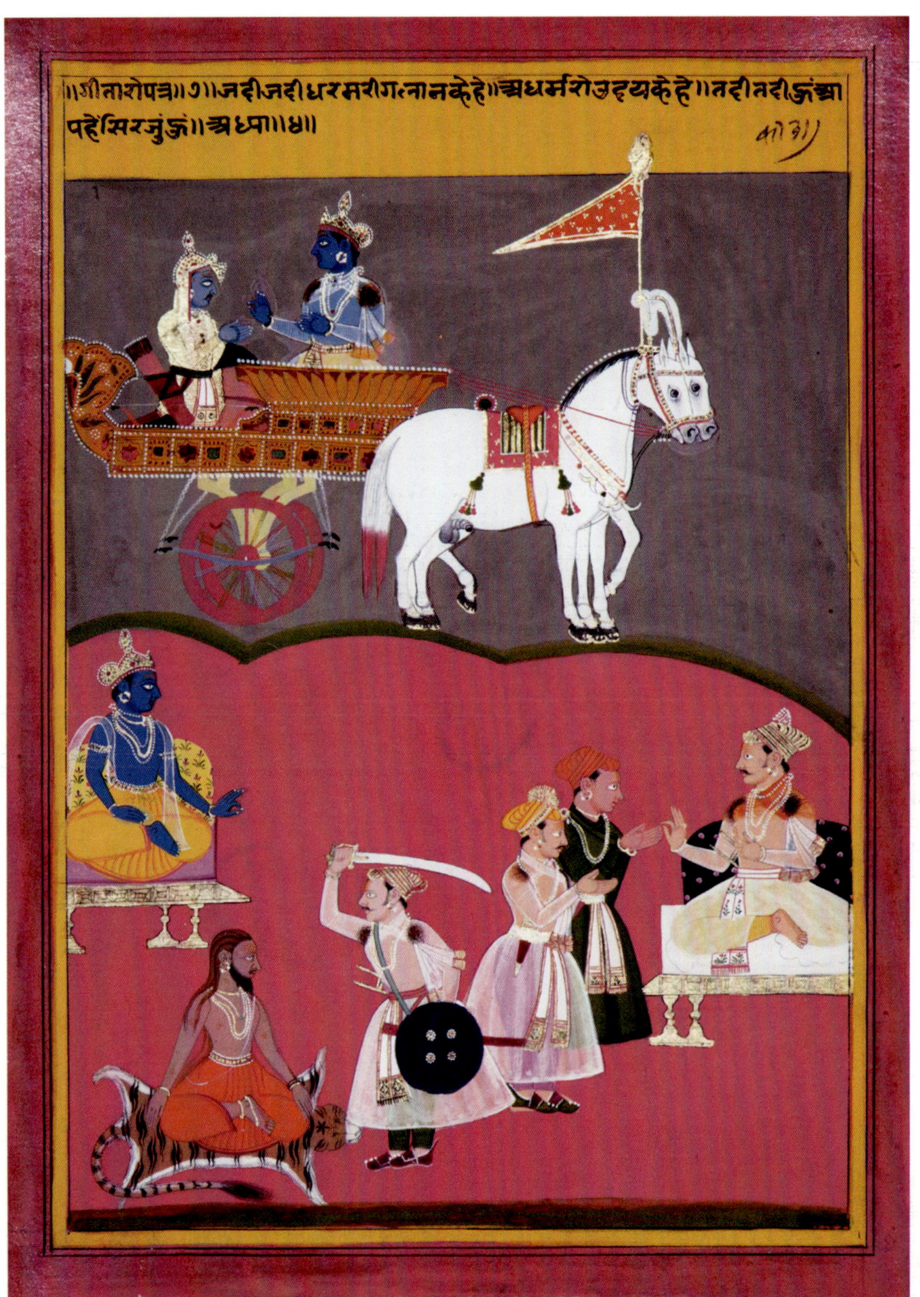

|7| श्री कृष्ण आगे कहने लगे, हे अर्जुन! जब-जब धर्म की हानि होती है और अधर्म की वृद्धि होती है तब-तब मैं अपने रूप को रचता हूँ।

|7| Sri Krishna further says: Hey Arjuna! Whenever dharma is threatened and adharma becomes stronger, I reincarnate myself.

|8| श्री कृष्ण आगे कहने लगे कि साधुओं के उद्धार, पापियों के विनाश और धर्म की स्थापना करने हेतु मैं प्रत्येक युग में प्रकट होता रहता हूँ।

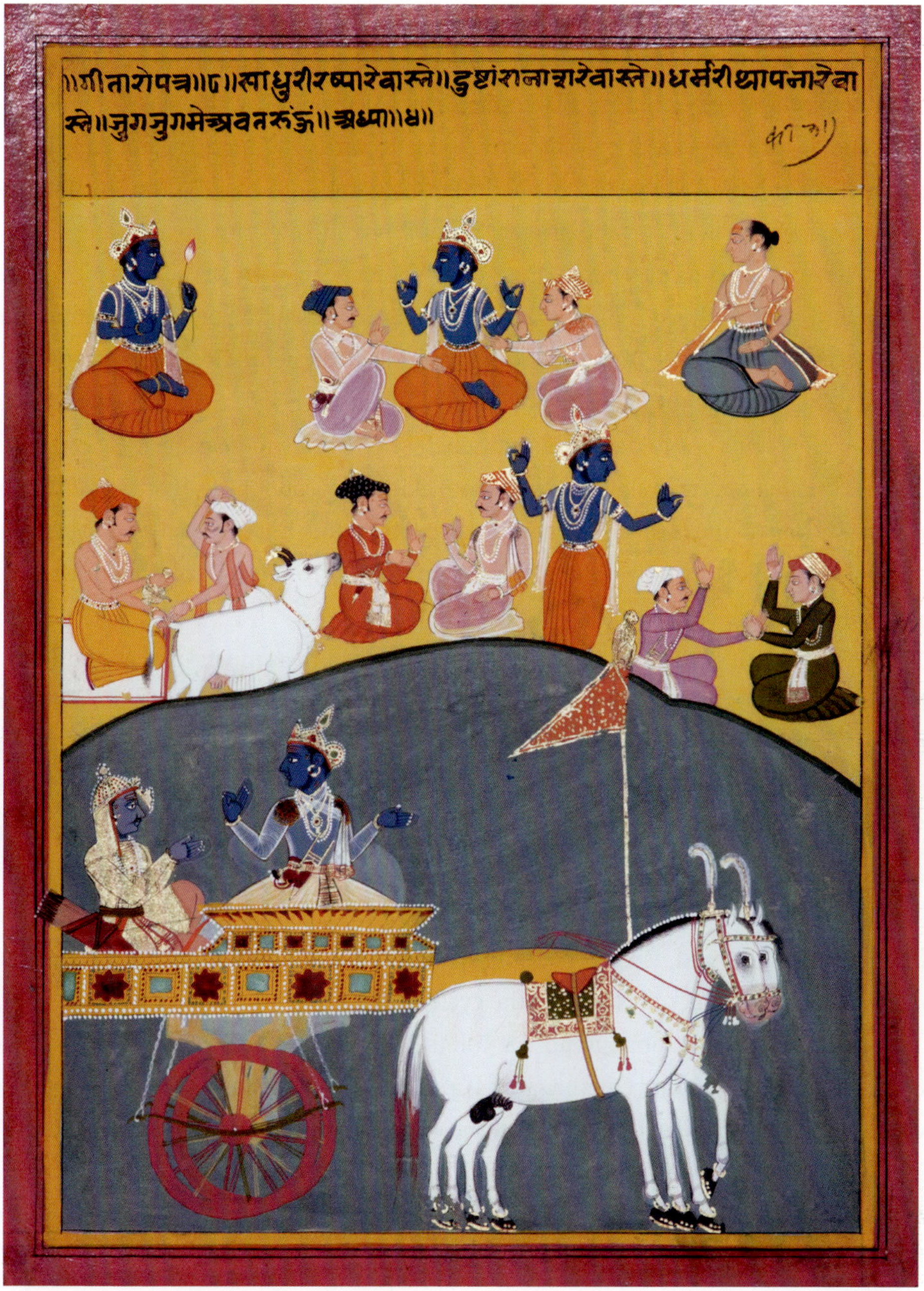

|8| Sri Krishna further says: Hey Arjuna! I am always reborn, age after age, to protect the good and the learned, and to destroy the wicked.

over the ages; he has witnessed good men unjustly destroyed. Arjuna, he knows, is neither the first nor the last man to struggle against the '*moha*', the delusions, of the material time. Even as one empathises with Arjuna's despondency, the eye catches sight of Hanuman peering out above the dark space towards the first Krishna and at the splendour of the sun. The viewer of Allah Baksh's painting is urged to think about the present instant and man's primal origins; about *itihas* and eternity.

In verse 9, Krishna teaches Arjuna that it is important to know that he is both human and divine. This is a difficult abstraction. Allah Baksh makes a fine attempt to find visual equivalents for Krishna's complex and sacred genealogy. He distinguishes between Krishna's divinity and Arjuna's earth-bound selfhood. Arjuna is placed near the base. His hands are folded in humility before Krishna's increasing self-revelation. The *Gita*'s dialogic form is slowly turning into a discourse about the divine. The chariot is isolated from all the busy activity by an undulating pink hill outlined by a pale green line, thereby, indicating how far removed Arjuna still is from understanding the sacred and its demands.

The upper half of the painting represents Krishna both as mortal and as god who is the beginning and the end of creation. On the left, he is the dark baby born to a human mother in an ornately painted room. Right below, he sits like a benevolent deity with a golden halo, receiving and blessing those who accept his divinity without fear or doubt. The scene at the top is surreal. Krishna pulls into his own being the soul of a dead man who has accepted his divine sovereignty. He sits still like a yogi, as if meditating on death's mystery without anxiety. A golden line of breath, emanating from the mouth of the man on the ground, is absorbed into Krishna's eternal body; the mortal becomes one with the immortal, only to begin the cycle of birth once again.

Goethe's engaging monograph on colour helps one to understand the strange images for verse 10. Colour, Goethe says, is "a significant outer sign of what is happening within" the self.[4] The effect of colour on the viewer is aesthetic and "sensory-moral."[5] The painting's space is not geometrically designed. It is organised by an intuitive and visionary sense of inward harmony and peace which, the verse says, are available to those who seek refuge in Krishna.

The space is divided into two distinctive colours by a thin, sinuous, yellow line that makes its leisurely way across the middle of the page. The artist paints images of

4 Goethe, *Essential Goethe*, p. 956.

5 *Essential Goethe*, p. 958.

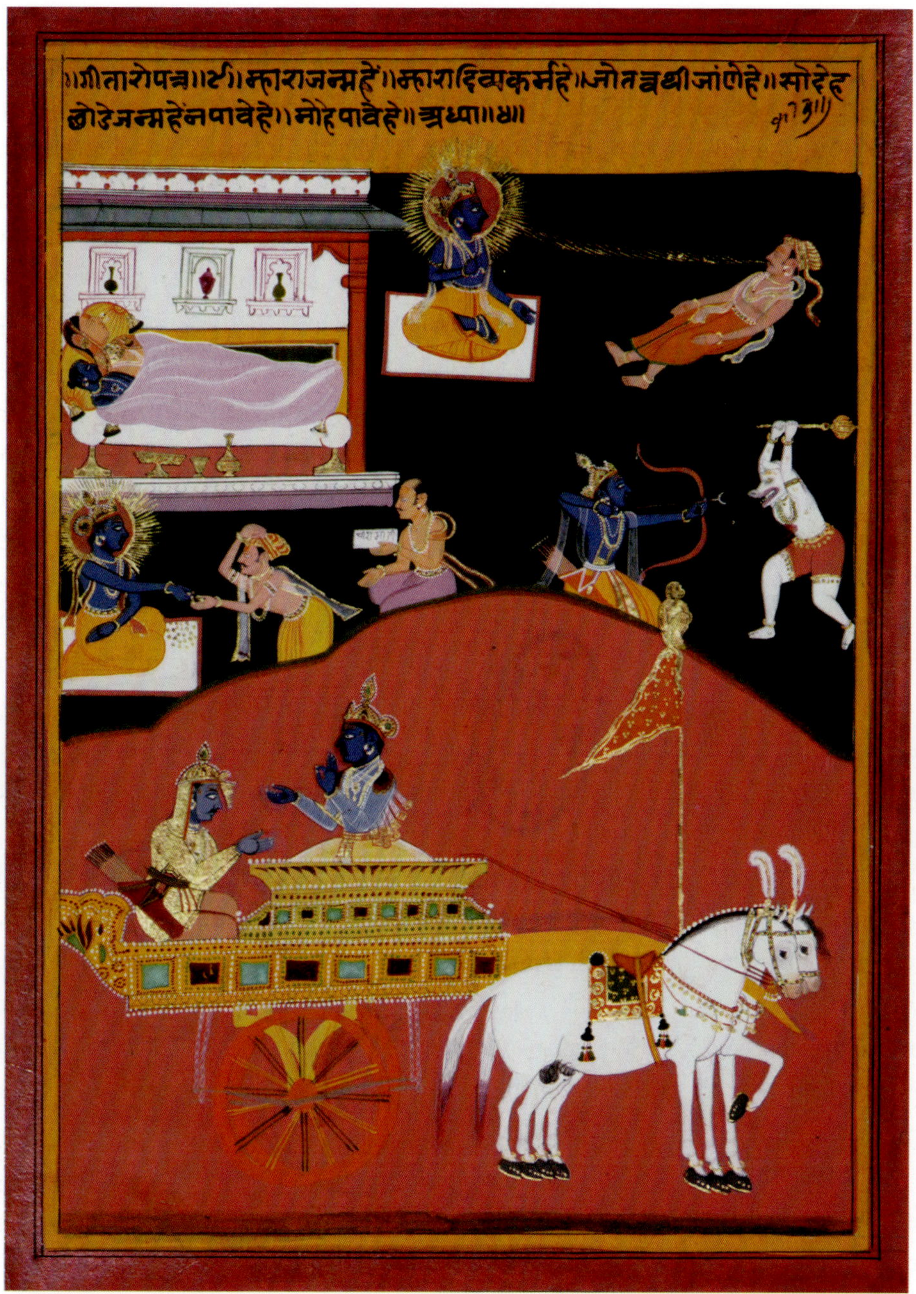

|9| श्री कृष्ण अर्जुन से कह रहे हैं कि जो मनुष्य मेरे दिव्य जन्म और दिव्य कर्म को तत्व से जान लेता है, वह देह त्यागने के बाद पुनर्जन्म नहीं लेता अपितु मुझे प्राप्त होता है।

|9| Sri Krishna says to Arjuna, the person who understands that my birth and life are divine is not reborn after death but is absorbed in me.

mundane human activities which are far removed from the agonies of war. The verse and the visual images suggest that human beings long to be reassured that the original unity of men and earth, sky and gods, which is now fragmented, can be regained through calm meditation on the divine. That is why the tonal contrast between the colours of the two halves does not create a sense of anxious dissonance.

From a distance, the flat surface of the painting is strangely surreal. Krishna's chariot is depicted as either standing on or submerged in a lake. The calm blue water reflects the calm blue sky. The battlefield is, for an instant, forgotten; so are the conflicts, as if they were momentary hallucinations. The soul must remain still and calm like the water and the sky. Then Arjuna will understand that what is *real* is Krishna's divinity. Since Arjuna is part of the same original unity, he too is an incarnation of the divine who must do his duty without the fear of committing sin.[6]

If the painting's lower half depicts the shores of eternity, its upper half leads to the shores of time and daily life. Here the sun does not rise upon a field of war, but on a group of worshippers. Krishna is placed near the eastern horizon where the pink ground meets the sky. He is at once the rising sun, a divine being and an earthly incarnation. While the fiery golden halo makes him numinous, the yellow robe, streaked with brick-red folds, gives him nobility. It is said that when the mind meditates on the colour golden-yellow, "the eye is gladdened, the heart expands, the feet are cheered, and immediate warmth seems to waft towards us."[7]

Looking at the figure dancing ecstatically in the sunlight, or the four men carrying golden bowls to offer to their gods, one feels that ordinary life goes on at its ritual pace even as wars are fought and evil renders the soul despondent. Spring always returns; human beings find their way back to a life of lyric celebration of the earth; life-rhythms are daily resurrected with the rising sun. How different this is from the revulsion that moved poets after the atrocities of the Second World War to declare that it will be impossible to write lyric poetry again.[8]

The idea that the world of imagination is the world of eternity is represented by the two 'visionary' poets sitting with Krishna. Long golden strings of divine songs rise from the mouths of the singers and dissolve in the glowing halo around Krishna. What

---

6 There are characters in the *Mahabharata* who refuse retaliatory violence though sanctioned by law.

7 *Essential Goethe*, p. 961.

8 Theodor Adorno, *Minima Moralia: Reflections from a Damaged Life* (1951), translated by E. F. N. Jephcott (London: New Left Books, 1974).

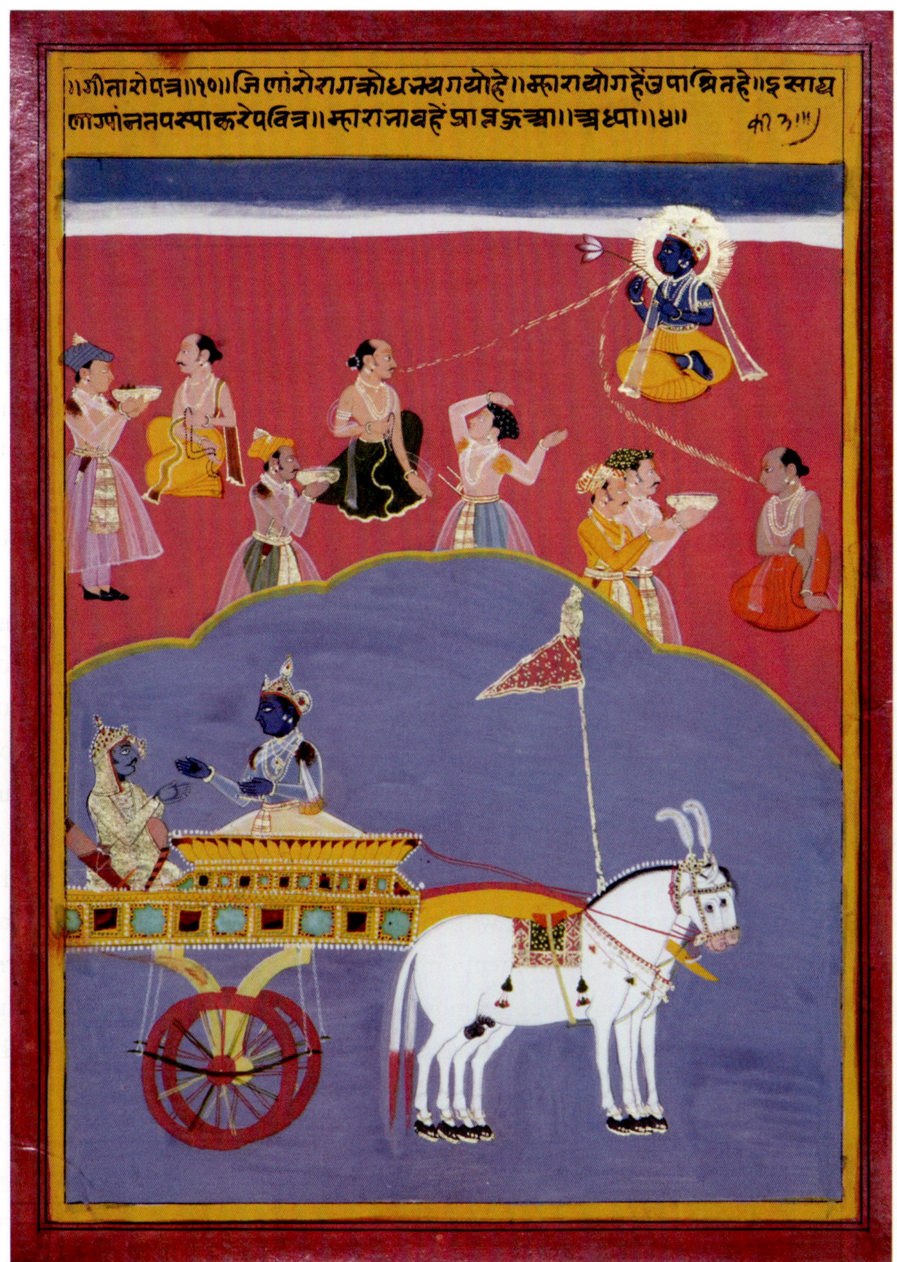

|10| श्री कृष्ण अर्जुन से कह रहे हैं कि जो प्राणी पहले से राग, भय और क्रोध से मुक्त होकर अपने मन को मुझ में लगा कर मेरे आश्रित हो जाते हैं। ऐसे भक्त ज्ञानतप से पवित्र हो मेरे स्वरूप को प्राप्त होते हैं।

|10| Sri Krishna says to Arjuna: Those who concentrate on me and take refuge in me can overcome desire, fear and anger. Such devotees, purified by the fire of wisdom, attain my state of Being.

is visually fascinating is the thought that the two poets are also singing Krishna into existence. Krishna is as much a creation of our myth-makers as he is of great mystic singers like Mirabai or Jaydeva. The poets in the painting are distinct, singular; yet they are 'bound' by a 'song-line' to Krishna. Such 'bonding', such 'bondedness', the painter suggests in visionary acceptance of what the verse says, can help us live, not only as sojourners passing through earthly time and space, but as the rightful dharmic inhabitants of an earth in which the same laws govern gods, human beings, animals, water, shadows, trees and asuras. When we understand this, the night of mourning shall dissolve and the morning of hope shall light our days.

Arjuna must look beyond his anxiousness, past the lake and up to the east where Krishna is visible in the rising sun. This vision of Krishna as the golden sun anticipates the awe-inspiring revelation of his divinity to Arjuna later. Here, he is not the unbearable, blinding light that will overawe Arjuna. The vision Krishna offers is gentle and benign. In his right hand, he holds a blue lotus which is reminiscent both of Sri Lakshmi, the life-bestowing and generous goddess, as well as the Buddhist saviour, Padmapani ("Lotus in Hand"), who is the Bodhisattva of "infinite mercy and loving compassion."[9] The open lotus is also the gateway to heaven and is rightly placed at the horizon where the earth and the sky meet.

After telling Arjuna that those devoted to him find peace in wisdom and are without desire, fear or anger, Krishna makes an important distinction between himself and other deities (verses 11, 12 and 13). He says that those who long for easy victories and quick rewards worship other gods. To be one with him demands the sacrifice of selfhood. The painting for verse 12 is a witty comment on this. Its crowded and fragmented space suggests the extensive division of labour among a variety of gods whom people worship to fulfil their needs and ambitions. Ironically, none of the worshippers seem aware of the presence of Krishna. Their concerns are too narrow; their minds are circumscribed by their immediate apprehensions or desires. An enlightened mind would have noticed that the world around them is radiant with red flowers on beautiful trees that are canopied by a clear blue sky.

Krishna's chariot stands on the green-fringed shore of the blue lake. The earth is covered with purple, red, yellow and white flowers. The image is a correlative of the idea that an awakened soul finds in nature sufficient ground for joy and a moral life. Having painted a space in the colours of renewal, passion and fecundity, Allah Baksh urges us to ask: What more do human beings want? Is an earth, embellished by beauty,

9 Zimmer, *Myths and Symbols in Indian Art*, pp. 90-97.

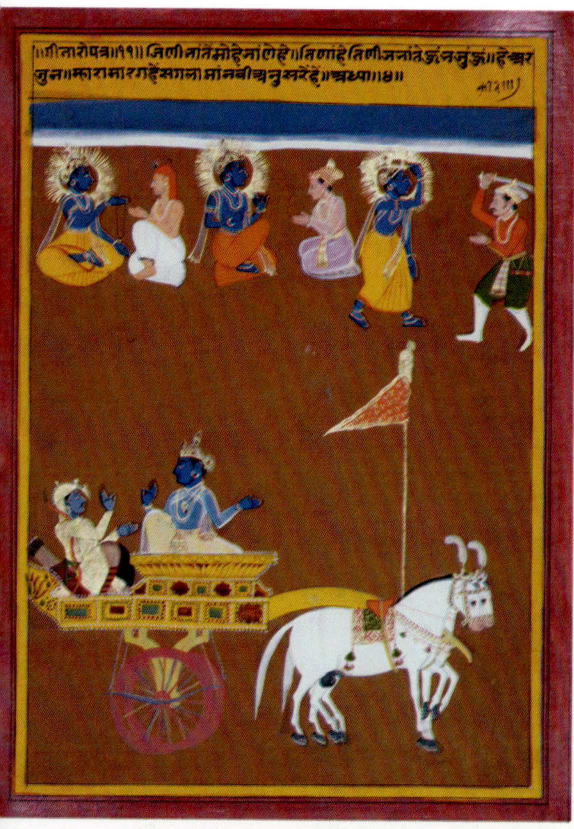

|11| श्री कृष्ण आगे कहने लगे कि हे अर्जुन! भक्तगण जिस प्रकार से भी मुझे भजते हैं, मैं भी उन्हें उसी प्रकार से भजता हूँ क्योंकि सभी मनुष्य सब प्रकार से मेरा ही अनुसरण करते हैं।

|11| Sri Krishna further says: Hey Arjuna! I am devoted to my worshippers in the same way as they are devoted to me.

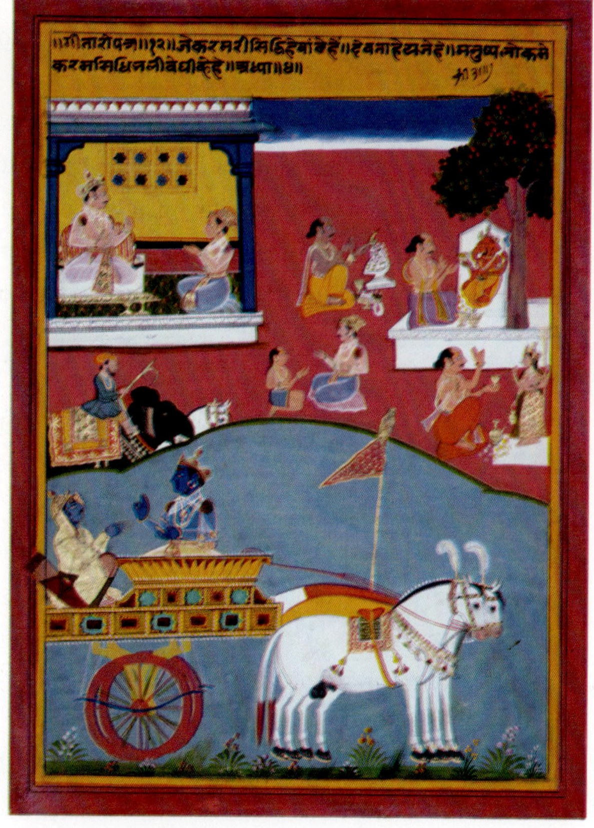

|12| श्री कृष्ण अर्जुन से कह रहे हैं कि इस मनुष्यलोक में कर्मों के फल की इच्छा वाले देवताओं को पूजते हैं क्योंकि इससे उनको कर्मों की सिद्धि शीघ्र मिल जाती है।

|12| Sri Krishna says to Arjuna: On this earth, the ones who long for the fruit of action only worship those gods who will grant what they desire quickly.

not enough? And, even more importantly: How can we so cultivate the inward eye that the perception of grace becomes a habit? If the purpose of Krishna's verse is to turn thought away from the vanity of ambitions towards the shaping of a non-egotistic soul, the artist's intention is to help us cultivate a mode of seeing which is aware of the divine in the tangible world.

The chariot is deliberately surrounded by a pale blue colour which lacks the emotional charge of the pinkish-red field above. The eye is instinctively distracted and the mind fails to concentrate on Krishna as the verses demand. Instead, like ordinary mortals, we try to 'read' and identify the different gods in the painting's upper half. A frenetic priest sits before a small gold-covered image of Devi or Lakshmi, the goddess of material and spiritual wealth. She holds emblems of power and wealth—a pot of elixir and a golden trishul. The priest is more desirous of earthly prosperity than of holiness. He holds up a golden goblet and sings hymns of praise in the hope of a boon. Golden vessels lie around him. With his back to Krishna, and his ears filled with the urgency of his own prayers, he pays no attention to Krishna's teachings.

A brahmin worships the idol of Ganesha in a simple white temple under a flowering tree. Ganesha has a mythic connection to the *Mahabharata*. When Vyasa needed a scribe, Brahma suggested Ganesha as only he could inscribe "the divine word…in the language of truth."[10] Ganesha is the god whose sharp mind clarifies the complexities of the text, clears its difficult concerns with dharma. Paradoxically, he can also place obstacles. In the popular imagination, he is also the beloved god of festivities who relishes an abundance of food. In this painting, he carries a bowl full of sweets in his right hand. The irony is that the priest no longer appears to recall Ganesha's connection to Vyasa's story and, hence, to Krishna's discussions about peace and non-cruelty, responsible and dispassionate action.

There are two other worshippers in the painting. One is praying to an idol of Krishna covered with silver ornaments and silk. He prays to an idol, but does not hear the divine word. The second worshipper is a reader of palms, an astrologer. He is diminutive, a caricature of the other priests and, hence, morally reduced. The scene dramatises the inanity of a superstitious life and its desperation. Indeed, the entire cluster of worshippers of different gods and seekers of astrological guidance lead constricted lives without imaginative courage.

There is another pictorial block at the top left depicting an opulent royal court. A princely figure, immaculately dressed, is full of regal pride and confidence. A supplicant,

10 *Adi Parva*, the *Mahabharata*, translated by Ganguli, volume 1, p. 2.

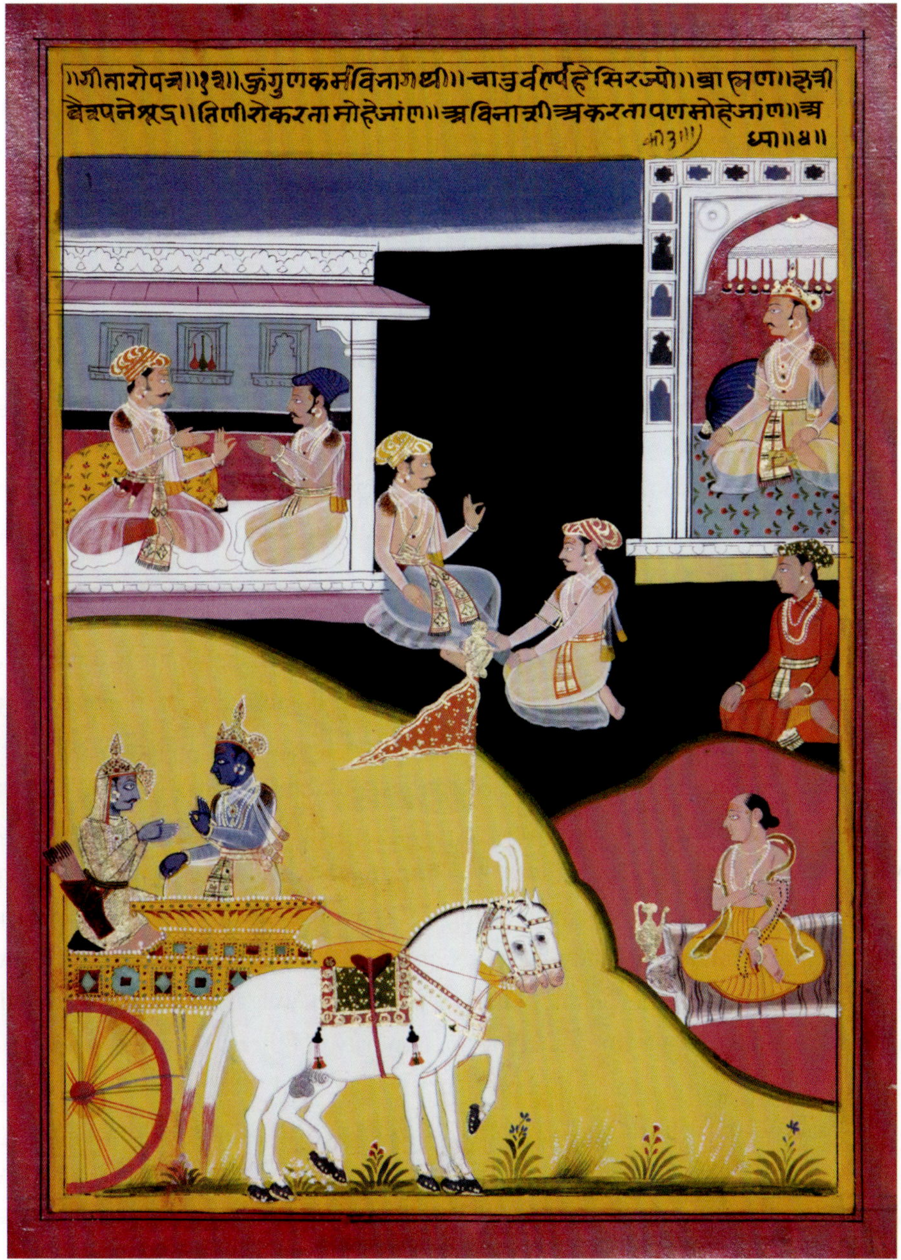

|13| श्री कृष्ण आगे कहने लगे कि हे अर्जुन! मैंने ही गुण और कर्मों के आधार पर चारों वर्णों की सृजना की है- ब्राह्मण, क्षत्रिय, वैश्य और शूद्र- फिर भी तू मुझ अविनाशी को अकर्ता ही जान।

|13| Sri Krishna says: Hey Arjuna! I created the four orders of society according to their nature and work—brahmin, kshatriya, vaishya and shudra. However, I perform no action and I am indestructible.

with hands outstretched, kneels before him asking for charity or favour. The scene is beautifully painted though, paradoxically, it presents a world of arbitrary authority and its whimsical capacity to bestow favours or demean. By placing Krishna's chariot below the palace in an open field, Allah Baksh shows the radical difference between the two. If the prince issues orders and decrees, Krishna patiently guides thought and sight through discussion; if the former dictates, the latter urges the imagination to discover the relation between dharma and everyday life where choices are made and consequences suffered. It is not surprising that an armoured elephant and a horse, intruders from the battlefield, separate the 'chariot of teaching' from the palace where a ruler's commands rather than wisdom prevails.

Hanuman is, once again, a bemused watcher. He listens to Krishna's discourses, and yet wonders at the folly of the worshippers above who perform the rituals but live according to borrowed truths; who know the formulae for living and grace, but will do nothing to solve the mystery of dharma.

Krishna's discourse about the four-fold division of a good society in verse 13 is controversial. He segments society according to varnas. Some English translations erase the word 'varna' and replace it by a more neutral classification of the social order, e.g. "the wise, the soldier, the merchant, the labourer" (Swami 34). But, in Krishandas's Mewari translation, the four human categories—brahmin, kshatriya, vaishya and shudra—are emanations of that unity of Being which Krishna himself represents. The four-fold division, Krishna insists, is neither hierarchical nor dependent on birth or gender. It is a formal way of structuring the economic and social order. However, Louis Dumont's influential study, *Homo Hierarchicus*, shows that, while the original classification may have been functional, in practice it was always hierarchical; the purity of some was always threatened by the impurity of others. It created inequalities and was, hence, contrary to the notion that all beings had their origin in the divine. In his great *Discourse on Inequality* (1754), Rousseau begins by asserting that evil is inequality. Gandhi, who knew Rousseau's text, argued that Krishna's varna system only made a distinction between the superiority of service over the superiority of status. "The moment superior status is arrogated," he says unconvincingly, "it becomes worthy to be trampled underfoot" (Desai 196-197).

The asymmetrical break-up of the pictorial space evokes visual dissonance. Allah Baksh does so to offer his own moral evaluation of Krishna's *varna* classification. Instead of creating harmony, for Allah Baksh it has left society fragmented and conflicted. While Krishna and Arjuna discuss the matter within a calm sunlit space full of flowers,

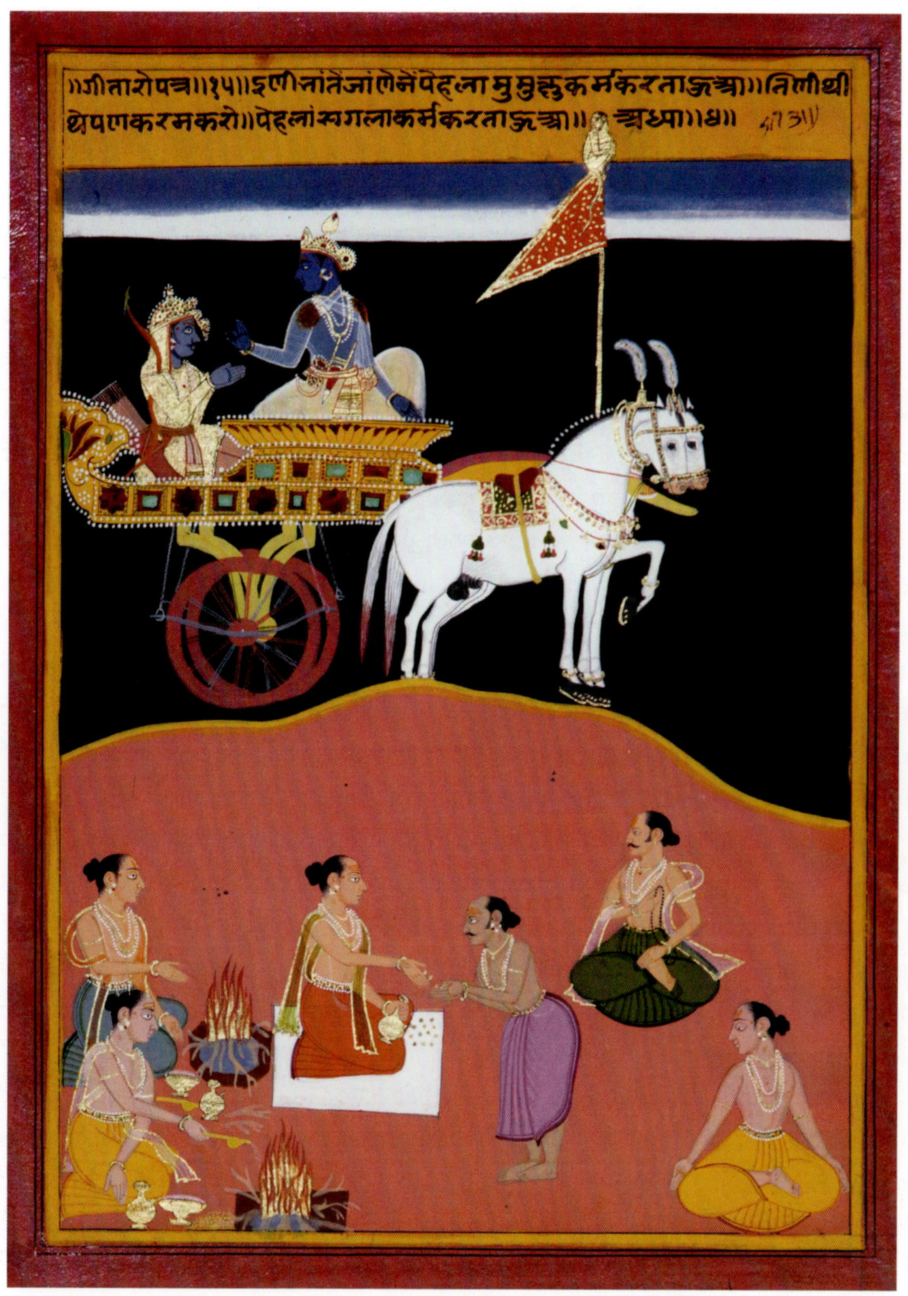

|15| श्री कृष्ण अर्जुन से कह रहे हैं कि पूर्वकाल में मुमुक्षुओं ने इस प्रकार जानकर ही कर्म किए हैं इसलिए तू भी पूर्वजों की तरह सदा से किए जाने वाले कर्म ही कर।

|15| Sri Krishna says to Arjuna: That is how wise men in the past acted; therefore, you should imitate what your ancestors have always done.

the social realm above them lacks any coherence of colour, geometric order or inter-relatedness. A brahmin sits on tiger skin within a pink bubble of his own. He stares into nothingness. His world is socially blank and morally unresponsive to things outside. The same lack of belonging isolates the kshatriya king at the top right. His palace is ornate, but is reduced in size and unceremoniously cut off by the painting's border. He stares blankly at a wall. He is well-dressed, but his body sags; his face shows no sign of vital intelligence. There is no courtly activity around him which demands his responsible attention. Isolated, he has no perceived relationship with other groups that make a harmoniously functioning society. The same sense of isolation marks the two men sitting in an austere white house on the left. Perhaps, they are merchants. Their animated gestures suggest that they may be exchanging news of the market. Their world is self-contained; cut-off from other social or moral concerns by a black and empty space; a space which promises no links with others, no conversation, no friendship, no interdependence. Three other men sit in an undefined and unlit space outside the home and the palace. One of them, who is isolated and placed between the brahmin and the prince, seems disconsolate. The other two are arguing. Hanuman sits between them as if in empathy. Is he wondering what place animals and other creatures occupy in the sacred division of the earth? In the *Mahabharata*, while they can be sacrificed for human good, animals are also important makers of moral communities.

The painting conveys no sense of mutuality between the four groups which, Krishna declares, were once part of a primal unity. Oblivious of each other, their separation in distinctive coloured spaces causes dissonance and should be read as the painter's implicit critique of caste (and, in his historical moment, religion) as a way of structuring society. By isolating Krishna and Arjuna in a separate space, is Allah Baksh hinting that there is an impermeable line between the moral ideal and the social practice?

In verse 16, the discussion shifts to whether action or ascetic withdrawal will help to fulfil life's ideal promise. The painting is beautiful and meditative. The *rasa* of its deep green colour is in harmony with the quiet and deliberative tone of the verse. The night is about to end, but the land still lies half-forgotten in darkness. There is a gleam of light on the horizon. Arjuna and Krishna, lost in the intricacies of their moral debate, are oblivious of the sun rising just over the edge of the earth. But, Hanuman, perched on the flag-pole, has already greeted the new day. The river on the earth below has absorbed the mood of dawn. Its water is a deep blue; the night-shadows below its surface have vanished. Pink and white lotus flowers—flowers of enlightened thought—have begun to open. They do not have to labour to achieve ethical perfection, or debate questions

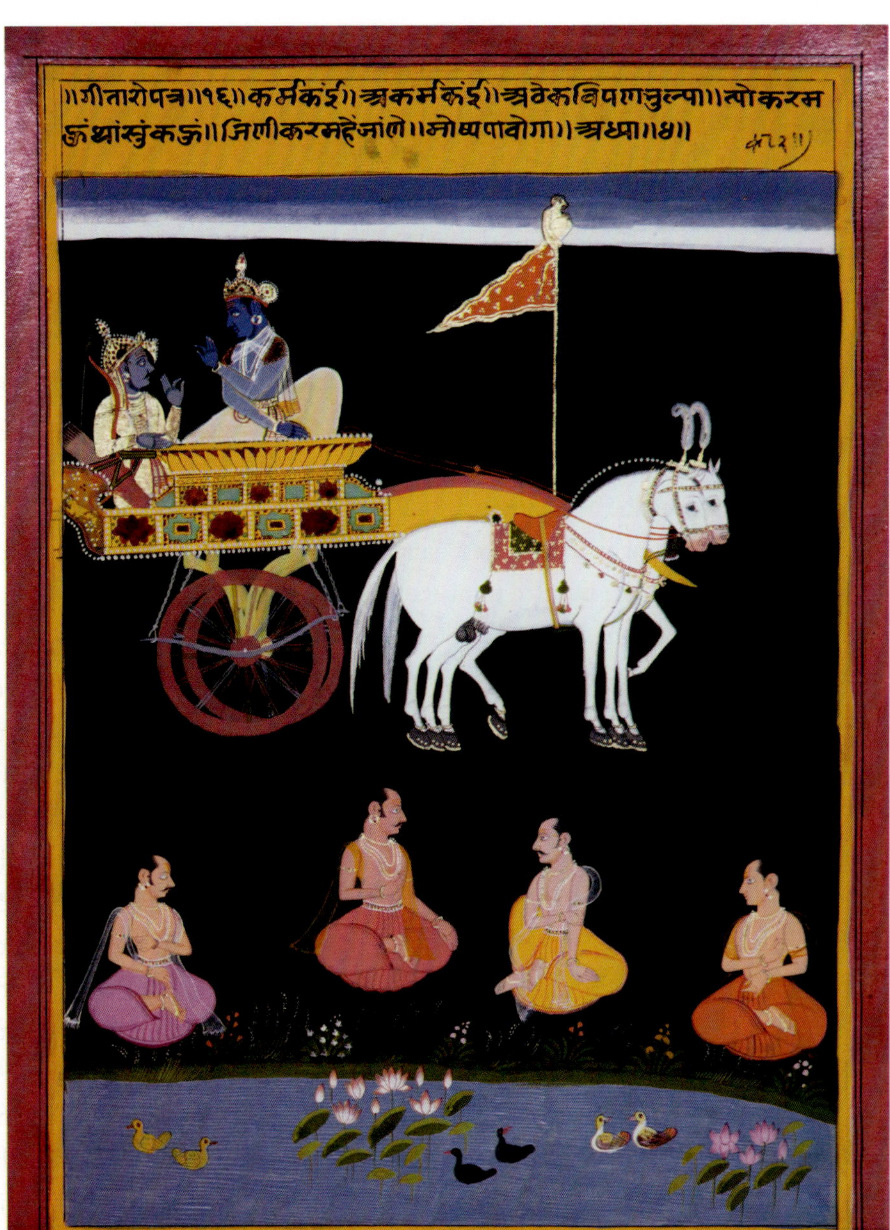

|16| श्री कृष्ण आगे कहने लगे कि हे अर्जुन! कर्म क्या है? अकर्म क्या है? इस बारे में बुद्धिमान भी भ्रमित है। इसलिए मैं तुम्हें कर्म के बारे में समझाऊँगा, जिसे जानकर तू मोक्ष पाएगा।

|16| Sri Krishna further says: Hey Arjuna! What is action? What is inaction? Even the wise are bewildered by these questions. That is why I will teach you what action is. Once you know it, you will find salvation.

of dharma. A similar sentiment about instinctive faith informs the New Testament: "Consider how the wild flowers grow. They do not labour or spin. Yet I tell you, not even Solomon in all his splendour was dressed like one of these" (Luke 12:27).

Three pairs of white, black and yellow ducks have noticed that the new day has arrived. Unburdened by the anxieties of duty, self or revenge, they are emblems of faith and affection, of the daily reaffirmation of a 'goodly' and hence 'godly' world. But, more importantly, this renewal of the morning imitates the first dawn and the first utterance of the word which contains all knowledge.[11] And, since what happened in the beginning was good, since it was a blessing and was the truth, it should be repeated once again and forever. Not surprisingly, Thoreau says: "I remember the book [the *Gita*] as an hour before sunrise."[12]

Four priests sit along the bend of the river. Flowers blossom around them. They are dressed in bright colours which find a resonance in the colours of the chariot and the sky above. The priests are the puzzled thinkers Krishna mentions. For them the sacred is not as ordinary as the sunlight or the flowers. Krishna is near them. Yet, instead of becoming active seekers, they are caught up in scriptural debates, as if that is action enough. They gaze at each other hoping, perhaps, that someone else will offer them revelation. But all they have to do is to look around and up. Since the priests seem to act as well as they can, the painter does not mock them. Their bodies are youthful and their gestures are alert.

Verses 17 to 20 continue to unravel the word 'action.' Krishna says: Since action is complicated, cultivate your discriminating intelligence if you want to understand the mystery and the paradoxes of life. Right action confuses even the wisest. They fail because, even when they do the right thing, they worry about results, rewards and victories. For those who regard life as a pilgrimage, right action follows old laws and always sustains the world. The painting shows a man who refuses to feed hay to a cow as custom demands and hurries out of the frame. He is an example of action which, Krishna says, is wrong. Another man gracefully invites a cow to eat a sheaf of golden hay placed before her. His outstretched arms and open hands rememorialise the old *natya* (drama) of hospitality. As an imitation of a ritual action, it is an example of what Krishna calls 'good work.' The wisest may be puzzled, the ascetics may sit still and gaze at the stars, but devotion to the other offered without any expectation of a reward can, as Yudhishthira finally discovers, open a door to paradise.

11 Eliade, *Cosmos and History*.

12 See Friedrich, *The Gita within Walden*, p. 25.

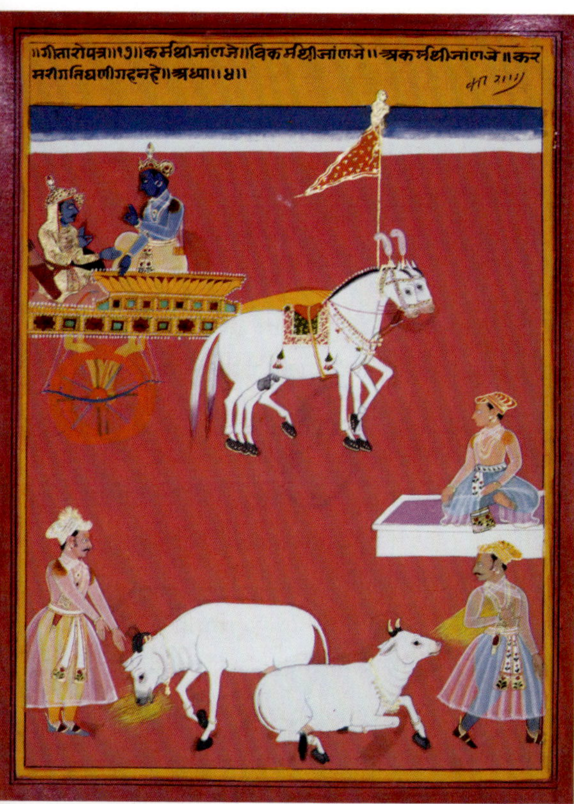

|17| श्री कृष्ण समझाते हुए कहने लगे कि कर्म का ज्ञान तुझे होना चाहिए, तुझे विकर्म का ज्ञान होना चाहिए और अकर्म का ज्ञान भी क्योंकि कर्म की गति गहन कही गई है।

|17| Sri Krishna explains to Arjuna: You should know what right action is; you should know what wrong action is; and, you should also know what inaction is. It is said that the law of action is mysterious.

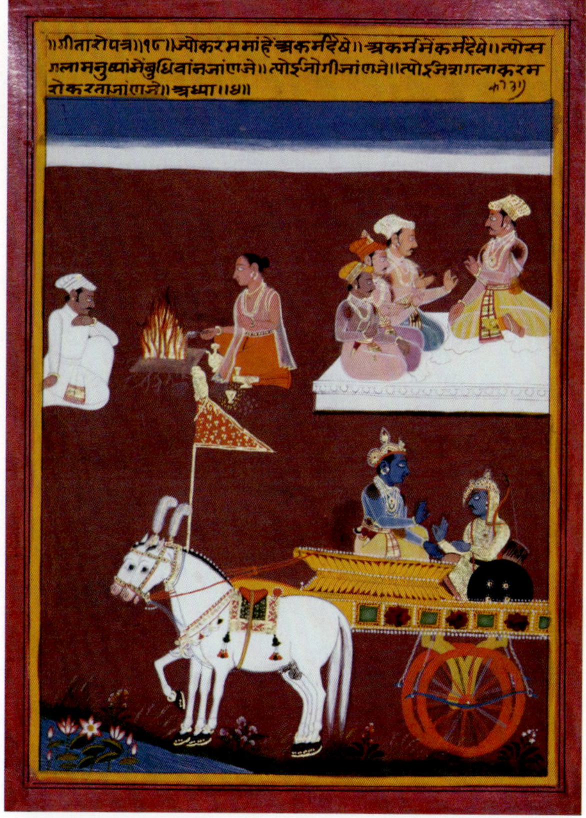

|18| श्री कृष्ण आगे कहने लगे कि हे अर्जुन! प्राणियों में बुद्धिमान वही है जो कर्म में अकर्म और अकर्म में कर्म देखता है। वह सारे कर्म करता हुआ भी योगी है।

|18| Sri Krishna says: Hey Arjuna! Amongst the living, the wisest is the one who can see inaction in action and action in inaction. He acts, but is still a yogi.

There are two aspects in the painting for verse 18 that are worth noting. Unexpectedly, the chariot is placed by the river. The shore is green and covered with flowers. The water sparkles with pink-tipped lotuses in full bloom. This creates a sense of holiness. Krishna and Arjuna are still debating the morality of action and ascetic withdrawal. Arjuna must come to recognise that the war he must fight is just. But, he has to chasten his soul so that it has no trace of pride or vengeance. Otherwise his action will be tainted by desire.

With his chin on his paw, Hanuman sits above a scarlet flag, indifferent to the debates around him; his body is burnished by a golden light. The earth remains unconsecrated; no gods tread on it and no meaningful actions are performed on it. The space between Hanuman and Krishna is barren with no sign of beauty or grace. The earth is unremittingly brown and uninviting. The blue water body with lotus flowers is much too narrow to offer any relief. It is as if no voice of wisdom will reach the ritual-makers who sit there; they will remain unenlightened. The priest's recital will never be heard. No sense of holiness radiates from this 'fire-sermon.' The ritual fire, scarlet and yellow against a bleak ground, produces disquiet; its intensity unsettles the eye and, hence, our emotional being. The ritual action being performed is mechanical and meaningless. The priest throws incense in the fire and chants holy words, hoping to win a boon. A sad vacancy is spread across the face of the man dressed in white who sits hunched up next to the fire watching the ritual. Red and golden flames rise from the altar up to a blank and empty sky. Given his placement and what he is doing, the man's white clothes compliment the cold white marble platform at the opposite end. Here 'white' does not persuade us to think allegorically about purity or innocence. A sense of purposelessness also marks the group sitting on the marble platform to the right. The white marble intensifies the feeling that what they are doing is vacuous, much like arid theological debates. That is perhaps why they form a closed circle, and their clothes are in pale and muted colours which neither excite the eye nor satisfy the mind with a sense of something having been achieved. Their gestures, mirror images of Krishna and Arjuna, are only trivial rhetorical assertions about small differences in an unresolvable argument. Notice the frenzy of their hands. In contrast, the conversation on the chariot is deliberate and thoughtful; it is not about the affairs of state or the subtleties of religious discourses, but about the very annihilation of the earth.

The painting for verse 21 is about Krishna's distinction between the body and the soul, desire and detachment. The pictorial space is so fragmented that it does not allow

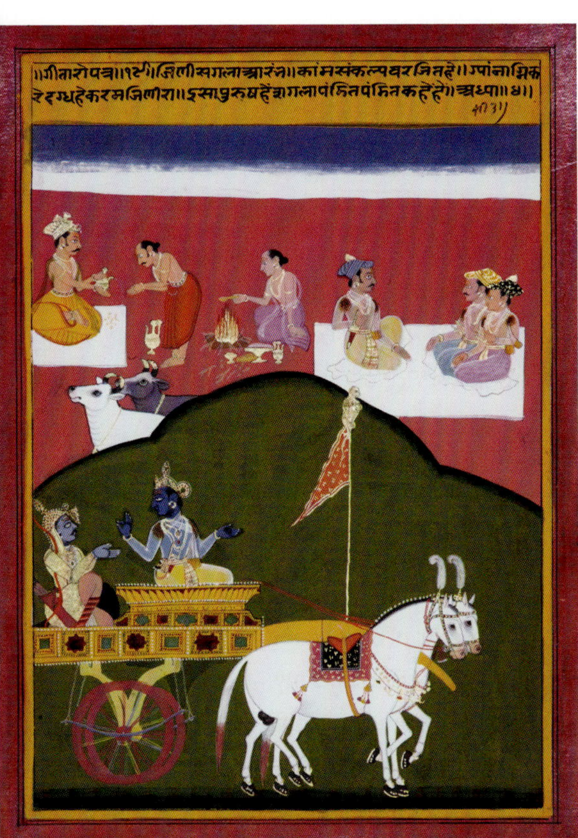

|19| श्री कृष्ण अर्जुन से कह रहे हैं कि जिसके सारे शास्त्रविहित कर्म कामना रहित और संकल्प रहित ज्ञानाग्नि में भस्म हो गए हैं, उसे ज्ञानी भी पंडित कहते हैं।

|19| Sri Krishna says to Arjuna: Knowledgeable men say that when one follows the scriptures and is free from desires and illusions, one's actions are tempered by the fire of wisdom.

|20| श्री कृष्ण आगे कहने लगे कि जो सारे कर्म और उनके फल में आसक्ति का त्याग कर संसार के आश्रय के बिना नित्य तृप्त है, वह कर्मों को अच्छी तरह करता हुआ भी कुछ नहीं करता है।

|20| Sri Krishna further says: If one surrenders one's claim upon action or its results, if one's is not dependent upon the world and is content, then one performs the right action and yet does not seem to perform it.

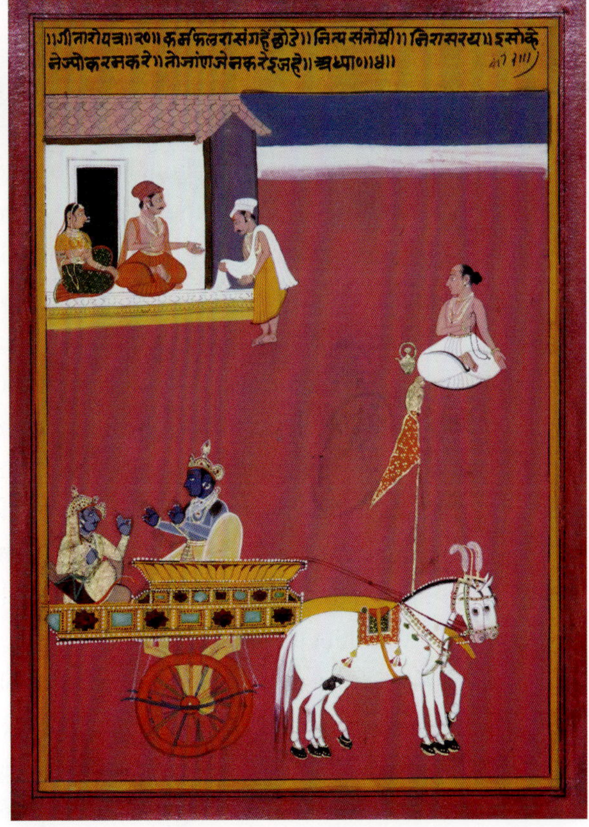

one to place either the chariot or the social scenes at its centre. If one does not regard the painting as an illustration of the division between the divine and the human, then one may be attracted by the scarlet flag fluttering against two shades of blue, before noticing the golden figure of Hanuman. One notices that the painting is structured around a golden axis which connects Hanuman, in the saffron-coloured sacred space above, with the entrance to hell and the red fire below. The two ends are separated by a pale blue space crowded with contradictory scenes of innocence and experience. Only Hanuman transcends that conflict. He is at once the image of the body's passions and its renunciation, of instinct which is able to work in the service of ethical reason, and of the earthly which is able to make a leap of faith.

Krishna's chariot is placed on a gently curving hill of green grass. It seems to emerge from behind a low knoll like a stately vision in the blue sky. Its sparkling yellow echoes the sacred colour of the textual-band above. The verse says, Krishna and Arjuna are discussing what human beings ought to do without being tainted by sin.

Clinging to the painting's border is a palatial home. It is ornate and wealthy. The outer edge of the roof is green. The colours create a feeling of disharmony. A bejewelled man, wearing a turban, sits on a marble platform in a room with pink walls. He is surrounded by golden urns signifying his material wealth. This man is being anointed or massaged by two other men standing on either side of him. The actions are in contrast to the elegant discourse about right conduct on the chariot above.

To the right, below the green hill, a man looks into a mirror as he wraps a yellow turban around his head. His self-admiring gaze is an example of narcissism. His thoughts and actions seem to be guided by desire or vanity.

Ironically, just below the man gazing at his own mirror-image, there is an innocent, vulnerable and gentle cow that looks up toward Krishna out of devotion and for protection. Pure white in colour, she is the image of the unselfconscious, inborn innocence and goodness of all earthly things; an emblem of what human beings, in their self–enchantment, forget. If she is Kamadhenu, the mythical cow of plenty, then she is the self-effacing provider of nourishment to all who dwell on earth. Her presence, so close to the mirror-gazing man, makes his efforts seem vain and absurd.

A burning funeral pyre, painted next to the cow, completes the life-cycle of most people as they move from innocence, through self-absorbed experience, toward death. The flames touch a red circle in which there is a man's face. The face is not sanctified by a halo, nor is it noble. His dishevelled appearance suggests an unenlightened death; a death which is full of regrets and helpless dissatisfactions; a life of unappeasable and

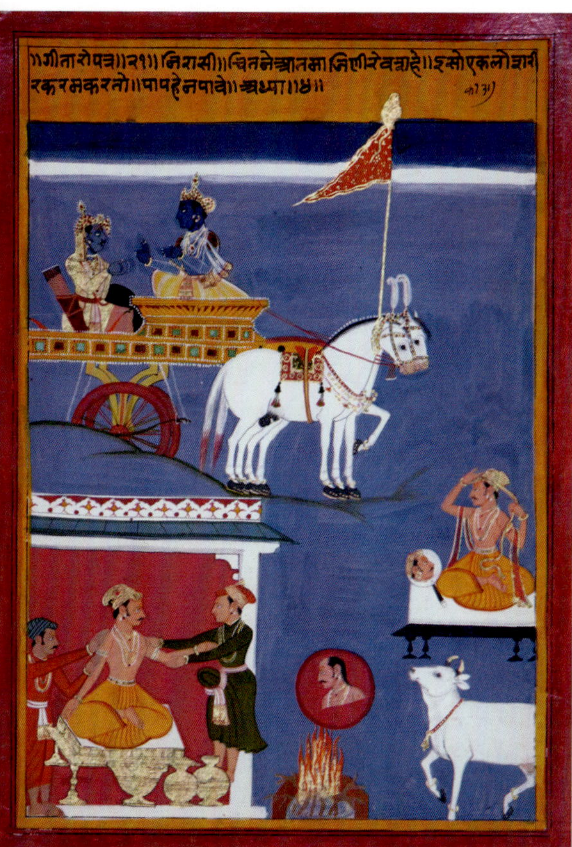

|21| श्री कृष्ण अर्जुन से कह रहे हैं कि जिसने संग्रह का भाव त्यागकर और इच्छारहित हो अपने चित्त को आत्मा में मिलाया है। ऐसा व्यक्ति शारीरिक कर्म करता हुआ भी पाप का भागी नहीं होता।

|21| Sri Krishna says to Arjuna: The one who desires nothing and is detached, who makes no distinction between his body and soul, is untainted by sin even though he acts.

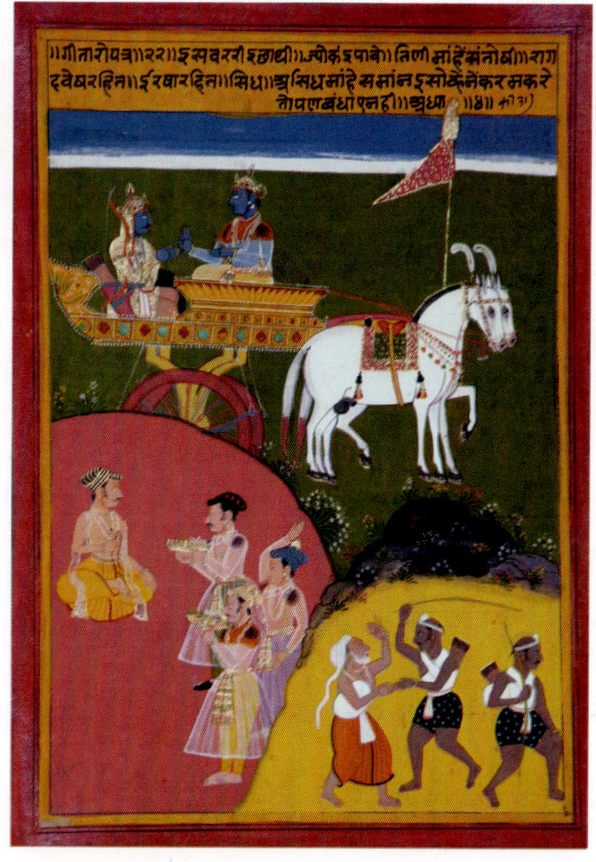

|22| श्री कृष्ण आगे कहने लगे कि हे अर्जुन! जो प्राणी अपने आप मिले लाभ से संतुष्ट है, द्वन्द्वों से परे है, ईर्ष्यारहित है और सिद्धि व असिद्धि में समान है, वह कर्म करता हुआ भी कर्म से नहीं बँधता।

|22| Sri Krishna further says: Hey Arjuna! The one who is satisfied and is not envious is unaffected by success or failure. He is not enslaved by the consequences of his actions.

unfulfilled longings. There are visual resemblances to suggest that the cluster of images are of the same man.

The painting for verse 23, once again, reveals Allah Baksh as a visionary painter of genius. The artist is astonished at the beauty of the earth. He merely recognises earthly glory intuitively as something abiding; it existed prior to the war and will survive. It is this loveliness, Krishna warns, which needs to be protected from the depredations of society. That is perhaps why the lower ground, on which the chariot stands, is covered with many coloured flowers. As the eye moves up, following the line of the golden flag-pole it finds itself in an ornamental grove. The trees are thickly canopied; the leaves—red, blue, yellow and green—are painted with the delight of one who has the freedom to choose colours without the constraints of realism. Some trees are in bloom. It is as if the artist's imagination sees the same world as the unenlightened eye and the unexcited mind does, but takes imaginative delight in seeing it differently and uniquely. We recall Arjuna's original question to Krishna: Why should I not withdraw, like an ascetic, into the forest where there is peace and beauty, instead of fighting for a kingdom? Is that not more worthy and in conformity with the ideals of dharma? The painting is a "hymn" to beauty which has the power to transfigure life.[13] Indian miniature painting, from different schools, is full of exquisite forms and colours which celebrate the joy of the earth when spring rains fall and the world seems to sing.[14] But there is something especially poignant about this work because the vision of beauty flashes upon the inward eye of the artist even as he knows that the verses are being uttered on a battlefield. For Allah Baksh, the *Gita* is a plea for ahimsa, for shanti and for action which will ensure peaceful survival.

At the centre of the grove, a ritual fire burns on a blue base; it is unthreatening and surely less dangerous than the fire in the hearts of excited soldiers on the battlefield. Does the fire, which burns with a golden glow and provides light and warmth in the grove, signal the mythic or alchemical idea that the sources of transforming illumination lie deep within each human soul? A priest sits calmly beside the fire tending it with ritual offerings. What is burnt in it leaves no other trace behind than ash which the breeze scatters, just like time scatters all destructive emotions and vanities, all envious thoughts and longings. The priest has unusually long and matted hair which is tied in a knot. His right hand touches the earth, a gesture of perfect detachment made in the

13 See Zimmer, *Artistic Form and Yoga*, p.230.

14 See B. N. Goswamy, *The Spirit of Indian Painting* (Gurgaon: Penguin, 2014), p. 412-430.

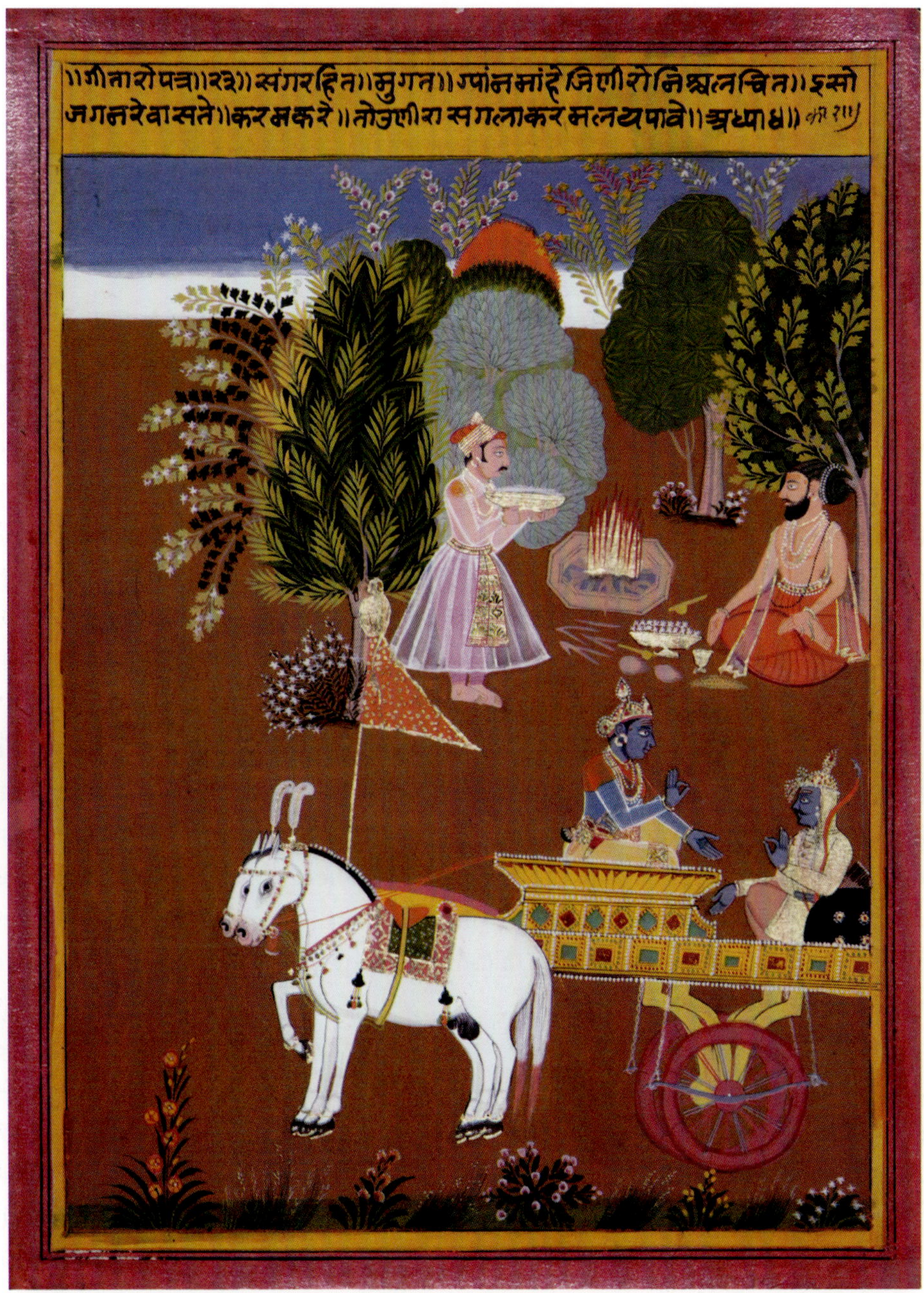

|23| श्री कृष्ण अर्जुन से कह रहे हैं कि जो संगरहित है, मुक्त है, जिसका चित्त ज्ञान में स्थित है और जिसका प्रत्येक कर्म यज्ञ है, ऐसे मनुष्य के समस्त कर्म विलीन हो जाते हैं।

|23| Sri Krishna says to Arjuna: The work of one who is detached, who is free and whose mind is focused on knowledge is like a sacrifice that leaves no trace behind.

spirit of peace and self-sacrifice. The most resonant story associated with this sign is of the Buddha's last ordeal before he attains nirvana. His steady calm is tested by Mara, the god of illusions and death. The Buddha calls upon the earth to bear witness to his meditative poise. His gesture makes no claim upon that particular spot under the bodhi tree where he sits. Nor does the ascetic in the painting assume that the tree under which he sits belongs to him. The presence of the ascetic and his gesture is the contrary of the violent claim to the throne by the Kauravas.

A princely man stands barefoot before the ascetic in a spirit of humility. He is offering what he thinks is precious to the sacrificial fire. He reminds one of what the philosopher Kierkegaard said that those who walk on the earth barefoot are constantly aware of their mortality, and of the vanity of all permanent claims upon its resources. As the eye travels down to the chariot, one realises that the four human figures, along with Hanuman, the horses and the fire, form a circle. It is tempting to read it as a circle of cooperation, interdependence and mutuality which existed once upon a time. In this context, it is illuminating to recall what Ramana Maharishi once said: The earth always exists in a state of *dhyana*, of pure attentiveness; the only demand that holiness makes is that we treat the earth with the same care.

Arjuna's right hand rests on his knee and echoes the *mudra* of the priest as a witness to his own desire for ascetic withdrawal. He has not yet given up that thought. But, we know that he will have to fight, that the veil of beauty created by the artist is transitory. On the other side of joy and beauty there is death.[15] Krishna's right hand is held up in a gesture of patience and generosity. The sign his left hand makes indicates that he is teaching Arjuna that what is required in the face of destructive evil is firmness of purpose.

The next ten paintings, inspired by verses 24 to 34, are concerned both with the idea of the sacrifice of the self as well as with various traditional rites of sacrifice. The space in these paintings is not fragmented as in the previous ones and a feeling of harmony prevails. They are not marked by the critical irony with which Arjuna's refusal to act was treated in some paintings earlier. Since the discussion between Krishna and Arjuna is not contentious, and Arjuna is only an intent listener, the emotional tone of the background colours is warm, graceful and calm. Blue-green, greyish-blue, pale yellow, or pink, the colours are restful, though neither scintillating nor exalting. They do not promise the miracle of redemption or sudden hierophany. But they do suggest that those who occupy these emotionally pleasing spaces are worthy of our reverent

15 Zimmer, *Artistic Form and Yoga*, p. 230.

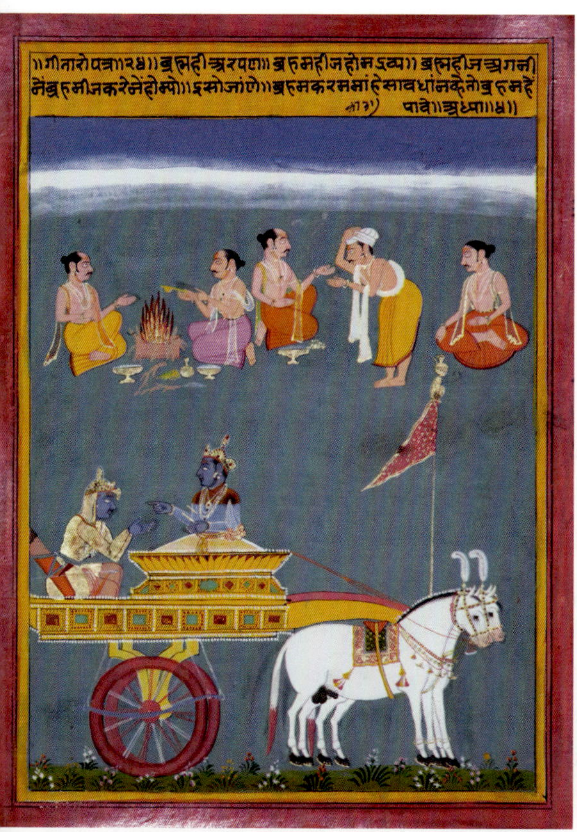

|24| श्री कृष्ण आगे कहने लगे कि हे अर्जुन! जिसके लिए अर्पण ब्रह्म है, हवि ब्रह्म है, अग्नि ब्रह्म है, हवन करने वाला ब्रह्म है और आहुति भी ब्रह्म है। ऐसा योगी ब्रह्म को ही प्राप्त होता है।

|24| Sri Krishna further says; Hey Arjuna! Sacrifice is God, the fire of sacrifice is God, the one performing the sacrifice is God and who is sacrificed is God. The one who performs sacrifice always attains God.

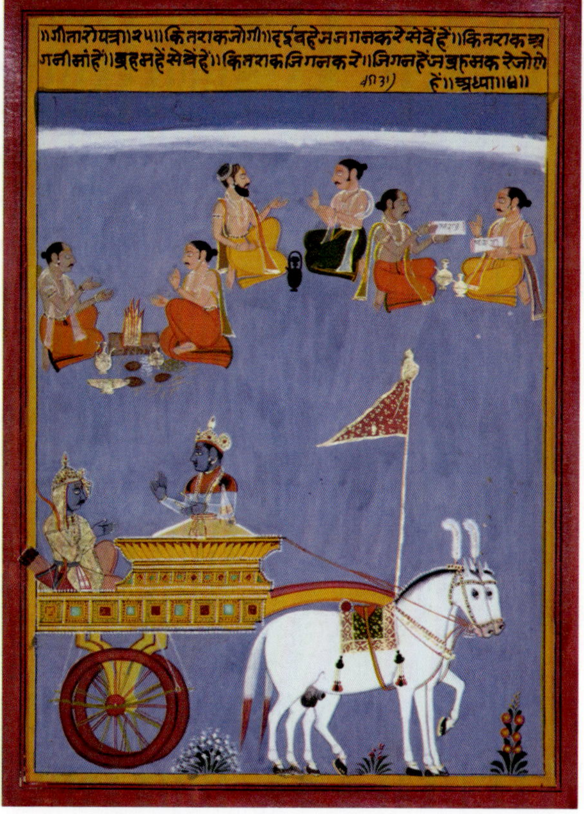

|25| श्री कृष्ण अर्जुन से कह रहे हैं कि कुछ योगी देवताओं का पूजनरूप यज्ञ करते हैं जब कि अन्य ब्रह्मरूपी अग्नि में ही यज्ञ द्वारा अपने आत्मरूप को अर्पित कर हवन करते हैं।

|25| Sri Krishna says to Arjuna: Some worshippers perform rites of sacrifice to the Gods, whereas other sages offer their soul at the altar of fire.

attention because they are genuine seekers of knowledge and followers of some yogic ideal which, they think, will help them evade misfortune and fill their souls with spiritual exaltation. They have, each of them, as the Buddhists might say, 'entered the stream' which will eventually lead them to nirvana.

In each of these paintings, Hanuman sits patiently gazing into open space. Allah Baksh does not use him as a participant commentator or as a foil to the actions of others. This is interesting since animals are an intimate part of the discussions about sacrifice, social morality and governance in the *Mahabharata*. Further, in most of these paintings, Krishna's chariot stands patiently on green grass with a sprinkling of white, orange or purple flowers. Once again, they are signs of a longing for peace and hope. The artist bears testimony to both, because without them moral judgement is impossible. Is the visual world being created an aspect of the moral philosopher's objection to the dharma of disinterested action? Can there be ethical action unless there is something desired, or something longed for? There is nothing mysterious about any of these paintings, nothing that is coded by esoteric knowledge.

The scenes Allah Baksh paints for verses 24 to 34 may have been part of the social and imaginative landscape of his time. What is remarkable is the range and variety of ascetics, mendicants, hermits, teachers, astrologers, sadhus or yogis who are drawn with sophisticated attention to their gestures, postures, clothes, instruments, ritual objects, actions or relations with each other. They are lively, busy figures whose bodies are well-proportioned, gestures are precise, postures are appropriate to the diversity of their tasks, and whose clothes, hair and turbans alert us to their social position or their attitude to ordinary life. All of them are observers of ceremonial routine. There is one who reads palms and makes astrological predictions. The yogic vow of another is so severe and extreme that, half naked, he hangs upside-down from a spindly tree. His feet are tied by a thin, frayed rope to a branch and his head is dangerously close to a fire. A singer of hymns, who plays a single-stringed instrument, is wondering if he too should sacrifice his world of sensuous music, as the verse suggests, and imitate the priest sitting on the tiger skin before him. Behind him, like a temptation and a reminder of stories about the gods who love music and dance, there are two beautiful apsaras with multi-coloured wings who have flown down from their sky-abode. One dances on the green earth while the other plays golden cymbals and sings. Both wear silver anklets with bells. They have distracted the mind of at least one of the hermits away from his vow of renouncing earthly delights. If there is irony directed toward them, it is because

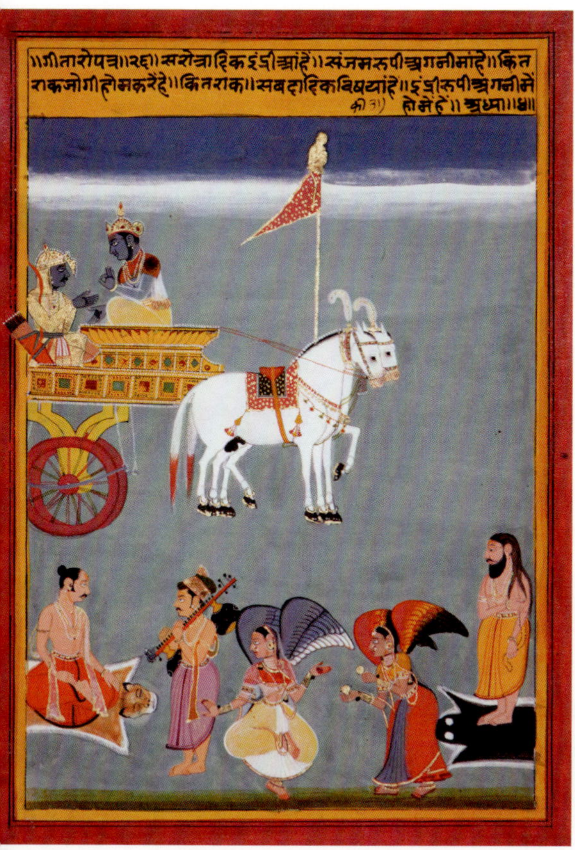

|26| श्री कृष्ण आगे कहने लगे कि हे अर्जुन! कुछ योगी श्रवण आदि इन्द्रियों को संयम की अग्नि में हवन करते हैं दूसरे योगी शब्दादि विषयों को इन्द्रियों की अग्नि में हवन करते हैं।

|26| Sri Krishna says: Hey Arjuna! Some wise men sacrifice their sense of hearing to the fire of restraint; others sacrifice their sense of sound.

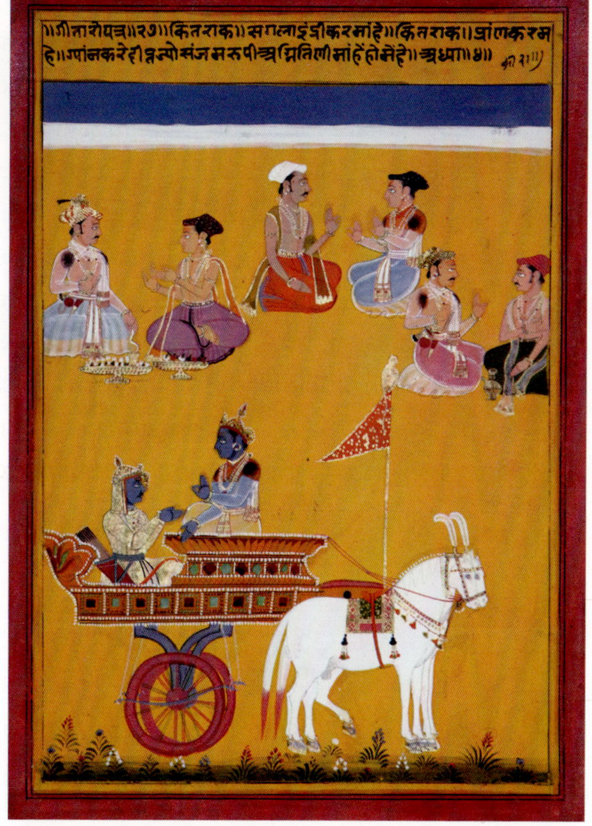

|27| श्री कृष्ण अर्जुन से कह रहे हैं कि कुछ योगी अपनी सारी इन्द्रियों व प्राणों की समस्त क्रियाओं को ज्ञान से प्रकाशित आत्मसंयम की योगाग्नि में हवन करते हैं।

|27| Sri Krishna says to Arjuna: Other sages sacrifice all their actions and their physical vitality to the fire of wisdom.

they are intent on achieving the emancipation of the self alone, while the attention of the *Gita* is on socially and morally responsible action.

There is an upsurge of lyric power in verses 33-42, though the accompanying illustrations are uninspired. These verses clarify that Krishna is now urging Arjuna to think harder and more critically about his own experiences which may help him resolve his dilemma. He is not naively saying: trust a teacher of traditional scriptures till you have realised the divinity within. Nor is Krishna equating faith with Being. Faith, he tells Arjuna, is not an aid to reflection; it is only the beginning of the quest. Faith in the benevolence of nature, however, is essential for understanding, because without it one would remain mired in despondency. In any case, without faith Arjuna would not have chosen Krishna as his charioteer. Reason, Krishna insists, must be satisfied; reason which each human being possesses. Only then could any decision be considered morally responsible. Reason and knowledge, along with faith, prepare the ground for wisdom. Given how subtly Krishna shifts the responsibility of moral action onto each human being, it is sad that these paintings, unlike the previous illustrations, make no attempt to explore the variety of ordinary ways in which human beings act justly and responsibly. Instead, in verse 36 one sees a diminutive Krishna overcoming an attack by two soldiers who do not have the stature to represent the formidable powers of ignorance and false reasoning. They are small and ungainly. Krishna is about to swat them away with his divine mace. The final painting for verse 42 is sorrowful. It depicts two soldiers fighting pointlessly with swords. Who are they—blind faith and hypnotised reason?

These scenes, unfortunately, are unconvincing as a visionary presentation of a crucial moral issue: How does one acquire, as verse 41 says "the sword of wisdom" to cut through illusions (Swami 36)? How can one live without desperation or despair so that one finds a sense of order and purpose? At the end of the *Mahabharata*, it is terrifying to learn that most of the protagonists wish that they had had the chance to live another kind of life.

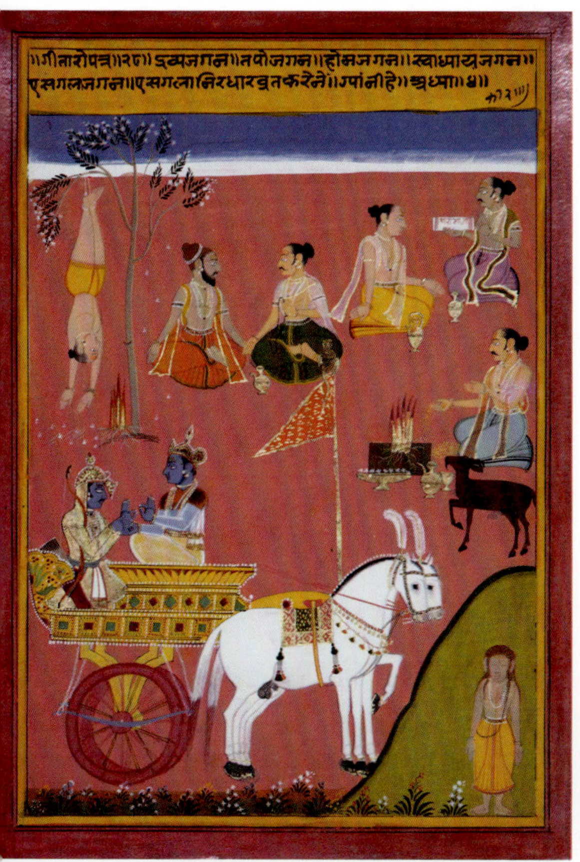

|28| श्री कृष्ण आगे कहने लगे कि कुछ योगी द्रव्य यज्ञ करते हैं, कुछ तप यज्ञ, कुछ योग यज्ञ, जबकि कुछ दृढ़ व्रत वाले यत्नपूर्वक स्वाध्याय और ज्ञान यज्ञ करने वाले हैं।

|28| Sri Krishna further says: Some sages practises rigorous asceticism, some meditate and some do yoga. A few take more difficult vows to renounce their scriptural knowledge and their spiritual powers.

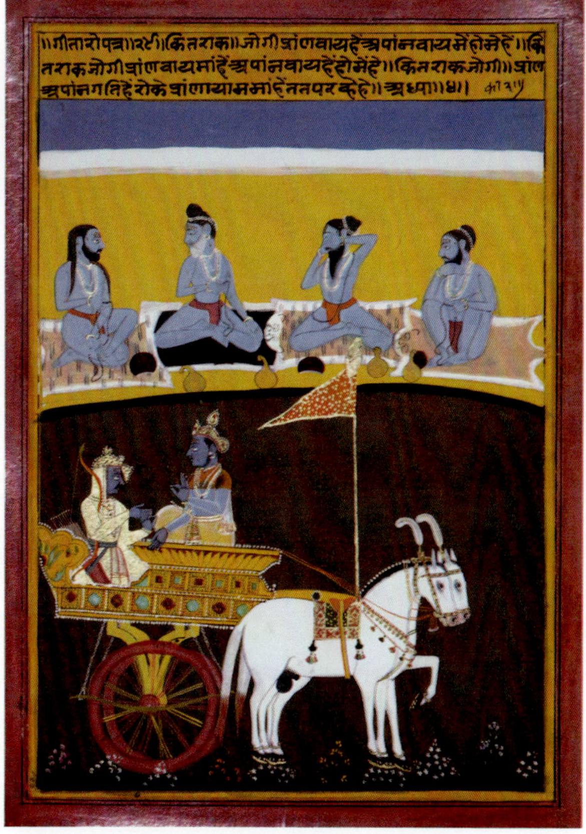

|29| श्री कृष्ण अर्जुन से कह रहे हैं कि अन्य कितने ही योगी अपान वायु में प्राण वायु को हवन करते हैं और कुछ दूसरे योगी प्राण वायु में अपान वायु को हवन करते हैं।

|29| Sri Krishna says to Arjuna: Some sages practise breath control—how they inhale or exhale; they sacrifice the air they inhale to what they exhale, and what they exhale to what they inhale.

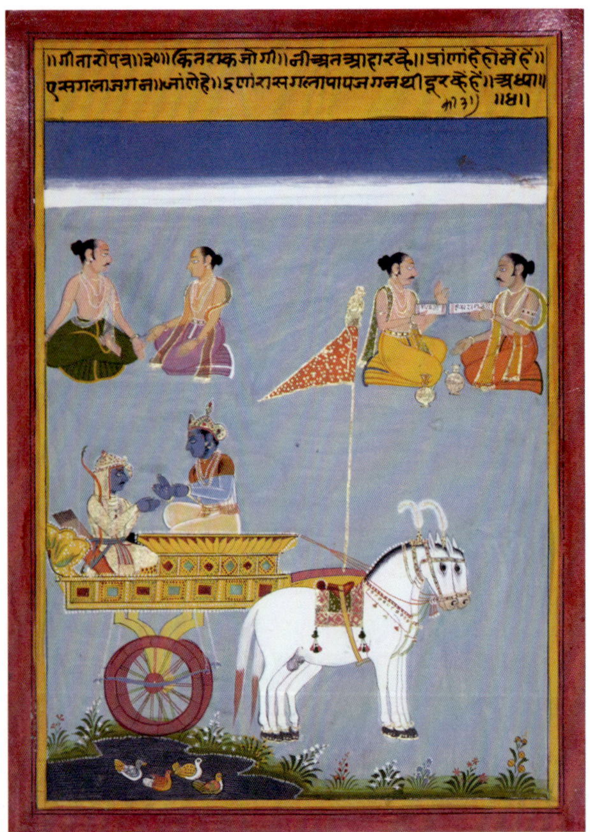

|30| श्री कृष्ण आगे कहने लगे कि हे अर्जुन! कुछ योगी नियमित आहार करने वाले प्राणायाम साधक प्राण और अपान की गति को रोककर प्राणों को प्राणों में ही हवन करते हैं। ये सभी साधक यज्ञों द्वारा पाप का नाश करने वाले और यज्ञों को जानने वाले होते हैं।

|30| Sri Krishna further says: Hey Arjuna! Some sages control their diet and their breath; they sacrifice their worldly life to attain a spiritual life. All of them understand that sacrifice washes away their sins.

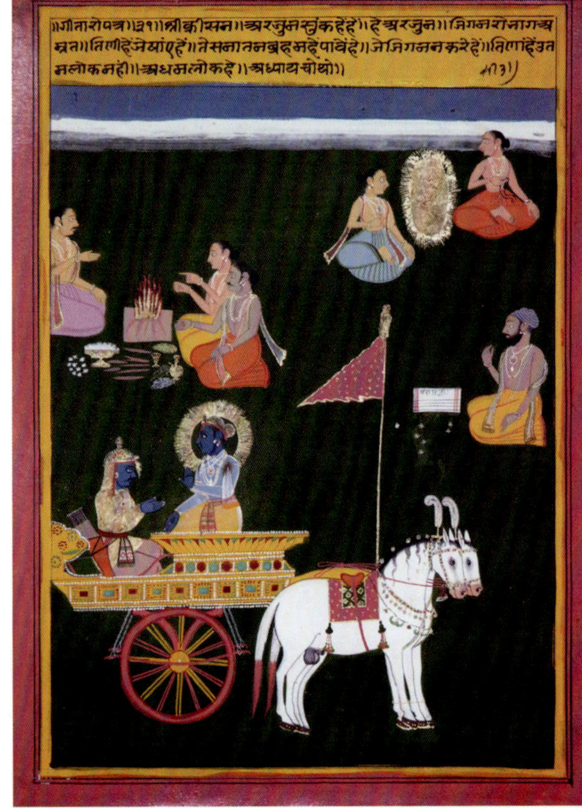

|31| श्री कृष्ण अर्जुन से कह रहे हैं कि यज्ञ से बचे हुए अमृत का सेवन करने वाले सनातन ब्रह्म को प्राप्त होते हैं लेकिन जो यज्ञ नहीं करता उसके लिए यह लोक भी सुखद नहीं है, फिर परलोक की तो बात ही क्या?

|31| Sri Krishna says to Arjuna: Those who taste the nectar of immortality left over from the great sacrifice attain heaven. If life on earth for those who refuse to make any sacrifice is far from happy, imagine what their life would be like in Hell.

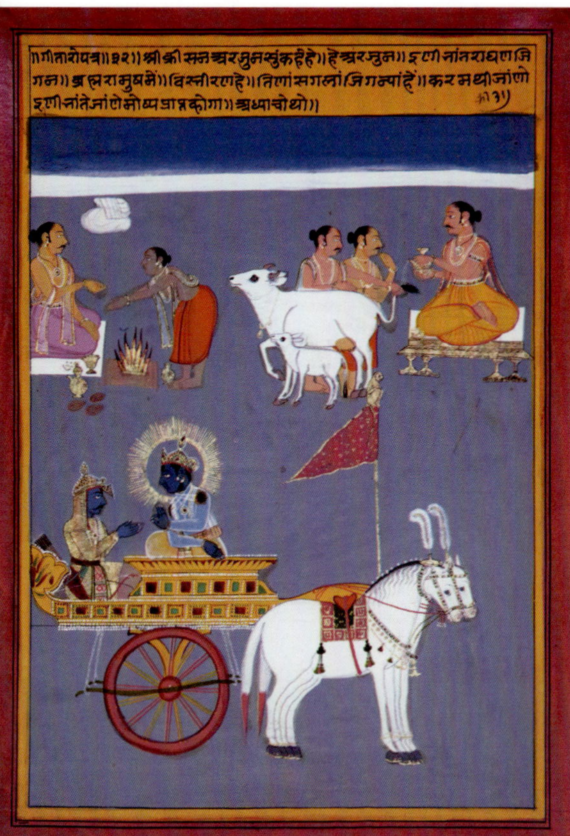

|32| श्री कृष्ण आगे कहने लगे कि इस प्रकार वेदों में अनेक प्रकार के यज्ञ वर्णित हैं, उन सबको तू कर्म से उत्पन्न जान। ऐसा जानकर तू कर्मों से मुक्त हो जाएगा।

|32| Sri Krishna says to Arjuna: All these sacrifices are described in the Vedas and all of them are born out of action. If you understand this, you will be free from all actions.

|34| श्री कृष्ण कह रहे हैं कि हे अर्जुन! तत्वदर्शी ज्ञानी तुझको तत्व ज्ञान का उपदेश देंगे, उनके पास जा, दंडवत प्रणाम कर, उनसे सरलतापूर्वक प्रश्न कर और उनके वचनों का सेवन कर।

|34| Sri Krishna says to Arjuna: Those who have seen the truth will teach you wisdom; go to them, bow before them, question them with humility and follow their teachings.

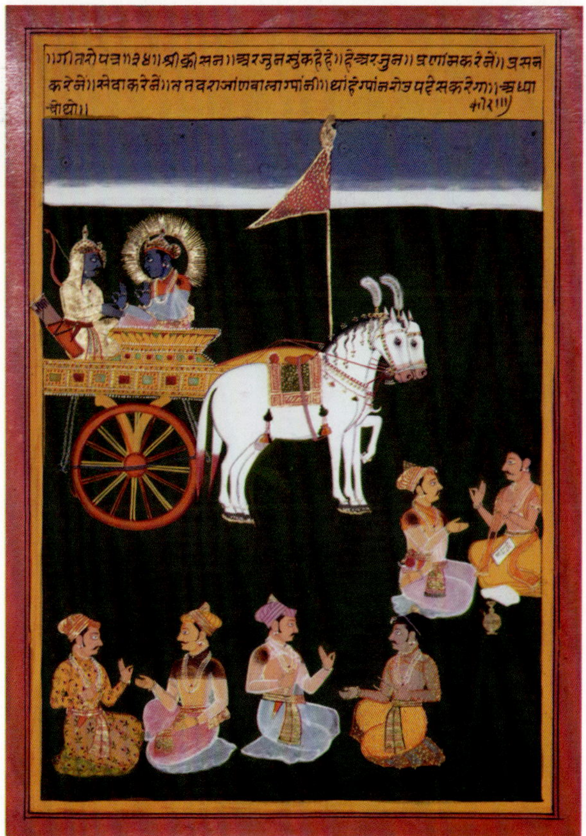

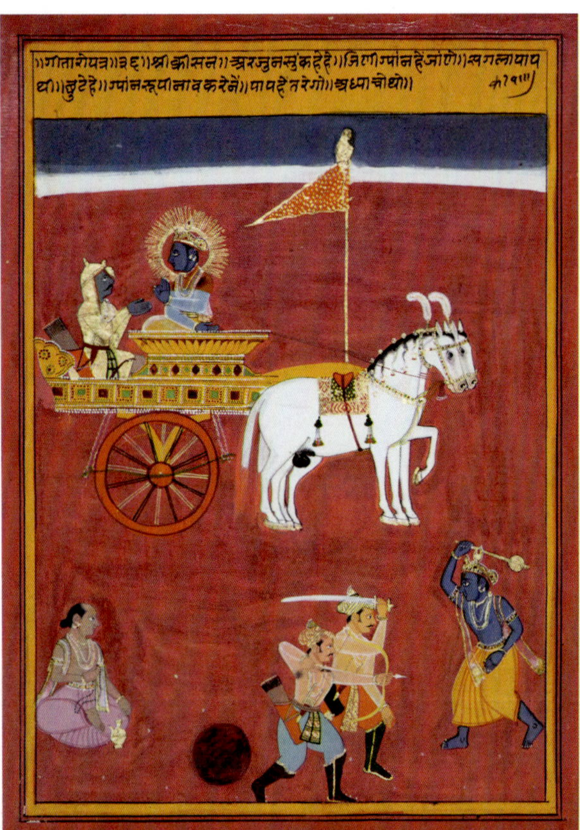

|36| श्री कृष्ण आगे कहने लगे कि यदि तू सब पापियों से भी अधिक पाप करने वाला है तब भी तू पाप-समुद्र से ज्ञान रूपी नौका द्वारा निश्चित ही पार हो जाएगा।

|36| Sri Krishna further says to Arjuna: Even if you are the greatest sinner, in the boat of wisdom you will cross the sea of sins.

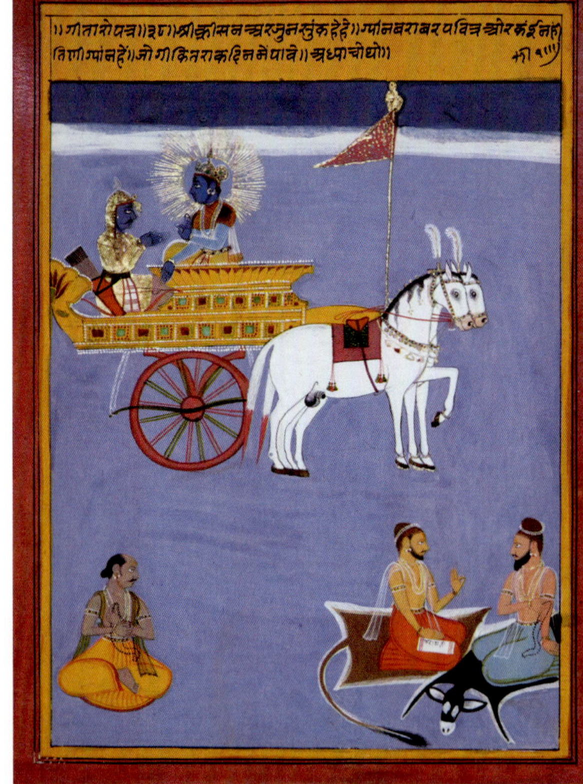

|38| श्री कृष्ण कह रहे हैं कि हे अर्जुन! ज्ञान के बराबर पवित्र करने वाला इस संसार में कुछ भी नहीं है। लंबे समय तक योगसिद्धि में लगा योगी उस ज्ञान को स्वयं ही अपनी आत्मा में पा लेता है।

|38| Sri Krishna says to Arjuna: There is nothing better than wisdom to purify you in this world. The one who practices yoga for a long time finds heaven in his soul.

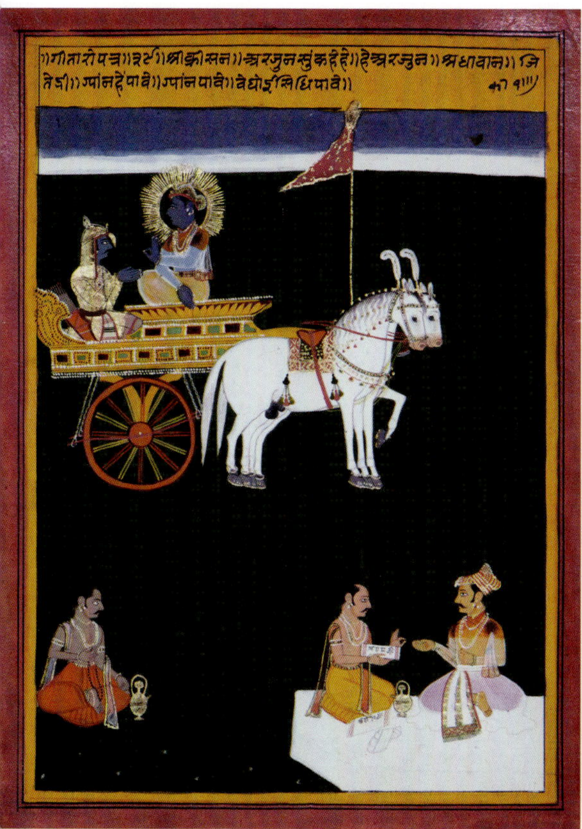

|39| श्री कृष्ण आगे कहने लगे कि जितेन्द्रिय, साधनारत, श्रद्धावान पुरुष ही ज्ञान को प्राप्त होता है और ज्ञान प्राप्ति से वह तत्काल ही परमशांति को प्राप्त हो जाता है।

|39| Sri Krishna further says: The one who can control his senses is disciplined, has faith, acquires knowledge and soon finds great peace.

|42| श्री कृष्ण आगे कहने लगे कि हे अर्जुन! इसलिए हृदय में स्थित अज्ञानजनित संशय को ज्ञानरूपी तलवार से छिन्न-भिन्न कर दे और योग में स्थित होकर खड़ा हो जा।

|42| Sri Krishna further says: Hey Arjuna! Therefore, destroy ignorant doubt which lies in your heart with the sword of wisdom and, confident in yoga, arise!

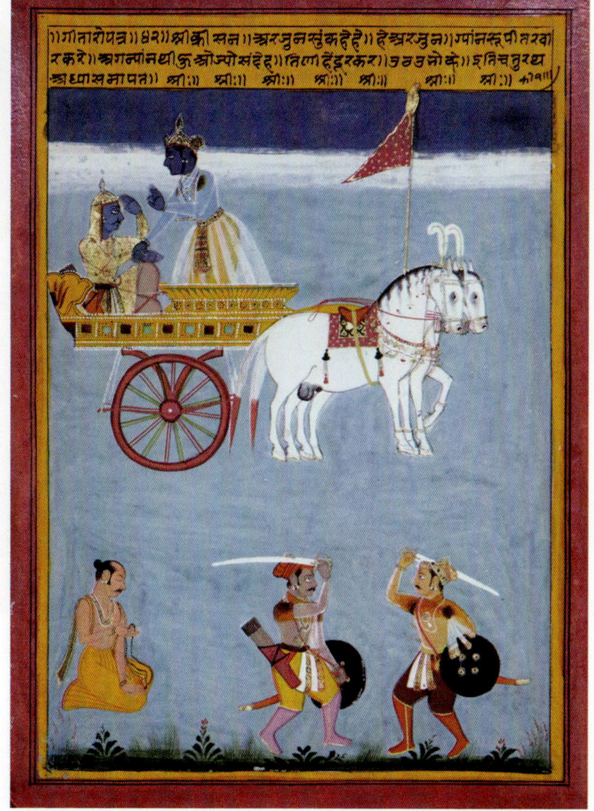

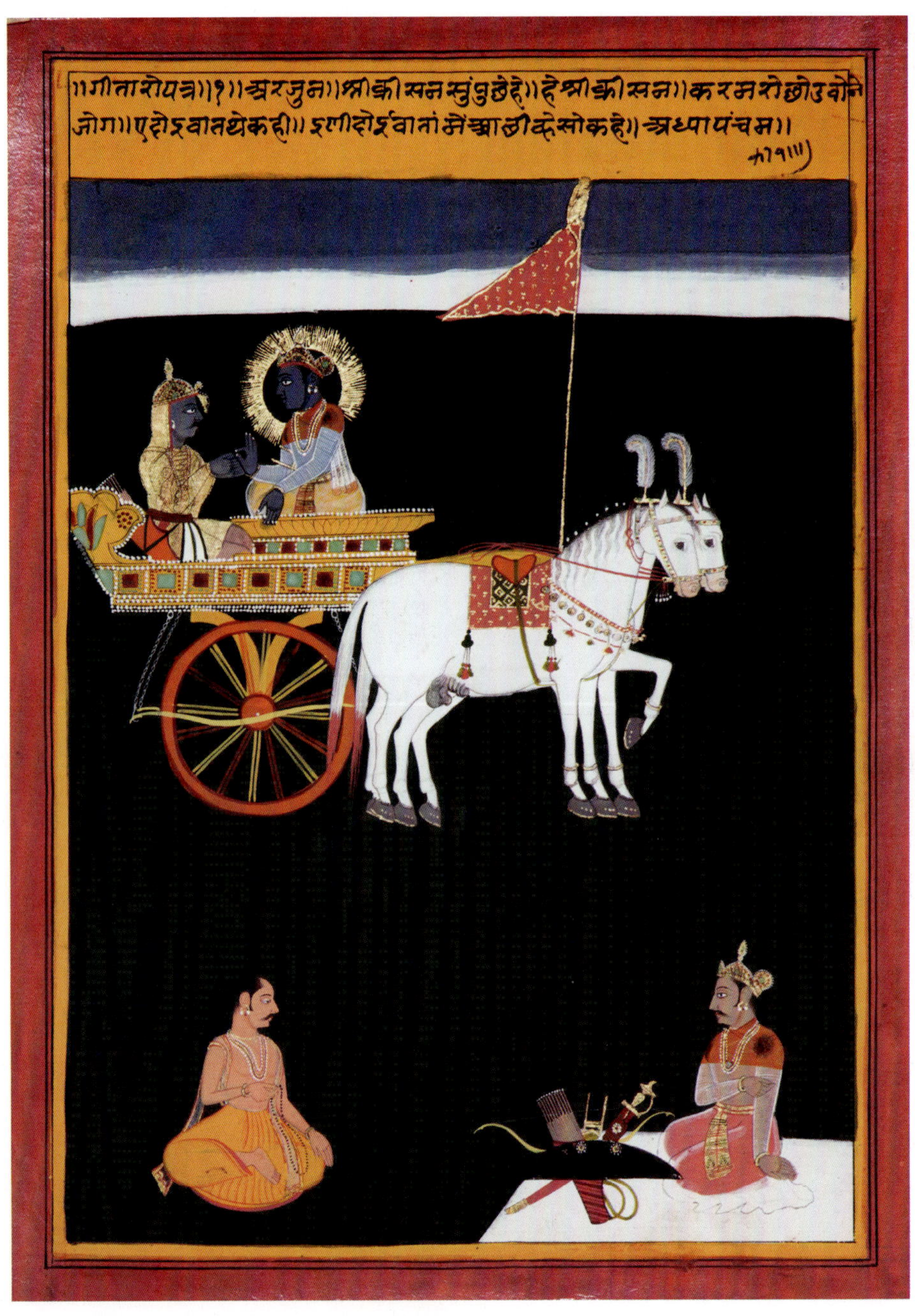

|1| अर्जुन ने पूछा कि हे कृष्ण! आप ने कर्म को छोड़ने की और कर्म योग की दोनों बातें कहीं। इन दोनों बातों में मेरे लिए अच्छी कौन-सी है सो कहें।

|1| Arjuna asks: Hey Krishna! You have spoken both about the renunciation of action and about performing yoga. Tell me which of the two are best for me?

CHAPTER 5

In the opening of Chapter 5, Arjuna asks Krishna to clarify the distinction between renunciation and selfless action. He seeks this clarification because previously Krishna had spoken eloquently about renunciation as a way to knowledge (*jnana*) and salvation. The *Jnaneshwari* imagines Arjuna pleading with Krishna to help him resolve the puzzles and paradoxes of life, to show him the path (*marg*) which has a "sure end, bearing certain fruit" and is "straight and easy to follow"(1:122). Krishna responds that both action and renunciation are valid and ultimately similar. Only the unenlightened speak of wisdom and right action as separate. Both, however, require the disciple of selflessness and complete detachment (Desai 211).

The painting accompanying verse 1 is inspired and sublime. It is a brilliant example of the artist's ability to envision the abstract and the realistic as two aspects of a single world-view.[1] Like other sublime works, the intense and overwhelming darkness against which its images are placed produces contradictory emotions: awe and veneration, empathy for its human subjects and fear for their fate.[2] A strange dread and a "mysterious presentment steals over us"[3] as we come upon it after reading the verse where Arjuna again displays intellectual tenacity and refuses to surrender his inalienable right to reason and debate; to think and doubt; to have faith and yet not let the integrity of his mind be swept aside by any demand even if it is made by God. He must act, he thinks, only after "the directing mind"[4] has critically examined all aspects and is convinced that there is no other ethical option left for a good man—a man who responds only to the "divinity seated within."[5] At this point, Arjuna's ethical coordinates are simple: a good act is that which is just, enhances the common good and expects nothing in return; evil is selfish, has contempt for the human community and leaves the world a little more defiled.

1 Kramrisch, *Vishnudharmottara*, p. 11.

2 Edmund Burke in *A Philosophic Enquiry into the Origin of Our Idea of the Sublime and the Beautiful* (1757) says that the beautiful inspires the sensation of love or affection. The sublime evokes a sense of moral superiority, spiritual immensity or aesthetic greatness.

3 Goethe quoted by Heinrich Zimmer, *Artistic Form and Yoga*, p.7.

4 Marcus Aurelius, *Meditations*, translated by Martin Hammond (London: Penguin, 2006), p. 17.

5 Aurelius, *Meditations*, p. 18.

Arjuna is a man of courage, who does not have to fight in order to win the empty accolades of crowds; he is a man of knowledge who has lived in close proximity to the divine, but he suddenly feels he cannot connect his reasoning self with his emotional world. He has faith, but he does not understand. He finds the question he has raised irresolvable. He cannot proceed and dare not decide. The tone of Arjuna's question is mild; he is conscious of his human stature. But his stance is firm as he turns to face Krishna. It is this quandary of the questioning mind that Allah Baksh visualises through concrete images, brilliantly structured spaces and the careful use of colour.

In the painting for verse 1, Arjuna and Krishna are engulfed in darkness suggesting that Arjuna's inquiries have brought their conversation to an impasse. Visually, however, what sustains hope is that Arjuna's cupped hands are extended toward Krishna in the conventional gesture of a seeker longing for benediction and the grace of clarifying knowledge. Krishna's left hand, held up in *mayur mudra*, rests in Arjuna's hand. It is a sign of divine confidence and ecstasy; the divine expects nothing less from any human being than the pursuit of his own heroic truthfulness. Arjuna is the ethical man worthy of being befriended by God. He is our spokesman. 'What should I do?' he questions on our behalf. The painting does not reveal the answer. But we notice that Krishna's left hand touches the wooden frame of the chariot acknowledging that both Arjuna and he are mortal-bound, human and limited (in myths a chariot is a symbol of the body traversing through time). It also indicates their concern is for the just and the good on earth while their aspiration is transcendental. Krishna's halo sparkles with golden light like the sun just below the horizon of the sky. This shimmering sun is symbolic of the confidence which the *Gita* inspires in the eternal presence of the good even when the night is grim and dark. In the painting, neither the dazzling light emanating from Krishna's head as a sign of supreme visionary intelligence nor the tranquillity of the blue sky penetrates the dark space. It is this radical opposition between illumination and opacity that bewilders us and produces "the ambivalent sensation of painful tension and enchanted estrangement."[6]

Unlike many other paintings in this folio, this one is not a work of beauty which invites us to admire God's benevolent and kindly creation. The black ground here is the objective correlative of the idea that Arjuna's material and spiritual state at present is inevitable. It is flat, empty, depthless, opaque and infinite. Its unrelenting darkness is profoundly disquieting. Thinking analogically about colours and music, Kandinsky

6 Zimmer, *Artistic Form and Yoga*, p. 5.

says that white is like "the harmony of silence" after a lyrical movement in a symphony which promises endless possibilities. In radical contrast, black is "dead silence"; it is the abyss of thought; the end of all possibilities.[7] If the melody continues after that, it comes from another world. In the earliest visual meditation on the colour black (1617), the Renaissance philosopher, Robert Fludd, painted a pure black rectangle on white to represent "nothingness", "negation" or the complete absence of light prior to creation. It is, Fludd says, the "absence" that would return at the end of creation.[8] Goethe asserts that black is so estranging that one wonders if the soul will ever emerge from its sense of privation and connect again with a more humane and meaningful world. The deep black colour in this painting looks impervious to light, impenetrable by reason, justice or the holy word. It leads reason to the edge of nothingness; to a boundary beyond which the mind can see nothing. It is the contrary of the blue sky above which is open, free and full of infinite possibilities.

Yet, the painting has figures which are drawn with clarity of line and form, purity of colour and a confident economy of design. The two men in the lower half are symbolic of the stark ethical choices Arjuna faces: ascetic renunciation or war. They sit facing each other separated by a blank space because there is no other choice, no other compromise. The ascetic on the left is poised and is drawn with geometric precision. His clothes are unostentatious and simple. He wears a deep yellow garment and holds prayer beads in his right hand. He is poised, calm, observant and uninvolved. The man on the right is more apprehensive. Quite evidently, he is a warrior-prince with a golden crown, ornaments of white pearls and a shimmering robe. He sits before a pile of weapons—a sword, a bow and quiver full of arrows, a dagger and a shield. Both men are still, waiting for a moment of decision. Curiously enough, both are placed in a triangular relation with Hanuman sitting atop the chariot's pole at the border marking the sky from the written word above the brooding darkness below. The precise design gives credence to a statement by the great Renaissance theorist of art, Alberti, that "no painter can paint without knowledge of geometry."[9] The triangle formed between the priest, the warrior and Hanuman is neither casual nor inconsequential. It is an abstract representation of a temple's spire and of spiritual aspiration.[10] It is also a sign of the self's inward and

---

7 See Wassily Kandinsky, *Concerning the Spiritual in Art*, translated by Michael T. H. Sadler, (New York: Dover, 1977).

8 Eugene Thacker, "Black on Black," in *The Public Domain Review*, 2015.

9 Quoted by Clark, *The Art of Humanism*, p. 80.

10 Kandinsky, *Concerning the Spiritual in Art*.

mysterious surge up toward a life of sanctity. As the eyes rises up from the ascetic and the warrior toward Hanuman, it feels that the possibility of resolution is not as bleak as the black colour had prophesied. Since the horses, painted with the customary élan, are unusually restive, it is clear what course of action Arjuna will eventually follow.

The painting is perfect. Nothing in it can be altered; there is nothing in it which has not been constructed by reason. It could only have been imagined by an artist who has meditated carefully, before marking his paper with charcoal, brush and colour, on why this particular verse was so consequential in Arjuna's search for an answer. He succeeds in conveying the tension in the mind of the noblest of heroes as he stands at the edge of reason. And, more importantly, he resolves Arjuna's dilemma in terms of his own practice as a painter. This work's sophistication suggests that the painter thinks of his art as an act of knowledge-making. Indeed, the discipline of crafting a work of such sublimity is possible only if the artist imagines that he is as dedicated to his art as Arjuna is to his skill as a fighter; that each line he draws or colour he selects is part of a spiritual discipline.

The voice of Krishna, responding to Arjuna's important query, is heard with dramatic suddenness and brevity in verse 2. It is clear, confident and consoling. The answer he gives in favour of action, at least here, is unambiguous. After Arjuna's anguish of reason and doubt, this is a moment of epiphany; an ecstatic reassertion of a knowledge which has been known, believed and intuitively understood from time immemorial. Allah Baksh's painting captures this astonishing instance of revelation. The painting's sunlit landscape does not merely succeed the previous one of darkness; it breaks through the very idea of temporal succession; a warm, golden light suffuses the earth as if for the first time. The sun is not some distant source of light; it has descended on earth and sacralised it just as Krishna has. The dark night of the soul has been overcome; the deathly silence of the black colour is no longer even a memory. The sudden spread of sunlight is a reassertion of a central idea in the *Gita* that everything in the world constantly flows and changes, contrary to the crucial theme in the *Mahabharata* that time decays. Krishna and Arjuna in the painting are more energised and animated. What we see has no mysterious shadows; material and spiritual life is clearly revealed; we realise, to our utter astonishment, that the simplest line in a primal colour, if rightly perceived, can mark a passage "into the fairest of all creations of Brahma."[11]

Krishna's answer dissolves the seeming opposition between the ideals of renunciation and of action with the same natural ease as the sun breaks through a dark, starless night; as if the answer is as obviously simple as the call of birds at dawn; as

11 Thoreau, *Walden*, p. 216.

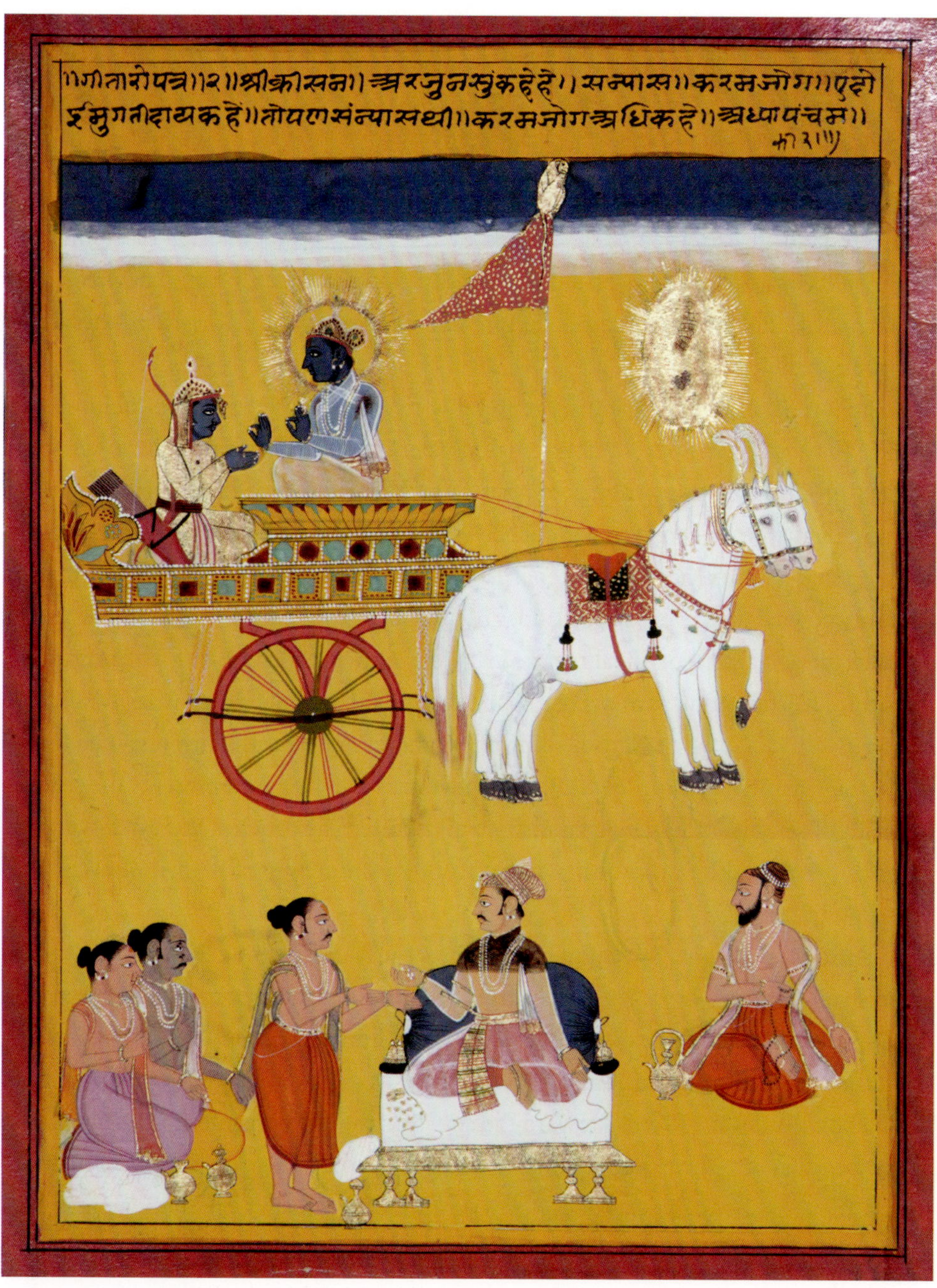

|2| श्री कृष्ण कहने लगे, हे अर्जुन! संन्यास और कर्मयोग ये दोनों ही मुक्तिदायक हैं। पर संन्यास से कर्मयोग अवश्य सुगम और श्रेष्ठ है।

|2| Sri Krishna replies: Hey Arjuna! Both renunciation and detached action lead to liberation. But the yoga of action is incomparably better.

inevitable and as hopeful. Both paths of action and of renunciation, he tells Arjuna, have their own grandeur; do not be disconcerted; both aspire toward transcendence. But, the decision should not be based on emotion and love, musty traditions and idle habits of thought. It must be made on the basis of truth arrived at after an imaginative struggle with ideas that will ensure the survival of all earthly beings. It is important to understand that each path, sanctioned by the gods, has its internal discipline and integrity, its protocols and rules, anxieties and sacrifices. After all, both knowledge and action are like lights from different lamps (*Jnaneshwari* 1: 124) How, then, should the choice be made?

The lower half of this painting represents two distinctive modes of being in the world. The first, the mode of action, is depicted by a worldly prince who sits on a golden throne distributing money to priests and keepers of tradition. The three priests receiving alms do not inspire confidence either as men of wisdom, renunciation or disinterested action. They seem keener to cultivate the goodwill of the prince than to acquire knowledge. The prince, too, does not inspire trust. Like the priests, he is also an actor in the social and political realm. Involved in the daily life-history of his people, the prince has taken the path of customary charity and routine ritual. Charity, after all, can also be an act of self-assertion and vanity; there is no salvation for one who thinks he can buy virtue. The bearded ascetic in the lower right corner represents the second: the path of renunciation. He is handsome and poised; he touches the earth with one hand as if he is asking it to bear witness to the genuineness of his withdrawal from worldly affairs.

Intention, Krishna tells Arjuna, determines the fate of the one who decides to lead a life of yogic renunciation. If a sanyasi tries to escape his duties, if he is merely lazy and delights in the masquerade of holiness, he entraps himself without any hope of release from the coils of *samsara*. The mood of the painting is gracious; the yogi's image does not invite scepticism. He looks toward the courtly scene with disinterest. Perhaps, he is not a specialist in vedic rituals, but he does not have to be. His prayer may be no more than a thought about the excellence of wise and just men. His meditations may lead him to think about human frailty and the temporality of all earthly things as Krishna repeatedly emphasises.

If this sun-suffused painting is a jubilation, an ecstatic calling out to the divine, the paintings that illuminate the verses 3 to 11 add to Krishna's growing authority as a comforter, guide and spiritual teacher. Each verse evokes a different colour which is not arbitrarily chosen. The *rasa* of colours cannot be experienced merely by classifying

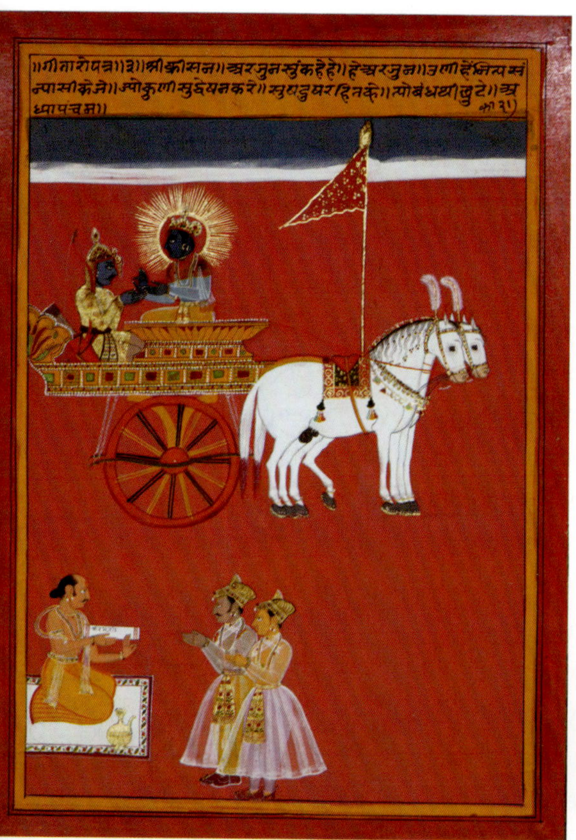

|3| श्री कृष्ण समझाते हुए कहने लगे, हे अर्जुन! वही व्यक्ति नित्य संन्यासी कहलाता है, जो किसी से द्वेष न करे न कोई इच्छा करे, सुख-दुखरहित हो। वह व्यक्ति बंधनों से मुक्त हो जाता है।

|3| Explaining further, Sri Krishna says: Hey Arjuna! Only the one who neither hates nor desires, who is detached from joy or sorrow can be called truly wise. Only such a one is liberated from bondage.

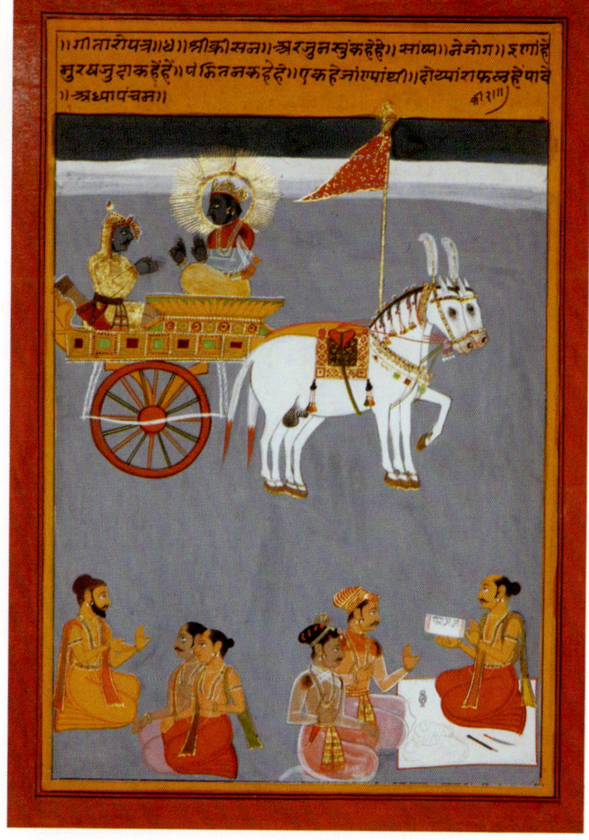

|4| श्री कृष्ण आगे कहने लगे कि हे अर्जुन! सांख्य (ज्ञानयोग) और कर्मयोग को अज्ञानी लोग अलग-अलग कहते हैं पर पंडित नहीं। इन दोनों में से किसी एक को जानकर भी दोनों का फल प्राप्त किया जा सकता है।

|4| Sri Krishna further says: Hey Arjuna! Only the ignorant distinguish between renunciation (sankhya) and the yoga of action; not the wise.

them, just as the moods of seasons cannot be appreciated by looking into an almanac, or the meaning of a poem understood by parsing its verbal units. Every distinctive colour used is part of a vocabulary of emotions; each shows how closely Allah Baksh is intellectually engaged in Krishna's unfolding argument. Each colour helps us to discover what is inherent in a given verse, and then sharpens our own understanding of what Krishna says, quickens it, makes us feel worthy of being participants in the discourse.

The reddish background of the painting for verse 3, immediately after the golden yellow, evokes the joy of a dew-washed sky at dawn. It creates a sense of Krishna's "perpetual nextness"[12] to Arjuna and subdues the blinding brilliance of the halo around his head. It also offers some hope of overcoming despondency. Hanuman sits on the chariot's pole gazing toward a blue infinity. Two noblemen, elegantly dressed in well-cut clothes, beautifully designed turbans threaded with gold and intricately embroidered waist-bands, stand humbly before a learned priest asking for guidance. The scene is in contrast to the one in the previous painting where two pundits were asking for charity from a prince. Here, the priest is a teacher who holds up the *Ramayana* as an example of moral action. Is the priest suggesting to the princes seeking advice that they should, like Rama, acquire knowledge and do their duty? The ethical intention of the *Ramayana* and the *Gita* is, however, more complex and ambiguous. Their emphasis is not on following the instructions of someone else (even if he is wiser); although, Krishna does say that if Arjuna follows him all will be well. Their stress, instead, is on discovering the self's inner goodness through a clear-eyed critical analysis. Knowledge, however, does not guarantee that the learned and the morally upright shall be invulnerable to sorrow, that they shall not be demeaned and destroyed. Krishna inspires devotion, not because he is a priest or a prince, but because he is unarmed imagination willing to help man negotiate the ethical labyrinth in which he is inevitably trapped; to find some answers to life and time's bewilderment.

The dark and sombre background of the painting for verse 5 suggests the steady erasure by time. The images of the acolytes, however, also show wisdom's mature ability to accept temporality with the same quiet dignity as a tree accepts the autumnal fall of leaves. Like a self-sustaining tree, a wise philosopher looks at both the object-world and the soul within, holds his own mind in reverence and seeks to live in harmony with others. Etymologically, Sanskrit recognises the relation between the eye that sees (*vid*) and the mind that knows (*ved*). Allah Baksh understands the relation between sight and knowledge as he paints Arjuna's armour reflecting both the light of the sun and the light

12 Stanley Cavell's comment on *Walden* quoted by Friedrich in *The Gita within Walden*, p. 91.

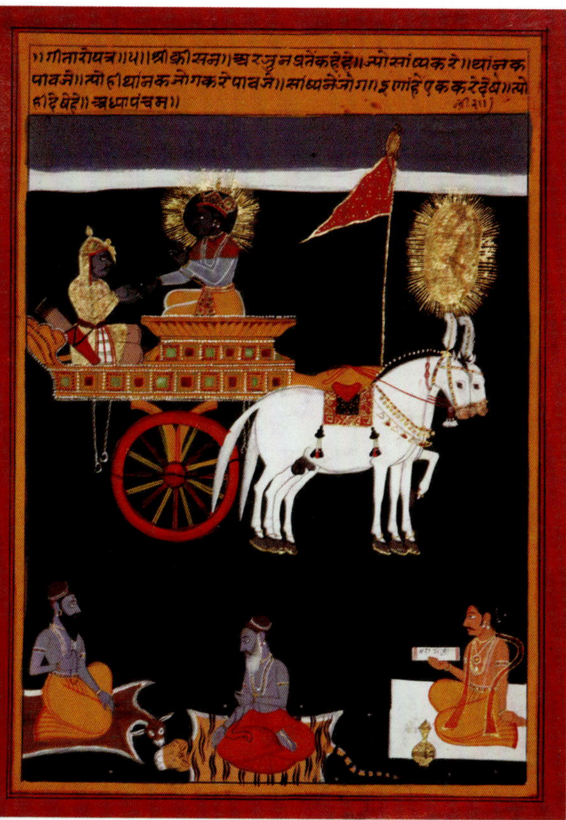

|5| श्री कृष्ण कह रहे हैं कि हे अर्जुन! सांख्य में जो स्थान प्राप्त किया जा सकता है, वही स्थान कर्मयोग से भी पाया जा सकता है। जो व्यक्ति सांख्य (ज्ञानयोग) और कर्मयोग को एक मान कर देखता है वही यथार्थ देखता है।

|5| Sri Krishna says: Hey Arjuna! One can achieve wisdom either through renunciation or through action. The one who sees that renunciation and action are the same perceives truly.

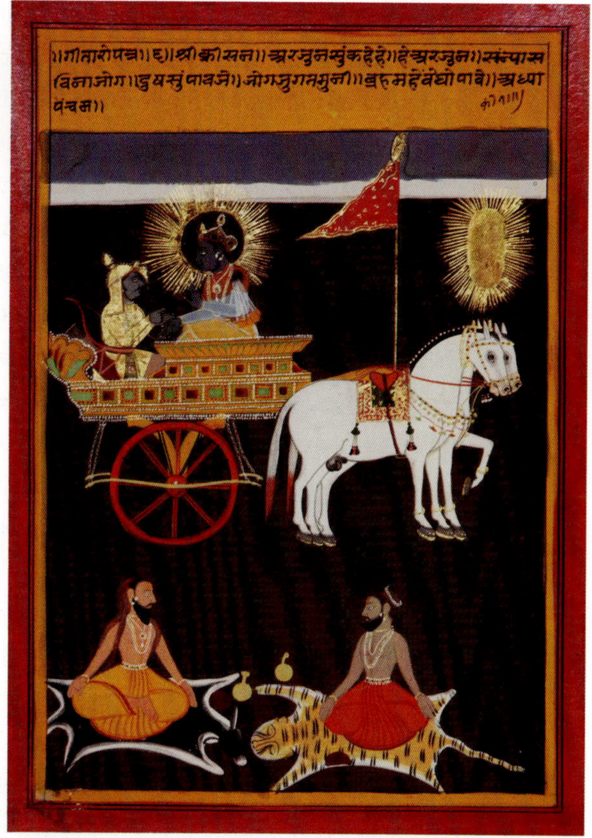

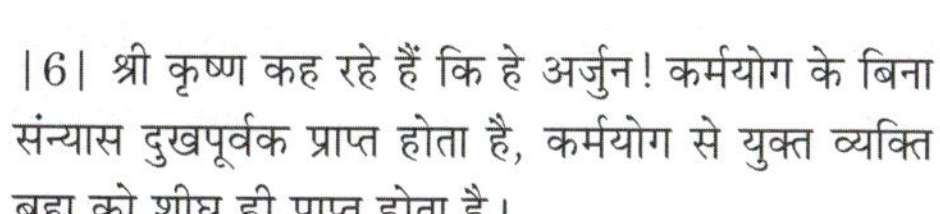

|6| श्री कृष्ण कह रहे हैं कि हे अर्जुन! कर्मयोग के बिना संन्यास दुखपूर्वक प्राप्त होता है, कर्मयोग से युक्त व्यक्ति ब्रह्म को शीघ्र ही प्राप्त होता है।

|6| Sri Krishna says: Hey Arjuna! Without action renunciation is difficult to attain. Through disciplined action, Brahma is quickly attained.

of Krishna's halo. The glow of the image makes it impossible to distinguish between the physical and the eternal. As a counterpoint to this image of knowledge leading to illumination, the painter shows two anchorites of different sects, one sitting on tiger skin and the other on donkey skin, staring at each other in sectarian anger. One is old; the other is still youthful. Tense, they are anything but the images of self-assured, self-knowing men of contemplative learning. A slightly over-awed, meek-looking pundit sits at a distance from the two. What are the three figures examples of? Is the presence of the two ash-smeared, bearded tantrics who live by shunning orthodoxies, and the pious *Ramayana* reading pundit, an acknowledgement of the fact that in India diverse systems of religious thought and practices are part of everyday life? Or, are they, given the arrogant postures of the tantrics, and their refusal to acknowledge the presence of the pundit and Krishna, examples of the idea that ascetic renunciation can also lead to self-righteous aggression and stupidity; that it can dishonour human beings just as surely as actions performed in bad faith can corrupt them?

In verses 5, 6, 8 and 9, Krishna insists that both the ascetic yogi contemplating the mystery of being human and the man of action trying to restore dharma must remain unaffected by the consequences of their choices. This idea is pictorially represented by a pool of water glowing in sunlight with lotus flowers and leaves, in the painting accompanying verse 8. Its symbolic implications can be gleaned from a comment in a letter by Mahatma Gandhi: A true man of knowledge or an honest man of action remains "unaffected even as the lotus remains unaffected by water though immersed in it."[13] For the one who has negated his narcissist identity there are different paths, Krishna says, to enlightenment. Just as "every craft seeks to make its product suit the purpose for which it is produced,"[14] the self's choice is only a method to obtain enlightenment (see paintings for verse 8). Given the aesthetic charm of these paintings, should one not say that an artist can be "the priest of beauty,"[15] while someone else can be the singing master of the soul, and yet another can incarnate the divine as a dancer; that each one of us is a pilgrim in search of enlightenment?

13 *Beloved Bapu: The Gandhi-Mirabehn Correspondence*, edited by Tridip Suhrud and Thomas Weber (Hyderabad: Orient Black Swan, 2014), p. 30.

14 Marcus Aurelius, *Meditations*, p. 49.

15 See Kandinsky, *Concerning the Spiritual in Art*.

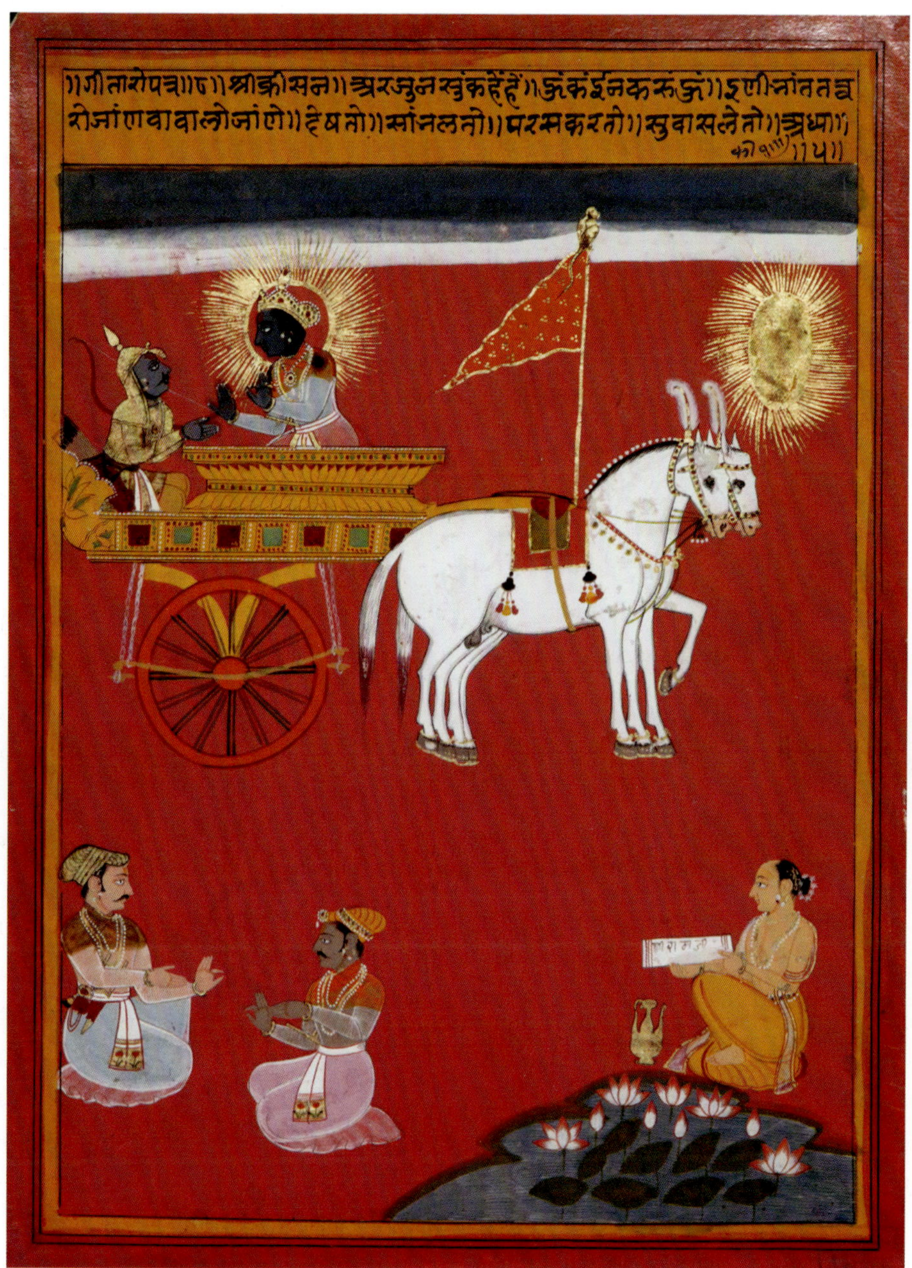

|8| श्री कृष्ण आगे समझाते हुए कहने लगे कि अपने स्वरूप से जुड़ा हुआ ज्ञानी देखते हुए, स्पर्श करते हुए, खाते हुए, घूमते हुए, सोते हुए, श्वास लेते हुए भी यही मानता है कि मैं कुछ नहीं कर रहा हूँ।

|8| Explaining further, Sri Krishna says that a wise man who is united with his true self always says to himself, as he sees, thinks, eats, walks, sleeps or breathes, that he is doing nothing.

The background of the painting for verse 10 is deep green-black—a colour restful for the eye and satisfying to the soul.[16] It provides a ground for moral coherence in the conduct of everyday life. The painting does not stage a scene of conflictual beliefs and aspirations which plunge societies into war. While the learned read the *Ramayana*, others worship a golden idol of Hanuman, Rama's greatest devotee. The entire scene suggests that a shared moral order in harmony with nature can always be restored by tolerant ritual practices, just as surely as spring (signalled by a profusion of white flowers) returns after a fallow season. Green is here the colour of renewal and reassurance.

The Mewari translation of verse 13 is, as usual, simple, bare and shorn of all the metaphoric flourishes of the original shloka. It simply says: "The one who renounces all action from his mind and heart is happy because he neither acts nor is the cause of action." It is interesting that it leaves out the one concrete image Krishna uses in the Sanskrit text to describe the human body as a city or a fortress of nine gates.[17] The translators and the commentators differ over whether Krishna defines the body as a city or a fortress. The two metaphors are radically distinct. The body as a city implies that the self-conscious man is both aware of and seeks to control a complex internal world in which the senses direct the attention of the self in varied directions and can create a feeling of bewilderment. The other metaphor of the body as a fortress suggests that the self is constantly besieged by diverse external chaos-creating sensual, emotional, social and political forces. Either way, the self requires the wisdom of one who is steadfast, who has attained perfect detachment from the body's pleasures and sorrows as well as from the temptations and sufferings of the external world.

16 See Goethe, "Theory of Colour," *The Essential Goethe.*

17 Abhinavagupta (p. 137) and Radhakrishnan (p. 179) think that Krishna describes the body as a 'city'; Barbara Miller thinks that 'fortress' is a more appropriate translation (p. 61).

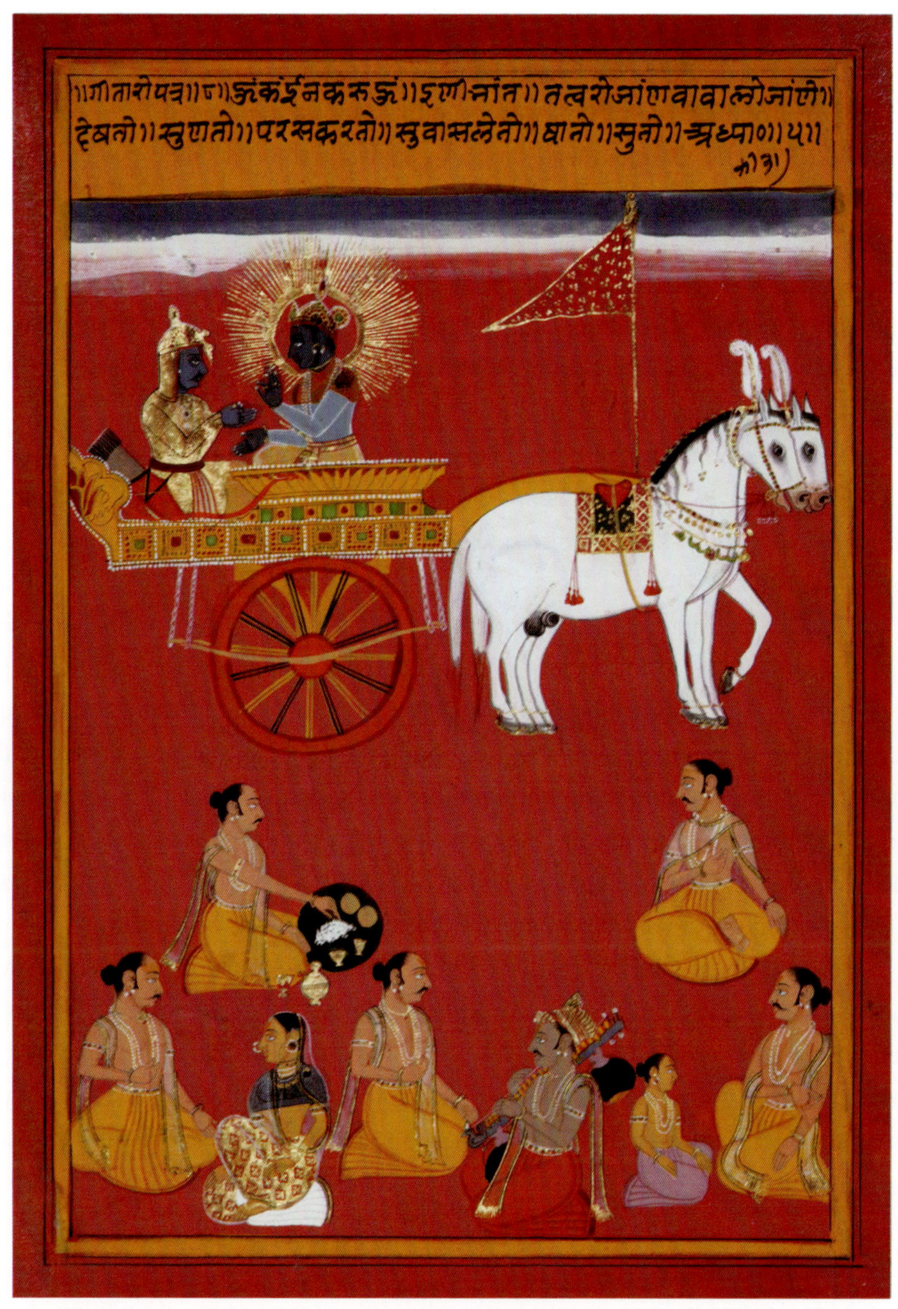

|9| हे अर्जुन! जो मन का स्वामी है, निर्मल आत्मा वाला जितेन्द्रिय है, जो अपनी आत्मा को सब प्राणियों की आत्मा में देखता है, ऐसा निष्काम कर्मयोगी कर्म करता हुआ भी कर्म में लिप्त नहीं होता।

|9| Hey Arjuna! The one who is detached, who can master his self, conquer his senses and see his soul in the soul of all beings, acts without being tainted by action.

The artist is, perhaps, thinking of the relation between knowledge and action when he again invokes the *Ramayana* in the paintings accompanying verse 13 onwards. The images are intriguing. Brahma himself not only holds up the *Ramayana* in two of his four hands, but also sits cross-legged on two copies of the epic. He is performing an elaborate *yagna* (a rite) with flowers, leaves, golden bowls and sanctified aromatic powers before a vedic fire. He has four heads with white beards and a body which is heavy enough to sustain their weight. Why is Brahma painted as a wise and old man? Is he only a symbol of some ancient tradition to which we turn out of sentimental affectation? Abhinavagupta commenting on this verse says, he is the wise guardian who sits inside the 'nine-gated' body and is entirely oblivious of time, age and decay?[18] Is he, thereby, an example for all human beings to live without any concern about aging and dying, time and change? Is he, as the *Jnaneshwari* says, the sovereign self which "pervades" the world, but is "quite unaware of the creation and dissolution of this world" (1: 128)?

Or, is he a reminder of the fact that by the time Krishna appears in the later days of *dwapara yuga*, the world's cycle is already heading down toward *kali yuga*? Or is he, more importantly, a commemoration of something crucial to the presence of Rama and Krishna—that in every age an avatar, or a good human being, appears to reassure the world that there will always be support for those who seek the path of virtue (that is why, perhaps, an avatar is also a *daridra narayana*, the helper of the poor and the troubled)? Is Krishna also urging Arjuna to look within himself for a memory, a thought, a dream or an aspiration which tells him where his dharma lies and how he should act?

Rama is, of course, the incarnation of the previous, less despairing *treta yuga*, when truth still had a value though evil had begun its rampage. The answer to why Rama is so prominent in these paintings is complex. Both Rama and Krishna are incarnations of Vishnu in different life-cycles of the earth; and both appear with the explicit blessing of Brahma, to intervene in the declining fortunes of the earth. The reason for Rama's presence in the painting is, therefore, two-fold. One, he is a rememorialisation in times of war of *satya yuga*, the golden age of truth when gods, human beings and all the creatures of the earth lived in harmony. And, two, his presence is a continuous warning to human beings to live a life of virtue and so prevent a further slide into a *tamasic* time of ambition, power and lust. That is what the verse says: control the inner senses before their contradictory impulses tear the self apart; and, resist, in all circumstances, the death-driving delusory forces of power and passion.

18 Abhinavagupta, p. 137.

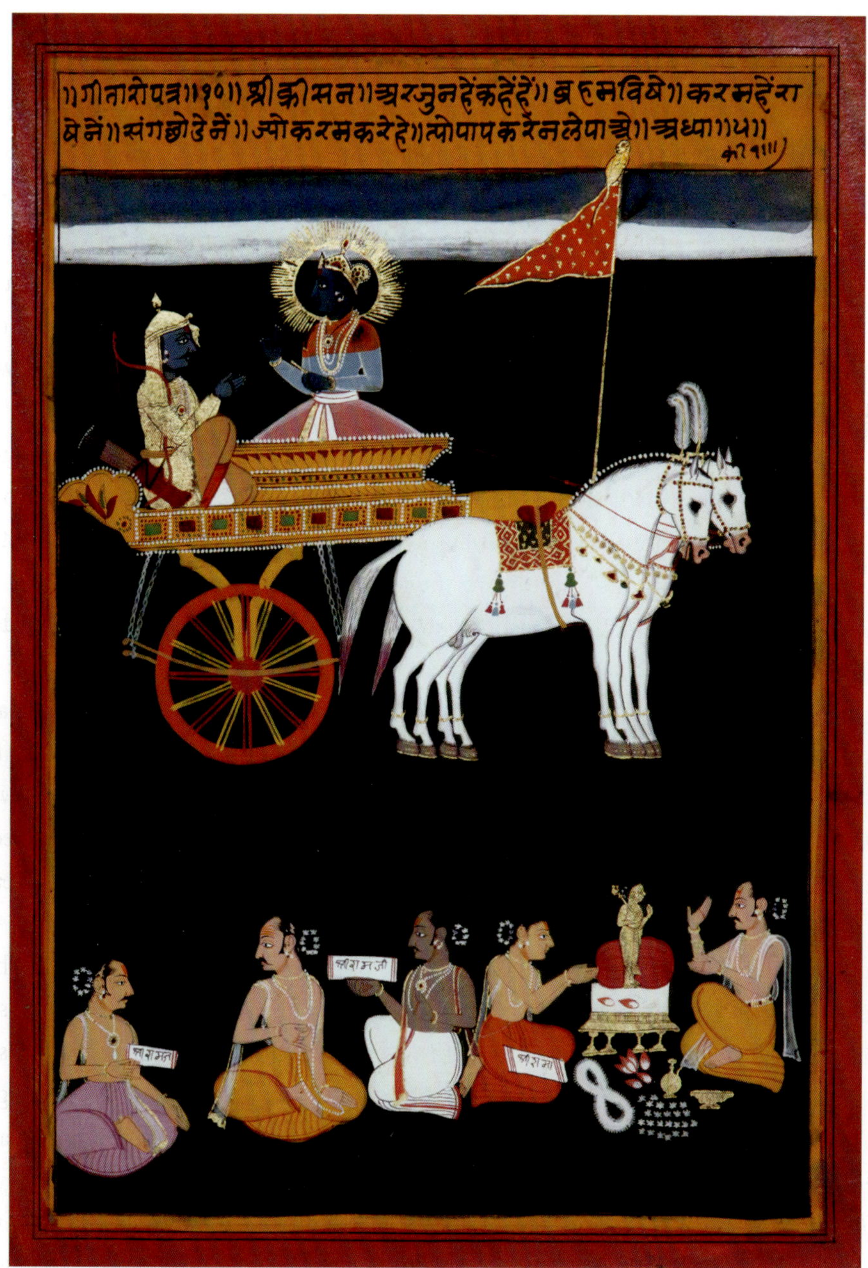

|10| श्री कृष्ण आगे कहने लगे कि हे अर्जुन! जो आसक्ति का त्याग कर सभी कर्मों को ब्रह्म को समर्पित करते हुए कर्म करता है वह कमल के पत्ते पर पानी की बूँद की तरह पाप में लिप्त नहीं होता।

|10| Sri Krishna says: Hey Arjuna! The one who acts after sacrificing all attachments and offers all his actions to Brahma remains untainted by sin like a drop of water on a lotus leaf.

In late 17th century Mewar, Rama and Krishna were the best known deities. Their stories were part of the everyday life-histories of nearly all sects. They were not only heroes, but their legends wove in and out of a variety songs, folk-tales, paintings, dance and music. Indeed, their presence was an overwhelming part of Mewar's moral and spiritual imagination. That is why their names are invoked for various purposes (as in *om namo Vasudeva* and *ramanaam satya hai*). Rama is the name (*naam*) that in the human imagination stands for the "formless…flawless…inner voice of conscience;" [19] it is the word that people recite when they make the effort to cross the river of trouble to the shore of safety. Krishna of the *Gita*, like Rama, is a name; the name of knowledge personified and of perfection imagined.

The shades of light blue in the painting for verse 15 are in response to the idea that devotion to Krishna can be as innocent as a child and as unselfconscious as the light of day; that a sheltering sky is always available to sustain a seeking soul. That is why Hanuman is seen gesturing toward the fiery sun just above the eastern horizon which matches the brilliance of Krishna's halo. The sun's brightness is not muted even by the light that makes the clear blue sky so visible. It is, of course, the physical sun that rises every morning. The metaphor of the sun, however, is complex. It also marks time's passage and the inescapability of death. The 'carnage' of temporality is one of the central concerns of the *Gita* and the *Mahabharata*; *kaal*, Vyasa says repeatedly, *cooks everything*, devours everyone. In the context of this particular verse and the accompanying painting, the sun is the image of the awakening intellect that lights up the soul; it is the visual equivalent of the illuminating wisdom of Krishna's song. As if to make the relation between dawn and spiritual illumination emphatically clear, Allah Baksh imagines another source of enlightenment. On the earth below, he paints the humanised form of the sun. Dressed in saffron, the Sun God is bare-foot and gentle. In his diamond-studded crown, he resembles Krishna. He holds a blossoming blue and red lotus flower in his right hand and looks benevolently upon a teacher and a child reading the *Ramayana*. Looking at them, one wonders if they are sitting on earth, floating on water, or soaring in the sky with Krishna and the sun. The visual mystery of the image is the artist's response to the notion that knowledge and action are irreconcilably different. Krishna denies that distinction. Learning itself cannot lead to enlightenment or dharma. Imitation of tradition can initially show the tracks that have led other seekers to enlightenment. Knowledge of the Vedas, he insists, is not a precondition for

19 Tridip Suhrud, "Afterword: Ramanama," in *Speaking of Gandhi's Death*, edited by Tridip Suhrud and Peter Ronald DeSouza (Hyderabad: Orient Black Swan, 2010), pp. 133-147.

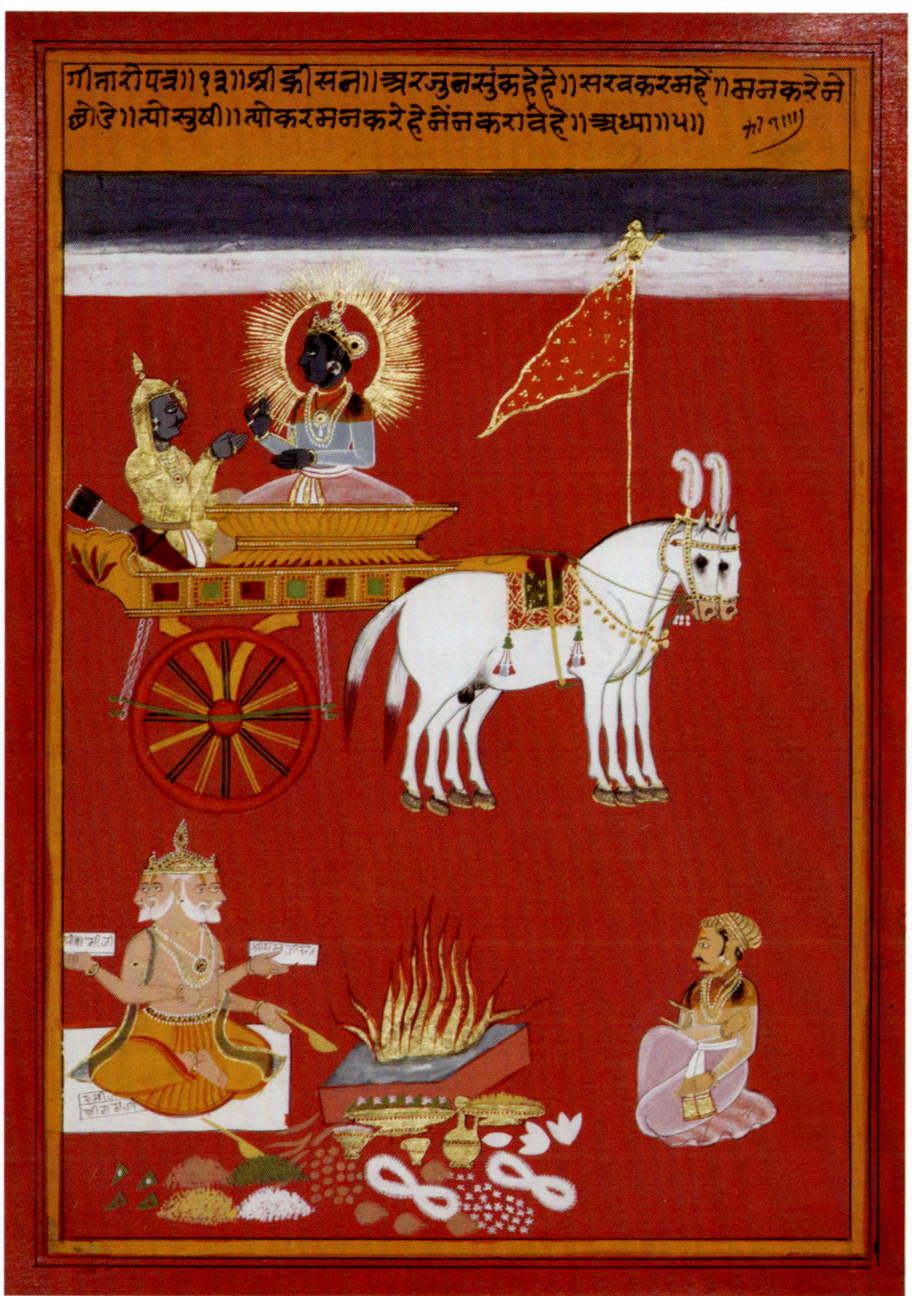

|13| श्री कृष्ण कह रहे हैं कि हे अर्जुन! जो पुरुष मन से सारे कर्मों का त्याग कर देता है वह सुखी है क्योंकि न वह कर्म करता है, न करवाता है।

|13| Sri Krishna says: Hey Arjuna! The one who renounces all action from his mind and heart is happy because he neither acts nor is the cause of action.

unravelling the mysteries of life. After all, both Arjuna and Duryodhana were taught by the same gurus, yet what they seek in life are radically distinct. However, in the painting, the two sites of teaching and learning give one confidence in the idea that knowledge can be acquired without the arrogance of power, wealth and scriptural erudition.

As names, Rama and Krishna are indistinguishable. In Gandhi's imagination, they also stand for Jesus, Allah or Ahura Mazda, names of righteous men of knowledge and action, compassion and truthfulness. If one could add that the name of a righteous man signals that he is "the embodiment of all created things and at the same time as their highest embodiment,"[20] then one can also understand why, in various paintings in the *Gita* folio, Krishna is also worshiped by goats, cows, horses and elephants. Like any Indian artist immersed in the scriptural and the folk tradition, Allah Baksh does not forget that, in the small tales of the *Mahabharata* and the *Ramayana*, animals not only assert their rights as creatures of the earth but are also moral exemplars through what they say and do. They may not be part of the *Gita*, but their inclusion in the paintings is a reminder that any attempt to resolve the perplexity of living must include the non-human for without it the fables of life would be incomplete and false. While these paintings are free from explanatory notes, they are always marked by thoughtfulness.

Allah Baksh responds to the idea that human beings can always have access to the sacred by painting (for verse 20) a garden, a pond and a bower with vines loaded with spring flowers. The garden has no walls, no restrictions. A young handsome priest sits with utmost calm on a marble platform under a colourful tree. "He is not elated," verse 20 says, "by pleasure, or depressed by pain" (Swami 40). A dark female singer, carrying a string instrument on her shoulder, has evidently wandered in to sing her songs of devotion. Is she seeking something, or is she one of the many women bhakti poets who form a rich part of India's spiritual tradition? Another woman pays her homage of fruit and flowers to the priest. Unlike the singer's simplicity, her clothes are threaded with gold and her offering is made on a golden platter. Both music and wealth have their charms; both are seductive; many a bhikshu has been charmed away by both. Many, of course, have also given up their thrones for their love of the divine. Bees hover in the garden. Bees are no respecters of boundaries and hierarchies, but often signal the unpredictable play of love, longing, renunciation or worship that human beings enact. Music and bees fill the space between the young priest, who seems calm and serene, and the young sensual girl who hides behind a veil of flowers to gaze at him.

---

20 See Walter Benjamin, "The Storyteller," in *Illuminations*, p. 104.

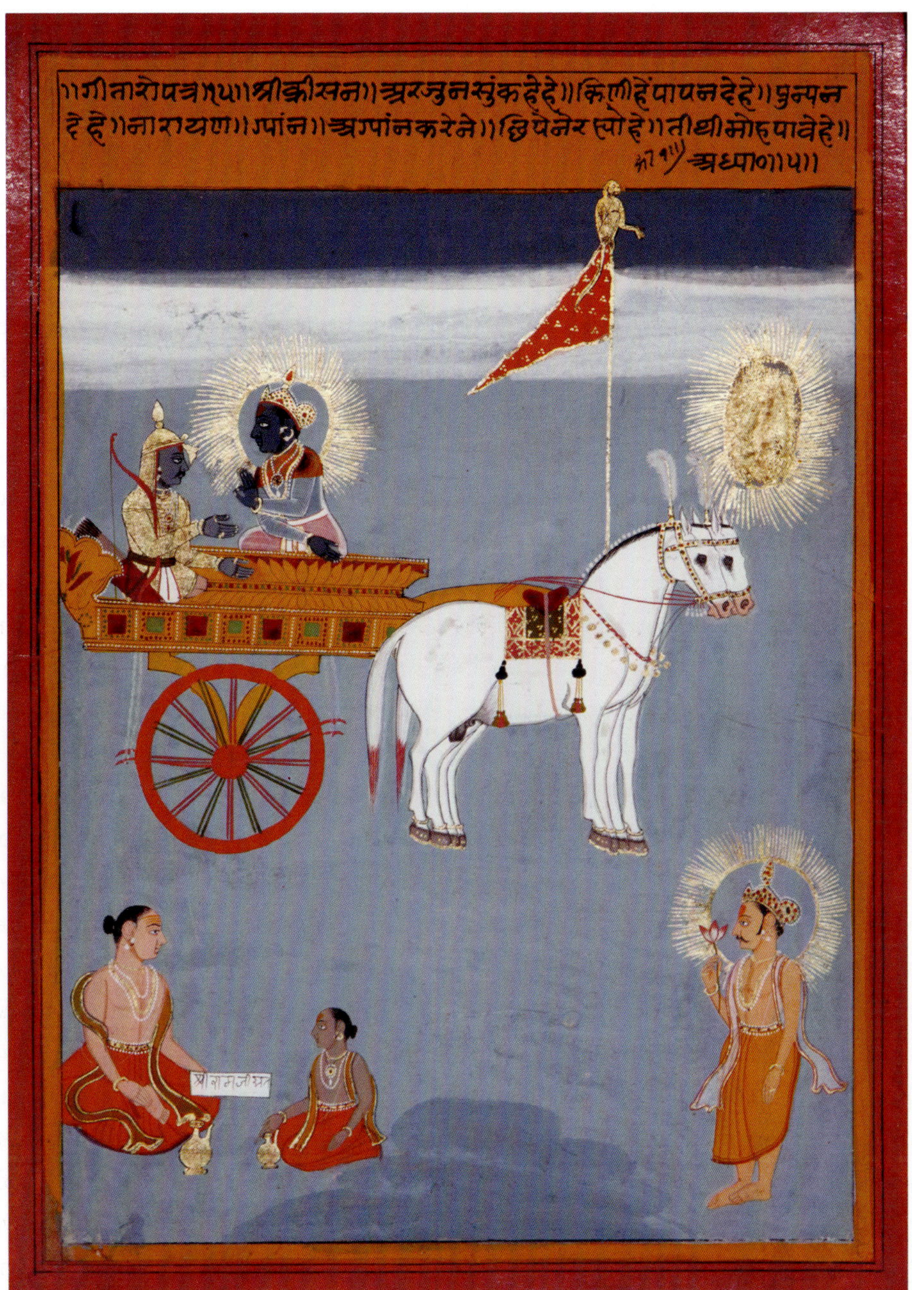

|15| श्री कृष्ण आगे समझाते हुए कह रहे हैं कि हे अर्जुन! प्रभु न किसी के पाप को और न ही शुभ कर्म को ग्रहण करते हैं क्योंकि अज्ञान से ज्ञान ढका हुआ है। इसी से सभी प्राणी मोहित हो रहे हैं।

|15| Sri Krishna further explains: Hey Arjuna! God neither takes the blame nor the credit for action. Ignorance veils knowledge and deludes people.

Life's exuberance is neither condemned nor negated. Krishna, the painter seems to suggest, only warns a seeker after wisdom not to be entranced by the temporal. Visually, the moment created is intense; it requires no narrative completion, for it has many possibilities for each of the figures.

In Pundit Kishandas's Mewari rendering, Krishna's response to Arjuna's 'calling out' to him is offered with, to use Anandavardhana's evocative word, "*sahridaya*"—"the same heart." Almost every verse in which Krishna speaks begins with "Hey Arjuna," a friendly, patient, gentle and persistent response which ensures that Arjuna never turns away from him in fear or rebellious rage. Each time Krishna names Arjuna, each time he calls, "Hey Arjuna" (and in so doing also reminds him of his human and social 'calling' as a Kshatriya), it is as if he is calling him for the first time with affection. "Is there any cause and any time which justifies violence?" Arjuna wonders. Socrates in *Gorgias* categorically declares that it is always wrong to use violence for any end whatsoever. Arjuna is not so sure. He is a Kshatriya whose traditional function in the social order is to be its armed protector. Unable to decide, he continues to debate with himself and Krishna; indeed, till the very end of the *Gita*, his rational self, distinct perhaps from his pious soul, is never completely convinced. "Would the good not be better served," he wonders, "if I did not, under any circumstance, imitate the Kauravas?"

Not everyone is privileged, like Arjuna, to be an active participant in a conversation between a hero and God, between man and the divine. It is, of course, possible, as painting after painting suggests that ordinary human beings can listen to this conversation and so work their way to enlightenment (as opposed, of course, to Dhritarashtra who also listens to the *Gita*, but remains obtuse). It is, however, important for every listener, who does not have the privilege of being 'called' by the divine, to know that, while it is possible for a conscientious human being in hours of despondency, uncertainty, reluctance or bewilderment to have access to the sacred, any resolution offered is always provisional; that the conversation with the divine ought to be an on-going one; that the idolatry of a single answer to life's endless problems always turns into brutal intolerance and stifles imagination's freedom. Arjuna knows that he is the exception, and is surprised that he is 'called'; that is what makes him so human, so enigmatic and so heroic. All that an ordinary human being can hope to achieve in contrast, as the paintings accompanying verses 23, 24, 26 and 27 suggest, is to listen carefully, learn to see the world's beauteous forms, acknowledge their enchantment and live by the integrity of his own soul. After all, most scriptures do not deny the world's beauty, nor negate the power of love, music, dance or poetry. Indeed, they acknowledge that all things of beauty can lead to the

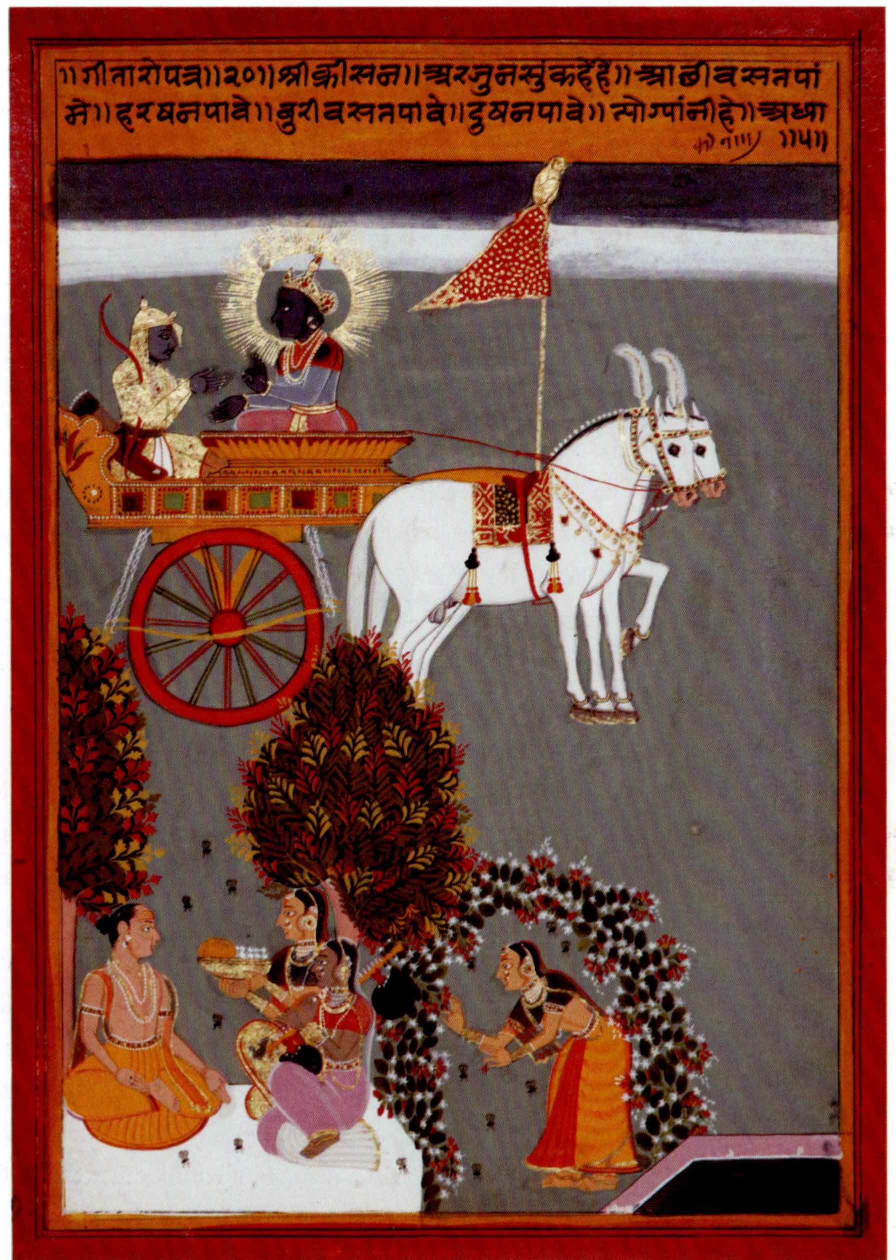

|20| श्री कृष्ण कहने लगे, हे अर्जुन! जो इच्छित वस्तु को पाकर हर्षित न हो और अप्रिय वस्तु पाकर उद्विग्न न हो ऐसा संशय रहित स्थिर बुद्धिवाला ब्रह्म में स्थित ज्ञानी होता है।

|20| Sri Krishna says: Hey Arjuna! The one who neither rejoices when he obtains the thing he desires nor recoils when he gets something unpleasant is a wise man who is free from delusions and abides in Brahma.

divine or be aids to reflection. Thus, in the painting for verse 23 a youthful yogi sits with his back to verdant, fruitful and beautiful trees, as he tells his beads. He looks, without apprehension, at the God of desire, Kama, who is hiding in the foliage of a dense, ornamental tree and is aiming an arrow, tipped with a pink lotus flower, at him. The yogi acknowledges Kama's presence and power, but a tall and slender tree stands between the two. As the eye follows the tree's upward movement, it is led to the presence of Krishna; the world of earthly desire and beauty is, thereby, transformed (perhaps disarmed too) into the eternal and supernal magnificence of the divine. The eye first notices the earth and its transitory splendour. Then, instead of being arrested there, it moves up seeking that point where secular space meets the horizon of the infinite sky and where clock-time dissolves into eternity; the visual perception and the visionary expansion are simultaneous; as is the verbal inscription of the verse and its resonance which says that a saint is one who "learns to surmount the promptings of desire and anger. . .and is happy" (Swami 40).

In contrast, the well-dressed nobleman nearby is burdened by his social and political symbols—turban, dagger, sash, ornaments and blue shoes. His feet lie heavy on the ground; his eye gazes uncomprehendingly at the scene being enacted with such ethereal gracefulness before him. He notices the trees, Kama and the yogi, but is unable to find a meaningful story or a reason in them which would transfigure his own consciousness. Unsurprisingly, there is only empty space around him.

In the next few verses, Krishna tells Arjuna that there is a simple alphabet of ethical achievement. Arjuna should know the world around him; understand his own social and sensuous desires, his longing for justice and the defeat of evil; and, having understood, he should act without wondering what he would achieve and without being scarred by grief if he fails. Do, Krishna tells him, what has fallen upon your lot; invest your entire being in it without expecting any returns; do it with self-conscious assertion and with a clear conscience. The paintings follow this pattern of spiritual awakening from within – of self-discovery by examining each doubt and difficulty. The paintings for verses 24 and 27 are a brilliant summing up of this understanding. The first painting (verse 24) shows an enlightened being. The halo around his head is brighter than the sun hovering above a meandering stream whose banks are lined with trees. The background against which he sits is dark. He gazes at

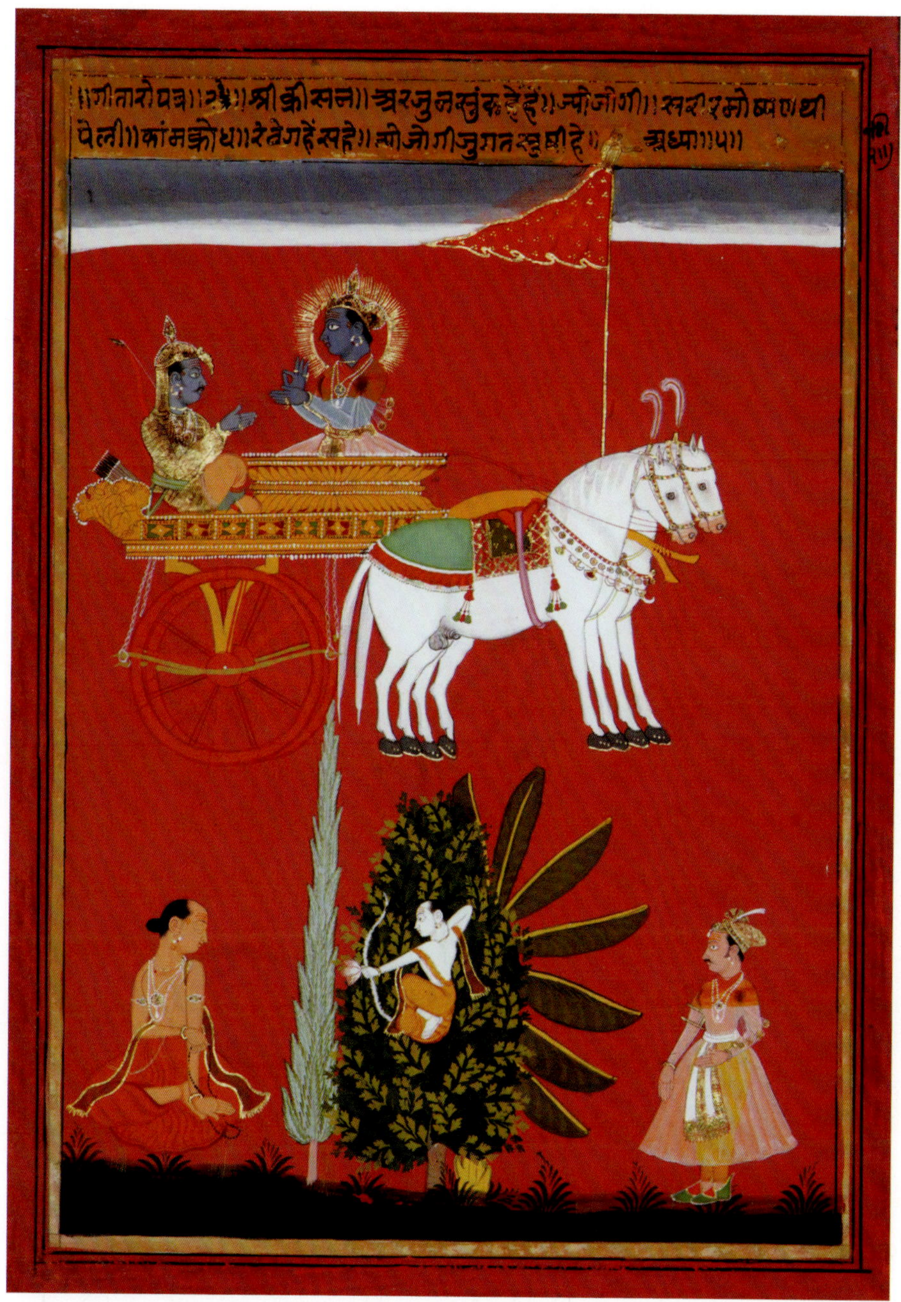

|23| श्री कृष्ण कहने लगे कि हे अर्जुन! जो योगी शरीर के क्षरण से पहले काम क्रोध के वेग को सहन करने में सक्षम हो जाता है, वही शूरवीर है, वही सुखी है।

|23| Sri Krishna says to Arjuna: Hey Arjuna! Only the yogi who succeeds in enduring desire and anger before giving up his body is heroic and happy.

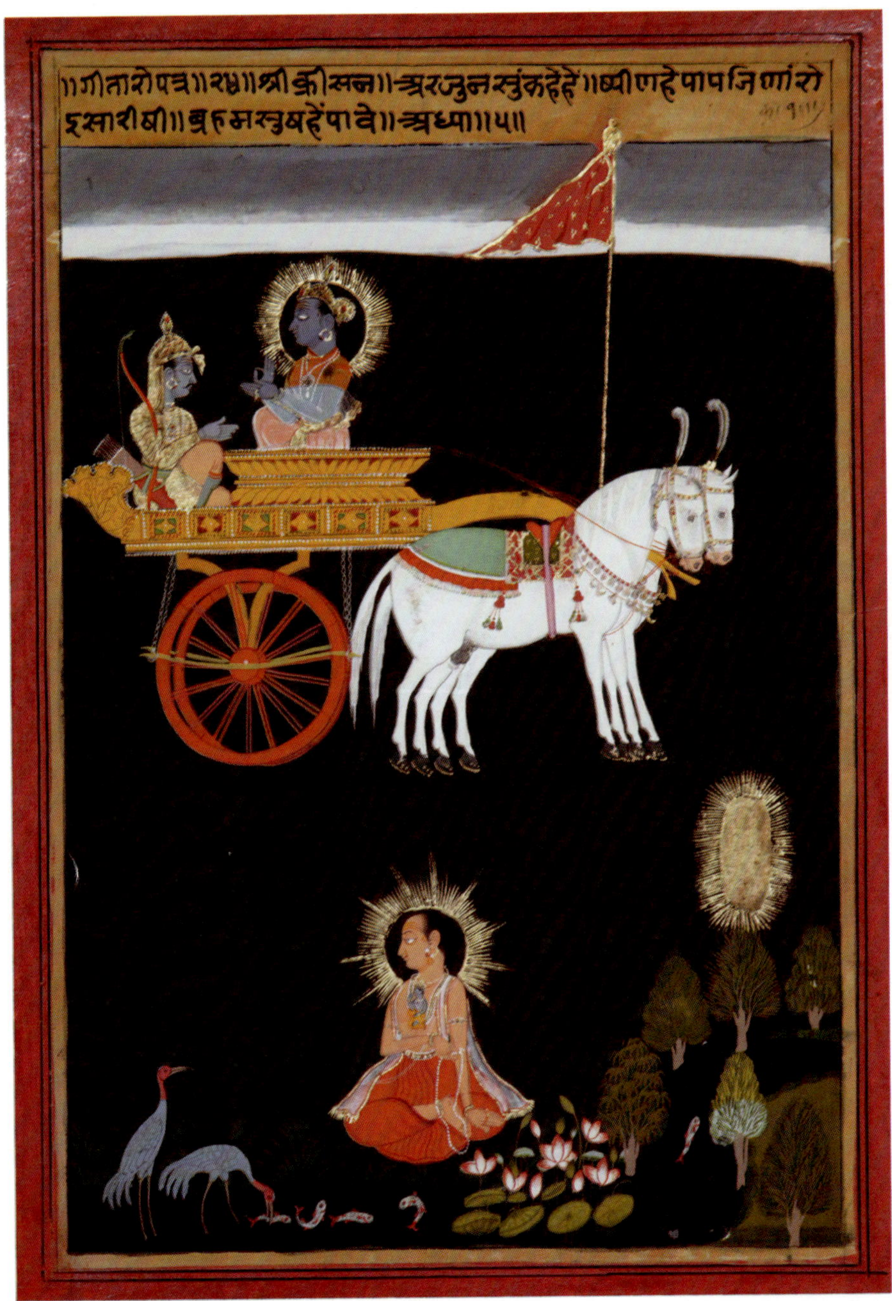

|24| श्री कृष्ण आगे समझाते हुए कहते हैं कि जो अंतर्ज्योति वाला निश्चय कर अपने आप में सुखी है और अपने में ही आराम करने वाला है ऐसा योगी ब्रह्म-सुख को प्राप्त होता है।

|24| Sri Krishna further explains: The disciplined man who concentrates on his inner self and is happy and content with himself attains eternal bliss.

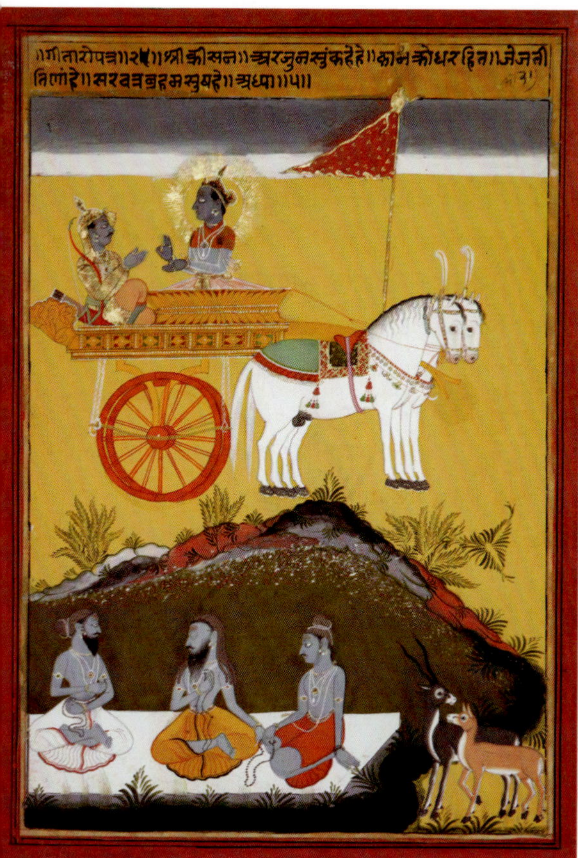

|26| श्री कृष्ण कहने लगे कि हे अर्जुन! जो काम-क्रोध से रहित, जीते हुए चित्त वाले आत्मज्ञान प्राप्त पुरुष हैं, वे सभी जगह ब्रह्म-सुख को प्राप्त होते हैं।

|26| Sri Krishna says: Hey Arjuna! Only the sage who conquers desire and anger, attains blissful union with the divine in all circumstances.

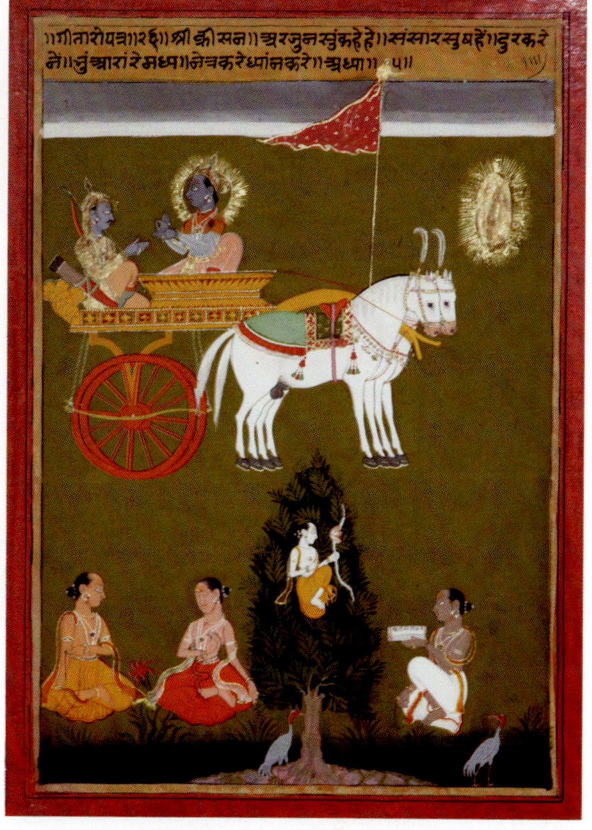

|27| श्री कृष्ण आगे कहने लगे कि संसार सुख को दूर कर के भ्रकुटि के मध्य दृष्टि को केंद्रित कर, अपनी साँस को सम कर जो ध्यान करता है वह मुक्त है ऐसा समझ।

|27| Sri Krishna further says: The one who controls his breath, distances himself from the joys of the external world and fixes his gaze between his eyebrows is liberated.

the sparkling stream which is teeming with fish and lotus flowers. The scene, however, is not unambiguously benign. Two red and blue headed storks stand near the stream, eating fish. Nature can be beautiful and cruel at the same time; its cycle moves through spring's fertility and winter's decay.

What is unique is the image of Krishna which sits in the ascetic's heart. Krishna has become part of the man's being. The ascetic no longer has to 'call' Krishna, summon him; Krishna is now inseparable from his own existence. That is why he is neither troubled by the sight of violence, nor despondent because the world around him has darkened. "Happy within his Self," the verse says, the "sage attains Eternal Bliss and becomes the Spirit Itself" (Swami 40).

In the painting inspired by verse 28, Krishna's chariot hovers over an open space. Its wheels are pale orange. Against the pink background, they are almost invisible, creating a sense that the chariot is floating above a grove of trees. The crimson flag flutters at the boundary of the earth and the sky. Hanuman is even further up and beyond the horizon of the sky where the gods abide. As the eye moves down, it comes to rest on a rich green canopy of trees sheltering an abundant range of animals, birds and flowers. A handsome worshipper, princely in his demeanour, sits meditating beside a river in which pink lotus flowers float. We have seen these are images before. The man's eyes are white as if they are turned inwards in concentration as the verse demands.[21] A saddled horse waits on the left. A peacock sits in the branches of the tree under which the man is meditating. Is the peacock a displaced image of Krishna himself, inspiring the man to know the world with his inward gaze fixed upon his own heart?

---

21 St. Augustine urges us "to read the Scripture with our eyes of the heart fixed upon our heart." Quoted by Julia Kristeva, *The Incredible Need to Believe*, translated by Beverley BieBrahic (New York: Columbia University Press, 2009), p. 4.

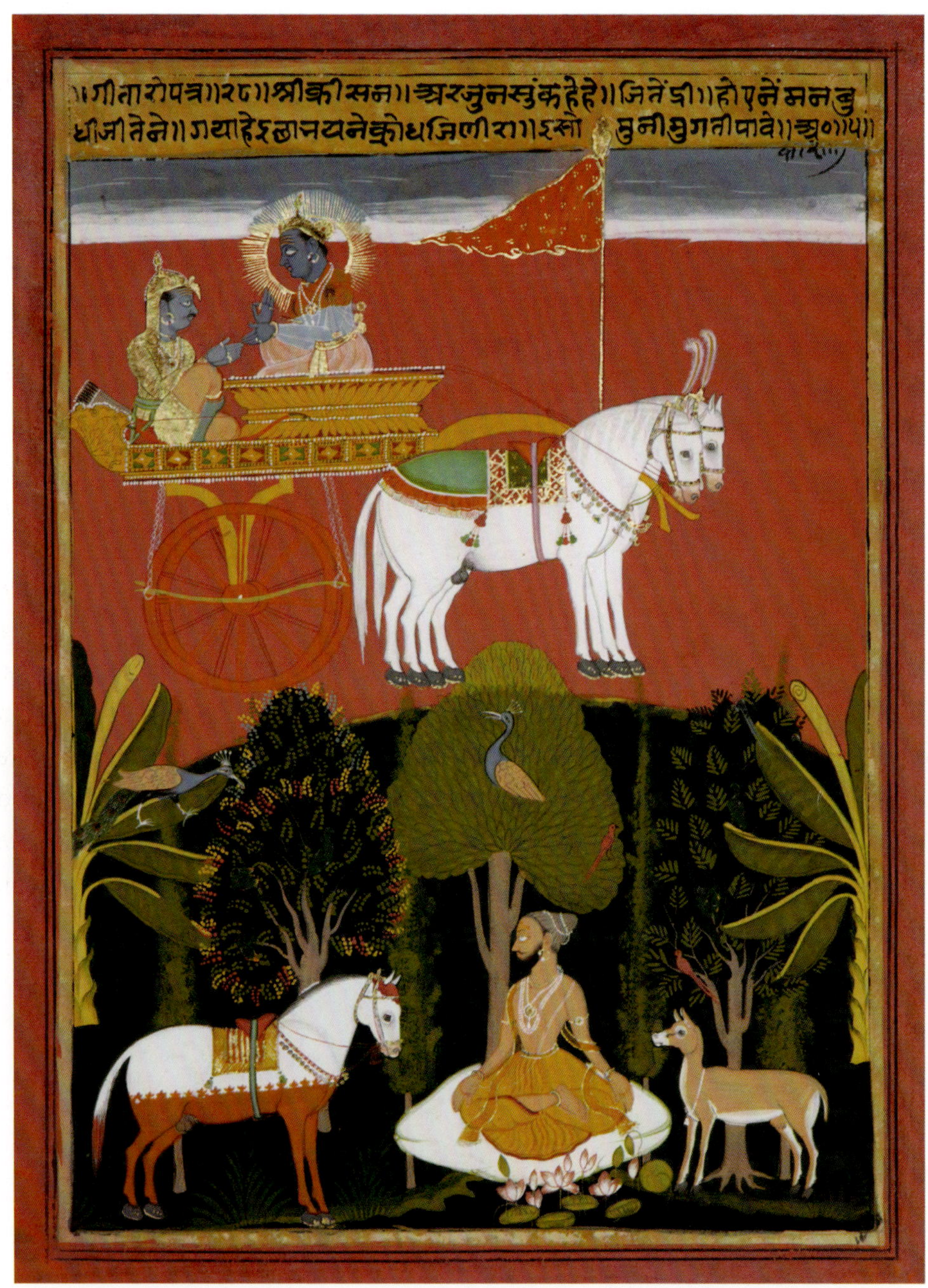

|28| श्री कृष्ण कहने लगे कि हे अर्जुन! जो इन्द्रियाँ, मन, बुद्धि को वश में कर, इच्छा, भय और क्रोध से रहित हो गया हो, उसे सदा मुक्त समझ।

|28| Sri Krishna says: Hey Arjuna! The sage who controls his senses, mind and understanding, the one who is free from desire, fear and anger is truly enlightened.

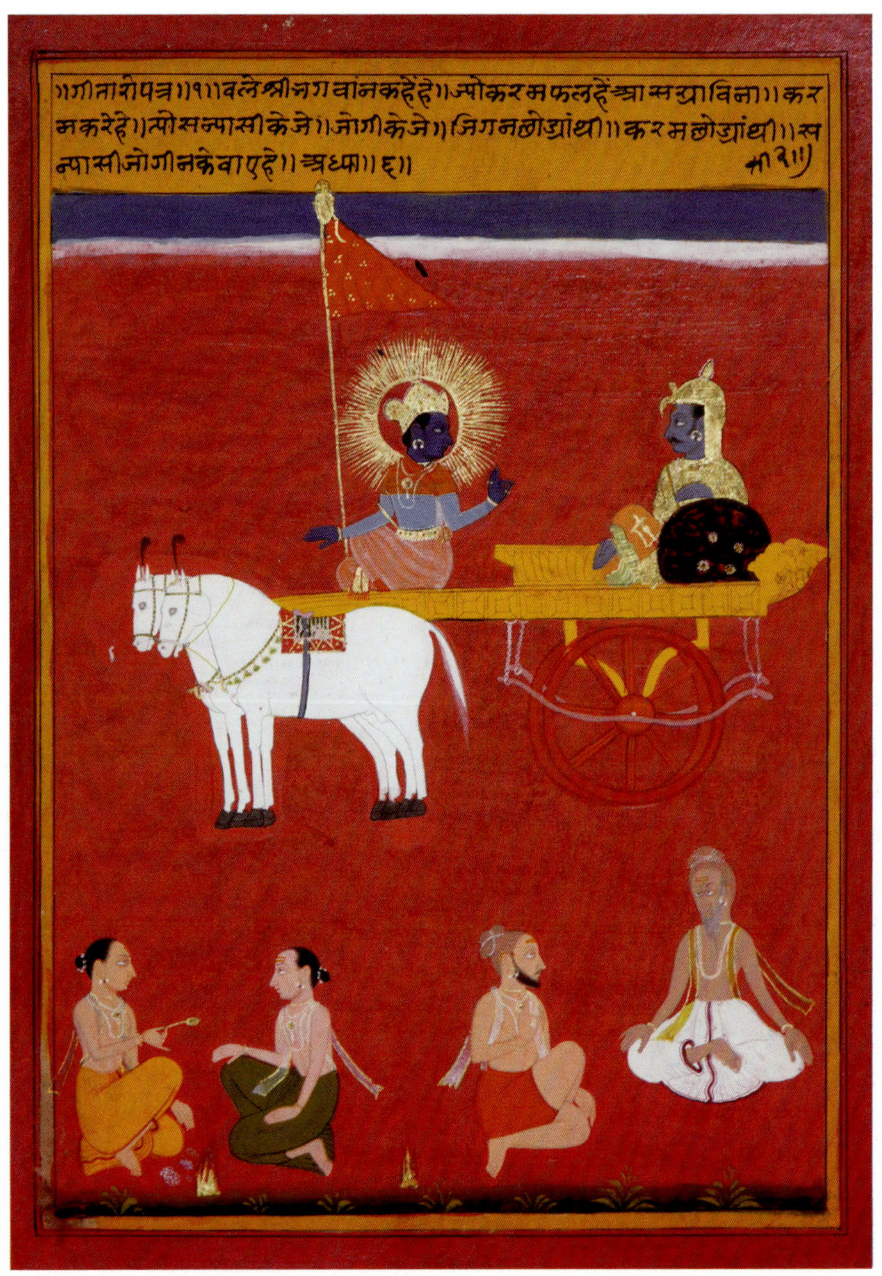

|1| श्री कृष्ण कहने लगे कि हे अर्जुन! जो कर्मफल के आसरे न रहकर कर्म करता है, वही संन्यासी है, वही योगी कहलाएगा न कि यज्ञ और कर्म का त्याग करने वाला।

|1| Sri Krishna says: Hey Arjuna! Only the one who performs his duty without waiting for the fruit of his action is a sanyasi and can be called a yogi—not the one who renounces ritual and action.

CHAPTER 6

In Chapter 6 and the paintings illuminating its verses, the process of revealing Krishna's divinity has begun. The form and direction of his chariot have changed. Allah Baksh intuitively understands that, in any repetitive ritual, when the design changes, the visual and emotional involvement of the participants is renewed. The chariot is now simpler, leaner, less ornate and more linear; the horses are closer to the conventional images of horses than to the visionary grace of the earlier ones. The distance separating Krishna and Arjuna is much greater. This indicates that the friendly intimacy between the two is slowly dissolving, and is being replaced by a more formal dialogue between the secular and the sacred, between a distraught man and the voice of divine wisdom. Henceforth, Krishna shall assume, with greater authority, the role of a teacher and an avatar.

There are two sites of dramatic activity in the painting for verse 1. The lower half offers literal pictorial translations of the verse about ritual and action. Duty performed, Krishna teaches, without being concerned about victory or defeat, is "spiritual" and the mark of a "true ascetic" (Swami 42). A wise, dispassionate yogi is like the earth which "naturally produces vegetation, without any awareness of itself, and does not look forward to the grain that grows." In contrast, the one who "merely observes rituals" is like a crow that "cannot recognize the moon" (*Jnaneshwari* 1: 140-141).

On the left, a priest tends to a ritual fire. His actions seem mechanical and merely prescriptive. Mahadev Desai's comment on the verse is perceptive: ritual fire is only a metaphor for good deeds, just as spinning the wheel for Mahatma Gandhi was a means of thinking about disciplined social and political action (Desai 225). Abhinavagupta's explanation of this verse relies on an odd analogy. A gambler, he says, may feel like a king while he is winning, but in reality he does not possess the throne.[1] The second dramatic scene is also a literal illustration of the verse. It shows a yogi who has turned his back on the second ritual fire. Neglecting his duty—which Abhinavagupta compares to the neglect of the 'household fire'[2]—he turns to face an old yogi. Can he be read ironically as a man who wants to acquire knowledge without having to work for it?

---

1 Abhinavagupta, p. 148.

2 Abhinavagupta, p. 147.

Verses 2 and 3 are concerned with renunciation and the equanimity of wisdom, both of which Arjuna must acquire if he is to fight and fight well. They are painted against green and sky-blue backgrounds. For Goethe, they are colours of quiet satisfaction, and are restful for the eye and the soul.[3] The figure of the yogi in each painting looks at the world with calm disinterest. In one, he is a young man with a long black beard. Spring is in the air, but he seems oblivious to it. In the other, he is old, the flowers on the ground have disappeared while the maturing of summer has turned the plants a deeper green. Both images are disturbing because the space surrounding the meditating men is empty and is devoid of the purpose, action or generosity which the presence of the yogis ought to arouse.

There is clarity, unity and continuity in Krishna's instructions about what a man, who aspires to be initiated into the difficult practice of yogic discipline, should do to prepare himself. The paintings accompanying verses 4, 5 and 7 are equally clear, simple and inspired. Their images correspond to Krishna's exposition about what constitutes genuine "self-control" for the attainment of "peace" (verse 7). They resonate with the emotional patience and calm a true seeker of enlightenment ought to cultivate. The poetic text is about a man whose original flame of divine imagination has grown dim in the dark labyrinths of *samsara*. He should first search for a clean place where he can, in the quietude of his soul, think upon the flame, tend to it, nurture it, till it begins to burn steadily again and regains its golden lustre (verses 4 and 5). In a witty comment, the *Jnaneshwari* says that the place chosen for the making of a hermitage should be so peacefully silent that it can even tolerate the occasional presence of a peacock (1: 151). It is worth noticing that Krishna's emphasis is neither on prayer nor on devotion to a particular god, but upon the self's own effort, its own search. Gods do not fulfil human needs and desires. The flame of imagination, Krishna insists, burns within each human being, and there is a method to finding it, reigniting it from its embers, and then watching it glow once again. The image of the inner flame suggests that the purpose of yogic withdrawal into the self is not to discover something new, but to recognise what is already present.

It is remarkable how the figure of the yogi is similar in the paintings for verses 10 to 19, 26 to 30. He sits cross-legged in the posture of meditation; his lower half has the roundness of an earthen lamp; his bare torso rises up like a slim, steady and radiant flame; his body is luminous. The spirit of the enlightened man, the *Book of Proverbs*

3 Goethe, *Essential Goethe*, p. 964.

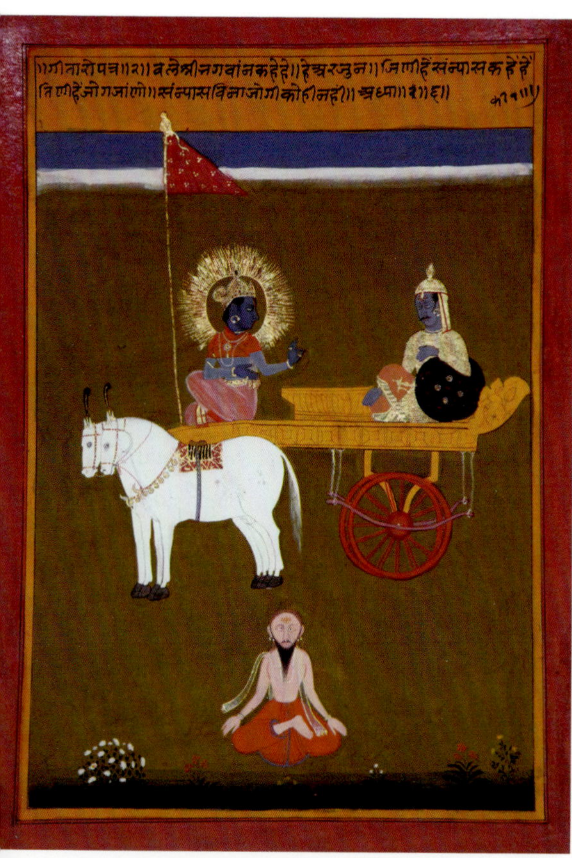

|2| श्री कृष्ण आगे कहने लगे कि जिसे लोग संन्यास कहते हैं, उसे हे अर्जुन! तू योग जान क्योंकि कोई भी संकल्पों का त्याग किए बिना योगी नहीं होता।

|2| Sri Krishna further says: Hey Arjuna! What people call renunciation is actually yogic discipline; one cannot become a yogi unless one has renounced all desire.

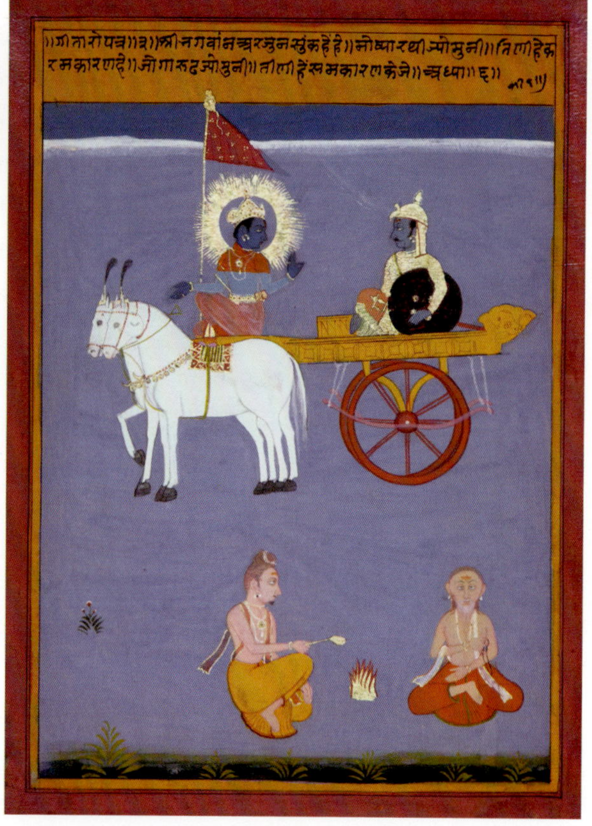

|3| आगे समझाते हुए श्री कृष्ण कहने लगे कि योग में स्थित होने वाले मुनि के लिए कर्मयोग ही साधन है और योगारूढ़ जो मुनि होता है उसमें संकल्पों का अभाव होता है।

|3| Explaining further, Sri Krishna says: Work or action is the only means for achieving wisdom; and a man seeking the maturity of wisdom is serene.

reminds us, "is the candle of the Lord."[4] The particular beauty of the image of the flame and the inner glow of the wisdom-seeking man is two-fold: it helps man to distinguish between what is his own and what belongs to the world; to understand that what he cherishes is always vulnerable.

The yogi's visual isolation is in keeping with Krishna's carefully articulated ceremony of inner attentiveness which a seeker must perform to gain control over the body's energies and help the mind keep its distance from the seductive charms and fearful storms of the world. The one who seeks enlightenment, Krishna says, must first look for a place where he can mediate in silence. This process, which initiates a search for a calm spot, would in itself block out the unpredictable temptations and the whirl of the world from his consciousness (verses 4 and 5). The painter rightly understands that this search begins only after a seeker experiences worldly turmoil. Hence, the background colour for verse 10 is not the pale blue of dawn, with its gentle gladness and freshness, but a sadder greyish-blue in which ashen evening shades have already begun to mingle. It is not the colour of despair, but it is coextensive with the emotions of one who knows sorrow and must somehow find his way toward calm acceptance.

In the painting, the place where the yogi begins his search is beautiful. A pale blue river, with lotus flowers, flows near his feet. There is a slight undulation of the green ground where the man chooses to meditate. It is far from the city which "is full of lost mornings and [where] the gods are silent..."[5] Here yogic meditation is nourished by silence. Knowing how to surrender the self and what to renounce is the first knowledge an ascetic must acquire, and do so on his own. In contrast, Orpheus, who cannot let go of his dead wife, Eurydice, descends to Hades to fetch her, opening for himself a door to desolation.

In the grey-blue light, the white horses, harnessed to the chariot, look ethereal, and the bright yellow wooden chariot seems to float in the uncanny space beyond and above the ascetic. There is a sense of 'purity' in the air—purity of space that Krishna says is the first requirement for the practice of yoga—and, there is beauty too, since the beautiful is never distinct from purity and truth. If painting is another form of writing which makes verbal abstraction visible, then, paradoxically, it also leads one beyond the physical to search for the invisible spirit that gives shape to the world. Indeed, in these

---

4 Quote by Radhakrishnan, *The Bhagavadgita*, p. 193.

5 Alain, *The Gods*, translated by Richard Pevear (London: Quartet Books, 1973), p. 80.

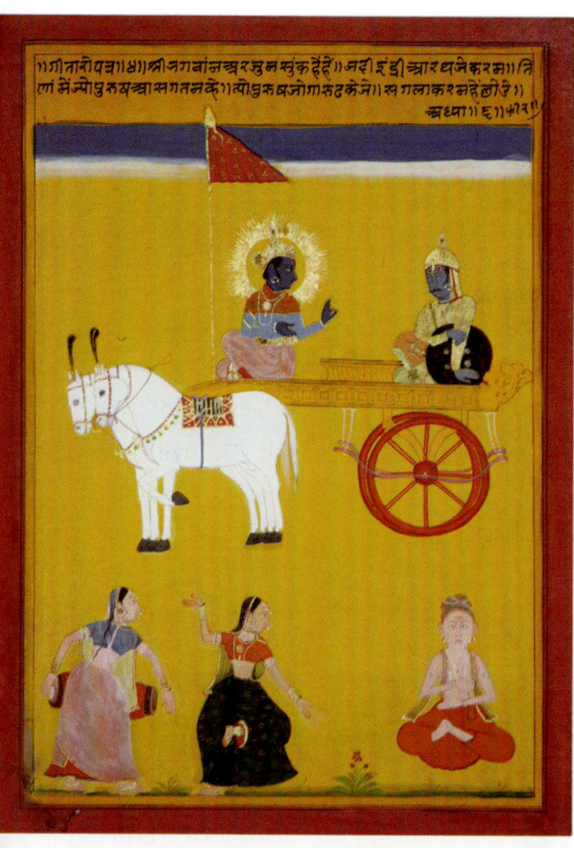

|4| श्री कृष्ण कहने लगे कि हे अर्जुन! जो कोई इन्द्रियों के विषयों में या कर्मों में आसक्त नहीं होता, ऐसे संकल्पों का संन्यासी पुरुष योगारूढ़ कहलाता है।

|4| Sri Krishna says: Hey Arjuna! The one who has no attachments and who acts without any desire is said to have achieved yoga.

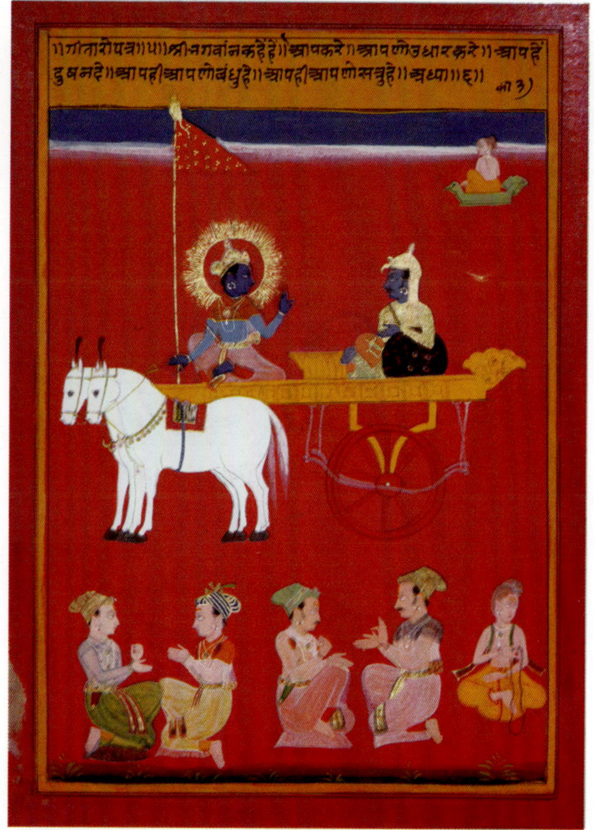

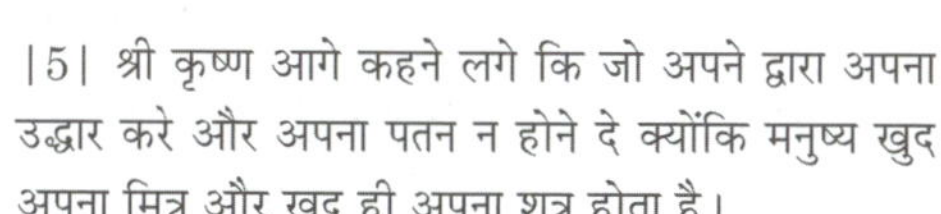

|5| श्री कृष्ण आगे कहने लगे कि जो अपने द्वारा अपना उद्धार करे और अपना पतन न होने दे क्योंकि मनुष्य खुद अपना मित्र और खुद ही अपना शत्रु होता है।

|5| Sri Krishna further says: One should improve oneself by one's own efforts, and one should never degrade oneself; one is one's own friend and enemy.

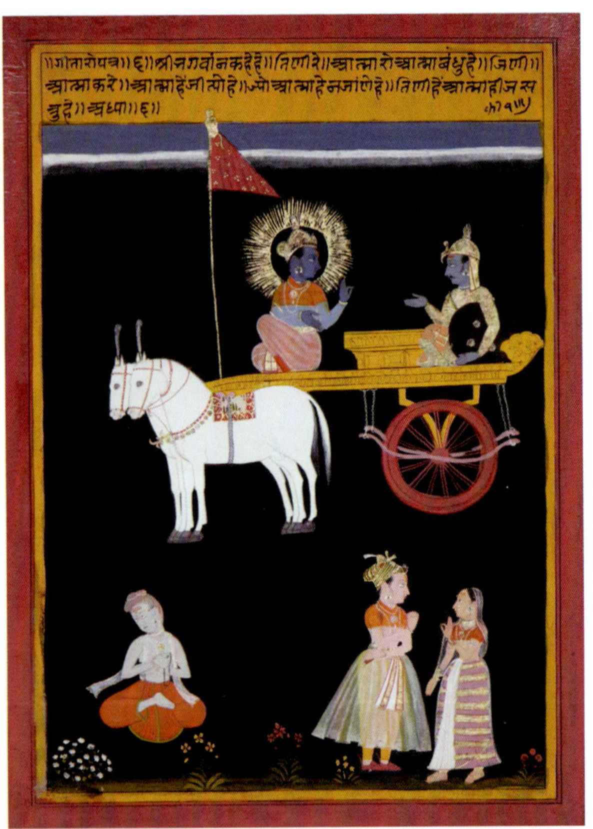

|6| श्री कृष्ण समझाने लगे कि हे अर्जुन! जिसने आत्मा से आत्मा को जीत लिया है वह स्वयं अपना मित्र है और जिसने आत्मा को नहीं जीता वह स्वयं अपना ही शत्रु होता है।

|6| Sri Krishna explains to Arjuna: The man who has won victory over himself by his own effort is his own friend; and the one who has not conquered himself is his own enemy.

|7| आगे खुलासा करते हुए श्री कृष्ण कहने लगे कि हे अर्जुन! जिसने स्वयं को जीता है उसे शांत और परमात्मा में लीन समझ, वह सर्दी-गरमी, सुख-दुख और मान-अपमान में समान रहता है।

|7| Explaining himself further Sri Krishna says: Hey Arjuna! The man who has mastered himself and is absorbed in mediating upon God is indifferent to heat-cold, joy-sorrow and honour-dishonour.

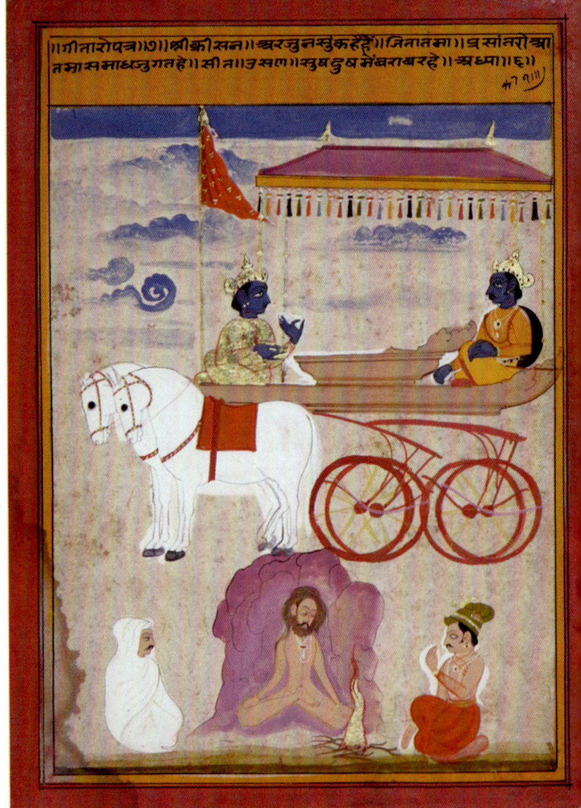

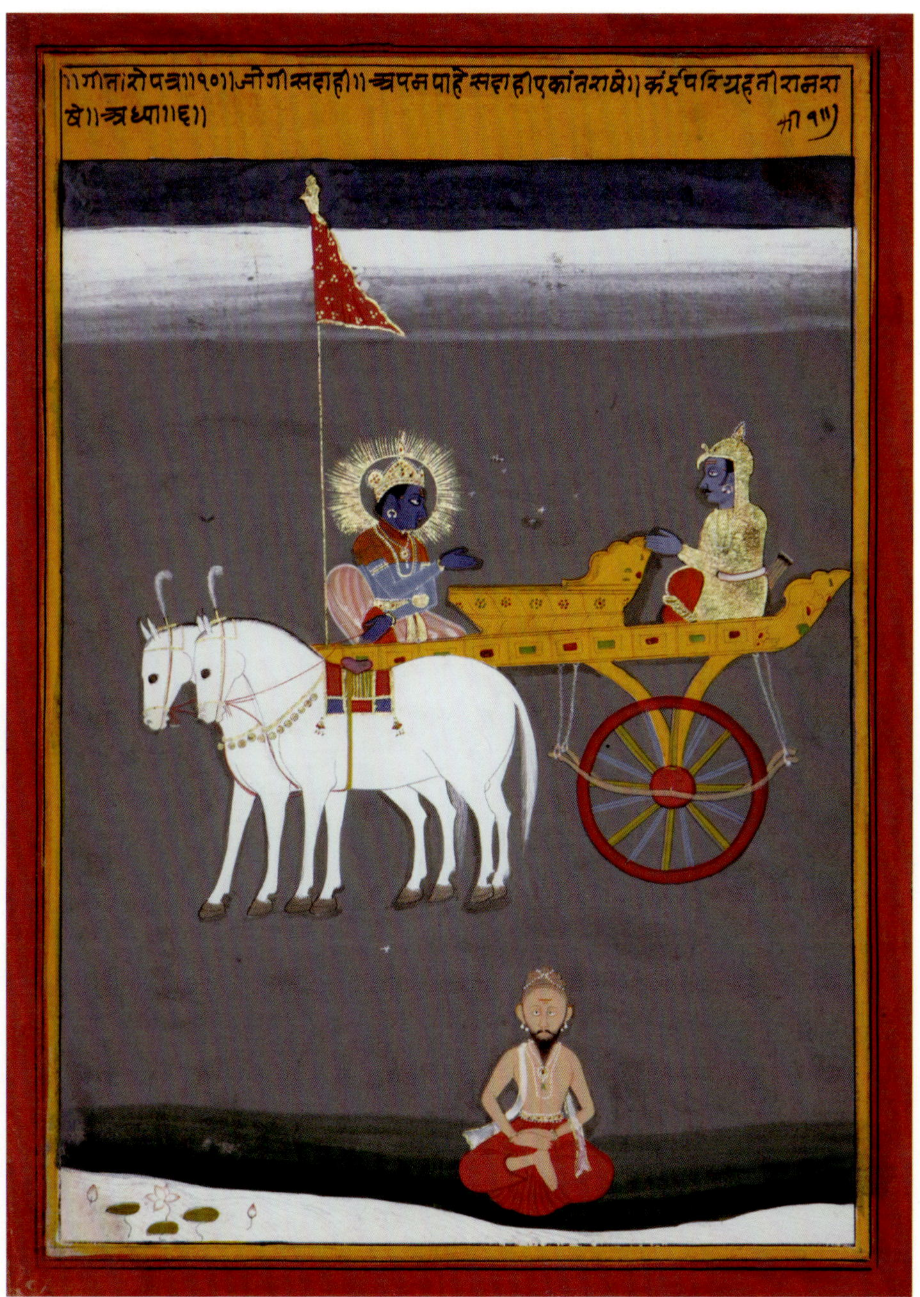

|10| श्री कृष्ण कह रहे हैं कि योगी को चाहिए कि वह आशारहित व संग्रहरहित हो अकेला ही एकान्त स्थान में बैठकर चित्त को आत्मा में स्थिर कर, आत्मा में ही लगाए रखे।

|10| Sri Krishna says: A yogi sits alone in a secluded place, rids himself of hope and conflict, and controlling his mind and body, concentrates on his inner self alone.

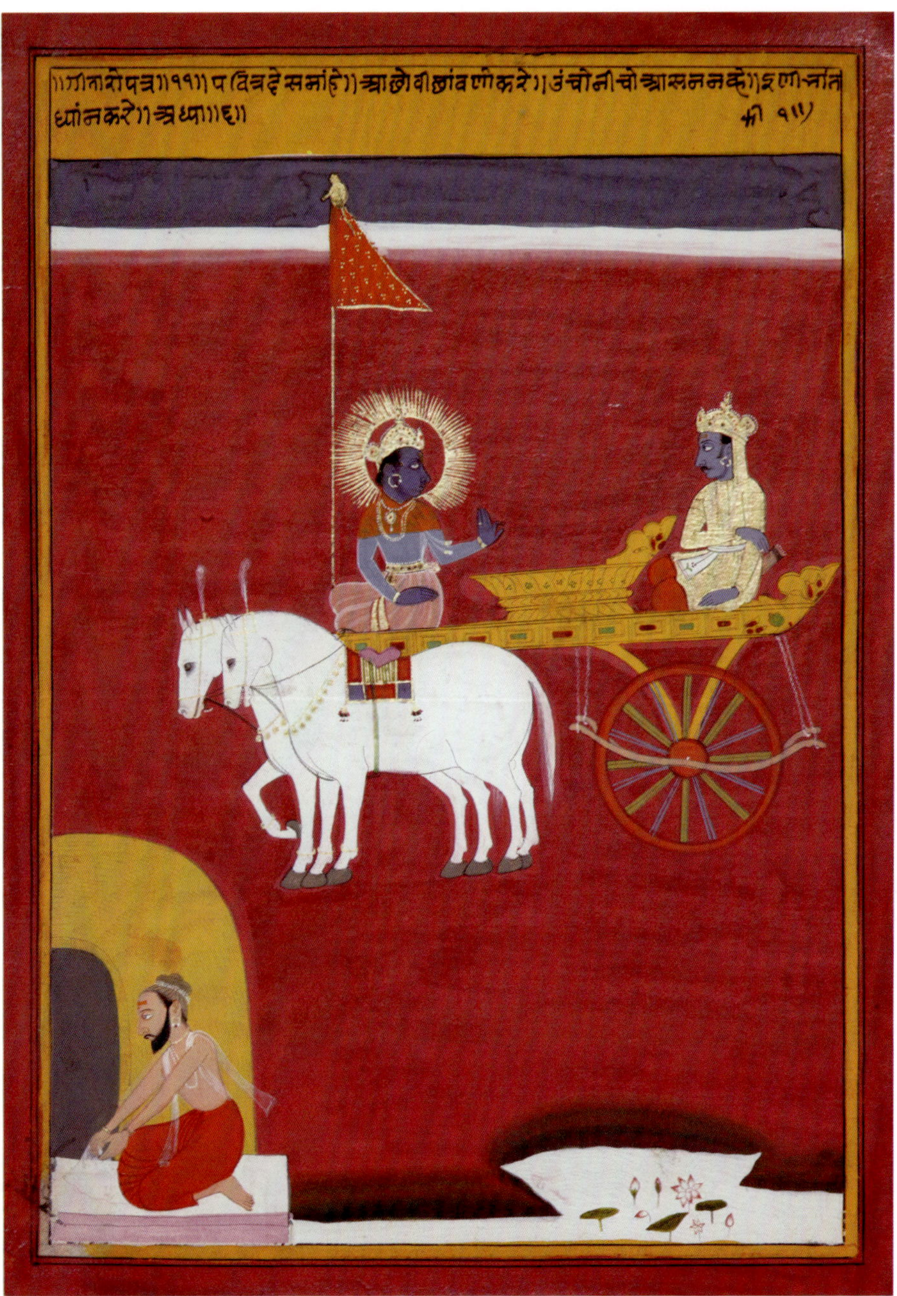

|11| श्री कृष्ण कहने लगे कि हे अर्जुन! योगी को चाहिए कि वह शुद्ध भूमि पर न अधिक ऊँचा न एकदम नीचा अपना आसन बनाए और उस पर बैठ कर एकाग्र मन से ध्यान करे।

|11| Sri Krishna says: Hey Arjuna! A yogi should sit in a correct posture on a sacred spot, which is neither too high nor too low, and concentrate on his mind.

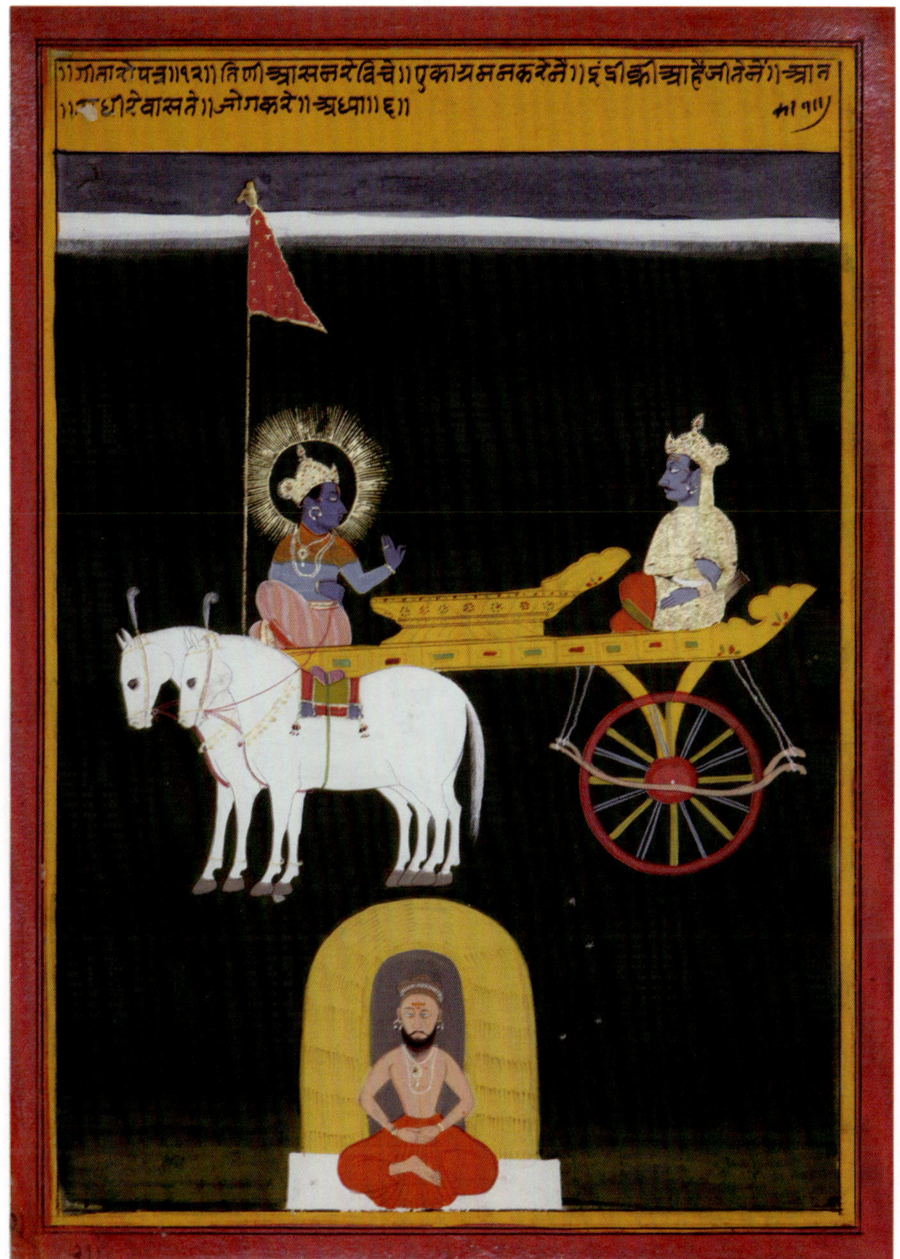

|12| आगे समझाते हुए श्री कृष्ण बोले कि योगी को चाहिए कि वह आसन पर बैठकर चित्त व इन्द्रियों को वश में करे, मन को एकाग्र करे और आत्मशुद्धि के लिए योगाभ्यास करे।

|12| Explaining further, Sri Krishna says: A yogi should, sitting on that spot, control his thoughts and senses, and practice discipline for the purification of his self.

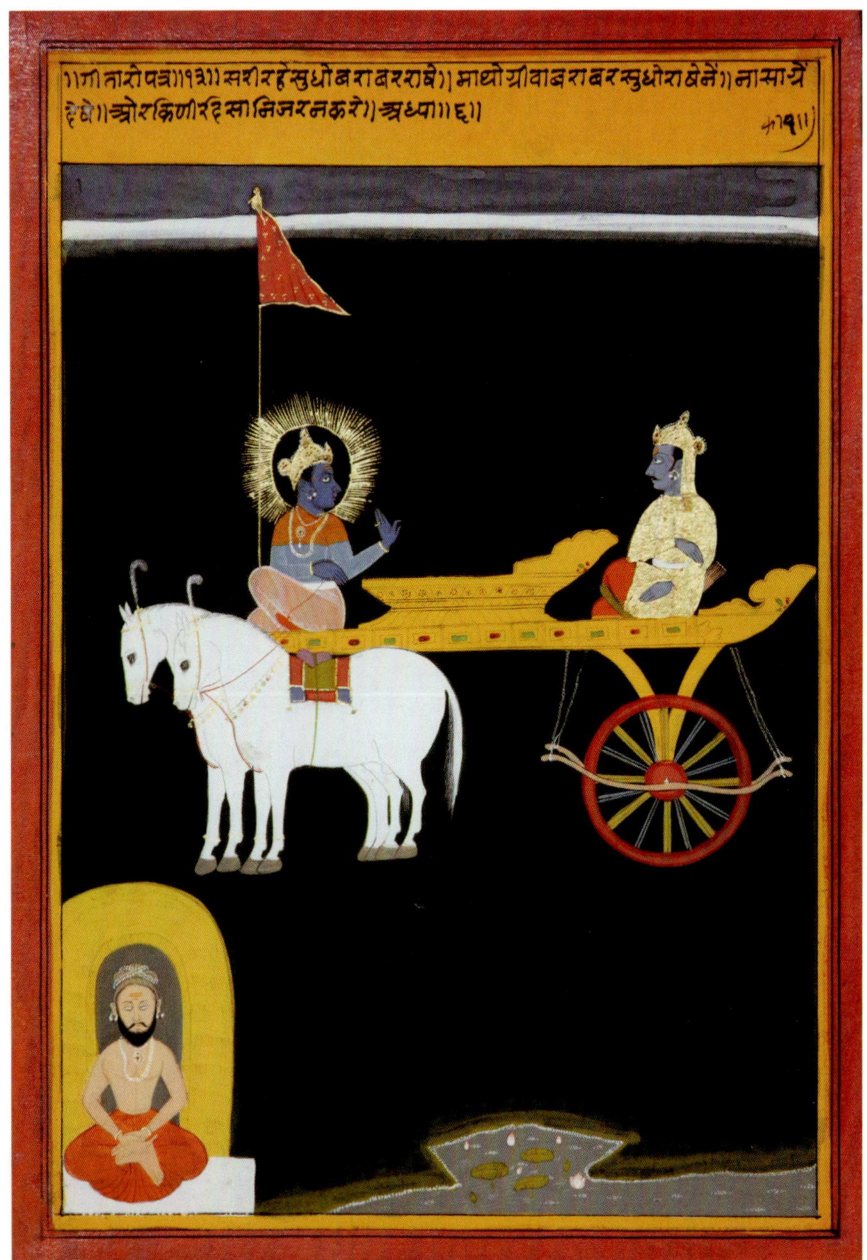

|13| और आगे समझाते हुए श्री कृष्ण कहने लगे कि योगी को चाहिए कि वह अपनी काया, सिर व गरदन को सीधा और स्थिर रखकर नासिका के अग्रभाग पर अपनी दृष्टि एकाग्र करे तथा दूसरी दिशा में न देखे।

|13| And explaining further, Sri Krishna says: A yogi should, keeping his body, head and neck upright and still, fix his gaze on the tip of his nose without looking in any other direction.

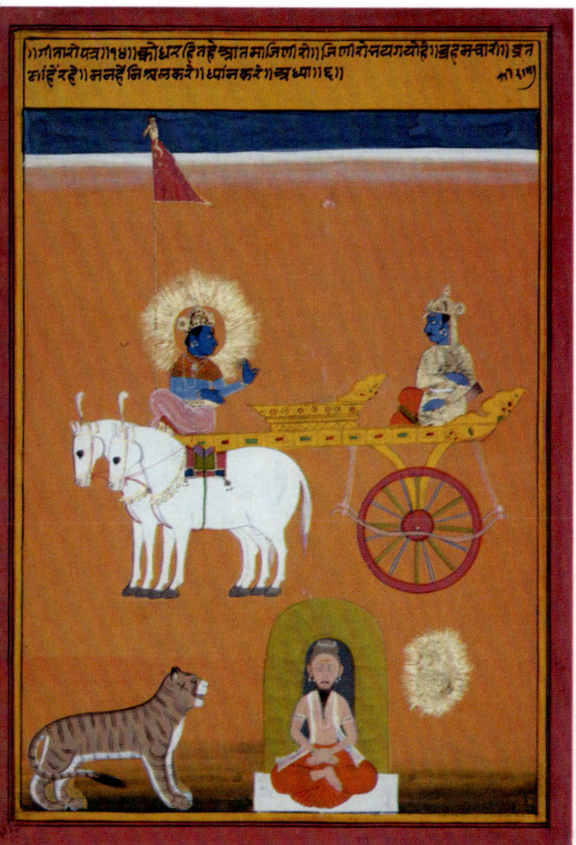

|14| श्री कृष्ण कहने लगे कि हे अर्जुन! क्रोधरहित है आत्मा जिसकी, जिसका भय समाप्त हो गया हो, ऐसा ब्रह्मचारी-व्रत में स्थित शांत होकर, मन को एकाग्र कर चित्त को मुझ में लगाकर ध्यान करे। उसे योगी जान।

|14| Sri Krishna says: Hey Arjuna! The one who has overcome anger, has dispelled fear, is firm in his vow of celibacy, and concentrates on me with a disciplined mind, is a yogi.

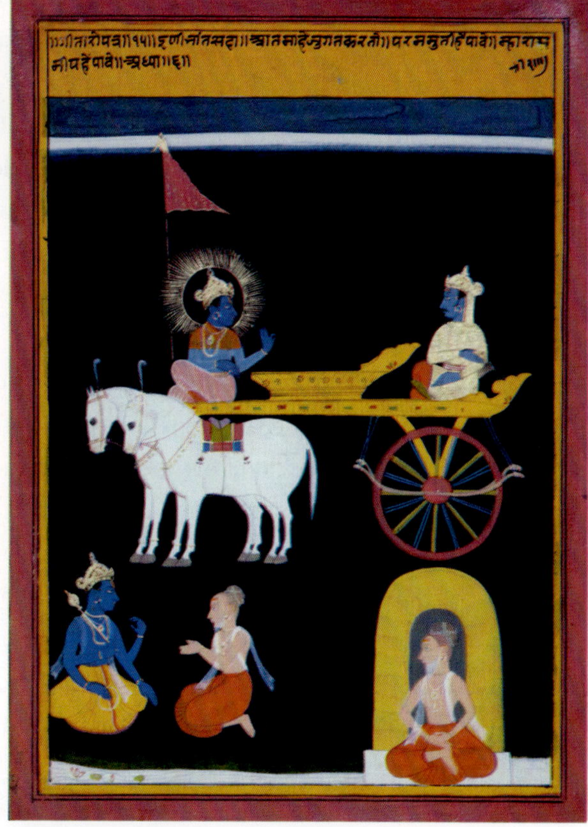

|15| आगे समझाते हुए श्री कृष्ण कहने लगे कि इस तरह मन को एकाग्र करने वाला योगी अपने मन को आत्मा में निरंतर लगाएगा। वह मुझमें रहने वाली शांति और मेरे सामीप्य को प्राप्त होगा।

|15| Explaining further, Sri Krishna says: A yogi who possesses a disciplined mind, whose thoughts are always concentrated on his inner self, can commune with me and attain the peace that is in me.

paintings (verses 10-19), the artist deliberately persuades us to look upward, follow the colour red of the ascetic's lower garment up toward the chariot's wheel, find its echo in Arjuna's clothes, before finally coming to rest on the scarlet flag near the line separating the earth and the sky. The emotional and spiritual effect of this ascendant visual movement is to produce a feeling of exaltation as it unites in a single spiralling movement the river, the green ground, the yogi, the chariot, Krishna, Hanuman and the sky. Metaphorically, it also sweeps into its outward expanding swirl the inner being of the man, the grace of Krishna and the divine. Perceptively, the poet-painter, William Blake, says: "the man who never in his mind & thoughts travel'd to Heaven Is No Artist."[6] Here the simplicity of design serves the highest moral and aesthetic purpose.

In these paintings, almost all the markers of realistic space are slowly erased. These erasures symbolically trace advances in the ascetic's spiritual journey to his inner being. In the painting for verse 11, he washes the entrance to a yellow stone-cave which is an archetypal marker of an opening into dream space and fluid time where the unconscious streams in with all its social grotesquery, ancestral voices and mantic prophecies. They are a melange of what the reasoning self knows and what the ego represses. Only the private self has the code to what they mean. That is why, Plato reminds us, the sign at the entrance to the cave at Delphi into the depth of one's own consciousness reads, 'Know thy Self.' Or, as Krishna tells Arjuna, to know the reality of the world, the first task is to cleanse the mind of social conditioning and bruising anxieties. This visual image, however, is inspired by one more thought. The cave of descent into the inner being is also the source of the stream with lotus flowers where the seeking self sits to meditate. It is, therefore, also a sign of new knowledge and new bhakti.

The paintings for verses 12 to 19 trace the ascetic's spiritual progress. He sits at the cave's entrance through which the self descends into darkness so as to shed all the vestiges of desire and discard the burden of inherited, borrowed and dead ideas. He learns, in the course of meditation, what Krishna tells Arjuna in his discourse, that there is a method of detaching the self from the gluttony of desire and the lethargy of the body. Krishna instructs Arjuna to think impersonally and impartially about the self's relation with the world. The painter visualises the yogi putting into practice those instructions: neither sleep too much nor too little (verse 16); neither indulge in pleasure for too long nor abstain from it all together (verse 17); be moderate and

6 William Blake, "Annotations to Reynolds," *Collected Works*, p. 458.

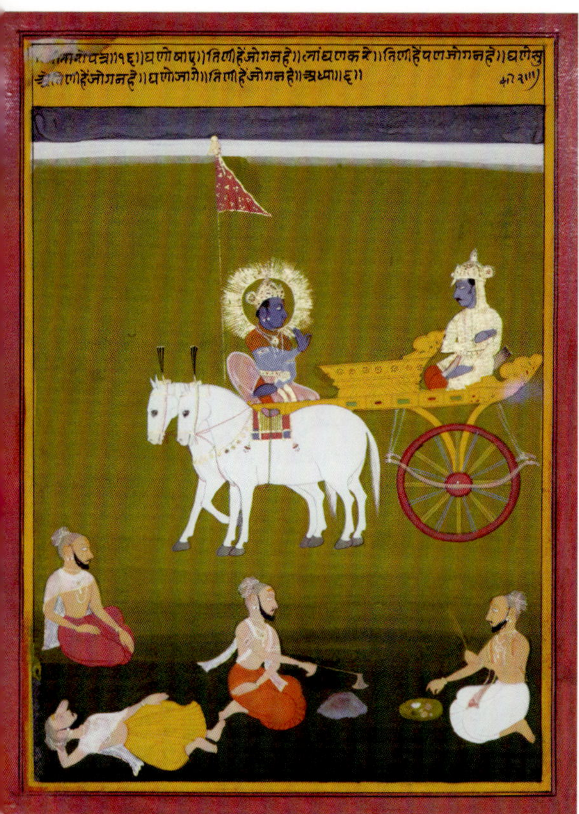

|16| हे अर्जुन! श्री कृष्ण कहने लगे कि योग न अधिक खाने वाले का, न बिल्कुल नहीं खाने वाले का, न अधिक सोने वाले का और न बिल्कुल नहीं सोने वाले का ही सिद्ध होता है।

|16| Sri Krishna says: Hey Arjuna! Yoga is not for the one who eats too much or eats nothing at all; and it is not for the one who sleeps a lot or does not sleep at all.

|17| श्री कृष्ण कहने लगे कि हे अर्जुन! योग उसके दुखों का नाश करता है जो आवश्यकतानुसार आहार-विहार करता है, जरूरत को ध्यान में रखते हुए कर्म करता है और जिसका सोना-जागना भी नियमित है।

|17| Sri Krishna says: Hey Arjuna! Yoga destroys the sorrow of the one eats or fasts when necessary, who acts with moderation, and whose sleep and wakefulness are regulated.

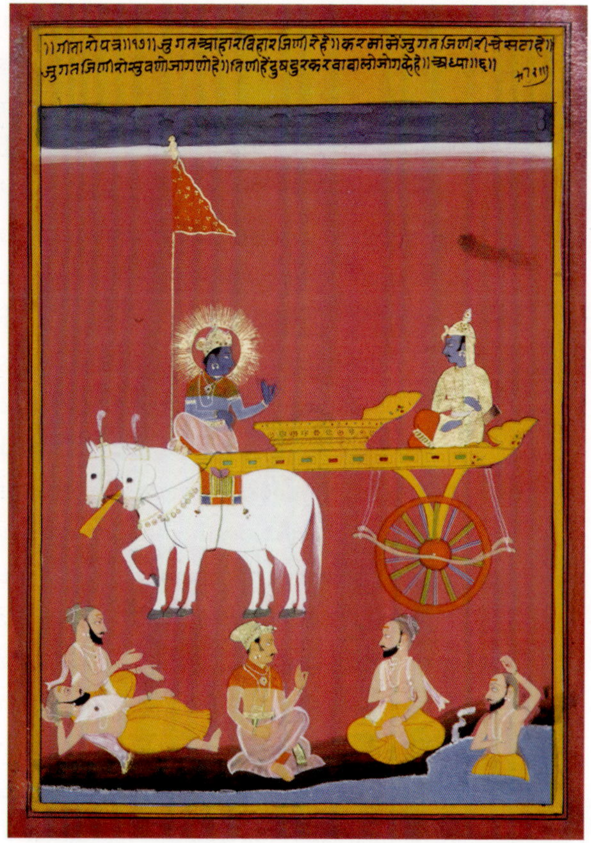

steady in all your dealings with the world so that you are ready to give up the social world and sit before a cave and mediate till the flame within you begins to glow (verses 18 and 19). If you can do that, Krishna says, the opaque and stony world enclosing you will be transformed.

The yellow stone of the cave is luminous, though the background is dark. Only the presence of Krishna and Arjuna, still talking in their chariot, arouses confidence. The yogi is calm as he disengages himself from the phenomenal world; dies to it; retreats into the depths of his own self as the natural world recedes and is no longer visible to the physical eye. As the meditation deepens, the yogi realises that the past holds no answer and the future must cease to be of interest. The real is here and now; it is neither fearful nor heroic; neither material nor spiritual. As he begins to know his real self within perpetual change, like the lotus flower blossoming in the stream (the image recurs in these paintings), the first sign that he is emerging into a fresh and personal understanding of himself in the world is the surge of background light and colour (painting for verse 14). The yogi continues to sit still against a gentle ochre-brown background lit by the morning sun. His eyes are shut; his hands are folded in his lap in a pose of quiet acceptance. A visionary tiger stands on his right. Since there is no correspondence between the image of the tiger and a real one, it is not a source of physical terror or fierce aggression. It is, however, a sign of the complete imaginative freedom the yogi has now attained, just as the lotus is a sign that he now knows that the beauty of the world is temporary but continuously renewed. Both the images, reflections of the world, are simultaneously empty of meaning and replete with the numen; neither insists on anything nor offers anything.

In the paintings for verses 15 and 19, the yogi's cave is placed vertically below the chariot's wheel, and their curving lines complement each other. If the cave is the conventional symbol of the earth and the sensual body of man, the wheel is the archetype of cyclical time and eternal change. Arjuna and the yogi are also located on the same vertical axis; their folded arms are mirror-images of each other and create a pattern of harmony. Since we see both Arjuna and the yogi simultaneously, this vertical arrangement is not designed to provoke any hierarchical differentiation between the two as in a Christian painting from the Italian Renaissance where the eye must travel upward from man to God, earth to heaven. Instead, there is a sense of a symbolic connection and equivalence between the two. After all, Krishna has been insisting that the man of action (the karma yogi) is the same as the sanyasi who withdraws from action. One should recall that Mahatma Gandhi once wrote a brief summary of Plato's

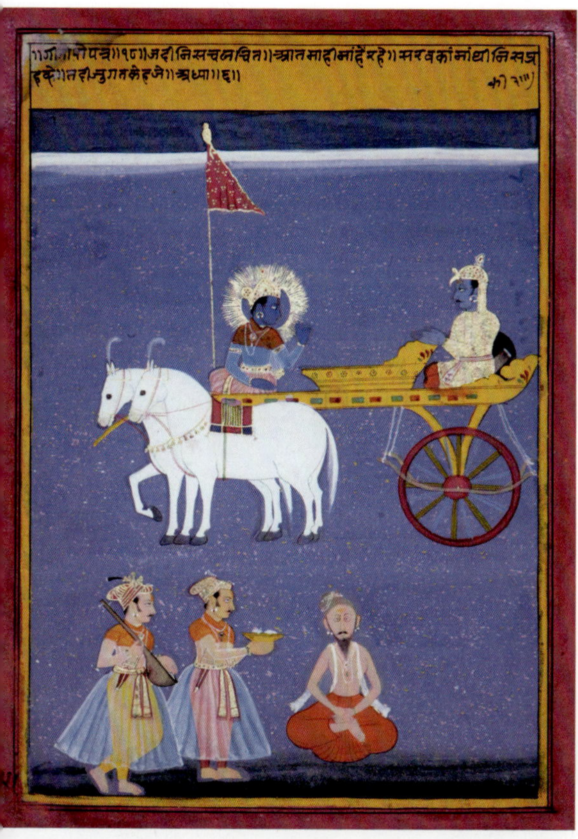

|18| योग को आगे समझाते हुए श्री कृष्ण कहने लगे कि जिस काल में अपने वश में किया हुआ चित्त, आत्मा में अच्छी तरह स्थित हो जाता है, उस काल में सभी कामनाओं से रहित पुरुष योगयुक्त कहलाता है।

|18| Explaining yoga a little more, Sri Krishna says: The man whose mind is disciplined and steadily focused on the self is called a yogi.

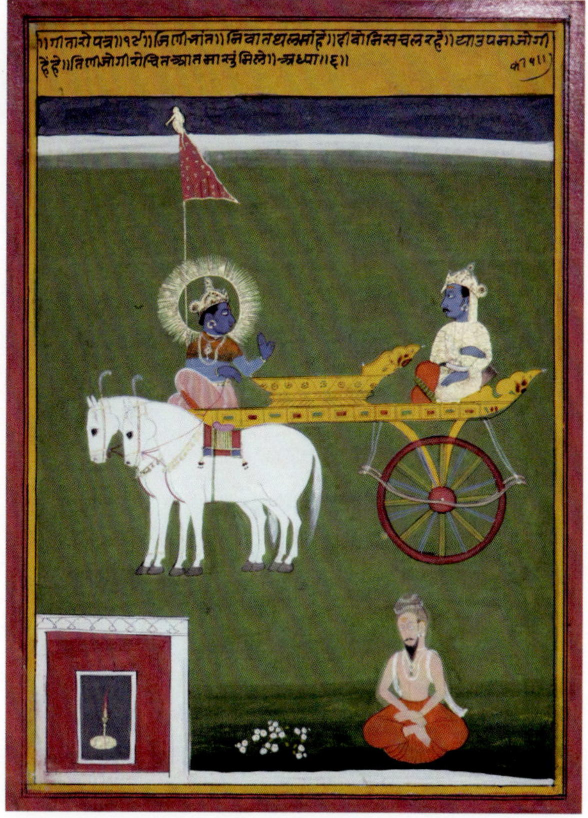

|19| श्री कृष्ण आगे कहने लगे कि हे अर्जुन! जैसे हवा रहित स्थान में रखे हुए दीपक की लौ नहीं हिलती है, यही उपमा चित्त को वश में किए हुए आत्मा से जुड़े योगी के लिए कही गई है।

|19| Sri Krishna adds: Hey Arjuna! A yogi, who has conquered his mind and who concentrates unwaveringly on his self, is like the flame of an earthen lamp which does not flicker in a windless place.

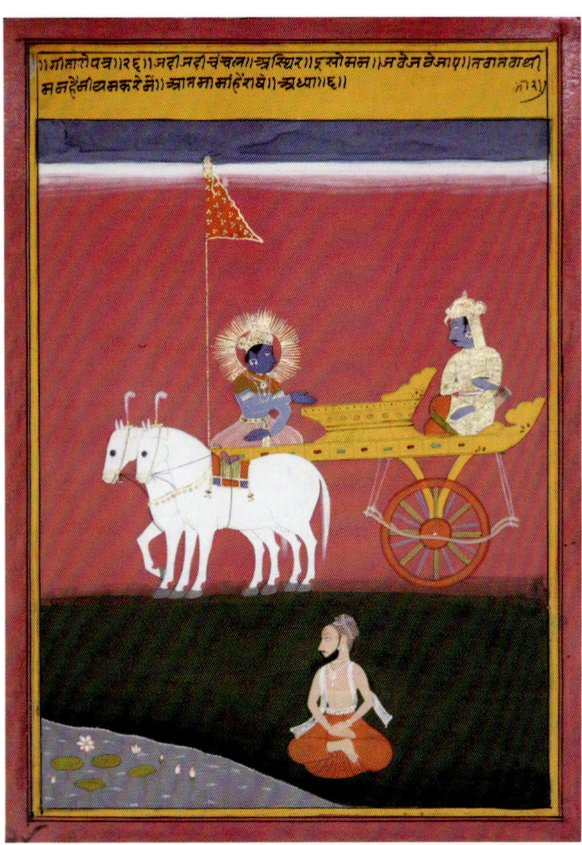

|26| हे अर्जुन! यह चंचल और अस्थिर मन जहाँ-जहाँ भागता है, उसको वहाँ-वहाँ से हटाकर फिर से आत्मा में स्थिर करना योग कहलाता है।

|26| Hey Arjuna! Whenever this fickle and wayward mind wanders away, yoga goes after it, subdues it, and brings it under the self's control.

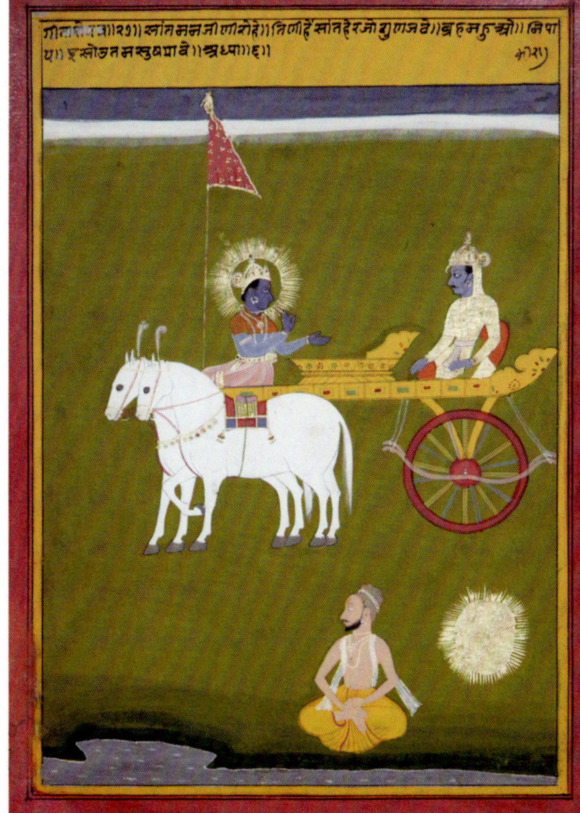

|27| श्री कृष्ण आगे कहने लगे कि हे अर्जुन! उत्तम सुख की प्राप्ति उस योगी को होती है जिसका मन शांत है, रजोगुणी जो पापों से मुक्त है और ब्रह्मभूत हो गया हो। ऐसा व्यक्ति उत्तम सुख पाता है।

|27| Sri Krishna further says: Hey Arjuna! That yogi achieves eternal bliss whose mind is at peace, who is without sin, and whose mind is fixed on Brahma. Such a yogi attains eternal bliss.

|30| हे अर्जुन! जो सभी में मुझे देखता है और मुझ में सभी को देखता है उसके लिए मैं कभी दूर नहीं होता और न वह कभी मुझसे दूर होता है।

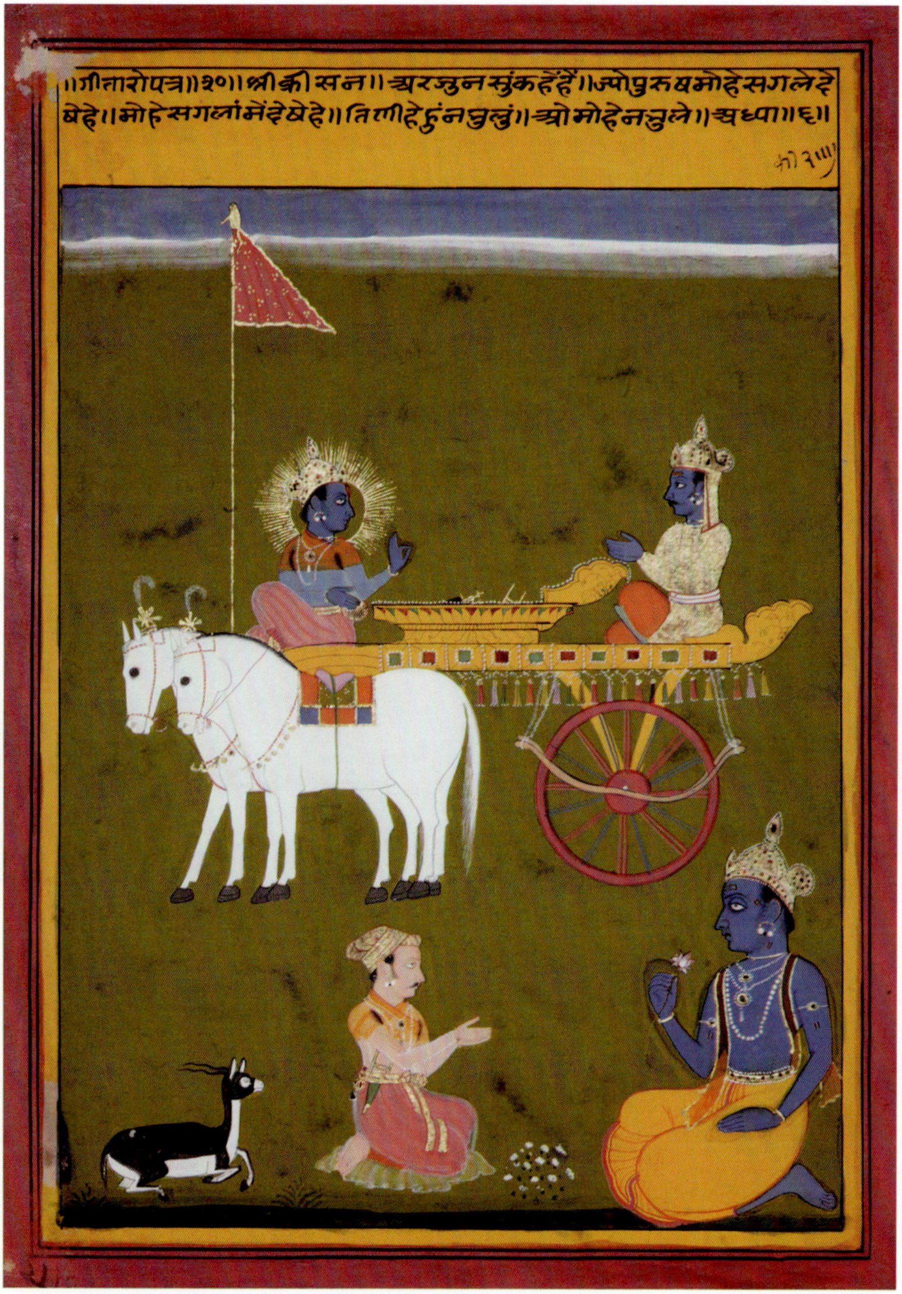

|30| Hey Arjuna! I am never far from the one who sees me in everything and everything in me; nor is he far from me.

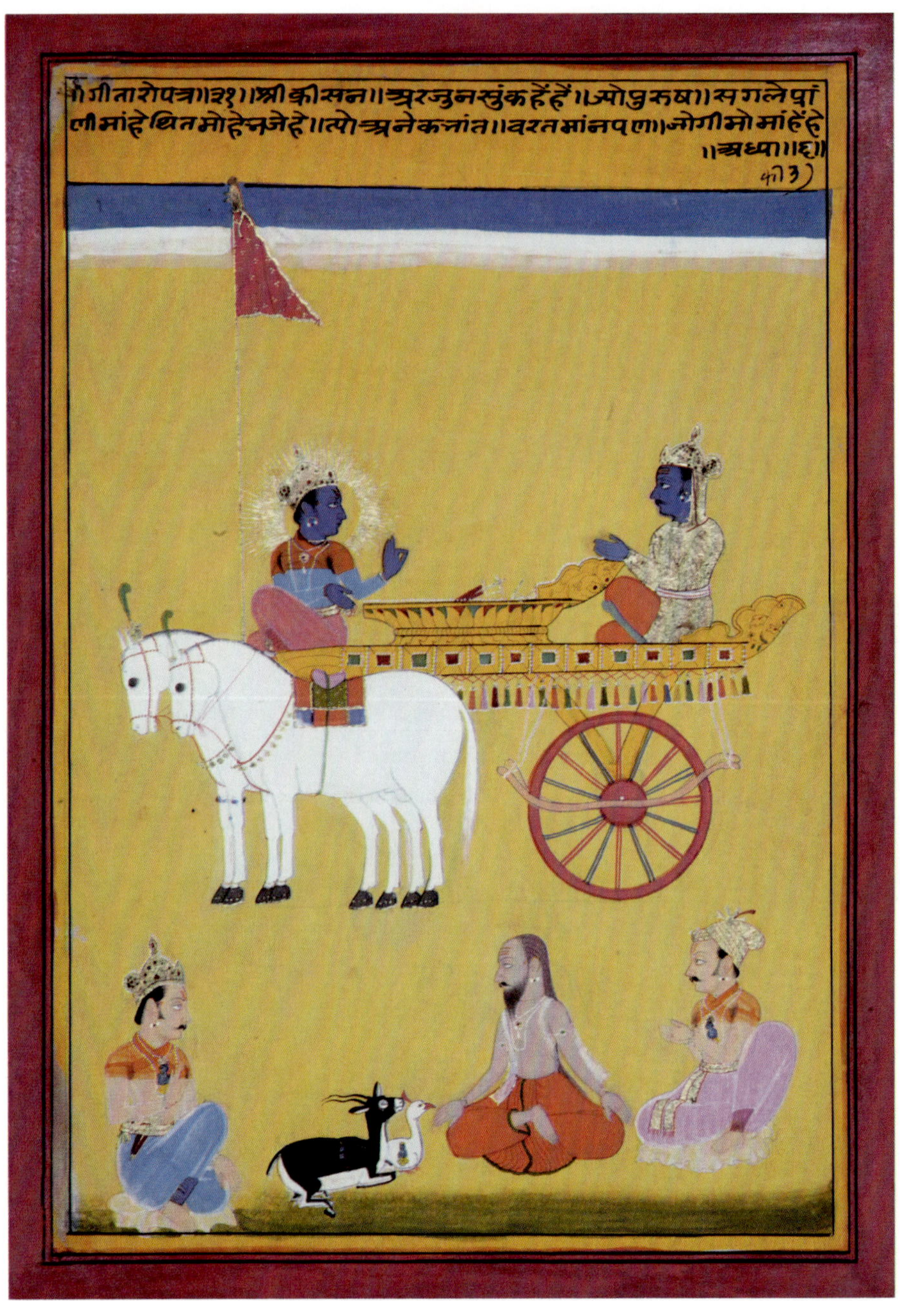

|31| श्री कृष्ण कहने लगे, हे अर्जुन! एकात्म भाव वाला जो मुझे सब प्राणियों में स्थित जानकर मेरा भजन करता है वह सभी प्रकार से वर्तमान में रहता है अर्थात मुझमें रहता है।

|31| Sri Krishna says: Hey Arjuna! The sage who sees unity in everything, who sees me in everything and chants my name, always lives in the present and so lives in me.

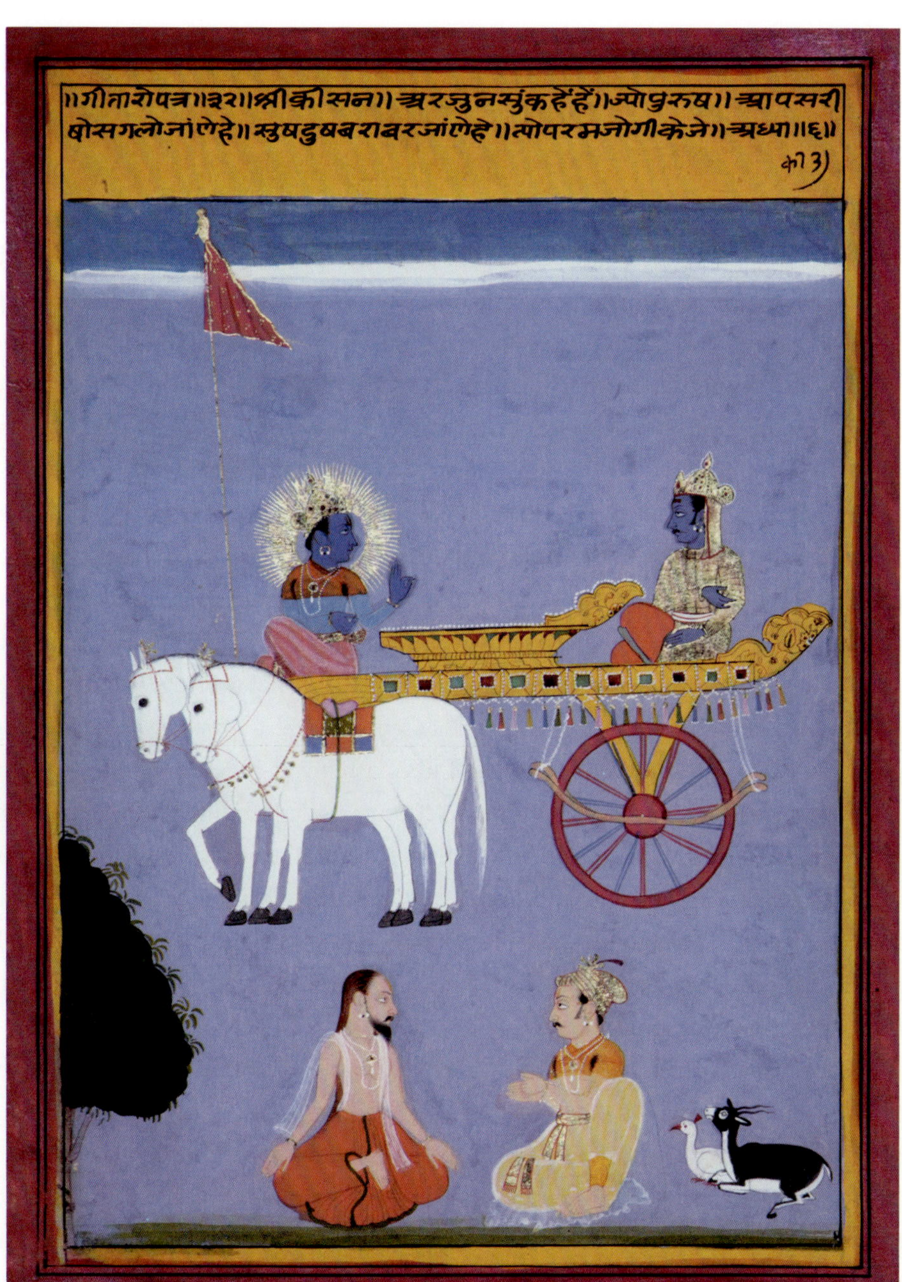

|32| श्री कृष्ण आगे समझाते हुए कहने लगे कि हे अर्जुन! जो अपने जैसा सभी को समझता है, सुख या दुख में समान रहता है, वही परमयोगी माना जाता है।

|32| Sri Krishna explains further: Hey Arjuna! The wisest yogi is the one who thinks that everyone, in joy or sorrow, is like himself.

Apology in which he called Socrates, a man of contemplative wisdom, a *karmavir*—a heroic warrior, a term he also used for Arjuna.

Arjuna must understand, as the yogi does, that an ethical action by a good person, has nothing to do with the salvation of the self because that is vanity; nor is it about the victory of a clan or faith because that would be sin; it certainly never has anything to do with the vengeful defilement of one's enemies because that would be folly. Right action is its own reward. This is why, as the yogi looks out of the cave to his right (verse 15), he sees a vision of himself sitting with his hands folded in humility before Krishna who has appeared on earth as an avatar. This process of self-knowing reaches its epiphanic moment in the painting for verse 30 where the yogi has understood his small human place in the cosmic process. Krishna is now beginning to acquire a larger visual presence. He is not yet the figure of awe (*vismaya*) he will become later. His appearance here is gentle, his manner kind. Dark-blue in colour, he kneels on the green earth amidst flowers. For the man, sitting before Krishna and talking to him, Krishna is still comprehensible; he can be addressed because he is still on our human side of language. It would be narcissism to assert that the yogi is one with the gods. In the *Mahabharata*, even Arjuna does not achieve that state. What the yogi has discovered is that the ordinary scale of his existence is his true manner of being in the world, and is sufficient. Here, in an act of genuine humility, a man shares the *darshan* granted to him by Krishna with a blackbuck (painting for verse 30). They are witnesses to the vision of Krishna; they can only offer the testimony of faith and not of reason. The visual paths of god, man and animal cross, and since they share the earth, together they offer an ideal vision of life. Of course, it is precisely this vision that the war threatens to wreck irrecoverably.

The paintings for verses 31 and 32 are luminous with the yellow light of the morning sun and gentle blue of spring. These sudden colours of joy are unexpected. Illumination comes at the most unexpected moments and unbidden; yet it only comes to the one who has prepared his soul to receive it. In the painting for verse 31, both the worshippers and the blackbuck and the white bird carry the image of Krishna in their hearts. The verse says: "The sage who realises the unity of life and who worships Me in all beings, lives in Me, whatever may be his lot" (Swami 45). The sage in both the paintings seems to tell those who care to listen about his singular and visionary experience. If they seek his guidance, all he can do is to repeat what Krishna says to Arjuna in the chariot above. And, perhaps, out of empathy for the seriousness of their quest, he can tell them of his own vision.

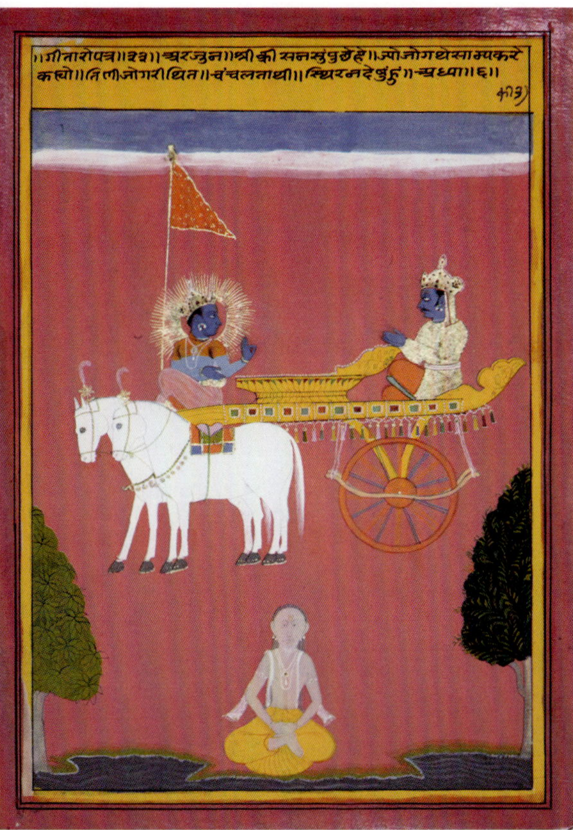

|33| तभी अर्जुन पूछने लगा कि हे कृष्ण! आपने समता योग बताया है पर मन की चंचलता के कारण मैं इसकी नित्य स्थिति को नहीं देख पा रहा हूँ।

|33| Then Arjuna asks: Hey Sri Krishna! You have told me everything about yoga. But since my mind is restless, I cannot see its foundation.

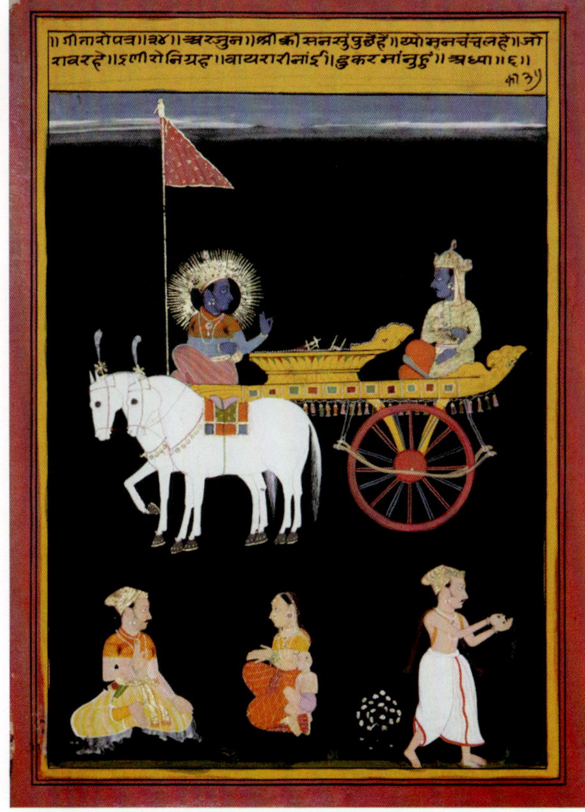

|34| तभी अर्जुन पूछने लगा कि हे कृष्ण! यह मन बड़ा चंचल है, बलवान है। मैं इसे रोकने का कार्य वायु को रोकने जितना दुष्कर मानता हूँ।

|34| Then Arjuna asks further: Hey Krishna! The mind is very restless and powerful. It is as difficult to control as it is difficult to control the wind.

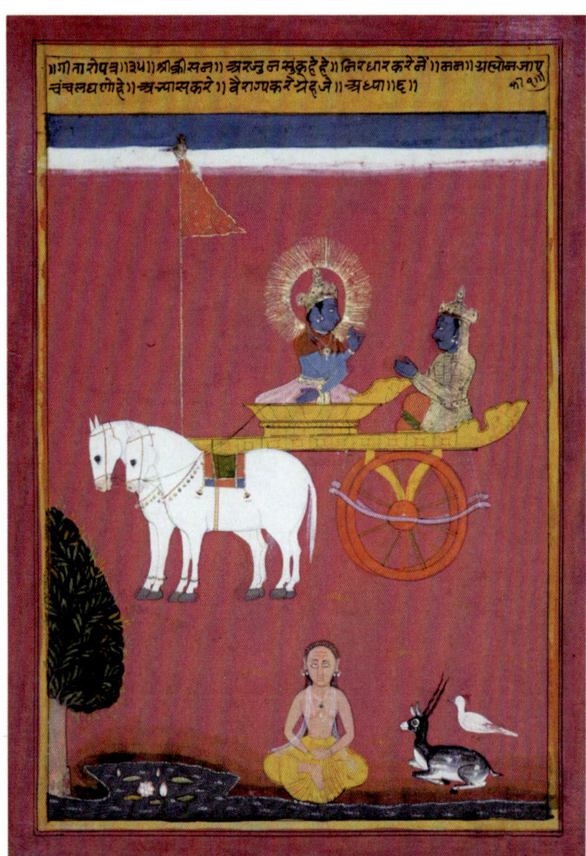

|35| श्री कृष्ण समझाते हुए कहने लगे कि हे अर्जुन! निस्संदेह मन चंचल है और इसको वश में रखना बड़ा कठिन है परन्तु अभ्यास और वैराग्य से इसे वश में किया जा सकता है।

|35| Sri Krishna replies: Hey Arjuna! No doubt your mind is restless, wayward. It is difficult to control it. But with practice and renunciation, it can done.

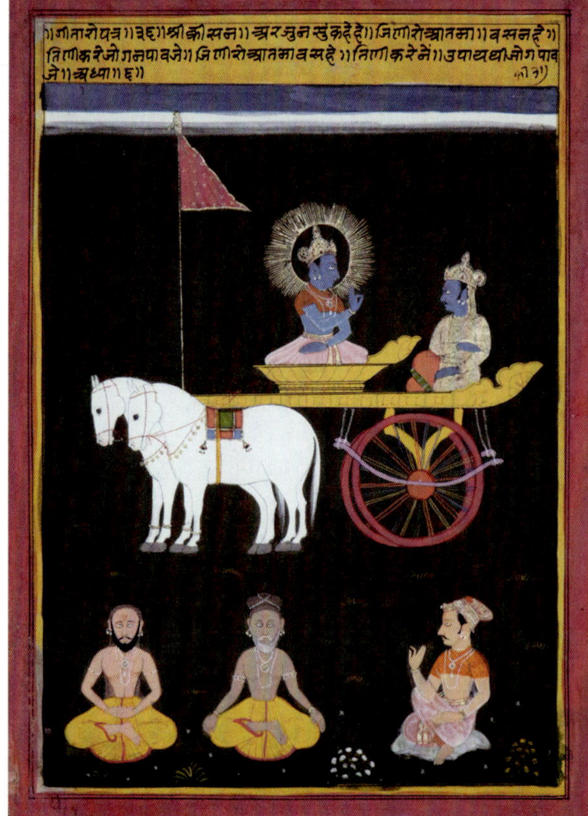

|36| श्री कृष्ण कहने लगे कि हे अर्जुन! जिसका मन संयमित नहीं, उसके लिए योग कठिन है किन्तु मन को वश में करने वाला इसे साधन द्वारा प्राप्त कर सकता है ऐसा मेरा मत है।

|36| Sri Krishna says: Hey Arjuna! Yoga is difficult for the one who has no self-control. But I believe that it is possible through constant practice and self-control.

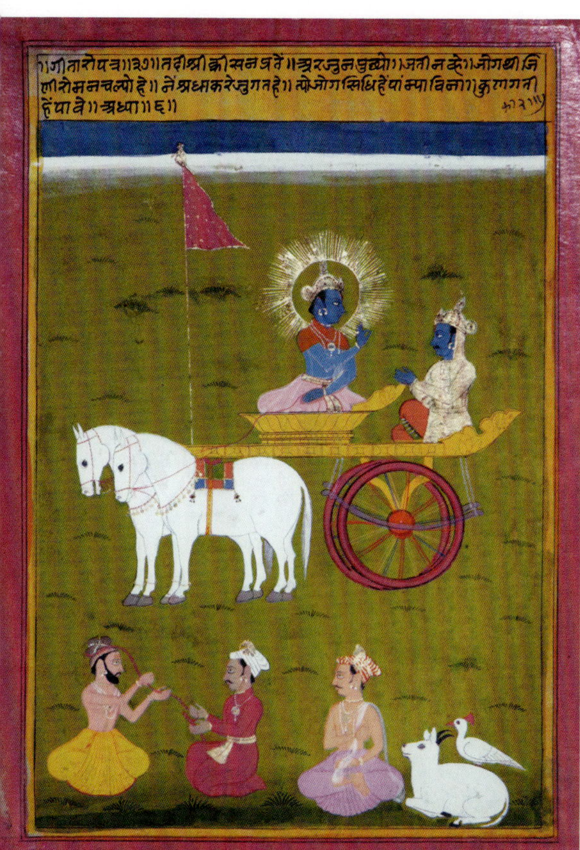

|37| अर्जुन मन की शंका दर्शाते पूछने लगा कि हे कृष्ण! श्रद्धावान होते हुए भी जो संयमी नहीं है, जिसका मन योग से विचलित हो गया है, तब वह योग सिद्धि न प्राप्त कर फिर कौन-सी गति को प्राप्त होता है?

|37| Arjuna, still full of doubt, asks: Hey Sri Krishna! What can a man do who has faith but no self-control; whose restless mind has wandered away from yoga?

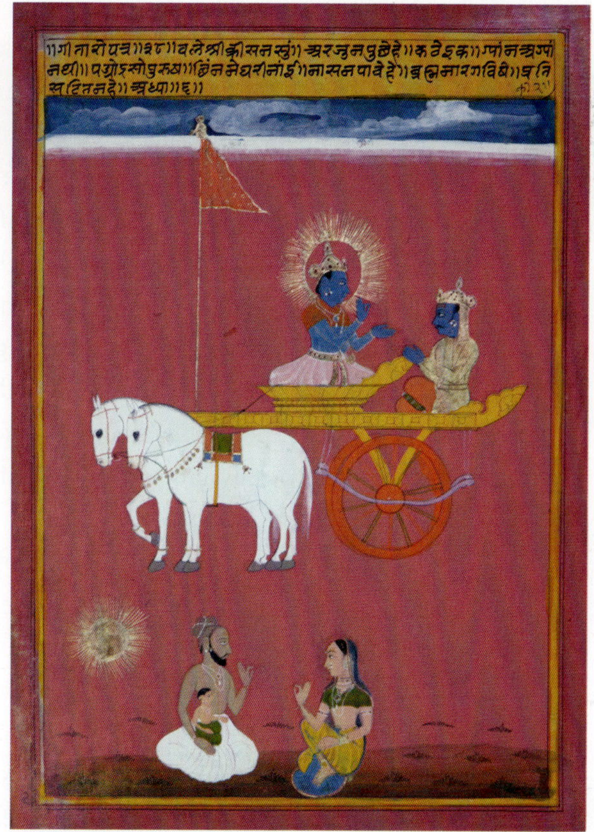

|38| अर्जुन ने आगे पूछा, हे कृष्ण! क्या ब्रह्ममार्ग से भ्रमित और अस्थिर पुरुष, छिन्न-भिन्न बादलों की तरह दोनों ओर से भ्रष्ट होकर नष्ट तो नहीं हो जाता?

|38| Arjuna further asks: Hey Sri Krishna! Is the one who has wandered off the path to Brahma, whose mind is scattered like a cloud, not destroyed?

One should note that the yogi in the paintings for verses 31 and 32 is not the youthful one we had seen in earlier paintings. There his body was erect like a steady flame. Now, it is the colour of grey ash, his hair is thin and hangs loose on his shoulders; his face has acquired the sad maturity of age and knowledge. If he is truly the man of wisdom who has seen Krishna in a vision, then he knows that he may never again be so blessed. To be truly at peace, he must accept that the vision of the divine is always fleeting. It is after all not the mission of the divine to be always available, whenever called; that is the groundless hope of those who have not understood. It is, therefore, visually appropriate that another yogi (paintings for verses 33-39) finds himself at a river bank mediating in the hope of gaining a vision of Krishna. The river is, perhaps, the same, but time has flown by. The trees on the river bank are darker with the shadows of age.

In these paintings, the cycle of leaving behind the days of family and society begins again for other men. If in one painting, a man is troubled by the fickleness of his mind and the unruliness of his heart, in another a yogi struggles with his thoughts protected by a blackbuck and a white bird. This sequence comes to a close in the painting for verse 39. The background is the deepest blue-black; the colour has an uncanny authority. It promises the end of the old time of uncertainty and the beginning of a new time of enlightened thought. Arjuna falls at Krishna's feet requesting him to finally clarify all his doubts because no one else can; to be assured, as Plato says in *Apology*, "that no evil can happen to a good man, either in life or in death" (Desai 237). Has the old yogi, who sits still beside a river, attained this knowledge? His body is shrivelled; his hair has turned white. Yet, his body glows with a bright inner light; the sun shines close to where he sits, illuminating his entire being.

The irony is that, if one thinks about the end of the *Mahabharata*, it is Arjuna, the principal listener of Krishna's song, who forgets it soon after the war. And, of course, there is no return; only another effort. Krishna preaches the *Gita* again, but its emphasis is different and its *dhvani* is not the same.

The paintings for verses 40 to 44 follow Krishna's account of a man who has lived a life of thoughtful regard for others while being detached from his own interests, but who is unable to find his eternal refuge among the gods. Krishna says that the life of such a man is not disciplined enough or disinterested enough. He shall, therefore, be reborn but in a morally upright, learned and prosperous family. People shall look up to him as a righteous man who now walks along the path to the divine. He shall never fall back into a life of selfish decrepitude; each step he takes, in every rebirth, shall be a

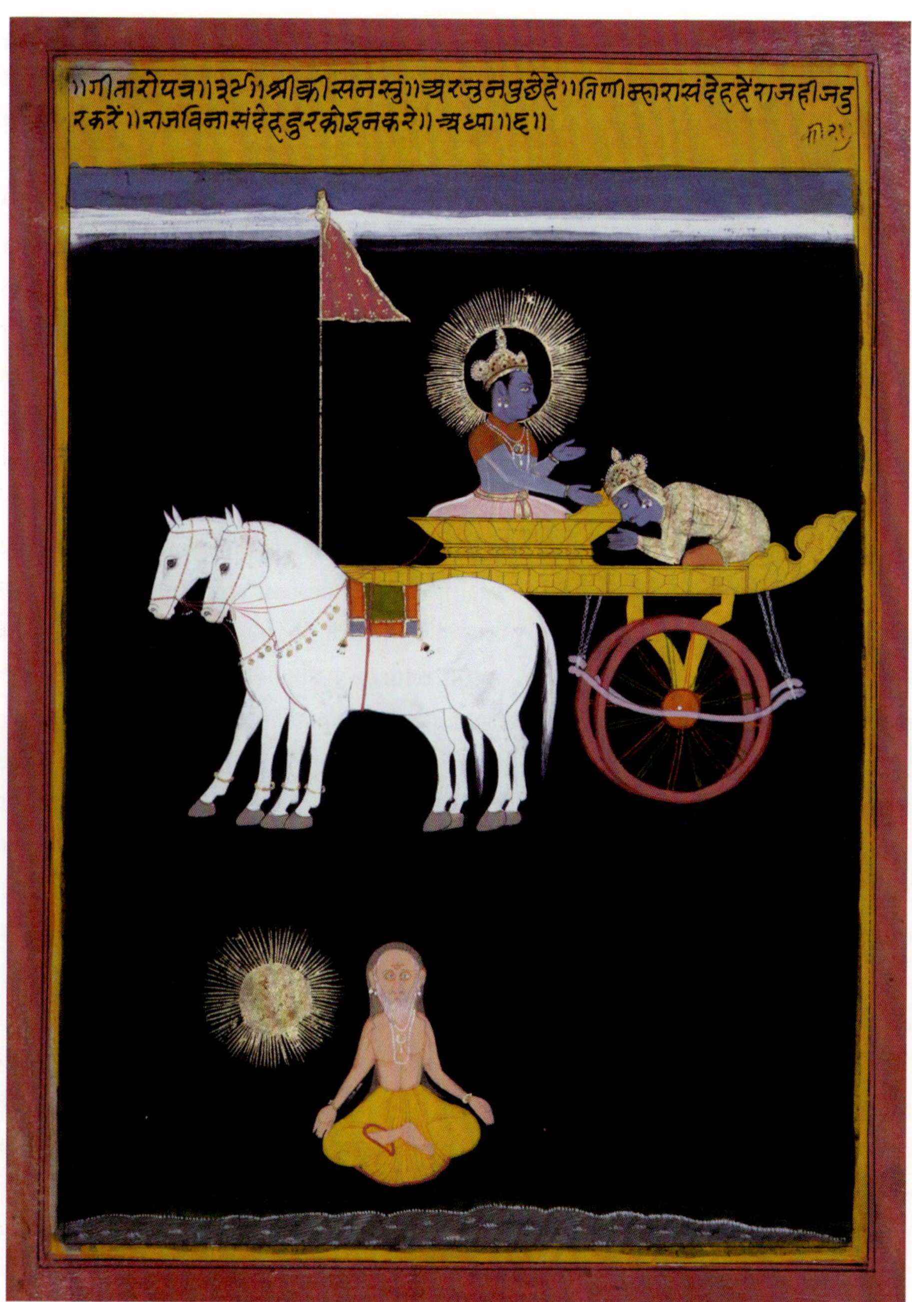

|39| अर्जुन आगे पूछने लगा कि हे कृष्ण! मेरे इस संशय को दूर करने में एक आप ही समर्थ हैं क्योंकि आपके अलावा दूसरा कोई इस संशय को दूर नहीं कर सकता।

|39| Arjuna also asks: Hey Sri Krishna! You are the only one who can dispel my doubt. There is no one else who can banish it.

step in 'pilgrim time' and toward the sacred. Thus, in the painting for verse 40, the yogi, whom the artist regards as such a man, is shown to be on two planes simultaneously. He is a flesh and blood man sitting on green earth. But, he is also on a soul-propelled flying boat, shaped like a green bird, above the ground and out of the constricting frames of time and space; a 'sky-rower' moving toward paradise.

The earth-bound yogi sits in deep mediation with his eyes closed. The bright yellow of his clothes is the first to catch the eye before one looks up toward the presence of Krishna with his golden halo. The yogi is oblivious to the presence of the two men sitting on either side of him seeking his attention or telling him stories of their sorrow. One is a prince with a golden crown and clothes woven out of gold and silk; the other a commoner wearing an ordinary turban and dress whose red colour is barely noticeable against the pink background. The two are representatives of the social and the political order of the time of the yogi and the artist. Perhaps, the yogi has had the experience and knowledge of the temptations of wealth and the despair of poverty. He seems to have now made, in the quietude of his soul, a disciplined resolve to be emotionally disengaged from both. Henceforth, his life-history shall be the contrary of the emotionally entangled stories of the heroes of the *Mahabharata* who escape from one worldly labyrinth, one nightmare of desire or power, only to be lost in another. Even if the yogi does not attain nirvana in this life, he shall not regard his life on earth as a curse, but see it as another chance to make, through sustained effort, his way to eternity. This is what Krishna says shall happen when people, weaving his moral counsel into the fabric of their lives, strive toward wisdom. The yogi sits between three speakers: a noble man, an ordinary man and god. He listens to all three with equanimity, and then, as the painting shows, makes his way to eternity.

The painting for verse 41 creates an earthly space where the yogi is reborn after having lived a good and disciplined life among the pure and the righteous. The painting's lower half, depicting life in time, is fragmented and crowded with ordinary people, families, houses, kings and animals, yet it retains its vibrancy and charm. The use of bright colours and lively images suggests that the life of the man represented is a blessing. He is an example, as Krishna says, of a kind man who shall not endure suffering because he has, in his previous birth, achieved knowledge and the blessing of the gods. His spiritual journey begins from the lower margin where a youthful drummer, sitting on green grass outside a house, announces, joyously, the birth of a child. The child grows up in a simple unadorned home. The walls of the house are a vivid red. He is taught by his father and cared for by his mother. There is a decorated white elephant in the lower

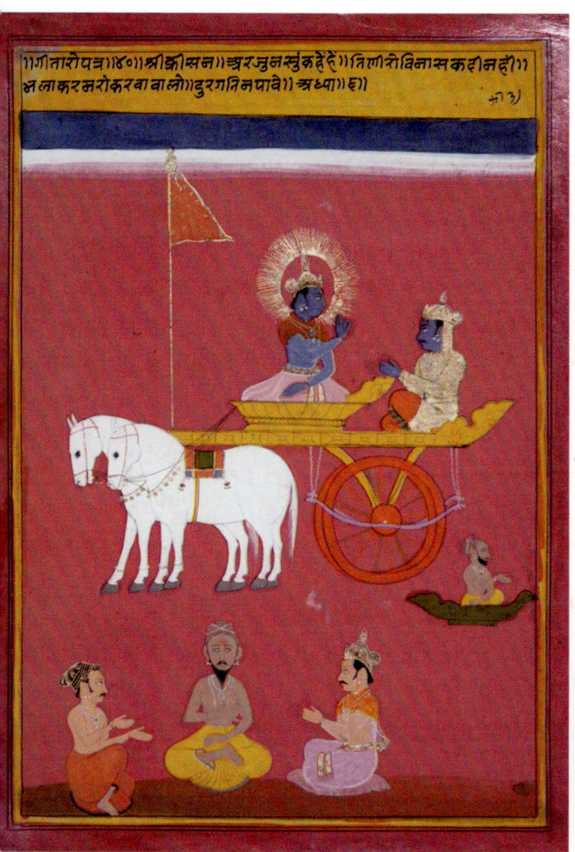

|40| श्री कृष्ण तब कहने लगे, हे अर्जुन! उसका न तो इस लोक में न परलोक में ही विनाश होता है क्योंकि कल्याण प्राप्ति के लिए कर्म करने वाला कभी दुर्गति को प्राप्त नहीं होता।

|40| Then Sri Krishna says: Hey Arjuna! The one whose actions are righteous never comes to a sad end; he is neither destroyed in this world nor in the next.

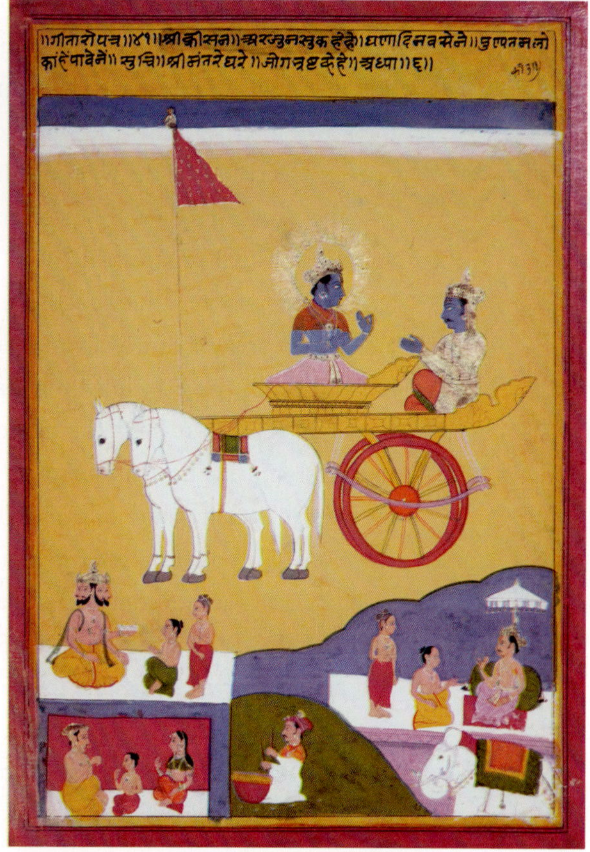

|41| श्री कृष्ण आगे कहने लगे कि योग भ्रष्ट पुरुष, पुण्य लोकों को प्राप्त कर अनेक वर्षों तक वहाँ निवास कर फिर वह पवित्र पुरुषों के घर में जन्म लेता है।

|41| Sri Krishna further says: A person who fails to achieve yogic perfection lives for many years in world of the righteous. He is then reborn in the house of those who are pure.

right corner. Is the presence of the elephant a reminder of the auspicious birth of the Buddha? Like the Buddha, has the child come with a long history of endeavour to live by the code of dharma? Such transcendence was promised by the image of the yogi in a soul-boat flying out of the constraints of time and space in the previous painting. The child's progress towards knowledge is indicated in the next pictorial frame on the right. It shows a mature and confident young man, dressed in the saffron robes of a savant, who is sitting before a benevolent king under a white parasol. The king's right hand is held up in a gesture of peace. His throne is set against a blue hill, suggesting that the kingdom is under the grace of a blue god. The boy's spiritual journey upward toward enlightenment is marked by his presence in the next space on the left where he kneels, with folded hands, before the four-headed Brahma who is instructing him about the life of the spirit, about dharma. As is common in these paintings, Brahma is reading the Vedas and the story of Rama, the archetype of a good man. Krishna's chariot is suffused by the pale yellow light of the sun. The colours that distinguish each space in the moral pilgrimage of the boy shine with their own internal light. The whole composition, illuminating the abstract poetics of Krishna, is the work of a highly charged imagination.

The painting for verse 42 continues the parable about a virtuous man and his spiritual progress. It shows a group of children as they watch in amazement another child practise an extreme form of yoga. These children are not the seekers of the divine; they will soon be lost in the shadows of life and time. The boy, however, tests his own spiritual attainment as he hangs upside-down from the branch of a tall tree. His hands are folded in prayer and his body is surrounded by a ring of fire. As each day goes by, their innocent vision of life shall be erased by the turmoil of common emotions. Only a select few, Krishna has just told Arjuna, shall recall a time when heaven was not some other place, and the *gunas* of Brahma were also the qualities of all earth's creatures. Since, our mind creates its own heaven and hell, it is always possible to remain disinterested in victory or defeat. One should add that, while the *Gita* never rejects asceticism, its purpose is to urge a life of ethical, unselfish and ahimsic action for the salvation of the self and the earth.

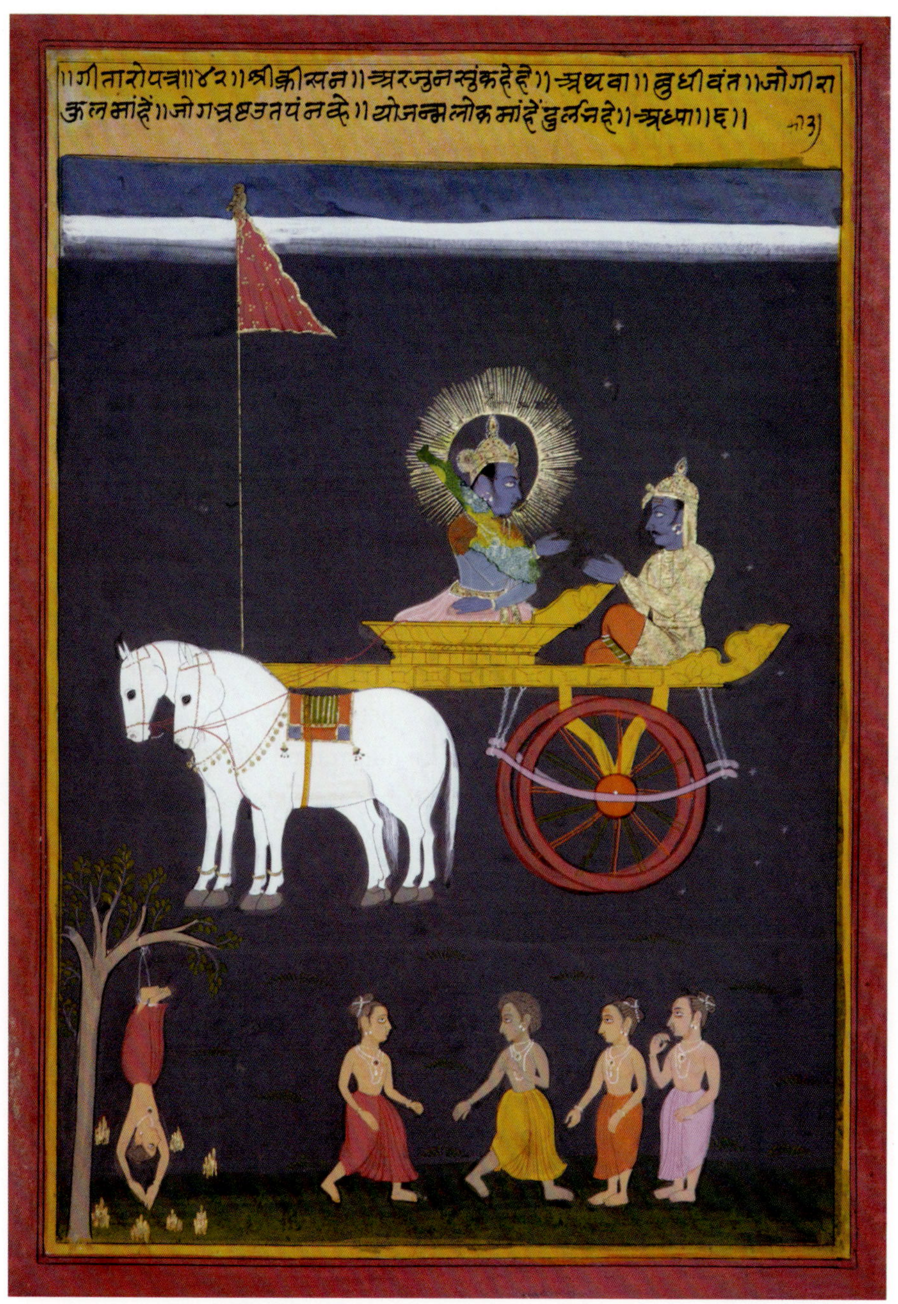

|42| श्री कृष्ण तब कहने लगे कि हे अर्जुन! अथवा वह अत्यंत बुद्धिमान योगियों के कुल में जन्म लेता है। निस्संदेह इस संसार में ऐसा जन्म मिलना अत्यंत दुर्लभ है।

|42| Sri Krishna then says: Hey Arjuna! Or he is born in the family of those who are very wise. Of course, to be born in such a family is extremely difficult in this world.

Since the boy is visually placed below Hanuman on the chariot's pole far above the limit of the sky, one can suggest that both are mirror reflections of each other; examples of unquestioning devotion to the divine. Only such a supplicant, Krishna indicates throughout this chapter, will reside permanently with the sky-gods; others may be granted fleeting visions of the holy in each of their successive births, but they shall have to return to their human forms and try again, with even greater rigour, to work their way through bhakti to paradise.

The painting for verse 44 shows that the life-cycle of the man Allah Baksh has been tracing in his illustrations for this chapter is now nearing liberation or enlightenment (*moksha*). The yogi is old. His face is tranquil. He sits with the spiritual sun beside him illuminating his journey through another birth. "After millions of years and thousands of births, he [the yogi] arrives at the shore of Self-realisation" (*Jnaneshwari* 1: 171). The earth is now covered with fresh blades of grass as a sign of a new spiritual resurgence. Krishna looks radiant as he sits on his golden lotus seat close to Arjuna. The paintings for this chapter end on a note of hope and the promise of advancement on the path to enlightenment for the yogi and, by implication, Arjuna.

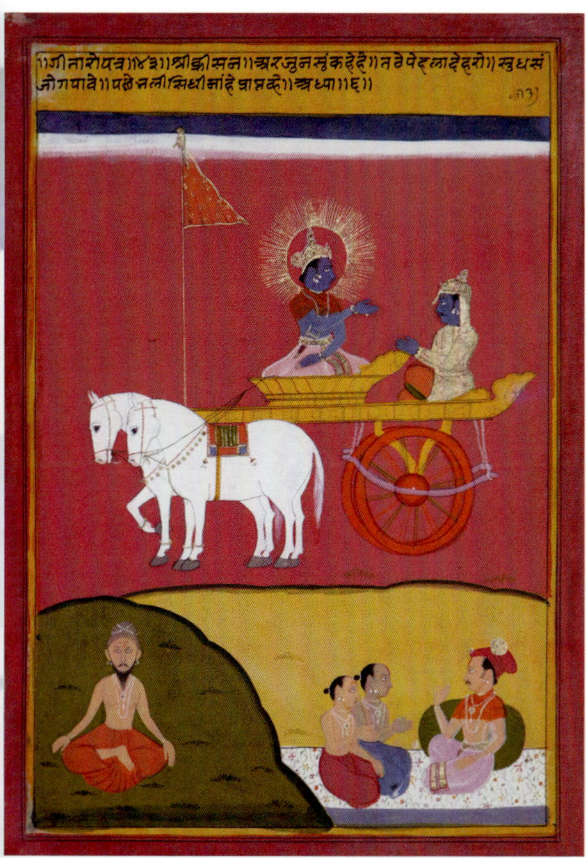

|43| श्री कृष्ण कहने लगे, हे अर्जुन! वहाँ वह अपने बुद्धि योग के पहले जन्म के संस्कारों को फिर से प्राप्त कर लेता है और इससे आगे वह फिर सिद्धि पाने का प्रयत्न करता है।

|43| Sri Krishna says: Hey Arjuna! There he regains the intellectual stage he had achieved in his previous birth and strives further to achieve perfection.

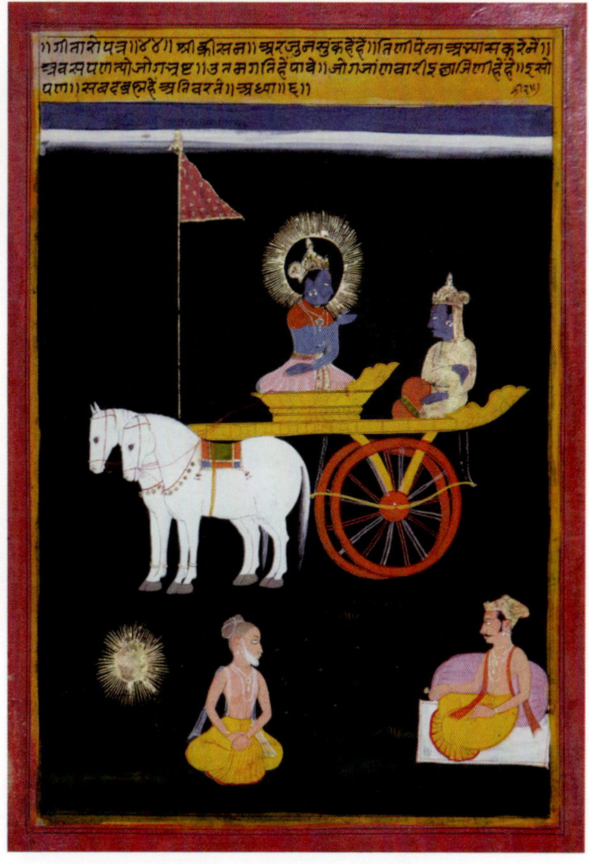

|44| श्री कृष्ण आगे बताने लगे कि जो पूर्व के अभ्यास के कारण न चाहते हुए भी योग की ओर आकर्षित होता है, ऐसा जिज्ञासु योगी शास्त्रों के नियमों से परे पहुँच जाता है।

|44| Sri Krishna further tells him: A man who practised yoga in his previous birth is irresistibly drawn toward it even if he does not want to be; such a seeker of knowledge goes beyond Vedic rules.

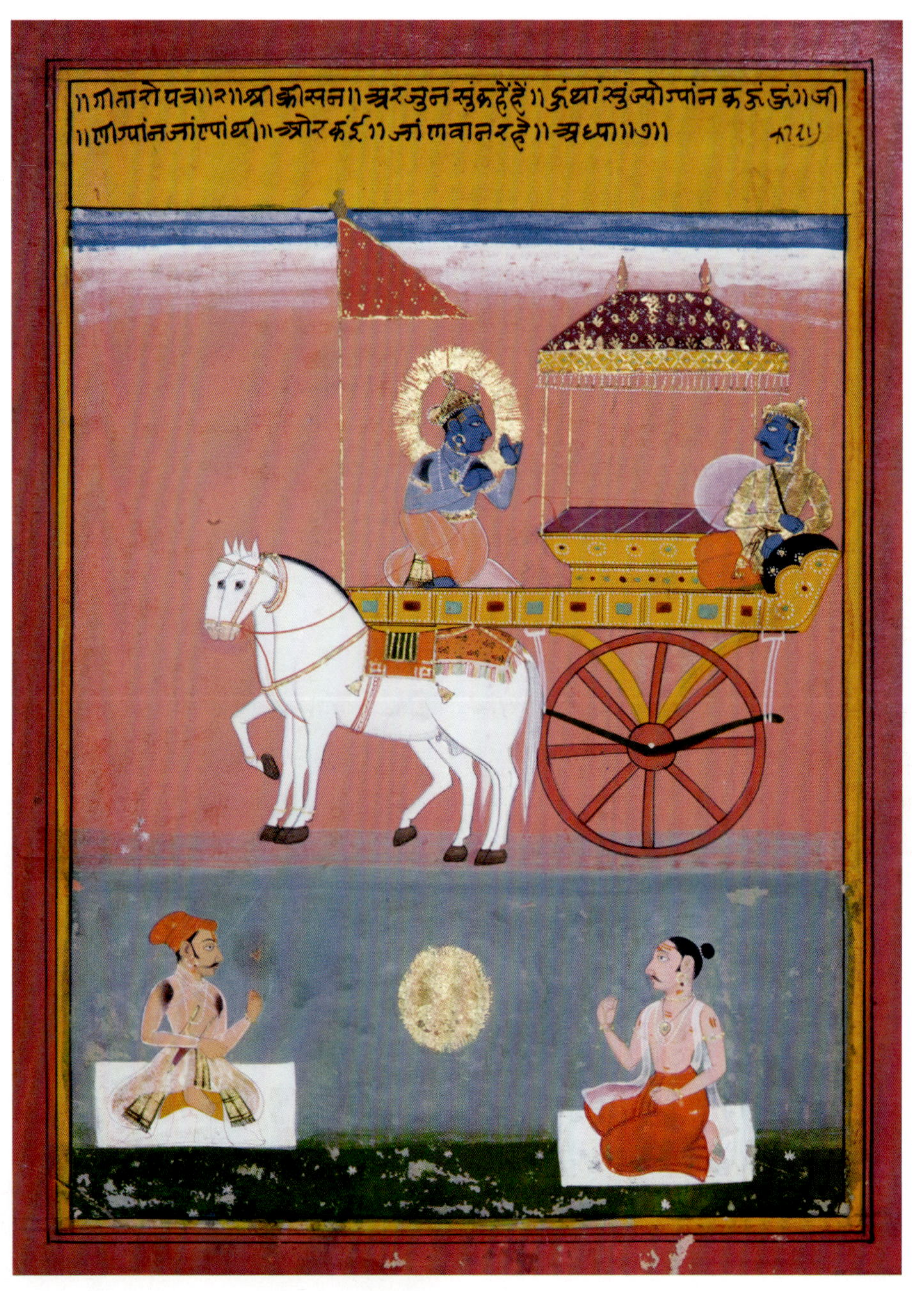

|2| श्री कृष्ण कह रहे हैं हे अर्जुन! अब जो मैं तुझसे ज्ञान कह रहा हूँ। उस ज्ञान को जानने के बाद और कुछ जानने को नहीं रह जाएगा। इसके सहारे तू मुझे भी पूर्णतया समझ जाएगा।

|2| Sri Krishna says: Hey Arjuna! The knowledge I am now going to reveal to you is complete. Once you understand it there will be nothing more left for you to know. With its aid you will also know me completely.

CHAPTER 7

In this chapter, the familiar idiom of a dialogue between two friends is gradually replaced by a more mystically inflected idiom. The tone also changes. Attention shifts away from a critique of past philosophic assumptions about knowledge and experience, the self and the not-self,[1] to the visionary awakening of the self. Instead of conveying anxiety, the verses are more ecstatic, heightened and charged with a feeling that something momentous is about to revealed; intimations of Being can now be heard with greater insistence. Of course, Krishna does not yet reveal his divinity, but it is clear that he is preparing Arjuna for a unique revelation.[2] But then, Krishna rarely identifies himself as divine in these initial chapters of the *Gita*. Only in Chapter 10 verse 39 does he acknowledge in passing that among the Vrishnis he is known as Vishnu. Later, in Chapter 11, Arjuna recognises him twice as an avatar of Vishnu.[3]

Arjuna has to be prepared to receive such knowledge; he must draw upon all the resources of his being—his knowledge (of the scriptures and yoga) and his disciplined past (as a warrior)—to accept the personal, social and moral responsibilities that come with the understanding of Krishna's holy presence. Indeed, the burden of Krishna's song is that while many human beings strive, often diligently and sincerely, to comprehend him and his divinity, only the rarest can understand it. Krishna, however, does begin to prepare the ground for understanding—the word 'ground' is appropriate since the revelation will be in historical time and its witness will be a mortal being. Kurukshetra will become, for the briefest moment, a place where eternity intersects with time.

The dramatic vignettes illustrating verse 2 evoke two related, but complex, feelings. One: our natural world is interfused with the holy. Two: amongst the seekers of the divine only those who are disciplined and capable of the greatest striving can apprehend it and achieve liberation. Others—rishis, ascetics or readers of scriptures—shall forever search, from age to age, and birth to birth, for an answer to

1 Desai insists that, to understand these verses, one does not have to be familiar with samkhya, *The Gospel of Selfless Action,* p. 241.

2 See J. A. B. van Buitenen, "Introduction," *The Bhagavadgita in the Mahabharata* (Chicago: University of Chicago Press, 1981), p. 12.

3 See van Buitenen, *The Bhagavadgita,* p. 27.

the question which, as Hamlet says, "puzzles the will" and not find it. They will never understand how the mundane itself can be a place of vision; how the words they have read before resonate with memories of older prophetic voices and future promises; how holiness can glow quietly out of lake-water like lotus flowers. Astute as usual, Gandhi hears behind Krishna's sad recognition of how difficult the path to salvation is, the voice of another teacher, another seeker: "Hard it is to be born a man; hard it is to live like one; hard likewise to hear the Right Law said: and rare is the birth of the Awakened" (*Dhammapada*).[4]

In the painting, a brahmin, with all the holy signs and emblems, sits meditating on a river bank. The scene is beautiful and peaceful. A golden sun glows in the blue water as if a supernal power has been incarnated in the natural world. Reading the image symbolically, one can say that just as the sun in the sky is reflected in the river, knowledge of the divine illuminates the mind of man. But, ironically, the brahmin is oblivious to this revelation of divine beauty visible even to ordinary perception. Instead, he is in conversation with a prince sitting at the opposite end. The prince holds a yellow flower in his hand. Unlike Arjuna, who is so puzzled and distressed by the potential for violence in life that he has put his weapons aside, the prince is armed with a dagger in his cummerbund. The concerns of the brahmin and the prince seem to be entirely worldly. Together they are the dyads of state-power and institutional religiosity, but not of enlightenment. Are they discussing political strategies or abstract philosophy? Visually they are so far apart that they cannot be conducting any meaningful dialogue. It is as if one can debate samkhya or yogic practice endlessly without noticing the mysterious gracefulness of the living earth. What Krishna demands in these verses is neither aesthetic appreciation of nature's beauty nor aggressive statecraft, but concentrated attention on every element in the universe so that one sees oneself as part of the holy ritual he enacts: "Earth, water, fire, air, ether, mind, intellect, and personality; this is the eightfold division of My Manifest Nature…my Superior Nature is the very Life which sustains the universe" (Swami 47).

The painting for verse 3 is ironic. It shows two groups of religious disputants. Both seemingly believe that the burden of human sorrow can be resolved by verbal or physical victories; that moral virtue can be established either by the power of rhetoric or the sharp edge of a sword. Indeed, it is the burden of Plato's *Gorgias* and *Apology* to show the folly of verbal jousting and the vanity of war; both are morally vacuous and

---

4 Quoted in Desai, *The Gospel of Selfless Action*, p. 241.

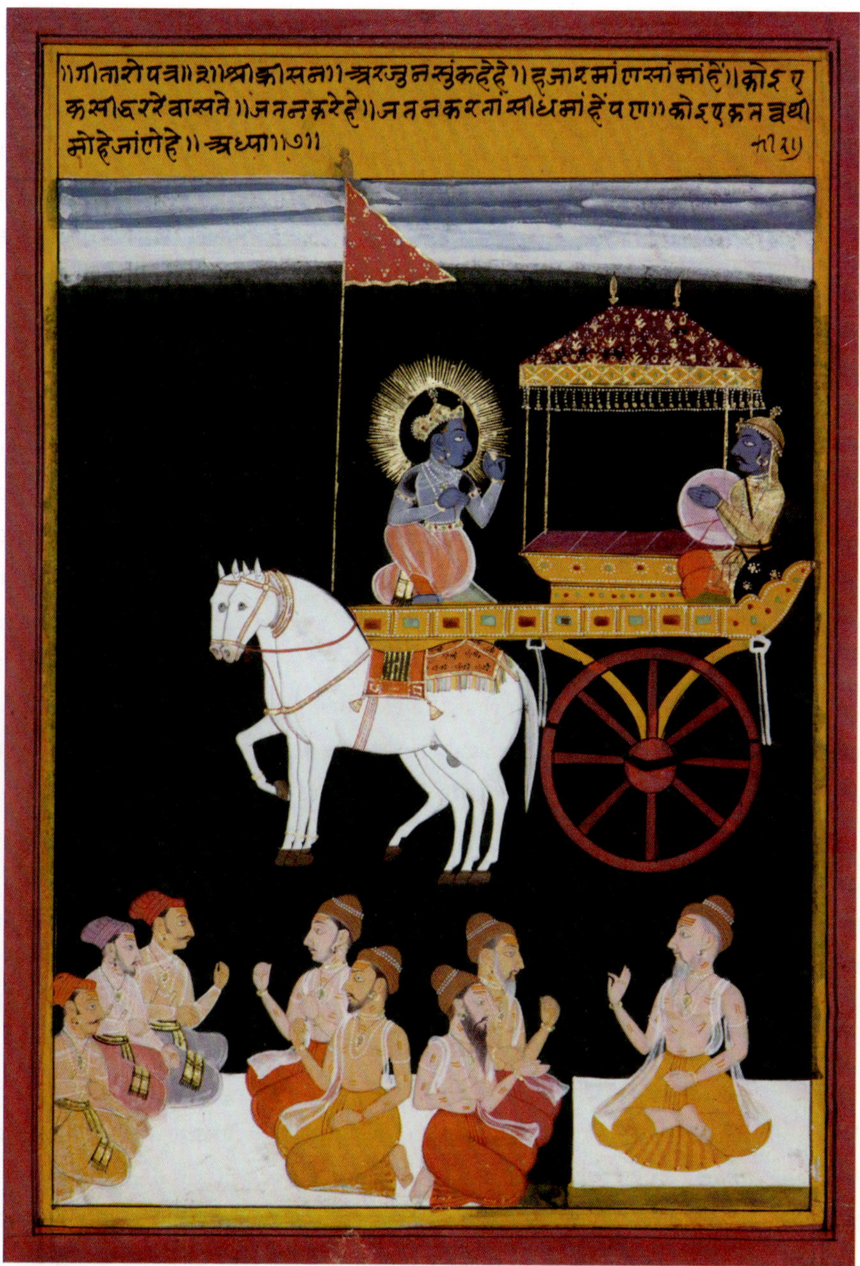

|3| श्री कृष्ण कहने लगे कि हे अर्जुन! हजारों मनुष्यों में से कोई एक योग-सिद्धि प्राप्ति के लिए यत्न करता है और ऐसे सिद्धि प्राप्त सफल पुरुषों में से कोई एक विरला मुझे तत्व से जान पाता है।

|3| Sri Krishna says: Hey Arjuna! One among thousands of human beings strives to achieve the perfection of yoga. And of the few who succeed, maybe one knows my reality.

can only lead to a spiritual cul-de-sac. The narcissism of small differences, Freud tells us, is the cause of profound emotional discontent and leads to annihilatory wars.

Both the aggressive groups have the outward signs of ritual earnestness. They perform the prescribed rites; sit in appropriate yogic postures or in silent spaces without distractions. Their clothes, beards and ages show that they belong to different sects and have participated in similar arguments often. The scene is noisy; the gestures of each have the sharpness of sectarian righteousness. The *Gita*, if anything, is non-sectarian. The burden of verses 4 to 10 is that every spark of light emerges from the original source of fire.[5]

How different these debaters of religious doctrines are from Arjuna's attentive devotion! How far superior is Krishna's discourse from their vain piety! However, despite the ironic criticism of religious discourses, the background colour of deep green mixed with black does not indicate despondency. Instead, it makes Krishna, Arjuna, the white horses, the purple canopy and the yellow chariot radiate with nobility and gracefulness.

In fact, the chariot's site in these paintings is above and separate from the ordinary and secular space below, indicating that the two belong to radically different orders of understanding. Allah Baksh, once again, creates a sense of hierarchical separation between the earthly and the divine. The images and colours suggest a qualitative change in the relation between Krishna and Arjuna. Krishna does not sit in close proximity to Arjuna. What he says no longer has the intimacy of a friend, but the formality of a teacher. As he looks back to talk to Arjuna, his right hand is placed on his heart while his left hand is held up in the mudra of blessing and instruction. Arjuna is a curious but startled listener, still unsure of what he will be told. Seated, he listens intently with folded hands as Krishna's teaching increasingly takes on the form of a special benediction and revelation.

Krishna's firm rejection of ritualism in verse 4 (along with the dry scholasticism of the commentators) is also reflected in the painting. Krishna tells Arjuna that he is earth, water, fire and wind. To notice such things means that ordinary people can apprehend the divine in the sensible world without rituals, gurus, esoteric yoga or scriptures. It is, thus, possible to read the human figures in this painting as the artist's ironic response to religious rituals performed for the fulfilment of personal desire, forgetting repeated injunctions against seeking rewards. A woman reads the

5 See van Buitenen, *The Bhagavadgita*, pp. 24-26.

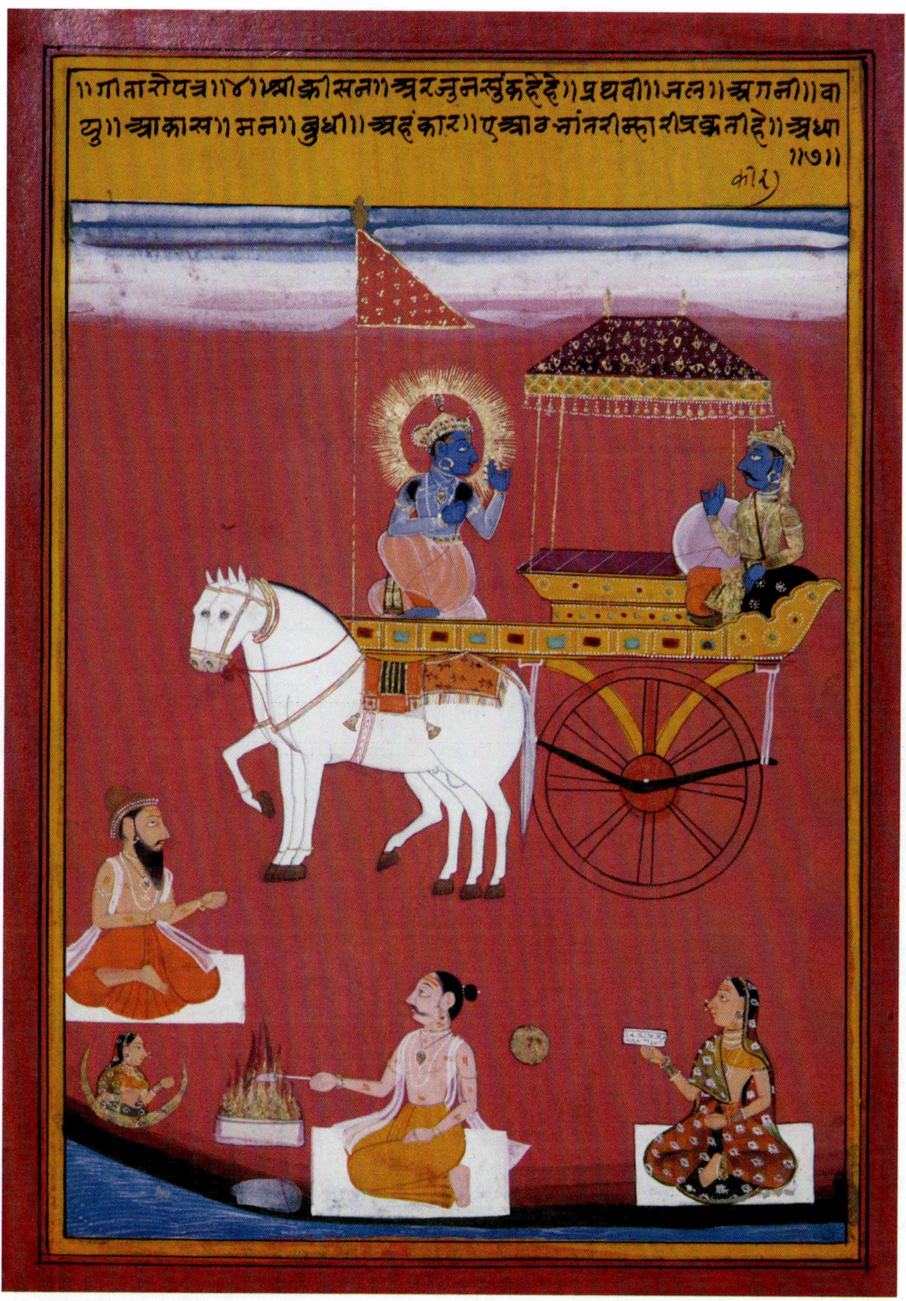

|4| श्री कृष्ण आगे कहने लगे कि हे अर्जुन! पृथ्वी, जल, अग्नि, वायु, आकाश, मन, बुद्धि और अहंकार- ये आठ प्रकार की मेरी प्रकृति है।

|4| Sri Krishna further says: Hey Arjuna! My material nature has eight parts: earth, water, fire, air, sky, mind, intellect and ego.

Ramayana for no recognisable purpose. Does she read it mechanically as a magical mantra? Does she not see the beauty of the river nearby as she chants the *Ramayana*? Self-absorbed, does she not notice, that with every return of the sun, the earth changes radically, and that it requires a renewed effort, a new beginning? Will she ever know that her own moral history is, as Krishna says, part of the world's ecology? To read and recite scriptures is of limited value, especially if the aim is to win god's grace. Indeed, as the Puranic story of the Asura, Hiranyakashipu, shows, scriptural piety may win the favour of gods for a specific desire and a limited time, but does not lead to *moksha*. Is not the aim of Krishna's teaching to help Arjuna cleanse the self and act without desire for power, revenge, or vanity?

The paintings for verses 4 and 6 deepen Allah Baksh's understanding of what Krishna means when he says that knowledge and action, free from all motives, should be the only ground of any religious beseeching. Mere ritualism or desire, he repeats, is the contrary of holiness. Priestly offerings by the privileged to persuade the gods to grant their wishes are signs of hubris and ignorance; they are also the causes of sectarian strife. T. S. Eliot is right when, meditating on the *Gita* and the Bible, he concludes: "The only wisdom we can hope to acquire/ is the wisdom of humility; humility is endless."[6]

Sitting near the woman, a priest performs a fire-ritual to appease the gods instead of working his way towards salvation. The priest does not realise that the crescent moon with a goddess floating near him is all the benediction he needs. He thinks he is conducting a prescribed fire-sacrifice; but an imaginative man knows, as Heraclitus says, that it is god who actually lights the fire.[7] Similarly, a visionary notices, that since each ripple in a river is a crescent moon with a goddess, its protection would lead him to infinity.

The painter's critical treatment of the ceremonies of priests, who seem oblivious of the profundity of Krishna's discourse, is neither contemptuous nor superior. He knows that irony is an instrument of moral correction; scorn is an ethical error. Krishna is often ironic about rites and scriptural recitation but never scornful; they may be futile, but they lay a foundation of knowledge from which men can work toward their liberation—even if it takes them "many lives" to do so (Swami 48). After all, he is a keen observer of human fearfulness which makes men clutch and defend what they have acquired. There is irony in his attempt to avert a war because he knows that the

---

6 Eliot, "East Cocker," *Four Quartets*, (London: Faber and Faber, 1944), p. 27.

7 Frye, *Words with Power*, p. 85.

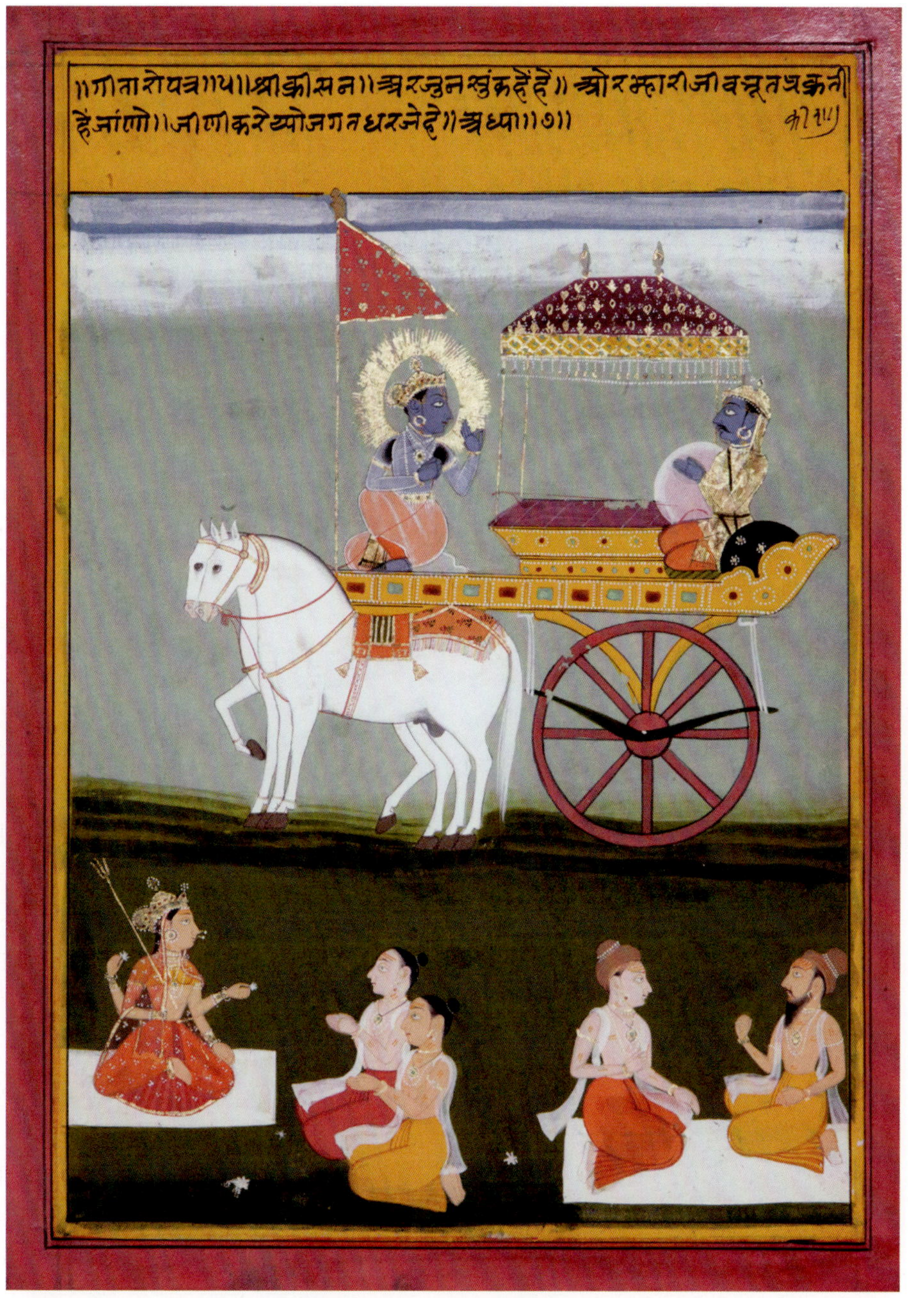

|5| हे अर्जुन! यह तो मेरी अपरा प्रकृति है, इसके अतिरिक्त परा प्रकृति को अलग से जान, जो जीवरूप है जिसके सहारे मुझसे यह जगत धारण किया जाता है।

|5| Hey Arjuna! This is my inferior nature. Apart from that know my superior nature too which is the life-force that sustains the world.

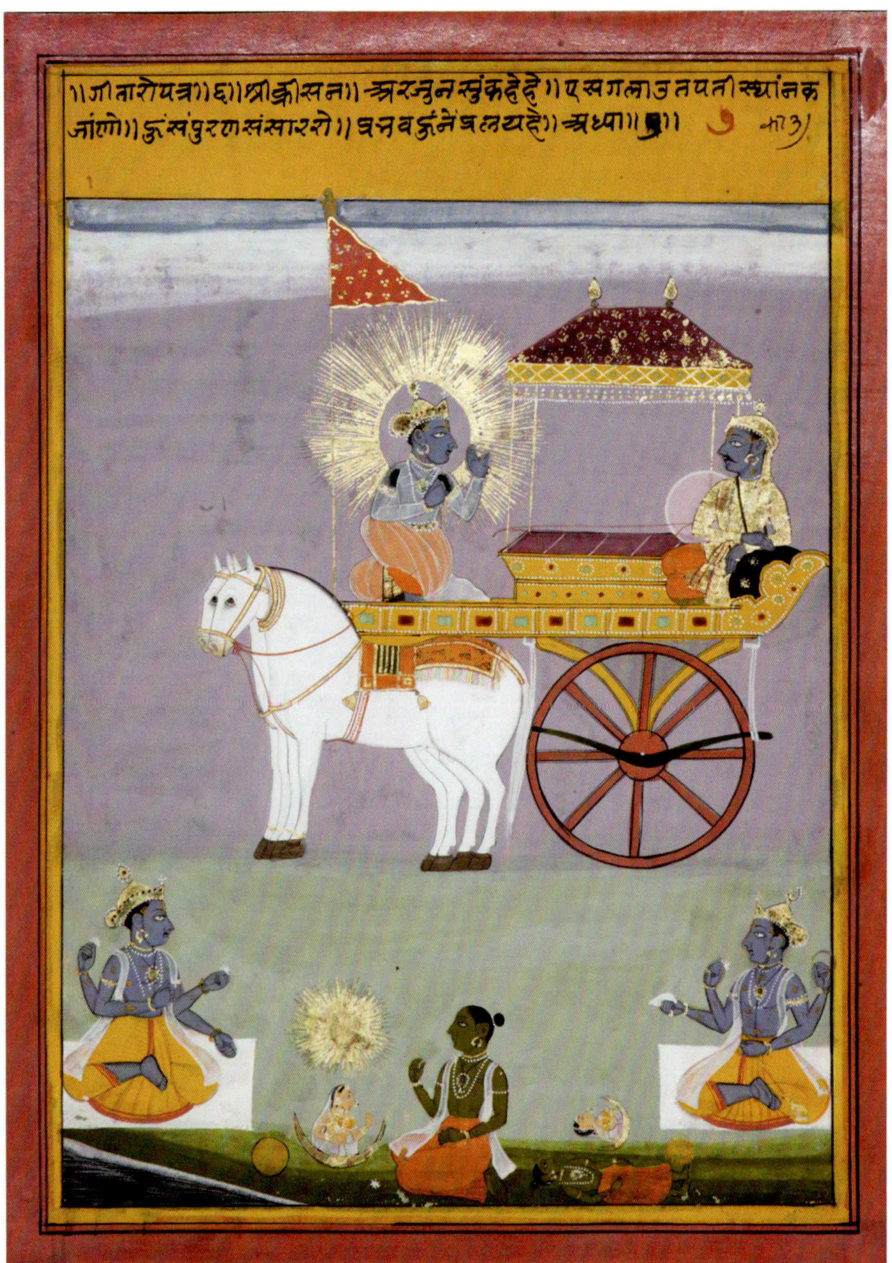

|6| श्री कृष्ण आगे समझाते हुए कहने लगे कि हे अर्जुन! सभी प्राणी मेरी दोनों प्रकृतियों से ही उत्पन्न होते हैं और मैं ही सम्पूर्ण जगत का उद्भव और प्रलय हूँ।

|6| Explaining further, Sri Krishna says: Hey Arjuna! All creatures are created out of both these aspects of myself. And I am the origin of the entire universe and the cause of its dissolution.

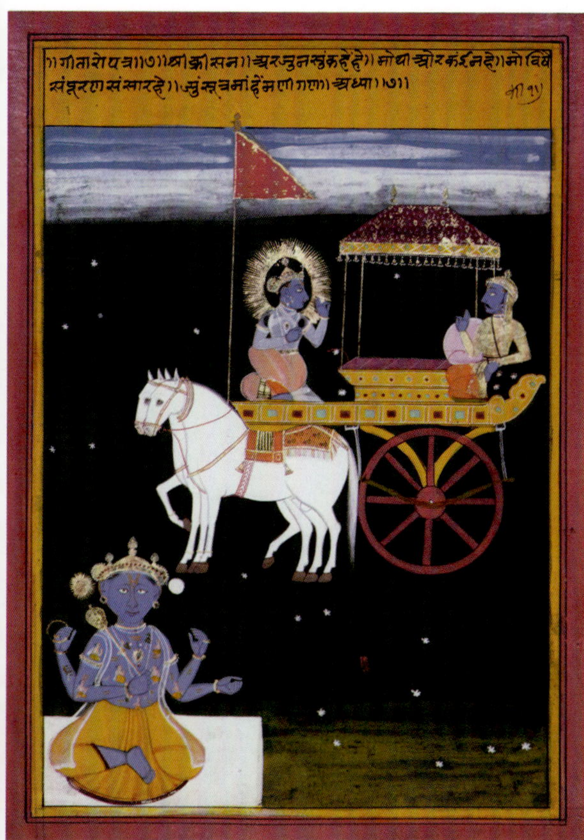

|7| श्री कृष्ण कहने लगे कि हे अर्जुन! मुझसे ऊँचा अन्य कुछ भी नहीं है। धागे में मणियों की तरह पूरे संसार का सब कुछ मुझ में ही पिरोया हुआ है।

|7| Sri Krishna says: Hey Arjuna! There is nothing higher than me. Everything is strung upon me like pearls on a string.

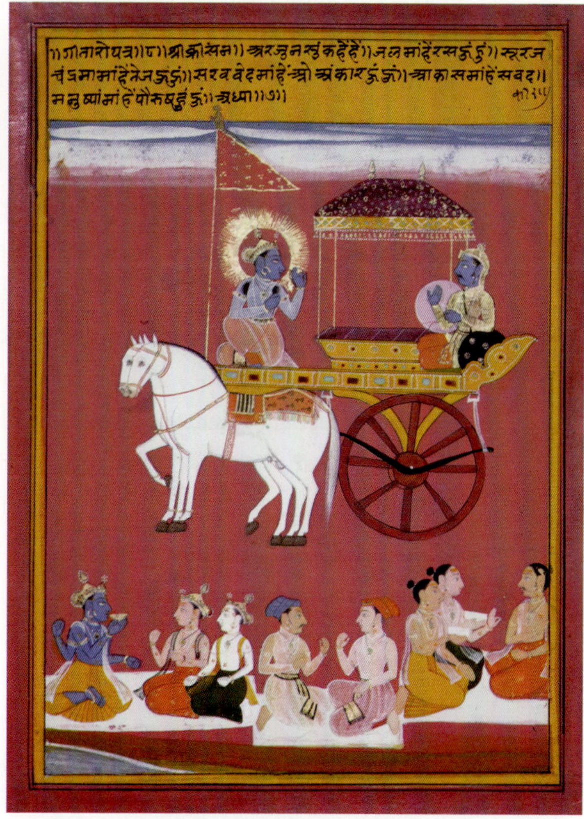

|8| हे अर्जुन! जल में मैं रस हूँ, चाँद-सूरज में प्रकाश हूँ। सभी वेदों में ओंकार हूँ, आकाश में शब्द हूँ और पुरुषों में मैं पौरुष हूँ।

|8| Hey Arjuna! I am the taste in the water, the light in the sun and the moon. I am the resonant OM in the Vedas, the sound in the air, and virility in man.

Kauravas are obdurate and will never accept the sage advice of the finest and the most learned of gurus on their side; the moral and the sacred require constant vigilance and selflessness which they lack. Krishna admits sadly that only a few understand that an assertive self-identity against the other is a dead-end; he is filled with sorrow at what he knows is about to happen. He can only warn Arjuna that human beings must accept the difficulty of their ethical positions and yet act virtuously; they must face the possibility of failure and yet not become vengeful. If they do so, they will simultaneously learn to subdue the ego's tendency to self-glorification, self-pity and vengeance and also learn to empathise with others.

The visual images for verses 6 and 9 are inspired and complex. Looking at them, a visionary sojourner on earth would find no difficulty in accepting the crescent moon as a beautiful boat for a goddess to travel across the sky or row down a river. Of course, in contrast, a literalist, a materialist or a sensualist would see the crescent as a phase of the moon useful either to chart the geometry of stars or configure an auspicious, wish-granting astrological position. Therefore, the image of the goddess in a crescent moon-boat is two-fold. First: for those who are only concerned with material well-being, the moon indicates the continual succession of instances when new desires are fulfilled or thwarted; man is, as verse 6 suggests, nothing more than another mortal creature amongst countless others in the ebb and flow of creation and destruction. As an image of the earthly lunar cycle which can be known mechanically and with the physical eyes alone, the crescent moon points to people who have forgotten their connection with the divine creative energy. This is an error both of knowing and of teaching; those who are concerned only with material success sink further into the demonic realms of superstition, greed, corruption and irresponsible power.

Secondly: the goddess in the crescent moon-boat reminds those who have faith that there is a benevolent eternity above the biological and geological order of things.[8] They understand what Krishna means when he says in an evocative lyric: "I am the Fluidity in water, the Light in the sun and the moon...I am the Fragrance of the earth, the Brilliance of Fire..." (Swami 8-9). Every instance in the life-cycle is equal to eschatology; reflecting on each moment from birth to death, Krishna recognises how all things have their proper place in flow of time; he is moved to ecstasy by each new beginning; and, finally, he feels only a sense of completion when a phase of life fades into darkness.

In the painting for verse 6, a worshipper sits facing a four-armed Vishnu. Between them there are remarkable images: a golden-hued, full moon; a river bank; a goddess

8 See Cirlot, *A Dictionary of Symbols*, p. 205.

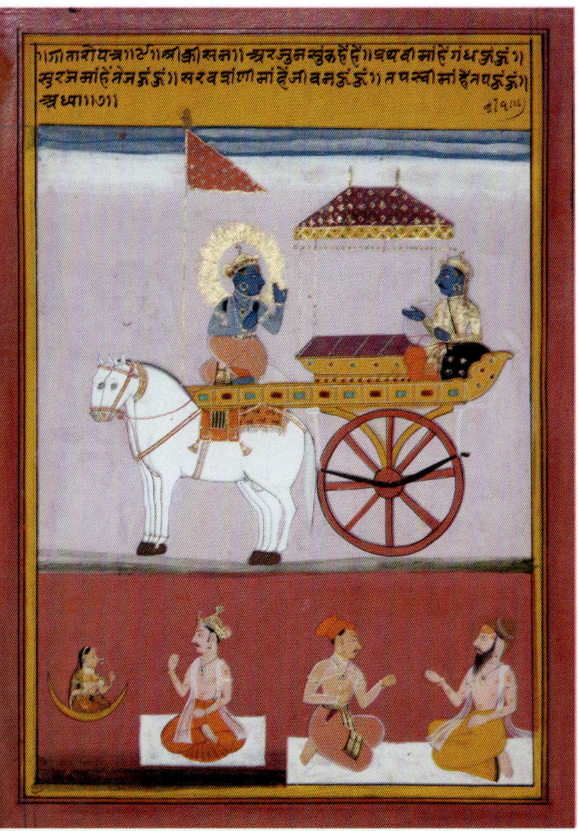

|9| श्री कृष्ण आगे बताने लगे कि हे अर्जुन! पृथ्वी में मैं पवित्र गंध हूँ, अग्नि में तेज हूँ, प्राणियों में जीवन और तपस्वियों में तप हूँ।

|9| Sri Krishna further says: Hey Arjuna! I am the pure fragrance of the earth, the radiance of fire, the life-force in all beings and the penance of the ascetics.

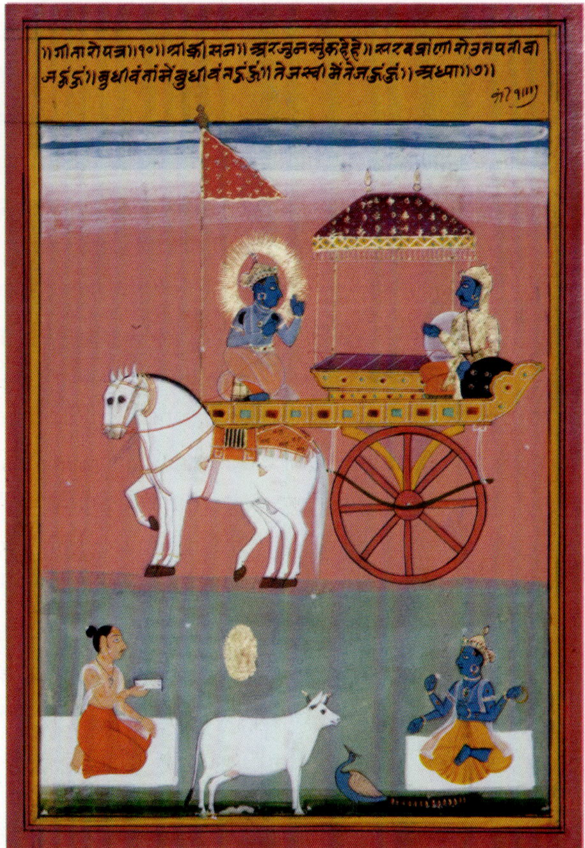

|10| श्री कृष्ण आगे समझाते हुए कहने लगे कि हे अर्जुन! सभी प्राणियों का मैं सनातन बीज हूँ। मैं बुद्धिमानों की बुद्धि हूँ और तेजस्वियों का तेज हूँ।

|10| Sri Krishna further explains: Hey Arjuna! I am the eternal seed of all beings. I am the intelligence of the intelligent, the brilliance of the brilliant.

with silver ornaments sitting in a crescent-moon boat gliding toward the worshipper surrounded by white flowers; and, above the goddess, a glorious sun burning with golden light. Vishnu is depicted holding a white flower in each of his three hands. His fourth hand touches the earth. This cluster of images, as the verse suggests, shows creation in its benevolent aspect. The hand touching the ground is reminiscent of the Bodhisattva calling upon the entire *shristi* to bear witness to the idea that life comes into being because there is mutual dependence and peace. Both these images are expanded in the second scene on the lower right. It is as serene as the one on the left even though it shows that the worshipper is dead. Once his life-cycle is complete, the same goddess who had accompanied his emergence on earth in her moon-boat guides his soul toward the sky. The fluid ease with which images on the left are redeployed is remarkable. If the first image of Vishnu, with the moon-boat floating horizontally in time, offers a welcoming benediction, this second image, with the moon-boat climbing vertically upward toward heaven, suggests that the fearless acceptance of death is the path to the divine. As if to indicate a radical change in the image of the divine from one who delights in the beauty of birth to one who calmly accepts the passing away of all things, Vishnu has placed one of his hands in his lap in a gesture of withdrawal from creation.

The other dramatic change in the scene on the right is that Vishnu holds a conch-shell in one hand, even as he smells the perfume of the white flower he holds in the other. Vishnu's conch-shell is symbolic of the enigma of creation, temporality and dissolution. The conch-shell's hard, bony exterior is formed after the death of living organisms in the sea. Its smooth and sensuous interior is the opposite of its gnarled surface; together they suggest a reconciliation of death and life, of origin and end. That is why in folk traditions, the inward spiralling form of a sea-shell is not only an "allegory of all origins and ends,"[9] but also of the crucial idea in the *Gita* that life and death belong to the same vortex of time. In the painting, this life-death cycle is also played out by the viewer. The eye travels from the figure of Vishnu sitting on the left beside the river of time to the sun and the moon marking the daily round of the acolyte's life; then to the worshipper's death; and finally to the other Vishnu on the right, before it circles back to the first Vishnu, only to trace the life-death cycle of another being. This cyclical movement, however, is not a dead-end because the upward movement of the second moon-boat with a Devi suggests that an enlightened being can break out the cycle of life and death and find a path to infinity.

9 Philip Kuberski, *The Persistence of Memory: Organism, Myth, Text* (Los Angeles: University of California Press, 1982), p. 79.

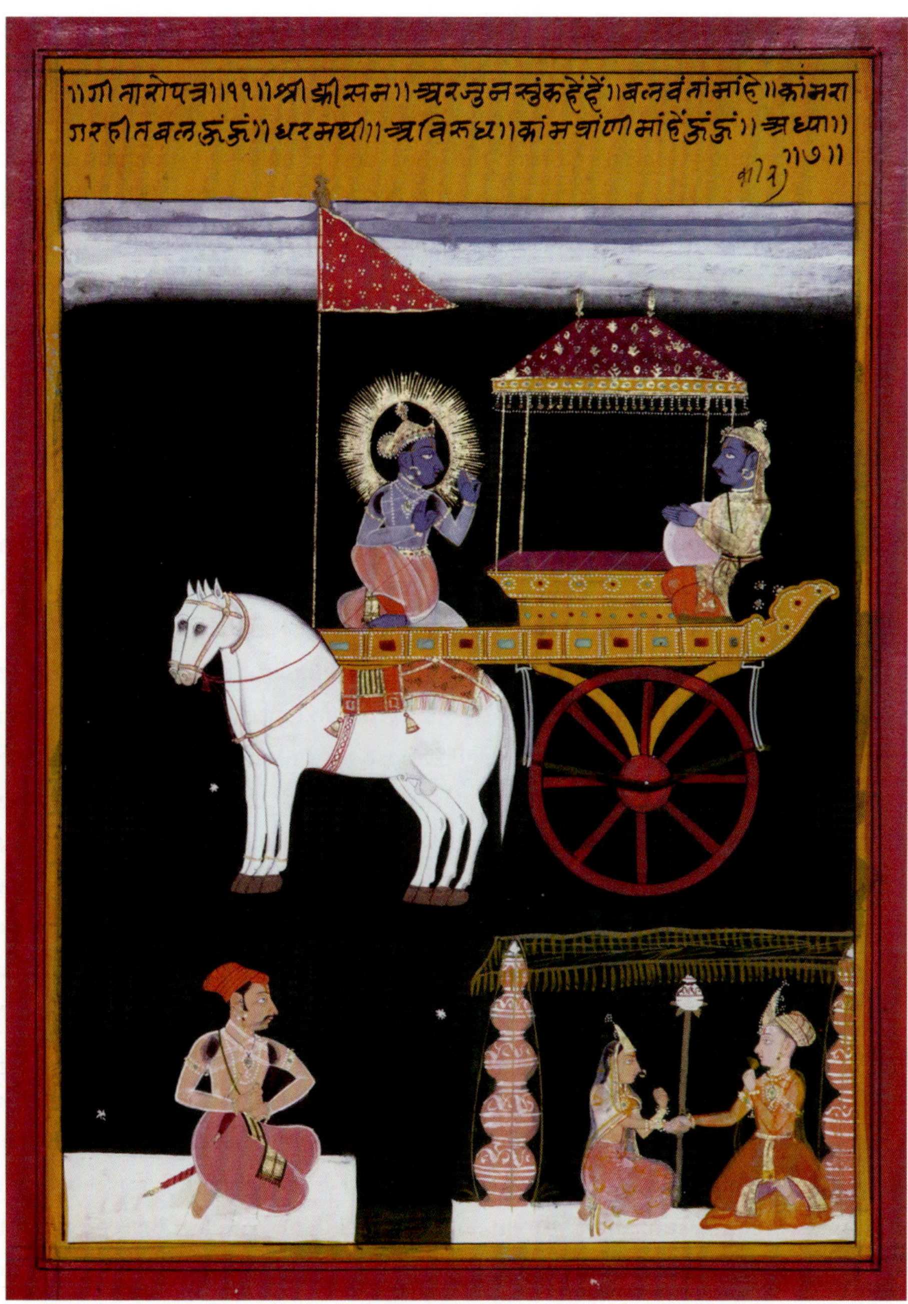

|11| श्री कृष्ण आगे समझाने लगे कि हे अर्जुन! मैं बलवानों में कामना रहित बल हूँ। सभी प्राणियों में धर्म के अविरुद्ध अर्थात अनुकूल हूँ तथा शास्त्रसम्मत काम भी मैं हूँ।

|11| Sri Krishna further explains: Hey Arjuna! I am the strength of the strong ones who are without attachment; I am the desire for righteousness.

Allah Baksh's images for verse 11 offer remarkable reinterpretations of Krishna's meditations on desire. Allah Baksh suggests that Krishna, unlike the samkhya philosophers, does not condemn desire in itself as evil.[10] He would, perhaps, have no difficulty in accepting Gandhi's gloss on the word "desire" in verse 11. Gandhi says that desire can lead to *moksha* if it is "undivorced from righteousness"; but "divorced from *dharma*" it leads to "perdition" (Desai 243). In the lower right corner of the painting, Allah Baksh shows a marriage being celebrated. The bride and the groom are gentle, youthful and happy. The young woman's pale luminous pink clothes deliberately echo the colour of Krishna's garment. The canopy above the couple is supported by pink clay pots filled with water as signs of joyous fulfilment. Together they honour the innocence of human longing, its non-predatory and instinctive destiny. There is, however, an armed, ominous figure sitting outside the marriage altar watching them. Is he the image of that demonic selfhood that can entrap a marriage in fearful notions of sin, tradition, law and power, reminding one of the fate of Rama and Sita?

The visual images for verses 12 to 15 capture the difficult, irreducible and conflictual condition in which, as Krishna says, all human beings find themselves. Since they live in historical time they are beset by the anxiety of desire and temptation. Those who are evil in spirit, or those who choose to walk the path of glamour and egotistic power, see the world 'through a glass darkly.' They may be pious and learned but, like the two youthful, bare-bodied priests in the illustration for verse 15, they are surrounded by spiritual darkness or *tamas*. The agitation of the young men is painted with an economy of line, colour and form which is only possible for someone who has mastery over the medium. Even though the verses urge that one should assume an attitude of dispassionate disregard for life's sufferings and rewards, one can feel the painful earnestness with which these two young men confront their emotional and spiritual confusions. It is as if the artist is insisting that they meditate on the difficulties of living, not in abstract terms of what human beings may face, but through their own lived dilemmas as unique individuals. Here the emotional state of the two men is rendered with precision and naturalness. They walk with bare feet on a green earth sparkling with white flowers, but they walk near a dark edge; walk between illusion and nothingness. As bewildered seekers after knowledge which can sustain and console them, they remind one of Dante at the entrance of hell who, in the middle of life's journey, is lost. Their feeling of uncertainty is intensified by the swirl of their dhotis and the swing of the white stoles on their shoulders. Krishna tells Arjuna that, while there

10 See Radhakrishnan, p. 254.

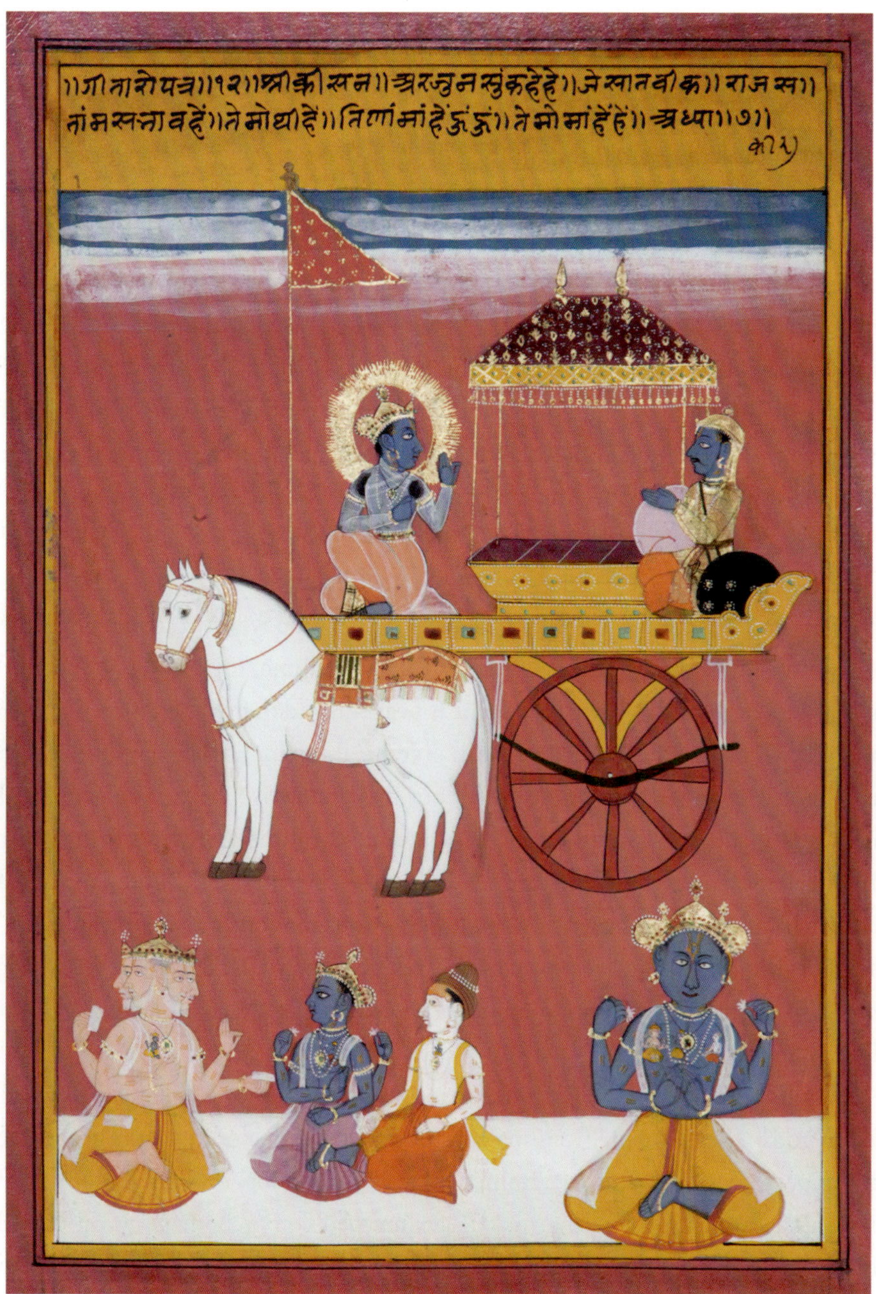

|12| श्री कृष्ण अर्जुन से कह रहे हैं कि ये जो सात्विक, राजसिक व तामसिक स्वभाव हैं, वे सभी मुझसे ही हैं। वे मुझमें हैं, किन्तु मैं उनमें नहीं हूँ।

|12| Sri Krishna says to Arjuna: All the qualities of purity, passion and inertia arise from me. They are in me, but I am not in them.

are many who begin their quest for enlightenment, most fail because they are distracted by the desire for knowledge, wealth or pleasure. Even the greatly learned Bhishma is morally damaged by the ease and the recognition offered by the Kaurava court. That is why one should remember that in the narrative ordering of the *Mahabharata*, while the *Gita* is preached before the war begins, it is recalled at the time when Bhishma is lying fatally wounded in the battlefield.[11] Are these young men, then, examples of those who walk mindfully on earth and are yet bewildered by its beautiful illusions and its delusory fears? The dark background colour suggests that they are aware of their existential condition, but the presence of the goddess and of Krishna seated on either side gives the entire scene an emotional force that is not despairing. One feels that, even as they are being pulled in different directions, there is vitality in their stride and alertness in their eyes. Maybe, they will find, as the verses insist wise men must, shelter under Krishna's benevolent gaze.

The painting for verse 13 shows two young worshippers sitting amongst the gods. Here, they are on the same green plane as the gods. Along with two images of Krishna (beside and behind them), they gaze at the eternal Brahma, the primal godhead from which the universe has its being. The scene is peaceful and there is no difference in scale between the human and the divine, no hierarchical distinction. What is emphasised is not the puzzlement of the young men, but their reflective spirit. The gods are less demanding. Instead of being remote, they are more intimate; instead being abstract idols in a temple sanctum, they are as visible as fellow beings. There is peace and equality between gods and men, and an intimacy because both carry within them the same imperishable energy. Herein, perhaps, resides the crucial difference between the *Gita* and the holy texts of Semitic religions where God is utterly separate, mysterious and unattainably higher.

The painting for verse 20 shows three mature couples kneeling before three different gods. They worship, Krishna says in the verse, "lesser Powers…according to their temperaments" (Swami 49). Immediately after, he adds, revealing once again his non-sectarian attachment to dharma, that when people pay homage to other deities with selfless devotion, they ultimately worship only him (verses 21-22). Appropriately, therefore, the illustration for verse 20 is celebratory. There is not a touch of the sensual in the drawings of the couples, though each couple is more richly adorned in gold and floral clothes than the figures in any previous painting. There is a sobriety about them, and a maturity, which will enable them to negotiate the right path through "the dense forest of

11 This point is crucially made by van Buitenen, *The Bhagavadgita*, p. 3.

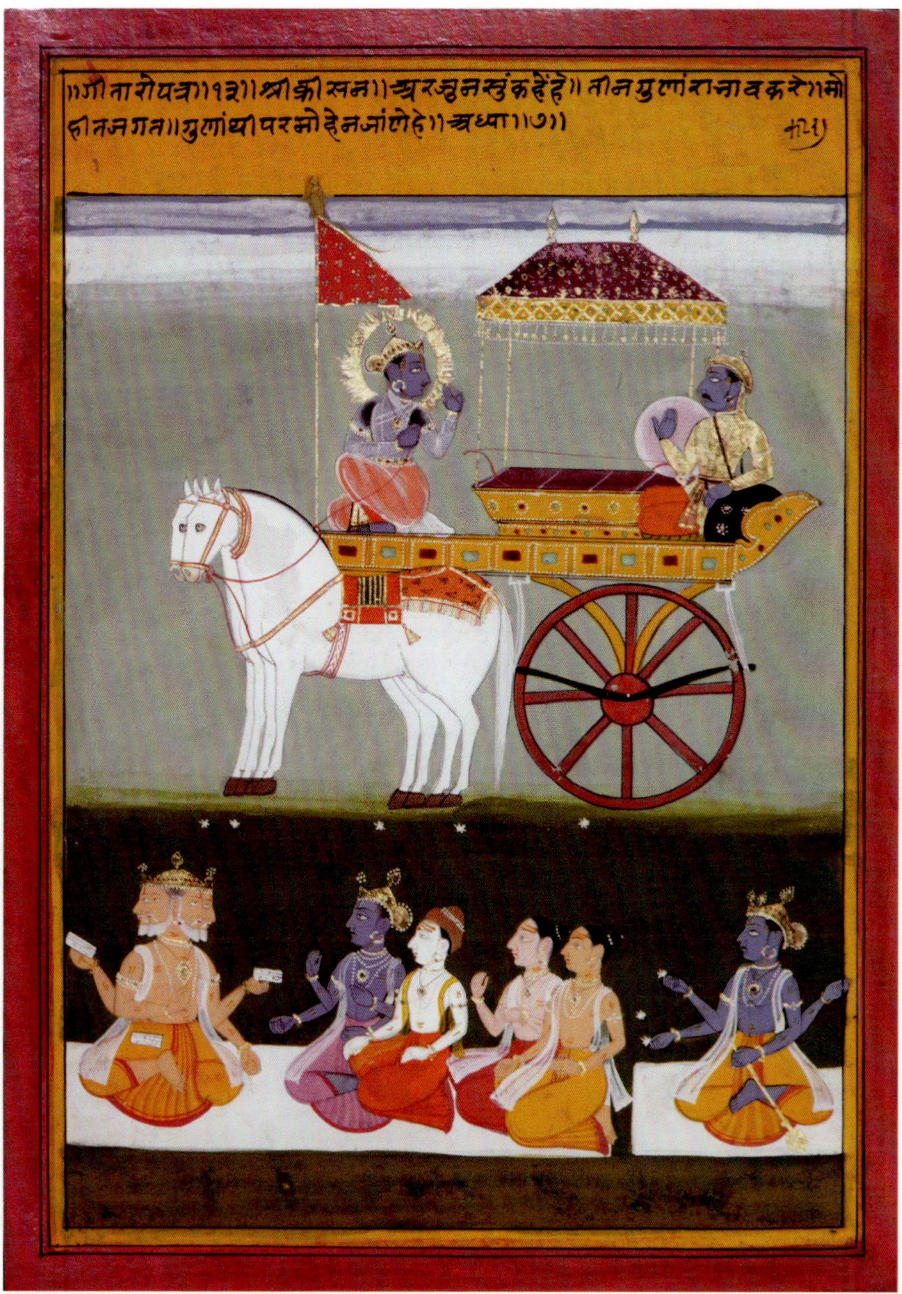

|13| हे अर्जुन! इन तीनों स्वभावों से पूरा जगत मोहित हो रहा है इसीलिए स्वभावों से परे मुझ अविनाशी को नहीं जान पाते।

|13| Hey Arjuna! The entire universe is deluded by these qualities. That is why they fail to know that I am imperishable.

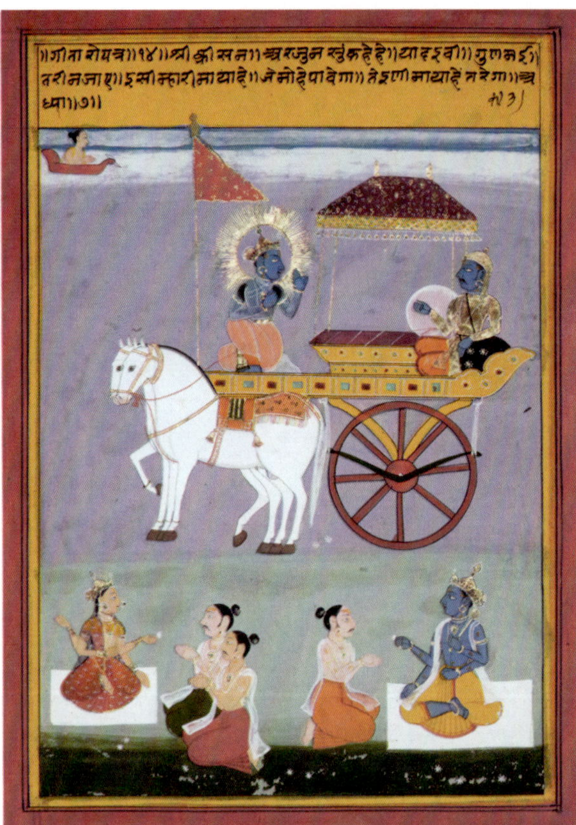

|14| श्री कृष्ण आगे कहने लगे कि हे अर्जुन! मेरी यह त्रिगुणात्मक माया बड़ी दुस्तर है पर जो मेरी शरण में आते हैं, वे इस माया को पार कर जाते हैं।

|14| Sri Krishna further says: Hey Arjuna! My divine illusion, created by these three qualities, is difficult to dispel; but those who take shelter in me can see past it.

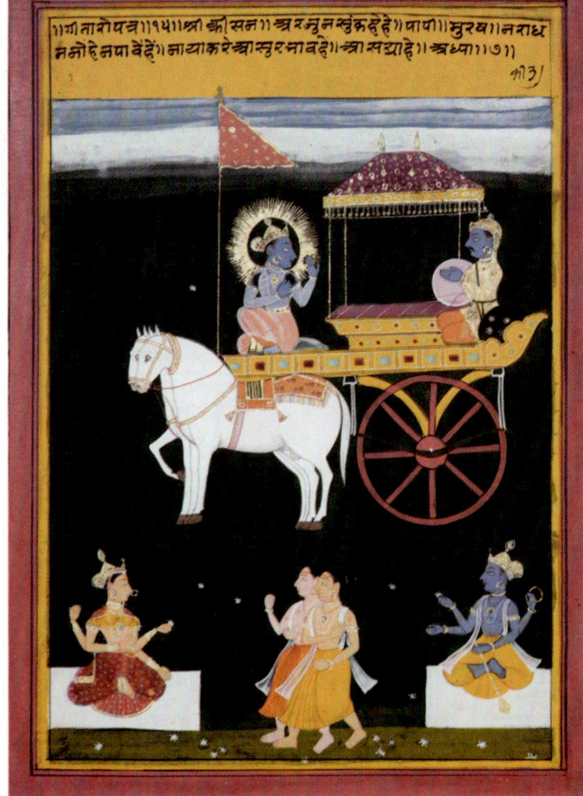

|15| हे अर्जुन! माया ने जिनका ज्ञान हर लिया है, ऐसे दुष्ट कर्म करने वाले मूढ़ नरों में पापी और आसुरी स्वभाव वाले मेरी शरण में नहीं आते।

|15| Hey Arjuna! Men who sin and do evil deeds because their minds have been deluded by illusions, do not seek shelter in me.

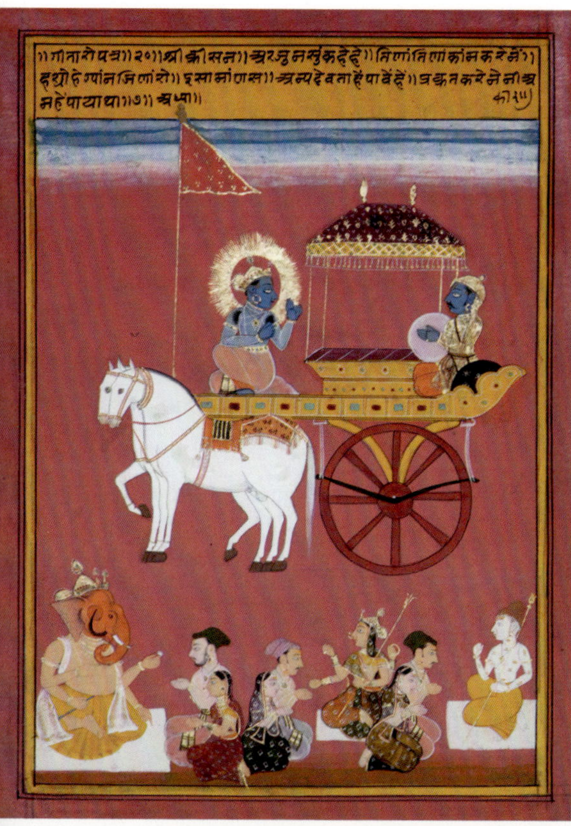

|20| हे अर्जुन! जिनका ज्ञान भोग की कामनाओं द्वारा हरा जा चुका है, ऐसे मनुष्य अन्य देवताओं को पूजते हैं अपने स्वभाव से प्रेरित होकर।

|20| Hey Arjuna! Those whose intelligence has been led astray by different desires, worship other gods according to their own temperaments.

|21| श्री कृष्ण आगे कहने लगे कि हे अर्जुन! जो-जो भक्त श्रद्धापूर्वक जिस-जिस देवता को पूजता है, उस-उस भक्त की श्रद्धा को मैं उस देवता में स्थिर कर देता हूँ।

|21| Sri Krishna further says: Hey Arjuna! I bestow unswerving faith on any one who worships any god with sincere faith.

sense-objects" towards righteousness (*Jnaneshwari* 1: 186). Indeed, their marital desires are treated with bemused affection. Ganesha in the left corner is especially enchanting (also see illustration for verse 23). He is larger than all the other figures and yet seems to be the gentlest. With the forefinger of his left hand he points to the earth calling upon it to bear witness to two ideas—ideas that the couple before him must also endorse—that co-operative generosity between all beings, and desire without coercive possessiveness, alone can sustain the world's generative continuity. The same gentle guidance seems to be offered to the other two couples by the Devi and a saintly figure. These lessons are, of course, about to be negated by the war in Kurukshetra—the earth of the Kurus will witness a fratricidal war because they claim that they have a greater right (*adhikar*) over it, and can enforce that right through any means. Gandhi makes radical use of both these ideas in the *Gita* to craft his politics of ahimsa, and his philosophic refusal to accept the doctrine that any action is acceptable if the ends are good.

This image of desire, natural and free, non-egotistic and joyous is created once again in a splendid illustration for verse 25. Here, Krishna himself gazes with erotic playfulness at his beloved in a green bower. The visual image helps us imagine Krishna in this verse saying: "I am desire in all creatures...that desire through which religion becomes the highest aspiration" (*Jnaneshwari* 1:180). The isolation of the couple within a bower of braided leaves and purple flowers intensifies the aesthetic atmosphere of love. War is forgotten, even if momentarily, so are all the injunctions against passion. What remains is the innocence of sensual longing in which the consciousness of human frailty and mortality are suspended and all thoughts of *sanyas* are discarded. The mood is similar to the one evoked by the poetic meter, *vasantatilaka*, or the spring's ornament, used by Bilhana's popular 11th century lyrics of love, *Caurapancasika*. Looking at this scene, one suspects that Krishna would perhaps empathise, despite the *Gita*'s warnings against being overwhelmed by passionate desire, when Bilhana sighs: "Even now,/gleaming white like a clear autumn moon,/her luscious face/could charm a saint's pure mind..."[12] The quiet enclosure, in one corner of the painting, is the contrary of the ascetic's cave in other paintings in this folio. Krishna and his lover are oblivious of the noise of time and of the two self-righteous representatives of dull tradition who walk away from the bower determined, perhaps, to rouse a censorious society against the lovers. Compared to the calm composure of Krishna and his consort, the two young men with top-knots seem more pre-occupied with the scriptures than with the song of a love god.

12 See Barbara Stoler Miller, *Phantasies of a Love-Thief: The* Caurapancasika *Attributed to Bilhana* (New York: Columbia University Press, 1971), p. 2.

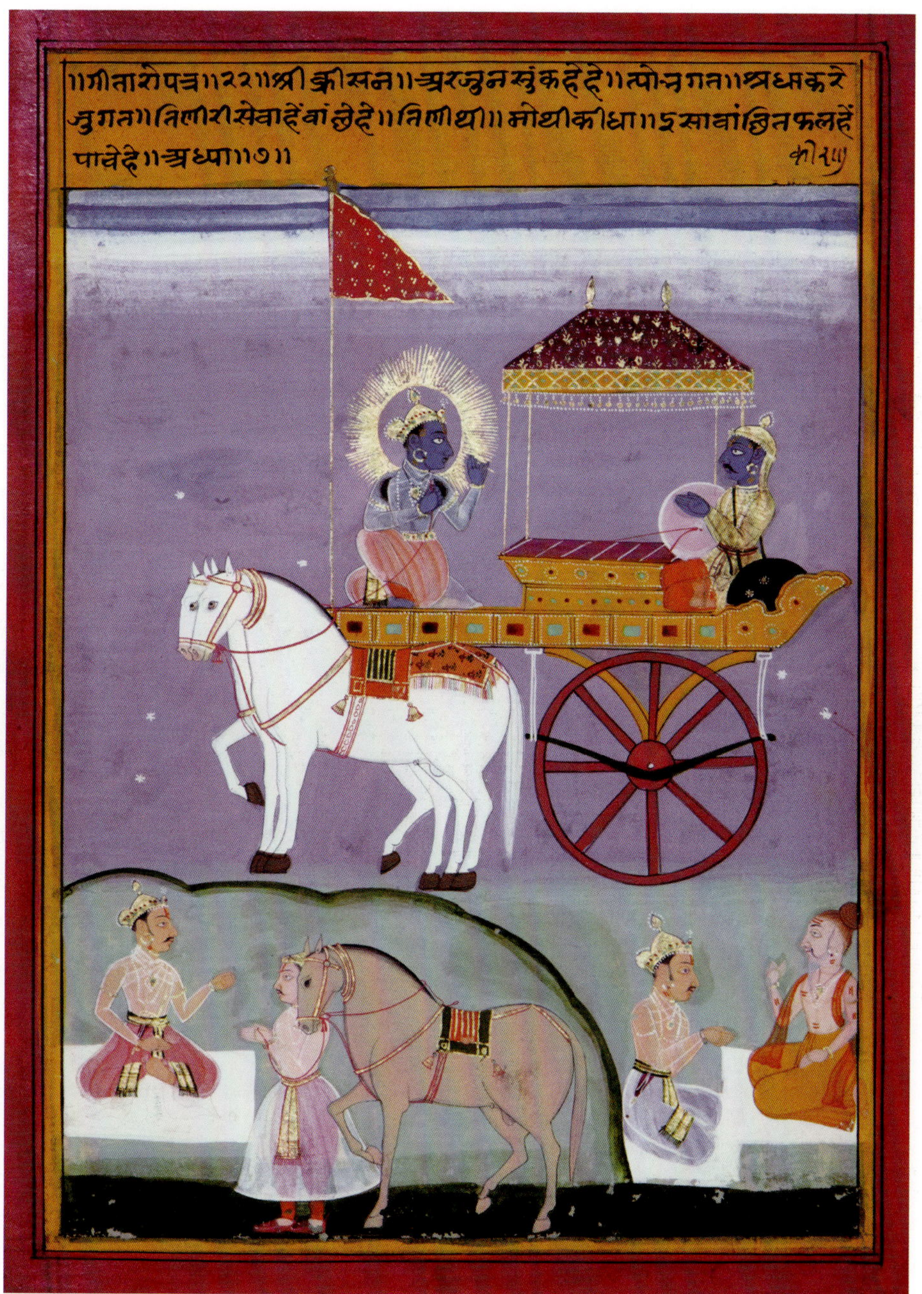

|22| हे अर्जुन! जो भक्त श्रद्धा से युक्त होकर उस देवता की आराधना करता है और उस देवता से वह मेरे विधान स्वरूप उन इच्छित भोगों को निस्संदेह प्राप्त करता है।

|22| Hey Arjuna! There is no doubt that if a man worships any god with complete devotion, he obtains his desires; this I myself grant.

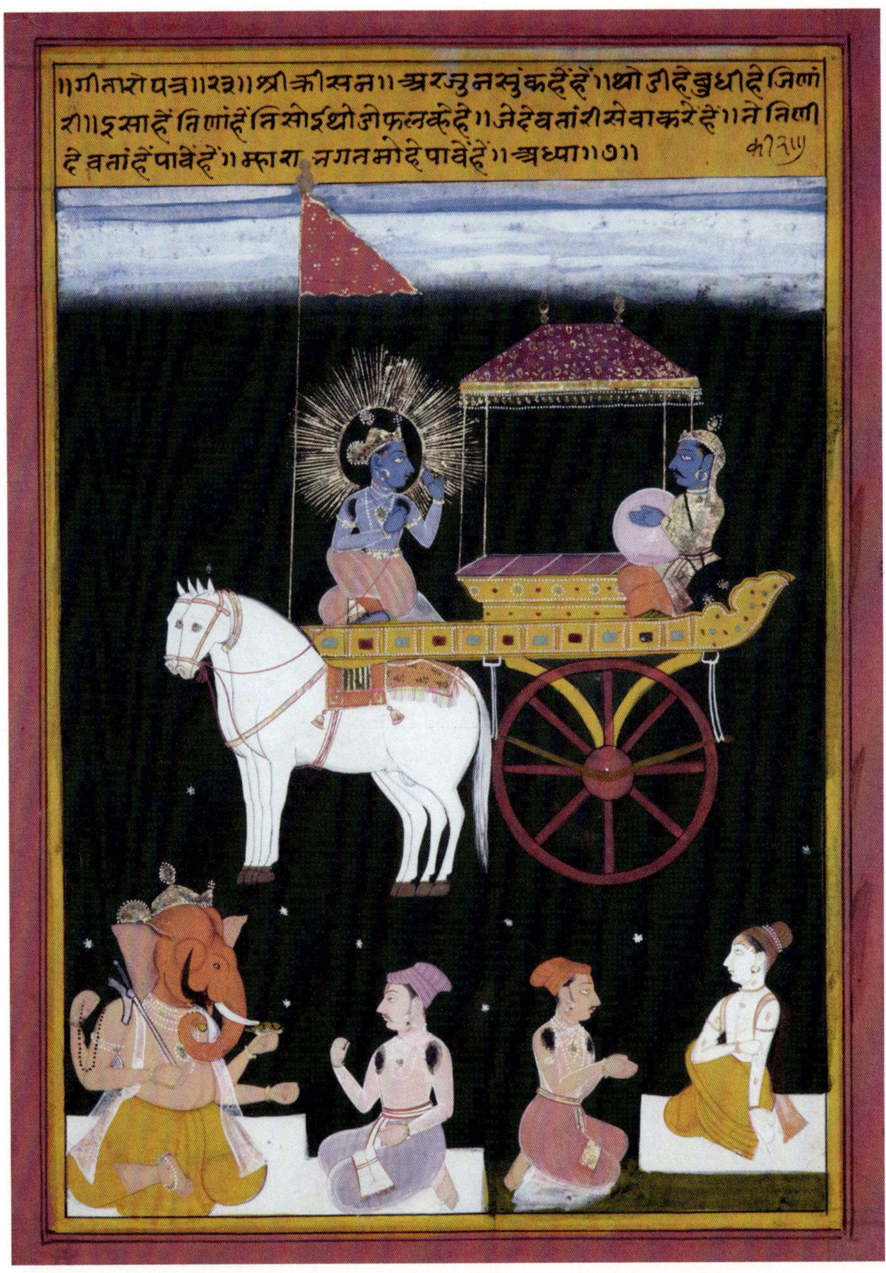

|23| श्री कृष्ण आगे समझाते हुए कहने लगे कि जिनकी बुद्धि अल्प है, उन्हें वैसे भी थोड़ा ही फल प्राप्त होता है। देवताओं को पूजने वाले देवताओं को प्राप्त होते हैं, और मेरे भक्त मुझे प्राप्त करते हैं।

|23| Sri Krishna further explains: Limited is the fruit obtained by those who are not very intelligent. Those who worship other gods go to those gods. Those who are devoted to me come to me.

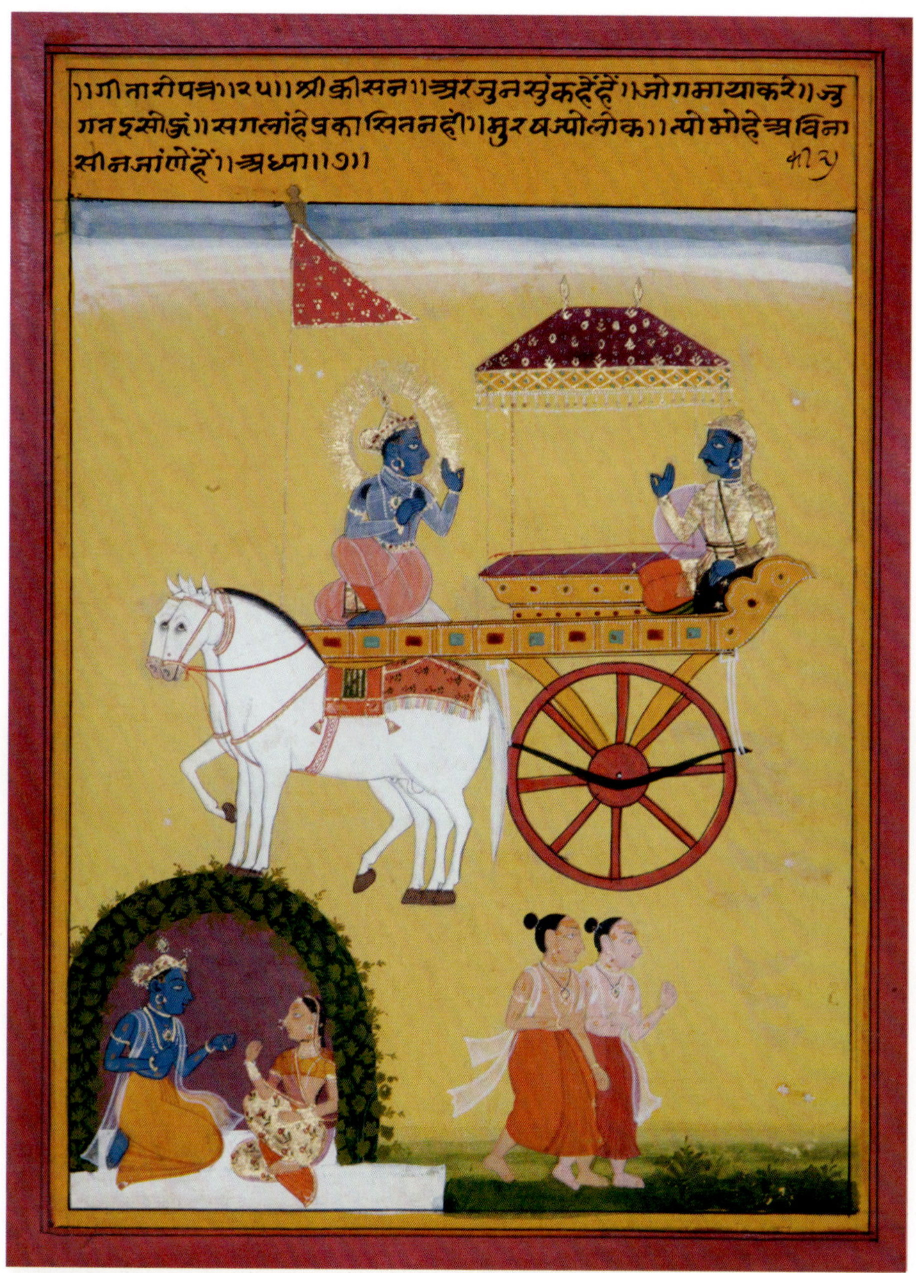

|25| श्री कृष्ण कह रहे हैं कि हे अर्जुन! अपनी योगमाया से ढका हुआ मैं सभी को प्रत्यक्ष नहीं होता इसलिए यह मूढ़ जगत मुझ अविनाशी और अजन्मे को जान नहीं पाता।

|25| Sri Krishna says: Hey Arjuna! Veiled by the illusion created by the power of my yoga, I am not visible to everyone. That is why this deluded world does not know that I am unborn and imperishable.

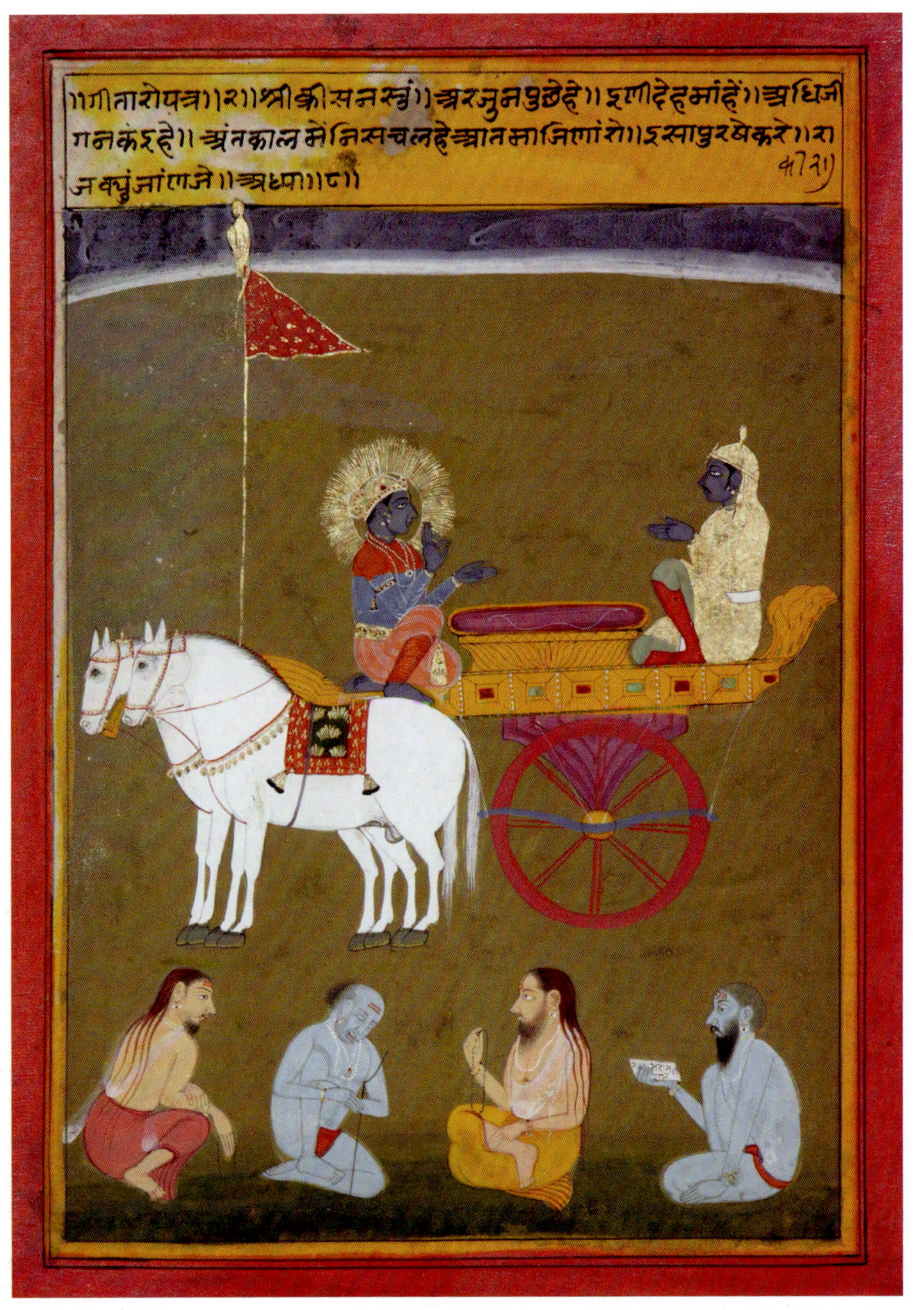

|2| अर्जुन तभी पूछने लगा, हे कृष्ण! इस देह में अधियज्ञ कौन है? और इस देह में कैसे हैं? लगातार आत्मा में स्थित पुरुष द्वारा अंतकाल में आप किस तरह जाने जाते हैं?

|2| Arjuna asks: Hey Krishna! How did the spirit of sacrifice become part of this body? And why? How can a disciplined man know you at the time of his death?

CHAPTER 8

Unfortunately, very few paintings for this chapter have survived. The chapter is concerned with Arjuna's difficult and abstract questions about Brahma, the self and karma. Many of the commentaries on them, instead of helping us disentangle the arguments, merely add to the metaphysical obscurities. Both Mahatma Gandhi and his scholarly secretary, Mahadev Desai, can always be trusted to help one see through mystification. Desai invokes Gandhi's comments to find meaning in the "apparent abracadabras" (Desai 251) of verses 1 to 7. Gandhi's explanation is simple and profound: Krishna tells Arjuna to regard man's life as perpetual "moral and spiritual" warfare (Desai 251). The world comes into existence when the Supreme Being sacrifices himself in the act of creation. Krishna says that he, too, has assumed, as an act of self-sacrifice, a perishable human form to help the world. Like any other mortal being, he shall finally merge with the Original Essence. If Arjuna is to escape this life-death cycle of suffering, he must "imitate" Krishna's selfless sacrifice and accept his role as a warrior in a righteous war. Not to do so is a temptation that he must resist (Desai 252).

The difficulties and abstractions of this chapter are reflected in the paintings. Allah Baksh seems almost daunted. He does not appear to be imaginatively and emotionally committed to the images: the horses are awkward in size, the usual beauty-making ornamentation is missing, the chariots are childishly drawn, the colours are uninflected, the same naked sadhus appear again and again, and the drawings are naively simple. Thus, when the verse talks about what people should think about at the time of their death, the ground is covered with images of corpses (verses 5, 6 and 20). The yogis who have renounced the world are merely ash-covered, unlike their images in other paintings in which their physical form is so attractive as to leave room for ambiguities and human uncertainties (verses 1, 2 and 14). Where the verses urge the self to keep the Supreme God in mind at all time, the paintings merely show Brahma and Krishna as having appeared on earth with no visual or dramatic indication of what their relation to the mortals is or can be. Thus, when Krishna speaks about the imperishable, the 'supreme spirit' against which the human and the earthly are inconsequential, the painting depects two diminutive worshippers sitting on a dull green ground before a larger-than-human Brahma (verse 3). It also shows Krishna at a remote distance enclosed within a golden sun. What is missing is the profound idea that the *Gita* is an intimate dialogue, and that the divine is in close visual contact with the human—an idea that Allah Baksh rarely ever forgets in other paintings. Indeed, these works are so disappointingly literal that they call for no interpretative effort.

Verses 6 to 20 continue to offer philosophic difficulties. One must again turn to Gandhi and Desai's attempt at clarification. On one level, Krishna's advice to Arjuna is simple and straightforward: Believe in me; fix your mind steadily on me without distraction; only perform morally good deeds without straying down the path of delusion, passion, ambition or rewards; lead a life of simplicity and virtuous conduct so that you can be without fear, anxiety and dissatisfaction. It is worth noting that for Gandhi, influenced by the Bible and Edwin Arnold's translation of the *Gita*, karma is equivalent to good deeds, and that the sacrifice demanded by Krishna is *the complete renunciation by the self of the fruits of the good deeds.* Arjuna, Gandhi insists, is not just being urged to act, but is *being urged to act only on behalf of the good*, with complete and disciplined disinterest in the final outcome of such an action.[1] Death will not be a stranger to such a person.

Thinking about his end, Montaigne wrote: "I want Death to find me planting cabbages, neither worrying about it nor the unfinished gardening."[2] Gandhi, who was familiar with Montaigne, takes this thought further. He merges the idea of selfless and disciplined action with that of self-sacrifice—a sacrifice which would be an imitation of the original sacrifice of the divine to create the world. He invokes Jesus, who says: "Whosoever would come after me, let him renounce himself and *take up his cross daily* and follow me" (the emphasis is Gandhi's).[3] Gandhi adds that for Krishna "life is a perpetual striving. There is always a tempest rising in us, and struggle against temptation is a perpetual duty" (Desai 252). The moral and spiritual renovation of the world, therefore, demands an ever-renewed war against the self's desires and a willingness to suffer. Gandhi's desire is to take the wisdom of the gods and weave it into the fabric of everyday life—to make everyone into a karma yogi, an actor in the fields of time.

1 See Bandyopadhyay, *Three Essays on the Mahabharata*, pp. 139-141.

2 Montaigne, *Complete Works*, p. 42.

3 This is not an exact quotation from the Bible. See Luke 9:23; Mark 8: 34 and Matthew 16:24.

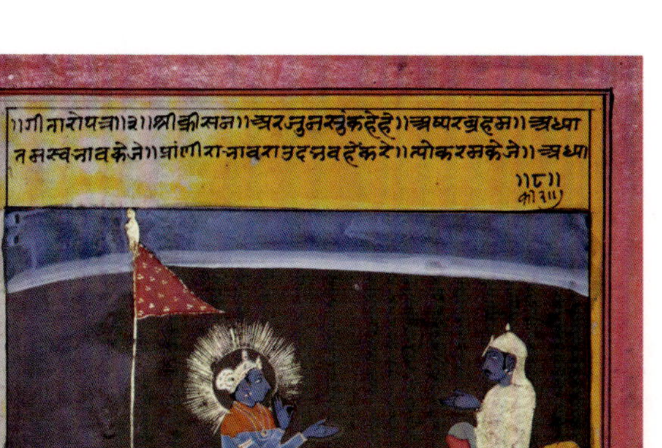

|3| श्री कृष्ण प्रत्युत्तर देते हुए कहने लगे हे अर्जुन! अक्षर ब्रह्म है और उसके स्वभाव को अध्यात्म कहा जाता है। प्राणी के भाव का उद्‌भव करे, वह कर्म तुझसे कहता हूँ।

|3| Sri Krishna replied: Hey Arjuna! The Eternal Spirit is imperishable and its dwelling place is the body. Its creative force is action. That's why I ask you to act.

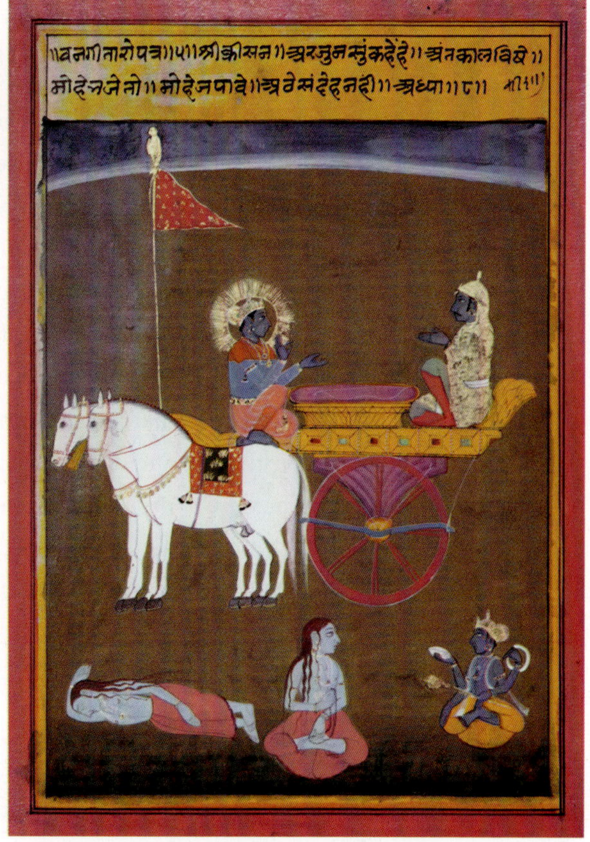

|5| श्री कृष्ण आगे कहने लगे, हे अर्जुन! जो पुरुष अंतकाल में केवल मेरा स्मरण करता हुआ देह त्यागता है, वह मेरे स्वरूप को ही प्राप्त होता है, इसमें कोई संशय नहीं।

|5| Sri Krishna further says: Hey Arjuna! There is no doubt that the man who thinks only of me at the time of his death becomes one with my Being.

The paintings, however, remain uninspired. In the painting for verse 6, none of the dead or dying men seem to have struggled for a virtuous life. They are all painted, appropriately, against a dark background. The young boy, sitting beside his father's corpse, seems quite bewildered; the young widow is dumb with sorrow as she gazes at the body of her husband; the rich man, dressed in orange and red, may have died while counting his gold. The earlier paintings were not so literal. They often had a double consciousness. If they were concerned with people who failed to strive for love or selfless action, they never forgot that another life, another possibility, was always open. But in this painting all we see is the same kind of literalism that informs much of popular contemporary religious art which is dull, flaccid and witless because it can only imagine gods as more self-satisfied and inane versions of our well-fed lives. The same laborious pedantry is responsible for the image illustrating verse 8 in which Krishna says that a worshipper should keep only the image of the divine in his mind and heart. The implications of this in the field of action for Arjuna are complex. Krishna does not mean that Arjuna should sit in seclusion with an imprint of his image in the heart—that would be idolatry. Instead, he wants Arjuna (and by extension all human beings) to live according to the ethical qualities that are inherent in him. Only then can he wage the difficult spiritual 'war' to become godlike and recreate a godly world (verse 7). Even if he were to perish in the attempt, he would still become immortal; he would be a continuous reminder to human beings of the possibility of living a life of good deeds on earth with others.

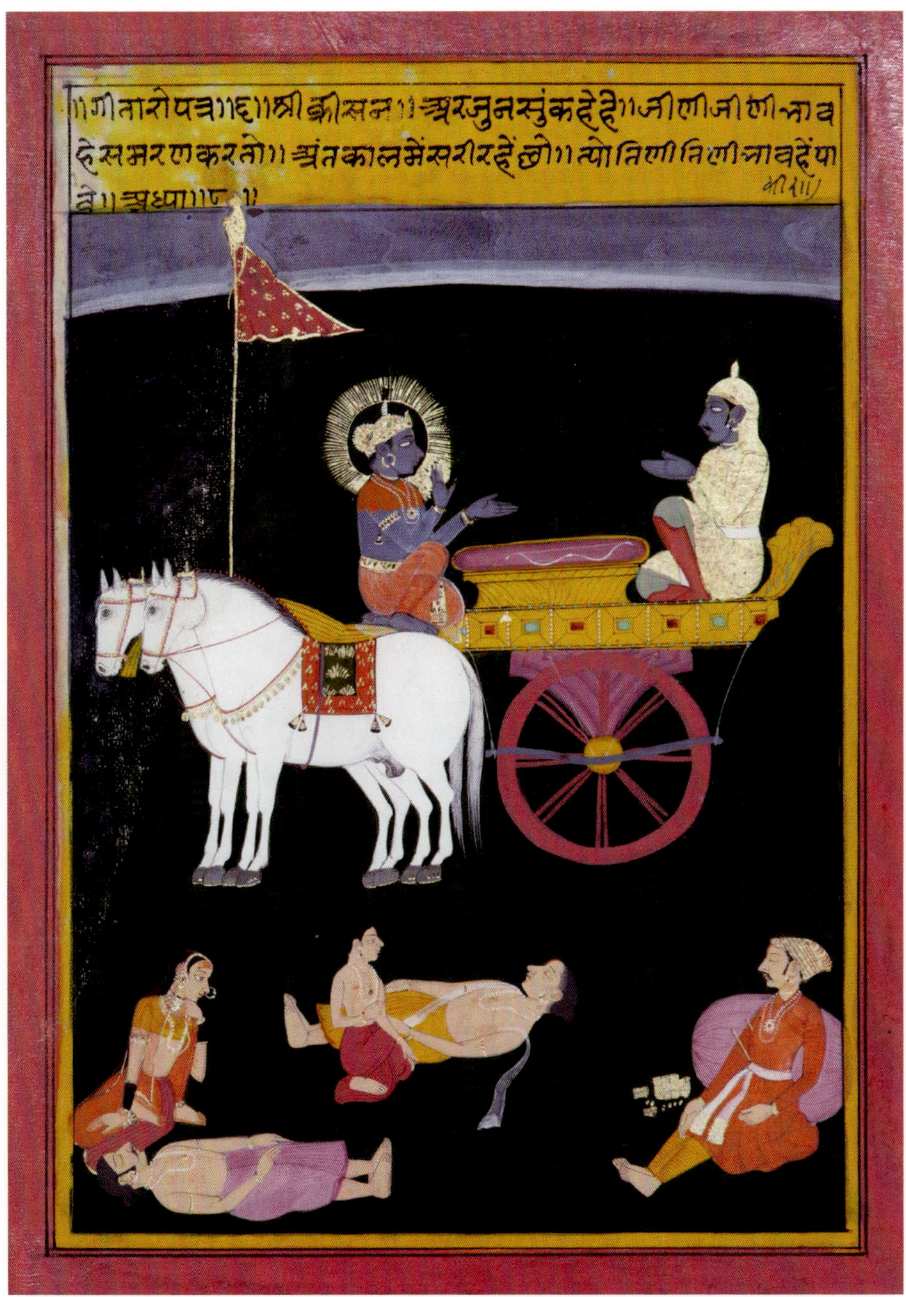

|6| श्री कृष्ण समझाते हुए कहने लगे कि अंतकाल में मनुष्य जिस-जिस भाव का स्मरण करता हुआ अपना शरीर छोड़ता है, वह उसी-उसी भाव को ही प्राप्त होता है।

|6| Sri Krishna further explains: A man only attains the form he continually thinks of at the time of his death.

The emphasis in these verses is not on extraordinary human beings. How can it be when Krishna says in verses 16 to 19 that the life of any man is an insignificant and unnoticeable moment in an infinite universe? "Multitudes of beings pass through a cosmic day... all are dissolved as the night of the universe approaches" (Swami 52). Krishna's concern is with any human being who lives a life of *attentiveness* to the earth. The three paintings for these verses locate Brahma at the centre and narrate the ordinary life-cycle of people hoping to sustain a world of goodness.

The verses 23-26 are suffused with strange and mystical elusiveness. They speak about the path the dead take depending upon the time of day they die and the positions of the sun and the moon. Does Krishna really mean that a simple man may have lived a life of devotion, but if he dies on a moonless, smoke-filled night his soul shall walk down an inauspicious path back to the world of impermanence, chance and sorrow (verse 25)? Can anyone be as lucky or blessed like Bhishma and choose his moment of death to coincide with the bright light of the sun and so attain salvation? Is Krishna actually telling Arjuna that a soul's chance of being one with the divine depends either upon atmospheric conditions or the position of the stars? But, surely death waits for nothing and no one. Indeed, up to this moment, Krishna has been saying clearly that only those who *choose good deeds or ethical action* can hope to find liberation. The idea, that man's final release from earthly entanglement is astrologically determined, is contrary to his prime argument that only unselfish, detached and impersonal action, which is indifferent to the final outcome, leads to *moksha*. Mahadev Desai honestly admits: "I do not understand the meaning of these...shlokas" (Desai 259).

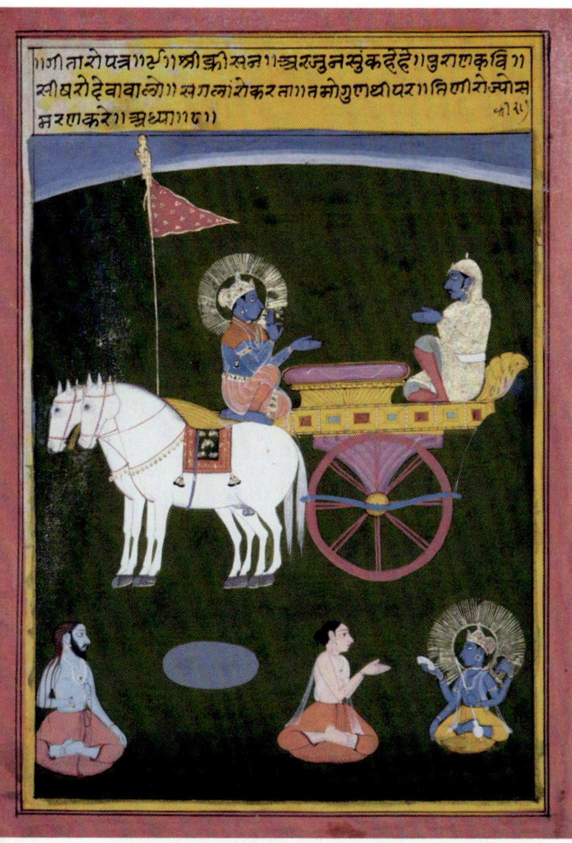

|9| हे अर्जुन! श्री कृष्ण कहने लगे कि वेदों का ज्ञाता जिसे अविनाशी कहता है और वीतराग संन्यासी जिसमें प्रवेश करते हैं और जिसकी इच्छा करते हुए ब्रह्मचर्य का पालन करते हैं, उस पद को मैं तुझे संक्षेप में कहता हूँ।

|9| Hey Arjuna! Sri Krishna says: Let me tell you briefly about the One whom the Vedas call imperishable and the One whom the disciplined and chaste ascetics wish to attain.

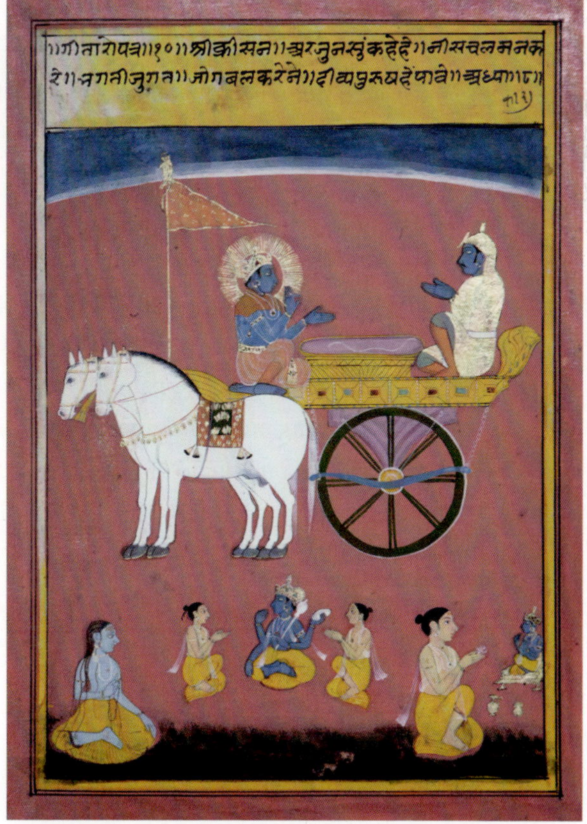

|10| श्री कृष्ण कह रहे हैं कि हे अर्जुन! भक्तियुक्त पुरुष जो प्रयाणकाल में निश्छल मन से योगबल द्वारा भ्रकुटियों के मध्य प्राण को स्थित करता है, वह दिव्य पुरुष को प्राप्त होता है।

|10| Sri Krishna says: Hey Arjuna! The man, who at the time of his death, is steady in his devotion and who meditates with discipline on the spot between his eyebrows attains the divine.

Allah Baksh makes a brave, but unsuccessful, attempt to find visually comprehensible images for these verses. The painting for verse 23 is child-like and reveals the painter's bewilderment at what is being implied. In a green and oval space, it shows images of a golden sun and a silver moon, equivalent perhaps of the solar and the lunar cycles astrologers speak about. The light from both is pale and uninspiring. There are two yogis, covered with bluish ash, one beside the sun and the other beside the moon. The yogi closer to the sun is leaving the frame of the painting never, perhaps, to return after his departure from the mortal world. It is not clear from the painting as to why he is the one who has been granted grace. The other yogi, standing next to the moon, looks forsaken. There is no apparent reason in the text to associate the light of the sun with wisdom and of the moon with ignorance. In folk and fairy tales the sun and the moon are, of course, charged with symbolic and mantic powers. However, it is the arbitrariness of symbols which gives to storytellers their imaginative freedom and power. Scriptural texts, on the other hand, are normative and try to offer a coherent response to the conundrums of life. Struggling to come up with an explanation for these verses, both Mahadev Desai and Radhakrishnan suggest that the moon's light is borrowed and is not as steady as the sun's brilliance; hence, the former can be regarded as a sign of both whimsical fancy and the lack of steady fortitude. The sun, on the other hand, is steady in its brilliance and self-generated intelligence. But this argument is really a case of transporting symbols from other texts so as to make these verses intelligible. The same uncertainty makes the paintings for these verses unconvincing and unattractive. In the painting for verse 25, a blue tantric, in a scanty loin-cloth, walks away from the moon on a dark night. It is unclear if he is going south and down to human life on earth again, or if he has chanced upon the right starry configuration and found the path to paradise. Interestingly, the painting for verse 26 shows the same blue-bodied devotee of Shiva stepping out of a shadowy moonlit night into a brightly lit sunny space where he finds Krishna in a halo of golden light. In the verse, Krishna says that the paths of light and darkness (or good and evil deeds) have always existed. These two paths are illuminated in the images for verse 26. Those who are wise, and whose ethical conduct is unwavering, always know how to discriminate between them. With these verses, the *Gita* is back to its primary moral propositions and clarity.

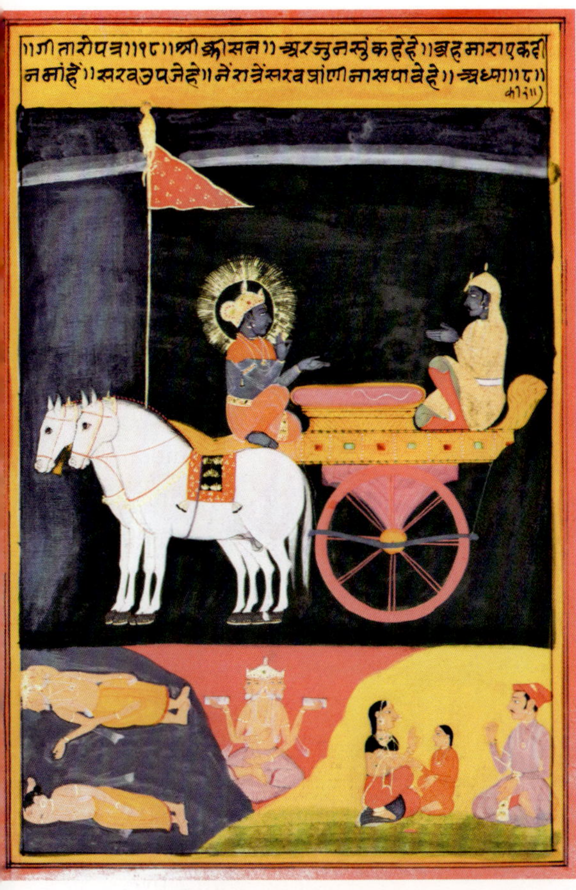

|18| हे अर्जुन! संपूर्ण चराचर ब्रह्म के दिन में उत्पन्न होते हैं और रात्रि के प्रवेशकाल में ब्रह्म के सूक्ष्म शरीर में लीन हो नाश को प्राप्त होते हैं।

|18| Hey Arjuna! When the day comes, all things emerge from Brahma's body; and when the night falls, all things dissolve into the same body.

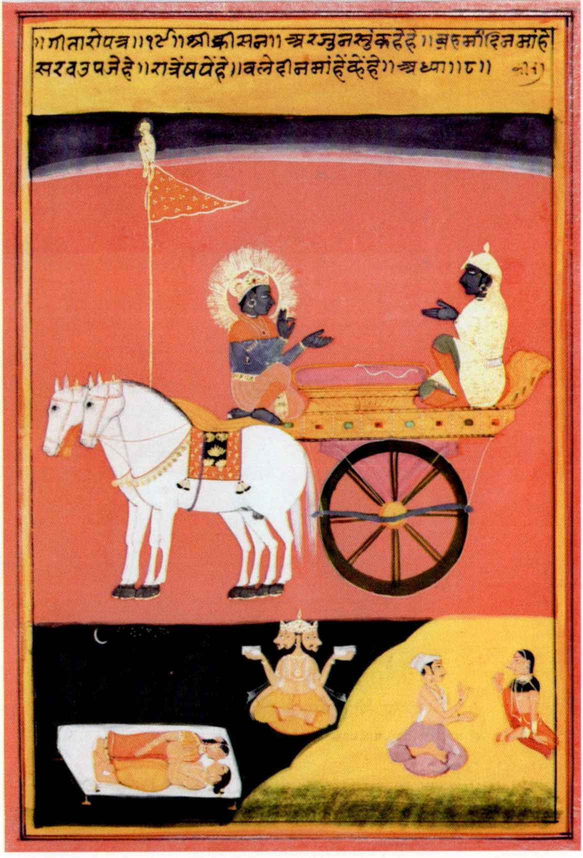

|19| श्री कृष्ण बताने लगे कि हे अर्जुन! भूत समुदाय प्रकृति के वश में होकर बार-बार जन्म लेकर रात्रि के आरंभकाल में लीन होता है और दिन के आरंभकाल में फिर से उत्पन्न हो जाता है।

|19| Krishna says: Hey Arjuna! An infinite number of beings are helplessly born in the world; they dissolve when the night falls and are reborn when the day breaks again.

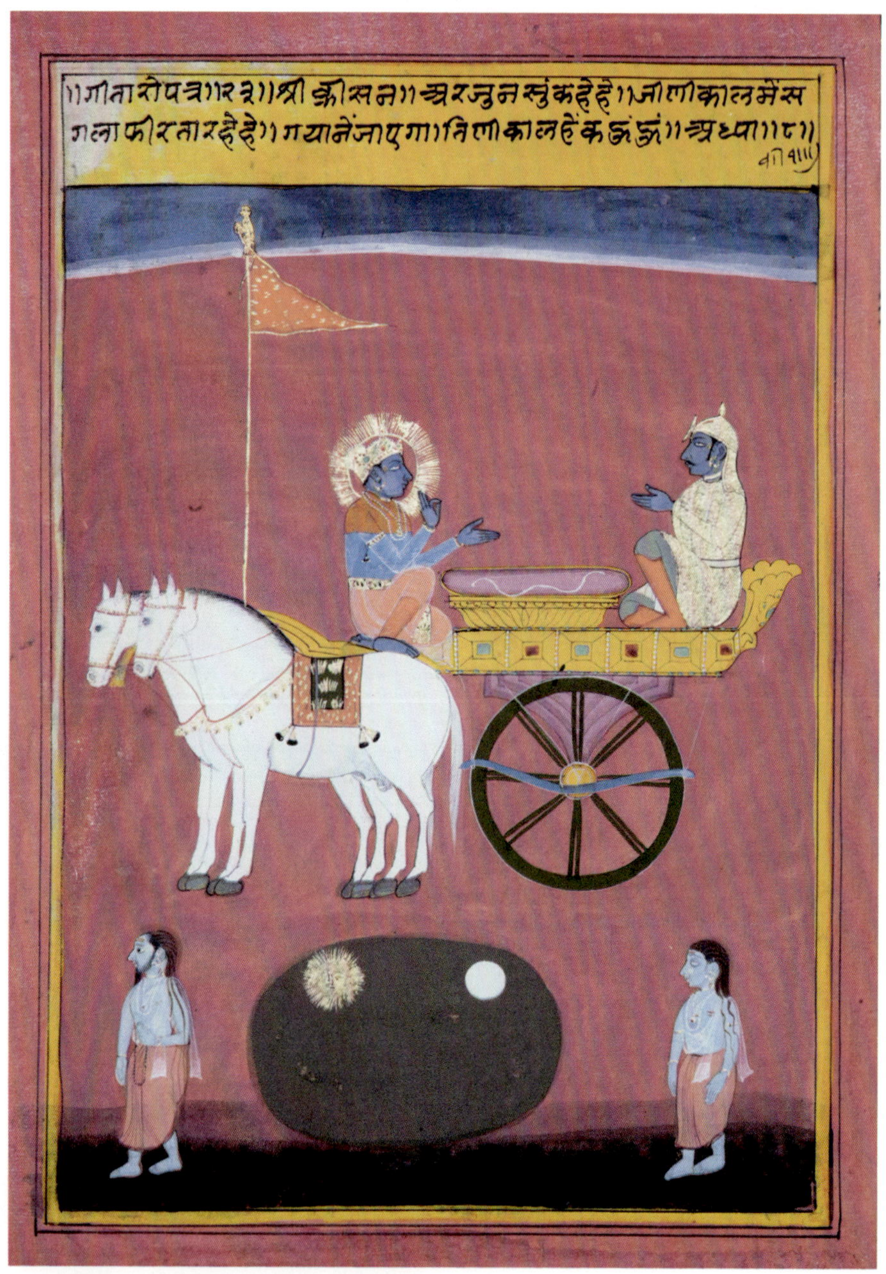

|23| श्री कृष्ण कह रहे हैं कि हे अर्जुन! जिस काल में प्रयाण करने वाले योगीजन वापस नहीं लौटते और जिसमें वापस लौट जाते हैं उन दोनों कालों को मैं तेरे लिए कहूँगा।

|23| Sri Krishna says: Hey Arjuna! I will tell you both about the time when yogis achieve enlightenment after they pass away and about the time when they are reborn.

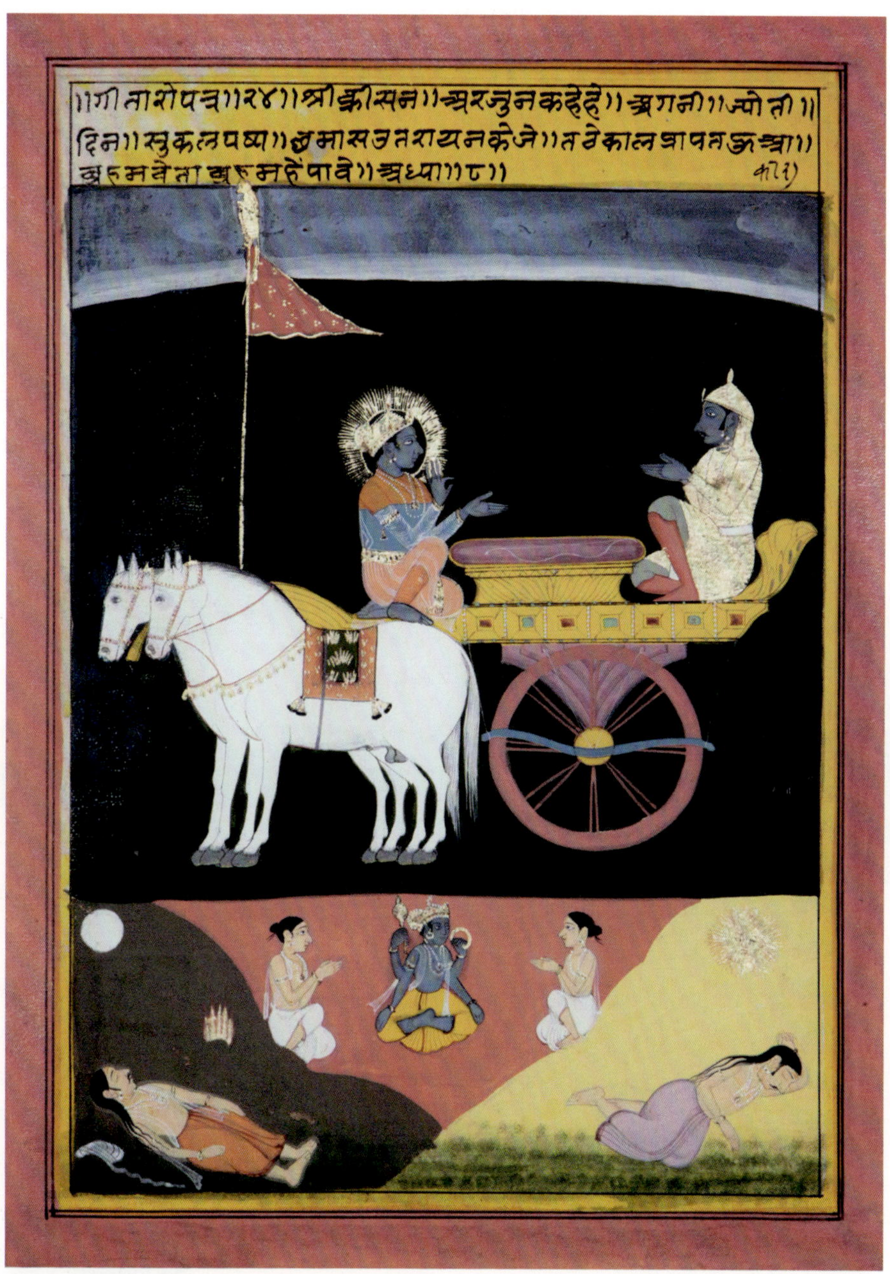

|24| हे अर्जुन! अग्नि अथवा ज्योति में, दिन में, शुक्लपक्ष में या उत्तरायण के छह महीनों में प्रयाण (मृत्यु का समय) करने वाले ब्रह्मज्ञानी, ब्रह्म को प्राप्त होते हैं।

|24| Hey Arjuna! Wise men who pass away when there is fire or light during the day or the bright light of the moon, or during the six months of the northern course of the sun, attain enlightenment.

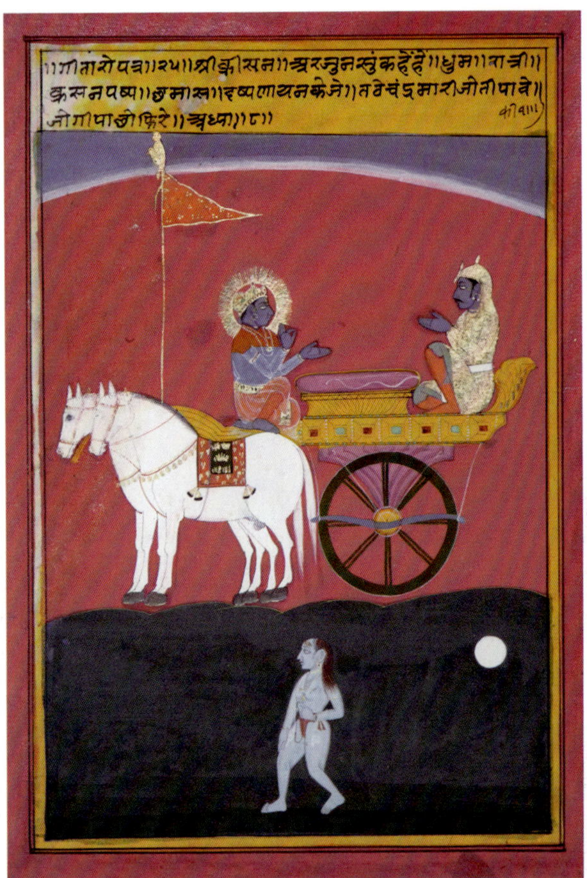

|25| श्री कृष्ण आगे कहने लगे, हे अर्जुन! इसी तरह धुएँ में, रात्रि में, कृष्ण पक्ष और दक्षिणायन के छह महीनों में प्रयाण करने वाला योगी, चन्द्र ज्योति को प्राप्त होकर वापस लौट आता है।

|25| Sri Krishna further says: Hey Arjuna! The yogis who pass away when there is smoke or at night, or when the moon is dark, or the sun is passing through the six months Southern course of the sun, return to earth.

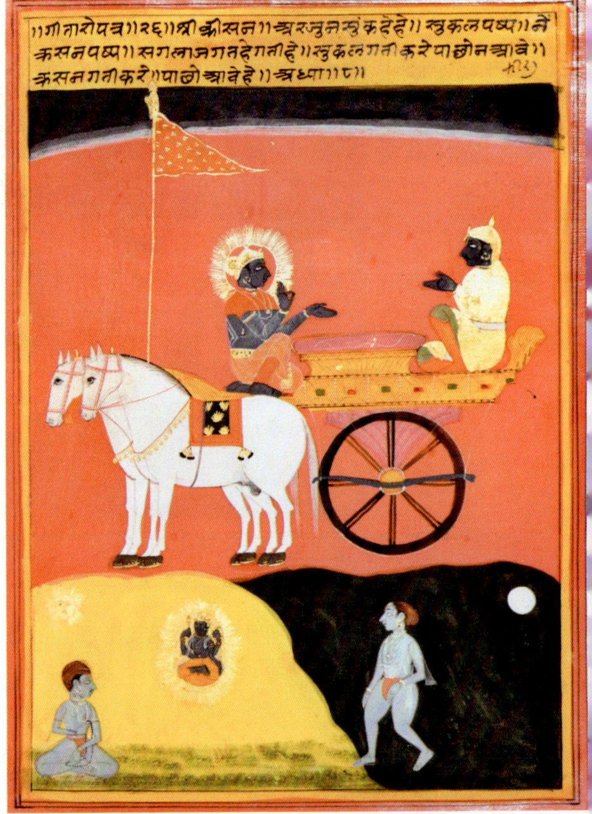

|26| श्री कृष्ण ने आगे कहा कि हे अर्जुन! शुक्ल और कृष्ण ये दो (मार्ग) गतियाँ जगत में सनातन मानी गई हैं। शुक्ल (प्रकाश) के मार्ग से जाकर लौटना नहीं पड़ता, जब कि कृष्ण (अंधकार) के मार्ग से जाकर लौटना पड़ता है।

|26| Sri Krishna says: Hey Arjuna! It is said that there are only two paths in the world: The path of light and of darkness. The one who chooses the path of light does not come back; the other, must return.

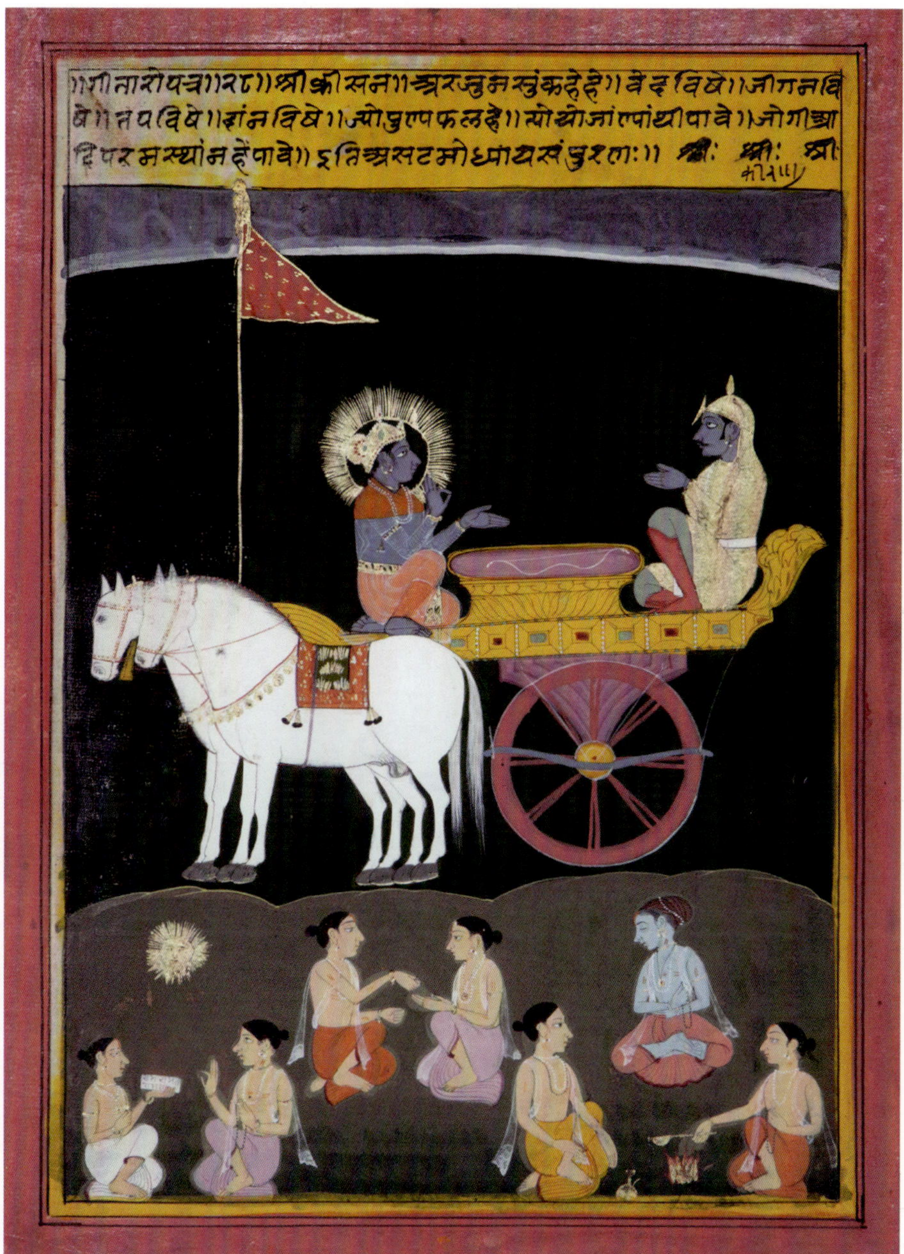

|28| श्री कृष्ण कह रहे हैं कि हे अर्जुन! इस तत्त्व को जानकर योगी वेदाध्ययन, यज्ञ, तप और दान से प्राप्त होने वाले जो पुण्यफल कहे हैं, उन सभी का उल्लंघन कर जाता है और परमपद को प्राप्त होता है।।

|28| Sri Krishna says: Hey Arjuna! The wise man who knows this transcends all the merit he may have accumulated through the study of the Vedas, rituals, austerities and acts of charity, and ascends to the supreme abode.

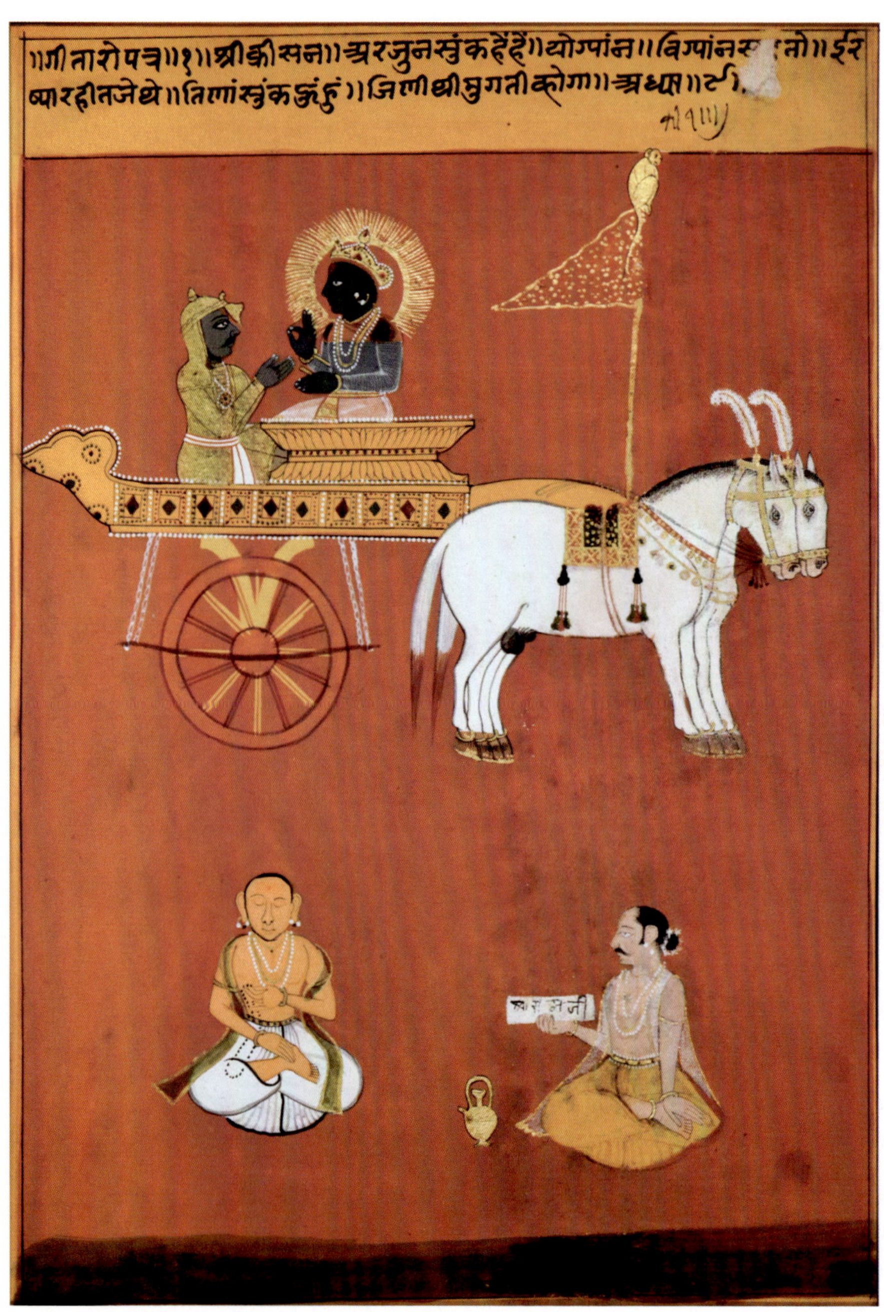

|1| हे अर्जुन! तुझ दोषरहित भक्त के लिए इस अति गोपनीय ज्ञान को विज्ञान सहित कहूँगा, जिसे जानकर अशुभ (दुख रूप संसार) से मुक्त हो जाएगा।

|1| Sri Krishna says: Hey Arjuna! Since you no longer doubt, I shall reveal to you that profound and mysterious knowledge which will release you from suffering.

CHAPTER 9

In this chapter, Arjuna is being prepared to receive knowledge, both about Krishna's divinity and the relation of the divine to all earthly things. Krishna reveals to Arjuna esoteric knowledge which only the wisest can understand. Knowledge of the divine, he says, can only be apprehended intuitively by one who is a sincere believer. Indeed, faith and knowledge are not distinct. The painting for verse 1 has images of an ascetic who is in deep mediation and a savant who knows the scriptures. Both are painted as men who attract equal respect. We begin to understand that Arjuna has arrived at his faith through his disciplined search for knowledge and the practice of yoga; indeed, it is his questing self which has laid the ground for belief; his has been a pilgrim's progress through the valley of doubt and despondency toward the revelation of the truth.

Krishna adds that the divine is the source of, and resides in, all created beings in the universe. The paintings for verses 4, 5, 6, 7 and 10 are exquisite illustrations of the idea that, for the man who knows the world imaginatively, all created beings glow with the *numen*, carry the spark of the holy, and make the divine 'visibly invisible.'

Against a sunlit landscape, the painting for verse 7 shows a saintly man preaching to animals and birds (the pictorial equivalent, perhaps, of the five monks who heard Buddha's first sermon at Sarnath). Each of them has the keenness and faith of those who have left the sorrows of the temporal world behind and are now willing listeners to the truth which will release them from the cycle of rebirth and death. It is as if they are being told: "Unto you it is given to know the mysteries of the Kingdom of God" (Luke 8:10).[1] Unlike the humanist thinkers of the European Renaissance, Krishna does not make an explicit distinction between the divine and human beings, animals and natural objects.[2] Nor does he, like St. Francis, preach to the animals. He does, however, acknowledge their presence as fellow beings, equal in holiness, making their compassionate and merciful way toward liberation. The knowledge-tradition of India does not place creation along a hierarchical chain of Being (paintings for verses 4-7). The holy wind from the heavens (verse 6) flows through all things.

---

1 *The Gospel of Selfless Action*, p. 263.

2 See Erwin Panofsky, *Meaning in the Visual Arts* (Harmondsworth: Penguin, 1955), pp. 23-24.

A sense of calm equality marks the animals in the painting. A mighty breeze, filled with intimations of immortality, blows through a green plantain tree standing proudly in a clean, blue space. The wind is symbolic of the divine creative energy which is uncontainable, unpredictable, unknowable, invisible and utterly impersonal. What is wonderful—and what is a cause for wonder—is that the painting forces us to regard the animals and birds not as insignificant and helpless beings in a sensual world, but to experience them as necessary for the making of a new visionary typography. The same is the case with the paintings for verses 7, 8 and 10 in which the gods themselves converse with the animals. As viewers, we are no longer indifferent on-lookers, who neither have the eyes to see more than what the "lethargy of custom"[3] permits, nor the heart to know what is beyond selfish desires, or the imagination to dream of anything other than what is outside the circle of dull habit. This awakening of the self, this radical transformation of perception and thought, Krishna says, is the beginning of visionary or spiritual wisdom. He praises Arjuna for having overcome scepticism and acknowledged that our demand for unity of perception and judgement is not about "the limitation of our humanness but of the human effort to escape our humanness."[4]

The great paradox is that, while the divine is in all sentient and non-living things, it is also transcendent. The divine is, therefore, immanent in the world and, at the same time, unattainable. In his paintings, Allah Baksh presents a world where the divine is interfused with each object and yet exceeds any single object. In "Auguries of Innocence," William Blake writes that a person of visionary intelligence can see eternity in a grain of sand.[5] Krishna in verses 16 to 20 says that he is the heat of the sun, the fuel used for fire, the chant and the offering. Thus, in the illustration for verse 20, Allah Baksh paints three priests lighting different ritual fires on a blue plain. The painter wants us to understand that it does not matter where the fire is lit or who lights it. A similar moral and spiritual intent is reinforced in other visual images too. In one painting (verse 22), Krishna comes down to earth to hear three Vaishnav singers.

3 S. T. Coleridge, *Biographia Literaria*, quoted by Abrams, *Natural Supernaturalism*, p. 378.

4 Cavell, in *Philosophy and Animal Life*, pp. 86-87.

5 *Collected Writings*, edited by Keynes, pp. 431-434.

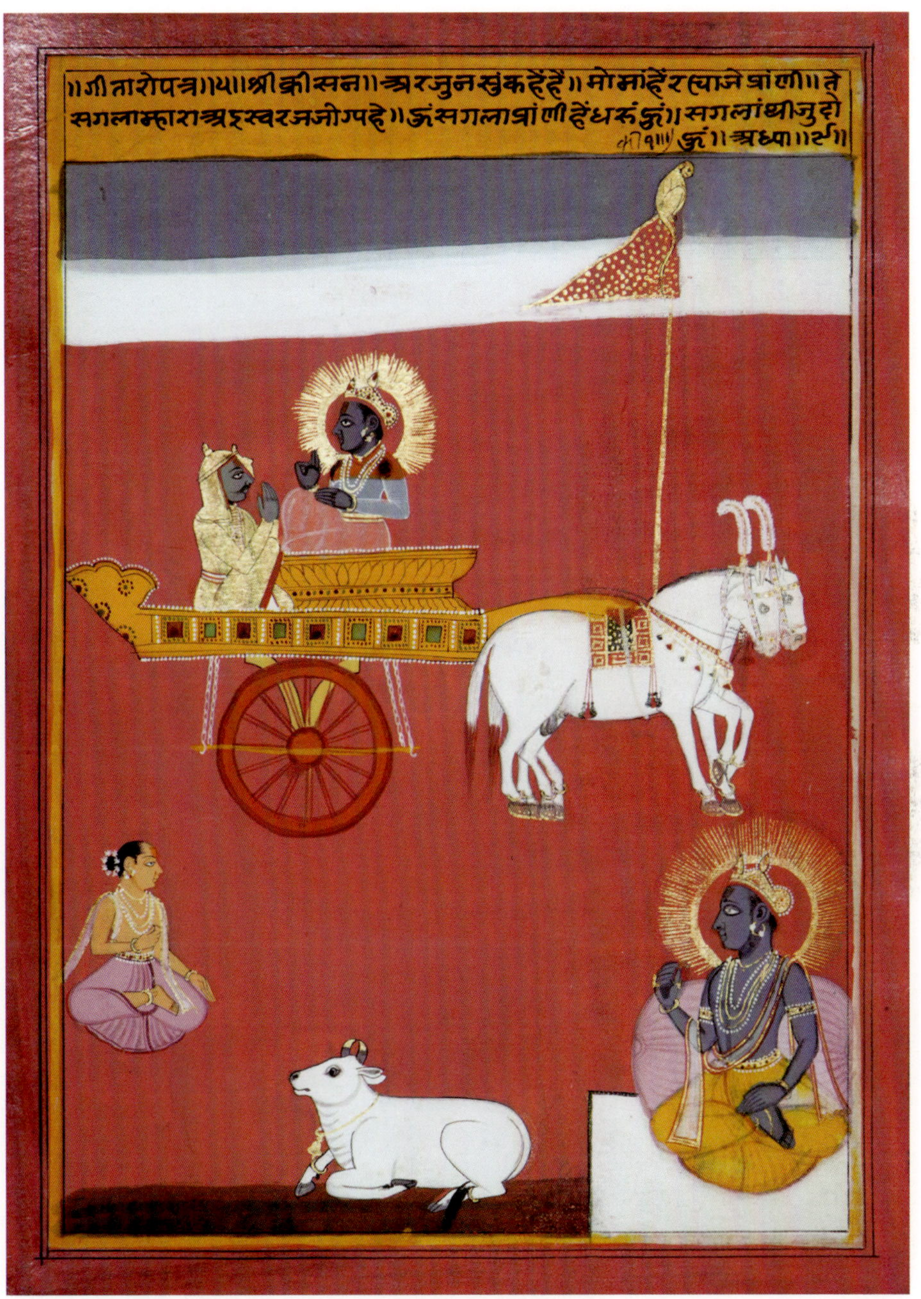

|5| श्री कृष्ण कह रहे हैं कि हे अर्जुन! सारे भूत मुझमें स्थित नहीं हैं किन्तु मेरी योगशक्ति को देख कि प्राणियों को उत्पन्न करने और उनका धारण-पोषण करने वाला होते हुए भी उनमें स्थित नहीं हूँ।

|5| Sri Krishna says: Hey Arjuna! All things are not in me. But see, such is my yogic power that, while I create and sustain all things, I am not contained by them.

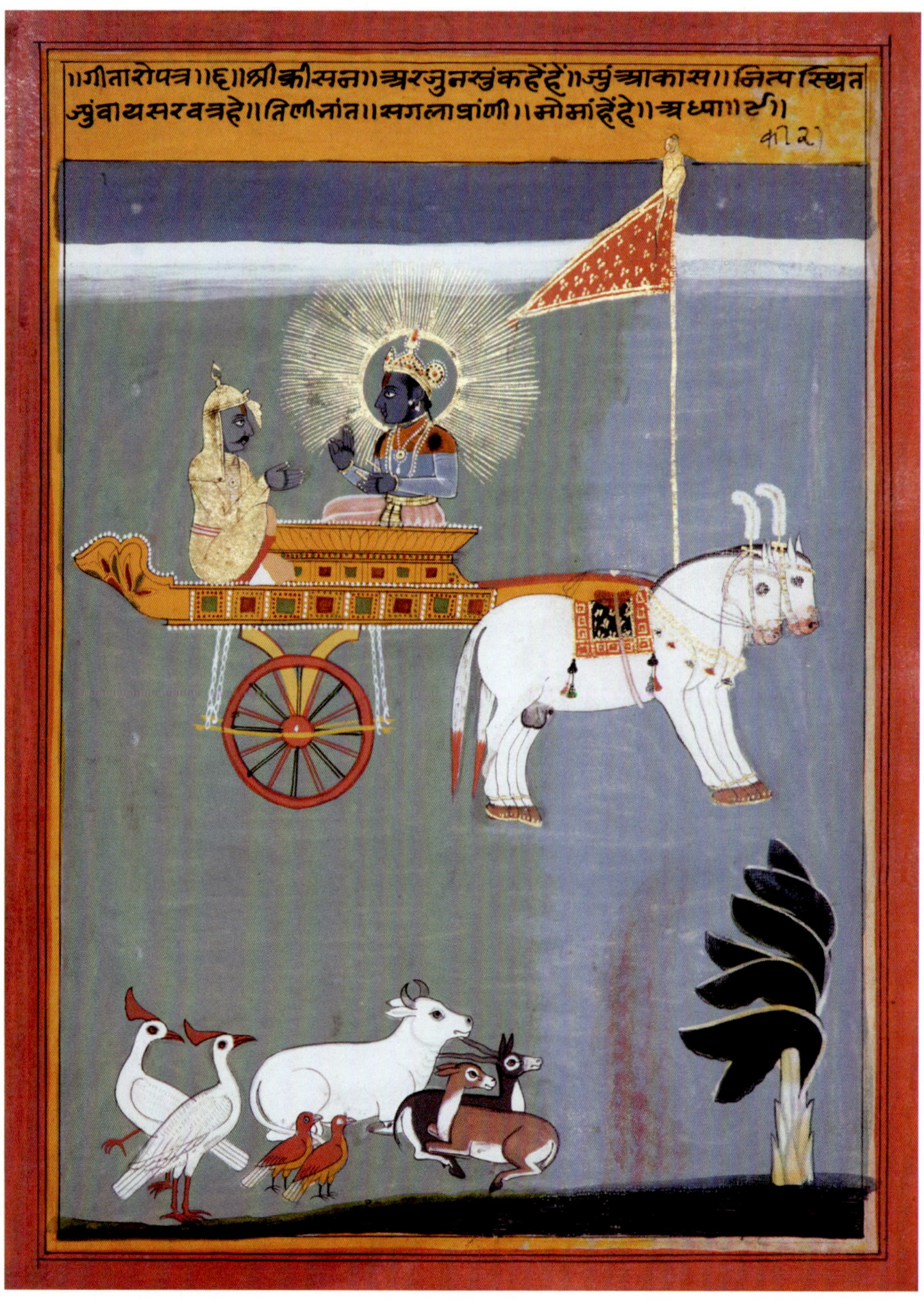

|6| श्री कृष्ण आगे कहने लगे, हे अर्जुन! जैसे आकाश में वायु सदा स्थित रहती है, वैसे ही सभी प्राणी मुझमें ही स्थित हैं, ऐसा जानो।

|6| Sri Krishna further says: Hey Arjuna! You should know that just as the wind is always present in the sky, all beings are always present in me.

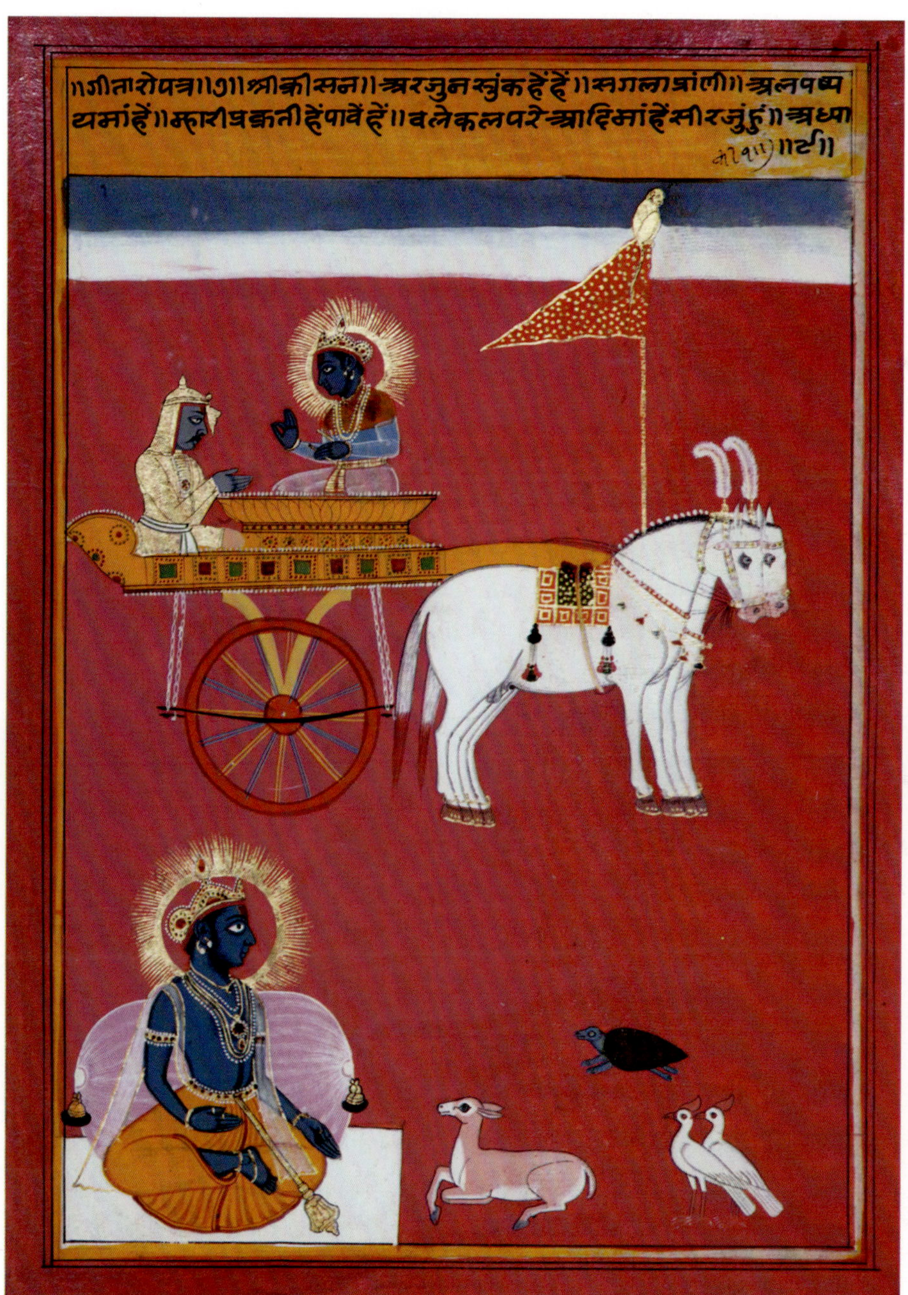

|7| श्री कृष्ण आगे समझाते हुए कह रहे हैं कि सभी प्राणी कल्पों के अंत में मेरी प्रकृति को प्राप्त होते हैं और कल्पों के आरंभ में उनको मैं फिर से उत्पन्न करता हूँ।

|7| Sri Krishna further explains: At the end of a cosmic cycle, all beings merge into my nature; and at the beginning of the next cosmic cycle, I create them again.

Illuminating verse 17, Brahma, Krishna and some priests sit on a floral floor beside a rocky hill and exchange stories about previous incarnations and earthly chronologies. In a corner, four-headed Brahma carries in two of his hands copies of the Vedas, while in the opposite corner he is absorbed in an intense discussion with Krishna. In the painting for verse 33, Krishna is talking to two learned pundits and, in the painting for verse 34, he is separately instructing two kings. In neither of these paintings is Krishna depicted as an idol that is so remote from earthly things and human emotions that he can only be worshipped. His divinity is familiar and approachable, and, at the same time, transcendent of earthly time and space.

The artist keeps in mind Krishna's assertion, that while the sins of those unique souls who drink the mystic soma of the scriptures are washed away and they ascend toward heaven (verse 20), such a spiritual journey is difficult and possible only for the rarest of earthly beings. Appropriately, the painter shows three men floating in the sky in a mysterious 'soul-boat' above the sun-encircled head of Krishna. There are also two other seekers of the divine, sitting high on a sacred mountain, who are no longer troubled by their knowledge of mortality. If they have been "purified from sin" (Swami 55), three others on the earth below, sitting before ritual fires, look like apprentices of the sacred. Their quest for knowledge has just begun; they are still earth-bound. They may be models of ritual performance, but we wonder what their ultimate fate will be? The painting is ambiguous. The *Jnaneshwari*, commenting on this verse, wonders if they hope to use the merit they acquire through such rites, merely to enjoy the "heavenly pleasures" the court of Indra promises; for to do good deeds only to fulfil desire is as sure a path to hell as to do evil. Or, do they, like Arjuna, long for nothing less than "the pure bliss of the Eternal" (*Jnaneshwari* 1:238)?

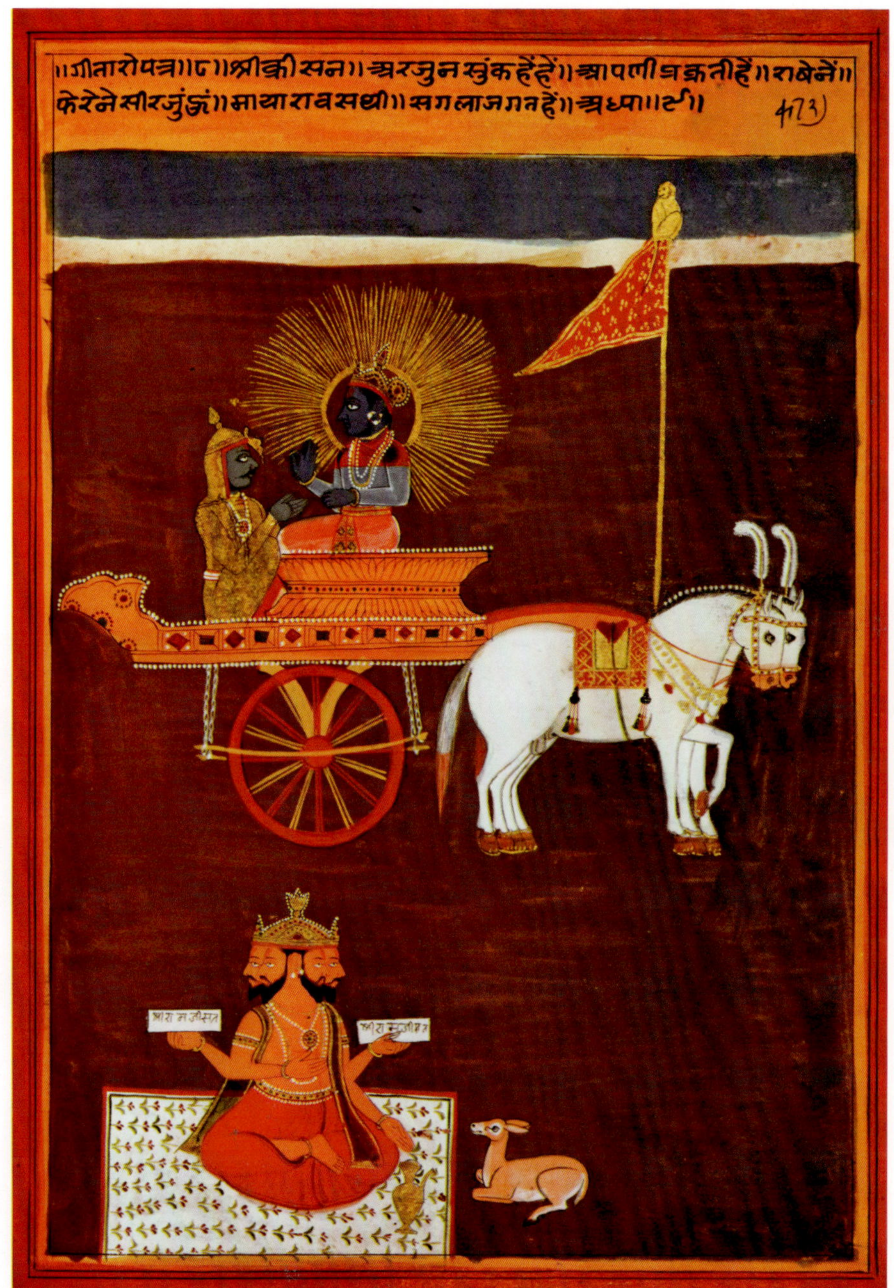

|8| श्री कृष्ण आगे कहने लगे कि हे अर्जुन! अपनी प्रकृति को वश में कर मैं उन सभी भूतों को पुनः-पुनः उत्पन्न करता हूँ, जो प्रकृति के वश में होने के कारण परतंत्र हैं।

|8| Sri Krishna says: Hey Arjuna! In complete control of my own Being, I create, again and again, all things which are under the control of nature.

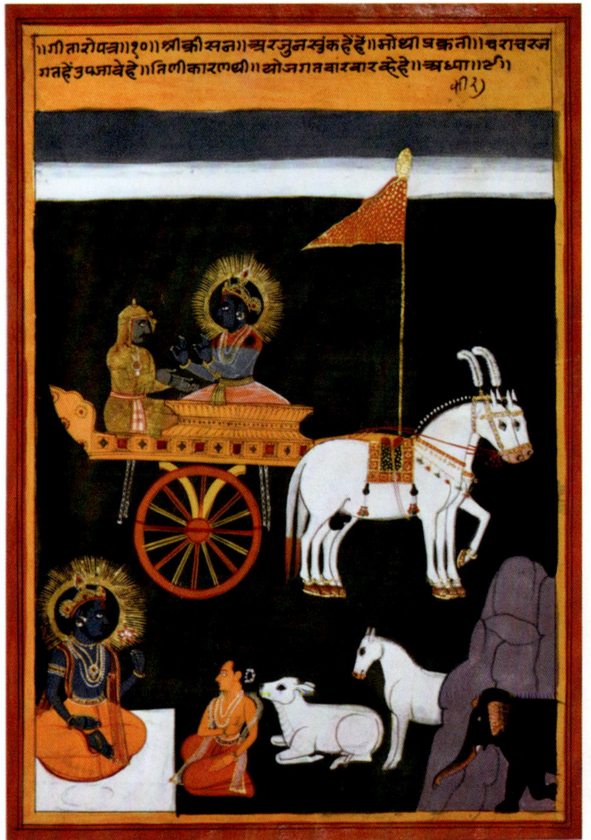

|10| हे अर्जुन! यह प्रकृति भी मुझसे है जो चराचर जगत को रचती है और इसी कारण से संसार चक्र घूम रहा है।

|10| Sri Krishna says: Hey Arjuna! I have created the entire universe and it revolves because of me.

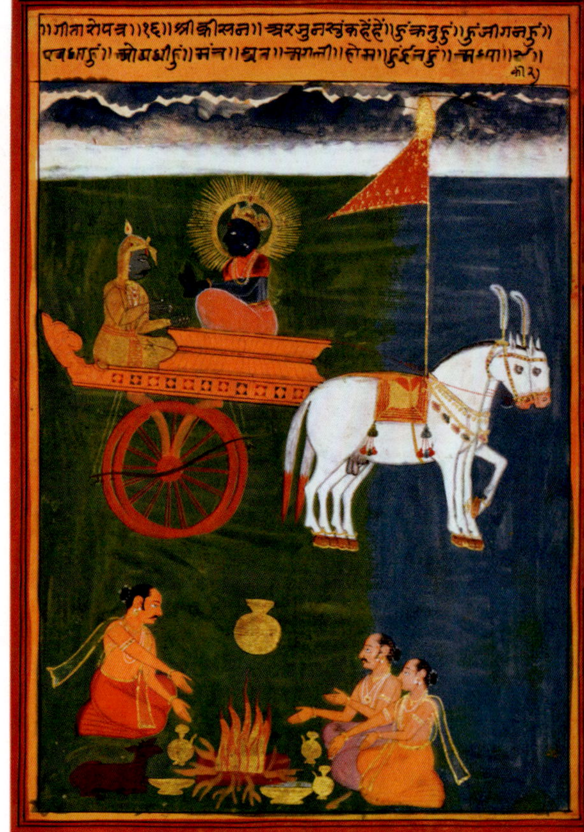

|16| हे अर्जुन! मैं क्रतु हूँ, यज्ञ मैं हूँ, स्वधा मैं हूँ, औषधि मैं हूँ, मंत्र मैं हूँ, घृत मैं हूँ, अग्नि मैं हूँ और आहुति भी मैं ही हूँ।

|16| Sri Krishna says: Hey Arjuna! I am the ritual and the sacrifice; I am the medicinal herb; I am the chant and the butter; I am the fire and the offering.

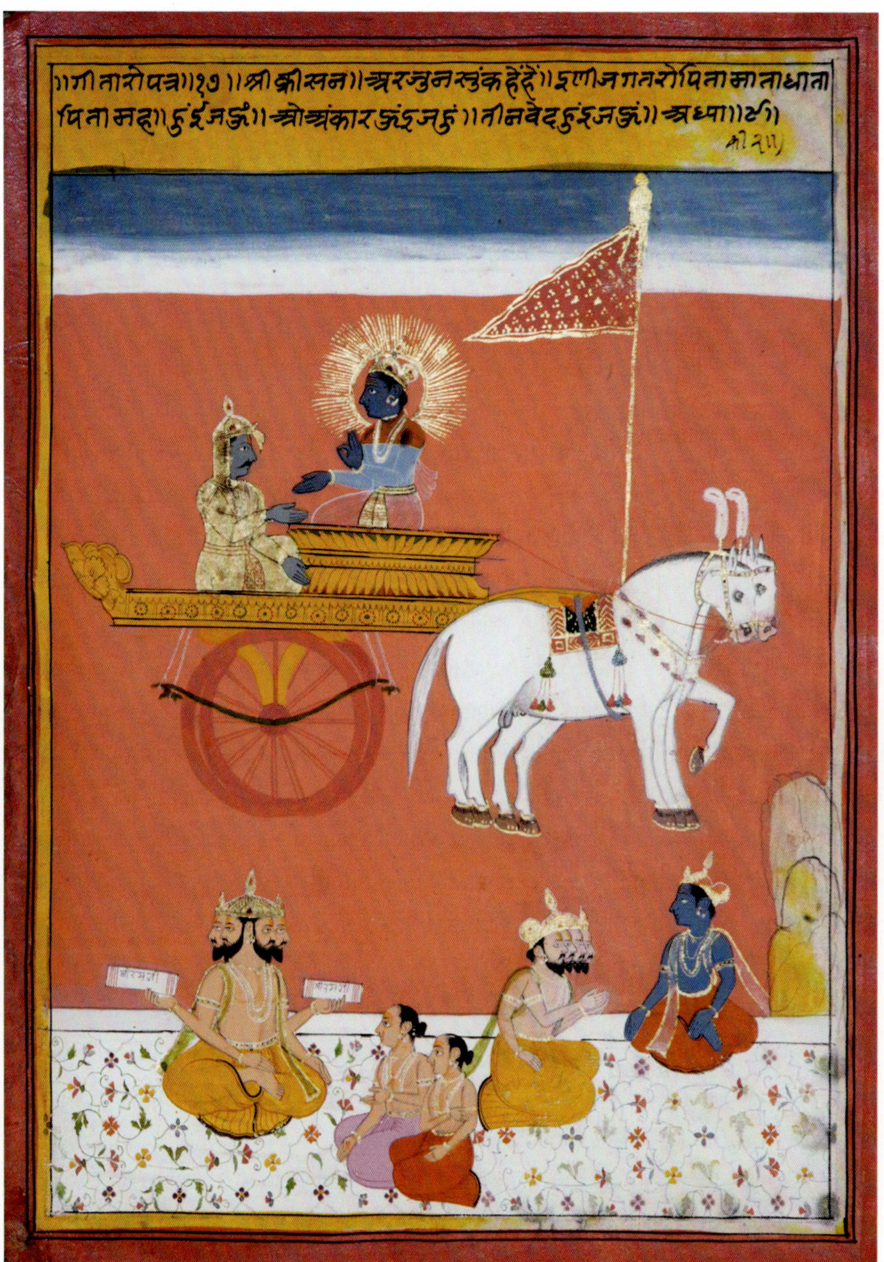

|17| आगे श्री कृष्ण कहने लगे, हे अर्जुन! मैं इस जगत का पिता, माता, पितामह और धाता हूँ। मैं जानने योग्य पवित्र ओंकार हूँ। ऋग्वेद, सामवेद और यजुर्वेद मैं ही हूँ।

|17| Sri Krishna says: Hey Arjuna! I am the father, mother, grandfather and creator of this universe. I am known as the sacred AUM; I am the *Rigveda*, the *Samaveda*, and the *Yajurveda*.

If the painting for verse 20 is in the spirit of inquiry and painted against a bright, sunlit blue space, the painting for verse 25 is a dark, brooding work. The verse speaks about the idea that human beings become what they worship or desire. The painting shows five isolated worshippers of various deities who, instead of travelling skyward, remain in their narrow self-created and confined spaces. Their sectarian exclusivity is made apparent by the different coloured enclosures in which they sit to perform self-absorbed rituals. Since the idols they worship are limited in power, their aspirations too, as the verse says, are limited. What they desire from the gods is not 'the peace that passeth understanding', but satisfaction of their small aims and ambitions. What they do not realise is that "sacrifices, charity, austerities or any such efforts of which a man is proud are worthless; they are as ineffective here as a blade of grass" (*Jnaneshwari* 1: 242). However, they do have, as the verse recognises, and the painting illuminates, the same potential for spiritual transformation as a seed has for growing and flourishing. But, like the seed, they could shrivel if they do not nourish and nurture their inherent intellectual and moral qualities (*gunas*). Instead, their belief that the divine is a remote, mysterious and an arbitrary giver of grace is a negation of Krishna's assertion that liberation can only be achieved by one who has the imaginative energy, the emotional freedom and the will to recognise that holiness inheres in everything that can be seen, touched, tasted, smelt and heard. Spiritual renewal is like the rising of the sun every day and like the coming of spring in every season. The divine is all around and in all things, but can only be recognised by the visionary eye, known by the enlightened mind or apprehended by a delighted heart.[6] Incapable, however, of imagining the immateriality of the divine, the idol worshippers in this painting reduce it to a collection of little things. That is why they are indistinct and obscure, intellectually frightened, superstitious creatures who think that god can be appeased like a tyrant through supplication. Each of them is diminutive; each seems to fade away like a phantom. Their idols are even smaller, more insignificant, inert, and inconsequential figurines of clay, stone or wood. The passivity of the worshippers can only result in the blankness of the soul; their daily, repetitive rounds of scriptural chanting can only lead them to old age and death. The Sufi mystic, Jalaluddin Rumi, says: "A man comes to be the thing on which he is bent" (Desai 271). We shape our tools and then our tools shape us; we become what we behold. Arjuna is being urged onward to unselfish action, moral exploration and decisions based on reason and imagination.

The second part of Krishna's teaching is that the divine exceeds the earthly; while it surrounds and suffuses everything, nothing contains it. It is interfused with all that

6 This is a restatement of *Atmabodha* quoted by Desai, *The Gospel of Selfless Action*, p. 265.

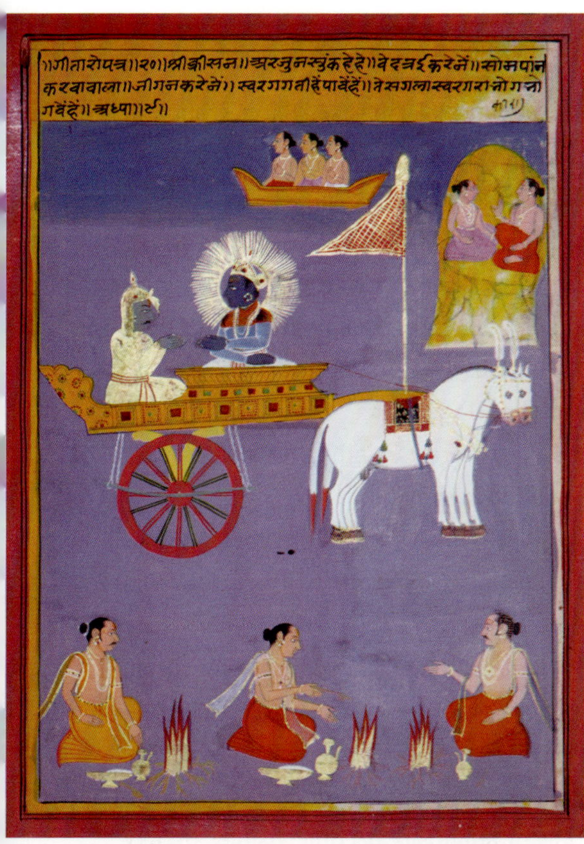

|20| हे अर्जुन! तीनों वेदों के ज्ञाता, सोमरस पीने वाले, पापरहित पुरुष यज्ञों द्वारा मुझे पूजते हैं, वे पुण्यफल से स्वर्गलोक को पाकर दिव्य सुख भोगते हैं।

|20| Sri Krishna says: Hey Arjuna! Those sinless ones who know the three Vedas and drink the soma juice, worship me with sacrificial rites, win the peace and joy of the gods.

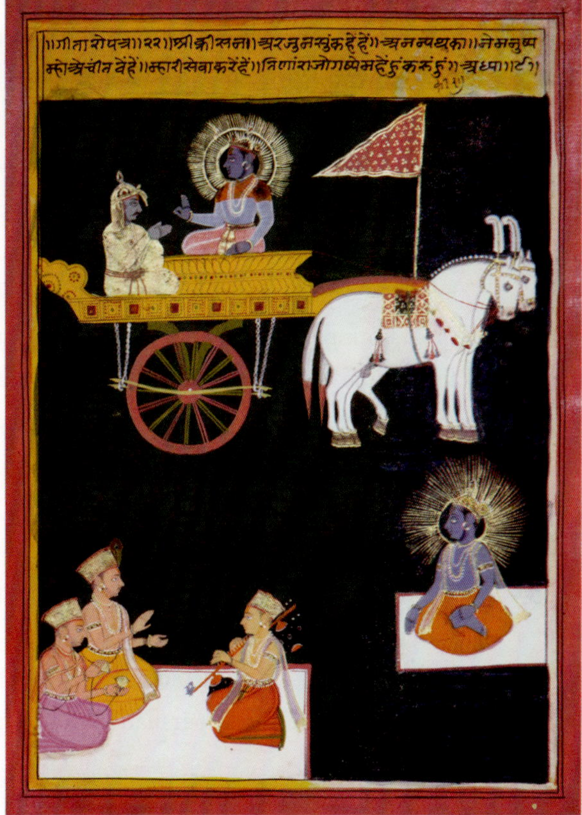

|22| श्री कृष्ण आगे कहने लगे, जो भक्तजन अनन्य भाव से मेरा चिंतन करते हुए मुझे पूजते हैं, ऐसे साधकों के योगक्षेम को स्वयं मैं वहन करता हूँ।

|22| Sri Krishna adds: I myself ensure that the attainments of those who worship only me with discipline and complete devotion are always protected.

exists and is yet utterly transcendent. In comparison, all that belongs to the earth is limited, frail and transitory. This knowledge, however, need not produce despondency or a sense of tragedy nor call upon human beings to overreaching rebellion. It should, instead, make way for tolerant civility and responsible action toward all.

Since the paintings and the verses of this chapter are preparing the ground for revelation, the background colours create an aura of holiness. The artifice is worth noticing. Most of the colours are bright crimson, lacquer red or vermillion, chosen to create a feeling of awe-inspiring grandeur, lucidity, valour and sacrality. The background colours in many of the earlier paintings were disconcerting, in keeping with Arjuna's tormented concern with the legitimacy of war and retribution: black, grey, rock-brown or sandy. From now on these colours shall appear only rarely to indicate that anguish is receding and despair is being replaced by the confidence of grace.

Such a slow emotional transformation in the *rasa* of the pictorial space, anthropologists of religious journeys tell us, happens to pilgrims who set out from home in search of spiritual comfort or truth. According to Victor Turner, the structure of a pilgrimage is as follows: in the beginning the path is characterised by secular chaos; there is expectation and longing, but also apprehension and fear; no activity is charged with any moral or religious frission. But as the pilgrim gets closer to the temple, holy shrine or grotto, the atmosphere begins to change. The turmoil of time seems to vanish; danger is left behind; greater signs and symbols of religiosity become visible; anxiety changes to anticipation; objects become carriers of fables; each step seems to be part of some ancient moral encounter; till, finally, at the door of the sanctum, the pilgrim becomes a participant in the parable of the god he has come to see.[7] If one arranges the paintings for this chapter and subsequent ones sequentially, one would recognise that the artist is following a similar emotional and spiritual path. The colours now only rarely evoke feelings of despondency unless a verse especially draws attention to human folly or ignorance, inertia or obdurateness. There is also a multiplication of the images of Krishna (paintings for verses 33 and 34). And in keeping with the paradox that the divine is present in all things and yet not contained by any, each image has the essential quality of being self-contained and utterly transcendent. There is sympathy in Krishna's eyes and compassion in his gestures, but there is also the stillness that comes with complete detachment from all the creatures of the earth. As observers we are forced to be silent; persuaded to listen calmly to our own inner voices; and realise

7 Victor Turner, *Dramas, Fields and Metaphors: Symbolic Action in Human Society* (Ithaca: Cornell University Press, 1974).

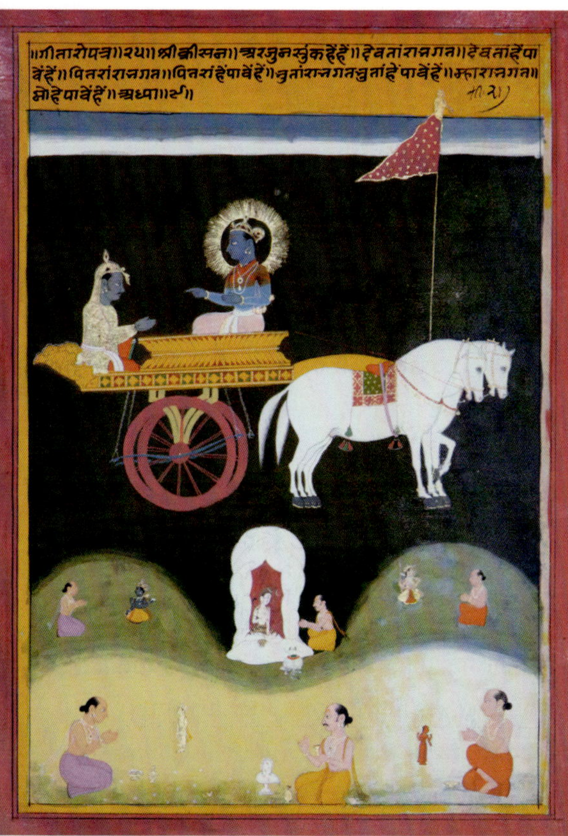

|25| श्री कृष्ण समझाते हुए कहने लगे कि हे अर्जुन! देवताओं को पूजने वाले देवताओं को प्राप्त होते हैं, पितरों को पूजने वाले पितरों को और भूतों को पूजने वाले भूतों को प्राप्त होते हैं और मुझे पूजने वाले मुझे ही प्राप्त करते हैं।

|25| Explaining further, Sri Krishna says: Hey Arjuna! Those who worship other gods, go to other gods; those who worship their ancestors, go to their ancestors; those who worship ghosts, go to ghosts; and those who worship only me, come to me. I accept all.

|33| हे अर्जुन! फिर पुण्यात्मा ब्राह्मण और राजर्षि भक्तों का तो कहना ही क्या! इस अनित्य और दुखद लोक को प्राप्त होकर अब तू मेरा ही भजन कर।

|33| Sri Krishna says: Hey Arjuna! How easy is it then for the sinless brahmin and the royal sages who are my worshippers! In this transient world of sorrow, you should worship only me.

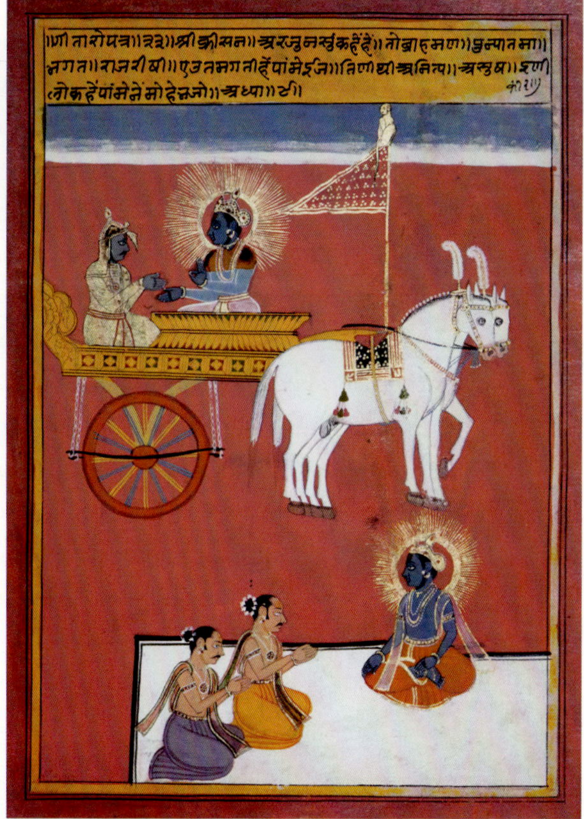

that the war about to be fought, like any other war, is a consequence of *tamas*; that it is a wilful decent into *duragraha* (the compulsion to do evil).

Since the world's reality is not denied in the *Gita*, the artist indicates its sensuous presence through a series of minimalist representations from the natural and social world. Thus, the beautiful images of cows, antelopes, birds, tortoises, wind-blown plantain trees, white flowers, pearls and handsome yogis are a testimony to the idea that nature and man are alive with the divine spirit. In the eyes of the painter, the forms of nature he draws are important not because of their verisimilitude, but because they are symbolic of the good that suffuses the world. Of course, Allah Baksh is aware that the *Mahabharata* is a record of how that original moral force is distorted and turns darkly evil. He wants, however, to pictorially recall, as Krishna also does in these verses, the world as it was in *satya yuga*: beautiful and good (paintings for verses 5, 7, 8 and 11). His picture-language asserts that beauty and moral innocence are the essence of all created things because the divine is in them.

There is, however, a greater truth to which Krishna's presence on earth bears witness; a truth which must survive the weariness of war. Sensing that truth, Allah Baksh wants us to know that the earth is the place "where Being passes into Appearance and unity into Variety"; the 'feel' of the original divinity in all things is always present even if we, at times, lose sight of it, or refuse to accept it in our scorning disbelief. Therefore, it is important in times of great violence to bear witness to the fact that beauty and calm understanding are also aspects of the truth of our world because otherwise we shall only face despair as Arjuna does. It is, however, not the artist's contention that the divine in history and time can only be recognised in beautiful forms because that would be a sentimental falsification. So, like Krishna's verses, he also invites us to recognise that the world's divinity always survives *asuric* terror. That is why Krishna is depicted, not only on the chariot speaking to Arjuna, but also seated on a white platform of earth. He is majestic and authoritative, but also full of sympathy and blessings. The artist bears witness to the paradox which Krishna reveals in this chapter: the Supreme Being gives structure to all that exists, adorns every aspect of the universe, and is present as a vital force in every moment as it unfolds. At the same time, the Supreme Being is detached, uninvolved and beyond the particular.

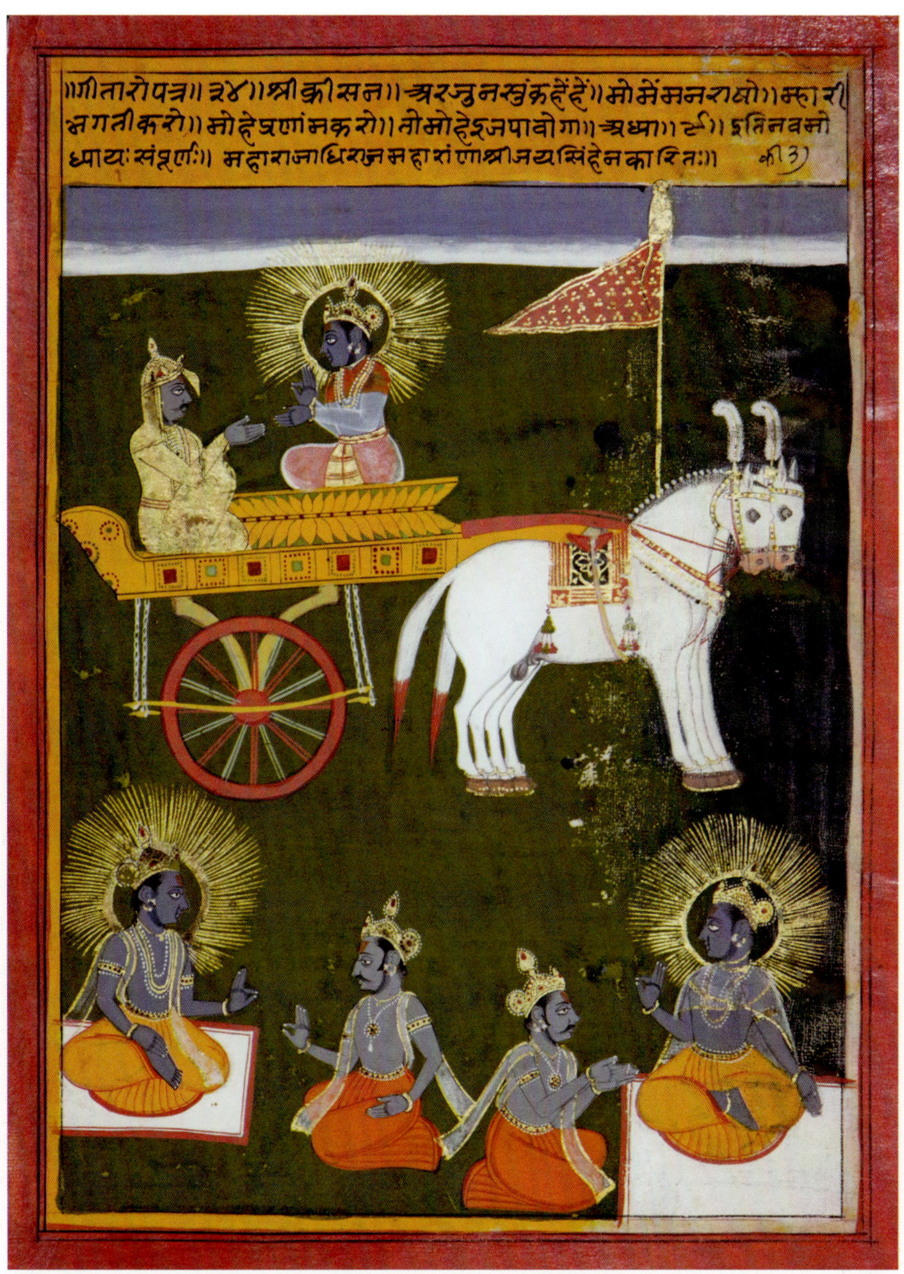

|34| श्री कृष्ण आगे कहने लगे, हे अर्जुन! तू मेरा भक्त बन, मुझमें मन लगा, मेरी पूजा कर, मुझे प्रणाम कर। इस तरह अपनी आत्मा को मुझमें युक्त कर, मेरे परायण हो, तो तू मुझे ही प्राप्त होगा।

|34| Sri Krishna further says: Hey Arjuna! Become my devotee, fix your mind on me, worship me, and bow before me; attach your self to me, make me the end you wish to attain, and you shall indeed become one with me.

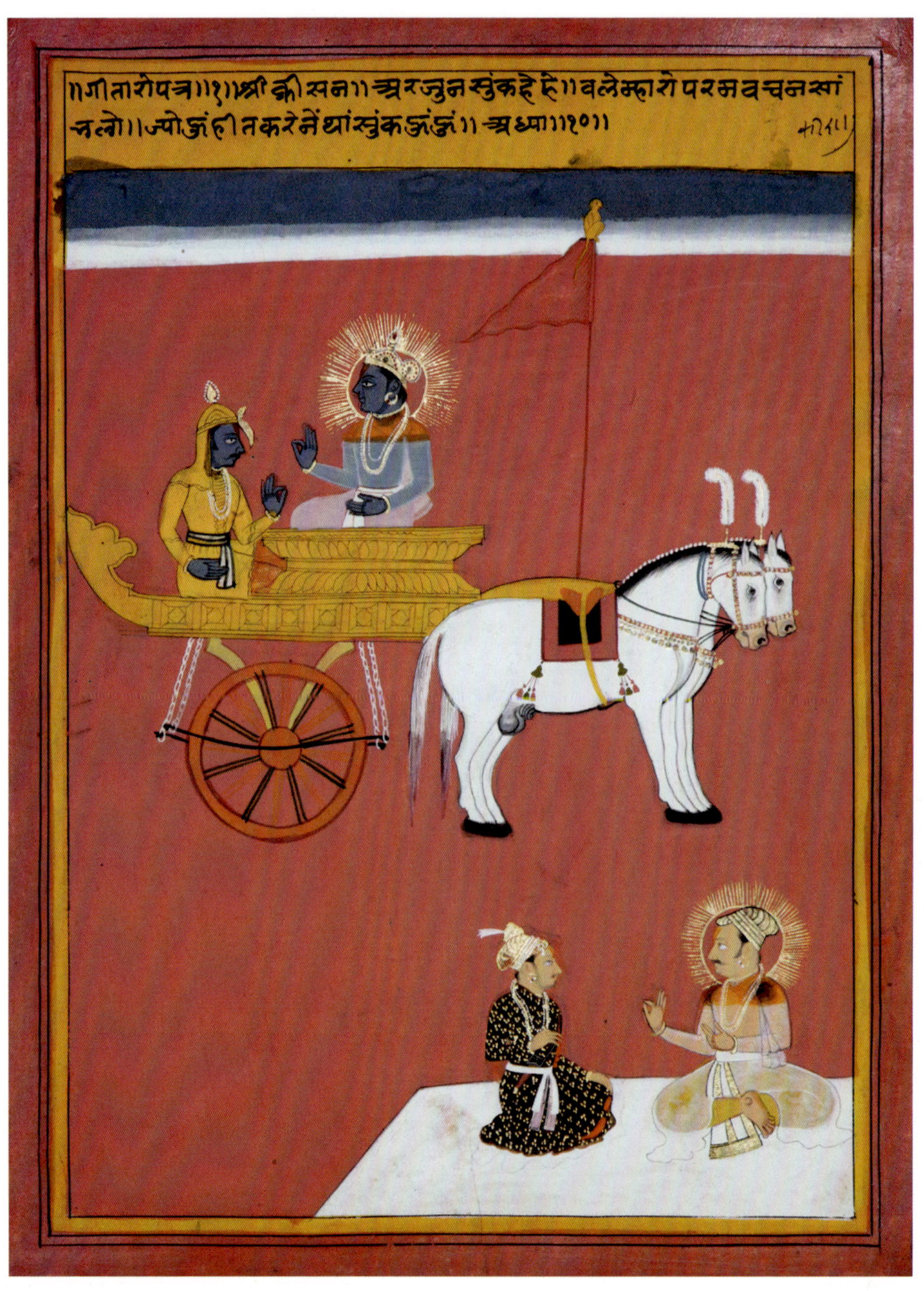

|1| श्री कृष्ण कहने लगे कि हे अर्जुन! मेरा यह परम वचन सुन, जिसे मैं तुझे अपना प्रिय मानकर, तेरे हित की कामना से कह रहा हूँ।

|1| Sri Krishna says: Hey Arjuna! Listen to my supreme advice. I am offering it because I love you. It is for your welfare.

CHAPTER 10

In Chapter 9, Krishna's persuasive song about his own divinity resolves some of Arjuna's questions and anxieties. Arjuna is no longer in doubt about the ethics of the action he must perform. The dialogic structure of the *Gita* and its dramatic quality are almost over in the previous chapter. Arjuna is now a devotee who is morally and psychologically ready, a rare seeker, who can face and endure Krishna's revelation about the world and his own divinity (see painting for verse 1). However, to complete his spiritual education, Arjuna still has to take one final and necessary step. Thus far, he has *thought* his way toward faith. He has understood that devotion to, or faith in, a personal God in itself does not lead to the good; committed action on behalf of dharma does. One can assume that, while he has acquired scriptural learning and endured the rigors of *tapasya*, his mind is still lost in the *avidya* of scholastic complexities. He is yet to be granted that final flash of illumination when he will *know* Krishna not only as the *other* of himself, but as his own self.

Scholars of religious experience say that during the journey toward enlightenment, those who assert faith can still fail; the ego can still become an obstacle; the self can still doubt or be afraid. Simone Weil tells us that for enlightenment, knowledge is useful and faith is essential. But neither is sufficient, since the revelation of the sacred has no precedent in the seeker's frame of knowledge; its only precedent is that "which is itself unprecedented."[1] To experience the unprecedented, Arjuna has to make a final effort to leave behind all the conventions and traditions of knowledge. There must be, as there always is, for any leap of faith, "a long deep process of unlearning...followed by a complete change of being."[2] Indeed, the sudden break of the sacred into the secular is a *never-before* occurrence and a *never-again* event. Further, there can be nothing similar to this epiphany in the future, otherwise it shall cease to be unprecedented. What is called for is the complete and final surrender of all that Arjuna has known.

Arjuna must understand that great visionary truth is not attainable through the effort of will or reason alone; it cannot be demonstrated; it cannot be found by repeating ancient precepts of the yoga sutras or upanishadic abstractions. Nor does wilfulness

1 Elaine Scarry, *On Beauty and Being Just.* (Princeton: Princeton University Press, 1999), p. 1.

2 Murdoch, *Metaphysics as a Guide to Morals*, p. 54.

lead to any moral improvement as in the case of Duryodhana. Arjuna's questions suggest that he has the sensitivity to pay heed to the world around him; to lead an attentive and examined life, and so empathise with the pain of others. Dhritarashtra, in contrast, lives thoughtlessly. Arjuna already knows that heroic expenditure of energy, whether on the battlefield or in ashramite regimes, rarely ever brings one closer to the truth, though it can establish earthly kingdoms and install gurus. He is a warrior with visionary aspirations. Since he is also a man of knowledge, he recognises the ruthless truth that on the battlefield "humanity must perforce prey on itself" (*King Lear*). Even if victory is attained there, fortune soon turns into blood and mire (as the *Stree Parva* so harrowingly shows). In the field of knowledge, however, there is only endless courtesy and the continuous assertion of *humanitas*—a word which in our time also includes ecological gratitude.[3] To become a fighter for the truth, Arjuna must become a visionary; one who can sing the kingdom the *Gita* imagines into existence. It is ironic, therefore, that the Pandavas do not succeed in creating of a compassionate kingdom despite the teachings of the *Gita*.

Krishna again talks about those human and social nuances of action and knowledge which will save Arjuna's world from being dug up from its roots so as to keep everything in it grounded in truth and enduring wisdom. Krishna's repetitiveness is structurally akin to repetition in any religious litany or religiously inspired music. No longer is the *Gita* a conversation between two friends. It is from now on a discourse by a great teacher to an awestruck disciple. Indeed, Allah Baksh responds to this change by drawing two teaching sites with simplicity and minimalism to illustrate the first verse. Against a crimson background, he paints two authoritative teachers and two keen learners. One is the sacred space of the chariot above the earth; the other is a privileged space of white marble in secular time. The two teachers have golden halos around their heads. The teacher in the secular space may or may not be teaching the *Gita*. But, without the presence of the chariot of learning above, where metaphysical concerns are being addressed, this teacher's ideas and presence would be empty of meaning, which is why he also has a golden halo. His teaching, in an open and unframed space, suggests that the teachers in the Indic tradition, those who have made breakthroughs like the Buddha or Mahavira have always been non-dogmatic inquirers. They do not sit in temples and madarsas. Krishna himself is a good example. Allah Baksh adds more images of non-sectarian teaching spaces in the painting for verse 2. What Krishna teaches emerges from, and is concerned with, the most serious of human questions being raised at the boundaries of existence.

3 Panofsky, *Meaning in the Visual Arts*, pp. 23-24.

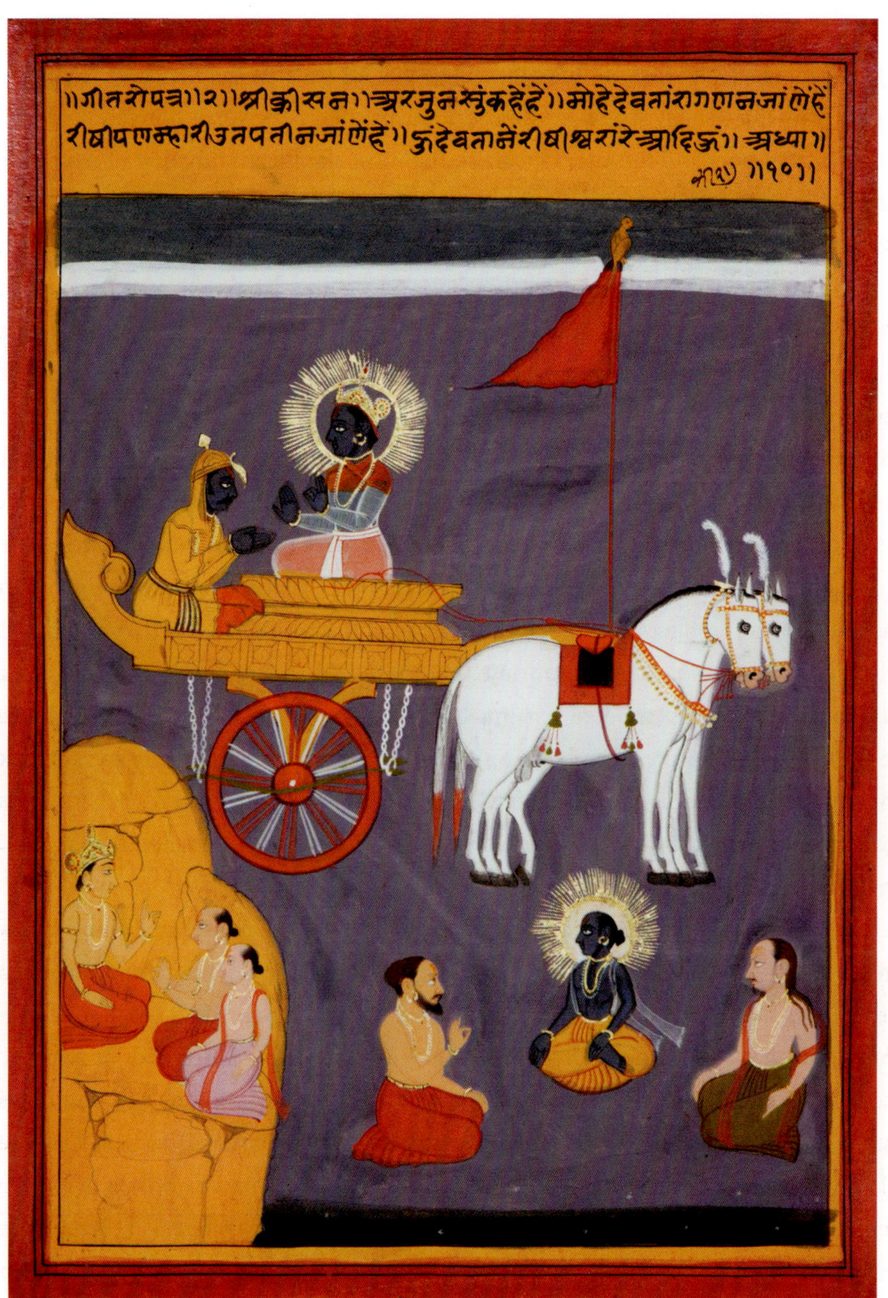

|2| हे अर्जुन! मेरी उत्पत्ति को न देवता जानते हैं, न महर्षिगण क्योंकि मैं सभी देवों और महर्षियों का आदि कारण हूँ।

|2| Sri Krishna says: Hey Arjuna! Neither the gods nor the great sages know my origin because I am the source of all the gods and the great sages.

For both the teachers in the painting, education is about those philosophic, emotional, social or moral issues that are life-affirming. That, at least, is the thrust of Chapter 10. Judging from the visually striking response of the painter to the verse, one can suggest that for the ancient poet and the later day artist, the most significant function of education is to enable beauty to be perceived. Such perception is a prerequisite of enlightenment. One, of course, never forgets that the context is a war of annihilation. Arjuna is still wearing his golden armour and helmet, and the chariot's horses are trampling restlessly on the battlefield. Surprisingly, there are no signs of bows and arrows, shields and swords in the paintings for this chapter. Moral education, after all, can only be imparted to those who are unarmed and without encrustations of preconceived ideas, even scriptural ones. A tyrant can neither be enlightened nor redeemed. Indeed, as Simone Weil rightly asserts, it is "not God who proves the Moral Law," but the one who questions, doubts and hopes.[4]

A unique text like the *Gita* demands that imaginative listeners be willing to suspend received ideas; make a new beginning; renew inquiry. Allah Baksh comprehends that. Krishna and the teachers in this painting glow with an inner light; they are not dull technicians of the soul. It is appropriate that these two scenes of education are placed at the beginning of the chapter. Arjuna still feels inadequate. Not because he has not shed his disquiet, but because he is unsure if he is intellectually ready to receive the momentous revelation which is at hand. This is apparent in verse 12 where Arjuna pleads with Krishna to reveal his power and glory, but only if Krishna thinks that he can endure such knowledge.

One should add that in none of the paintings that follow, which are primarily about verses concerned with forms of knowledge, is it suggested that teaching must be restricted to the princes, the wealthy and some sections of society. Indeed, that would once again create a sense of exclusion and otherness in human communities and, of course, by extension, between species, resulting in the continuation of pointless and annihilating conflicts. That is why the artist, deeply sympathetic to what Krishna says to Arjuna about the original beauty of a world created by a compassionate god, paints lyrically charged scenes of teaching and learning. Amongst the keenest listeners of religious texts in these paintings are birds and animals, gods and demons, kings and commoners. Their presence as teachers and thinkers rememorialises a fundamental assertion of the *Gita* that the world at the beginning was inclusive and non-violent.[5] The places of teaching and learning in these paintings are quiet or full of the murmuring sounds of fountains

4 *Lectures on Philosophy*, translated by Hugh Price (Cambridge: Cambridge University Press, 1978), p. 71.

5 See Gandhi, *Sita's Kitchen*, pp. 68-70.

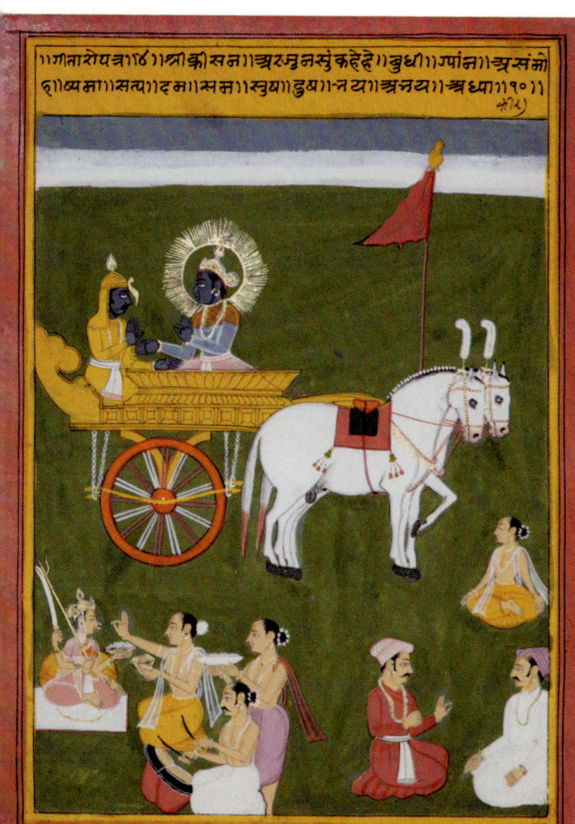

|4| श्री कृष्ण और समझाते हुए कहने लगे, हे अर्जुन! बुद्धि, ज्ञान, असम्मोह, क्षमा, सत्य, इन्द्रियनिग्रह, मनोनिग्रह, सुख-दुख, उत्पत्ति-प्रलय, भय-अभय सारे भाव मुझसे ही उत्पन्न जान।

|4| Sri Krishna further explains: Hey Arjuna! Intelligence, wisdom, non-illusion, forgiveness, truth, self-control, tranquillity, joy-sorrow, birth-death, fear and fearlessness all spring from me.

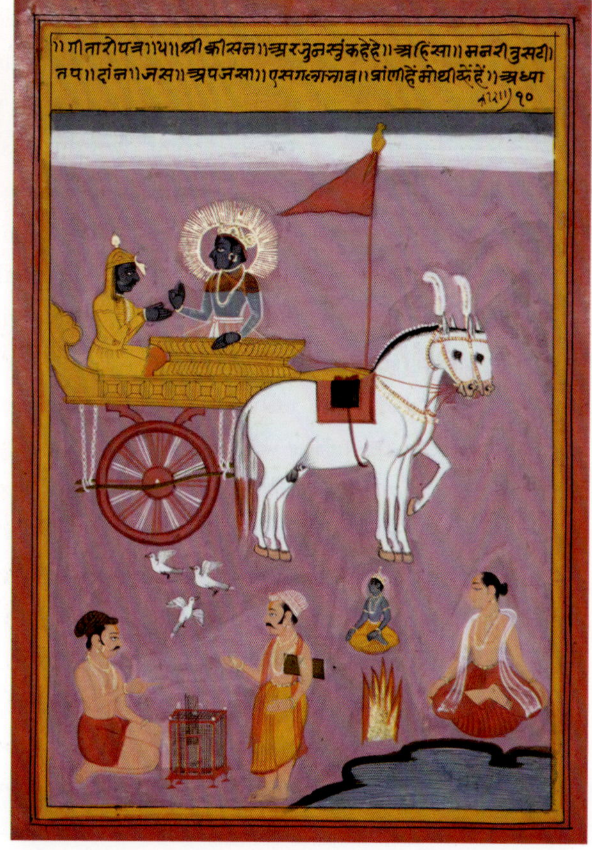

|5| हे अर्जुन! कृष्ण आगे कहने लगे कि अहिंसा, समता, तुष्टि, तप, दान, यश व अपयश इन सभी भावों को भी मुझसे ही उत्पन्न जान।

|5| Sri Krishna then says: Hey Arjuna! Nonviolence, equanimity, contentment, austerity, charity, fame and disgrace all spring from me.

(verse 40); they are at the banks of lakes fringed with wild flowers; they are sanctuaries lit by a golden sun or a mystic moon.

In painting after painting, Krishna speaks like an inspired teacher, his hand gestures are more and more energetic; his posture changes constantly. In the illustration for verse 19, even the painter is momentarily entranced. Here, as Arjuna finally admits that all his scepticism has dissolved and that he is ready for the final revelation of the truth, the painter does not surround the chariot with the usual choreography of scenes from ordinary life. Indeed, it is the only painting in which the chariot is enclosed in a vast crimson halo beneath a sky whose shades of blue lead the eye up and beyond the infinite horizon, indicating that, while Krishna is the animating principle of all things on earth, he is uncontainable.

Throughout this chapter, Krishna directs Arjuna's attention not to grand and universal ideas about god and eternity, Being and Time, but to small, transitory and commonplace things so that the heart can overcome its dread and the imagination can find its source of ecstasy. Krishna has said all this before, but here he offers, through reiteration, a simple formulation which does not require the mystifying exegesis of many of the *Gita*'s commentators. He tells Arjuna that there are innumerable non-heroic acts, ideas and actions that carry within them the radiance and the vitality of life. Each of them, in their own quiet, slow and meditative ways clarifies thought, sustains the order of the world, reveals its beauty and, hence, its truth. Allah Baksh would surely have accepted Weil's assertion, made at the time of another annihilatory war, that beauty is "an imitation of celestial harmony."[6] While the *Gita* recognises that there is a profound relationship between truth, beauty and peace, and that violence is perversion, none of the protagonists in the epic can escape war. Krishna says that he is mercy and pity, justice and compassion (verses 4, 30 and 34); he is the impulse behind all the arts of life which can be obtained by anyone who is calm, detached, controlled and has discriminating intelligence (verses 4 and 5 and 10); he is the maker of music and poetry which weakens the urge to war (verses 22, 26 and 35); he is every tree and every bird and so makes the surrounding world visible; he is both the singular letter uttered and the complex sentence spoken (verse 33); he makes each prayer possible and every myth imaginable (verses 25 and 30). In each of these, he says, human beings can find a peaceful alternative to a life of arrogant self-regard—of which war is the final and most heinous consequence. Nowhere does he say that he is the cause of violence; nor does he say that he can prevent the war. Instead, he implies, that it is

6 Weil, *Notebooks*, p. 246.

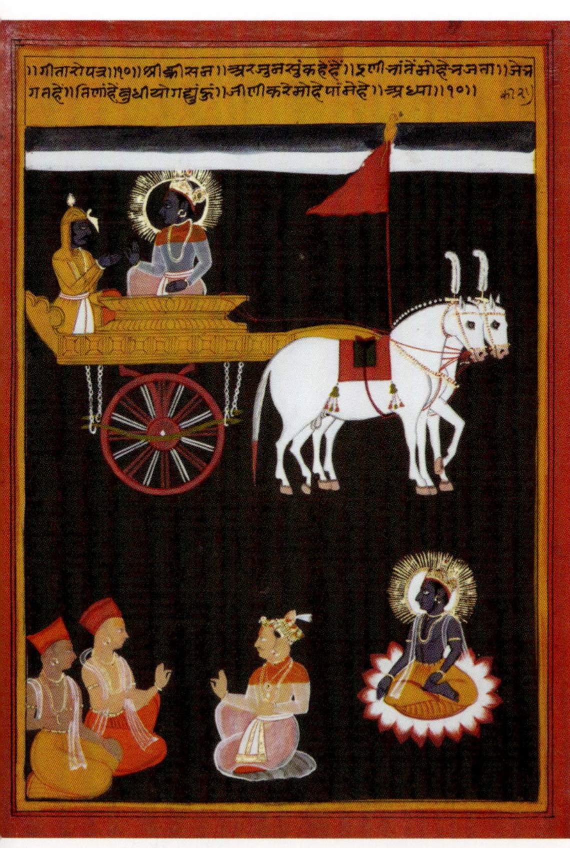

|10| हे अर्जुन! ऐसे नित्य-निरंतर मुझे भजते हुए जो भक्त हैं उनको मैं बुद्धियोग प्रदान करता हूँ, जिसके माध्यम से वे मुझे ही प्राप्त होते हैं।

|10| Hey Arjuna! I offer disciplined intellect to those devotees who always worship me; with its help they can always reach me.

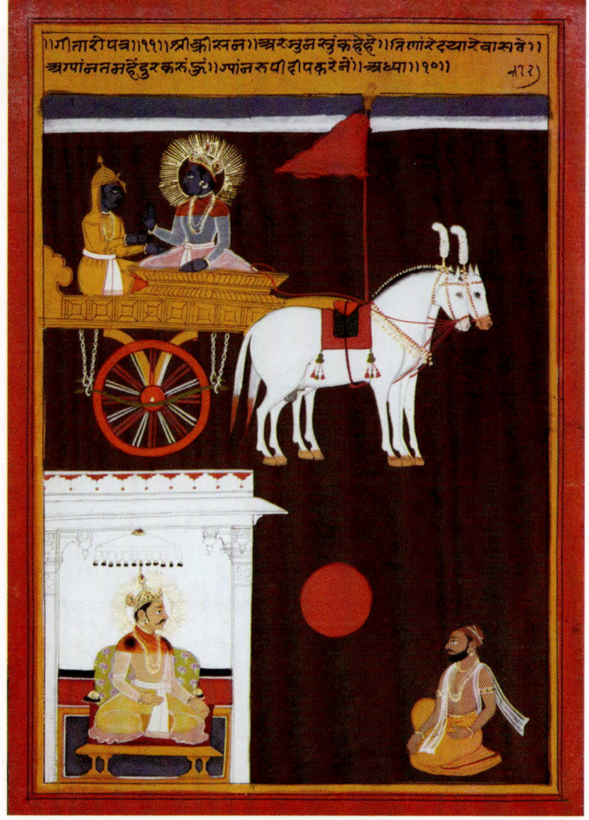

|11| श्री कृष्ण आगे कहने लगे कि उन पर दया करने के लिए उनके आत्मभाव में स्थित हुआ, मैं ही उनके अज्ञान जनित अंधकार को ज्ञान रूपी दीप से नष्ट करता हूँ।

|11| Sri Krishna further says: Out of compassion for them, I dwell in their hearts so that I can dispel the darkness of ignorance with the lamp of wisdom.

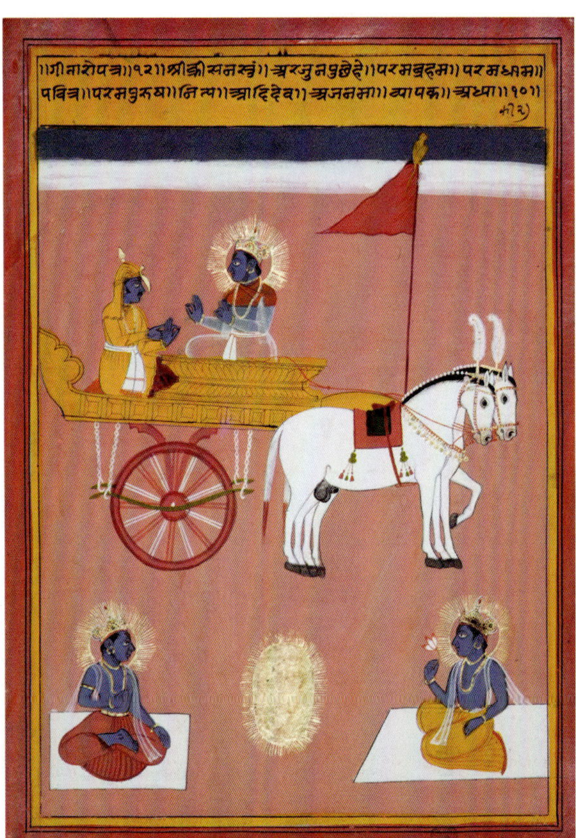

|12| यह सुन कर अर्जुन बोला, हे कृष्ण! आप परमब्रह्म, परमधाम, परम पवित्र, नित्य, दिव्य पुरुष, आदिदेव, अजन्मा और सर्वव्यापक हैं।

|12| Then Arjuna asks: Hey Krishna! You are the supreme Brahman, the eternal home, the purest of the pure; you are the immortal, divine self, the primal God, the unborn; you are omnipresent.

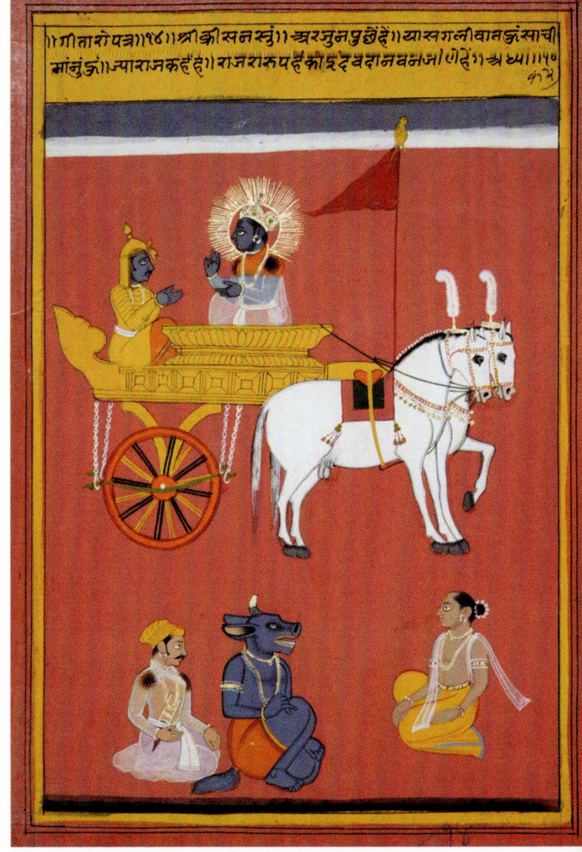

|14| अर्जुन कहने लगा, हे कृष्ण! आप मुझे जो कुछ भी कहते हैं, मैं उस सब को सत्य मानता हूँ। आपके स्वरूप को न तो देवता जानते हैं, न ही दानव।

|14| Arjuna continues: Hey Krishna! I accept all that you have told me as the Truth. Neither the gods nor the demons know your divine manifestation.

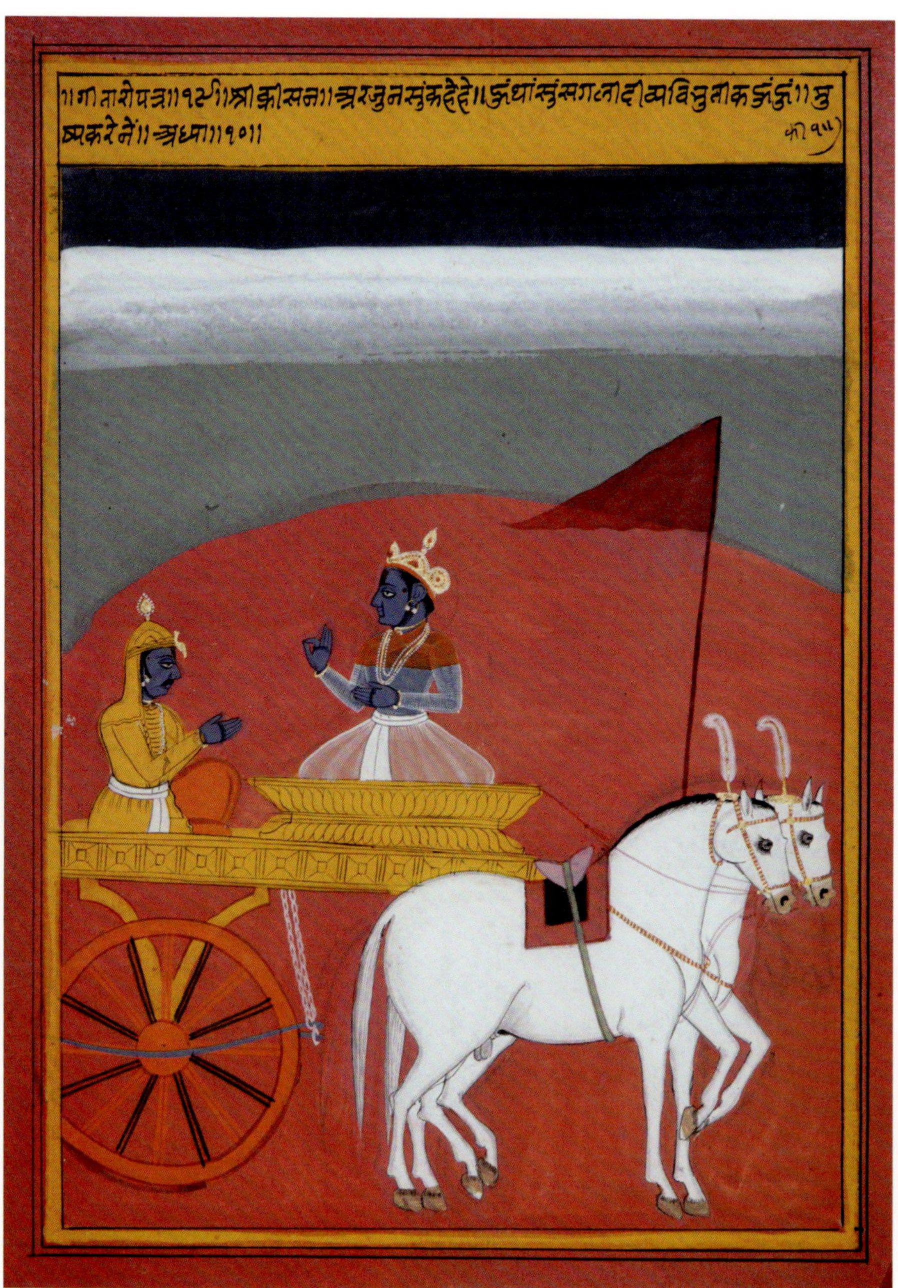

|19| प्रत्युत्तर में श्री कृष्ण कहने लगे, हे अर्जुन! अब मैं अपनी सारी दिव्य विभूतियों को तुझे प्रधानता से कहता हूँ क्योंकि मेरे विस्तार का कोई अन्त नहीं है।

|19| In response, Sri Krishna says: Hey Arjuna! I will recount to you only some of my divine attributes because there is no limit to my sacred powers.

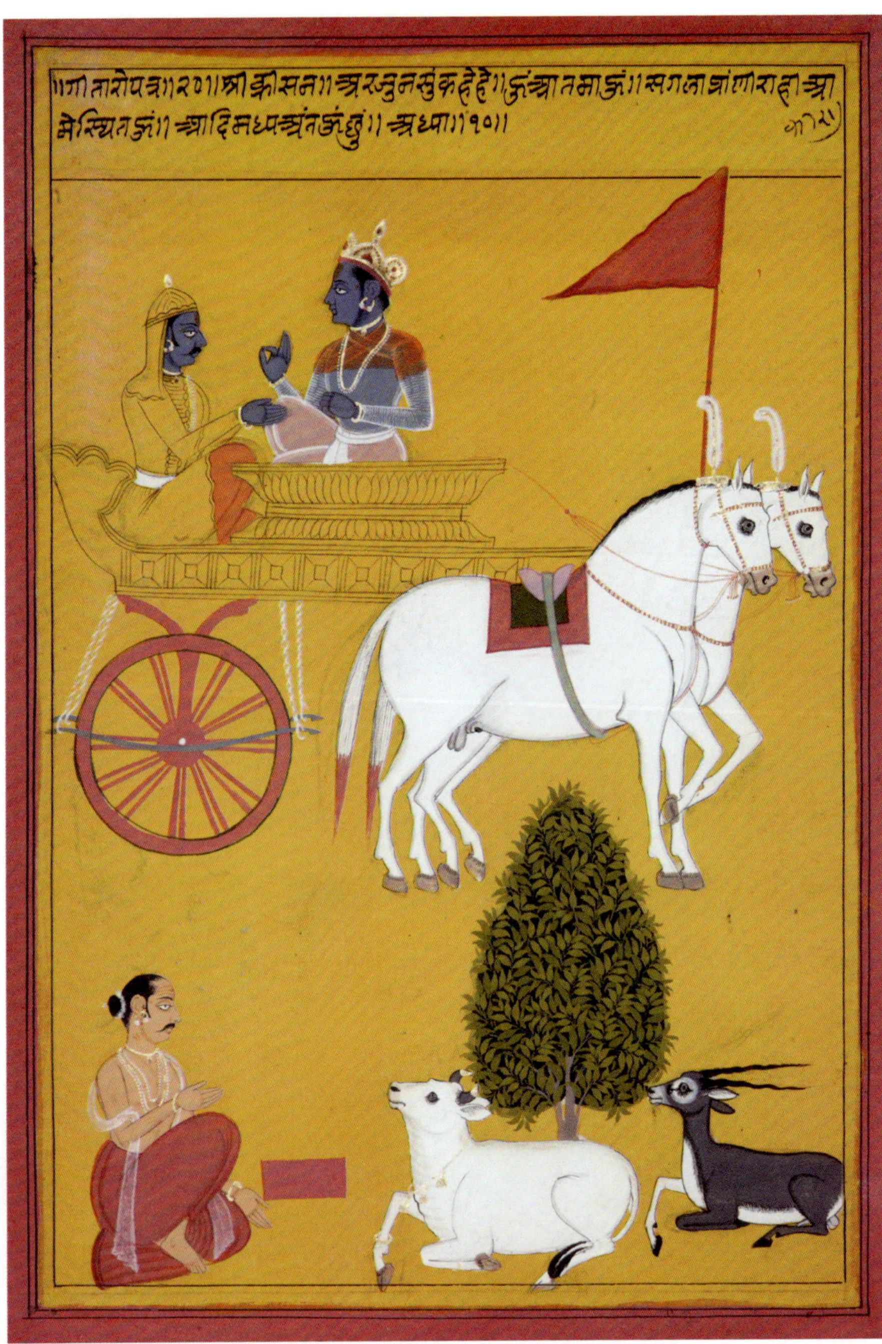

|20| हे अर्जुन! मैं सभी जीवों के हृदय में स्थित आत्मा हूँ, सभी प्राणियों का आदि, मध्य और अंत मैं ही हूँ।

|20| Hey Arjuna! I am the self that abides in the hearts of all creatures; I am the beginning, middle and end of all beings.

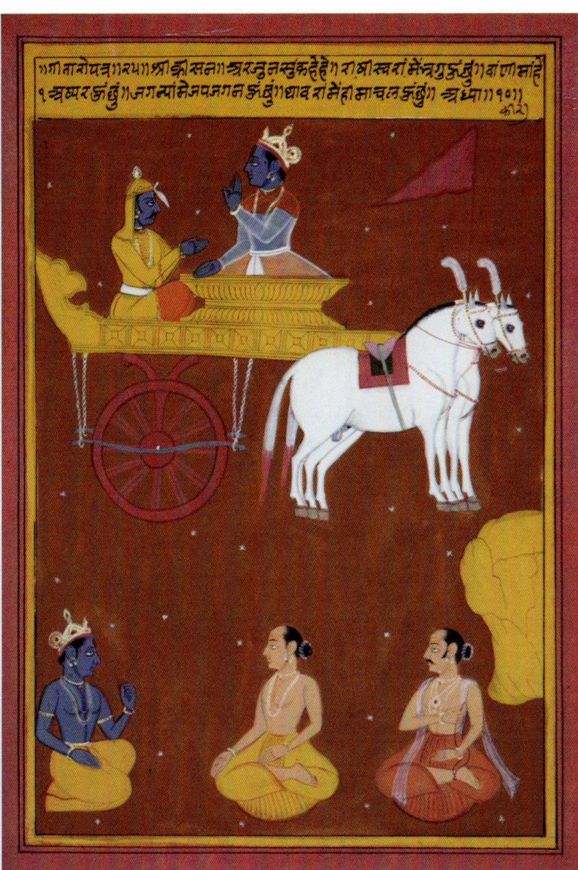

|25| श्री कृष्ण आगे कहने लगे कि मैं महर्षियों में भृगु हूँ और वाणी में एक अक्षर 'ऊं' हूँ। यज्ञों में जपयज्ञ और स्थावरों में हिमालय हूँ।

|25| Sri Krishna further says: Among the great seers, I am Brighu; among words, I am the sound 'OM'; I am the prayer in rites of sacrifice; and among the things that endure, I am the Himalayas.

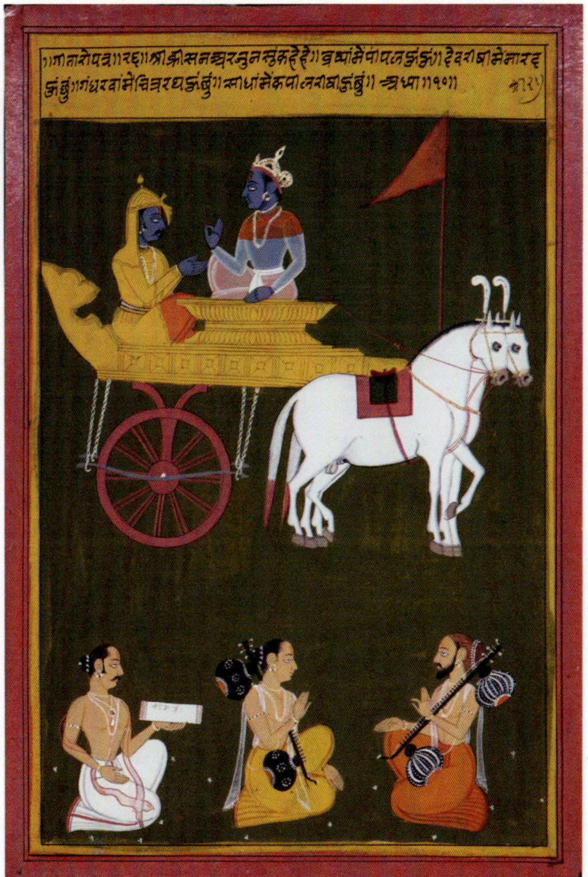

|26| हे अर्जुन! सारे वृक्षों में मैं पीपल हूँ, देवर्षियों में नारद, गंधर्वों में चित्ररथ और सिद्धों में कपिल मुनि हूँ।

|26| Hey Arjuna! Among trees, I am peepul; I am Narada among the divine seer; among the heavenly musicians, I am Chitraratha; and among the ascetics, I am Kapila Muni.

only the self which forgets, however momentarily, that it is a portion of the eternal, and feels the emotions of frustration, rage and violence. When these feelings become the instruments of action, they lead the self further away from the divine toward a useless death. In the *Mahabharata*, it is symbolically significant that Karna dies with his feet and chariot stuck in the blood-soaked mud of the battlefield and Duryodhana sinks to his death in a reed-filled swamp. Both are examples of an imperious will which blocks out all sentiments of empathy toward others and acts obstinately, obsessively and single-mindedly to fulfil its desires.

Allah Baksh's painting for verse 30 is especially worth noting because it is about one of the few mythic stories that wander into the abstractions of the *Gita*. Shockingly and quite unsentimentally, Krishna says that, just as he is part of the earth's gentleness or joyousness, he is also part of its predatoriness or carnivorousness. He is the Lion who kills for food and the snake-eating Eagle, Garuda; he is Time that devours everything. However, his destructive aspect is neither that of a wanton hunter nor of a self-indulgent killer. In each manifestation, his violence is necessary for the earth's ecological existence; it neither causes grief nor exultation because, in life's cycle of birth, death and renewal, it is essential, primal and non-discriminatory. The Lion, the Eagle and Time do not, therefore, contradict the fundamental non-violence of life; its radical ahimsa.[7] They do not negate life, like the hunter who kills for pleasure and without self-restraint, whose actions cause suffering and raise moral questions about evil. It is to clarify this distinction between thoughtless, callous and intentional actions performed to inflict pain, and the non-intentional violence for survival in nature that Krishna invokes the popular tale about Prahlad and his father, Hiranyakasapu. A version of the story, which is recorded in the *Bhagavata Purana*, was often told by Mahatma Gandhi to illustrate his ideas about *bhakti-marga*, or the path of devotion, with its emphasis on other ways of living and satyagraha. It is important to note that Prahlad's name means 'filled with joy.'

The story of Prahlad's relation with his demon father is filled with great violence. Hiranyakasapu, king of the *Daityas* (demons), exiles the gods and takes over the control of heaven and earth. Here evil is defined simply as obdurate selfhood, boundless greed and blind disregard for the legitimate rights of others—hence the connection with Dhritarashtra and Duryodhana. His son, Prahlad, is a demon too but disregards his kin-identity when it comes into conflict with dharmic goodness or truth. In the *Mahabharata*, Prahlad's story is a comment on Karna who fails to repudiate friendship and clan loyalty when Draupadi is molested in the court by the Kauravas, and so

7 Gandhi, *Sita's Kitchen*, pp. 78-79.

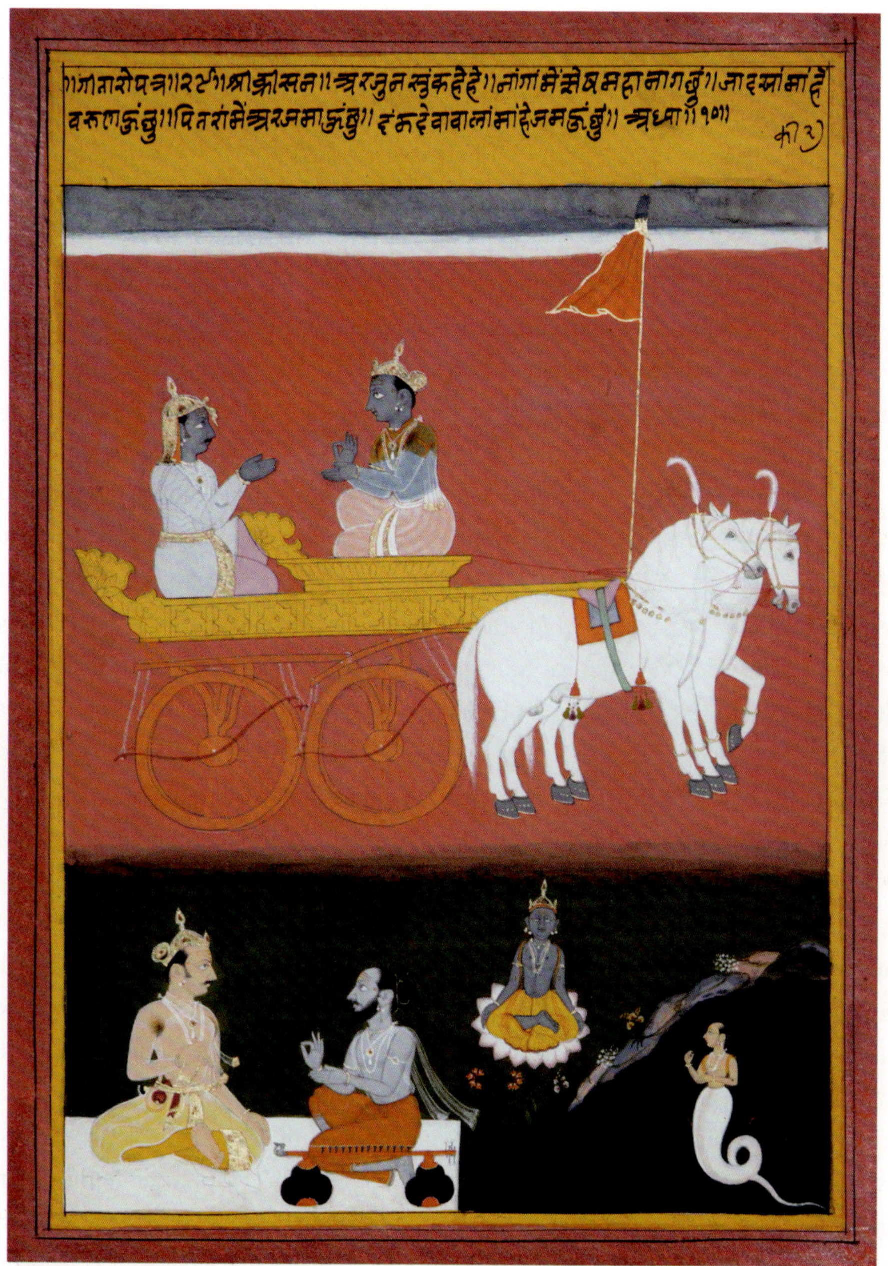

|29| श्री कृष्ण आगे कहने लगे कि मैं नागों में शेषनाग हूँ, जलचरों में वरुण हूँ, पितरों में अर्यमा और दंड देने वालों में यम हूँ।

|29| Sri Krishna further says: I am the thousand-hooded snake among the snakes; among the water-dwellers, I am Varun; I am Aryaman among the ancestors; and among the chastisers, I am the God of Death.

becomes complicit in their evil. Hiranyakasapu has been given a boon by the gods that he cannot be killed either by one who is born from a living womb, by a man, an animal, by day or night, indoors or outdoors, in a temple, on land and water, or by a man-made weapon. His attempts to get rid of Prahlad are described in brutal detail in the textual sources. He is finally killed when Vishnu, in the form of Narasimha (half man and half lion), bursts out of a stone pillar in the portico of Indra's palace and rips him apart with his long claws. Throughout this story of atrocities, Prahlad calmly devotes himself to the worship of Vishnu and refuses the adversarial vision which divides the world into good and evil, self and the other, god and demon etc. He only makes the distinction between truth and untruth, real and unreal. When he is offered a boon, unlike his father, he refuses to accept it. To ask for a boon, he says, is to become a merchant.

The analogical relation between Prahlad and Arjuna is consistent with the emotional tone (*bhava*) of Allah Baksh's paintings of the *Gita*, as rage is a threat to the soul's integrity. Even Vishnu, as Narasimha, finds it extremely difficult to regain the equanimity of his divine being after he rips open Hiranyakasapu. Only Prahlad's soothing prayer pacifies his anger and saves the cosmos from complete annihilation. The irony is that the possibility of ahimsa that Prahlad represents is now in the past. *Satya Yuga*, the age of Truth, is long over, and Krishna does not encourage Arjuna to imitate Prahlad's saintly calm. He tells the tale only to prevent Arjuna from the coarsening exultation that often follows victory after a violent conflict. In the painting for this verse, it is not surprising to find that what is violent in Prahlad's story is excluded; the emphasis is on calm meditativeness. The colours are neither flamboyant nor sentimentally pious. Paradoxically, the demonic figures radiate tranquillity. They are not painted for us to admire the beauty of their form; they are, instead, placed before us for us to subdue our own urge to be roused to anger quickly and turn to violence to avenge wrongs. Perhaps, Zimmer's comment about the emotions many Indian sculptural figures produce is helpful in comprehending the distinctive quality of a painting like this one. These figures, he says, do not compel aesthetic attention. At rest within themselves, "they are pure Being, undivided by self-knowledge."[8]

Krishna concludes the chapter with this resounding declaration: "Whatever is glorious, excellent, beautiful and mighty, be assured that it comes from a fragment of my splendour" (Swami 61). The beauty of these paintings is inspired by the sonority of the verses and is a warning to us that, under all circumstances, war is a derangement and an affliction.

---

8 Zimmer, *Artistic Form and Yoga*, p. 13.

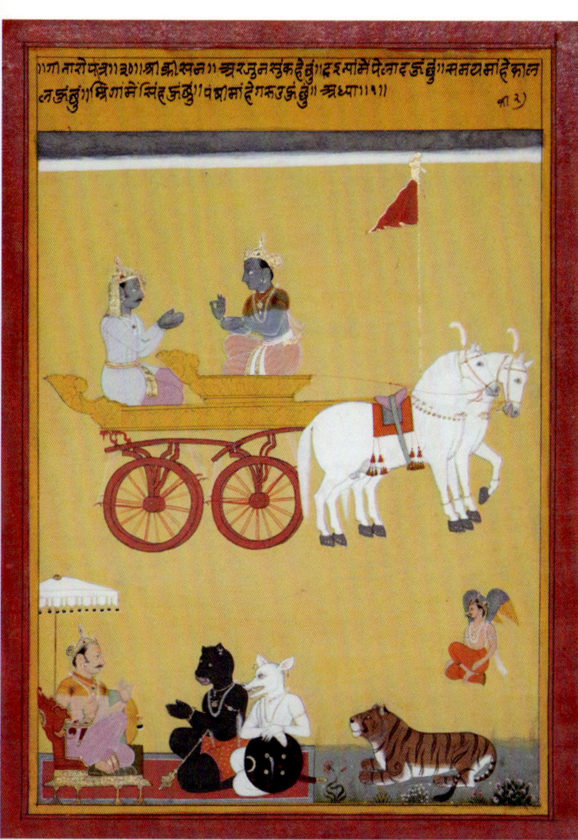

|30| श्री कृष्ण आगे कहने लगे कि हे अर्जुन! दैत्यों में मैं प्रह्लाद हूँ, समय में काल हूँ, मृगों में सिंह और पक्षियों में गरुड़ मैं ही हूँ।

|30| Sri Krishna further says: Hey Arjuna! Among the demons, I am Prahlad; I am the eternal Present of time; among the animals, I am the lion; and among the birds, I am Garuda.

|33| श्री कृष्ण आगे कहने लगे कि मैं अक्षरों में अकार, समासों में द्वंद्व समास हूँ। मैं ही अक्षय काल हूँ और सभी ओर मुखवाला सभी का धाता हूँ।

|33| Sri Krishna further says: I am the first letter of the alphabet; I connect compound words; I am indestructible time; I am the all-seeing one who looks in every direction.

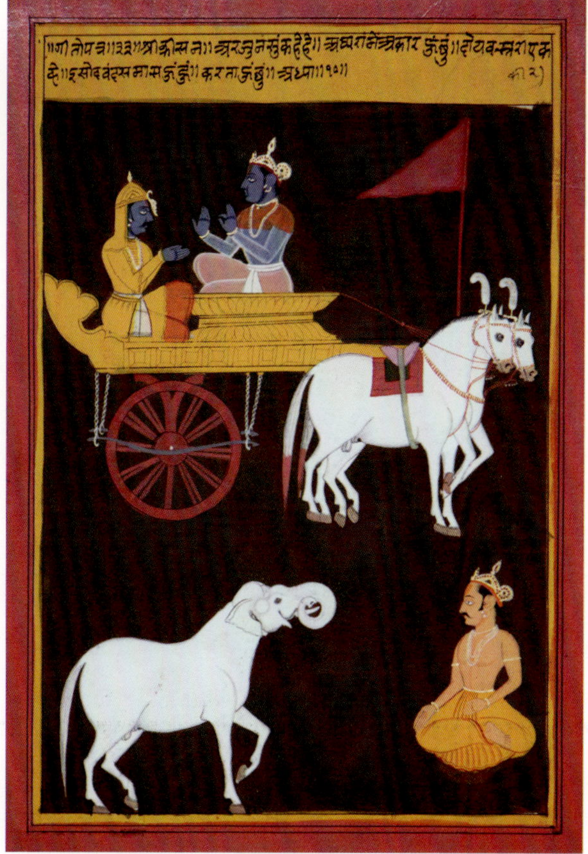

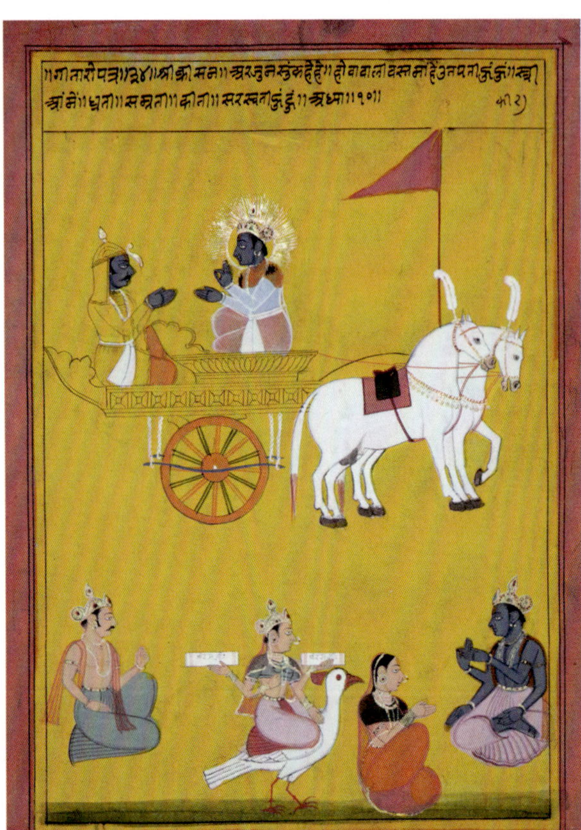

|34| हे अर्जुन! सब का नाश करने वाली मृत्यु मैं हूँ और होने वाली वस्तु के उत्पन्न होने का कारण भी मैं हूँ। नारी में कीर्ति, श्री, वाक, स्मृति, मेधा, धृति और क्षमा भी मैं हूँ।

|34| Hey Arjuna! I am Death, the destroyer of everything; I am also the source of all things that come into being; in women, I am glory, beauty, speech, memory, intelligence, resolve and forgiveness.

|35| आगे समझाते हुए श्री कृष्ण कहने लगे कि सामवेद में वृहत्साम मैं हूँ, छंदों में गायत्री तो महीनों में मार्गशीर्ष हूँ और ऋतुओं में बसन्त मैं हूँ।

|35| Explaining further, Sri Krishna says: I am Brihatsaman (ritual chant) in the Samaveda; I am the metre in the Gayatri mantra (sacred song); among the months, I am the sacred month of December and among the seasons, I am spring.

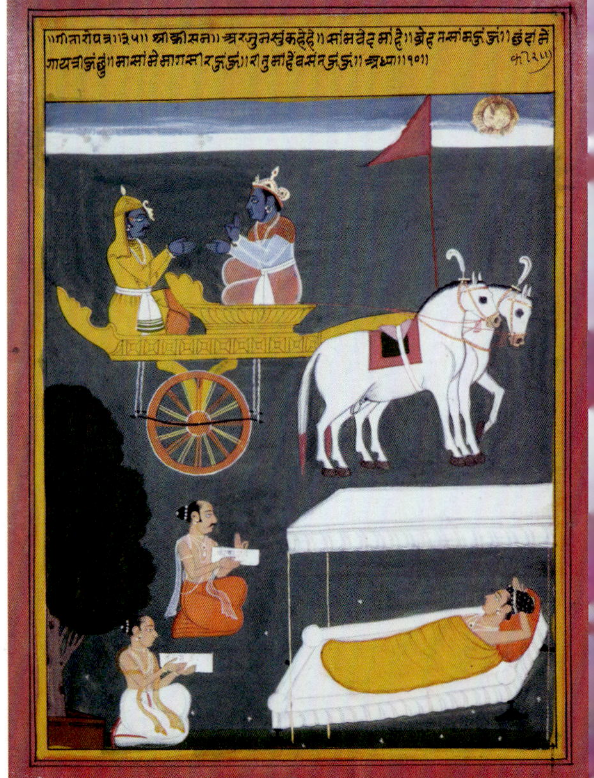

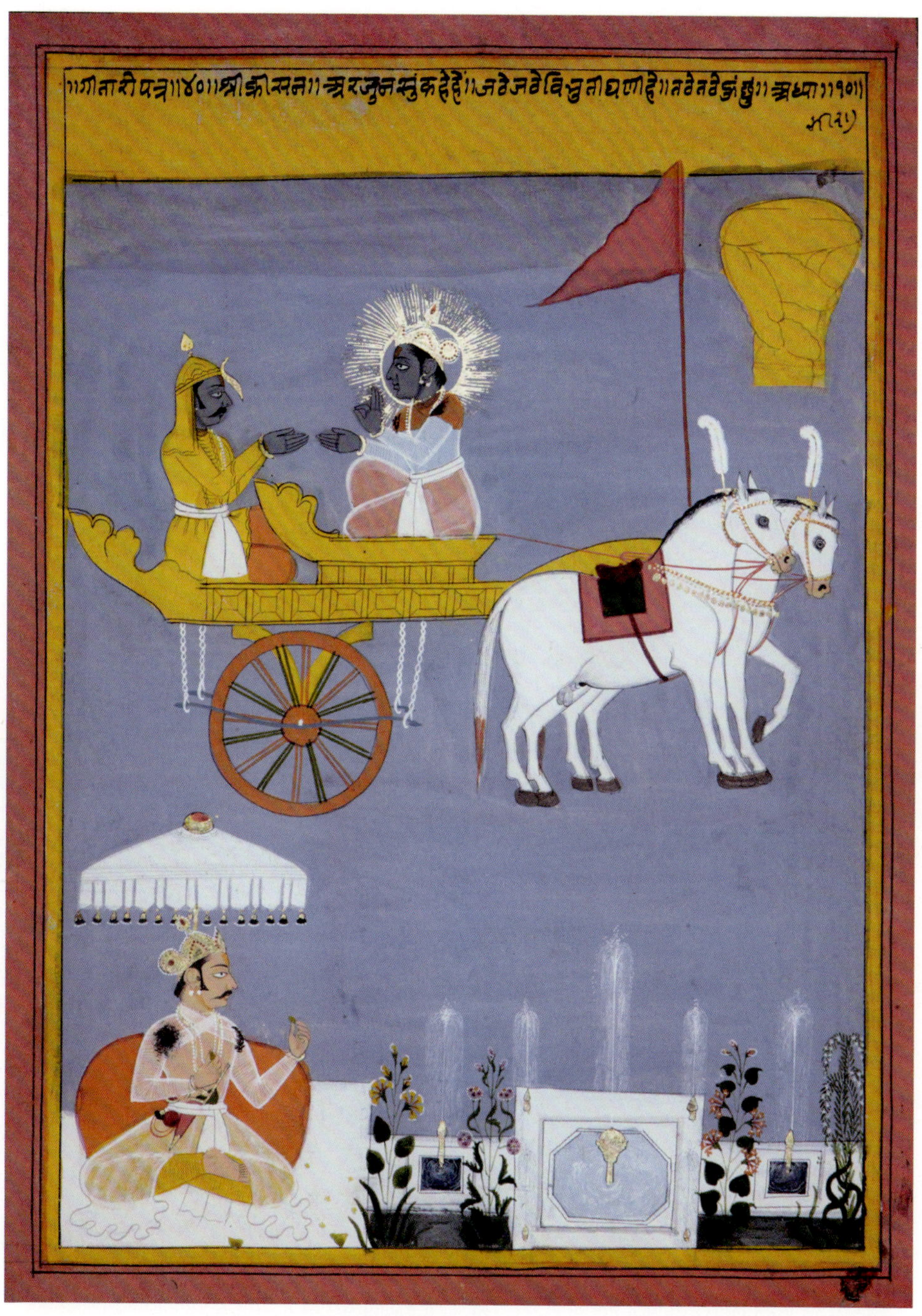

|40| हे अर्जुन! मेरी विभूतियों का कोई अंत नहीं। मैंने थोड़े में अपनी विभूतियों का विस्तार कहा है यह समझ।

|40| Hey Arjuna! There is no limit to my divine attributes; I have only hinted at a few.

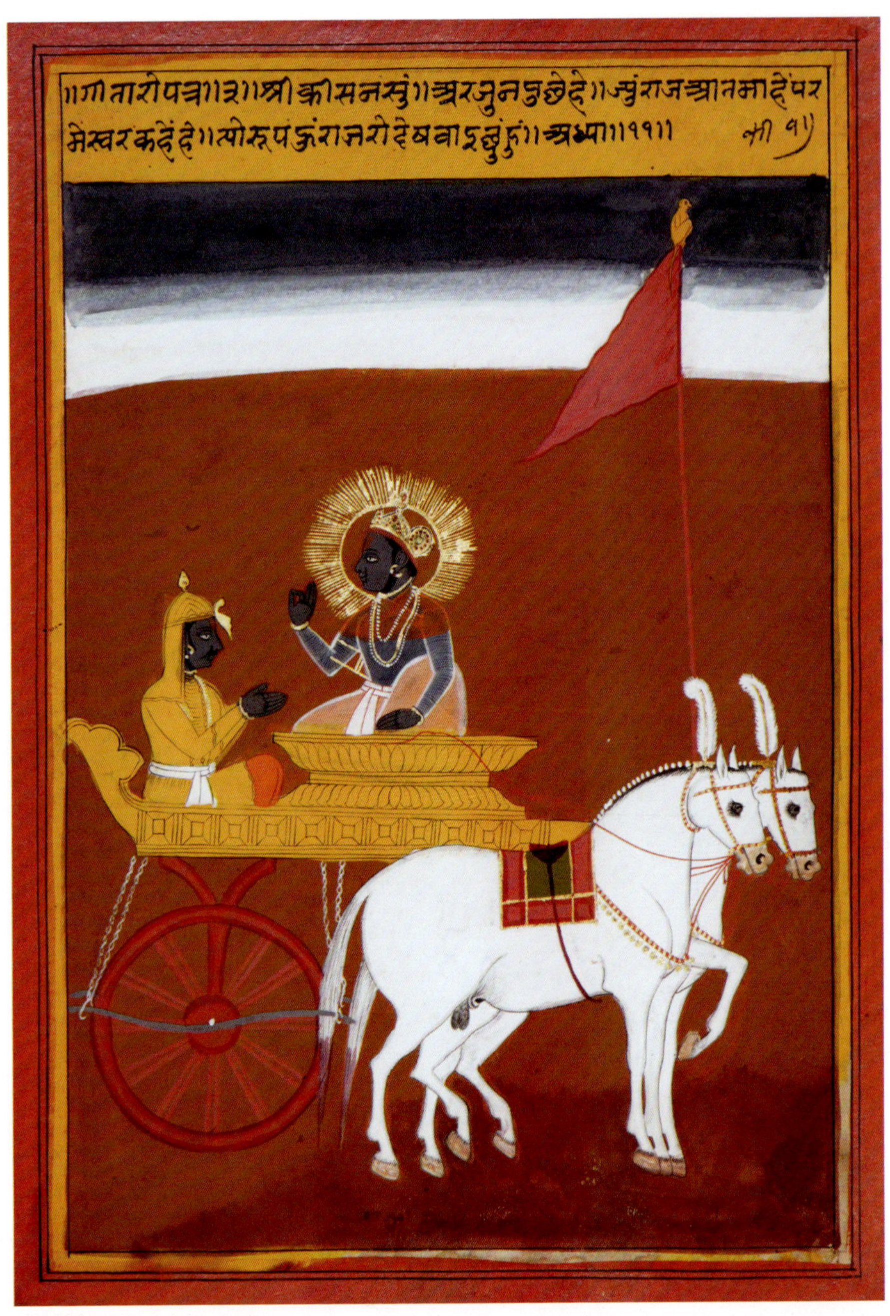

|3| अर्जुन कहने लगा, हे कृष्ण! आप अपने को जैसा कहते हैं आप वैसे ही हैं परन्तु मैं आपके ऐश्वर्यशाली रूप को देखना चाहता हूँ।

|3| Arjuna says: Hey Krishna! You are just as you have described yourself. I now want to see the majesty of your divine form.

CHAPTER 11

Chapter 11 of the *Gita* is justly famous. Critical commentary often treats it as auspicious because Krishna reveals, at Arjuna's request, his cosmic form. What Arjuna seeks, like any anxious moral pilgrim whose sense of the rightness of the world has been disoriented, is a sign that belongs not to the familiar world but is wholly other, utterly transcendental, and an incontestable guide to action. In Rudolf Otto's well-known theoretical formulation, what Arjuna sees is simultaneously majestic and incomprehensible, terrifying and beautiful, indifferent and merciful.[1] Only Arjuna can endure the frightening blaze of revelation which is brighter than a thousand suns because he has prepared himself intellectually for it, and because Krishna grants him, as his friend and devotee, visionary eyes. Having come face to face with the transfiguring glory of Krishna, Arjuna is transformed; his face acquires an unearthly glow; he becomes what he beholds.

Sanjaya too has been granted visionary powers, but he is not privileged to see Krishna's terrible majesty; he only hears what Arjuna describes. What we know of Arjuna's experience and Krishna's sacred splendour is through Sanjaya's description. Never again in the vast mythology of Krishna does he manifest himself as an impersonal and dread-inspiring force who is capable of ruthless destruction. In all the other innumerable stories about Krishna's human manifestation, he is the very source of joyous play, sensual delight, endless song, beauty, intoxication and bewitchment; he is the god of plenitude whom each bhakt sees and knows intimately.

In the *Mahabharata*, Krishna's theophany at Kurukshetra is his second one.[2] The first was in Dhritarashtra's court, before all the warriors, gurus and princes, where he had pleaded for a modest settlement to avert the war. The Kauravas were so blinded by their own selfish purpose, ambition and hate that they had shut their eyes to Krishna's numinous presence in their midst. One can choose not to meet righteousness face to face.

Krishna's revelation of his divine identity is not only the epiphanic centre of the song, it is also the moral core of the *Mahabharata*. Without the *Gita*, the war at

1 See Eliade, *The Sacred and the Profane*.

2 See Hiltebeitel, *Ritual of War*, p. 126.

Kurukshetra would be no more than a predictable melodrama of inexorable cycles of violence. Instead, it makes us think seriously about the pity of war. More importantly, it rememorialises the idea, often exemplified in many shorter narratives in the *Mahabharata*, that non-violence is the originary principle of the world and ought to define life on earth. Unfortunately, the cosmogonic promise of a harmonious, peaceful and delightful world, which the Krishna *lila* myths celebrate with music, song and dance, has long been forgotten. War now, Krishna asserts sorrowfully, will have to be fought since every effort at a peaceful resolution has failed. The brutal adharma of the Kauravas has to be defeated. Adharma, which depends upon vanity, self-interest, envy, chance, exclusion, violence or power, is the basis of most of the actions the Kauravas perform. Arjuna is the only one who can fight on behalf of dharma since he has now "renounced attachments" and has "ill will towards none" (Desai 303).[3]

Arjuna is not seeking to affirm his destiny as a fighter in a traditional caste hierarchy. It is worth recalling what Spinoza said: a prophet's function is not to teach people pride in their exclusiveness, but "true virtue" which all possess. God, he says, does not choose one people over another; "he is equally gracious to all."[4] The *Gita* neither upholds the interests of a particular class nor sanctifies an individual's desire for personal salvation; both would take us further towards the abyss of kali yuga.[5] The *Gita* only urges Arjuna 'to yoke' himself (since that is what the word 'yoga' literally means)[6] to his personal dharma. Indeed, the *Gita*'s uniqueness lies in its opposition to the ritualists as arbiters of dharma regarding them only as debaters of the Veda.[7] Instead, the *Gita* is a call, a calling out to each individual, to pay devout and compassionate attention to all living and non-living beings, even as it urges war *now* as the only way of holding the world together and restoring it, once again, to its original, peaceful sanctuary and sanctity. This paradox of the *Gita* is as intricately enmeshed in the *Mahabharata* as are the small tales of ahimsic justice in the epic which should be read as ethical annotations on the *Gita*.[8]

Allah Baksh and Sanjaya face the same problem. How can they visualise theophany for us mortals who are so far removed from the mystical? How can Allah Baksh make

3 This is according to Desai's translation in *The Gospel of Selfless Action*, p. 303.

4 Benedict de Spinoza, *A Theologico-Political Treatise and a Political Treatise*, translated by R. H. M. Elwes (New York: Dover, 1951), pp. 49 and 56.

5 Simona Sawhney, *Modernity of Sanskrit* (Ranikhet: Permanent Black, 2009), pp.98-108.

6 van Buitenen, *The Bhagavadgita*, p. 17.

7 van Buitenen, *The Bhagavadgita*, p. 18

8 Gandhi, *Sita's Kitchen*, pp. 78-79.

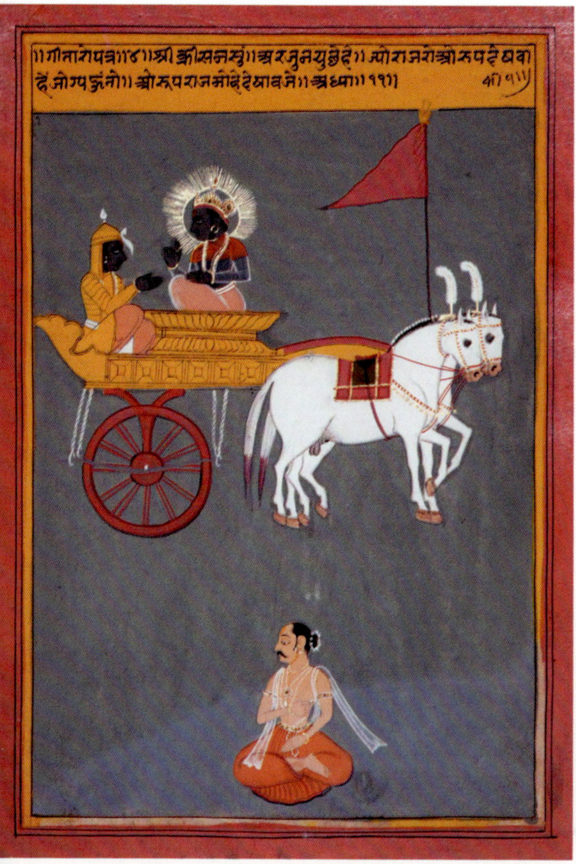

|4| अर्जुन ने आगे कहा कि हे कृष्ण! यदि आप यह समझते हैं कि मैं आपके रूप को देखने में समर्थ हूँ तो आप मुझे अपने अविनाशी स्वरूप का दर्शन कराइए।

|4| Arjuna further says: Hey Krishna! If you think I can see it, reveal to me your imperishable form.

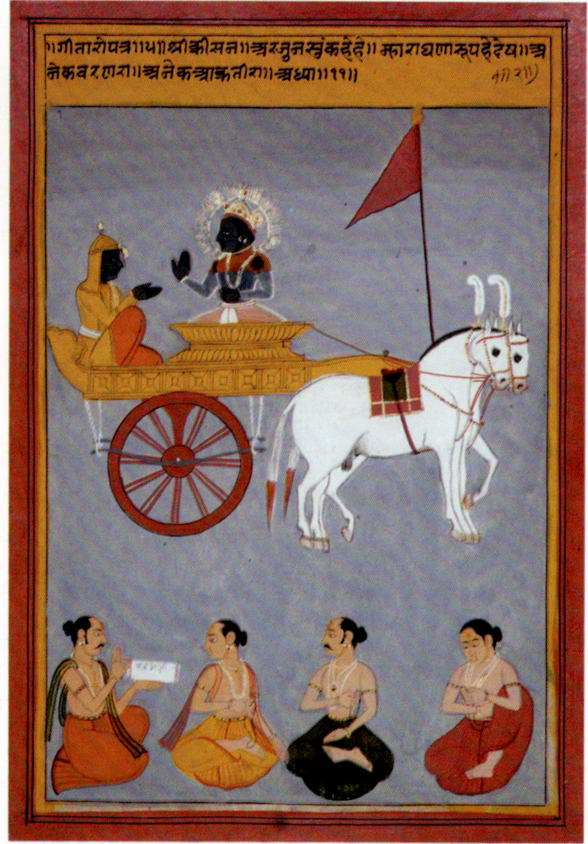

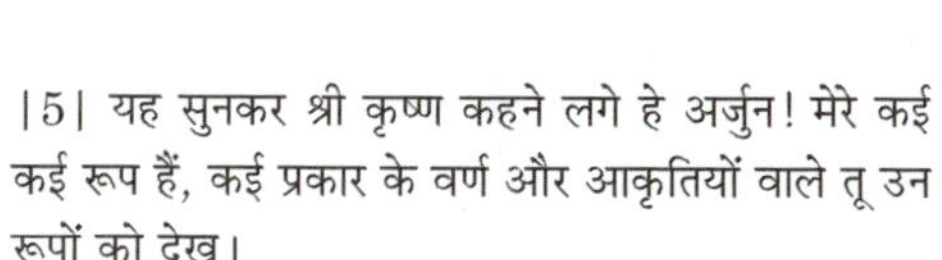

|5| यह सुनकर श्री कृष्ण कहने लगे हे अर्जुन! मेरे कई कई रूप हैं, कई प्रकार के वर्ण और आकृतियों वाले तू उन रूपों को देख।

|5| When he hears that, Sri Krishna says: Hey Arjuna! Behold my various and diverse shapes and forms.

an unimaginable god visible, especially a god who changes shape endlessly? How can he pictorially imagine that which is "inherently beyond the comprehension of mere mortals;"[9] what is the possible form in which the absolute Being becomes visible to human eyes? When Arjuna comes face to face with the divine, what does he see? Since only Arjuna sees the divine form of Krishna, how can an artist paint that which is impossible and unrepresentable; that which, according to Arjuna's vision, contains in its manifestation all the suppleness and fluidity of life in time, all that has been known, all that will come into existence, all that human beings have ever imagined and feared, all that inhabits the three cosmic realms? Arjuna makes no effort to reconcile what he sees; the *Gita* does not offer a singular and composite image of what is revealed. The text only describes, again and again, a shifting, changing, mobile divinity which is as infinite in its forms as creation itself. The only thing Arjuna knows is that the divine has manifested itself, and that nothing in his past learning or experience has prepared him for what he sees (painting for verse 8).

As soon as an artist gives Being a shape, he risks being accused of presumption, idolatry and falsification because what is revealed to Arjuna is inconceivable and unprecedented, personal and gentle, remote and ferocious. For the painter there is an additional moral problem: he cannot claim that the image of Krishna's numinous majesty is the definitive one because that would be nothing more than egotism and, therefore, spiritually fraudulent. Allah Baksh's solution to the problem is brilliant. He begins by first painting for verses 4 and 5 priests, ritualists and debaters either as isolated and lost or as empty moral gossipers who would, as Sri Ramakrishna says, rather talk about paradise than do anything to get there. They avoid action and karma, therefore, not only live in vain but also for the self alone.[10] It is, however, only in verses 47, 48 and 53 that Krishna dismisses scriptural piety and tells Arjuna: "Not by the Vedas, not by penance nor by gifts, nor yet by sacrifice, can any behold Me in the Form that thou hast seen" (Desai 301-303).

The painting for verse 4 is poignant. Imagined against a bare, blue ground, it shows a pundit sitting alone and gazing vacantly out of the frame on the left. He is lonely, because once ritualism is rejected in favour of the quest for a personal deity there is no social or moral need for priests. His body sags, his arms and hands make no meaningful gestures; his body seems heavy. In contrast to the bright sparkle in the eyes of Arjuna

9 Joan Cummins, *Vishnu: Hinduism's Blue-Skinned Saviour* (Ahmedabad: Mapin, 2011), p. 221.

10 van Buitenen, *The Bhagavadgita*, p. 21.

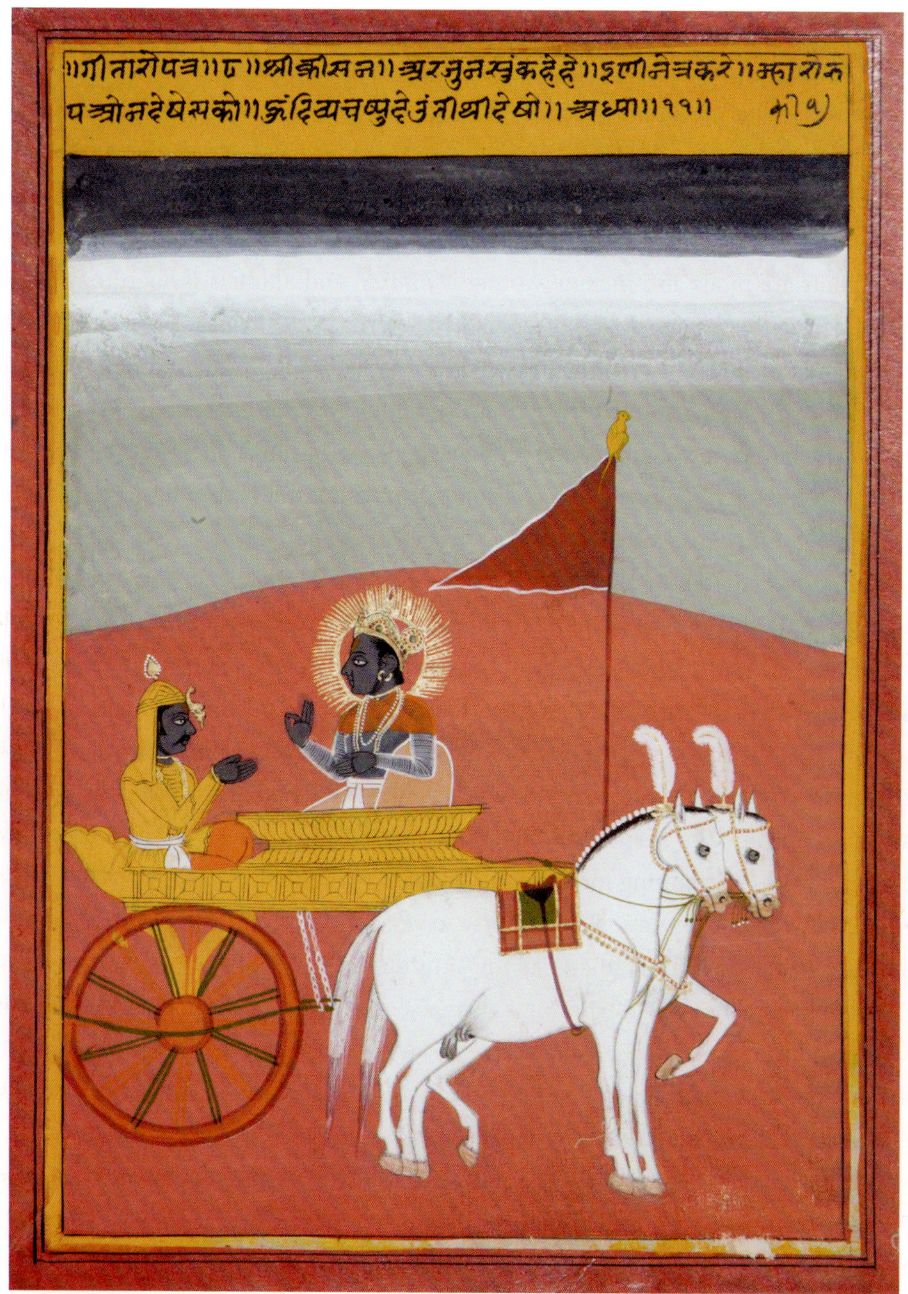

|8| हे अर्जुन! पर तू तेरे सामान्य नेत्रों से मुझे देखना चाहे तो यह संभव नहीं। अत: ले मैं तुझे दिव्य चक्षु देता हूँ इन से तू मेरी योगशक्ति को देख।

|8| Hey Arjuna! It is not possible for you to see me with your natural eyes. Let me give you divine sight so that you can see my power and majesty.

and Krishna above, his eyes are despondent and unseeing. The painter is clearly responding to Krishna's assertion that each soul has to come to an understanding of his own personal dharma and act accordingly for the sustenance to the world. If one does so, all will be well.

In the paintings for verses 3, 4 and 5, Allah Baksh paints different sites of scriptural exchanges. The discourses, as in many other paintings, are conducted in peace; their participants are pious and include women, children and animals though they are far removed from the ecstatic bhakti of a personal god that Krishna has led Arjuna toward. Each of them is engaged in rituals of devotion, though none of them seem to be free from desire. Their aspirations are not transcendental. Arjuna's engagement, in contrast, is not a ritual one; and, significantly, though the Pandavas have their gurus, brahmins and clan priests, Arjuna turns to a charioteer for wisdom. It is the charioteer in these paintings who sits on a golden lotus-shaped seat.

The most remarkable aspect of the paintings for this chapter, however, is Allah Baksh's unique and personal meditation on Krishna's revelation of his inconceivable, extraordinary, cosmic body—Vishwarupa—where all mortals and immortals, living and non-sentient forms reside. Except for Krishna's dark-blue colour and larger than human physical proportions, the figures Allah Baksh paints have hardly any iconographic precedent, no tradition which he imitates. He has the freedom, like any bhakta, to imagine the shapes the divine may take as it manifests itself in the world. Beginning with the painting for verse 10, he offers more than 22 distinctive images of Krishna's divine self-revelations from verse to verse. In each of them, Krishna occupies the entire visual space and radiates an uncanny aura.

Allah Baksh knows that painting Krishna's cosmic form is 'impossible' because he has no beginning, middle or end; he is everywhere (verses 11-16), yet he has to be framed within a limited space. The text says that Krishna's form is so awe-inspiring, so fierce to look upon that Arjuna, in danger of losing his senses, finally pleads for relief. Krishna is sitting on his chariot in the middle of two armies, his face glowing with *tejas*, his eyes fiery, his mouth curled with time's malice, his body armoured, as he urges Arjuna to war with his arms outstretched. He is truly fearsome.

In contrast, however, the emotional tone and moral depth of these paintings are radically different. In no image does Krishna have a mocking face, fiery eyes, fearful jaws where fires of dissolution burn, or sharp white teeth which tear and grind all living beings without remorse or mercy. Indeed, the painted images are not literal visual correlatives of what the verses say. In keeping with the dominant sentiment of Allah

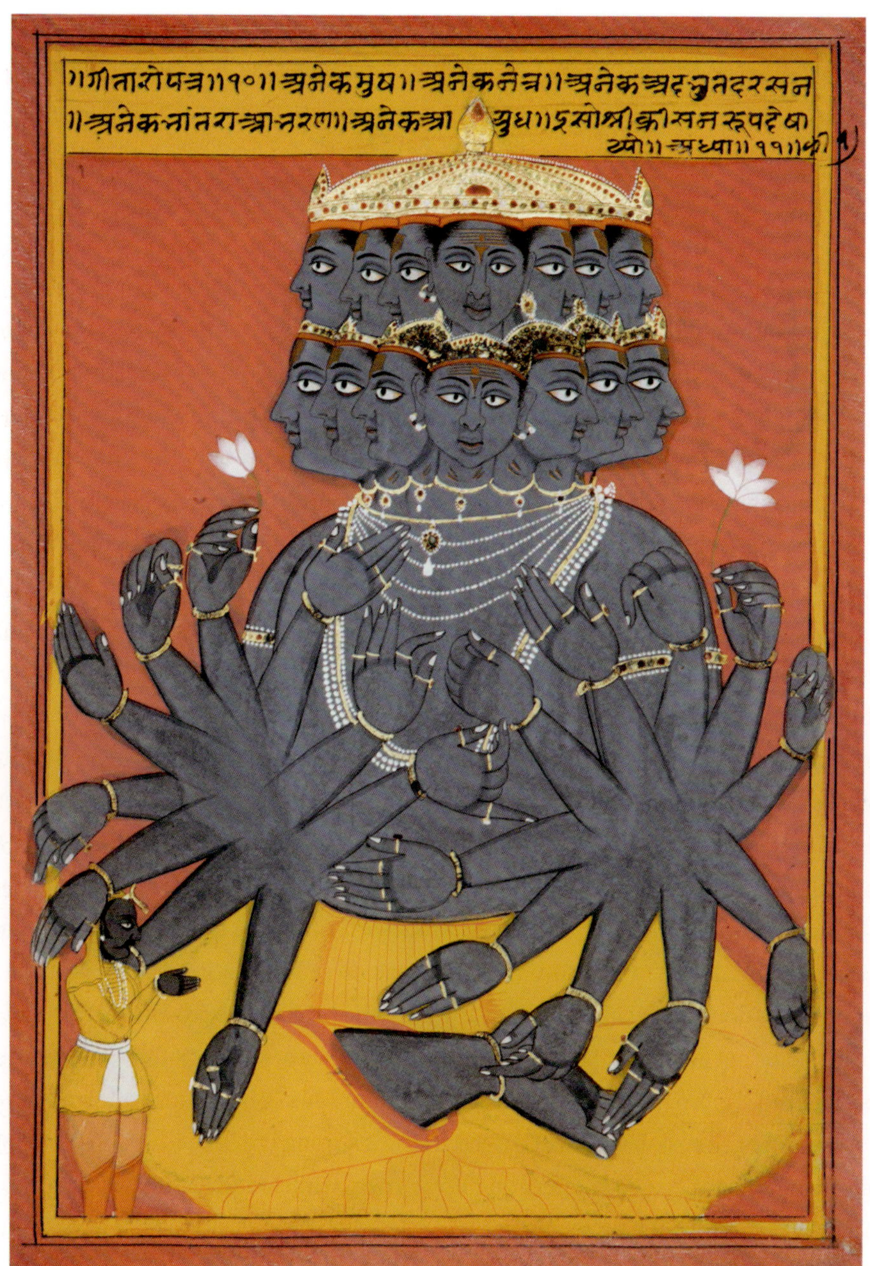

|10| ले अर्जुन! देख, यह कह कर श्री कृष्ण ने अनेक मुखों, नेत्रों से युक्त, कई तरह के दिव्य आभूषणों से युक्त, अनेक दिव्य शस्त्र धारण किए हुए अपना रूप दिखाया।

|10| Here Arjuna! See, saying this, Lord Krishna revealed his divine form with countless mouths, many eyes, innumerable celestial ornaments and infinite divine weapons.

Baksh's *Gita* folio, Krishna is not terrifyingly unapproachable, but strangely serene and beautiful, gentle and calm. Krishna carries no lethal weapons nor is Arjuna sheathed in armour. There are no swords and hangman's nooses, no goblets full of blood and no writhing bodies often seen in other representations of Krishna's Vishwarupa. Instead, Krishna sits cross-legged like a yogi, dressed in a saffron-golden garment streaked with flowing red lines. In all his appearances, he holds white lotus flowers in his multiple hands as emblems of the transcendence which is always possible for people to achieve even if they are mired in the suffering of *samsara*. In every painting, he also carries a pinkish-white conch shell, one of the nine auspicious treasures of Kubera, the god of wealth, and the source of the sacred sound OM.[11] In some paintings, Krishna does carry a mace, but it is never raised aggressively. His hands, instead of being threatening, are held up in different mudras of peace, mercy, pity, comfort and grace. His Vishwarupa inspires Arjuna to leave his fate entirely to Krishna trusting in his sense of justice and on behalf of the good. Krishna's wide open eyes are like white lotus petals. He gazes somewhere far into the horizon and looks upon everything with equal indifference and impartial justice. His remoteness from life's daily turmoil produces in Arjuna not dread but peaceful devotion as he stands with his hands folded in the lower corner near Krishna's feet. These paintings radiate with Arjuna's ecstatic acknowledgement that he has seen what no man has ever seen before and, in utter humility, he declares gently and with adoration: "O Lord! Most adorable! I salute Thee, I ask Thy blessing. Only Thou can'st be trusted to bear with me, as father to son, as friend to friend, as lover to his beloved" (Swami 67). As he looks up at Krishna's face, he no longer feels the need to converse and debate. He is sure that Krishna's sacred revelation has established the limit of all the doubts and moral conundrums of the profane world. His sorrow will not be resolved or put aside, but he now knows where his duty resides if the world's order is to be restored. Appropriately, once Krishna, resumes his "gentle human form" (Swami 68) sitting on his lotus-shaped seat on the chariot, Arjuna is depicted as a warrior in his golden armour, and armed soldiers on grey, brown, white and blue horses appear once again in the paintings for verses 33 and 34.

11 Cummins, *Vishnu*, p.103.

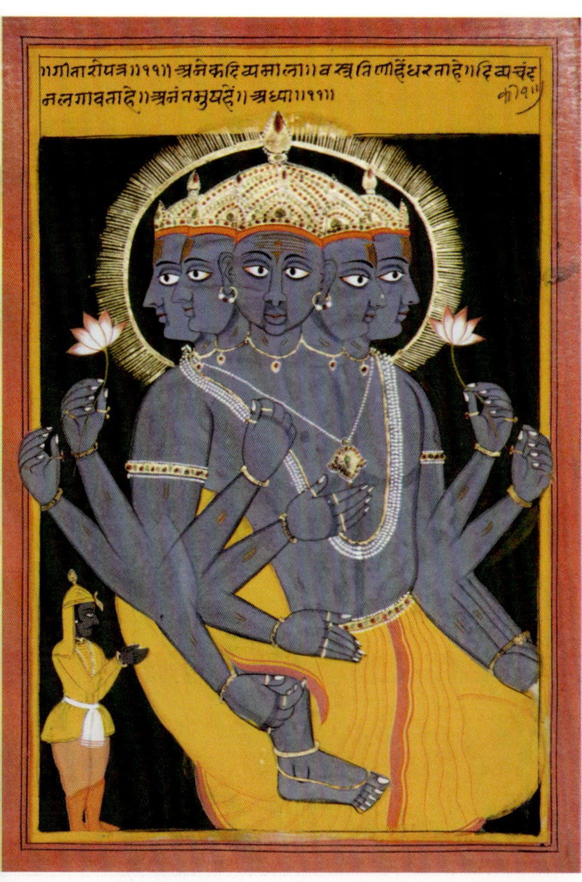

|11| अनेक दिव्य मालाओं और दिव्य वस्त्रों को धारण किए हुए, अपनी देह पर दिव्य सुगंध का लेप किए हुए रूप में, सभी दिशाओं में मुख वाले देव को अर्जुन ने देखा।

|11| Arjuna saw that Krishna wore an infinite variety of heavenly garlands, sacred clothes; his body was anointed with divine perfume; and that He had faces which looked in every direction.

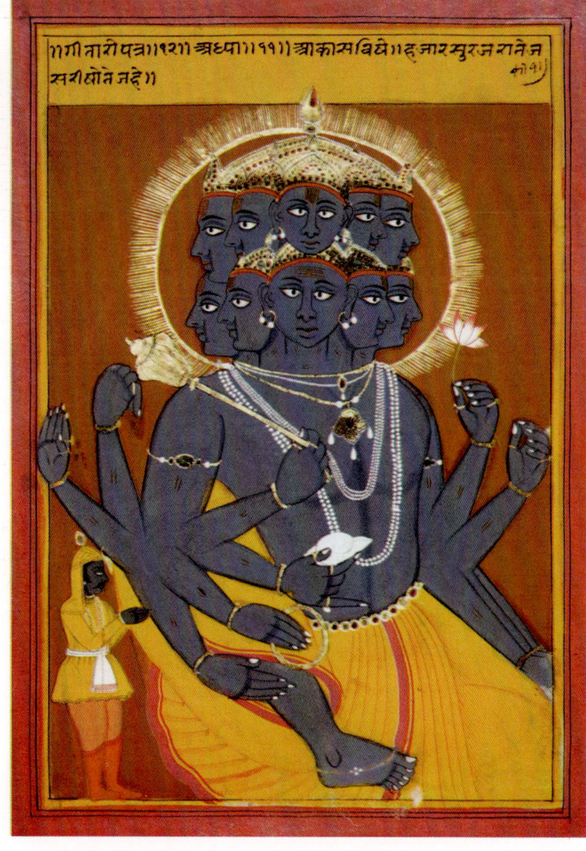

|12| संजय ने कहा कि आकाश में यदि हजार सूर्य एक साथ प्रकाशित हों तो भी उनका तेज उस महान स्वरूप के बराबर कदाचित ही हो।

|12| Sanjaya says: Hey King! His splendour was brighter than a thousand suns in the sky.

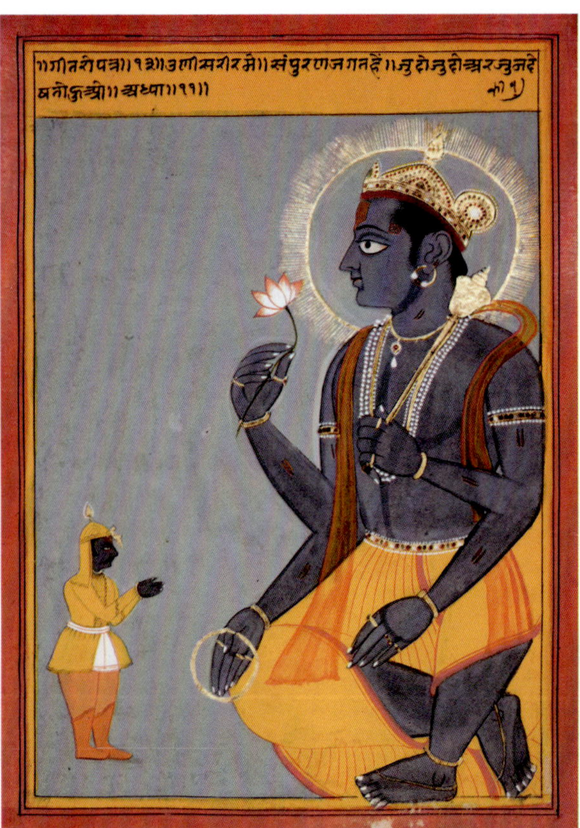

|13| संजय ने कहा कि पांडुपुत्र अर्जुन ने विराट स्वरूप में अनेक प्रकार से विभक्त संपूर्ण जगत को देखा।

|13| Sanjaya says: Then Pandu's son, Arjuna, saw the infinite universe gathered in the majesty of Krishna's body.

|14| संजय आगे बोला, हे राजन! उसके बाद आश्चर्य-चकित और रोमांचित होकर अर्जुन ने विराट स्वरूप को सिर नवाया और हाथ जोड़ कर कहने लगा।

|14| Sanjaya says: O King! Then, filled with amazement and wonder, Arjuna bowed his head before that majestic form, and stood with folded hands.

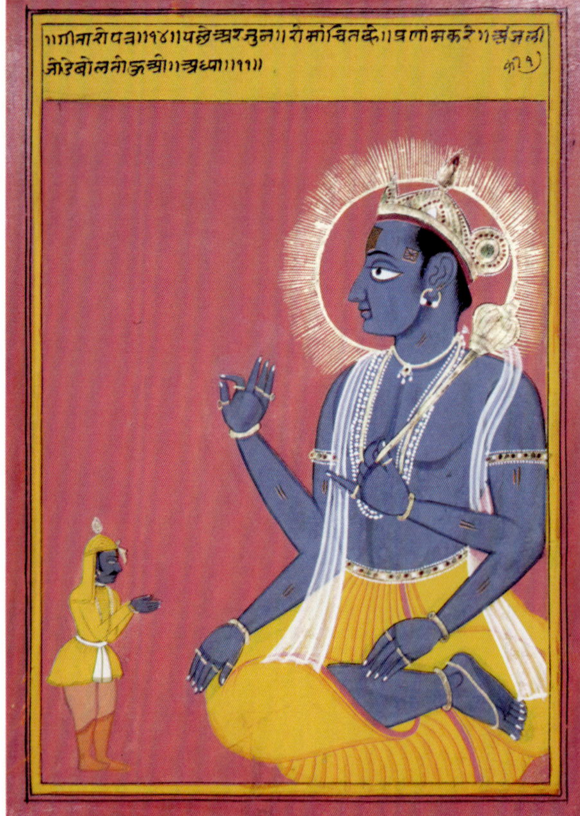

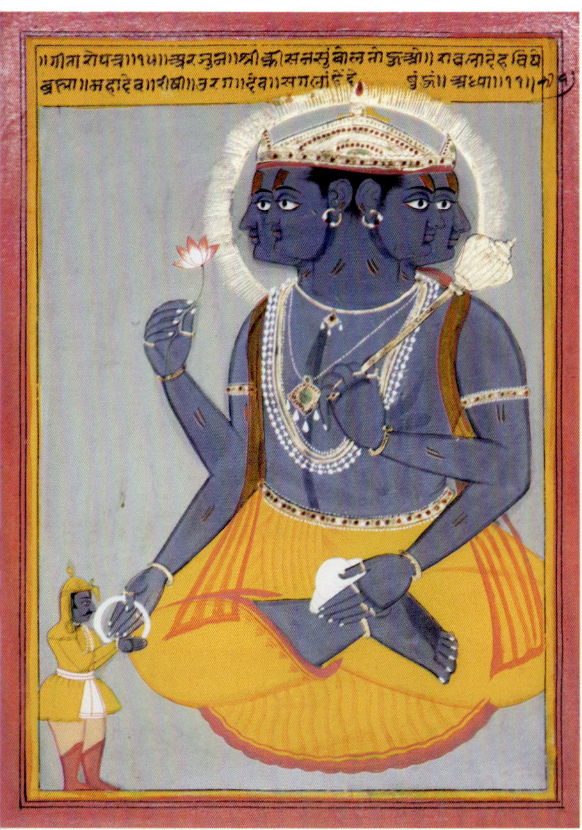

|15| अर्जुन बोला, हे कृष्ण! मैं आपकी देह में सारे देवताओं, समस्त प्राणियों के समुदायों सहित कमलासन पर स्थित ब्रह्म को, महादेव को, सभी ऋषियों और दिव्य नागों को देखता हूँ।

|15| Arjuna says: Hey Krishna! With my divine sight, I can see all the gods, all the diverse variety of creatures, Brahma seated on a lotus flower, Shiva, all the sages and celestial serpents.

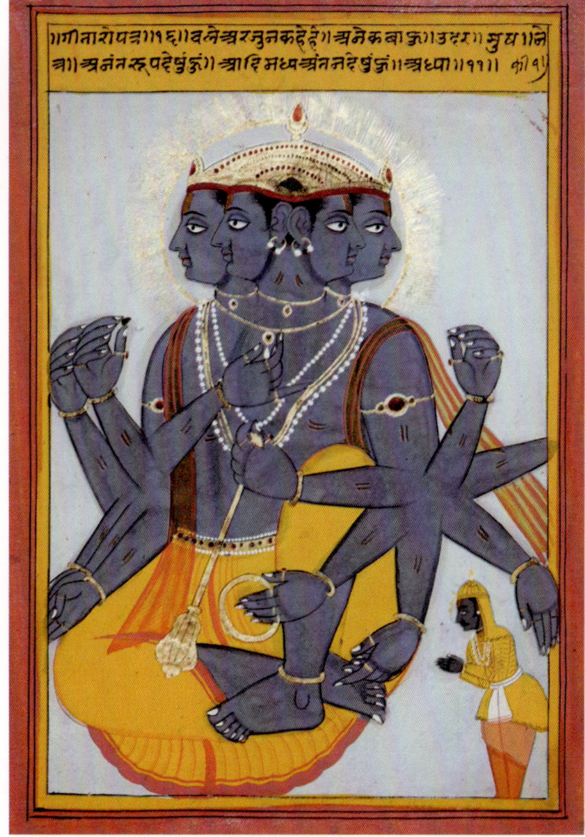

|16| अर्जुन आगे कहने लगा कि हे कृष्ण! मैं अभी आपको अनेक बाहुवाला, कई उदर, मुख, नेत्रों सहित अनन्त रूपों में देख रहा हूँ। मुझे न आपका आदि दिखाई देता है, न मध्य और न अंत।

|16| Arjuna adds: Hey Krishna! I see your countless arms, many bellies, faces and eyes; I see your infinite forms; but I do not see your beginning, middle or end.

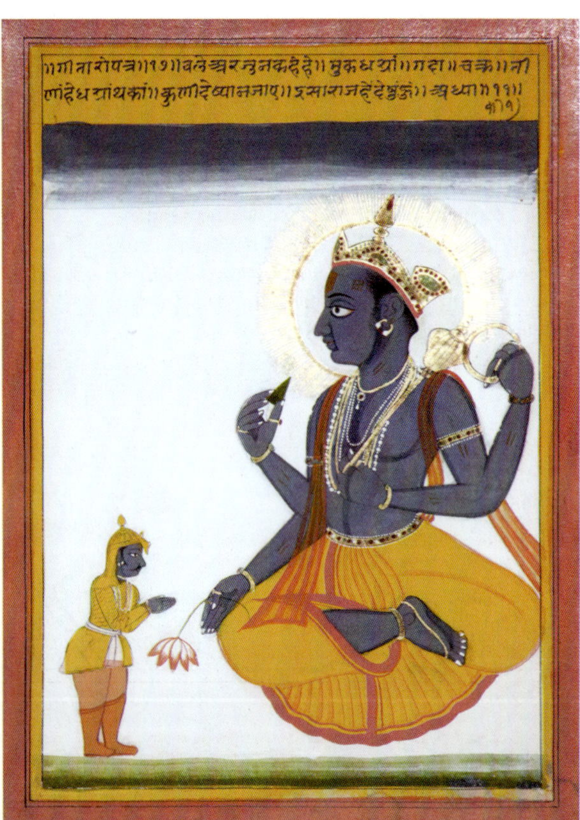

|17| अर्जुन आगे बोला, हे मुकुट, गदा और चक्र युक्त देव! आप सभी ओर से प्रकाशवान तेज पुंज, प्रज्वलित अग्नि और सूर्य के समान नजर आ रहे हैं, जो किसी से भी देखा न जाए। मैं ऐसे आपको देख रहा हूँ।

|17| Arjuna further says: Hey Lord of the crown, mace and disc! Wherever I look, you are surrounded by dazzling light; you are brighter than the glowing fire, more radiant than the blazing sun.

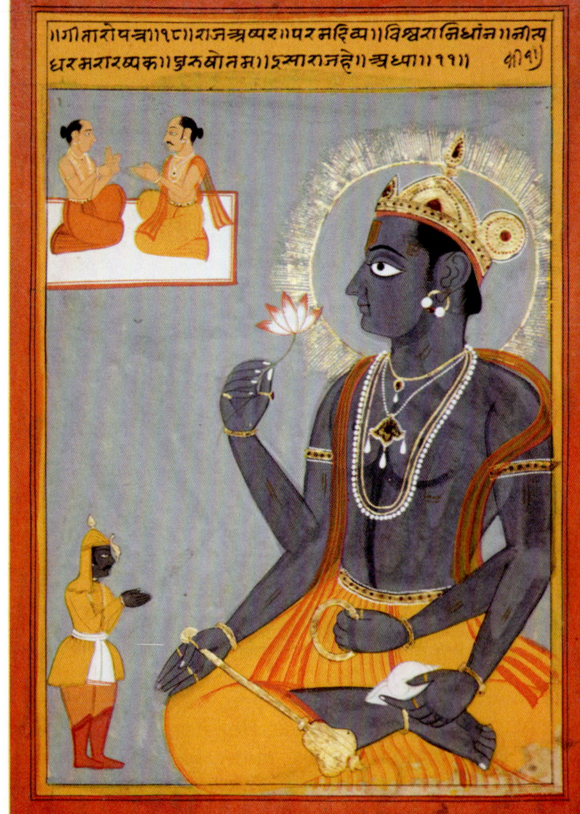

|18| अर्जुन आगे बोला कि हे कृष्ण! आप परम अक्षर और विश्व के परम आश्रय हैं, आप नित्य धर्मरक्षक हैं और आप ही अविनाशी सनातन पुरुष हैं मुझे ऐसा प्रतीत होता है।

|18| Arjuna further says: Hey Krishna! I believe that you are eternal and the final resting place of the universe; you are the steadfast guardian of dharma and you are the everlasting spirit.

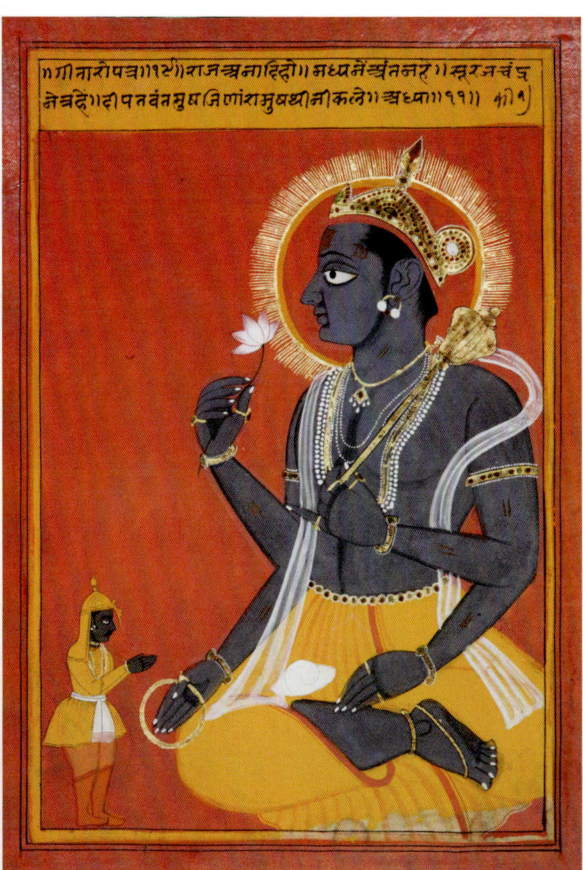

|19| अर्जुन आगे कहने लगा, हे विराट स्वरूप देव! आप अंतरहित अनंत सामर्थ्य वाले अनंत भुजाओं वाले, सूर्य-चन्द्र रूपी नेत्रों वाले, प्रदीप्त अग्नि के समान मुख वाले हैं। मैं आपको अपने तेज से इस विश्व को तपाते हुए देखता हूँ।

|19| Arjuna goes on to say: Hey God of majestic form! You are boundless; your power is infinite; you have infinite eyes; your eyes are like the sun and the moon; your mouth is a blaze of fire; the warmth of your radiance is spread over the universe.

|20| अर्जुन बोला, हे कृष्ण! स्वर्ग और पृथ्वी के मध्य का संपूर्ण आकाश, सारी दिशाएँ एक आप में व्याप्त नजर आती हैं। आपके इस अद्‍भुत रूप को देखकर तीनों लोक डर रहे हैं।

|20| Arjuna says: Hey Krishna! I can see that all that lies between heaven and earth and in every direction resides in you; at the sight of your awe-inspiring form, the three worlds tremble with fear.

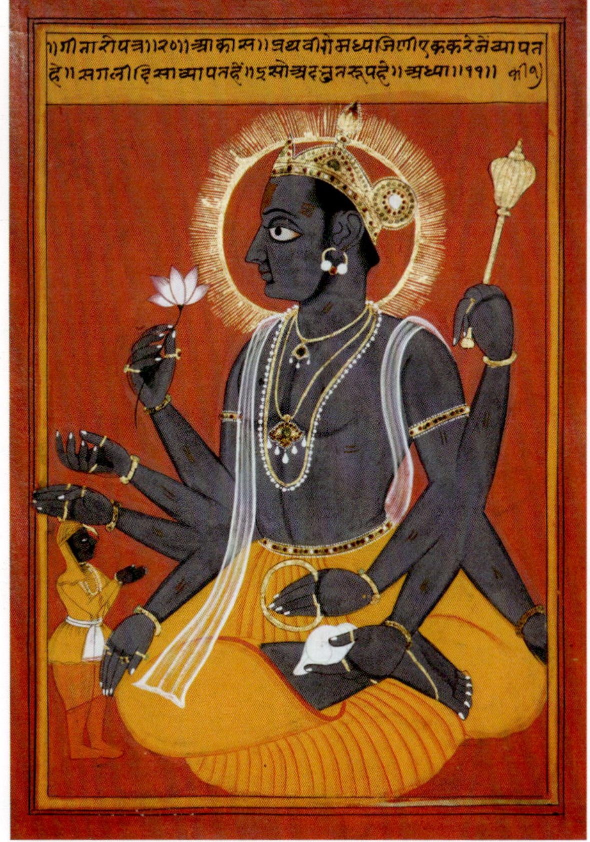

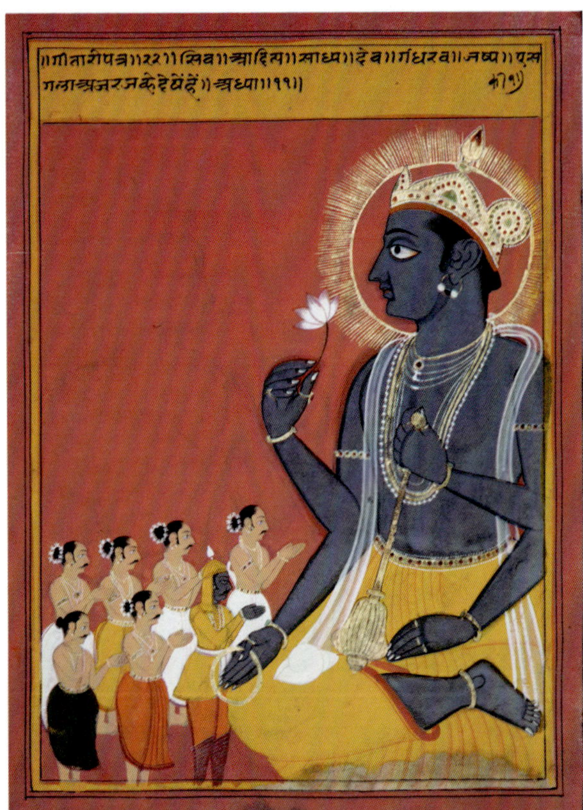

|22| अर्जुन कहने लगा, हे कृष्ण! रुद्र, आदित्य, वसु, साध्यगण, गंधर्व, विश्वदेव, अश्विनी कुमार, मरुद्गण, पितरों के समूह, यक्ष, असुर, सिद्धों के समूह, सभी आश्चर्य से आपको देखते हैं।

|22| Arjuna says: Hey Krishna! Rudra, Aditya, Vasu, Sandhya, Gandharva, the Guardians of the Universe, Ashwini Kumar, Marudgana, innumerable ghosts, Yakshas, Asuras, groups of Siddhas, all gaze at you in amazement.

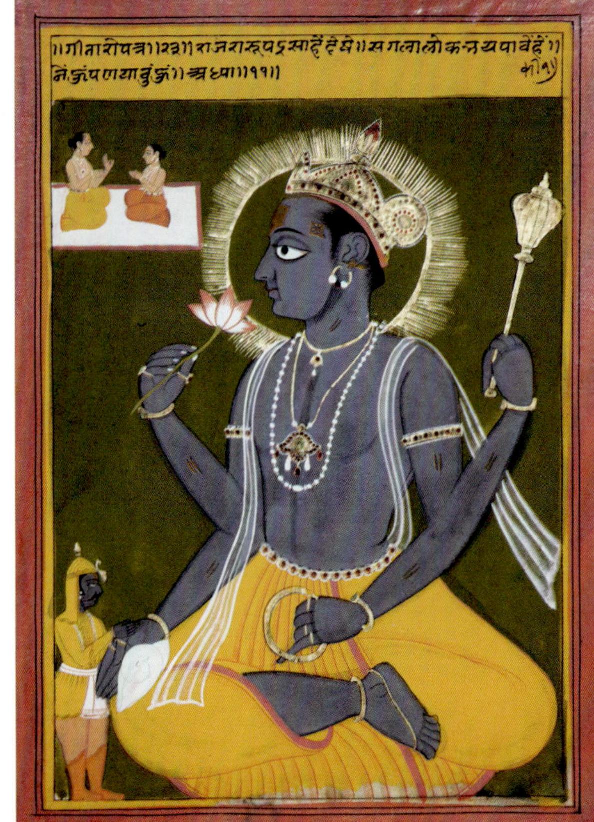

|23| अर्जुन आगे बोला, हे कृष्ण! आपके ऐसे रूप को देखकर सभी लोग व्याकुल हो रहे हैं और मैं भी डर रहा हूँ।

|23| Arjuna says: Hey Krishna! Seeing your majestic form, the entire world is filled with dread; so am I.

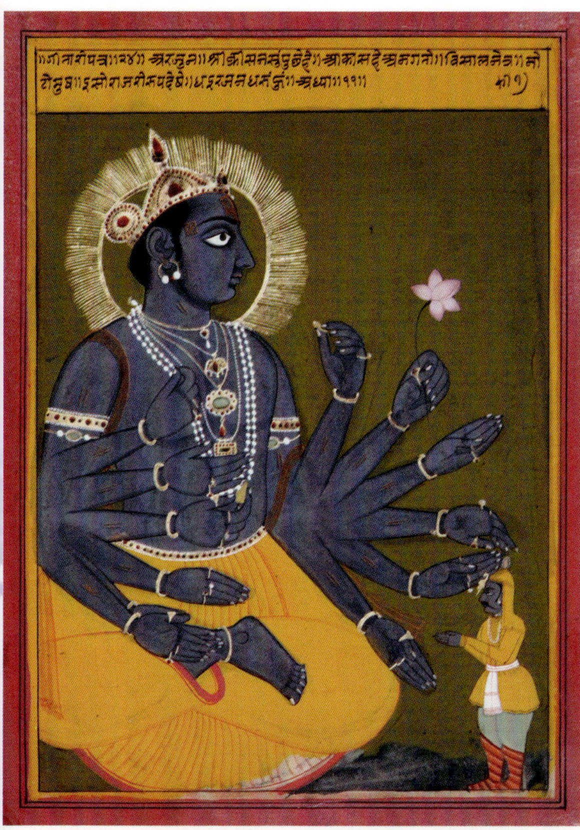

|24| अर्जुन कहने लगा, हे कृष्ण! आकाश को छूता हुआ, बड़ा खुला मुख और विशाल प्रकाशवान नेत्र से युक्त आपको देखकर मेरी अंतरात्मा भयभीत है और मैं धैर्य और शांति नहीं पा रहा हूँ।

|24| Arjuna says: Hey Krishna! When I see your great form touch the sky, your mouth wide open, your eyes burning with fire, I am terrified; I have neither courage nor peace.

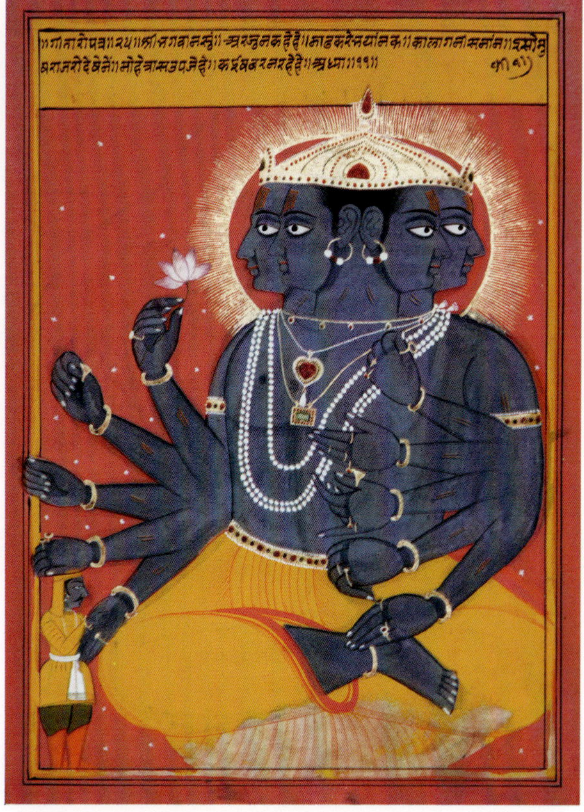

|25| अर्जुन बोला, हे कृष्ण! विकराल दाढ़ों और प्रलय की अग्नि की तरह आपके प्रकाशित मुखों को देखकर मैं दिशाहीन हो गया हूँ। भय के मारे मुझे कुछ भी खबर नहीं है।

|25| Arjuna says: Hey Krishna! When I look at your fearful jaws and the fires of dissolution burning in your mouth, I no longer know where I am; I am so afraid that I have lost my bearings.

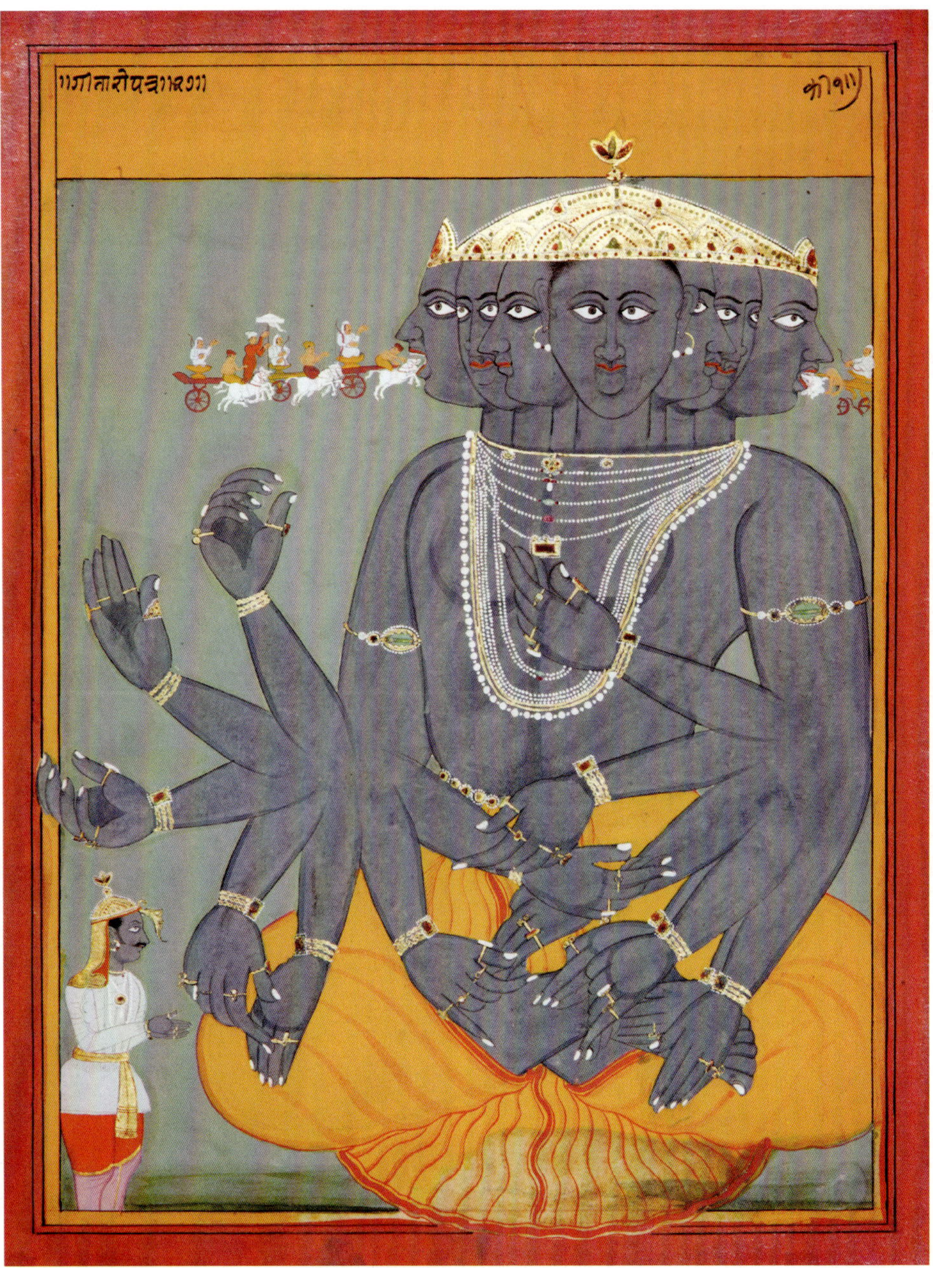

|26| अर्जुन बोला, हे विराट स्वरूप वाले कृष्ण! धृतराष्ट्र के सभी पुत्र, उनके पक्ष के राजाओं के समूह, भीष्म, द्रोण, सूतपुत्र कर्ण और हमारे पक्ष के प्रमुख योद्धा आपके भयानक मुख में प्रवेश कर रहे हैं।

|26| Arjuna says: Hey God of majestic form! All the sons of Dhritarashtra, the kings allied to them, Bhishma, Drona, Karna and all the warriors on our side are entering into your terrifying mouth.

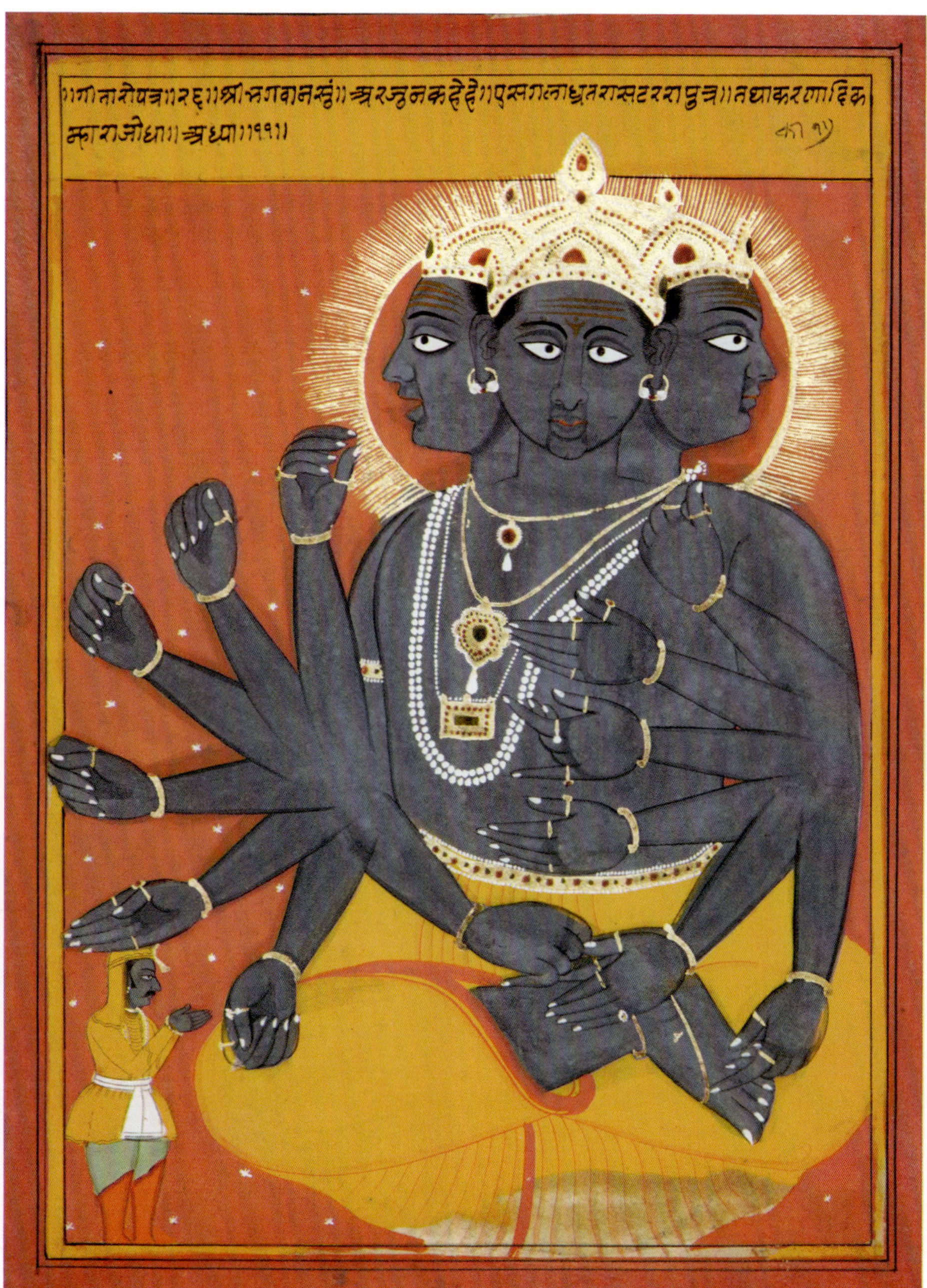

|27| अर्जुन आगे कहने लगा, हे देव! मैंने सभी को आपके विकराल दाँतों के मध्य फँसे सिर से चूर-चूर हुए देखा है।

|27| Arjuna further says: Hey God! I can see their heads and bodies crushed between thy terrifying fangs.

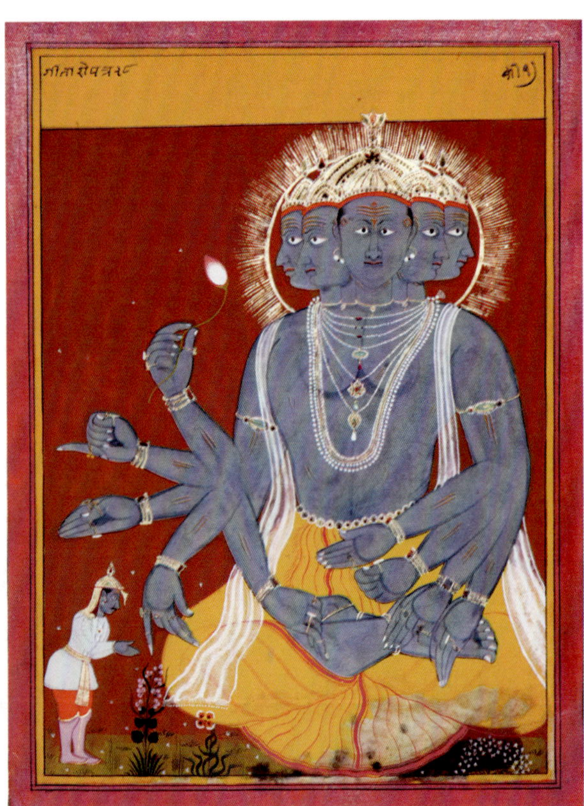

|28| अर्जुन कहने लगा, हे कृष्ण! जैसे नदियों की वेगपूर्ण धाराएँ समुद्र में जा मिलती हैं, वैसे ही उन नरलोक के वीरों को मैंने आपके प्रज्वलित मुखों में घुसते देखा है।

|28| Arjuna says: Krishna! I can see these warriors rush into your radiant mouths just as flooded rivers plunge into the sea.

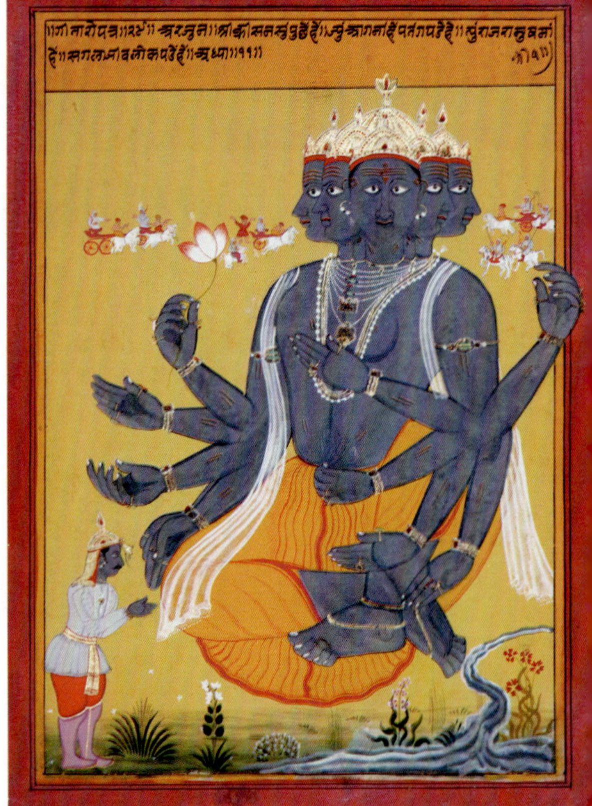

|29| अर्जुन आगे कहने लगा कि जैसे पतंगे अपने नाश के लिए पूरे वेग से अग्नि में घुसते हैं, वैसे ही जगत के सभी प्राणी अपने नाश हेतु पूरे वेग से आपके मुखों में प्रवेश कर रहे हैं।

|29| Arjuna says: Just as moths fly impetuously to the fire to be destroyed, all the creatures of the world rush into your mouths to their destruction.

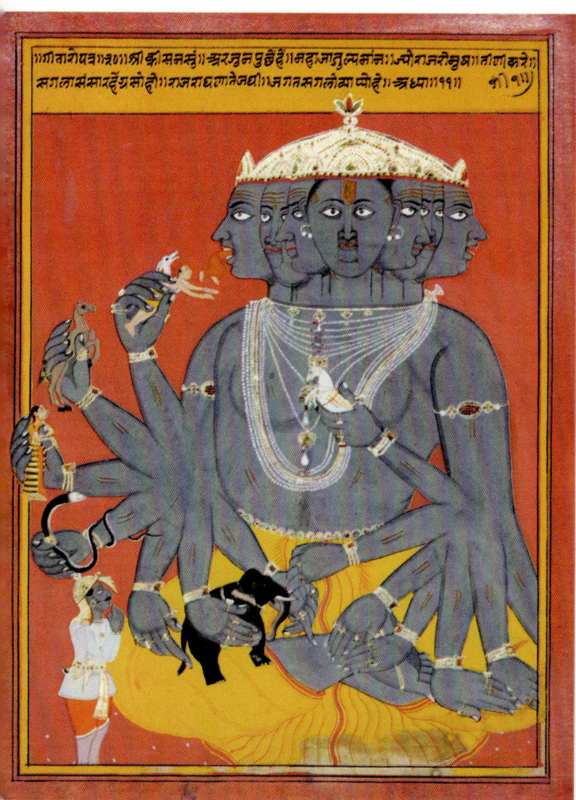

|30| और आप भी प्रज्वलित मुखों से सारे लोकों को सभी ओर से निगल रहे हैं। आपका उग्र तेज जगत को तपा रहा है।

|30| And you also devour all the worlds as they enter your radiant mouths from every direction. Your fierce fires are scorching the entire universe.

|32| श्री कृष्ण बोले, हे अर्जुन! मैं लोकों का नाश करने वाला काल हूँ। इस समय इन लोकों को नष्ट करने के लिए प्रवृत्त हुआ हूँ। तेरी विपक्षी सेना के सारे योद्धा तेरे (युद्ध किए) बिना भी नहीं रहेंगे।

|32| Sri Krishna says: Hey Arjuna! I am world-destroying Time. My purpose now is to annihilate everything. Even without you, all the warrior ranged against you will cease to exist.

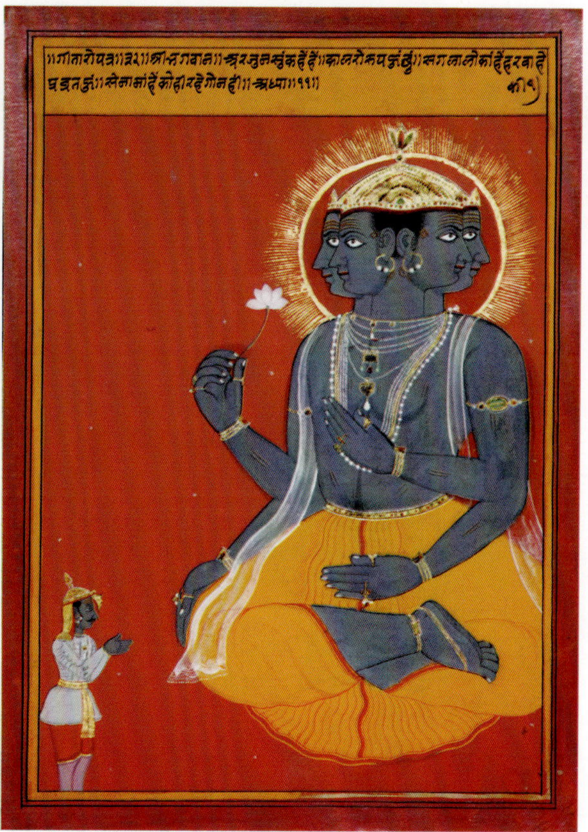

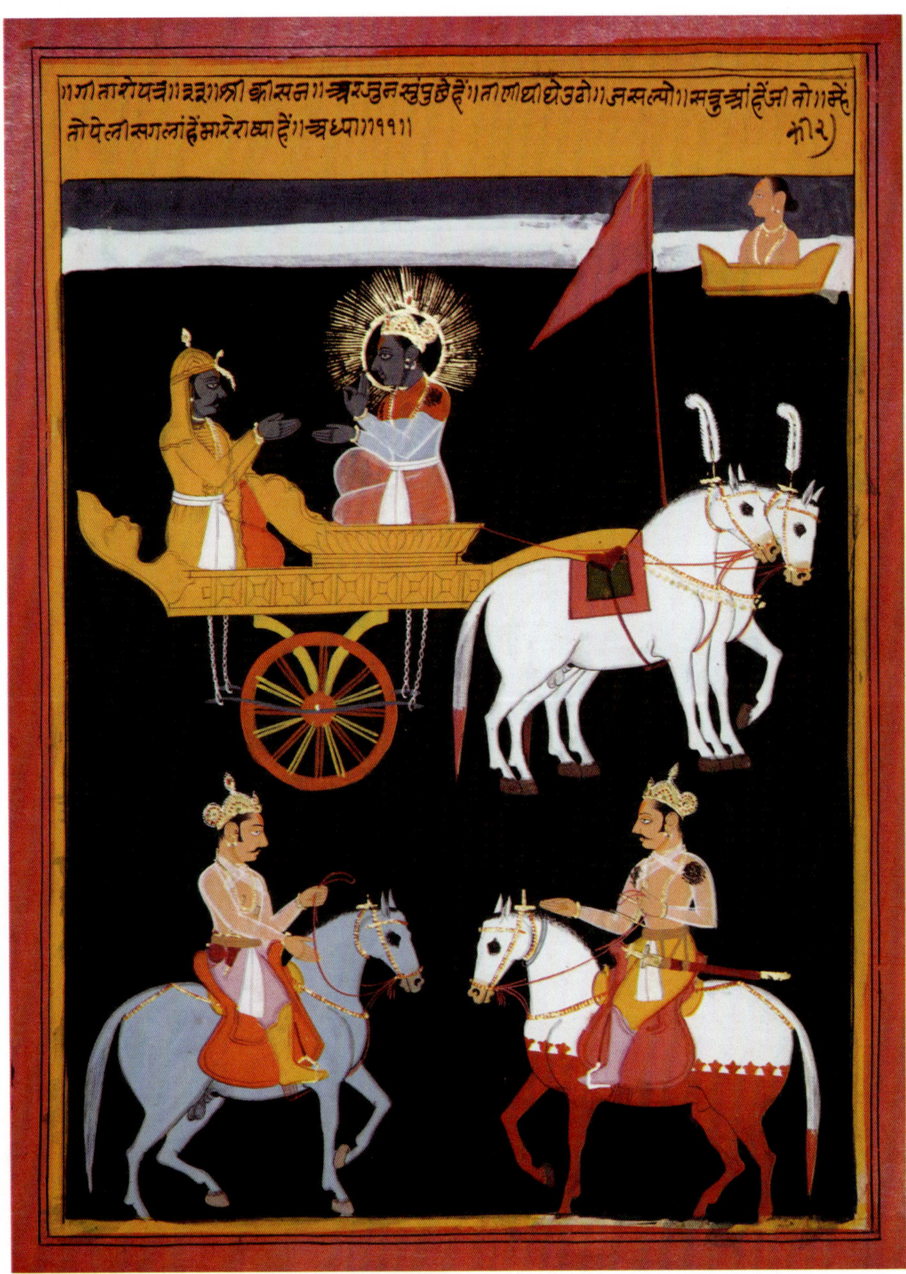

|33| श्री कृष्ण आगे कहने लगे, हे अर्जुन! इसलिए तू उठ! यश प्राप्त कर! शत्रुओं को जीतकर राज्य का उपभोग कर। तेरे सारे शत्रु तो पहले ही मेरे द्वारा मारे जा चुके हैं तुझे तो बस निमित्त मात्र बनना है।

|33| Sri Krishna further says: Hey Arjuna! Therefore, arise! Win renown! Defeat your enemies and enjoy your kingdom. All your enemies have already been killed by me. You only have to be my instrument.

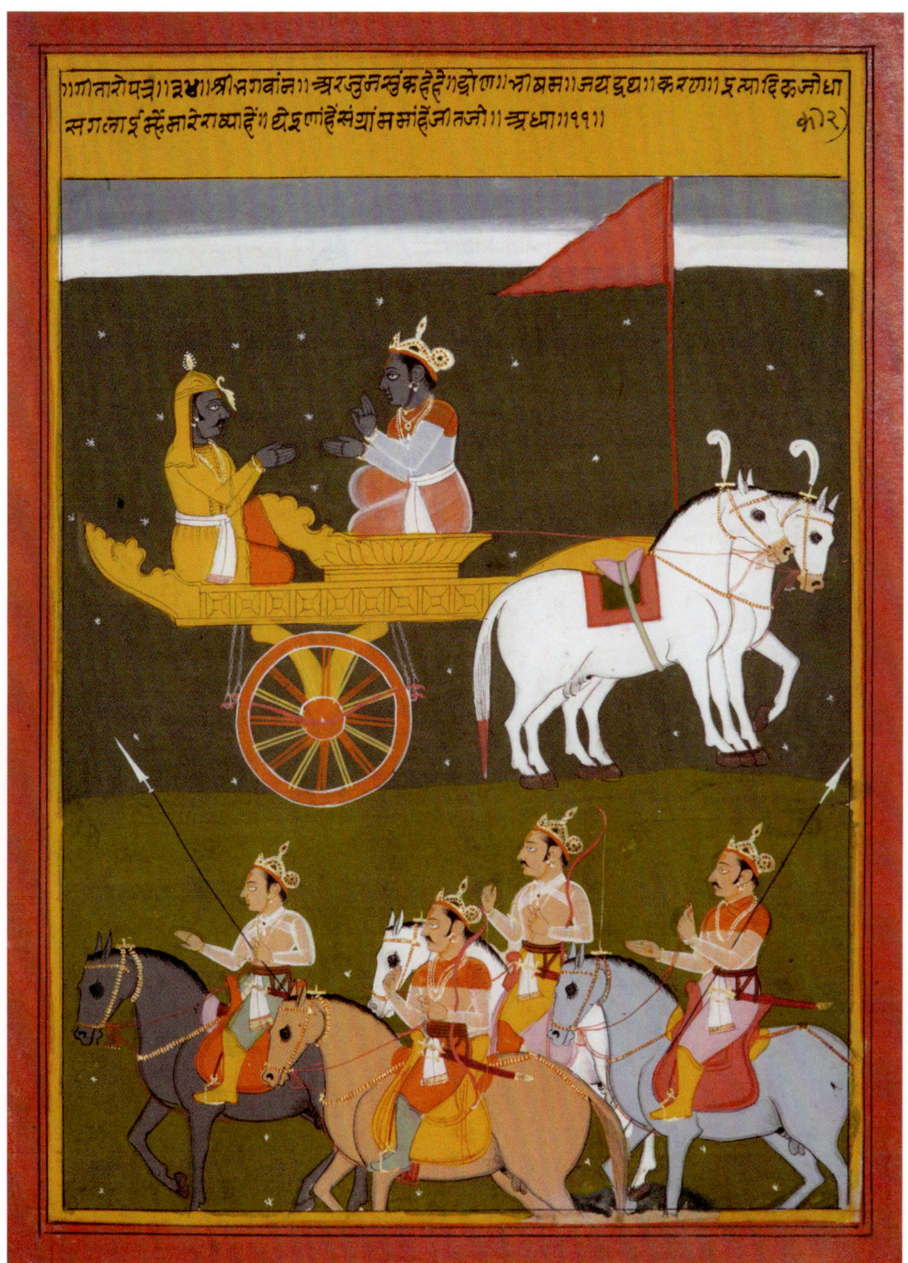

|34| अब हे अर्जुन! तू द्रोण, भीष्म, जयद्रथ, कर्ण तथा अन्य शूरवीर योद्धा जो मेरे द्वारा मारे गए हैं, को मार। भयभीत न हो। तू युद्ध में जीतेगा। अत: युद्ध कर।

|34| Now, hey Arjuna! Since Drona, Bhishma, Jayadratha, Karna and other brave warriors have already been killed by me, go and kill them. Do not be afraid. Go and fight. You will win this war.

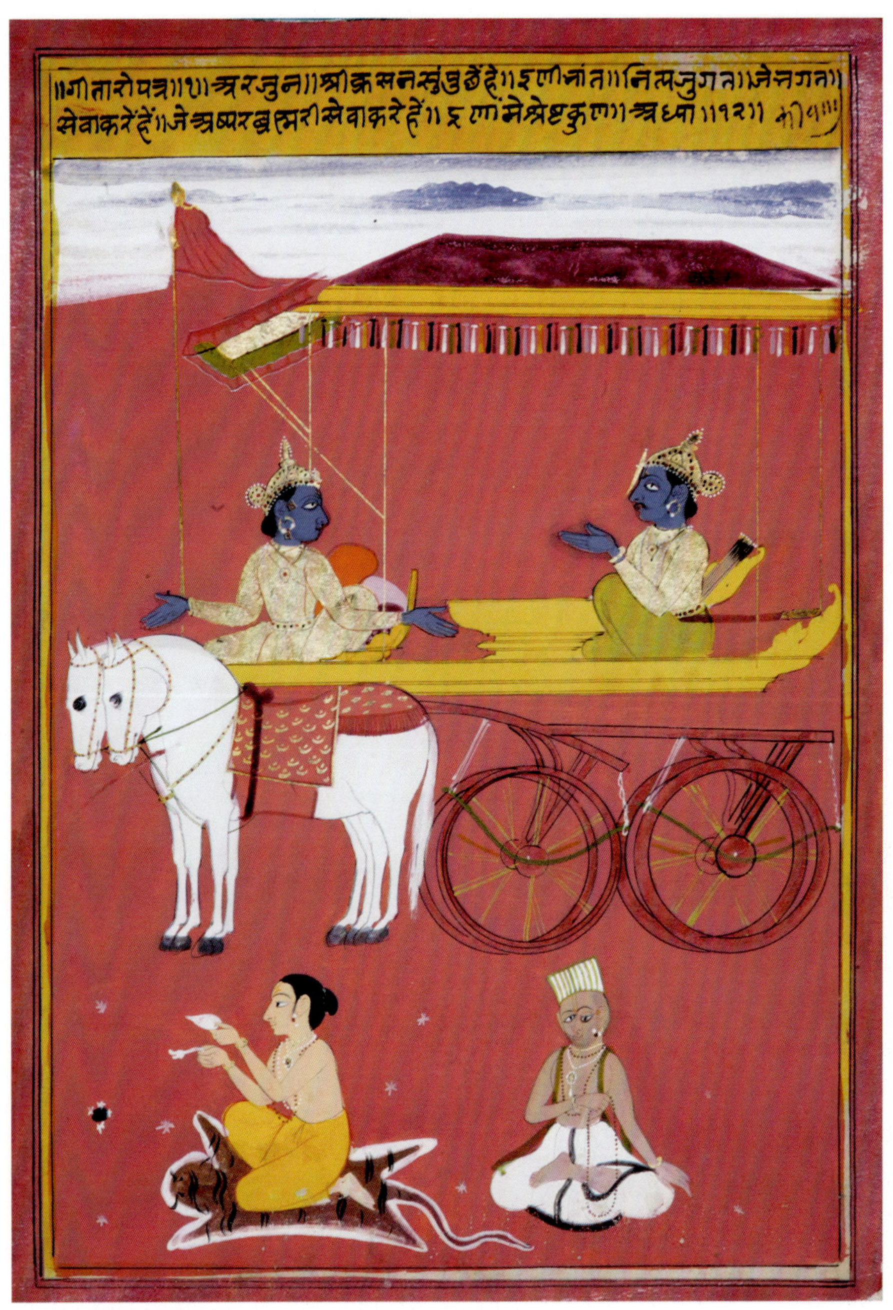

|1| अर्जुन पूछने लगा, हे कृष्ण! जो भक्त आपके रूप की निरंतर उपासना करते हैं और अन्य जो अविनाशी ब्रह्म को भजते हैं, इन दोनों में श्रेष्ठ कौन है ?

|1| Arjuna asks: Hey Krishna! Who is your best devotee, the one who constantly worships you or the one who worships the indestructible Brahma?

CHAPTER 12

After witnessing the theophany of Krishna, Arjuna is a radically transformed man. Instead of asking anguished questions, he seeks further clarifications about action, devotion, desire, and God's *caritas* (love and mercy). This, in itself, is unusual for a kshatriya who is supposed to live by a heroic code. He should now pick up arms, but does not. Instead, Arjuna wonders if it more worthy to be devoted to a personal or an impersonal god. War is still far away. How can one know, he asks, if the voice heard or the vision seen is divine, a guide to cosmic good, and not a chimera which will lead to moral disaster? What are the visible signs or verbal inflections which can help him decide? After all, in the past, even Arjuna had misheard and misperceived dharma, only to be struck dead. Yudhishthira's wisdom had rescued him. Surely, Arjuna remembers that Indra had granted the kshatriya ruler, Kuru, the boon that men who undespondently plough a field in peace will not be deemed inferior to those who recite the Vedas. Both can gain heaven. Does Arjuna not know that the name 'Krishna' includes in it the syllable '*kr*' ('to do') and the word '*krishi*' (ploughman), and that Sita is an earth goddess (Bhu Devi), born in the furrows of a field?[1] Mahatma Gandhi discards the idea that masculine valour is a sign of godly grace and declares that the *Gita* teaches "the utter nothingness of earthly power."[2]

Allah Baksh's paintings, responding to Arjuna's philosophic quandary, refuse to acknowledge the imminence of war. There are still very few images of soldiers and horsemen. Arjuna continues to sit unarmed on the floor of the chariot listening intently or asking questions with humility. Significantly, he does not occupy the raised, yellow lotus-shaped seat on the chariot since that is Krishna's and sacred. Krishna's discourse is accompanied by the gestures of an animated teacher and not of a commanding god or a stern moralist. At times, his arms are spread wide as if taking in the entire world (painting for verse 1); at other times, he leans back (painting for verse 6), his elbow resting on a seat, as he patiently explains that he rescues everyone who is devoted to him. Often his hand gestures promise fortitude and fearlessness to those who

1 Hiltebeitel, *Nonviolence in the Mahabharata*, p. 100.

2 Quoted by Hiltebeitel, *Nonviolence in the Mahabharata*, p. 144.

are "incapable of hatred toward any being" (Swami 70)—a lesson that is extremely important for Arjuna as a warrior (paintings for verses 2, 3, 9 and 18). And whenever he does assume the pose of an instructor and a guide, he self-consciously upholds his left hand in a non-threatening *mudra* so as to include himself as the subject and object of his teaching (paintings for verses 3, 15 and 17). Indeed, in these paintings Krishna's popular associations with peacocks, dance and music are never forgotten—a reminder that Krishna is the god of love and not just Arjuna's charioteer in Kurukshetra (paintings for verses 7 and 9).

Since this chapter is concerned with how one can conceive of a personal god, or how difficult it is to approach a transcendental being, Allah Baksh gives every kind of worshipper serious consideration. The space below the chariot is now crowded with all those who have their own ecological stake in a world without war—hermits, householders, animals and birds. Since Krishna says that all forms of truth-seeking lead only to him, in each painting he is a presence between the moral and intellectual pilgrims on earth and in the sky. Generally the rishis, scholars, priests and temple goers are painted with affection and reverence, though the ascetics who follow extreme forms of yogic practices are treated with well-tempered irony. Thus, the old sage, with a white beard, in the painting for verse 4, is a particularly gentle being. His clothes are white and he sits alone in a cave mediating upon a beautiful tree with green and red leaves. He has subdued all his senses and regards all things with the same disinterested and impartial eye. His body has taken on the contours of the hill-side indicating his restful sense of being part of the earth's rhythms. In contrast to the noise of human beings on the battlefield, his presence in the enwombed space resonates with sacred silence. Jorge Luis Borges says that it is "enough for one man to be irrational for others and the universe itself to be so as well."[3] This painting suggests that the *Gita* offers a more hopeful counter: It is enough for there to be one man who lives a life of non-cruelty (*anrsamsya)* to establish that non-violence is the fundamental basis of all existence and that the gods *will* it to be so. India's saintly literature and art tradition is full of stories and images of yogis who are so deeply and unthreateningly immersed in the earth's seasons that creepers wind their way up their bodies while birds play in the leaves. It is clear that for the artist, Krishna's discourse in this chapter is a warning against destructive rage and retaliatory vengeance.

3 Jorge Luis Borges, *Selected Non-Fictions*, edited by Eliot Weinberger (New York: Penguin, 1999), p. 246.

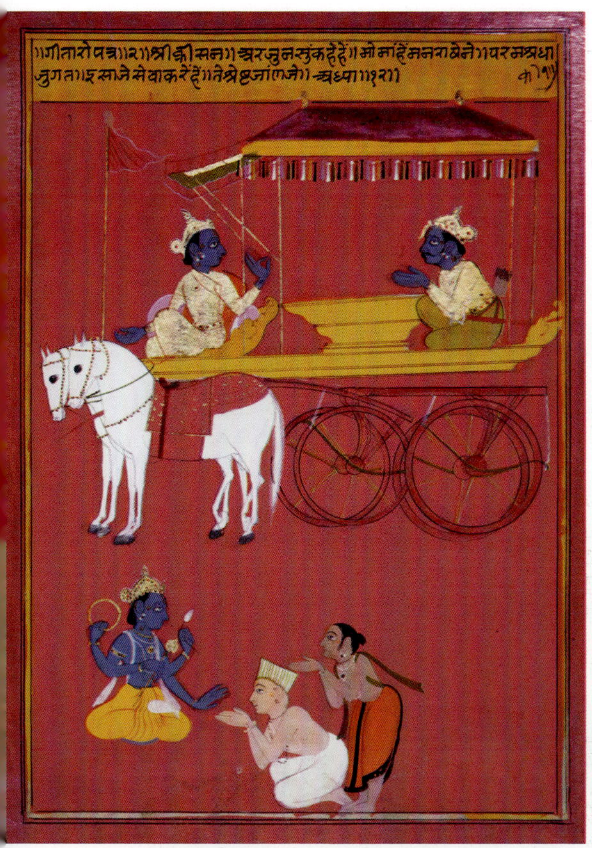

|2| इस पर श्री कृष्ण बोले, हे अर्जुन! जो मुझमें मन स्थिर करके निरंतर मेरे ध्यान में लगे हुए, पूरी श्रद्धा से मेरी उपासना करते हैं उन्हें श्रेष्ठ मानना।

|2| Sri Krishna says: Hey Arjuna! Those who have true faith in me and worship me with a steadfast mind are the very best.

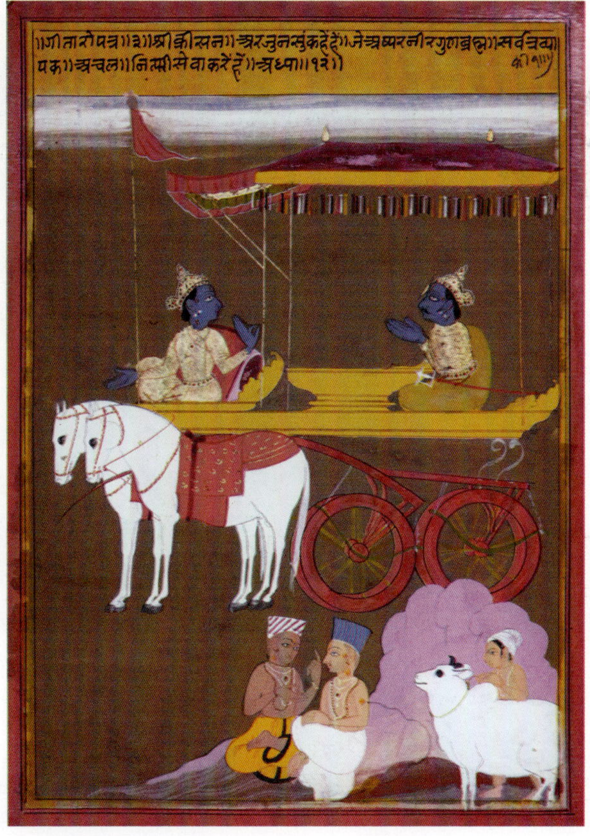

|3| श्री कृष्ण आगे कहने लगे कि जो अक्षर, सर्वव्यापी, अचल, नित्य, निराकार ब्रह्म की उपासना करते हैं। मन बुद्धि से परे अकथनीय स्वरूप की आराधना करते हैं।

|3| Sri Krishna further says: Hey Arjuna! Those who discipline their mind and thoughts and worship the indestructible, the unmanifest, the immutable, the eternal Brahma, also worship me.

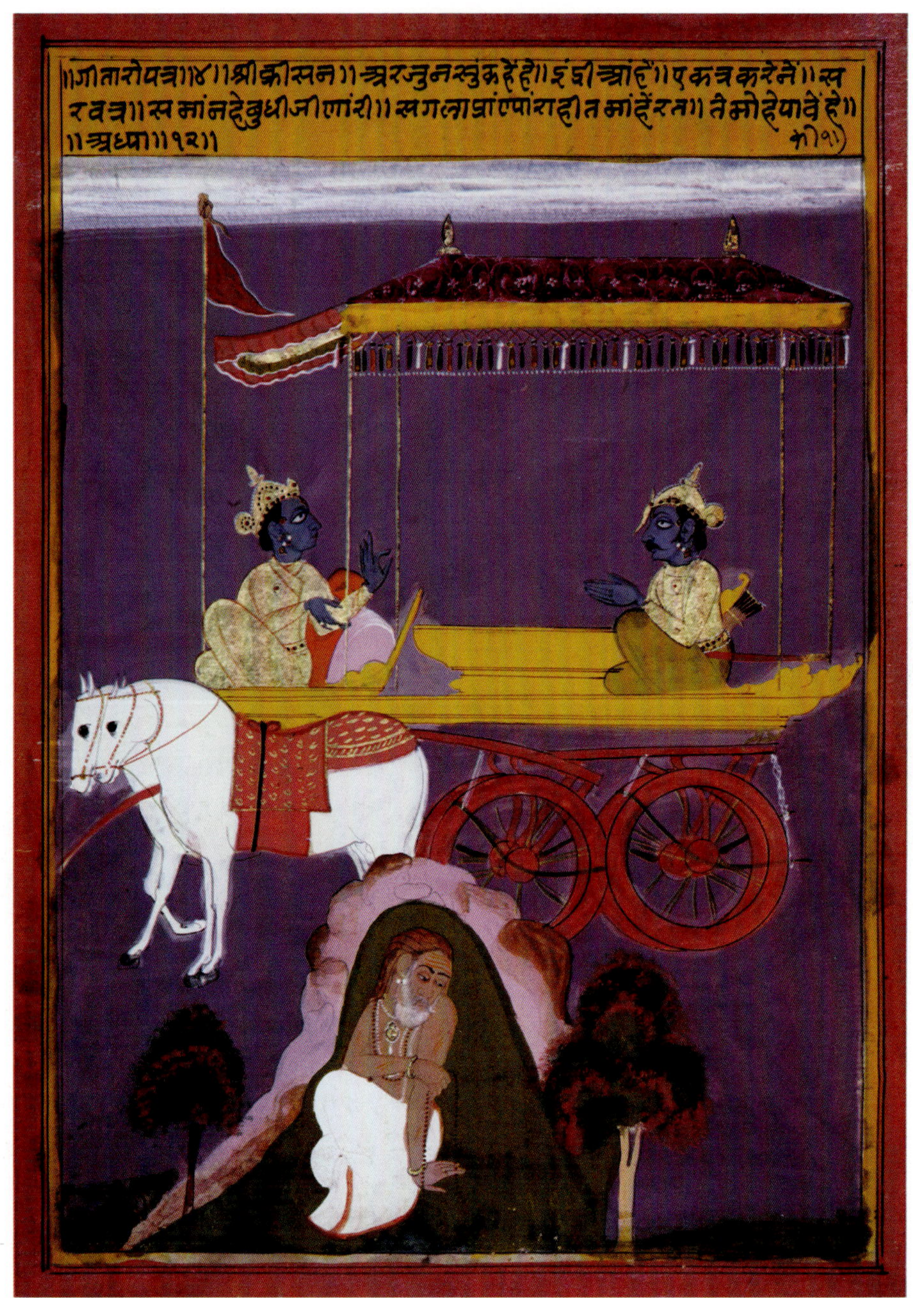

|4| श्री कृष्ण आगे कहने लगे, हे अर्जुन! जो इन्द्रियों के समूह को अच्छी तरह वश में कर, जो समबुद्धि पुरुष सभी प्राणियों के हित में रत रहते हैं, वे मुझे प्राप्त होते हैं।

|4| Sri Krishna further says: Hey Arjuna! Those who are wise control their senses and work for the welfare of all creatures also reach me.

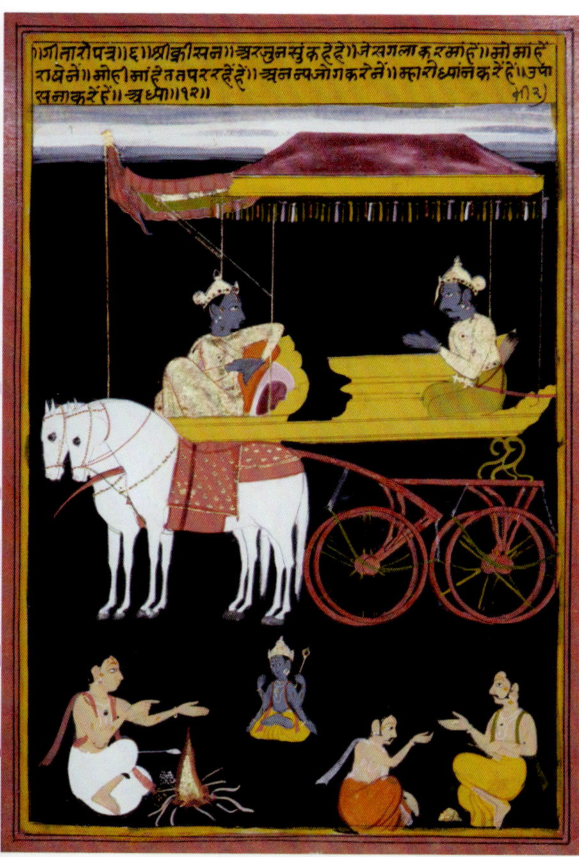

|6| श्री कृष्ण आगे समझाते हुए कहने लगे, हे अर्जुन! जो समस्त कर्मों को मुझमें अर्पण कर अनन्य भक्तियोग से मेरा ही ध्यान करते हुए उपासना करते हैं।

|6| Sri Krishna explains further: Hey Arjuna! Those who renounce all their actions, and meditate only on me, worship me, find me.

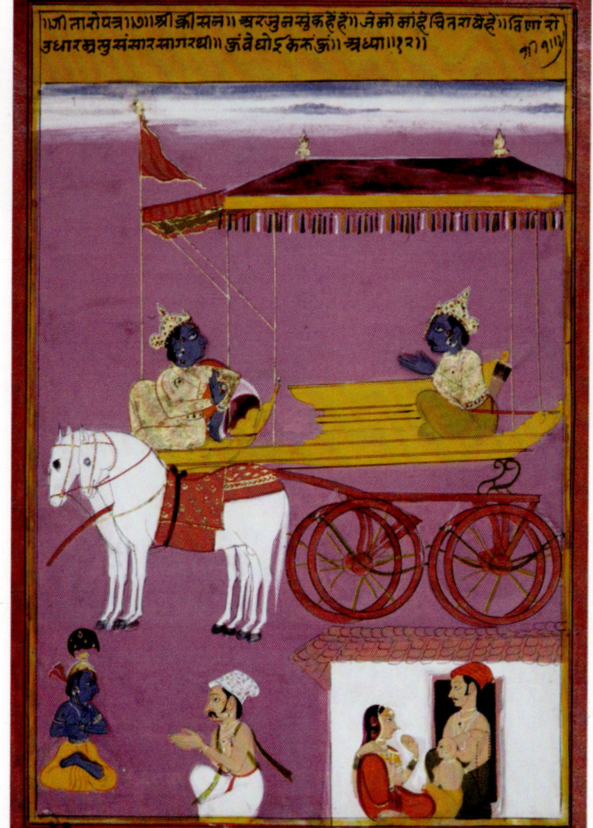

|7| हे अर्जुन! ऐसे मुझमें चित्त लगाने वाले भक्तों का मैं शीघ्र ही मृत्युरूप संसार सागर से उद्धार करता हूँ।

|7| Hey Arjuna! I redeem such people quickly from the ocean of life and death.

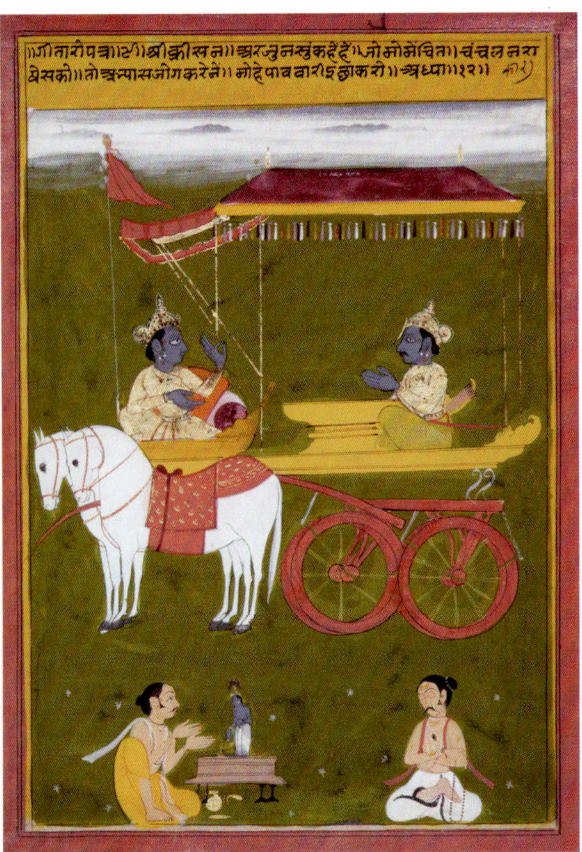

|9| श्री कृष्ण आगे कहने लगे, हे अर्जुन! यदि तू चित्त को स्थिरता से मुझमें लीन करने में असमर्थ है तो अभ्यास रूप योग के द्वारा मुझे प्राप्त करने की इच्छा कर।

|9| Sri Krishna further says: Hey Arjuna! If you cannot concentrate only on me then try to reach me through the practice of yoga.

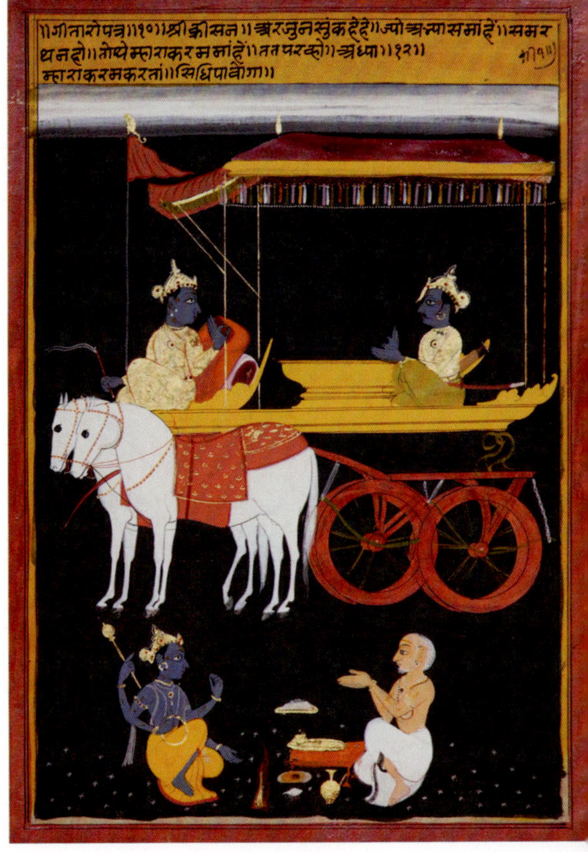

|10| श्री कृष्ण आगे समझाते हुए बोले, हे अर्जुन! यदि तू अभ्यास करने में भी असमर्थ है तो मेरे लिए कर्म करने में तत्पर हो जा। मेरे लिए कर्म करने से भी तू सिद्धि को प्राप्त होगा।

|10| Sri Krishna explains further: Hey Arjuna! Even if you fail to concentrate on me, you must still act for my sake. If you act for my sake, you will attain your goal.

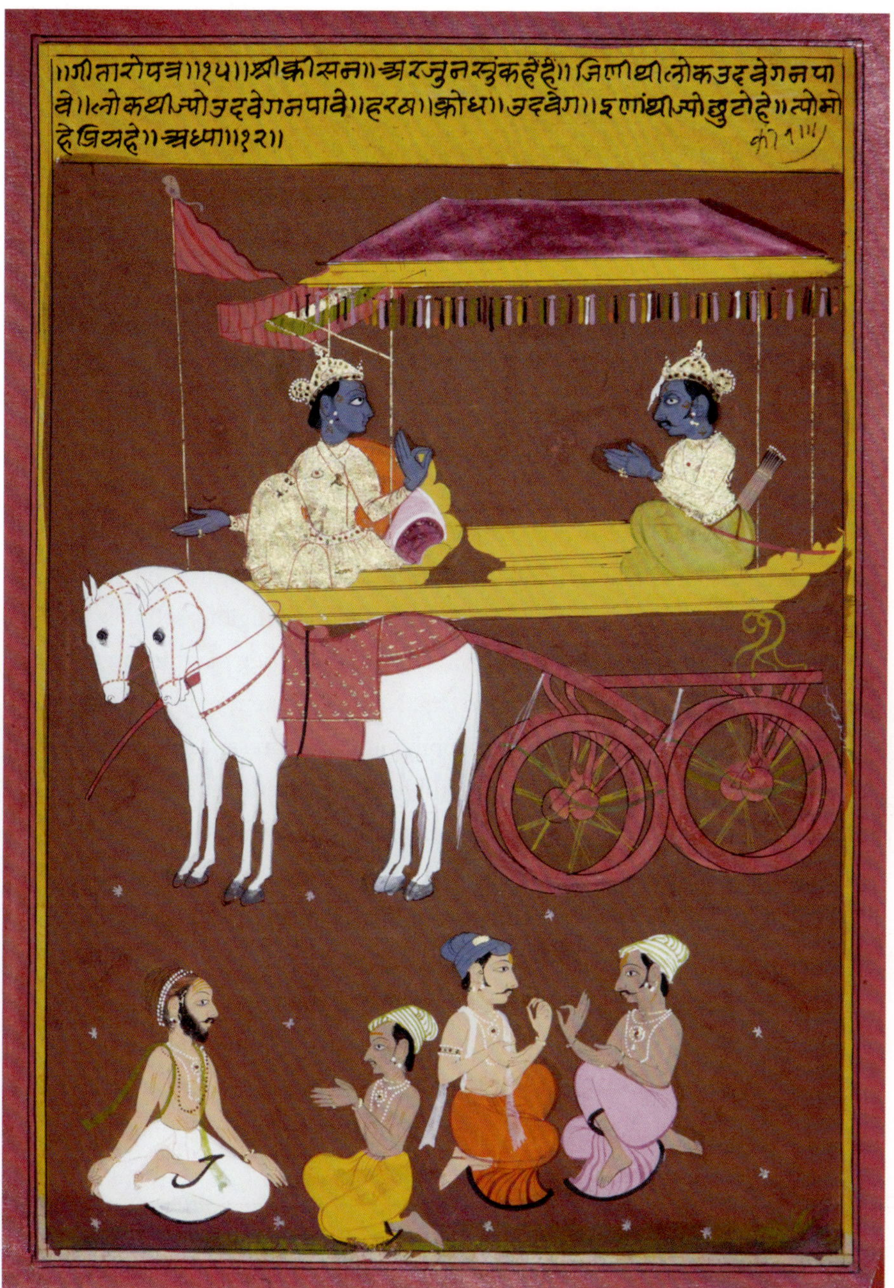

|15| श्री कृष्ण आगे कहने लगे कि जिससे कोई प्राणी उद्विग्न नहीं होता और न जो किसी से उद्विग्न होता और जो हर्ष, ईर्ष्या, भय से मुक्त है, वह मुझे प्रिय है।

|15| Sri Krishna further says: The one who is not hated by anyone, who hates no one and who is free from joy, envy and fear is dear to me.

In the paintings for verses 6, 7, 9, and 10, Krishna is a witness to his own worship and a delighted participant. In none of these paintings does he appear in his frightful Vishwarupa, but in a form ordinary people are capable of imagining and enduring. The background colour of each painting is a bright, restful, warm and spiritually exalting scarlet, green violet, purple or blue. White flowers are scattered on earth, indicating nature's unplanned beauty-making powers. Each painting adds to a huge thesaurus of ordinary men and women who ask the same questions as Arjuna does: what is the nature of the divine; which personal god should they follow; how can they establish a relation with the transcendental 'Other'? They are also non-violent and unselfconsciously tolerant of distinct social, ecological and religious practices. Thus, in the painting for verse 1, there are two worshippers of different religious schools. The one sitting on tiger skin is a Shiva acolyte; the other may belong to a local sect judging from his striped cap. Neither of them regards Krishna as his personal god and both seem oblivious of his presence above. Their presence testifies to the idea that there are different modes of seeing and becoming 'good', thereby, demonstrating Krishna's basic assertion that every pilgrim-path leads to the same truth and that god makes no distinction between his devotees. Further, in the painting for verse 3, a cow and a cowherd are amongst the eager listeners to a religious discussion reminding one that in the Krishna myth his most entranced followers are not only the upper-caste kshatriyas or brahmins, but also those who till the land and milk the cows. Allah Baksh's Krishna-world is democratic; it mingles the sacred with the secular, and enables the earthly to recognise the divine as immanent.

These paintings lead one back to listen to Krishna's song again and realise that, after the dread-inspiring revelation of Chapter 11, the music is gentler; the tonal response to Arjuna's concerns is quieter and more humanely measured. Krishna's answers are not primarily about whether one should unconditionally worship a personal god whose images are

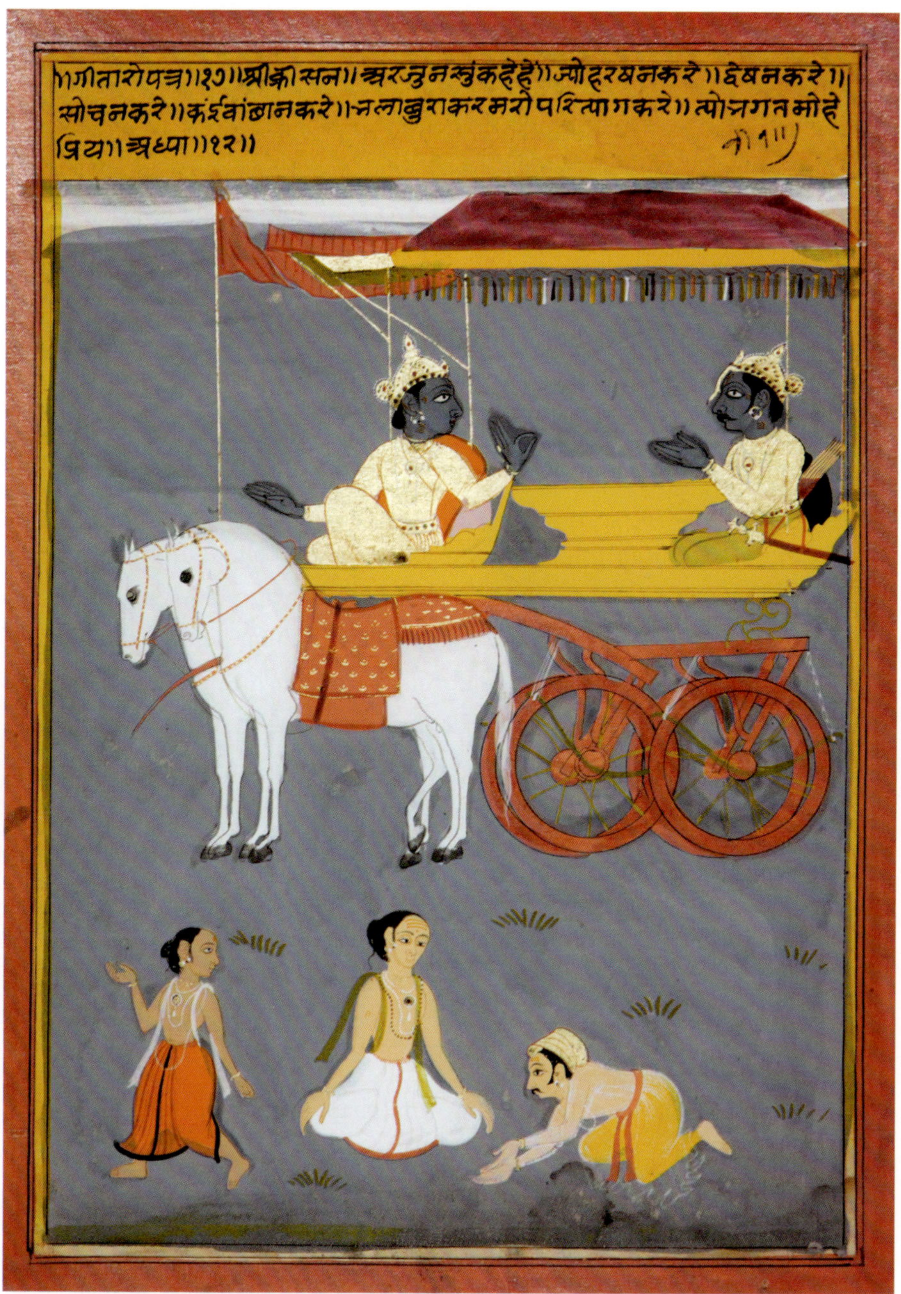

|17| हे अर्जुन! जो न हर्षित होता है न द्वेष करता है, न शोक करता है, न कामना और जो शुभ-अशुभ का त्यागी है, ऐसा भक्त मुझे प्रिय है।

|17| Krishna says: Hey Arjuna! The one who neither rejoices nor hates, who neither laments nor desires, who renounces fortune and misfortune, is dear to me.

manifest or abstract, inconceivable or impersonal. Those questions have been answered earlier. To worship an abstract Being, he says, is to follow a difficult path. But no matter which god people worship, ultimately they worship only him. Of course, Krishna is urging Arjuna to place his entire faith unquestioningly in him as a friend, guide and god. However, Arjuna's religious concern is philosophically more urgent. He knows that unconditional surrender to god in itself *does not define the good.* One should recall that there are characters like Ashwatthama, Karna or even Bhishma in the *Mahabharata* who are devotees either of an absolute god or a personal god, but whose actions cannot always be regarded as good and worthy of imitation.

Critics have used this chapter to claim that Krishna's frighteningly powerful and awe-inspiring vision has finally convinced Arjuna of his traditional destiny as a warrior who must fight without being concerned with victory or defeat. Does Arjuna really surrender his questioning and thinking selfhood to a display of divine power? Allah Baksh does not appear to think so. That is, perhaps, why in the painting for verse 19, he presents a less threatening Vishwarupa of Krishna. There is, however, no closure to the dialogue. The idea that there is a sense of an ending neither helps us to hear the tragic cadences of the *Gita* nor locate the source of its lyrical power. The real question is: how does one know if the decision arrived at for action at the behest of a personal or an impersonal God is just and good; if it is necessary for the maintenance of cosmic harmony, especially if the action is violent?

For Mahatma Gandhi, reading this chapter is important. It is a touchstone for ahimsa, he says, and teaches us how to "hear" God. It is "the essence of *Bhakti*." Since it is brief, a devotee can memorise and "call [it] to his aid in moments of trial" (Desai 304). Gandhi, however, does not tell us how its recitation would resolve personal or moral difficulties. Does it function like a chanted mantra to remind satyagrahis not to despair because even difficulties are part of the cosmic design? Can it rescure them "from the ocean of life and death" (Swami 69)?

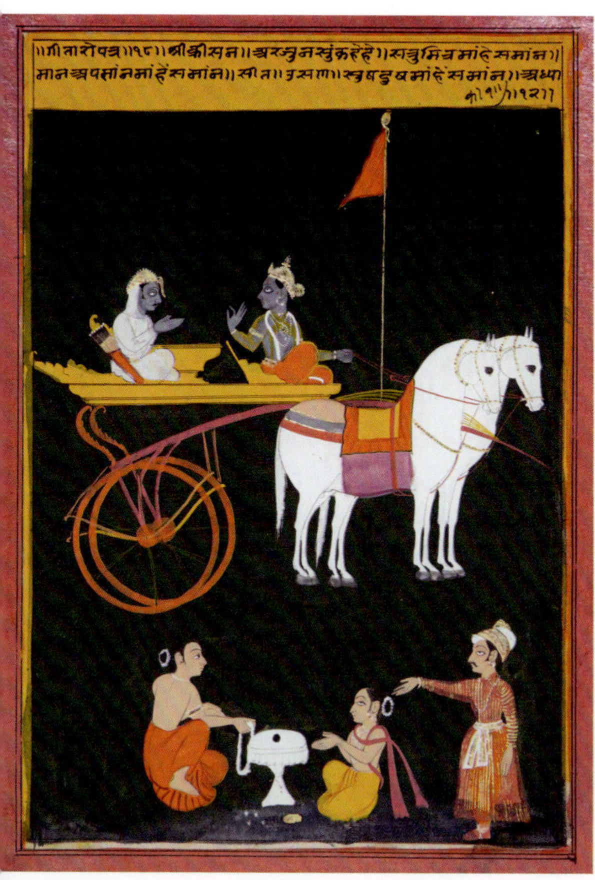

|18| हे अर्जुन! जो शत्रु-मित्र तथा मान-अपमान में समान रहे, जो सर्दी-गरमी व सुख-दुख के द्वंद्वों में समान रहे ऐसा आसक्ति रहित भक्त मुझे प्रिय है।

|18| Hey Arjuna! The one whose steadfast mind treats oppositions like friend-foe, honour-dishonour, heat-cold, joy-suffering alike is dear to me.

|19| हे अुर्जन! जो निंदा स्तुति में समान रहे, वाणी का संयमी, जो मिले उसी में सुखी रहने वाला हो। जो स्थिर बुद्धि रहने के स्थान में भी आसक्ति रहित हो ऐसा भक्त मुझे प्रिय है।

|19| Hey Arjuna! The one who is indifferent to praise-blame, enjoys silence, is content with his fate, has no fixed home but has a steadfast mind and is my devotee is dear to me.

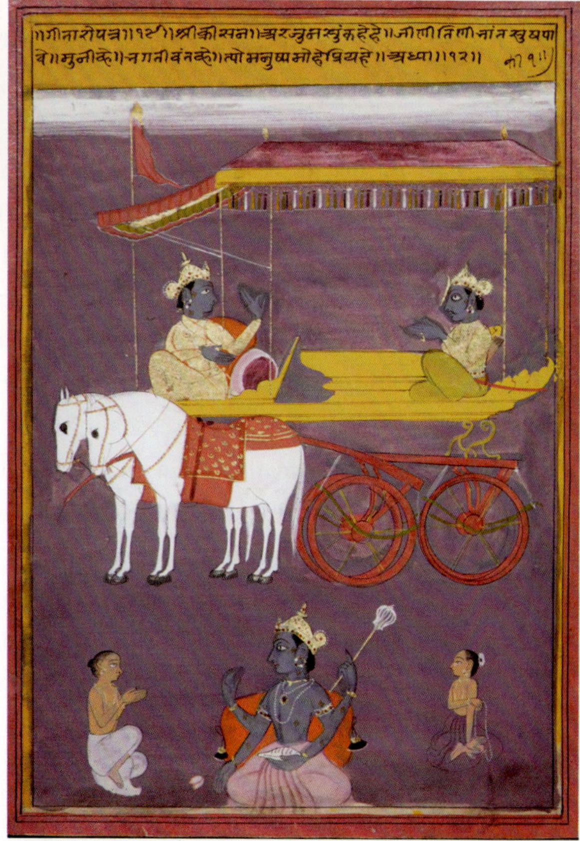

One way of understanding the chapter's intent and the visual images is to read them both beside Gandhi's favourite scriptural text, *1 Corinthians*: 13. What rings through its prophetic song, with elegant precision and clarity, is that even if we "speak with the tongues of men and of angels, and have not charity" our words shall "become as sounding brass, or a tinkling cymbal"; even if we have "the gift of prophecy" and the faith to move mountains, even if we "see through a glass darkly" and come "face to face" with God, even if we have faith and hope, but do not have "charity" it shall bring us no spiritual and moral "profit" (1 Corinthians). What echoes with similar lucidity in these verses of the *Gita* and Allah Baksh's simple images is Krishna repeatedly saying that his "beloved" devotee is one who longs for "peace", practices self-control and "expects nothing"; who does not hate, looks after the welfare of all beings and "does not harm the world" (Swami 69-70). The test of the voice of God is that he only urges ethically good deeds; actions which create a ground for others to act in the name of dharma. It is clear that faith in a personal god, that mere beseeching, however ardent, is not enough. Krishna's friendship and love has to be earned. That is why, the actions of all the ritualists of different sects in Allah Baksh's paintings are of limited ethical worth (painting for verse 20). Their passive non-violence is to be applauded, but none of them can achieve the wisdom of salvation. In these paintings, only Arjuna can sit face to face with Krishna because, amongst all his devotees, only he has the critical intelligence, the moral imagination and the will to act. He can become the man of vision; he can become, as Krishna says in the final words of the chapter, "My most beloved" (Swami 71).

One must note that the colophon of the painting for verse 20 declares, for the second time in this *Gita* folio, that the entire series of paintings was commissioned by Maharana Sri Jai Singh Ji.

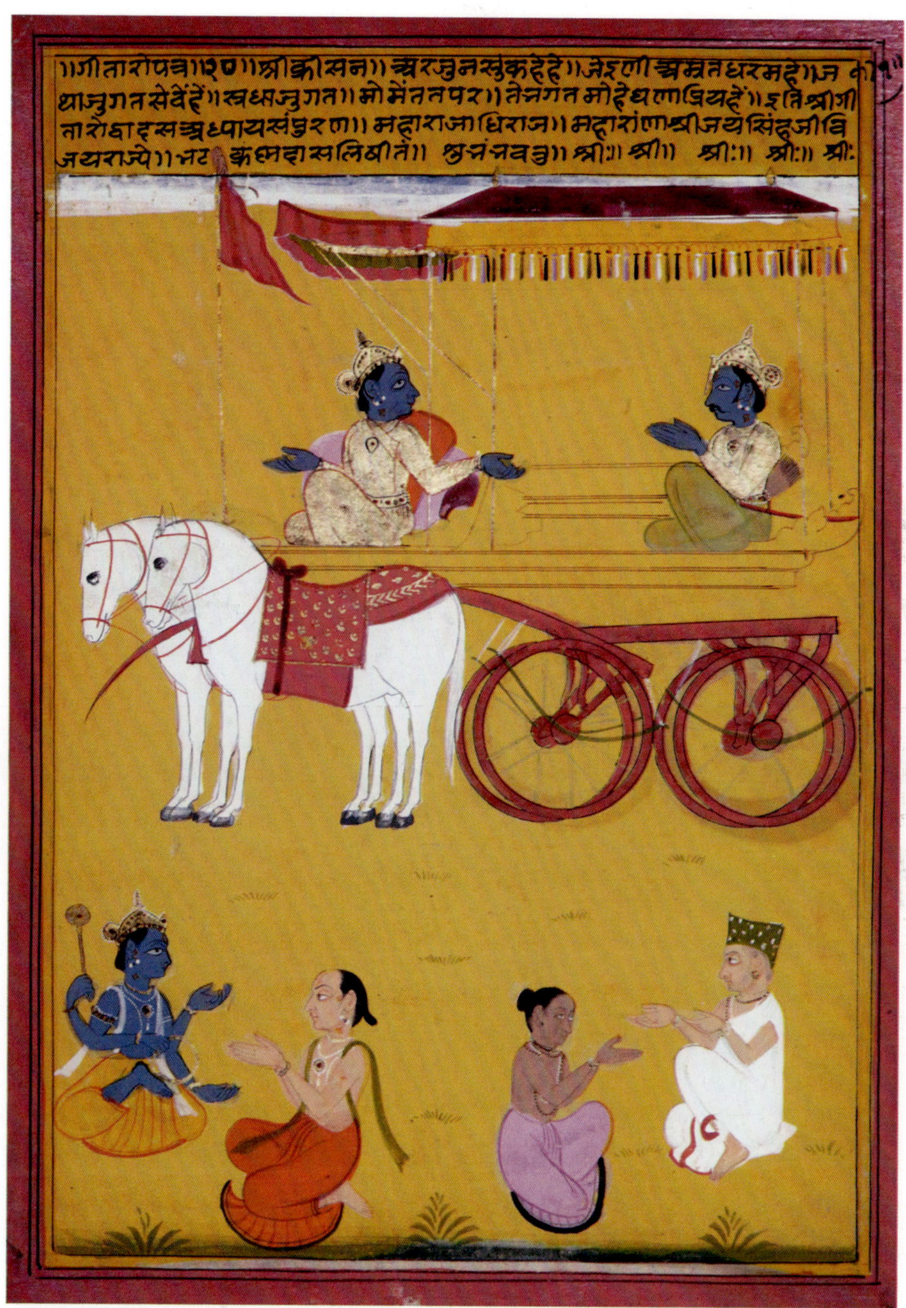

|20| हे अर्जुन! जो श्रद्धा से इस उपरोक्त अमृतज्ञान का प्रेम भाव से सेवन करता है, ऐसा भक्त मुझे प्रिय है।

|20| Hey Arjuna! The one who cherishes this spiritual wisdom and follows it with devotion is dear to me. This has been written for Maharajadhiraj Maharana Sri Jai Singh Ji by Bhatt Kishandas. Sri, Sri, Sri, Sri, Sri.

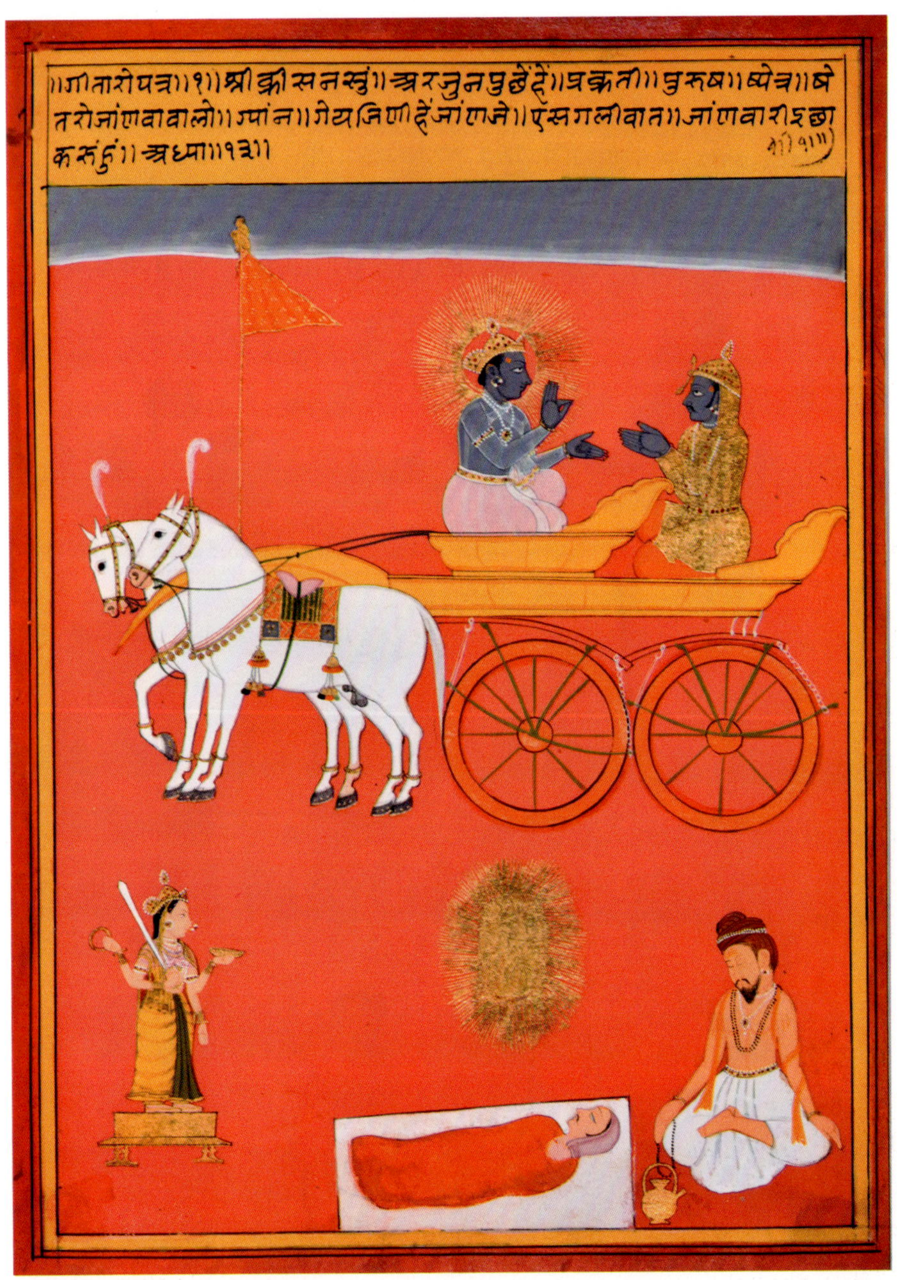

|1| अर्जुन पूछने लगा कि हे कृष्ण! मैं आपसे प्रकृति, पुरुष, क्षेत्र और क्षेत्र को जाननेवाला, ज्ञान और ज्ञेय को जानना चाहता हूँ। आप इन सारी बातों का खुलासा कीजिए।

|1| Arjuna asks Krishna! I want to know from you what is nature, man, field and the knower of the field, knowledge and what is worth knowing. Please explain all these things to me clearly.

CHAPTER 13

Krishna's answer to Arjuna in the opening verse is only seemingly arbitrary. Most *Gita* editions do not include Arjuna's question about the difference between *prakriti* and *purusha*, the field and the knower of the field, the body and the mind. The editors, who include it, do not always give it a number because, according to tradition, the *Gita* has 700 verses.

Allah Baksh follows the tradition and assumes that Krishna's reply is the first verse. Krishna makes a distinction between the sacred or the primal field where the divine has its being, and the field that exists in time and is of the earth. He also distinguishes between Eternal Man and man in the field of time. For the Eternal Man, knowledge of the three *gunas* or qualities of *sattva* (reason or intellect), *rajas* (emotion) and *tamas* (passion) is intuitive or instinctive; no disturbing shadow falls between the self and what it knows. The three *gunas* in the Eternal or Primal Man are not in conflict; they do not negate each other. Indeed, the Eternal Man's mode of acquiring knowledge and what he knows is holy and ethical. While the three qualities "are the primal cultivators of the land...*rajas* sows the seed, *sattva* preserves it, and *tamas* alone gathers in the harvest" (*Jnaneshwari* 2: 32).

In historical time, however, the field refers to the physical and temporal body and the earth. This physical body is an emanation of the divine body, but it is aware that since it is manifest in time, it is radically different and separated from the eternal. No longer guided by the eternal imagination, it becomes a place of tension, a destructive battlefield where there is perpetual conflict between the three *gunas* because each seeks domination over the other. If *sattva* begins to assert its singular power, *rajas* atrophies and *tamas* decays; compassion ceases to be an essential ethical requirement. If *tamas* overpowers reason, the consequences are either emotional violence or abysmal ignorance. And, if *rajas* guides action, then the self either becomes an abject fool of desire or an ignorant idolater; reason sleeps and the monstrous invades the personal or social space. Either way, the self that desires, has ambitions, or becomes slothful is fragmented, loses its integrity, and falls further and further away from enlightened action till it dies a useless death. Thus, the metaphor of the field in time suggests that the physical body of man is fertile or barren; it grows and decays; it is subject to the downward, spiralling whirl of time. Krishna tells Arjuna that the learned argue about who controls the field. None of them know or understand. In verse 5, he says "Seers have sung of It in various ways, in many hymns and Vedic songs, weighty in thought, and convincing in argument" (Swami 72).

Attempts by the wise to find out who controls the field, and their arguments about it, remain inconclusive. Is the field the home of the spirit or is the soul a perpetual stranger in it—"a sojourner on a long journey" (*Jnaneshwari* 2: 31-32)? However, Truth exceeds all speculations and the only one who can answer the question, Krishna tells Arjuna, is Krishna himself. That means, Krishna is the original knower of the field and what he knows is Himself. Analogously, in the field of time, man must become the ethical man who seeks knowledge, and what he seeks to know is himself as an emanation or incarnation of the divine. That is why, as we look at the recurring images of Krishna and Arjuna talking to each other in the chariot in these paintings, we begin to see them as reflections of each other; god and man in conversation become indistinguishable.

Allah Baksh's paintings offer remarkable visual correlatives for these abstract issues. He illustrates the first two verses with visionary daring. He creates an image for Arjuna's implied question and another for Krishna's answer. These images are drawn against coloured backgrounds with distinctive symbolic and emotional charge. The emotional quality of painting 1 is strangely surreal. It is not merely a record of physical death. Painted against a vibrant, energetic, sanctified red earth, it makes death part of a significant rite; part of a meaningful journey toward the divine which is possible for an intelligent soul to make. A dead body lies on the ground. A golden sun has descended on earth and shines over the body as if it is illuminating the path of the departing soul towards enlightenment. A bearded priest, with matted hair, sits near the head of the corpse. Unlike other priests, he is not merely a mechanic of religious rites. There is compassion in his eyes. More remarkably, a goddess shimmering with gold stands on a golden platform near the feet of the body. She is both an image of primal beauty and of the inherent qualities of purity or truth, sympathy or selflessness. The goddess carries a golden bowl filled with grace-giving nectar; a rememorialisation of the original plenitude of the divine. Religious sources tell us that the "mythical destiny" of the resplendent Devi is that she is "endowed with self-regenerative energy" and stands for "the beginning and end of every biological form."[1] There is sadness, of course, in the

1 Madhu Khanna, "Nature as Feminine: Ancient Vision of Geopiety and Goddess Ecology," in *Prakriti: The Integral Vision*, edited by Baidyanath Sarasvati (New Delhi: Indira Gandhi National Centre for the Arts, 1995), p. 109.

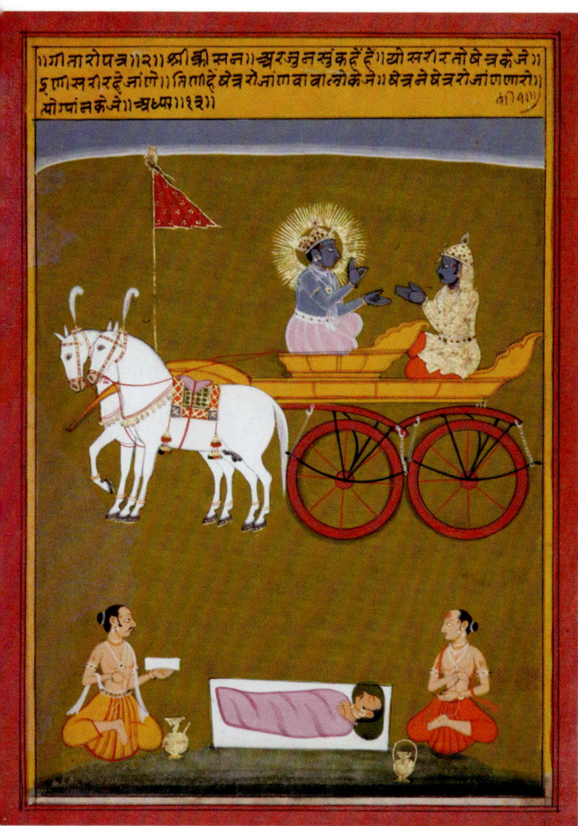

|2| श्री कृष्ण कहने लगे, हे अर्जुन! यह शरीर क्षेत्र कहलाता है और जो इसको जानता है उसे तत्वज्ञानी क्षेत्रज्ञ कहते हैं।

|2| Sri Krishna says: Hey Arjuna! This body is called the field. The one who knows it is called a field-knower.

|3| हे अर्जुन! मैं सारे क्षेत्रों में क्षेत्रज्ञ भी मुझको जान। और क्षेत्र-क्षेत्रज्ञ को तत्व से जानना ही ज्ञान है ऐसा मेरा मत है।

|3| Hey Arjuna! I am omniscient and know all the fields of the self. The one who knows the field of the self and who knows himself is a man of knowledge.

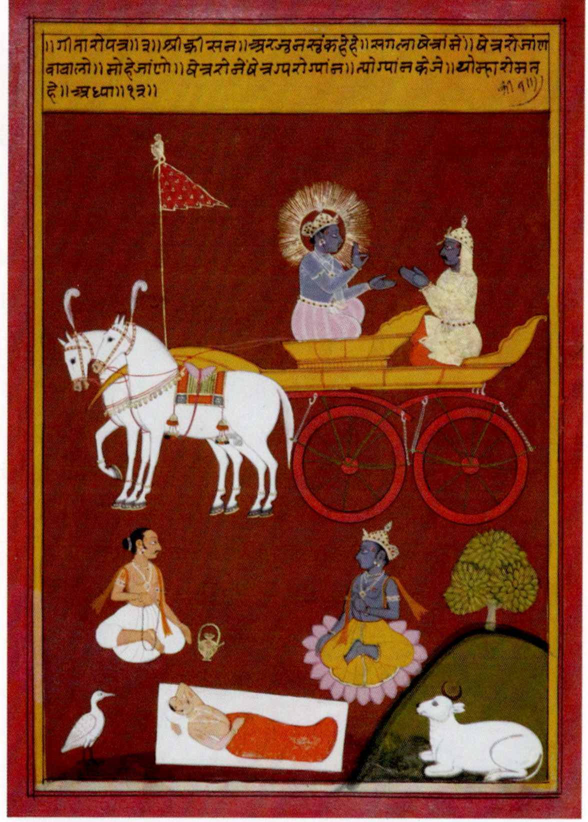

entire scene being enacted, but there is also exaltation, because time past, present and future are perceived simultaneously; each emerges from and falls back into eternity. As T. S Eliot says in *Burnt Norton*, a poem with profound echoes of the *Gita*:

> Time present and time past
> Are both perhaps present in time future
> And time future contained in time past.[2]

We are urged to recall what Krishna has said to Arjuna thus far about the original covenant between the sacred and the profane, the divine and the earthly, which life's history may sometime shatter, but which is never erased. If life were only in the present, it would be unredeemable as the painting for verse 2 depicts.

In the painting the ground or the field on which the chariot stands is green. Krishna has let go the reins of the horses. He turns around to face Arjuna, who sits with humility on a lower seat with folded hands and listens to the instruction. Arjuna is still unarmed, though he is wearing his golden armour. A golden halo around Krishna's head signifies his divinity. In contrast, and contrary to what the green colour ought to evoke, the scene below, on the lower ground, is almost despairing. It presents a small drama of unredemptive mortality. A corpse, in a purple winding cloth, lies on the ground. Two priests, one sitting near the head of the corpse and the other at its feet, are performing the last rites and chanting religious verses. There is no indication that the lifeless body once had any connection with the divine; it is no more than part of the natural phenomena; a mere thing which has neither been moved by Arjuna's anxiety nor wondered "who holds up the stars in the heavens" (*Jnaneshwari* 2: 33).

In verses 3 and 5, Krishna says that the wise can distinguish matter or the temporal self from the Eternal Self which controls it. The wise know how matter is composed, changes and decays. They also understand that both the Eternal Self and the particular self were once interfused and can once again be united in imaginative harmony if life, in historical time, is ethically lived. The painting for verse 3 is brilliantly composed and intelligently thought out. It has all the emblems of secular materiality and of eternity. Both the temporal and the eternal are separate and distinct, yet occupy the same earth-brown ground or field. They are so arranged that what they create is a new harmony between the divine and the earthly, time and eternity. A gentle, white cow sits peacefully

2 T. S. Eliot, *Four Quartets* (London: Faber and Faber, 1944), p. 13.

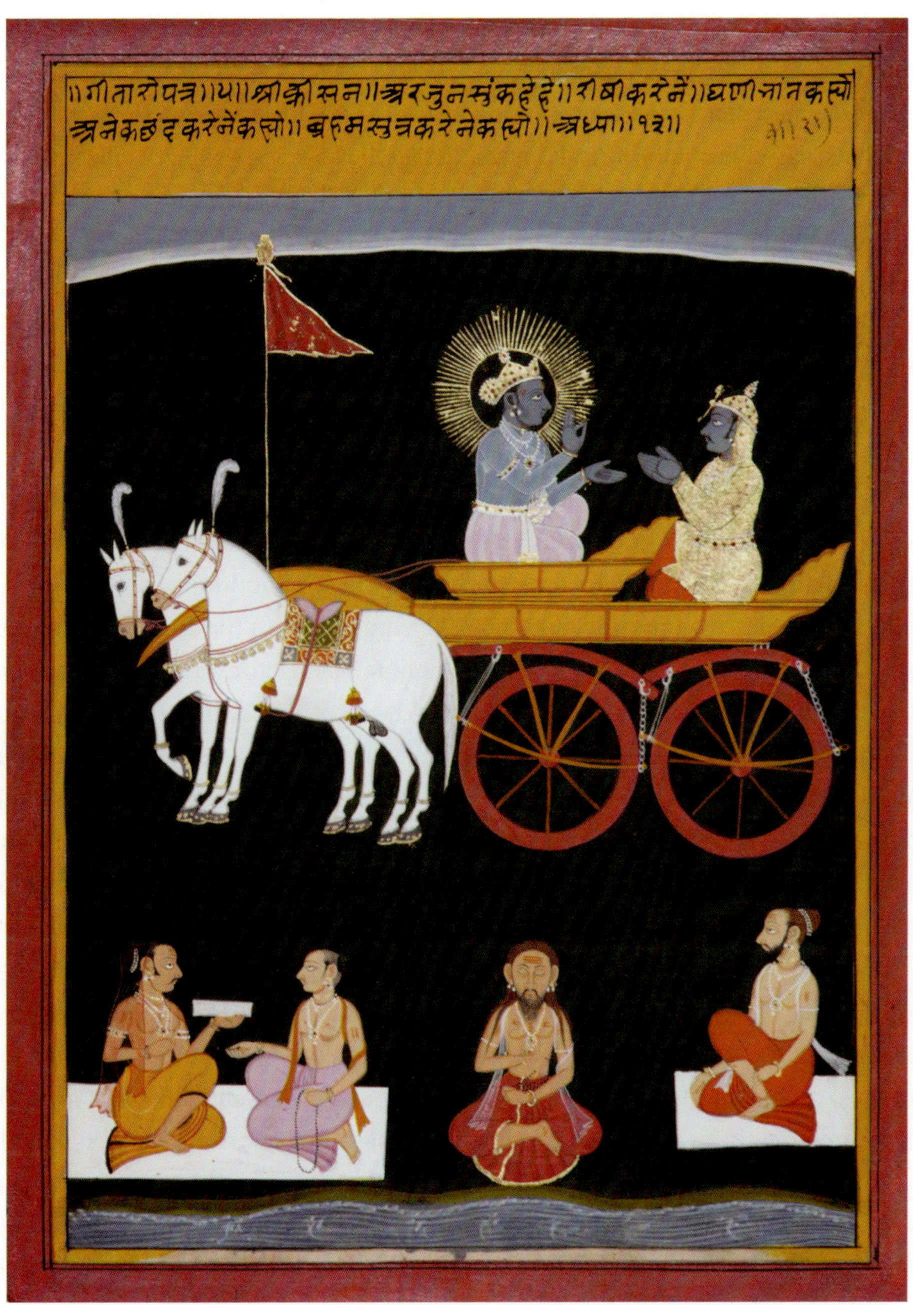

|4| श्री कृष्ण कहने लगे, हे अर्जुन! ऋषियों ने इसे कई प्रकार से कहा है। उन्होंने विविध छंदों (वेद मंत्रों) द्वारा कहा है। ब्रह्मसूत्र के पदों द्वारा भी इसे कहा है।

|4| Sri Krishna says: Hey Arjuna! The sages have said this in many ways. They have recited it in different meters and have sung about it in the Vedic hymns.

below an axial tree which may be growing either on top of a gentle green hill or at the edge of a circular and secure garden. Either way, the tree and the cow are symbolic of the idea that a green, fertile, and generous earth was the original image of a heavenly place and that it still abides in historical time for those who have the visionary capacity to see it. In the context of the impending war, Allah Baksh asserts that one can always find spots of earth and time which are still the living home of beauty, innocence, abundance and peace; that war is a negation of the intrinsic and natural order of things. A home of peace and beauty is not some prelapsarian fantasy, "a mere fiction of what never was."[3] It is always available to each of us in ordinary life as a possibility, provided we live according to some elemental and minimum ethical precepts. But this visionary insight is not available to the passive and lethargic mind. This is ironically made apparent in the figure of a sleeping man lying on a white sheet who seems, at first glance, to be dead. He is oblivious to the beauty and the divinity that is all around him. He is a representative example of ignorance; of the self whose ethical imagination is lost in some dark dream. A white bird looks inquisitively at the man. The scene is reminiscent of Dharma disguised as a Yaksh crane questioning Yudhishtrira near a pond in *Vana Parva* about the right conduct in the world. As a carrier of philosophical puzzles, the bird is indifferent to the scene of time and death; oblivious of human desires and ambitions. Yet, visually, it demands attention. In trying to comprehend the beauty and significance of its presence, the self becomes less obsessed with its own egotistic concerns and so longs to understand what transcendence means. Iris Murdoch reminds us that, for Plato, since beauty exists prior to time, its presence in our world makes the good, and hence eternity, accessible to the senses and the reasoning mind.[4]

Krishna sitting beside the man particularly well painted. His presence on earth eloquently suggests that the moral and spiritual world is always within our grasp. He sits cross-legged on a white lotus flower whose petals flare around him like a mandala. His saffron dhoti glows against the white petals like a radiant sun. However, only the wise have the discriminating intelligence to see that the earth is an aspect of eternity. Is the learned man, who sits across from Krishna, such a man? He is certainly a man of the scriptures, but is he a man of good deeds? He has scholastic knowledge, but has he struggled to arrive at the kind of illumination and deep conviction which Arjuna seeks? Perhaps, he looks upon the external landscape, recognises its splendour and bemoans

3 Abrams, *Natural Supernaturalism*, pp. 26-27.

4 Iris Murdoch, *The Fire and the Sun* (Oxford: Oxford University Press, 1977), pp. 35-36.

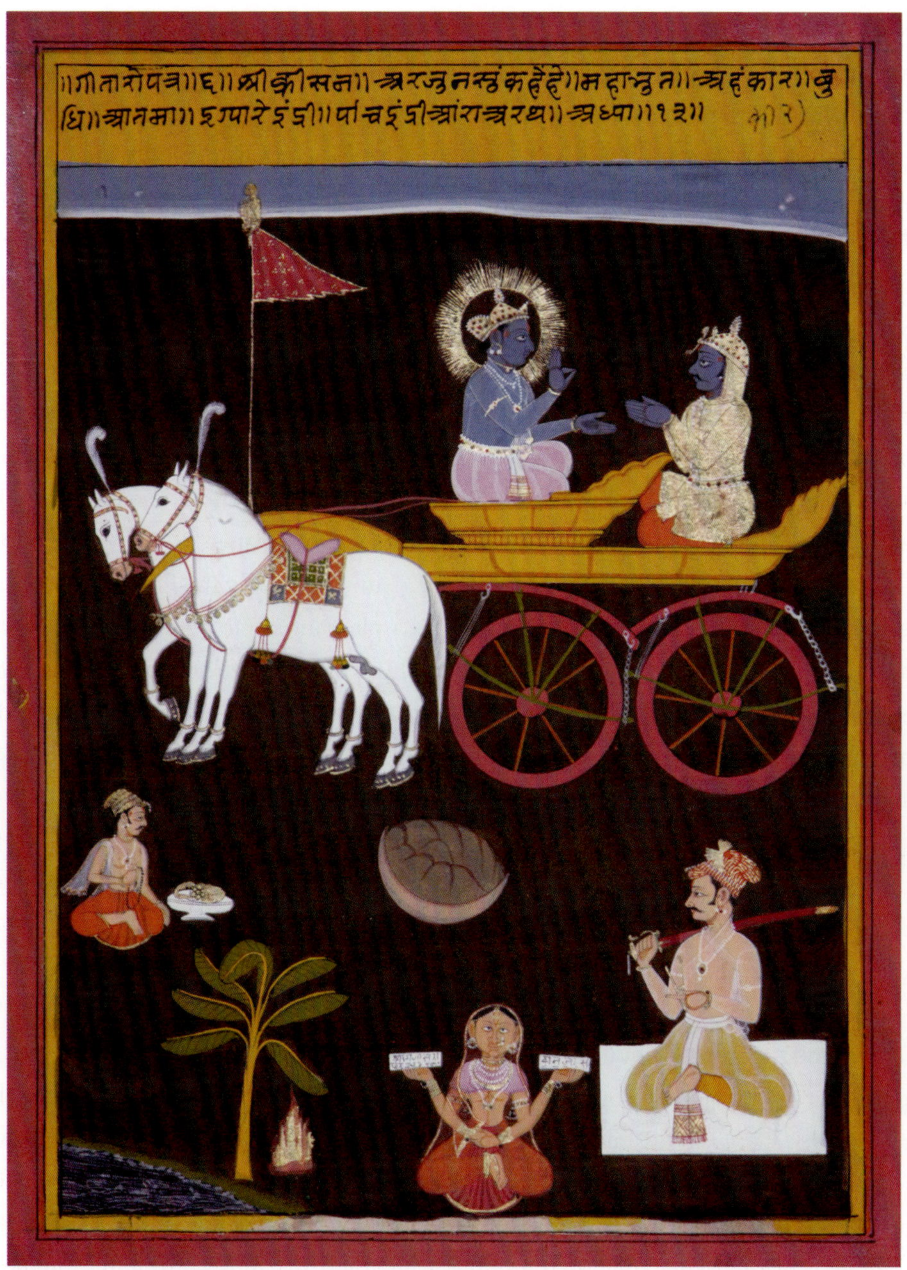

|5| हे अर्जुन! पंच महाभूत, अंहकार, बुद्धि, आत्मा, दस इन्द्रियाँ और एक मन तथा पाँचों इन्द्रियों के विषय (शब्द, स्पर्श, रूप, रस और गंध) विकार के क्षेत्र हैं।

|5| Hey Arjuna: The following are the sources of degeneration: five great elements, ten organs of perception, five senses, intellect, consciousness, ego, heart and five sources of feeling (hearing, sight, touch, taste and smell).

its transience. But does he see it with his inward eye? His knowledge does not arise from that confrontation with death and suffering which makes Arjuna tremble with dread. For that he must become, as Krishna tells Arjuna, a karma yogi; a man who acts, who takes the risk of losing his entire self to make the world eternal and godly once again.

The images of rivers in the paintings for the verses 5, 6 and 9 suggest the ceaseless flow of time and the passing away of all created things. In mythic lore, rivers are places of *tiraths*, pilgrimages in search of enlightenment. Acceptance of mutability without fear and trembling, Krishna has been telling Arjuna, is the ground of wisdom. It is also the reason for ethical action. The painter imagines small moral vignettes on river banks as he contemplates the idea of temporality and wonders who can, in the flow of time, "spy/ Some shadows of eternity."[5] But, since the river is beautiful, what it signifies about the dissolution of our identities ought not to cause sorrow. It should, instead, lead us back, as the *Gita* says, to imagine the formless form of the divine.

Thus, the painting for verse 5 in which Krishna describes the 'field' in material, psychological and metaphysical terms depicts a pleasant scene by a river just before sunrise. A sliver of white light shimmers in the horizon where the dark green field and the deep blue sky meet. Hanuman sits on the line separating the earth and the sky. His small body flashes with gold as if the light of understanding has, at last, broken through the night of ignorance. In one of his *Vinaya Patrikas*, Tulsidas writes:

> To those who look to Hanuman
> The fulfilment of promise is certain,
> like a diamond-cut line in stone.[6]

Krishna and Arjuna are silhouetted against the dark-green field. They glow with spiritual light. Their clothes and armour seem translucent. How untouched they both are by the rage of war! There is a hushed sense of anticipation around them, as if an epiphany is at hand; a flash of understanding about how interfused the earthly field and the divine actually are. A river flows across the lower edge. Every ripple in its waters catches the white light of the rising sun. As the *Jnaneshwari* says: the mind of the man without wisdom is like these eddying, circling waves; it carries on an unending conversation with itself; it encourages hope, arouses passions, is touched by fear, imagines strange

---

5 Henry Vaughan (1621-1695), "The Retreat," lines 13-14.

6 John Starton Hawley and Mark Jurgensmeyer, *Songs of the Saints of India* (Oxford: Oxford University Press, 1988), p.167.

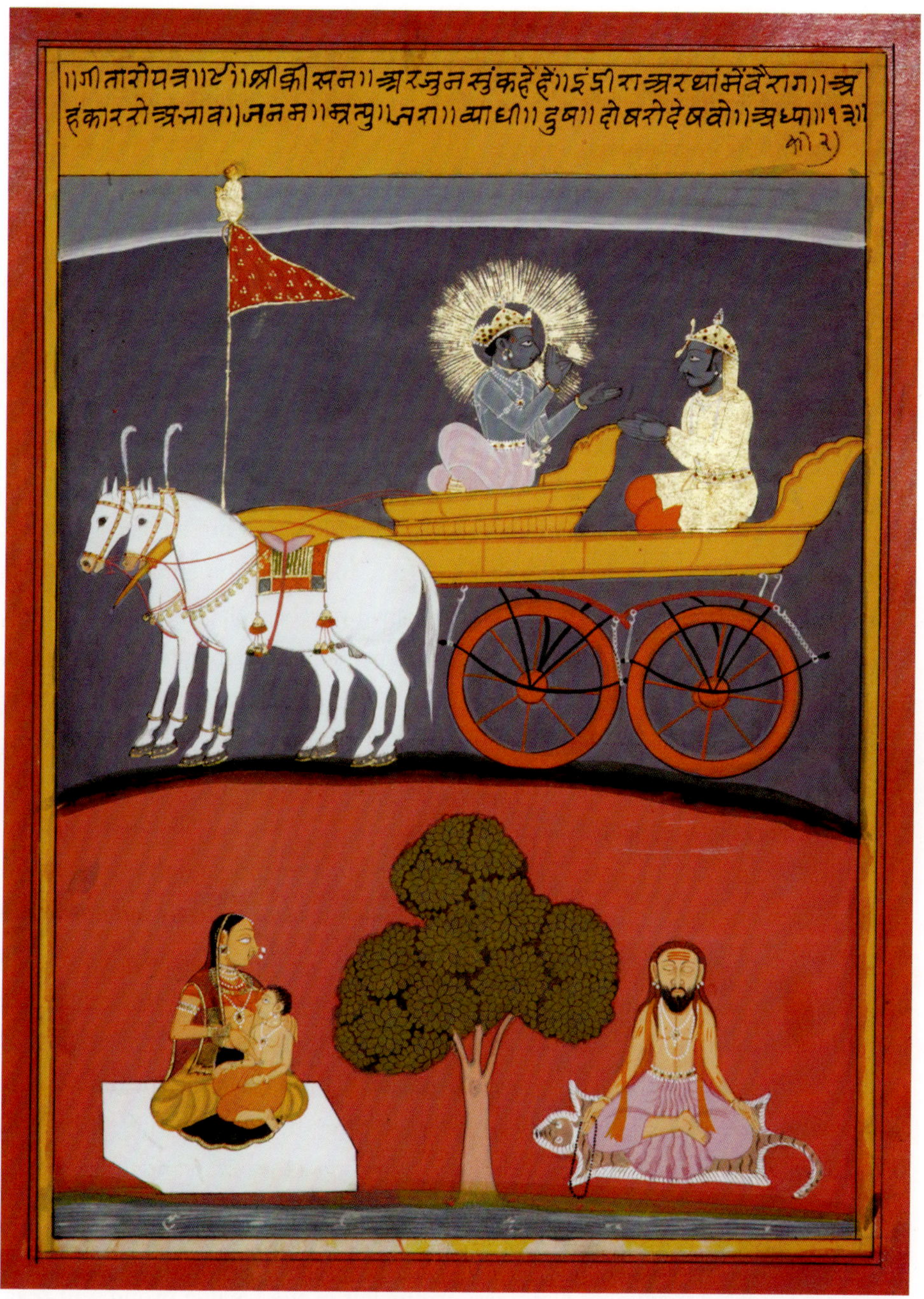

|8| हे अर्जुन! इसी तरह इन्द्रियों के विषयों से वैराग्य, अहंकार का अभाव, जन्म, मृत्यु, जरा-व्याधि, दुख और दोषों के बार-बार विचार करने को ज्ञान कहा है।

|8| Hey Arjuna! Further, knowledge means non-attachment to sense-objects, non-egotism, and thoughtfulness about birth, death, old-age, suffering and sin.

things and then shatters them. But, beneath all this swirl of desire and failure, the wise man seeks a steady centre of awareness, as in the depths of river water; a unity and a purpose in life which rises from some sacred spring, tumbles into time, and moves toward the great ocean.

In the painting, a Shaivite priest is telling his beads and reciting a mantra. His eyes are closed. His left hand rests on his lap. Another yogi, in a red dhoti, sits calmly with his legs crossed and gazes at the Shaivite. Such a posture is assumed by any man whose intentions are harmless, and who appears as if he has achieved, at least for a moment, peace and understanding (*Jnaneshwari* 2: 33). Two pundits sit on a white sheet discussing the *Ramayana*.

In the painting for verse 6, a Devi with four arms, looks searchingly far into infinite space beyond the river. She holds two holy texts in her hands. Her poised body rises like a serene flame in a lamp. A golden fire burns beside her. A breeze blows through a plantain tree growing on the river bank. Again and again the emphasis in these paintings is on the idea that the earth was and can always be a place of joy and beauty. What they commemorate are not some half-remembered fragments of life's grace, but a consistent faith in the fact that life must conduct its dialogue with love; that the mind must seek its analogies with beauty; that the business of war, and its association with unreasonable power and brutal death, is a violation of the abiding covenant that dharma and life have made with each other.

Other images intensify the feeling of glory which ought to light our days on earth. A crescent moon shines above the Devi's head. The image cluster combines the five great elements (earth, air, water, fire and the sky) that verse 6 says make up the entire sacred and profane cosmos. In a comment about this verse, the *Jnaneshwari* says that the hands of a good man are always empty, free and gentle (2: 47). Writing about the same verse, Mahatma Gandhi says that pride is subtle because it masquerades as humility and is, therefore, the last sin to be conquered. Interestingly, he quotes Marcus Aurelius: "Nothing is more scandalous than a man who is proud of his humility."[7] The composite sensory image is shaped by Allah Baksh's notion of ideal beauty; the moral idea which he visualises is that everything created inevitably dissolves. To the left of the Devi, a proud and regal man, wearing a scarlet turban, sits with a sword on his shoulder. He is the image of non-redemptive violence and arrogance.

7 Quoted by Desai in *The Gospel of Selfless Action*, p. 314.

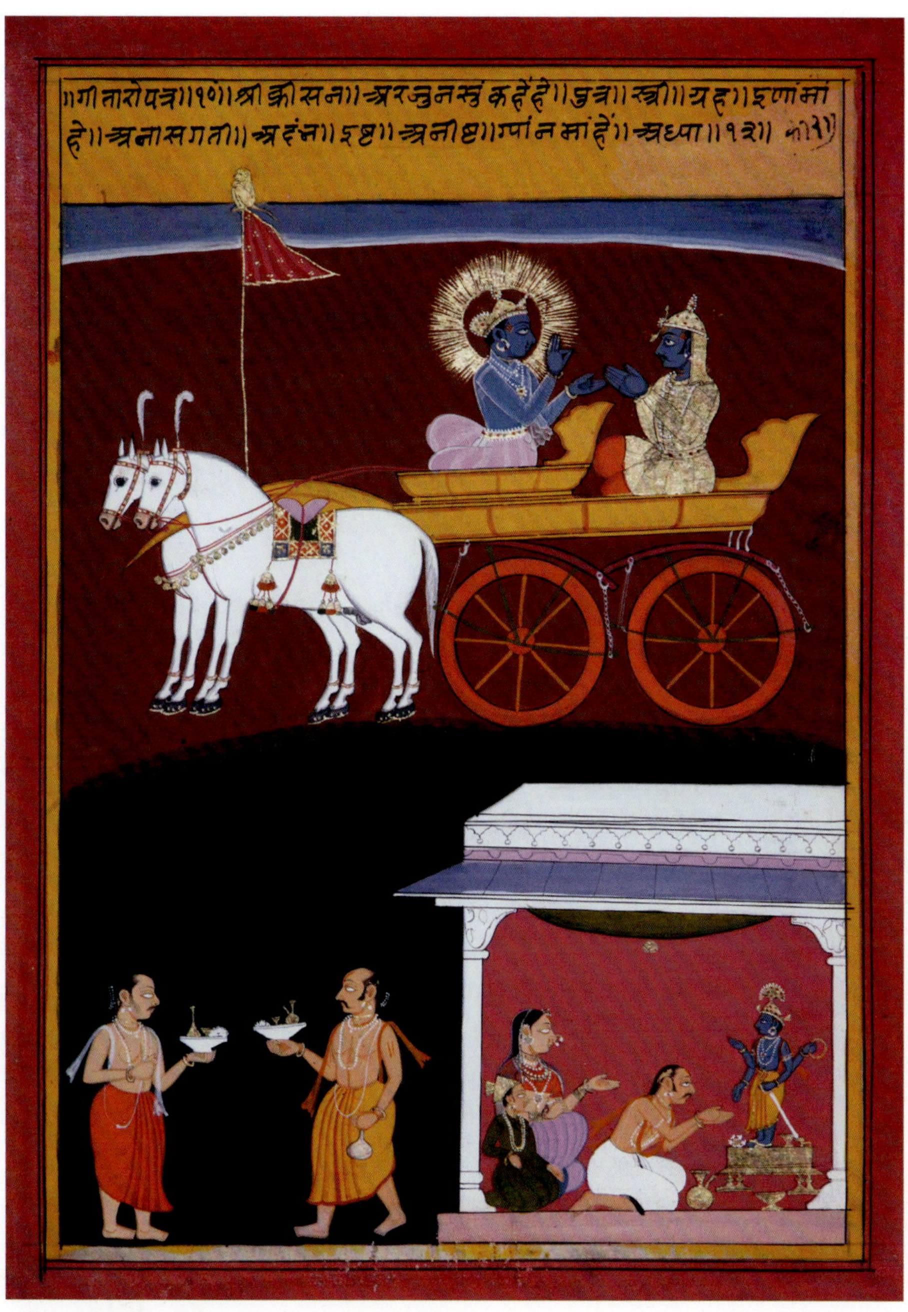

|9| हे अर्जुन! इसी तरह पुत्र, स्त्री, घर और धन में अनासक्ति, ममता का न होना प्रिय तथा अप्रिय की प्राप्ति में सदा चित्त को समान रखने को ज्ञान कहा है।

|9| Hey Arjuna! Further, knowledge means non-attachment to son, wife, home and wealth; dispassionate regard for success or failure.

As Krishna continues from verses 9 to 18 with a description of his divinity and a list of the virtues which must be cultivated by the wise, Allah Baksh paints new and imaginatively designed images, in sparkling and vibrant colours, so as to help the viewer reflect upon the ideal and how it is tarnished in historical time. Thus, he paints (for verse 9) a verdant tree at the centre of the earth. Its wide canopy, selflessly and non-violently, offers comfort and shade to everyone. The artist invokes the image of an ordinary and sheltering tree to help us comprehend the ideal of disinterested generosity and harmlessness. The beautiful woman nursing her child near the river is not a member of the royalty. Her clothes are not embroidered with gold and silver, and her hair is not braided with pearls. She is the visual analogue of the ideal qualities Krishna itemises in verse 9: the renunciation of sensuality, absence of pride and right understanding of birth and death (Swami 72-73). The blue waters that wash her feet also flow past yogis and gods of different sects.

As if to complete the cosmic cycle, Krishna also speaks about age, sickness and death in verse 9. The artist responds to this concern with temporality by including the figure of a Shiva-worshipping yogi in a painting of idyllic charm. The yogi sits on tiger skin; his body is covered with ash, symbolic of the unappeasable violence of death. He sits in deep mediation on the other side of the tree, across from the mother and child. Is their presence an ideogram of the life-cycle completed? Or, is the yogi an example of the other path, the path of renunciation toward wisdom and peace which Krishna has already discussed and rejected? Anyway, the figure of a nurturing, tender and affectionate mother on a fertile earth must also be thought about alongside that of the utterly distraught and dishevelled women and wives in *Stree Parva* at the end of the war, who scuttle across a red and blood-soaked field of pain in search of their children and husbands. Her presence, both before and after the war, like that of the Devi in other paintings, makes Allah Baksh's reading of the *Gita* part of a tragic story, and gives it a poignancy not always recognised by its more religious interpreters.

In these paintings, rituals, dreams and knowledge flow into each other. Thus, in the enigmatic painting for verse 13, when Krishna says that the Eternal Spirit which dwells within him has form and is also formless, a golden sun or cosmic egg (both archetypes of creative origins) shines in all its effulgence on a river bank. A priest sits gazing at the golden light which has shape but no boundary. Since there is no other figure around, we are urged to look to the glory of Krishna for an answer. The painter is an empathic witness of all that is being sung, read or discussed. Instead

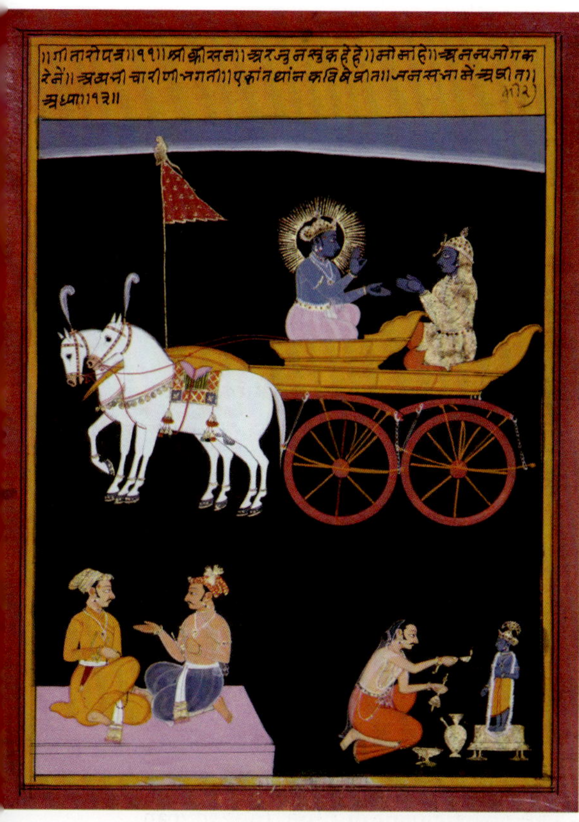

|10| हे अर्जुन! मेरे अनन्य योग से अव्यभिचारिणी भक्ति के साथ एकांत में निवास करना और विषयासक्त जन समूह में प्रेम के न होने को ज्ञान कहा है।

|10| Hey Arjuna! Further knowledge means unwavering devotion to me disciplined by yoga; living in solitude without attachment to worldly affairs.

|12| हे अर्जुन! जो जानने योग्य है, जिसे जानकर पुरुष परमानंद को प्राप्त होता है अब उसको कहता हूँ। वह अनादि परब्रह्म न सत् कहा जाता है न असत्।

|12| Hey Arjuna! I shall now tell you what you need to know in order to attain immortality. It is the supreme Brahma which is neither Being nor non-Being.

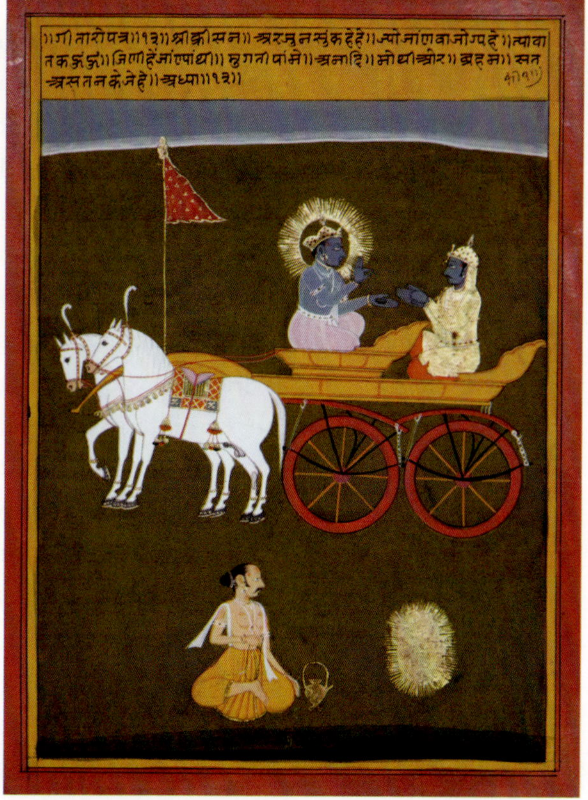

of ascetic silence, the world is full of words; sacred and ethical words, words of peace and of beauty. Each of them is given a form in the painting. Allah Baksh understands that the *Gita*'s profundity lies in its two-fold assertion: one, that the conditions of harmlessness or of non-violent living (ahimsa) can only be fulfilled by each of us through compassion, pity and selflessness; two, that in our times, it is seemingly impossible to achieve the ideal ethical qualities essential for a life divine. Anticipating what Krishna will soon say, the painter's images show that, in the field of war, a man must find the inspiration within himself to overcome egoistic aggression and self-promoting narcissism. "Inspiration," the poet Octavio Paz says, "is that strange voice that takes a man out of himself to be everything he is, everything he desires; another body, another being."[8] The artist is also aware of how quickly the ideal erodes in time, and how easily inspiration is defeated by social and moral obduracy.

In verses 14 to 18, Krishna describes himself through a series of paradoxes as the Absolute, the Universal, the Eternal or the Truth; yet, he also pervades time and guides every process of becoming in time. He is, he goes on to say, personal and impersonal; he exists and does not exist; he is the manifest in the universe and is also unmanifest; he is everything, he is in everything and is yet an illusion; he remains unchanged and is yet a participant in time. Indeed, in these abstract verses, he *describes* all the awe-inspiring qualities which he had revealed to Arjuna so as give them a human scale even though the mystery of his Being remains impossible to comprehend. Thus, he once again tells Arjuna that he is all knowledge and is yet impossible to know; he acts in time and yet remains unchanged; he is all words and speech and is yet the silence before birth and after death; he is everything and yet does not exist; he is imminent in all things and is yet utterly remote. Allah Baksh finds creative images which help us think about Krishna's inherent and divine qualities and attributes. His chariot moves through a background of vibrant and glowing colours. As he sits facing Arjuna, his posture radiates the confidence of wisdom; his gestures are gentle and kind. They indicate knowledge imparted with grace. Arjuna's hands are held before him in a mudra which shows how receptive he now is to what is being offered.

8 Octavio Paz, *The Bow and the Lyre*, pp. 162-163.

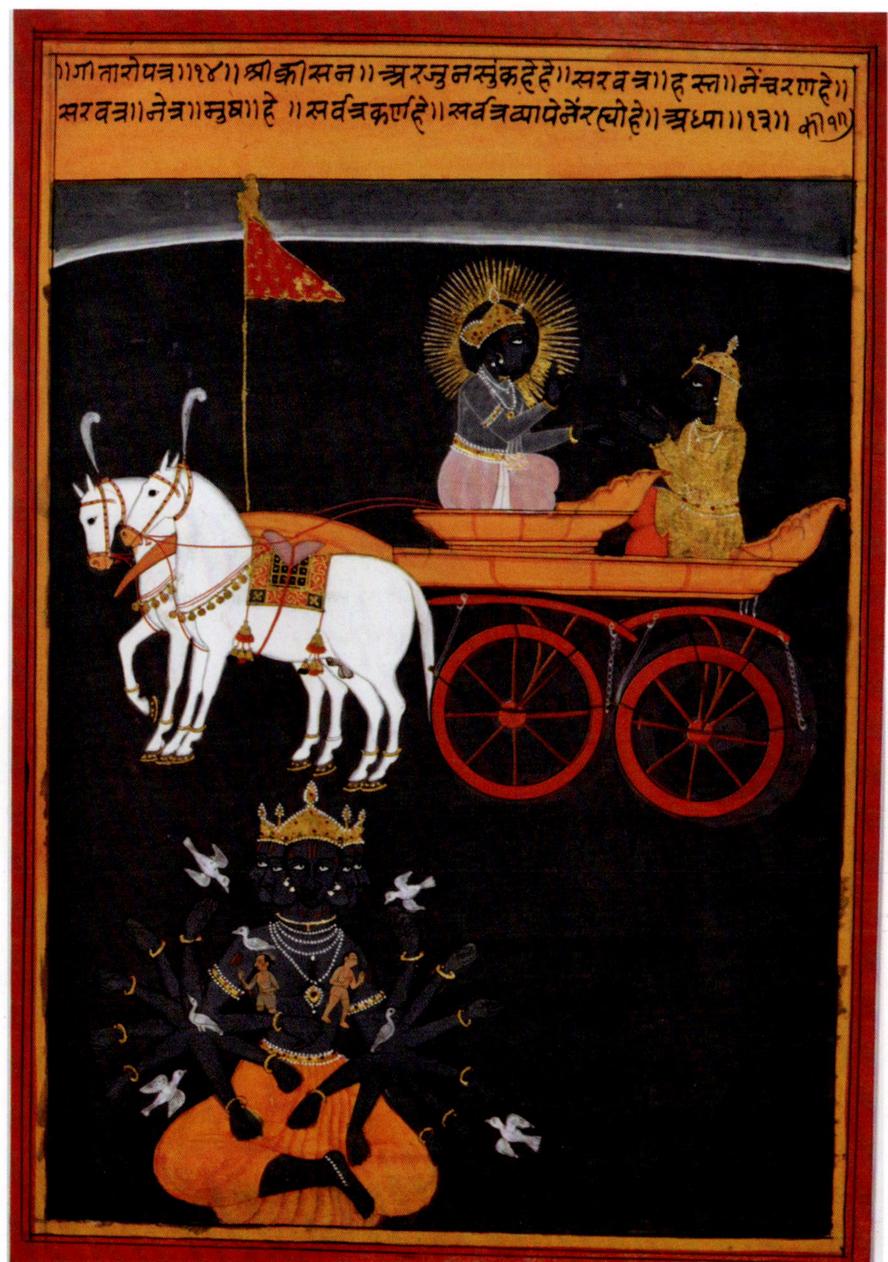

|13| हे अर्जुन! उसके सब तरफ हाथ-पैर हैं, सब ओर नेत्र, सिर और मुख हैं, सब ओर कान हैं क्योंकि वह संसार में सभी को व्याप्त करके स्थित है।

|13| Hey Arjuna! He has many hands and feet, he can look in all directions; he has many heads and mouths; he can hear everything because the entire universe is situated in him.

The visual image for verse 14 is akin to the multi-headed and multi-armed figures that Allah Baksh had painted for Krishna's Vishwarupa, but is much reduced in size. Seated cross-legged in the lotus position, Krishna is calm and serene. His dark blue body both emerges out of and fades into the pale blue background as if to make us think about the idea that he is simultaneously perceptible to our senses and is like the invisible ether that pervades all space. He carries no weapons in his sixteen arms. Four of his hands lie idle in his lap signifying that he has renounced all thoughts, words and deeds which can cause harm or threaten peace. His other twelve arms, flashing with golden bracelets, form a circle of flickering lights in the emptiness that surrounds him. His eyes are radiant like the white pearls that adorn his body. They gaze at us, but do not seem to be aware of our presence. Four white birds fly toward him from the four cardinal directions. They are images of time and also archetypal messengers of that peace which should be the instinctive principle of all that inheres in the world. Three more white birds find shelter in his arms, as do two men whom he cradles near his chest. His body offers refuge to whoever needs it or desires it.

Krishna's Vishwarupa in the painting for verse 16 is smaller and less regal; gentler and kinder than his revealed form earlier in Chapter 11. Youthful, powerful and handsome, he is seated against a lemon-yellow background as if the earth is soaked in the light of the morning sun. He has only four arms instead of the multiple arms in the previous vision. He gazes out toward the east and the sunrise. His front left arm rests on his knee. In his other left hand, he holds a white chakra or disc which touches the ground. This is a radical departure from the traditional iconography in which Krishna holds a serrated chakra as an emblem of destruction above his head and in his right hand. Here, the chakra is an emblem of the cycle of time. As if to emphasise its peaceful intent, a white bird sits on Krishna's left wrist. He holds the bud of a white lotus flower as an image of life's potential to reveal the beauty of mortal existence; ready to open "like sudden time in a world without time."[9] Another white bird rests in the nook of the left arm. The iconicity of Krishna is completed by the other symbols of his presence that he carries in his right arms: a golden mace rests on his shoulder and a white conch-shell is held in his right hand; symbols of protection, death, and the soft resounding sound of creation.

9 Wallace Stevens quoted by Abrams, p. 423.

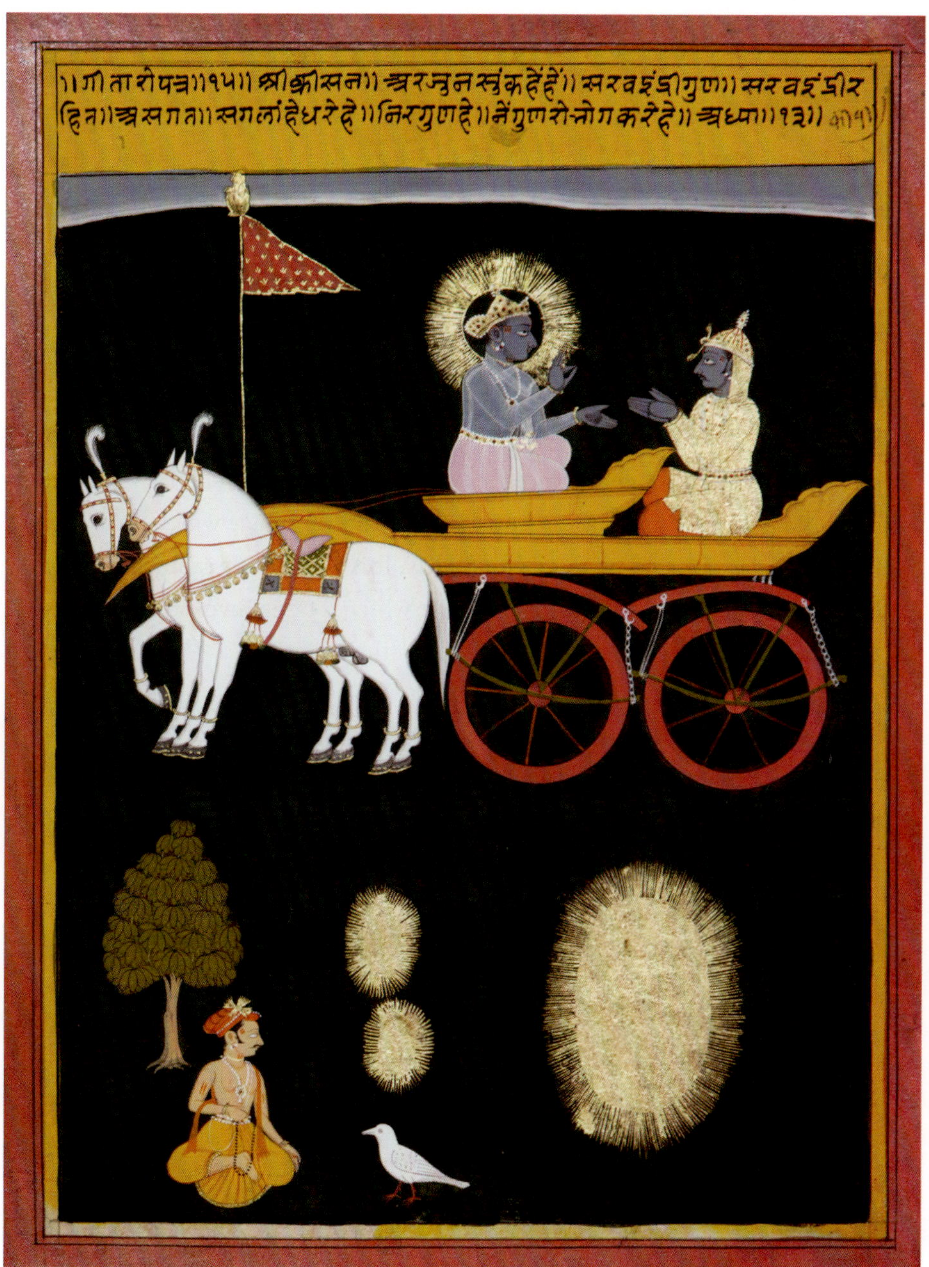

|14| श्री कृष्ण कहने लगे, हे अर्जुन! सभी इन्द्रियों के विषयों (गुणों) को जाननेवाला होने पर भी सब इन्द्रियों से रहित है। सब का पोषण करते हुए भी अनासक्त है तथा गुणों को भोगने पर भी निर्गुण है।

|14| Sri Krishna says: Hey Arjuna! He has knowledge of all the senses and is yet unattached to any of them. He enjoys all the qualities (gunas), but is unaffected by them.

Now in a moment of revelation and calm understanding, Arjuna knows what Krishna means when he says that he is "the Light of lights, beyond the reach of darkness" (Swami 73). In the painting for verse 17, Allah Baksh takes us beyond the vision of Krishna's Vishwarupa and invites us to concentrate on the image of a golden cosmic egg sparkling like another sun beside our earthly sun, like the light beyond any light we know. However, this light is not as terrifying, as unendurable, as the blinding flash which is brighter than a thousand suns. Instead, it is a milder and mellower image which is carried into our field of vision by four white birds. It is the luminous image of the experience of eternity in a moment of time which is often invoked by mystics to explain their experience of the paradox of timeless time.

In a series of epiphanic paintings for verses 22, 24, 29 and 31, Allah Baksh suggests that if these glimpses of "God dwelling in the heart of Nature" (Swami 74) can be placed beside each other, the terrestrial field can be apprehended for what it actually is: a field of paradise where the gods sit in daily communion with all the things that pass through time on earth. In the painting for verse 24, for example, painted with complete simplicity and sincerity, and in radiant colours, we may recognise Brahma, Vishnu, Shiva, and Devi sitting in a garden. Is the garden an image of the home we may have left behind? Is it the image of the home we hope to recover in future time?

In these paintings, Krishna embraces all of creation—mankind and nature—he cherishes them and is indifferent to them. In the fields of vision, each has a place in the divine ritual; in the fields of time each perishes and leaves no trace. This knowledge Arjuna must accept with a grateful and obedient heart; it may help him find some order, some moral purpose in the destruction which shall soon be unleashed.

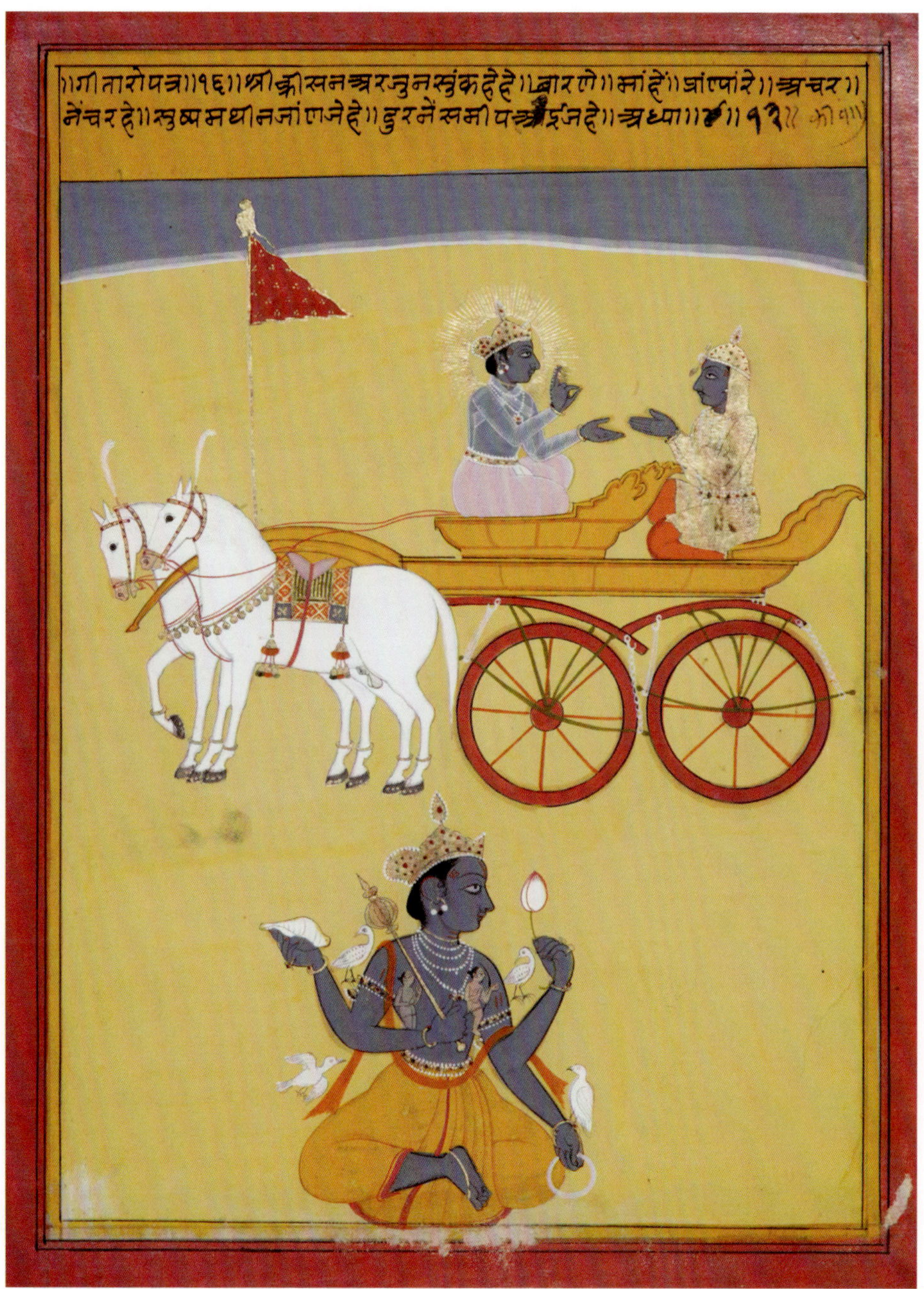

|15| हे अर्जुन! कृष्ण आगे कहने लगे कि वह समस्त चर-अचर प्राणियों के भीतर व बाहर है पर सूक्ष्म होने से वह जाना नहीं जा सकता है। वह अति समीप भी है और दूर भी।

|15| Hey Arjuna! Sri Krishna says that the Brahma is within all beings, yet outside; He is too subtle to be known; He is very near, yet far.

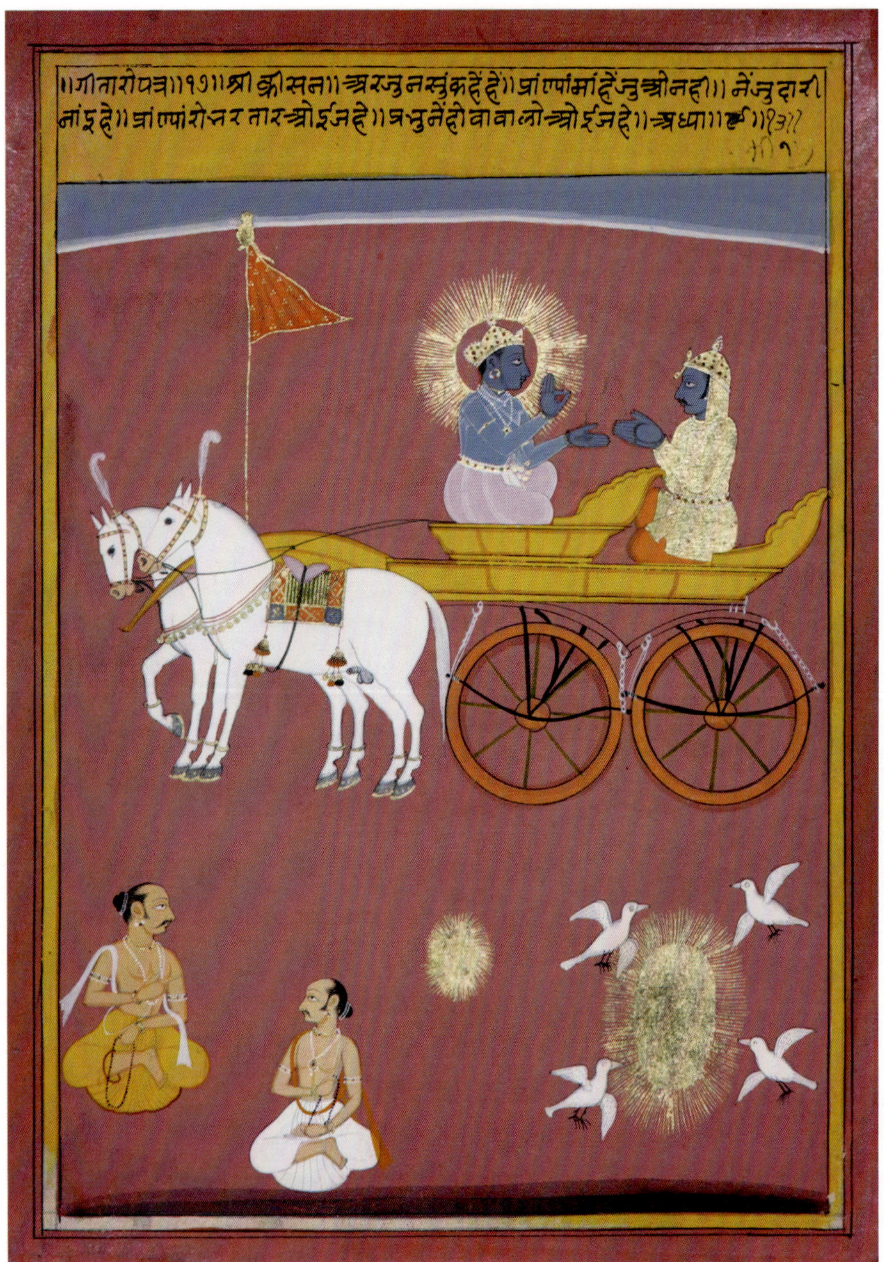

|16| वह अविभक्त होने पर भी सभी भूतों में विभक्त हुआ-सा प्रतीत होता है। वह जानने योग्य है। वही सभी भूतों का पोषण, संहार और उत्पन्न करने वाला है।

|16| Sri Krishna says: The Omniscient Self appears to reside in all beings, yet is outside them. You should know that self because it is the creator, the upholder and the destroyer of creation.

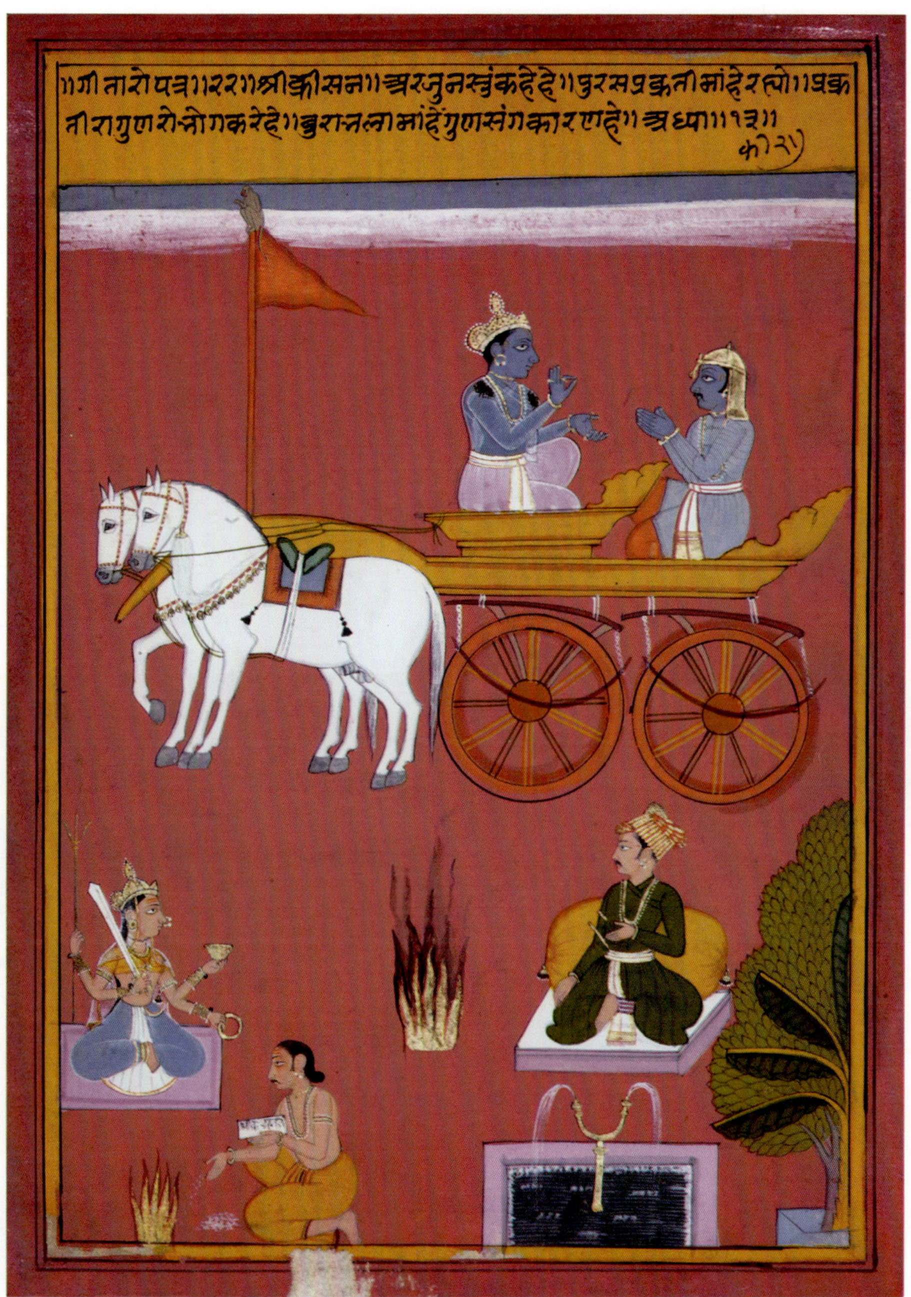

|21| श्री कृष्ण आगे कहने लगे, हे अर्जुन! प्रकृति में स्थित पुरुष ही प्रकृति से उत्पन्न गुणों को भोगता है और इन गुणों का संग ही अच्छी-बुरी योनियों में जन्म का कारण बनता है।

|21| Sri Krishna further says: Hey Arjuna! Dwelling in nature, man experiences the qualities of nature; and these qualities are the cause of good-evil actions.

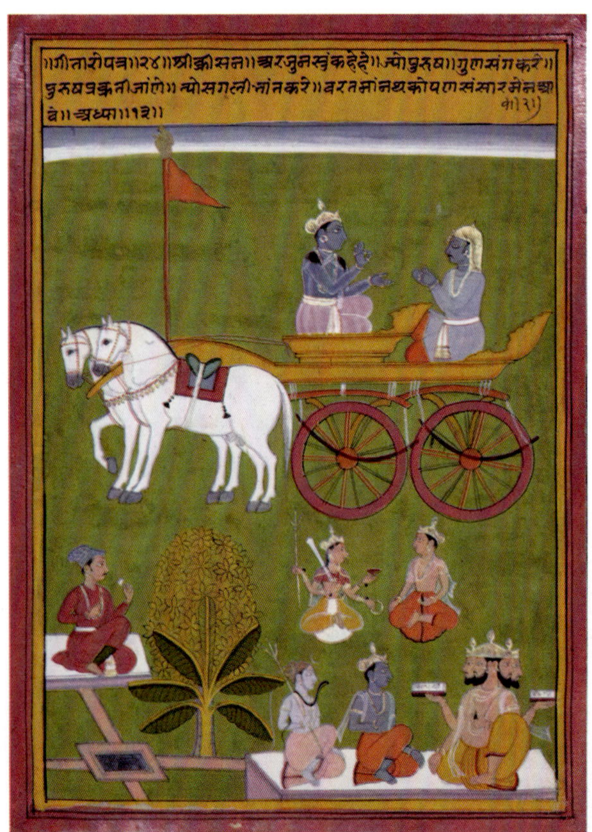

|23| हे अर्जुन! इस प्रकार जो, पुरुष और गुणों के सहित प्रकृति के सभी तत्वों को जानता है, वह सभी प्रकार के कर्म करता हुआ भी फिर जन्म नहीं लेता।

|23| Hey Arjuna! He who knows the Supreme Self and knows all the qualities of nature and can perform all actions he wants, shall never be born again.

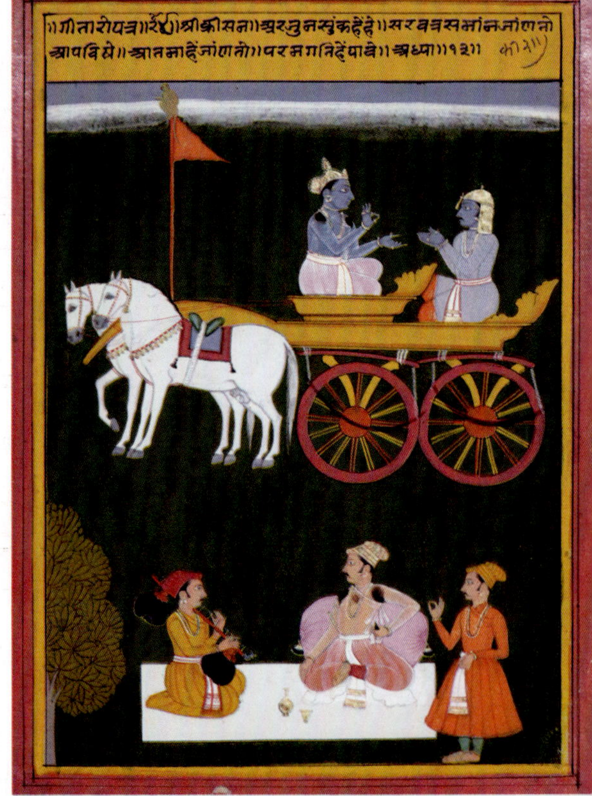

|28| श्री कृष्ण आगे बताने लगे, हे अर्जुन! क्योंकि जो सब में सम भाव से स्थित परमेश्वर को समान देखता है, वह अपने द्वारा अपने को नष्ट नहीं करता और परमगति को प्राप्त होता है।

|28| Sri Krishna further says: Hey Arjuna! He who sees the imperishable Being standing in everything and does not injure the Being in himself reaches the highest bliss.

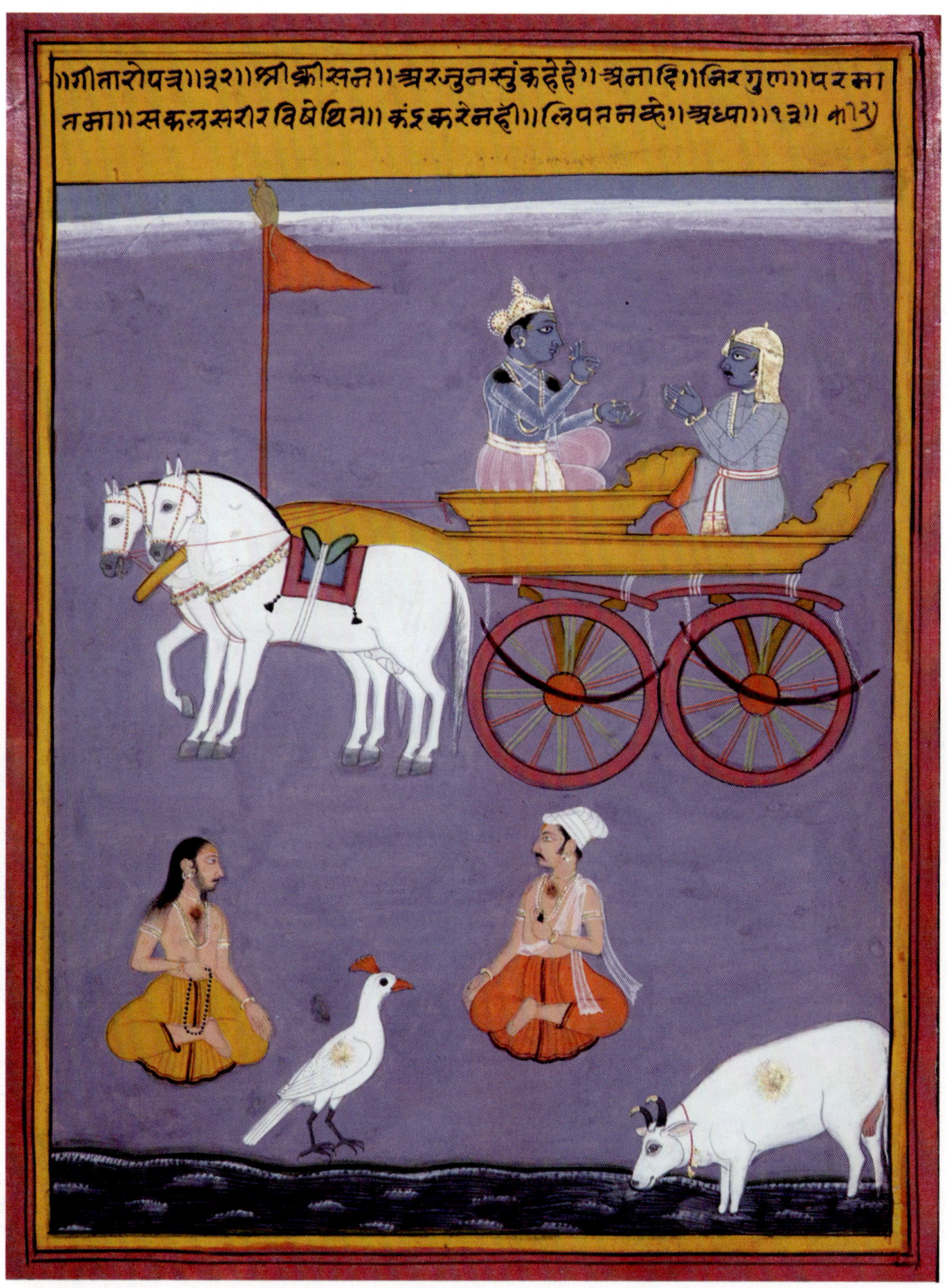

|31| हे अर्जुन! अनादि और निराकार होने से वह अविनाशी परमात्मा शरीर में स्थित होते हुए भी न कुछ करता है और न करने में लिप्त होता है।

|31| Hey Arjuna! Because the Supreme Being has no beginning, is formless and indestructible, it neither acts nor is defiled by any action.

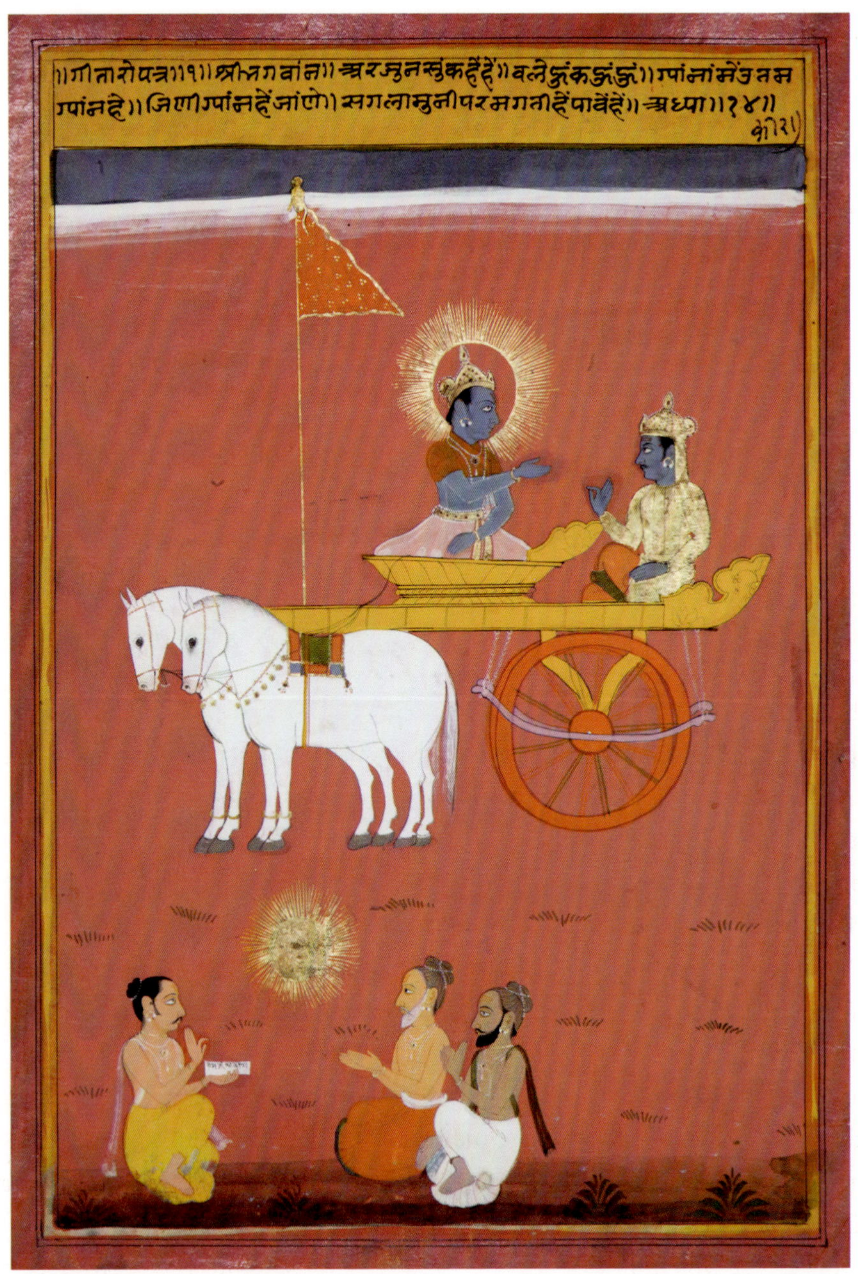

|1| श्री कृष्ण कहने लगे, हे अर्जुन! अब मैं तुझे ज्ञानों में अति उत्तम ज्ञान को फिर से कहता हूँ, जिसे जानकर सभी मुनि इस संसार से मुक्त हो कर परम गति को प्राप्त होते हैं।

|1| Sri Krishna says: Hey Arjuna! I shall now teach you the profoundest knowledge once more; all the sages who know it have attained liberation from the world and reached the highest perfection.

CHAPTER 14

Krishna declares in verse 3 that the three primal gunas are created: "in the eternal Cosmos of My womb" (Swami 76). They function with cooperative intelligence and what they create is good, peaceful and true.[1] In historical time, however, they begin to change and "fetter the free Spirit in all beings" (Swami 76). Only the visionary poet or mythmaker has the creative imagination or the spiritual memory to apprehend or recall the relation between them in eternity. The result is a breakdown of the original concord and a change in the qualities themselves. *Sattva* loses its luminosity and is tarnished by self's yearning for happiness. *Rajas* turns into passion and the self's infatuation with the sensuous and the pleasurable alone. T*amas*, uninfluenced by goodness and austere self-control, plunges the self into ignorance, folly and lethargic modes of thinking which perpetuate cycles of violence and revenge, anger and misery.[2]

Earlier, Krishna had made an important distinction between seeing the world through the physical eyes and seeing it through the eyes of wisdom. The first helps us understand the random scattering of discrete objects and events that appear and disappear over time, while the mind struggles to find a common thread. The second leads to the revelation that life is meaningful and has a unity and purpose. The first reveals the working of things on earth; the second the working of the gods.

In incandescent verses, Krishna explicitly reveals to Arjuna the mystery of the universe which shall so transform him that, instead of being only a man of knowledge, he shall become a man of wisdom. What follows is a visionary history of how the transcendental qualities of mind, body and life in eternity become slowly trapped in earthly existence and decay. The rememorialisation of origins is important if man "freed from birth and death, from old age and misery" is to drink the "nectar of immortality" again (Swami 77).

Allah Baksh's paintings for this chapter are fascinating as he finds image after image to indicate life's joyous, fresh, youthful origin and its present decrepitude and sorrow. It is significant that in none of the paintings are Krishna and Arjuna armed. While Arjuna

---

1 Eliade, *The Sacred and the Profane*, pp. 88–89.

2 See Radhakrishnan, *The Bhagavadgita*, pp. 376–378.

wears armour of gold, there are no weapons in the chariot. Contrary to the popular notion that the *Gita* is a song urging a warrior to fight, Allah Baksh thinks of it as a great song which calls upon all to remember that in the beginning there was peace and coexistence in the entire universe. The painting for verse 1 creates two sites of teaching: one on the chariot above, the other on the ground below. Both indicate the difference between a privileged *bhakt* like Arjuna who acquires wisdom in a flash of illumination, and ordinary seekers of knowledge who have to undergo a life-long process of learning and are never sure if they will achieve the transcendence of wisdom. In keeping with the tone of Krishna's patient words and demeanour, the scene of teaching in daily life is peaceful, uncontentious and calm. A bright and golden sun lights up the space. A young brahmin is delivering a discourse on the *Ramayana* thereby suggesting that education is not ethically neutral, but is an initiation into acts of faith and devotion, moral and social norms.

As the presence of the dialogical scene above between god and man suggests, this education is never without sceptical questioning, doubt and continuous refinement of knowledge. The two ascetic listeners of the *Ramayana* deserve notice. One is black-bearded and young; the other is old. They are listening, with devout concentration, to their teacher. They have probably heard the *Ramayana* before. Repetition of the epic, thereby, re-actualises the life of a good man and a divine being in historical time. Like these paintings, which take us through the *Gita* shloka by shloka, persuading us to look intensely for their meaning ourselves, the repetitive reading of the *Ramayana* also proceeds at the same slow, sincere and attentive pace. Indeed, such knowledge makes the reader and the listener feel proximate to the gods, helps them endure suffering and assuages their fear of death. But it does not mean that they shall achieve the wisdom Krishna offers Arjuna.

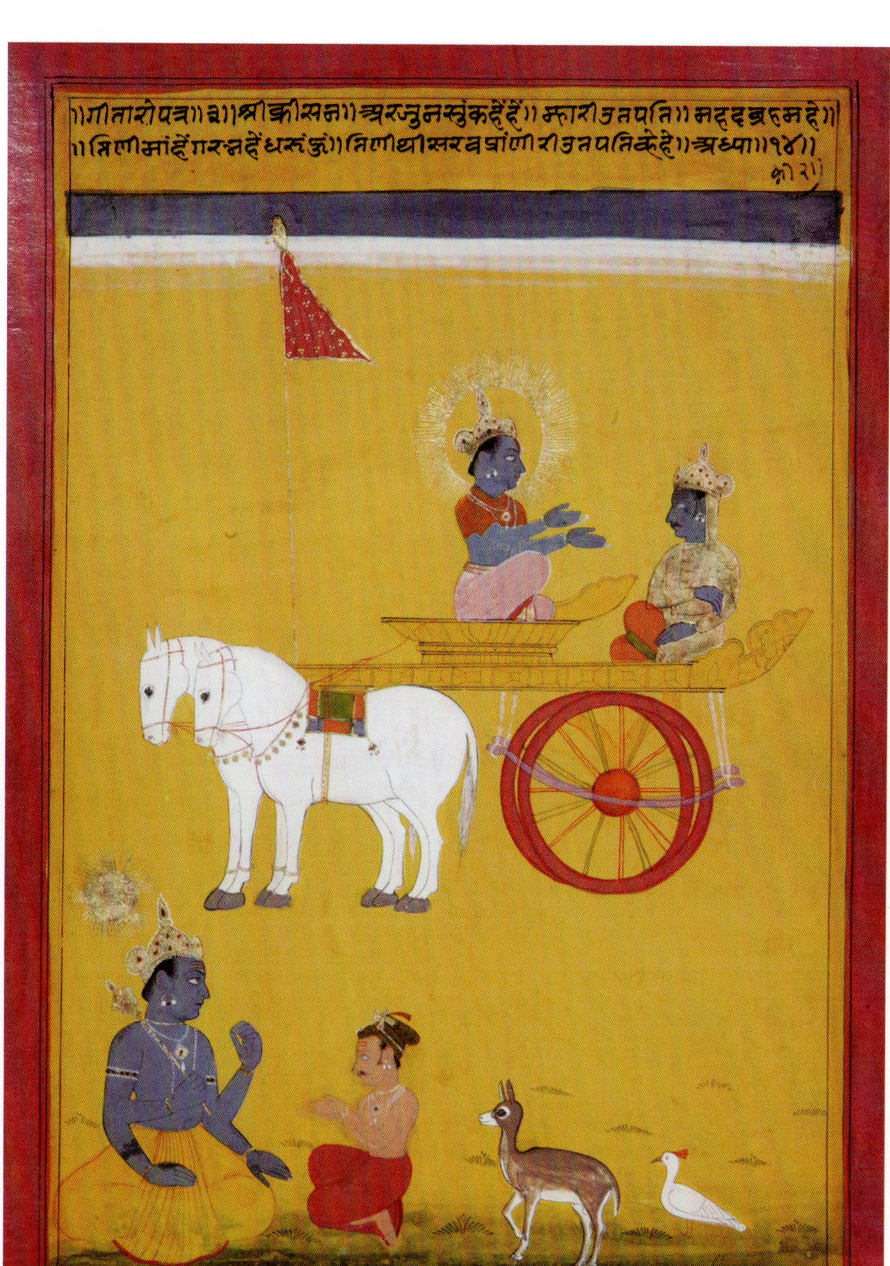

|3| श्री कृष्ण आगे बताने लगे कि मेरी उत्पत्ति नाद ब्रह्म से है, जिसमें मैं जीव रूप गर्भ धारण करता हूँ। इसी गर्भ से सभी प्राणियों का जन्म होता है।

|3| Sri Krishna further says: The eternal cosmos is my womb; I obtain my living form there. All creatures are born from that womb.

The paintings for verses 3 and 4 are meditations on Krishna's central revelation that he is the source of all things that exist. Allah Baksh may have been familiar with the images of the Buddha delivering sermons to all created beings. His paintings show that ethics cannot only be human centric since all creation has the same divine origin and is equally vulnerable to pain and mortality. Commitment to the good, Krishna firmly and clearly tells Arjuna, cannot be based on a moral hierarchy in which gods and human beings are given a higher value and, therefore, greater power than animals or birds or trees. This issue is raised repeatedly, and with increasing despair, in the *Mahabharata* narrative, till the very end, when the mongoose chastises Yudhishthira for the unspeakable violence of the horse sacrifice. Who has given him the right, the mongoose asks, to sacrifice animals so pitilessly?

The paintings for verses 3, 4, and 5 are beautiful parables of the sacred equality between the divine and all worldly emanations. It is appropriate that such a lesson about the divinity of all things should be taught on the battlefield where the story of most extreme rupture in the universe is about to be enacted. Blue-bodied and four-armed Krishna appears before an ordinary man, a cow, a fawn and a white bird indicating that a consideration of animals and other living things on earth must always be part of any argument about moral life. There is nothing threatening about this image of Krishna. His mace rests on his right shoulder; his hands are held in *mudras* of restfulness and self-reflexive peace (painting for verse 3). The image of the deity conversing with earthly creatures is gentle. The mood of reverence is created through a blend of bright yellow, red, green and white colours.

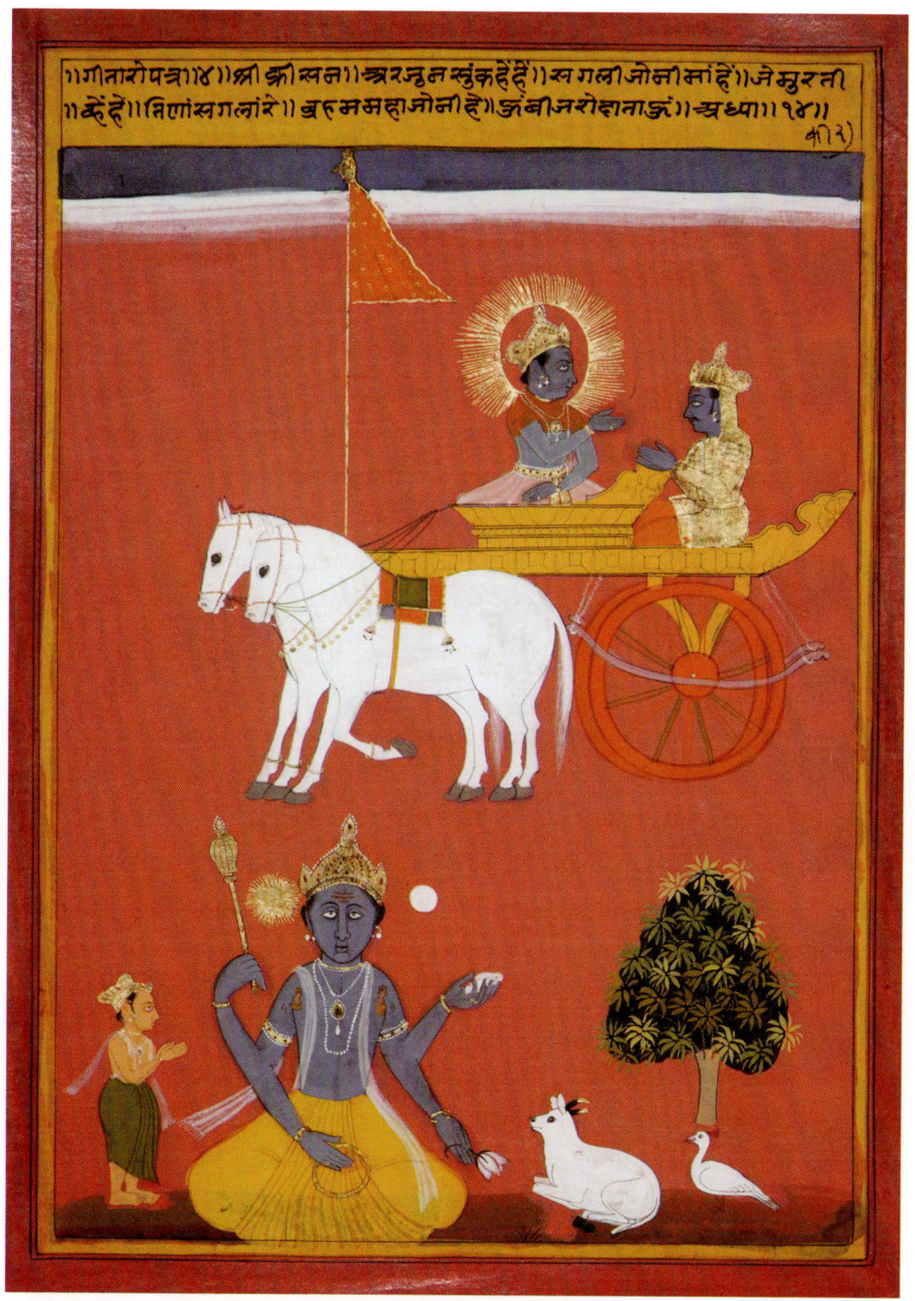

|4| श्री कृष्ण कहने लगे हे अर्जुन! सारी योनियों में जितने भी देहधारी प्राणी उत्पन्न होते हैं, कुदरत (प्रकृति) उन सभी की गर्भ धारण करने वाली माता है और मैं बीज प्रदान करने वाला पिता हूँ।

|4| Sri Krishna says: Hey Arjuna! I am the seed-giving father and nature is the womb of all creatures born.

The same is the case with the next painting for verse 4 where Krishna carries the emblems of the entire creation itself: the sun and the moon, the lotus and conch-shell, the disc and the mace. The image itself is more hieratic than the previous one; Krishna is less a human presence and more an object of worship. His remoteness is, however, moderated by the presence of a cow and a decorative tree. But this iconic and sacerdotal distance between the divine and the earth's creatures is replaced in the next painting (for verse 5) by the presence of Brahma, Vishnu, and Shiva who appear as youthful and excited makers of a new universe. Brahma is reciting the *Ramayana* to Shiva as a prophecy of life to come when the highest qualities of the mind, heart and body would become rarer, and only god-inspired visionary poets would recall them. This lovely tableau about the gods reading and listening to their own words (or, to change the metaphor, watching over their own creation) can also be read as the painter's parable about visual and verbal attentiveness to the world.

In verses 8–20, Krishna gives a condensed spiritual history of how the original concord between mind, life and body is violated, and how a rift appears between the gods, human beings and all other animate creatures. He describes how human beings forget their own connection to eternity and, in their narcissism and egotism, begin to believe that they themselves are the sources of all action. Allah Baksh, following Krishna's account, paints a visual narrative about how the "free Spirit" (Swami 77) of man, through ignorance, lethargy and misconceptions (*tamas*) gets lost in the labyrinths of sorrow.

The painting for verse 8 is an interesting work which meditates on words like activity, passion, yearning and pleasure that define the verse. On the lower right, a mature man dressed in diaphanous white clothes may be giving advice to the young man facing him. Perhaps the older man, holding a black pot and surrounded by various silver plates and cups, has also offered the young man a betel-leaf or a fragrant blossom to stimulate desire or give him confidence. This is surely the inference of the scene with its sensuously painted blue room with a white couch on a floor strewn with flowers. The man on the couch may be the same one who needed encouragement in the scene on the right. Both have the same head-gear, a pearl necklace with a red stone, large dangling gold ear-rings, and wide-eyed youthfulness. A garland of yellow flowers lies discarded on the couch. A woman sits at his feet massaging him.

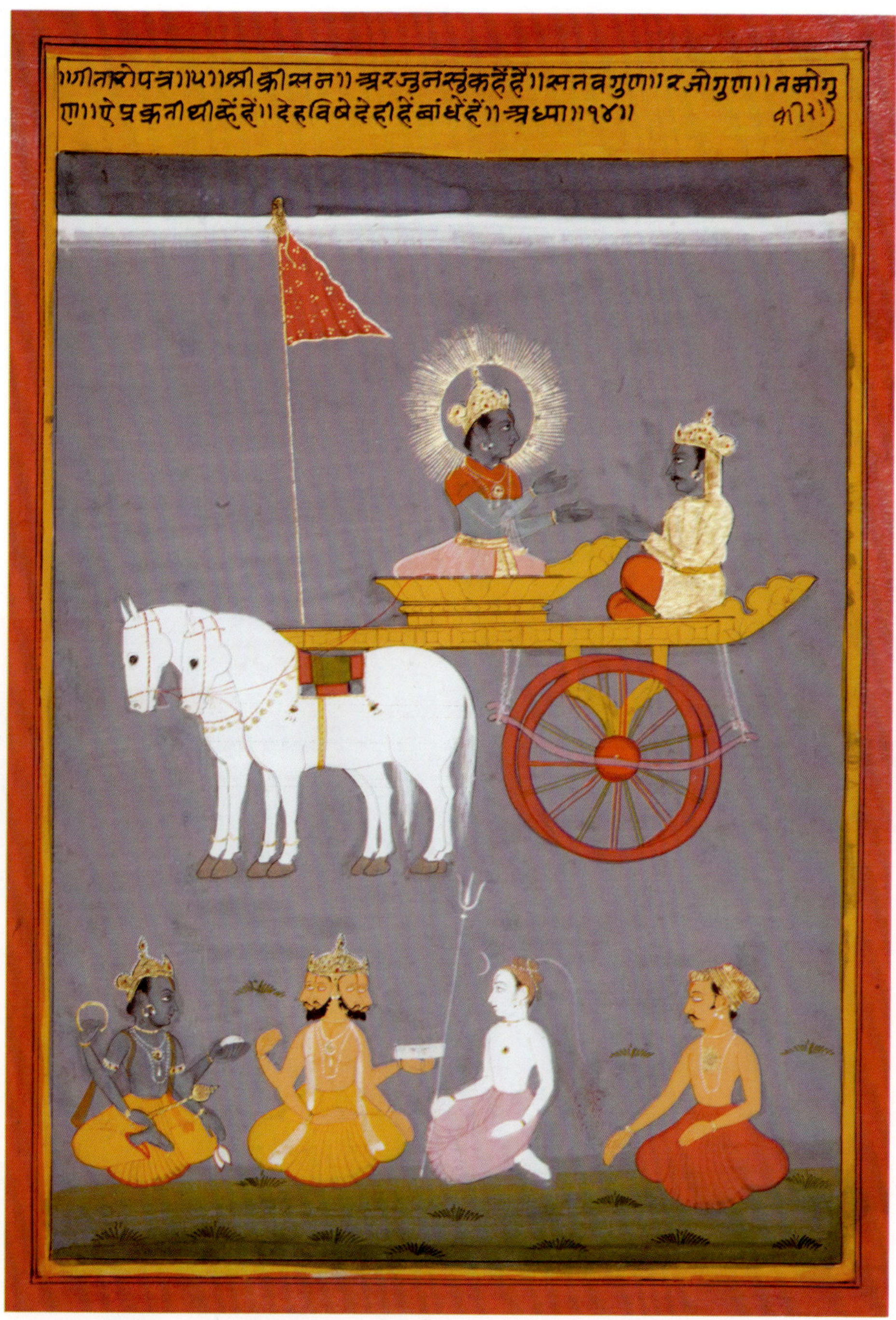

|5| हे अर्जुन! प्रकृति (कुदरत) से उत्पन्न सत्व, रज और तम ये तीनों गुण अविनाशी देह को देह में बाँधते हैं।

|5| Hey Arjuna! Truth, Passion and Ignorance bind the indestructible self to the body.

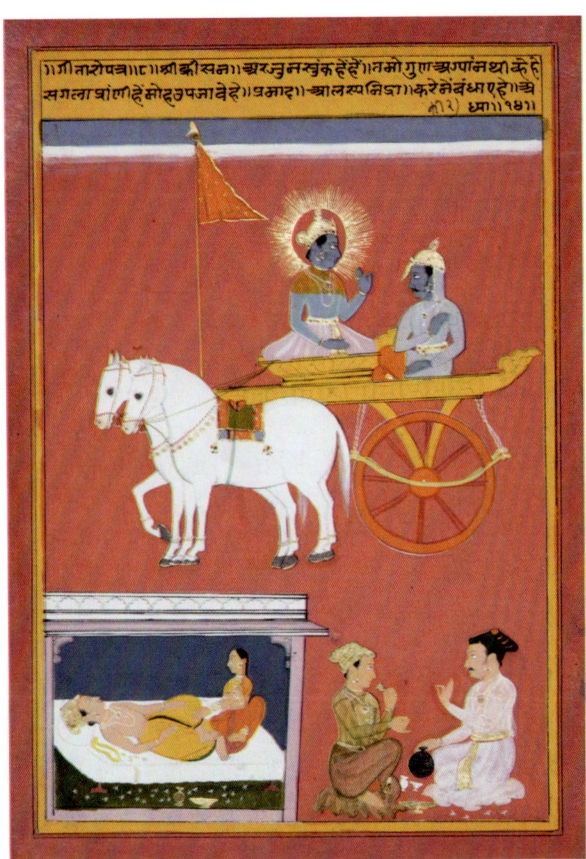

|8| श्री कृष्ण आगे कहने लगे, इसी तरह सभी देहधारियों को मोहित करने वाले तमोगुण को तू अज्ञान से उत्पन्न जान। तमोगुण प्राणियों को प्रमाद, आलस्य और नींद से बाँधता है।

|8| Sri Krishna further says: Ignorance is the source of inertia and delusion. It binds all creatures to folly, indolence and sleep.

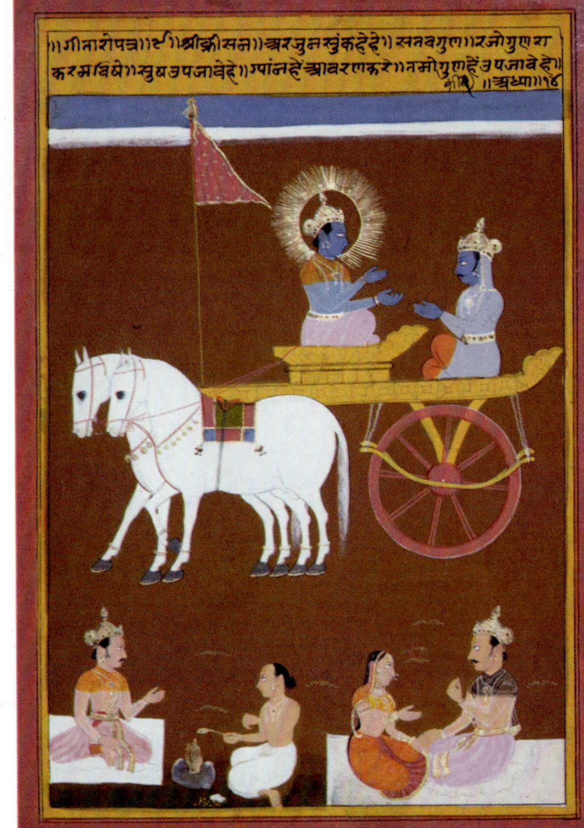

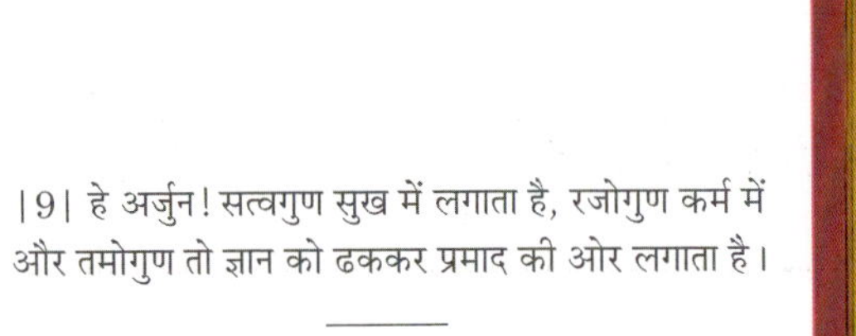

|9| हे अर्जुन! सत्वगुण सुख में लगाता है, रजोगुण कर्म में और तमोगुण तो ज्ञान को ढककर प्रमाद की ओर लगाता है।

|9| Hey Arjuna! Truth leads to happiness, Passion to action, and Ignorance obscures knowledge and leads to error.

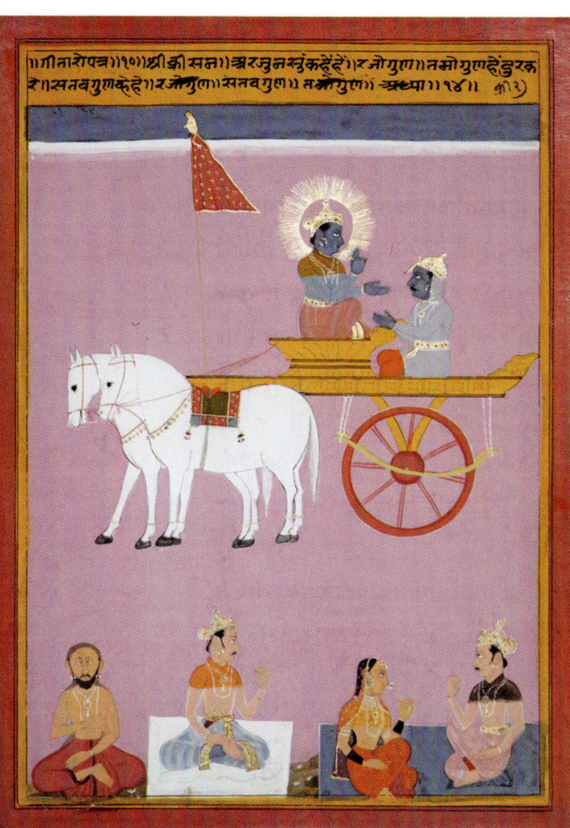

|10| हे अर्जुन! रजोगुण और तमोगुण को दबा कर सत्वगुण, सत्वगुण और तमोगुण को दबाकर रजोगुण एवं सतोगुण और रजोगुण को दबाकर तमोगुण प्रधान होता है।

|10| Hey Arjuna! Truth prevails when Passion and Ignorance are suppressed; Passion prevails when Truth and Ignorance are suppressed; and Ignorance prevails when Truth and Passion are suppressed.

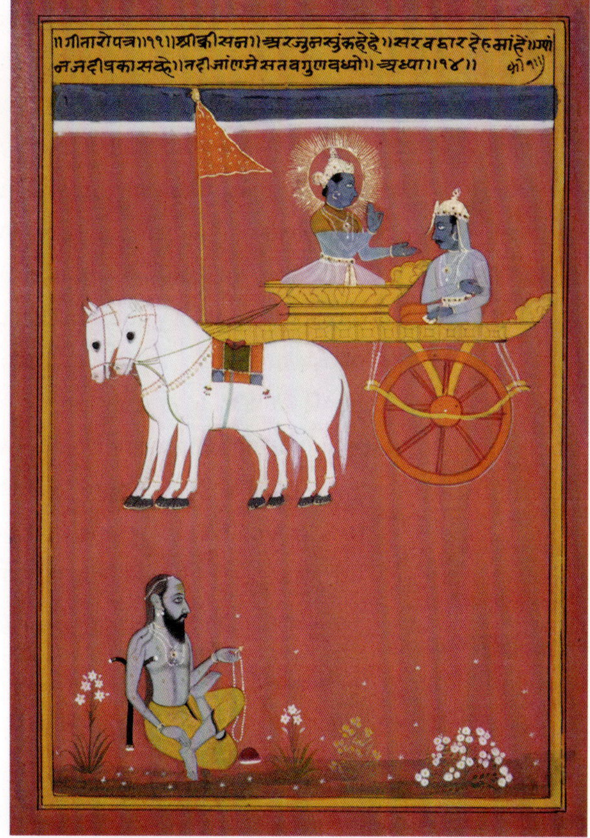

|11| श्री कृष्ण आगे कहने लगे, हे अर्जुन! जब इस देह के सभी द्वारों से ज्ञान का प्रकाश प्रदीप्त हो तब यह जानना चाहिए कि सत्वगुण बढ़ रहा है।

|11| Sri Krishna further says: Hey Arjuna! When the light of knowledge shines through all the gates of the body then be sure that Truth prevails.

This scene of intimacy is a visually literal rendering of Krishna's warning that when passion "binds the soul" the reasoning mind yields to "indolence and lethargy" (Swami 76). Self-adoring lovers create a beautiful artifice around them which ignores time and its prophecies of chance, suffering and death. Lost in their own singular and private story, in an exclusive and enclosed space, they no longer connect with the real and the eternal. The qualities of love and wonder are essential, but if they satisfy only private desire they become destructive.[3]

Allah Baksh also paints other forms of unthinking activity which lead, Krishna says, to "Darkness, stagnation, folly and infatuation" (Swami 77). Once again, Krishna does not give complete sanction to action based only on faith, but insists on moral preparation for it. The illustration for verse 13 is specially worth noticing in the context of the *Mahabharata*. It is painted against a black background—a colour appropriate for *tamas*. In a lower right corner, a man and a woman play a game of dice. We know the fatal consequences of addiction to gambling in the *Mahabharata* where Yudhishthira, tempted by victory and avarice, twice surrenders his intellect to the ghosts of chance. The metaphor of gambling introduces the idea that life is subject to disruption by chance and misfortune, and warns against gambling one's home away and with it one's accumulated past gunas as one's future journey into wisdom is dependent on it. It is imperative, therefore, that one like Arjuna makes thought and learning part of his daily habit and character.

3 See Northrop Frye, *Fearful Symmetry: A Study of William Blake* (Boston: Beacon Press, 1967), p. 234.

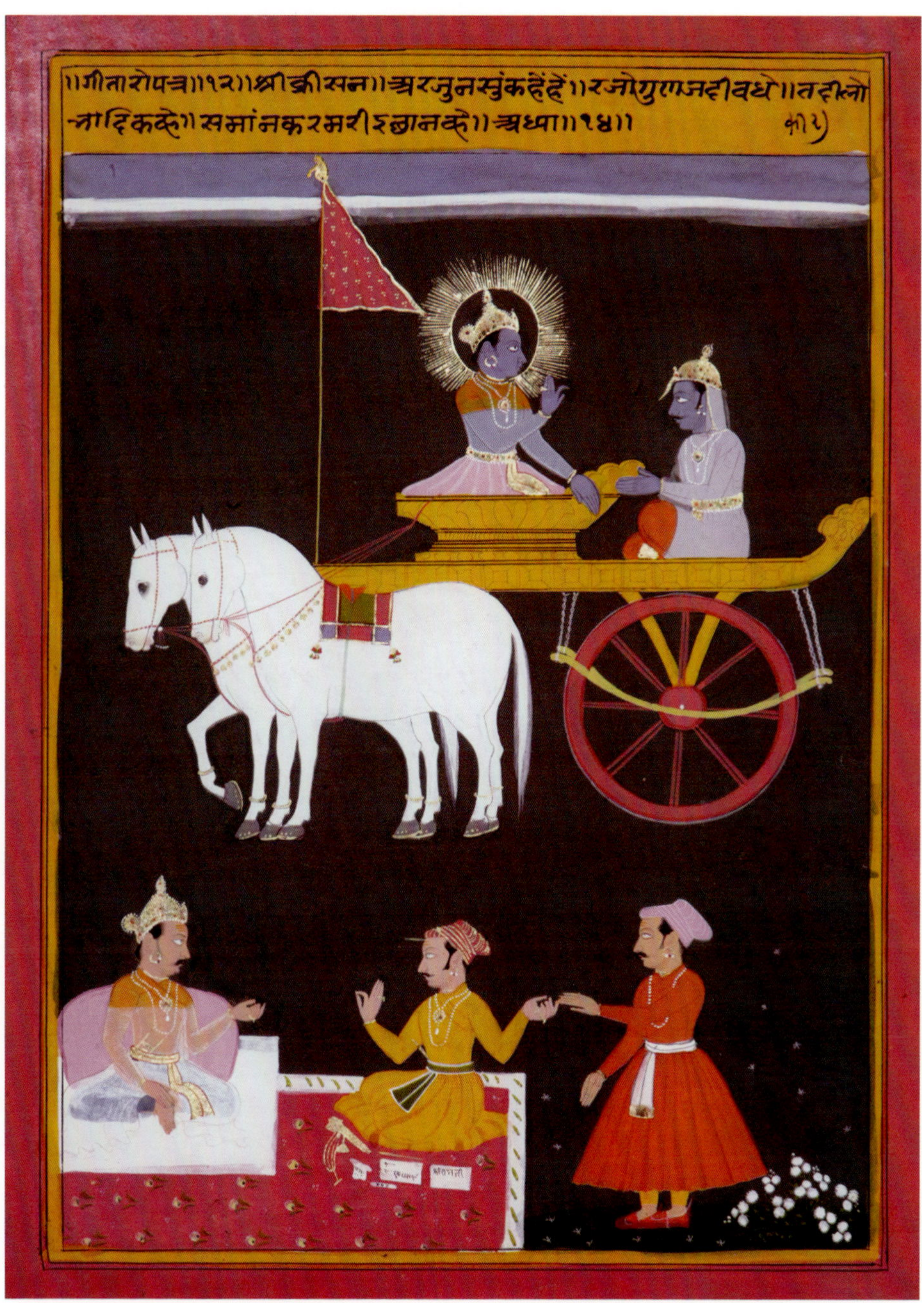

|12| हे अर्जुन! रजोगुण के बढ़ने पर यह जानना चाहिए कि लोभ की प्रवृति, कर्मों का आरंभ, अशांति और विषय भोगों की लालसा ये सभी उत्पन्न होते हैं।

|12| Hey Arjuna! Passion predominates where there is greed, unrest, craving for action, and longing for rewards.

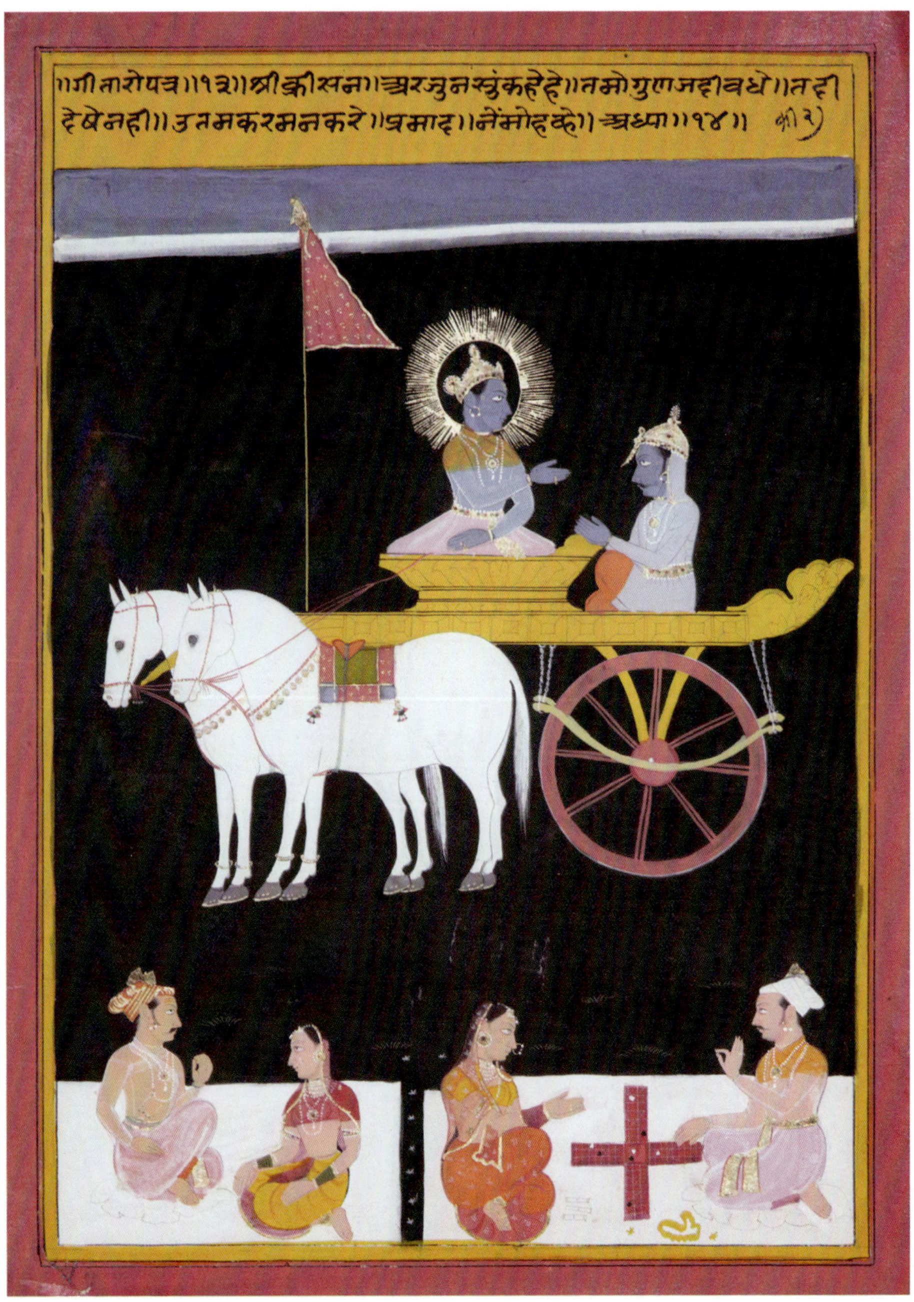

|13| श्री कृष्ण आगे कहने लगे, हे अर्जुन! तमोगुण के बढ़ने पर अँधेरा, आलस्य, असावधानी और मोह ये सभी उत्पन्न होते हैं।

|13| Sri Krishna says: Hey Arjuna! Where there is Ignorance there is darkness, inertia, negligence and delusion.

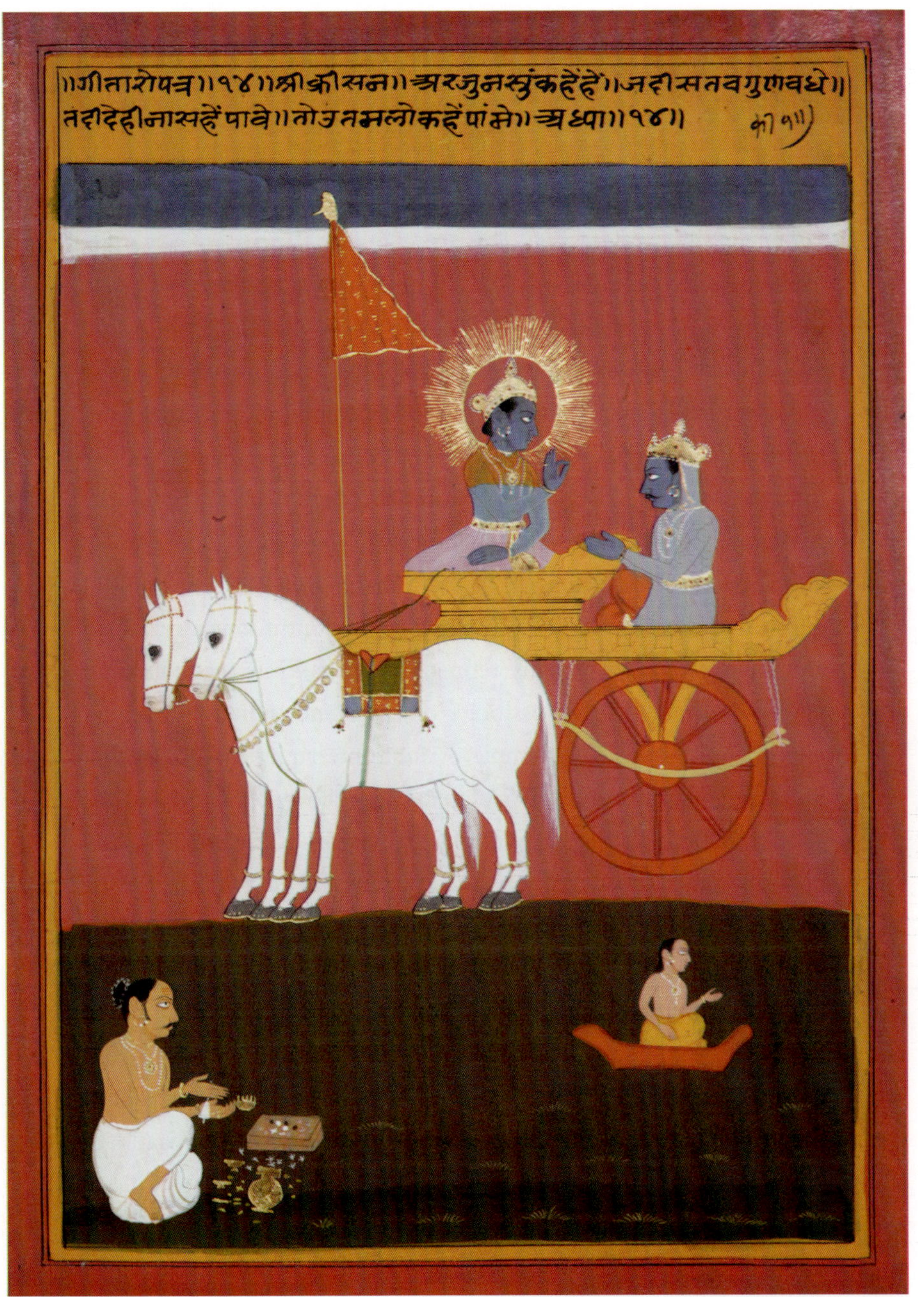

|14| हे अर्जुन! जब सत्वगुण की वृद्धि हो और मनुष्य मृत्यु को प्राप्त हो तब वह उत्तम कर्म करने वालों के निर्मल लोकों को प्राप्त होता है।

|14| Hey Arjuna! When a man of Truth dies, he enters the pure realm of those who live by the highest ideals.

Both verse 14 and the painting suggest that, if one is knowledgeable and devout, one can set out on the path of salvation: "When Purity prevails, the soul on quitting the body passes on to the pure regions where live those who know the highest" (Swami 77). The painting depicts a priest performing his morning prayers in the lower left corner. He sits facing the east and holds a ritual lamp to dispel the night's shadows and welcome the morning. Above him, closer to the rising sun, is another ascetic who sits in a self-navigating boat floating toward a new day.

The *Gita* is, like the rest of the *Mahabharata*, a great book of questions where problems of existence are continuously reframed and answers are perpetually refined, as life is finite, passing from *yuga* to *yuga* with the possibility of error and vulnerability built into it. In verse 21, for example, Arjuna interrupts Krishna's calm, measured and beautifully articulated, lyrical flow (verses 19 and 20) about the three distinctive *gunas* human beings possess to ask: "My Lord! By what signs can he who has transcended the qualities be recognised? How does he act?" (Swami 77-78). Arjuna's dramatic intervention is brilliantly placed. It shows that his decision to fight the war is not merely pragmatic. He does not simply decide to go to war because someone has acted unlawfully. Instead, he seeks from Krishna a greater assurance based on what has been revealed about the primal nature of the universe prior to history. Arjuna wants to know if the suffering of war will set the world right again; if peace will not be a brief interregnum before other woes cause pain; if life on earth will be remade so as to resemble what it was in *satya yuga*. For, otherwise, would it not still be nobler to renounce everything?

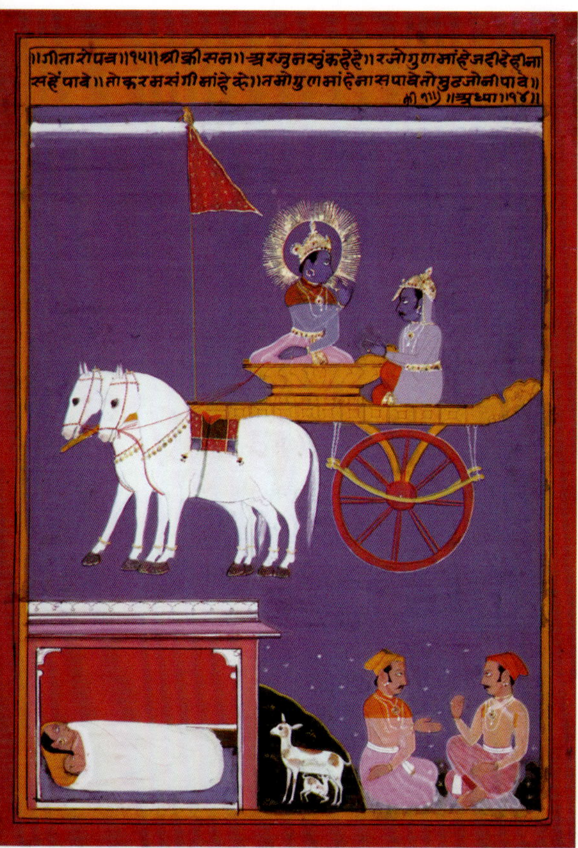

|15| श्री कृष्ण समझाते हुए कहने लगे कि रजोगुण की वृद्धि हो और मनुष्य मृत्यु को प्राप्त हो तब वह कर्मों में आसक्त मनुष्यों में जन्म लेता है और तमोगुण की वृद्धि में मृत्यु हो तो मूढ़ योनियों में जन्म लेता है।

|15| Explaining further, Sri Krishna says: When a man of Passion dies, he is reborn among those who love action; and when an Ignorant man dies, he is enters the womb of the ignorant.

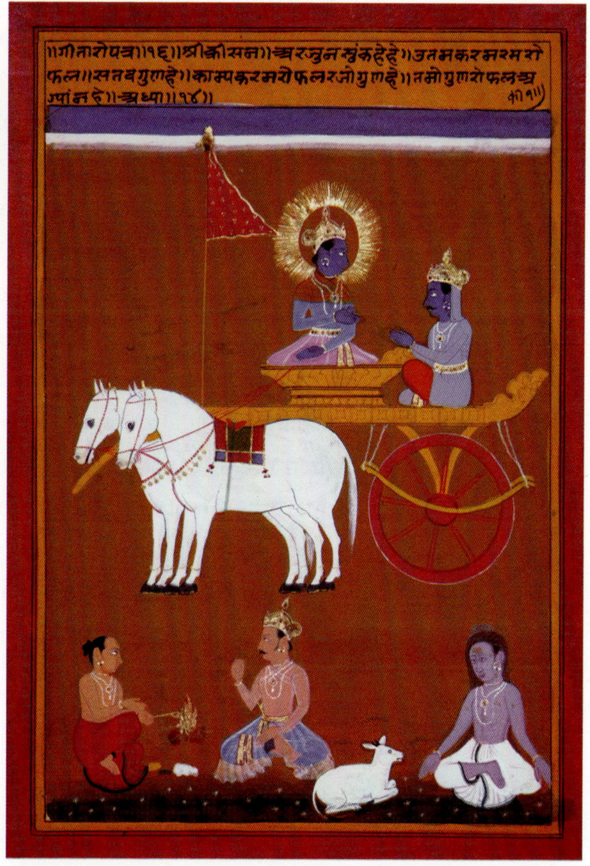

|16| हे अर्जुन! सात्विक कर्म का फल निर्मल कहा गया है। राजसिक कर्म का फल दुख और तामसिक कर्म का फल अज्ञान माना गया है।

|16| Hey Arjuna! The fruit of Truth is said to be gentle and pure; the fruit of Passion is sorrow; and the fruit of Ignorance is dark inertia.

The artist understands how ethically important Arjuna's questions are not only for him but also for the gods. In his visual comment on verses 19, 20 and 21, Allah Baksh shows Shiva, Vishnu and Brahma sitting on a flower-strewn earth like three yogis, against a dark background faintly lit by the silver light of a crescent moon—a reminder of the cycles of time, fertility and sacrifice. Are they actively discussing Krishna's response? Sitting patiently on the far left behind Shiva, overhearing the gods and bearing witness to their presence, is an aged, white-bearded sage (painting for verse 21). His long hair is ringed with white flowers. His forehead is marked by three ochre-coloured horizontal lines, indicating that he is a Shiva acolyte. His right hand lies calmly in his lap, while his left is placed on his chest in a pose of restful attentiveness. His eyes shine with intelligence and are gentle; he finds the hierophany of the gods neither frightening nor threatening. The artist suggests that the gods are always visible to any human being who is ethically good and whose relation with the universe is kind and merciful. Is the presence of the old sage, who is clearly non-heroic, an answer to Arjuna's question at the beginning of the chapter: What signs reveal a good man who has all the *gunas*?

The painting continues to demand our attention. The three gods are presented in their gentler aspect, an aspect prior to their descent into human time when the three *gunas,* which the gods too have, were in harmony. In the painterly commentary, the gods appear on earth, or are imagined by the wise man, as they existed in eternity; or, indeed, as they still exist in that eternity which we can apprehend in our acts of goodness, charity or love. Each of them is of the same bodily proportions and, therefore, unlike many

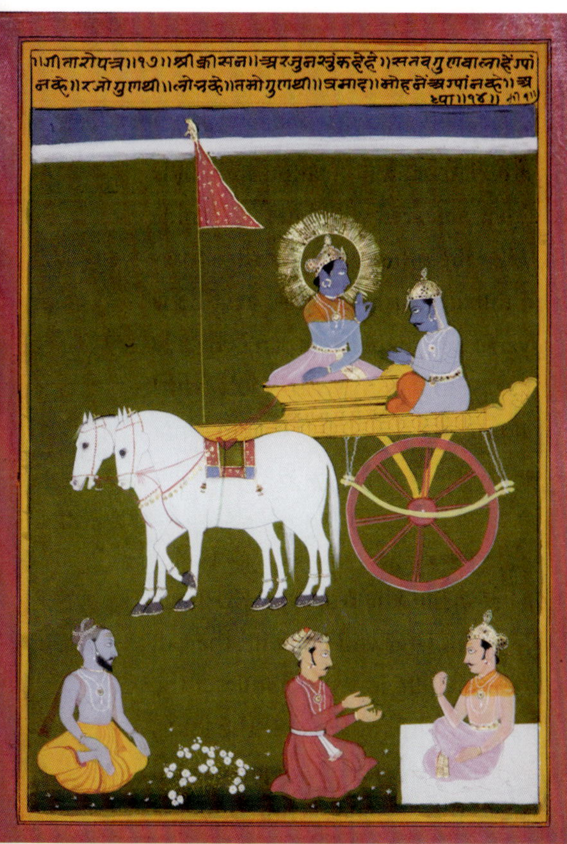

|17| श्री कृष्ण आगे कहने लगे कि सतोगुण से ज्ञान उत्पन्न होता है, रजोगुण से लोभ और तमोगुण से मोह, अज्ञान और प्रमाद उत्पन्न होते हैं।

|17| Sri Krishna further says: Wisdom is born of Truth; greed is born of Passion; and delusion, inertia and error are born of Ignorance.

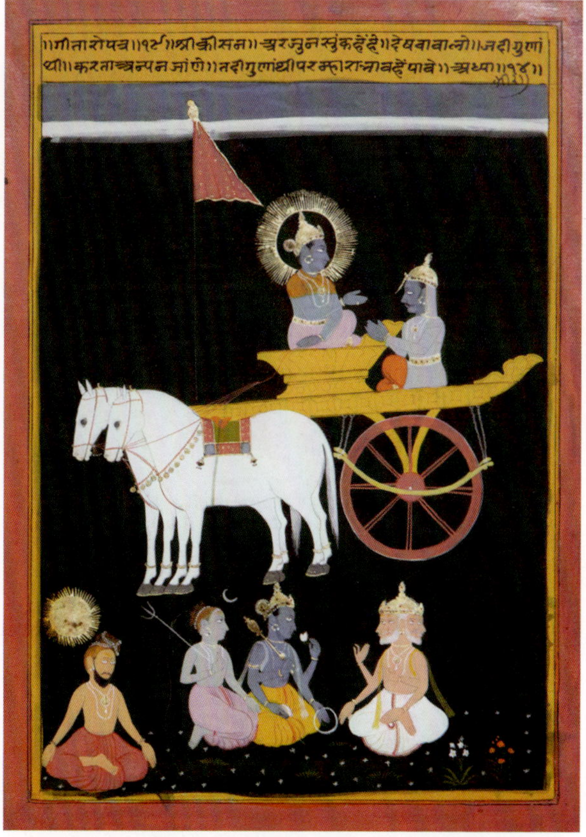

|19| हे अर्जुन! जब देखने वाला अन्य किसी को कर्ता नहीं देखता और गुणों से परमात्मा को जान लेता है तो वह मेरे स्वरूप को प्राप्त होता है।

|19| Hey Arjuna! When the seeker finds no other agent of action and recognises the divine qualities of nature, he becomes part of my cosmic Being.

an argument in Puranic myths about who is the supreme god, here none can claim superiority over the other nor chronological priority.[4] Each of the three gods (four if we also include Krishna) has his emblem of identification and holds it without inspiring any fear of destruction. Shiva, smeared with blue ash, holds a trident unthreateningly in his right hand. Like the other gods, he sits cross-legged in the posture of a yogi. His left hand touches Vishnu's knee as if he is bearing witness to a peaceful and a good universe where the gods can converse about ethics and fate. Vishnu holds the chakra, symbol of the inexorable whirl of time, change and fate, close to the ground. It is unlike the chakra that Krishna holds aloft on other occasions to hurl in rage against his enemies. Since Vishnu wears a saffron-coloured garment with red stripes, the viewer's eye catches its resonance with the gold and saffron coloured lotus-shaped seat of the chariot above before coming to rest on the sun-bright crown and halo around Krishna's head. Vishnu's conch shell lies in his lap; only much later will it sound the call to war. In his left hand, Vishnu holds a half-open white lotus symbolic of the peaceful union of water and the sky, and an emblem of knowledge. The lotus, in sacred tradition, is "the highest form or aspect of the earth."[5] Four-headed Brahma is the calm patriarch of the universe who watches, with supreme tranquillity, over the past, the present and the future of the universe. Two of his faces look back at the beginning of time, the history of the gods and the earth; two look forward to a future of the gods and men.

Further, if we glance back at the the yogi sitting across from Brahma, we notice that he looks east towards Brahma. Brahma gazes back at him. Is the yogi in these paintings the great visionary poet, Vyasa, who knows all, sees all, and who has the power of words to reveal eternity? It is not difficult to imagine Vyasa in the *Gita* too. He is the erudite yogi who intervenes often in the story and is a sorrowing witness to the earth's fate. The mirrored image of man and god suggests that, had our understanding not been darkened by the illusions of heroism and the dramatics of war, we would have understood that "God and Creature are consubstantial, Eternity and Life are one and

4 Zimmer, *Myths and Symbols in Indian Art and Civilization*, pp. 128-130.

5 Zimmer, *Myths and Symbols in Indian Art and Civilisation*, p. 52.

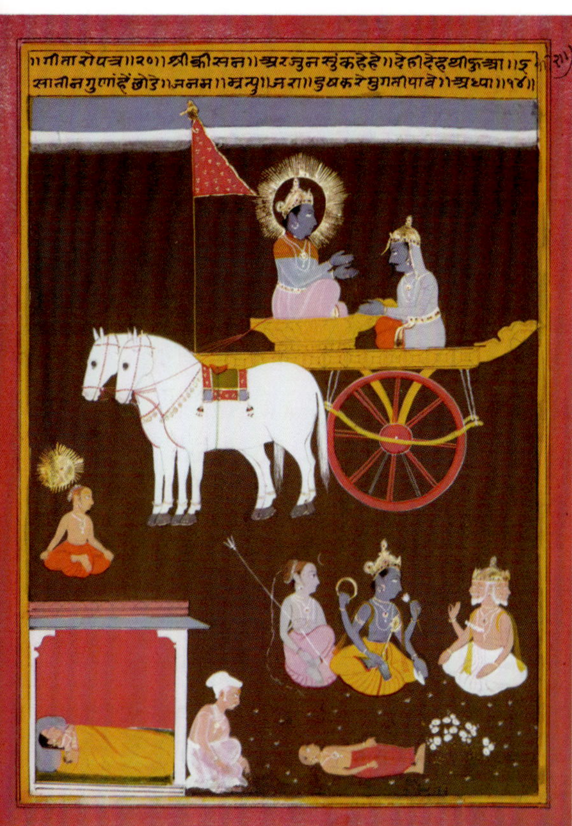

|20| श्री कृष्ण आगे कहने लगे कि प्राणी देह की उत्पत्ति के कारण रूप तीनों गुणों का उल्लंघन कर जन्म, मृत्यु, वृद्धावस्था और दुखों से छूट कर मुक्ति को प्राप्त करता है।

|20| Sri Krishna further says: The self which transcends the three Qualities which are the real cause of physical existence, is freed from birth, death, old age and suffering.

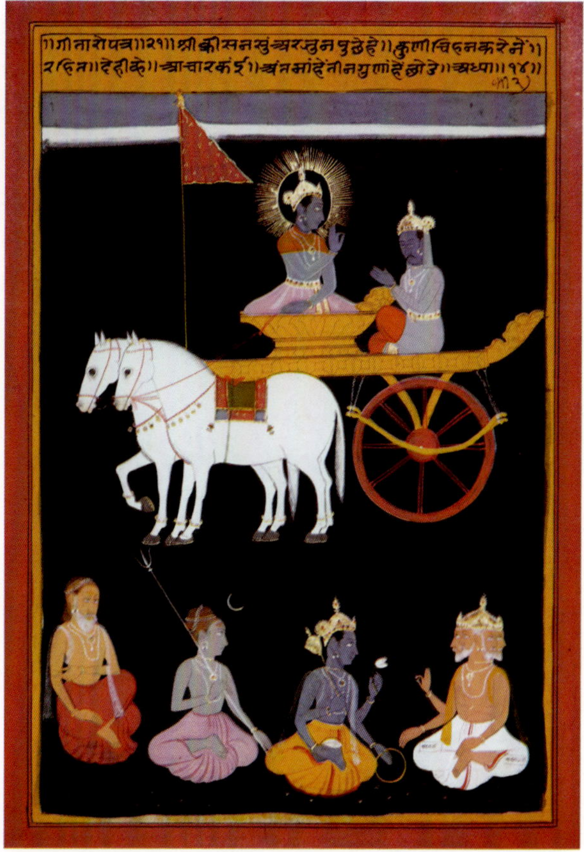

|21| तभी अर्जुन पूछने लगा कि हे कृष्ण! इन तीनों गुणों से ऊपर उठा प्राणी कैसे लक्षणों वाला होता है, उसका आचरण कैसा होता है और वह किस साधन से तीनों गुणों को छोड़ता है?

|21| Then Arjuna asks: Hey Krishna! What signs distinguish the one who has transcended the three Qualities? How does he act? How does he find release from the three Qualities?

the same."[6] These exquisitely visualised scenes radiate bliss; their beauty suggests that the good lies all about us, close by, and is easily available for our apprehension. Destruction, we now understand, is the consequence of human folly and ignorance; of *tamas* becoming our guiding quality. Indeed, Krishna's teaching from verses 1 to 20 is about the choices human beings make to give direction to their lives. If, like Duryodhana, the choice is folly, then, the misery they bring upon themselves and others is infinite because "Folly is an endless maze."[7]

The painting for verse 24 does not present a man of action or a warrior as the subject for our approval. Instead, in keeping with the spirit of non-violent renunciation that has defined Allah Baksh's work, it shows an ascetic sitting on a clean, white, marble platform in a beautiful forest grove. On one side, a stream with water-fountains runs past the flowering trees. A sacrificial fire burns on the other side. The yogi is a witness to each of their existences. Light and heat, flowing water and inert marble, the ever-changing shapes of the flames and the upsurge of fountains, the rustle of the leaves and the rooted-stillness of the tree trunks delight the one who has wisdom and, at the same time, leave him untroubled and undisturbed. He knows that "the peace and light and bustle, and inertness of our common experience are illusory" (Desai 332). Such a person grows closer and closer to the original concord between *sattva, rajas* and *tamas,* prior to and transcendent of time and change.

The field of war is the negation of visionary clarity.

6 Zimmer, *Myths and Symbols in Indian Art and Civilisation*, p. 199.

7 William Blake, "The Voice of the Ancient Bard," *Complete Works*, p. 126.

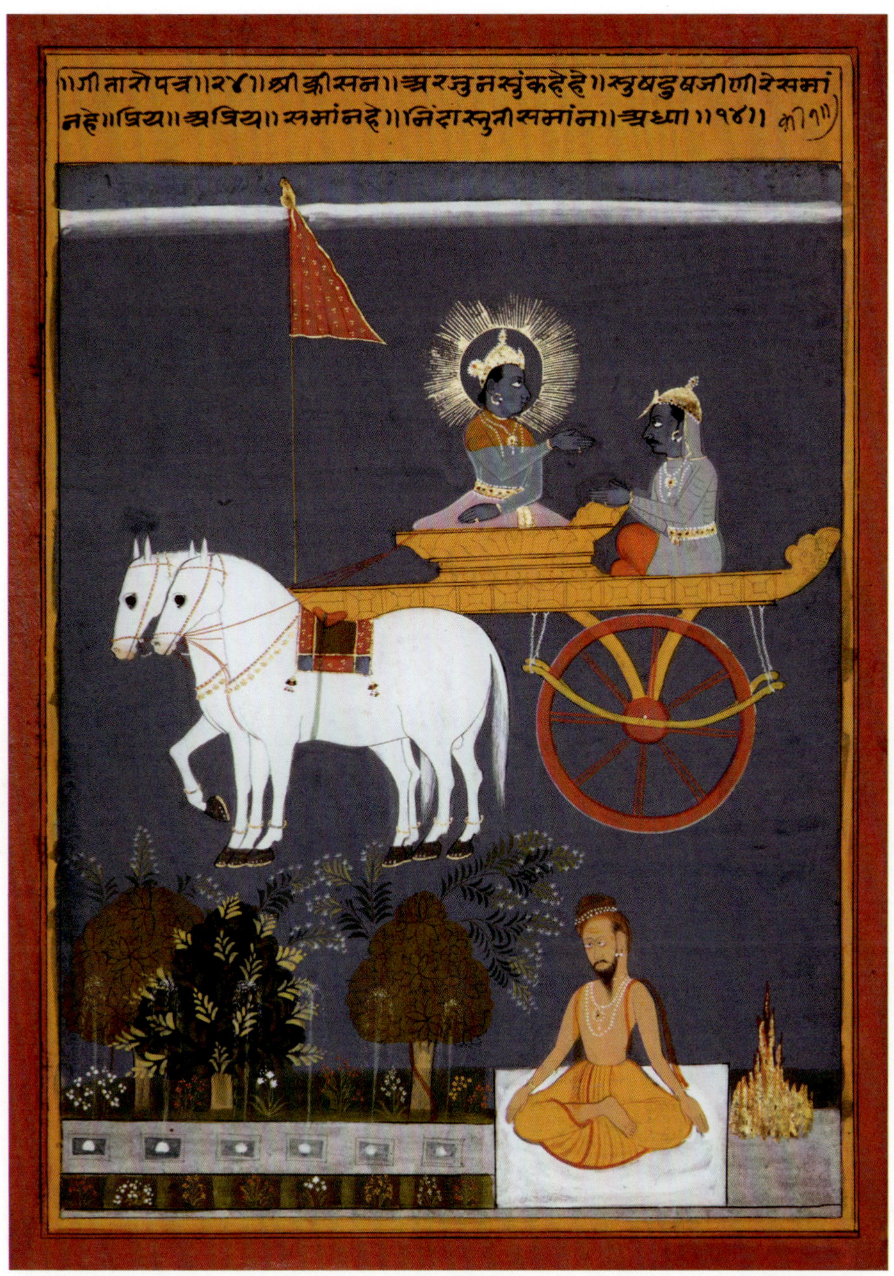

|24| श्री कृष्ण आगे कहने लगे, जो स्व में स्थित है, जो दुख-सुख को समान समझता है, मिट्टी और स्वर्ण में समभाव वाला और प्रिय-अप्रिय में एक जैसा धैर्यवान और निंदा-स्तुति में भी समान भाव वाला है।

|24| Sri Krishna further says: He is steadfast in his own self, indifferent to joy and sorrow, thinks that stone and gold are the same, has neither likes nor dislikes, and is unperturbed by praise or censure.

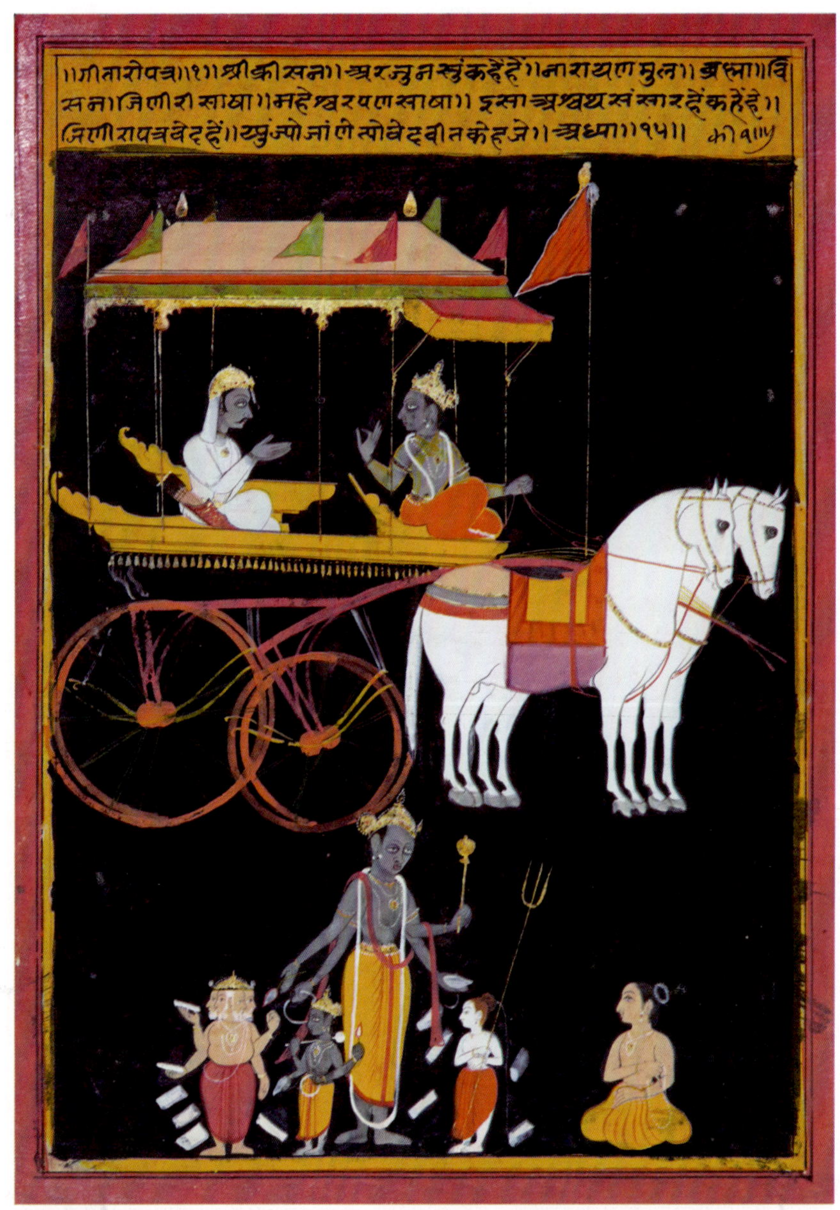

|1| श्री कृष्ण बोले, हे अर्जुन! ऊपर जिसका मूल नारायण है, नीचे प्रकृति जिसकी शाखाएँ हैं। ऐसा संसार रूपी पीपल अविनाशी कहा गया है और वेद जिसके पत्ते कहे गए हैं। जो प्राणी इस संसार रूपी वृक्ष को तत्व से जान लेता है वह वेदविद् कहलाता है।

|1| Sri Krishna says: Hey Arjuna! Its roots are in the sacred space above, its branches are in the earth below. They say that the imperishable asvattha tree is like the universe and its leaves are the Vedas. The one who knows the reality of this universe-resembling tree knows the Vedas.

CHAPTER 15

In the opening verse, Krishna invokes the image of the *asvattha* tree, or the mythic tree of life, which grows at the centre of the universe, to differentiate between two modes of perception and knowledge. The first is the knowledge of the world of ordinary phenomena gained through the senses. For the perceiver, the *asvattha* tree is out there, distinct and separate from his own self, with roots that dig down into the earth and branches that reach for the sky, and spread so wide as to give shelter to a variety of living creatures. In the mythic world, it is also a stately tree under which stories are told and yogis sit in meditation; in its shade the Vedas are recited, the *Mahabharata* is narrated and the Buddha achieves nirvana. It is, therefore, a tree which directs attention to the profound interdependence of all forms of life on earth. To know the tree in its totality requires a patient unfolding of a long literary and spiritual tradition. The word *asvattha* means that which both changes and yet perpetually renews itself. For the imaginative thinker or the seeker of wisdom, the *asvattha* tree is an image of *samsara*, or the cycle of life, death and rebirth of earthly existence.[1] It is rooted in heaven, while its boughs and leaves trail down to the world. Its origin, like that of all things, is in the divine. Unique, and yet part of a unity, it is of this world and yet transcendent. The Upanishads say that since it draws its nourishment from the qualities of heaven, its branches are ether, air, fire, water and earth; its leaves are the scriptures.[2] The one who can think about the *asvattha* tree both as a natural tree rooted in the earth and as a tree of mystery growing downward from the sky, is the man of wisdom who can imagine his "resurrection into eternity."[3]

Allah Baksh's paintings for verses 1, 2 and 3 are remarkable for their beauty of form and lucidity of thought; their pleasing simplicity and restful tranquillity. In each of them, a wise observer of the gods sits with yogic poise at the margins. He is a counterpoint to Arjuna's restless and compassionate soul. In the first painting, he is dressed in colours of spiritual attainment—golden-yellow, blue or brick-red—he inspires confidence in the

1 Swami Chidbhavananda, *The Bhagavad Gita*, p. 750.

2 Cirlot, *A Dictionary of Symbols*, pp. 229-230.

3 Frye, *Fearful Symmetry*, p. 211.

idea that the world will abide. That the artist is self-conscious about the threat of war is suggested by the unrelentingly dark background against which the yogi is painted. His gaze is calm and confident; his hair is knotted behind his head with a ringlet of white flowers that sparkles against the black space. He sits watching the scene before him with hands that rest peacefully in his lap. In the second and the third, his arms are folded across his chest in a gesture of the in-gathering of energies. The wise men who are witness to the scenes of Krishna and Arjuna above understand from their position that human ego and desire are not the centre of significance.[4] In fact, in the visual space, even Arjuna is not at the centre. It is Krishna, and below him an iconic Vishnu, who form the axis of the paintings.

What the contemplative man sees is a cosmogony of the gods; a vision of perfection at the beginning of time. In the illustration for verse 1, a tall, noble and gracious Vishnu stands at the axial centre. He wears a saffron-yellow garment streaked with ochre and a red stole signalling purity and creative energy. There are two large garlands of white flowers around his neck. His crown is golden. His feet are turned outward to suggest stability. In his four arms, he holds the emblems of creation, harmony and compassion: a golden mace, a white lotus bud, a conch-shell and a golden chakra. In some myths about Vishnu, he is the presiding deity over the entire creation from the beginning till its final dissolution. In this painting, his gaze is fixed on some far horizon, beyond the ends of the earth and detached from all that may be happening around him. Standing near his feet are three of the primal gods of creation, sustenance and dissolution: Brahma, Vishnu and Shiva. Their stature is human for they seem to be active participants in the temporal world. Keeping in mind how the reading of Indian scripts begins from the left, Brahma, the four-headed creator of the universe, stands at the painting's left margin. He carries the scriptures in two of his hands. The scattered pages on the ground draw our attention to the complex analogy between the leaves of the *asvattha* tree and the scriptures.

4 See Murdoch, *The Fire and the Sun*, p.36.

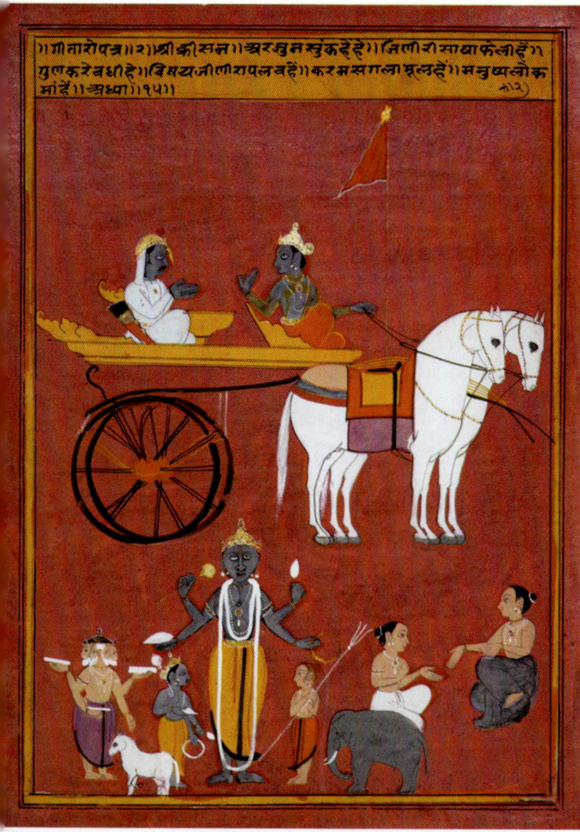

|2| हे अर्जुन! इस संसार वृक्ष के तीनों गुणों की विषय और भोग रूप कोपलों वाली शाखाएँ नीचे-ऊपर सभी ओर फैली हैं और केवल मनुष्य योनि ही कर्मों के अनुसार बाँधने वाली है।

|2| Hey Arjuna! This universal tree draws its nourishment from nature's qualities; its buds are our senses; its branches are spread above and below us, and human beings are entangled in them according to their actions.

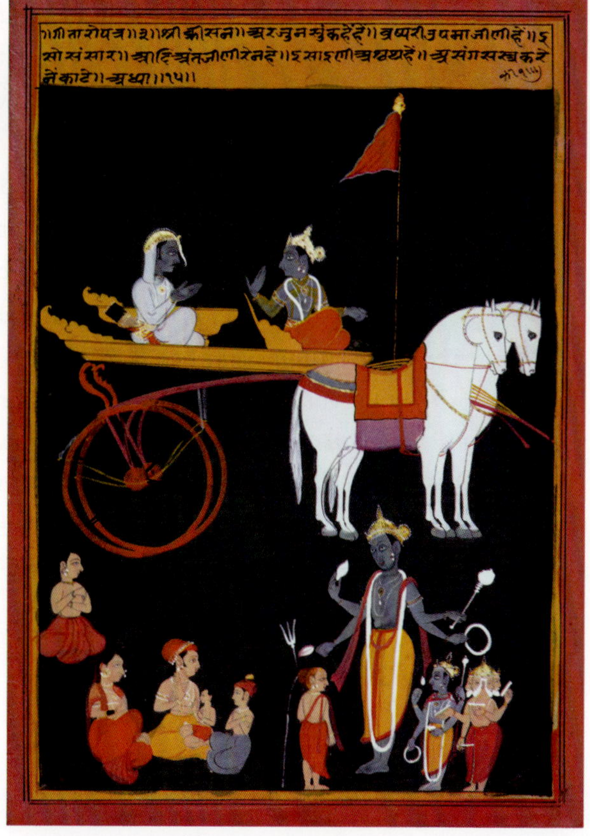

|3| हे अर्जुन! इस संसार-वृक्ष का जो स्वरूप है ऐसा नहीं पाया जाता क्योंकि न इसका आदि है न अंत। इस दृढ़ मूल वाले वृक्ष को वैराग्यरूपी शस्त्र द्वारा काटना चाहिए।

|3| Hey Arjuna! The true form of this universal tree is not found in this world because it neither has a beginning nor an end; such a deep-rooted tree can only be cut down by the axe of detachment.

Imagination's "modifying power"[5] learns to distinguish the empirical tree that reason knows from its divine analogue. Unlike the physical tree, the *asvattha* tree has no life-history. As it hangs vertically downward, its trunk is the *axis mundi* around which the world revolves. That is why, mythopoeically, the inverted tree is *not* analogically *like* god, but *is* God. T. S. Eliot understands this well and, in *Burnt Norton,* identifies the place where the tree grows as one where daily time becomes incarnation.[6] Given this cluster of associations, it is not surprising that in the spiritual traditions, from the Upanishads and the Vedas, to the Christian and Gnostic texts, the Kabala, shamanic dreams and alchemical speculations, mythic romances and folklore, the inverted tree is symbolic of wisdom; a sign of the divine promise of fertility, spiritual renewal and resurrection. Its fruit of immortality is difficult to acquire, and it is almost always protected by a dragon, a seraphim, a riddling spirit or a trickster God.

What Krishna is asking of Arjuna is a radical transformation of the common, the ordinary and the traditional, the *tamasic* way of being in the world where he is only a kshatriya warrior. If he can do that, Krishna tells him, he shall no longer be troubled by "the riddle of the world."[7] Instead, with the help of "the sharp axe of non-attachment" (Swami 79), he can cut his way through the forest of illusion and open a path to "the Primal God from whence this ancient creation has sprung" (Swami 79). The painting accompanying verse 4 is a brilliant illustration of the mind which can cast aside customs and habits to gaze on the refulgent vision of Vishnu, sitting in the golden blaze of light. He is a projection of the disciplined mind of the yogic sage himself; a vision of the awakened self; as real and as ephemeral. Judging from the yogi's detached posture, an arm crossed over his chest and one leg folded under his body, he neither seeks to surrender himself to the divine like a priest nor become one with god like a mystic.

---

5 Coleridge's phrase defining imagination, in Abrams, p. 379.

6 See Frye, *Words with Power*, p. 162.

7 Coleridge's phrase in Abrams, p. 378.

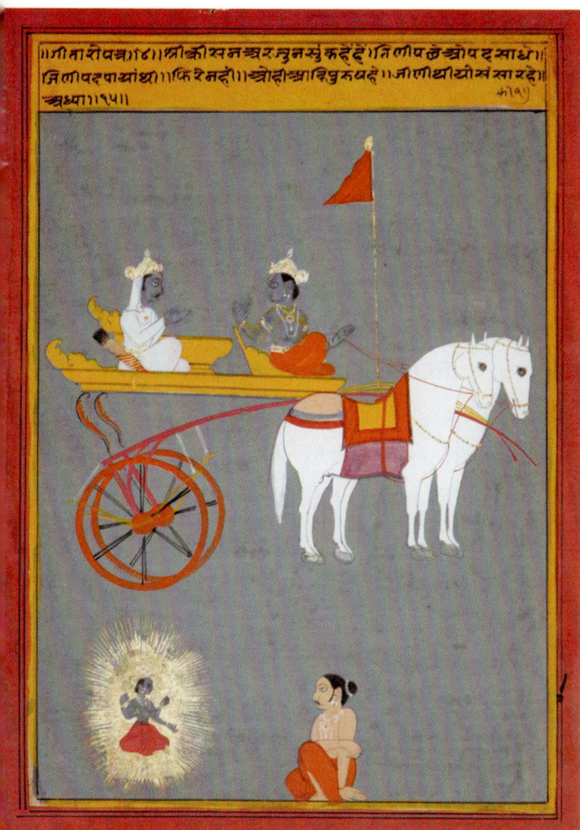

|4| हे अर्जुन! फिर उस परमपद परमात्मा को खोजना चाहिए, जिसकी शरण में गए हुए प्राणी संसार में लौट कर नहीं आते। ऐसा निश्चय कर कि इस पुरातन संसार वृक्ष की प्रवृत्ति का विस्तार हुआ है, मैं उस आदिपुरुष की शरण में हूँ।

|4| Hey Arjuna! Search for that heaven from which there is no return. Seek shelter under this vast universal tree; believe that you are under the blessing of the primordial Being.

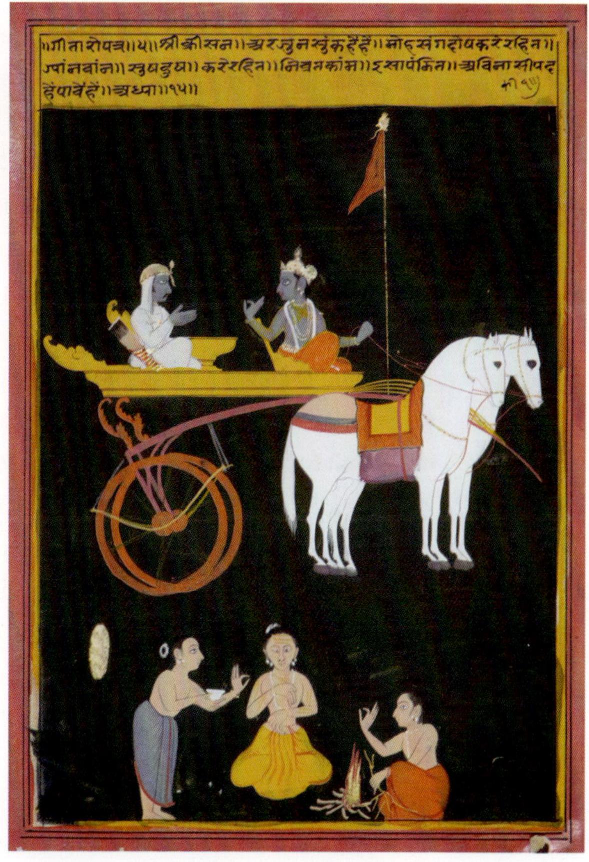

|5| हे अर्जुन! जिसका मान और मोह नष्ट हो गया है, जिसने आसक्तिरूप संग-दोष को जीत लिया है, जिसकी कामनाएँ खतम हो चुकी हैं, ऐसा सुख-दुख से मुक्त ज्ञानी ही उस परमपद को प्राप्त होता है।

|5| Hey Arjuna! The one who has destroyed pride and delusion; is indifferent to friendship-enmity; has vanquished desires; is free from joy and sorrow is wise and has reached the highest stage.

The next few verses reflect a change of tone in Krishna's voice, from that of a stern moralist to an enlightened teacher who is ready to reveal mystic knowledge, which is wonderfully expressed in verse 8: "When the Supreme enters the body or leaves it, He gathers these senses together and travels on with them, as the wind gathers perfume while passing through the flowers" (Swami 80). Verse 9 of this chapter informs us that Krishna "is the perception of the ear...and the enjoyment of the things that they perceive is also His" (Swami 80). That is why in addition to abstract images, there are references to music, or rather holy singers in a state of ecstasy in the paintings for verses 7 and 9. Both sets of images are simple, minimalist and precisely tuned to the verses. While there are a few Indian religious sects and scriptures which frown upon the delights of music and dance, generally both are blended into holiness, since they honour the gods and are life-affirming celebrations of human existence.[8] Indeed, the Vedas (especially the *Samaveda*) express their 'truths' in music and song.[9] The heavenly court is depicted in most verbal and visual representations by the Hindus, Buddhists and Jains, as a place where there is an eternal celebration by musicians and dancers. When there is singing and dancing on earth, more often than not, the gods assemble in heaven to listen and watch. Thus, harmony and rhythm, gestures and songs, are celebrations of the world coming into being in its infinite variety and boundless creativity. Every time people sing and dance in later time, they commemorate, or inexhaustibly repeat, the sacred moment of creation; recall their lost connection with the paradisal or mythical model of society and action.[10]

There is an overwhelming sense of peacefulness in the painting for verse 7 where a noble man sits on a square marble platform and listens attentively to a female singer. In the painting for verse 9, a young female minstrel wanders from place to place playing on a single-stringed instrument. Her head is demurely covered with her sari and she is not as ornately dressed as the woman in the earlier work. Since both music and dance invite the participation of an entire community, they negate the politics of war and suffering. What the senses perceive, Krishna says, is part of Himself, and what they reveal belongs to Him.

8 See Frits Staal, *Discovering the Vedas: Origins, Manners, Rituals, Insights* (Gurgaon: Penguin Random House, 2008), p. 318.

9 See Staal, p. 107.

10 See Eliade, *The Sacred and the Profane*, pp. 68-69.

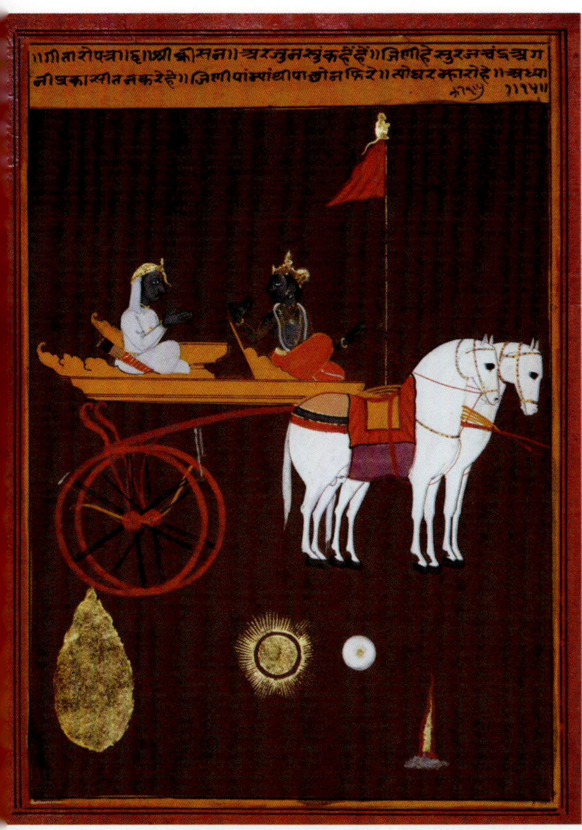

|6| हे अर्जुन! जिसे न सूर्य, न चन्द्र, न अग्नि ही प्रकाशित कर सकते हैं, जिसे प्राप्त होकर प्राणी वापस संसार में लौट कर नहीं आता, वही मेरा घर (परमधाम) है।

|6| Hey Arjuna! Neither the sun nor the moon nor fire can illumine my home; nor can anyone who reaches it, return to the world again.

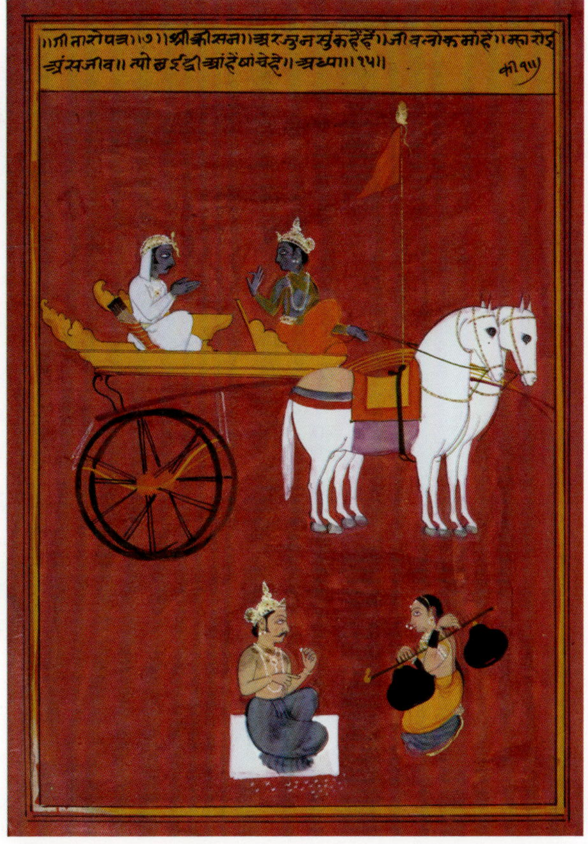

|7| श्री कृष्ण आगे समझाते हुए कहने लगे कि इस देह में बसने वाला जीवात्मा मेरा ही सनातन अंश है और वही प्रकृति में स्थित मन सहित पाँचों इन्द्रियों को आकर्षित करता है।

|7| Explaining further Sri Krishna says: A small part of me is the timeless essence in this body; it draws around itself the mind and the five senses.

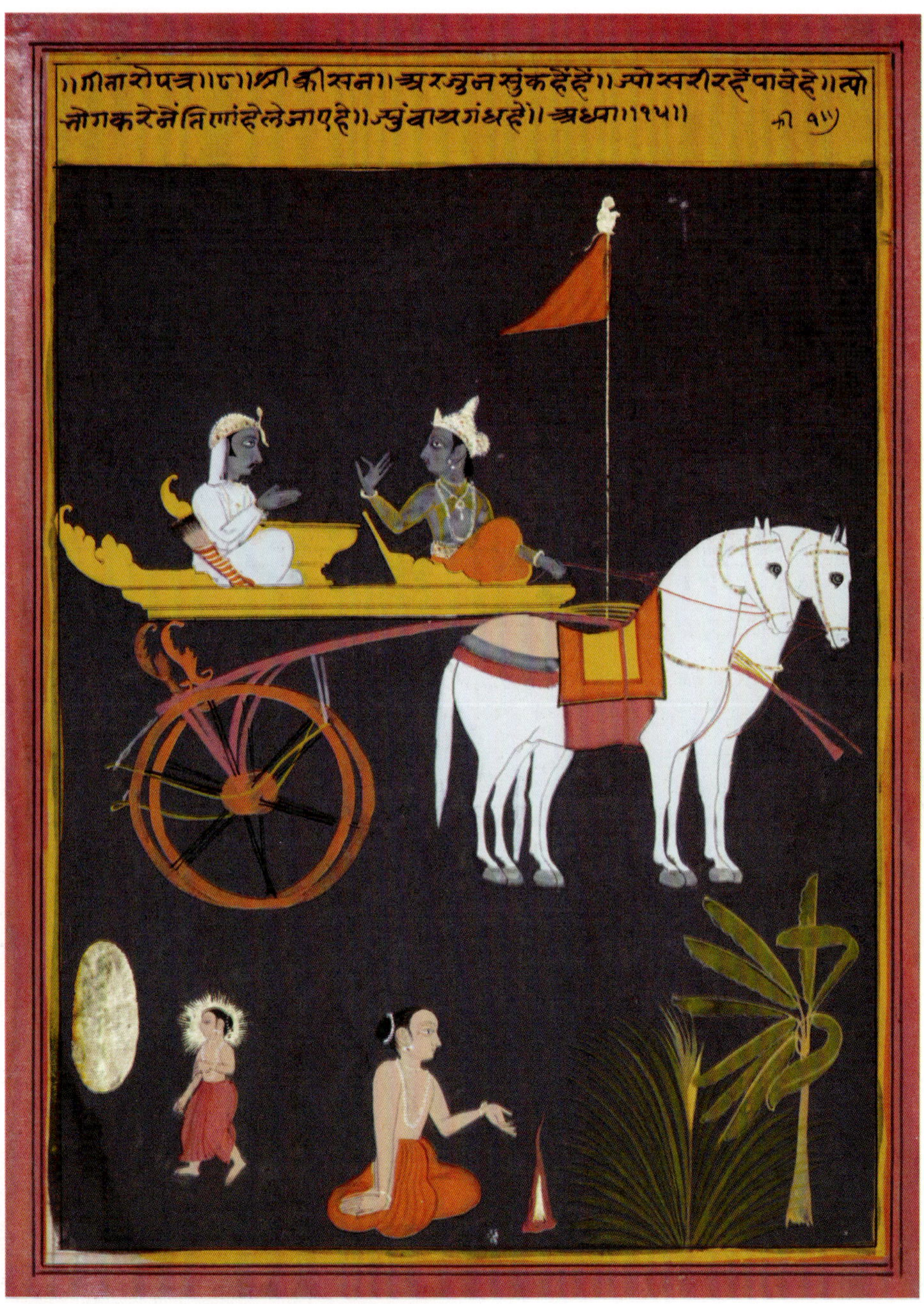

|8| हे अर्जुन! जैसे वायु गंध को ले जाती है वैसे ही देह का स्वामी जीवात्मा जिस देह को त्यागता है, उससे सभी इन्द्रियों को ग्रहण करके अपने साथ नए धारण करने वाली देह में ले जाता है।

|8| Hey Arjuna! Just as the wind carries perfume away, when the Lord sacrifices a body, He gathers all its senses together and takes them with him to a new body.

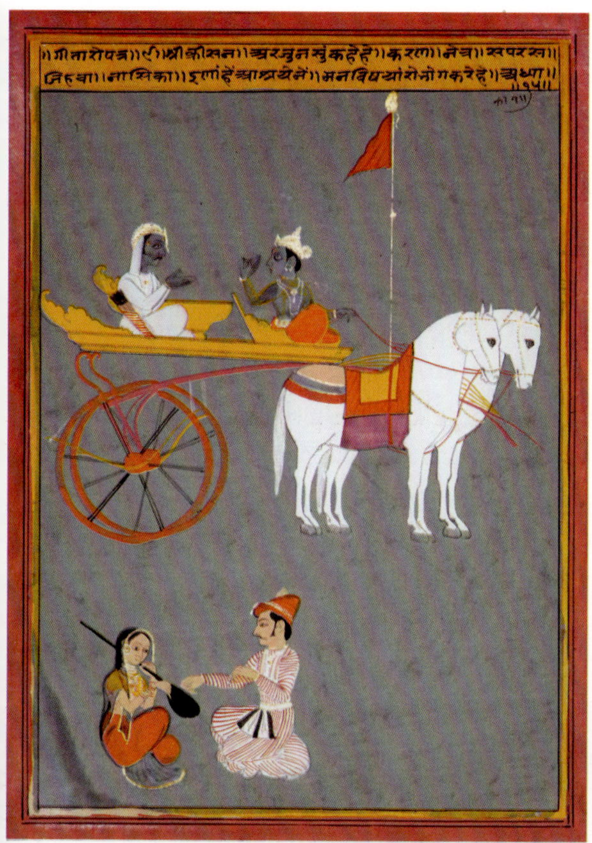

|9| श्री कृष्ण आगे कहने लगे कि यह जीवात्मा कान, आँख, त्वचा, घ्राण, रसना और मन का सहारा लेकर इन्द्रियों के विषयों का भोग करता है।

|9| Sri Krishna further says: Since He is the life-source of ears, eyes, touch, smell, taste and mind, He savours the senses.

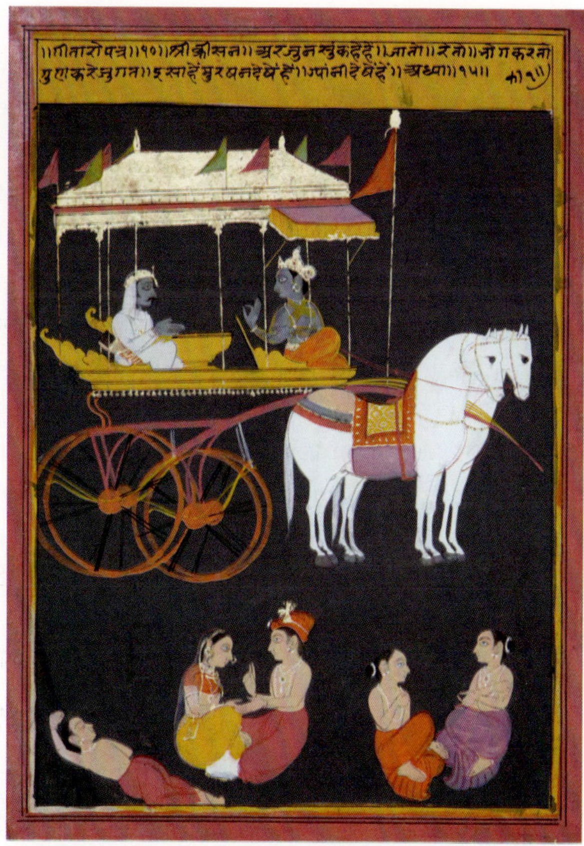

|10| हे अर्जुन! देह त्यागते हुए, देह में रहते हुए, विषयों का भोग करते हुए अथवा तीनों गुणों से युक्त हुए को भी अज्ञानी नहीं देख पाते, केवल ज्ञान रूपी नेत्रों वाले ही देख पाते हैं।

|10| Hey Arjuna! The ignorant can neither see Him leave the body, nor see Him as a living presence in the body, though they have the natural qualities. Those who have visionary eyes can see Him.

Looking at the other paintings for this chapter, one realises that for Allah Baksh, painting each verse, and finding visual correlatives for Krishna's abstract arguments has been an imaginative and spiritual exploration. The archetypal symbols in the paintings have correspondences in the gentler tone of Krishna's spiritual poetics. Only the ignorant and the unintelligent, as verses 10 and 11 assert, are incapable of understanding this basic principle of life. The paintings for these verses show self-absorbed, self-obsessed men and women, against dark or uninspiring backgrounds, who will continue to be lost in the circle of infinite time.

Allah Baksh's images for verses 12 and 13 about Arjuna's intellectual journey into the interior of the self and its relation to the reality outside are more ascetic and abstract. Arjuna has still not picked up his bow and arrows. Since he has now surrendered his entire moral being to Krishna, the paintings for these verses show him, with his eyes transfixed on Krishna, sitting like a devotee with folded hands waiting for final instructions. Krishna himself is now more confident that Arjuna will act, become the warrior of wisdom. That is why, he holds the reins of the horses in his left hand as he turns back to speak to Arjuna, and raises his right hand in a *mudra* of quiet certainty. The chapter ends with Krishna addressing Arjuna as the "Sinless One" to whom he has revealed "mystic knowledge" (Swami 81).

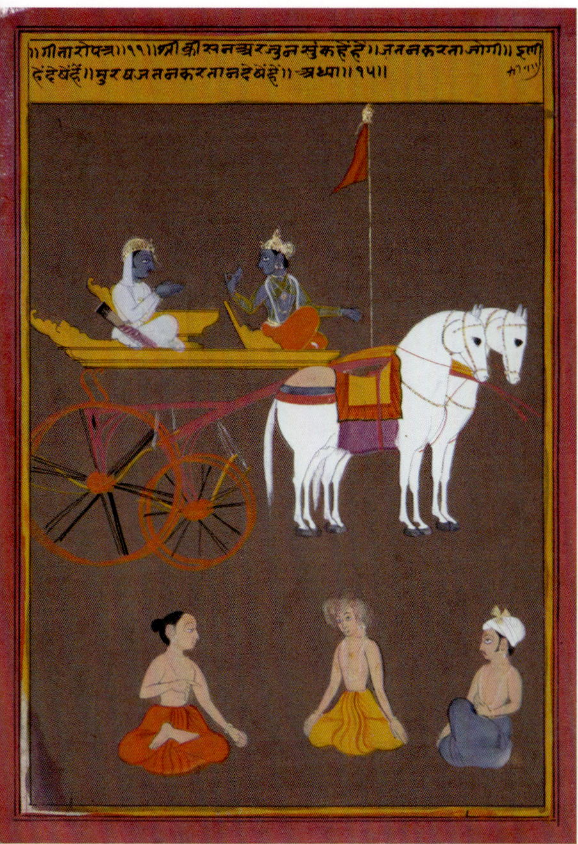

|11| श्री कृष्ण आगे कहने लगे कि यत्न करने वाले योगीजन अपने हृदय में इस आत्मा को प्रत्यक्ष देखते हैं किन्तु अशुद्ध चित्त वाले अज्ञानी यत्न करने पर भी इसे देख नहीं पाते हैं।

|11| Sri Krishna further says: Those who strive with yogic discipline can see Him within themselves clearly in their heart; but the ignorant who are impure cannot see Him even if they strive.

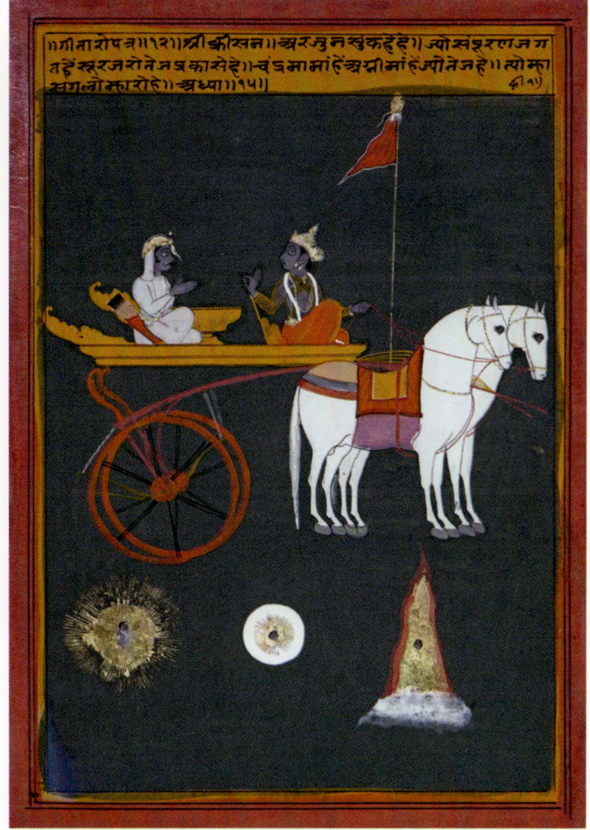

|12| हे अर्जुन! जो तेज सूर्य में स्थित होकर पूरे जगत को प्रकाशित करता है, जो तेज चन्द्र और अग्नि में स्थित है, उसे तू मेरा तेज ही समझ।

|12| Hey Arjuna! Know that my radiance is the radiance of the sun and the radiance of the moon and the fire.

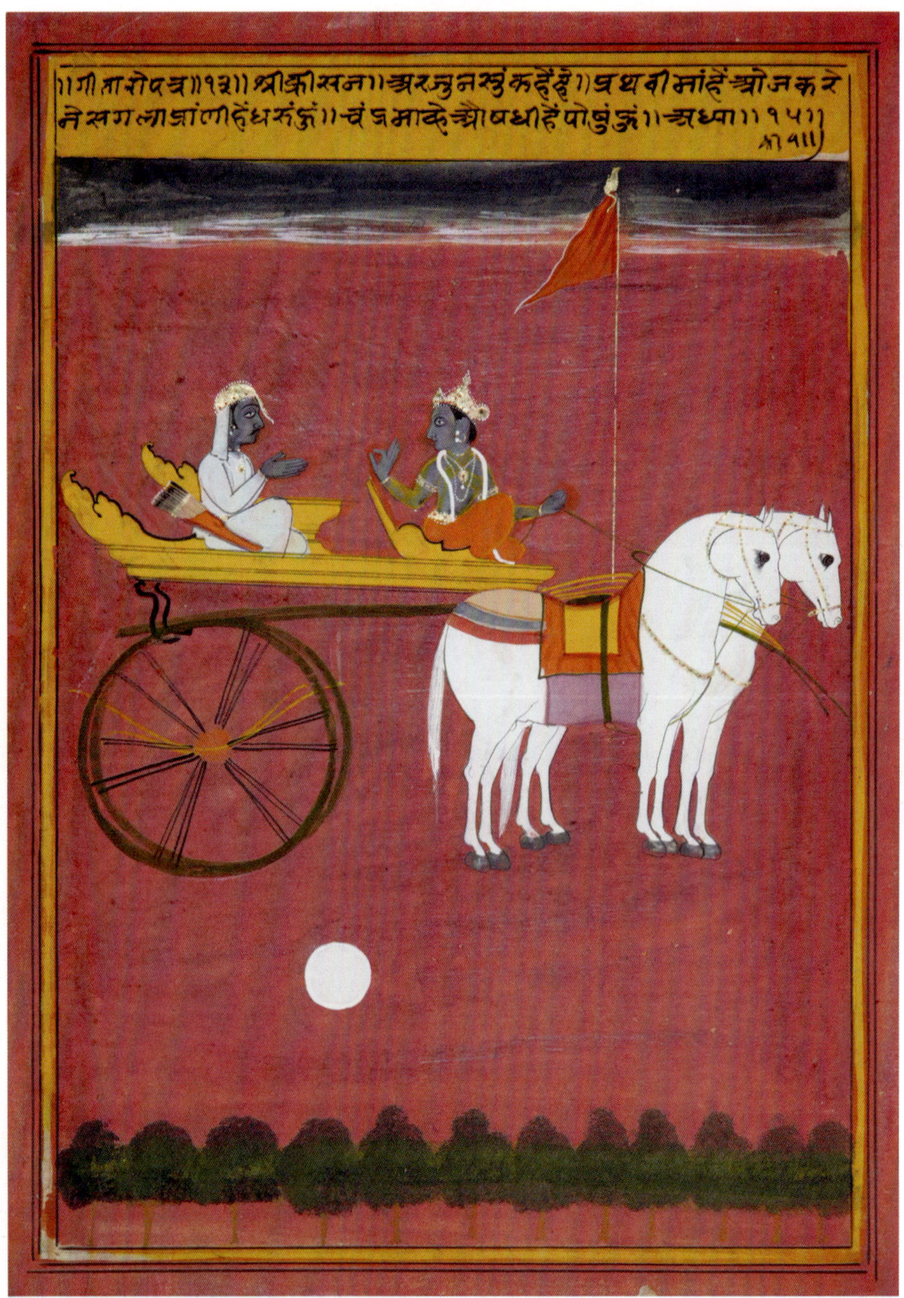

|13| श्री कृष्ण आगे कहने लगे कि मैं ही पृथ्वी में प्रवेश कर अपनी शक्ति से सारे प्राणियों को धारण करता हूँ और रस रूप चन्द्रमा होकर सारी औषधियों को पुष्ट करता हूँ।

|13| Sri Krishna further says: I enter this earth and with my strength sustain all the creatures; and becoming the ambrosia of the moon, I nurture all the healing herbs.

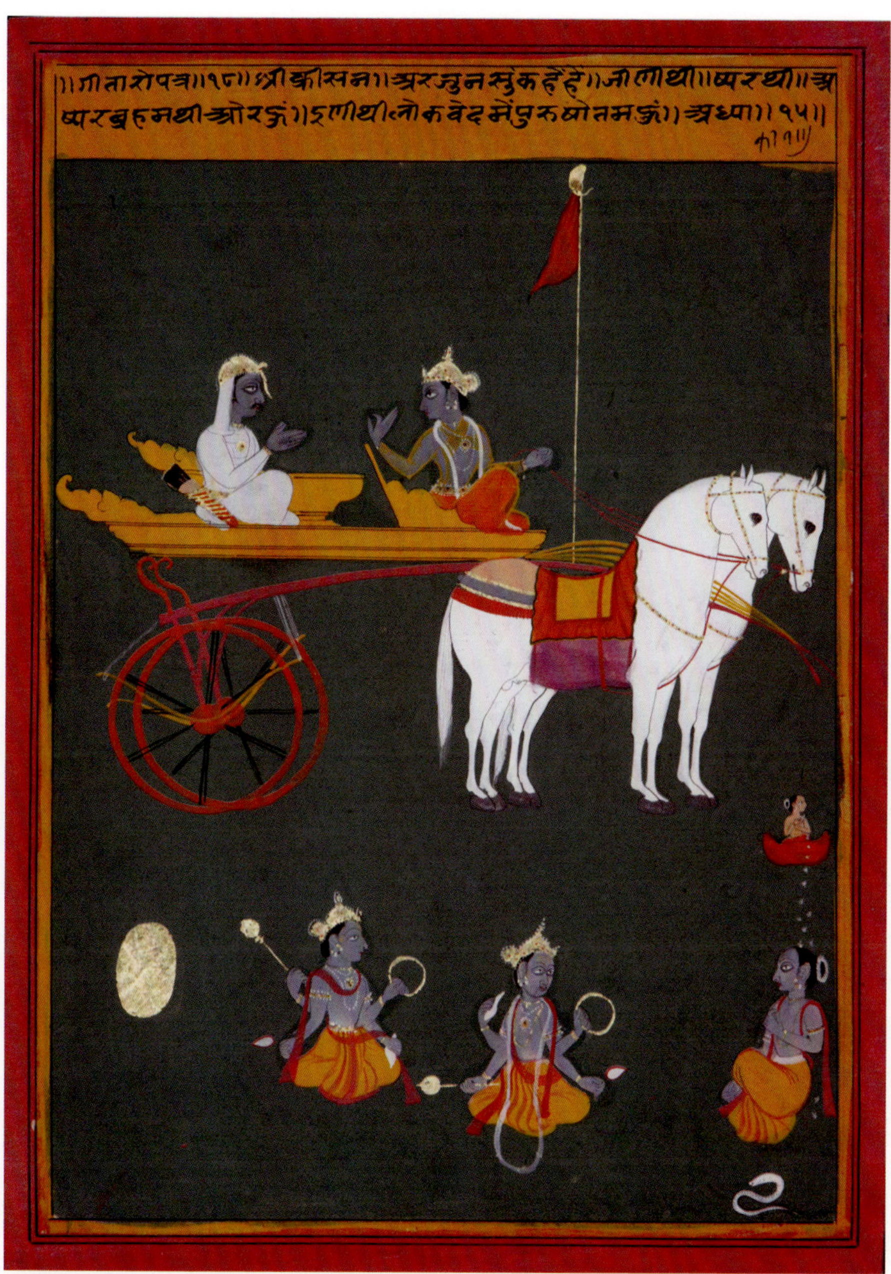

|18| श्री कृष्ण ने आगे कहा, क्योंकि मैं क्षर से परे और अक्षर जीवात्मा से भी उत्तम हूँ, इसलिए लोक में और वेदों में पुरुषोत्तम नाम से विख्यात हूँ।

|18| Sri Krishna further says: Because I transcend the perishable and am higher even than the imperishable, I am known by the people and in the scriptures as the Supreme Being.

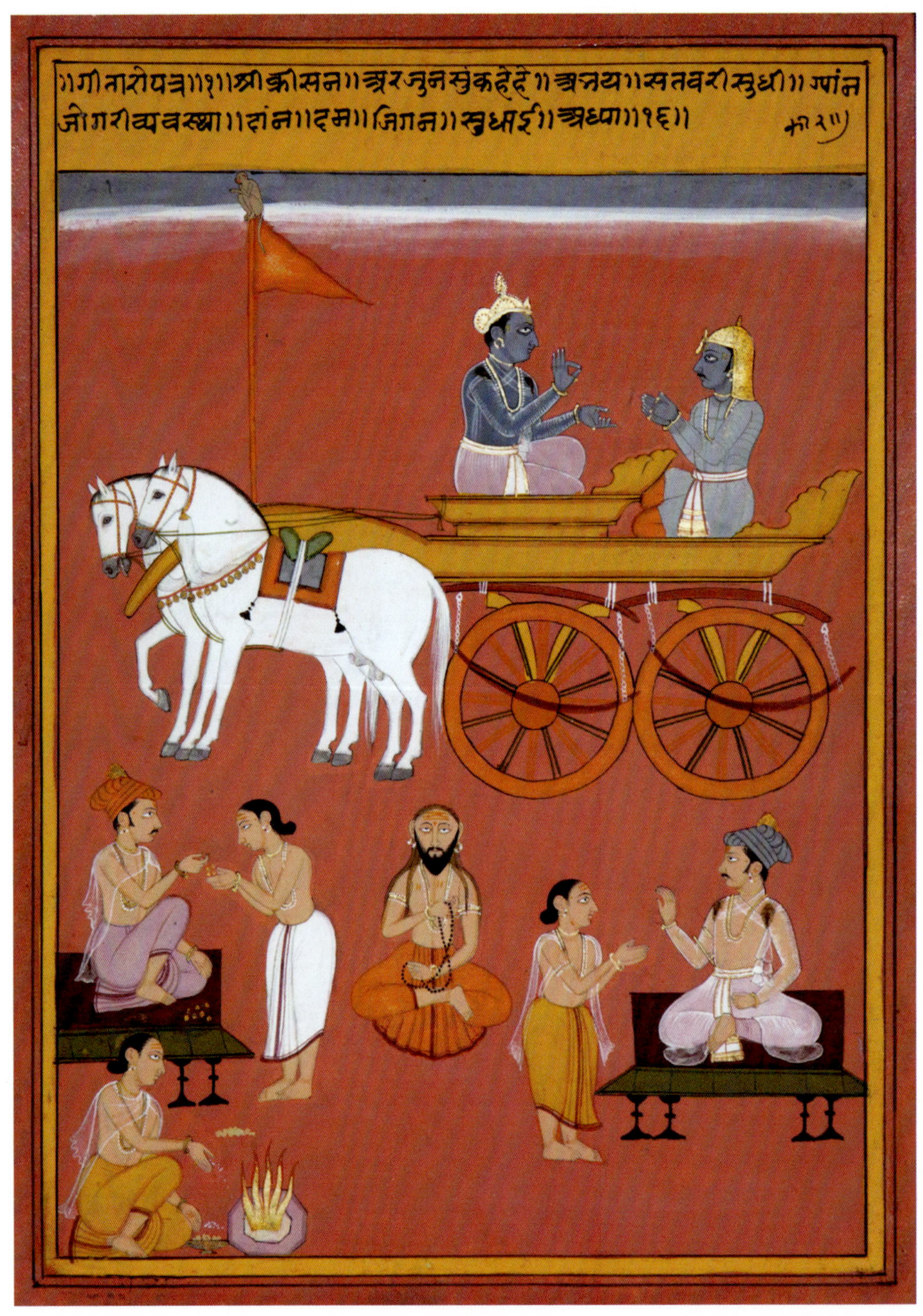

|1| हे अर्जुन! अभय, चित्त की शुद्धता, ज्ञानयोग में निरंतर दृढ़ स्थिति, दान, दम, यज्ञ, तप और सरलता।

|1| Hey Arjuna! Fearlessness, purity, disciplined knowledge, charity, determination, sacrifice, penance and simplicity.

CHAPTER 16

In the paintings of the previous chapter, Krishna held the reins of the horse and looked back to speak to Arjuna as if anticipating immediate action. In the painting for verse 1 of this chapter, he has dropped the reins, and looks directly at Arjuna so as to pay him his finest attention. There is nothing casual about this special staging of Krishna's discourse. His confidence and Arjuna's poise as an intelligent listener and seeker is a fine objective correlative of the simplicity and clarity with which the verse makes a distinction between godly and demonic human beings and civilisations. The moral purposefulness and spiritual grace in Krishna's teaching is visually conveyed through the soft colouration of clothes and the absence of armaments. There is in Arjuna, the painting suggests, a profound and abiding resistance to violence. Of course, by now Arjuna has understood what the traditionally determined destiny of warriors is. He knows that he has the fearlessness and the strength to overcome his adversaries. He also knows that fearlessness is not only physical; even fools can go where angels fear to tread. However, he does express a legitimate moral fear. What moral courage and what qualities of the soul must he cultivate to evade the internal logic of force which demands that he should not only be strong, but be the strongest of all in order to avoid defeat? He does, after all, know that even the most blessed warrior has to assume the cunning and the deceptions of his enemies; has to trespass moral boundaries, and in the process be so radically changed as to become a stranger to the social and moral order he has been chosen to protect. How can he find that "margin of mercy"; how can he fight, and yet never cease to hear words that resonate with peace and love?[1] Without them, he would become the mirror image of the injustice he has set out to oppose.

The distinction Krishna makes between the morally good and the asuric is for all beings. While the qualities he assigns to those who either struggle for perfection or do evil are unambiguously stated, they still require a complex reading. Krishna is, after all, not a vendor of shastric palliatives which can soothe anxiety. He is, instead, a "bright preacher of life."[2] Summarising the chapter, Mahatma Gandhi says that the *Gita* does

1 See Georges Dumezil, *The Destiny of the Warrior*, translated by Alf Hiltebeitel (Chicago: University of Chicago Press, 1969), pp. 106–107.

2 Blake uses the phrase to describe Jesus in "Jerusalem," 77:21, *Complete Works*, p. 718.

not spring a surprise on us by simply telling us to go find our course of action in the scriptures (Desai 350). It demands, instead, that we think through the difficulties of moral action as Arjuna does. Krishna, Gandhi claims, is speaking to those who seek "power, glory and easy life."[3] That is why Krishna opens this discourse with the word *abhayam* (fearlessness). The troublesome idea of ahimsa, which forbids acts of violence and is relegated to the tenth position in the second verse, is hence of less importance. Maybe, ahimsa also requires fearlessness, but if *abhayam* is disassociated from it, then the problem of violence in war is resolved. It becomes ethically unavoidable for a just society. Krishna becomes someone who endorses the idea that ethical ambiguity is at the core of the *Mahabharata*. This is problematic. It makes Krishna indistinguishable from many of the gurus in the epic who propose that "nothing is wholly good or wholly evil."[4] Even Anandavardhana does not claim that ahimsa is the essential moral quality, though he does assert that *shanta rasa* is the principle subject of the *Mahabharata*.[5]

The burden of Krishna's song in this chapter is that the distinction between the preacher of death, whose actions lead to "the gate of Hell" (Swami 84), and the one who struggles self-consciously to be with gods is categorical and unambiguous. Commenting on this idea, the *Jnaneshwari* says that for Krishna the distinction between divine longing and demonic *tamas* is as sharp as the one between the resplendent sun and the night of ignorance: "At the rising of this sun the dark night of thieves passes away and the travelling yogis set out on the path of spiritual experience" (*Jnaneshwari* 2: 168).

Allah Baksh's paintings are confident meditations on the idea that there are no hierarchal distinctions between the twenty-six morally imperative qualities Krishna lists in the first three verses. The illustrations for verses 1, 2 and 3 suggest that for Allah Baksh the nine virtues listed are not only part of a mandala of ethics Krishna is making, but also ceremonies of colour and language. The word mandala invokes the idea that for Krishna no moral virtue has priority; each is an aspect of the divine. In the paintings, Allah Baksh assumes that since physical valour is a value Arjuna already has, it does not need a visual correlative. Arjuna's *abhayam* does not require him to be vengeful. He shows sufficient courage when he refuses to give his consent to violence before considering every other alternative. For the artist, Arjuna's strength of character lies in being an unarmed, humble but intense seeker of truth.

3 Radhakrishnan, *The Bhagavadgita*, p. 396.

4 Radhakrishnan, *The Bhagavadgita*, p. 396.

5 See Alf Hitebeitel, *Non-violence in the Mahabharata*, pp. 140–141.

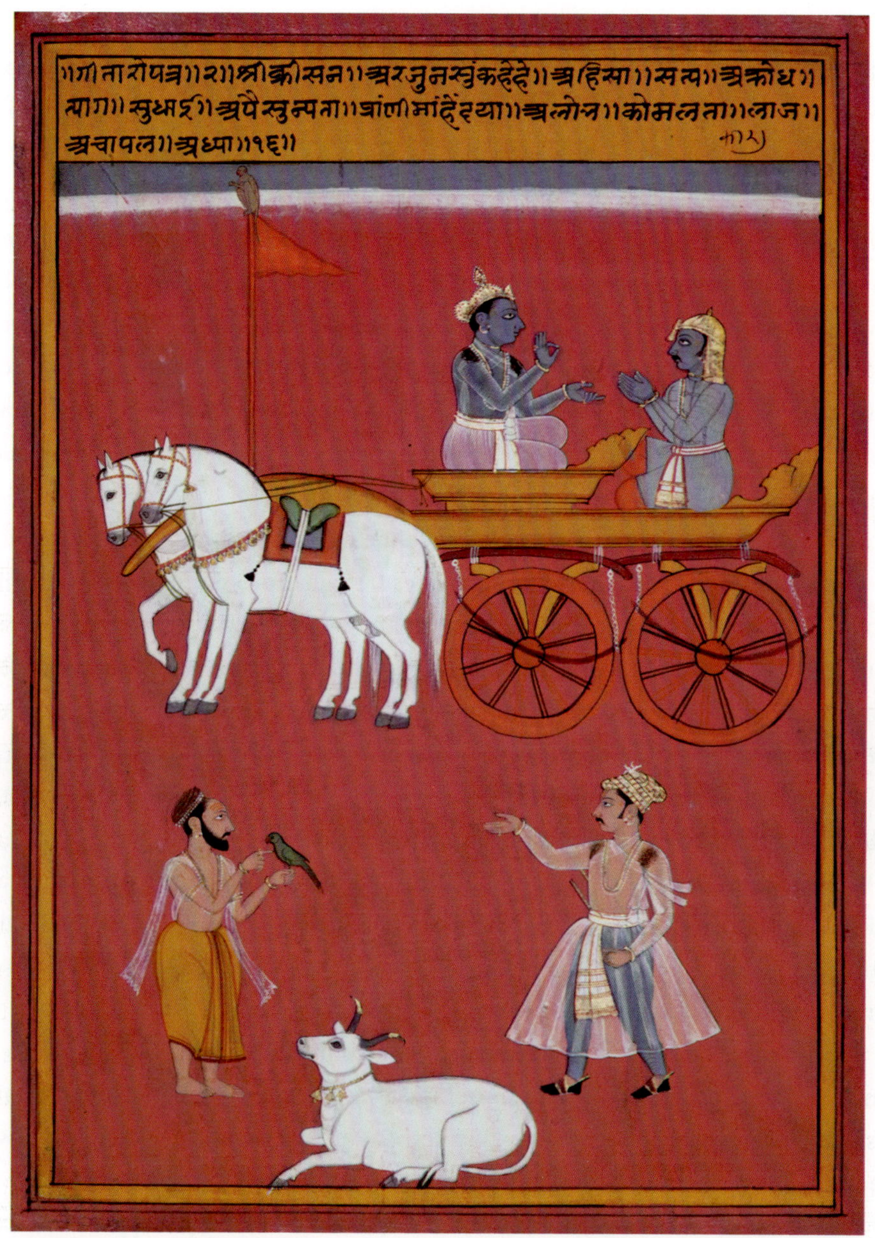

|2| श्री कृष्ण आगे कहने लगे कि अहिंसा के अलावा आपको सत्य, अक्रोध, आसक्ति का त्याग, कर्तापन के अभिमान को छोड़ना, शांति, निंदा न करना, दया, इन्द्रियों के विषयों से संयोग होने पर भी अलिप्तता, कोमलता, अलोभ, लज्जा और अचंचलता का भी अभ्यास करना चाहिए।

|2| Sri Krishna further says: In addition to non-violence, truth, equanimity, renunciation, humility, refusal to disparage, compassion and the lack of covetousness, you must cultivate gentleness, modesty and constancy.

Interestingly, the six male figures painted in four groups in the visual scene for verse 1 are examples of the other desired virtues listed: purity, concentration, charity, self-control, scriptural study, austerity and uprightness. Each of them modifies fearlessness. At the centre is a yogi. He is placed just below Krishna. Together they form the vertical axis around which the other figures are painted. The ascetic is wearing an ochre dhoti. His hair is plaited, and he is sitting in *dhyana mudra* (concentration)reading his beads. His presence combines many of the virtues Krishna says a good man should have. Far removed from the realm of passions and desire, he knows his religious texts and looks inwards to control the movements of his soul. He is surely a man of knowledge and peace, but not yet the man who has achieved that highest wisdom which would release him from the wheel of time. Allah Baksh locates two dramatic scenes in rectangular spaces on either side of the yogi. Both are examples of the qualities Krishna says define the good: ahimsa and forgiveness, self-control and sacrifice, charity and courtesy, peacefulness and absence of anger amongst others. A man in a purple garment and a red turban signifying his social status is giving alms to a poor brahmin in a simple white dhoti standing before him with folded hands. The gesture of the man seeking alms is similar to that of Arjuna asking for knowledge. On the right, a nobleman, gently and with modesty, accepts the blessings of a pious man. Both the scenes from a mundane life of commerce and kingship radiate gentleness and calm, virtues that require self-control. They are not less important than fearlessness. The third scene that completes the mandala of desirable ethics shows a lone priestly figure conducting a fire sacrifice. The entire painting is an example of *shanta rasa*, the emotion of peace and tranquillity, and is far removed from the anxious destiny of a warrior.

The painting for verse 2 continues, in its colours and figures, the emphasis on ahimsa and truth as virtues which require, and always temper, courage. A godly world, Krishna says, is non-violent, not only instinctively out of ecological necessity, but with splendid self-awareness. There is a persistent sense of folkloric innocence and naivety that defines the choice of images for verse 2. A white cow, with gold-tipped horns and golden bells, sits on the ground as if she is eternally under the magical protection of human beings and gods. As she looks up, one is charmed by her humility; but more engagingly, by the eagerness with which she waits to see if we will accept her peaceful presence as a gift to the earth. She is one of those inconspicuous creatures human beings pass by blindly as their gaze is fixed on some remote enterprise and thought, or is preoccupied with the problem of how to overcome ancient enemies. The earth abides

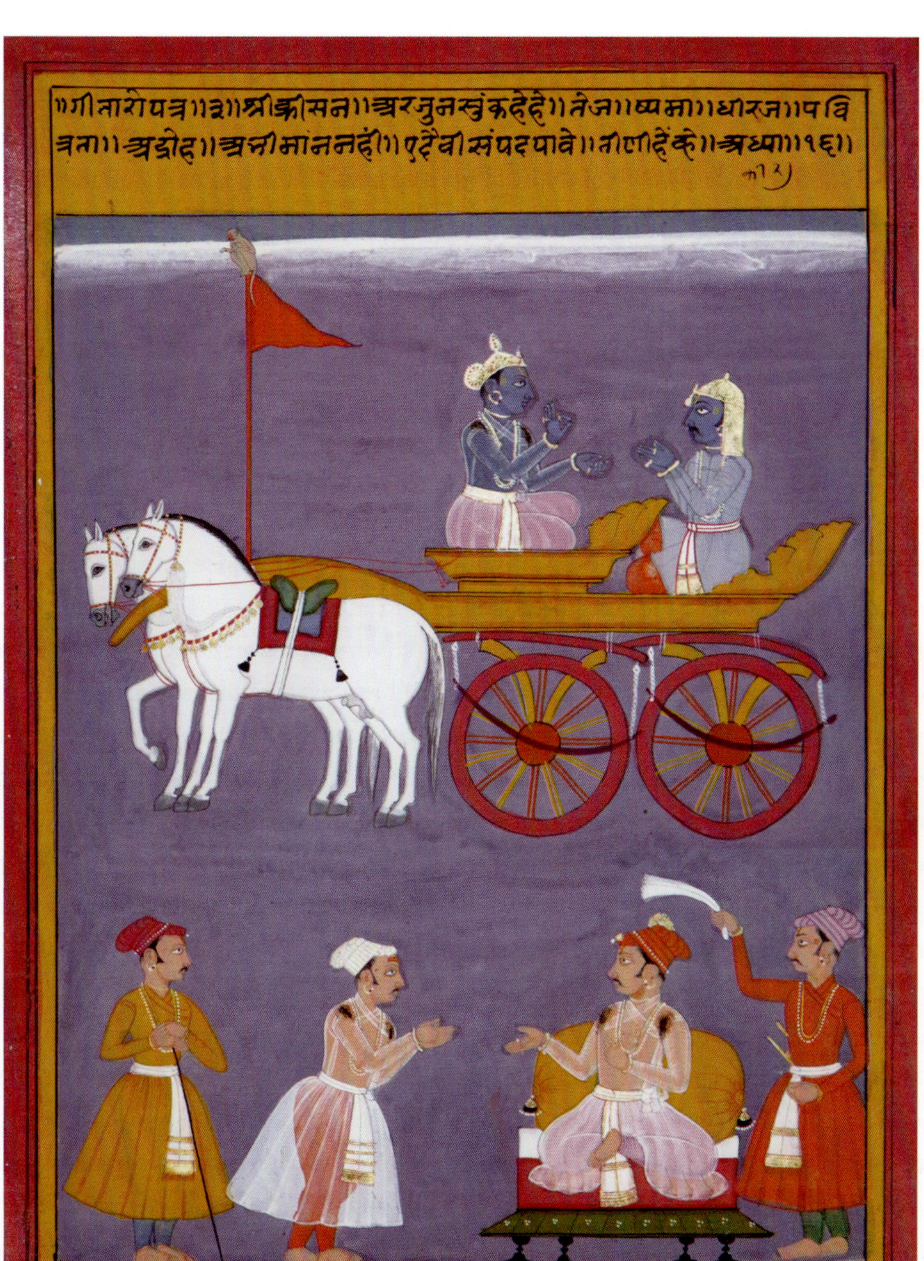

|3| हे अर्जुन! तेज, क्षमा, धैर्य, पवित्रता, अद्रोह, अभिमान की शून्यता, ये सभी गुण दैवी संपदा को लेकर जन्मे पुरुष के लक्षण हैं।

|3| Hey Arjuna! Valour, forgiveness, fortitude, purity, lack of envy and the absence of arrogance are the characteristics of one born with the blessing of the divine.

because she, like other small creatures, lives on it. The same holds true for Hanuman on the chariot's pole and the green parrot. The cow, the parrot, the horse, the yogi, Krishna, Arjuna and Hanuman are painted on the same scale and with the same reverential attitude. Surely, the ethicality of the *Gita* must be read in the context of all the things and circumstances that surround human life on earth; including all the antecedent and future times.

The figure of the bare-bodied ascetic with white flowers in his hair, a confident posture and kindly eyes is a parable of the many *gunas* of a good man: renunciation, compassion, non-cruelty or unostentatiousness. A green parrot is perched on his left hand while his right hand points to it as if they are engaged in a conversation. Together, man and bird, belong to the same timeless world; archetypes of an action performed time after time; performed to infinity for the welfare of all creatures. The aesthetic beauty of the image and its ethical truthfulness is in fine consonance with what Krishna says about the moral qualities required to lead us to enlightenment. Thinking about war and its call for heroism, the artist stakes a claim for the future of mankind in ahimsa as one of the non-negotiable truths and asserts that beauty is its affirmation.

The kindly figure of the ascetic is in harsh contrast to the noble man standing across from him. The noble man is dressed in a flashy blue *jamma* covered with a transparent white costume. A dagger is tucked into his waistband. He wears a gold-trimmed turban with a glittering diamond on his head. He has a sense of his own special and delusive entitlement to the social and natural world. His left arm is outstretched in a gesture which seems imperious, angry and demanding. The wrathful energy of his forward movement is captured by the backward swing of the two white ribbons tied to his dress and the sash around his waistcoat. He is one of the men with an overbearing ego whom Krishna disparages later: "I am rich, I am well-bred; who is there to compare with me? I will sacrifice, I will give, I will pay—I will enjoy. Thus blinded by ignorance...they sink into the horrors of hell" (Swami 8).The logic of power is that it neither leaves a margin of mercy nor gives the other a right to live in his integrity. The ethics of renunciation, on the other hand, helps to cutivate a ground for everything to flourish. Following Santideva's characterisation, that people in power are only aware of their desires, it is tempting to think of the enraged and armed man as one of "the guards of the prison of being [who] stand in the house of the mind, in the cage of greed."[6]

From verse 4 onwards, Krishna defines the characteristics of evil men whose obtuseness has no end. While a godly man, Krishna says, can walk toward paradise if

6 *The Bodhicaryavatara of Santideva*, p. 160.

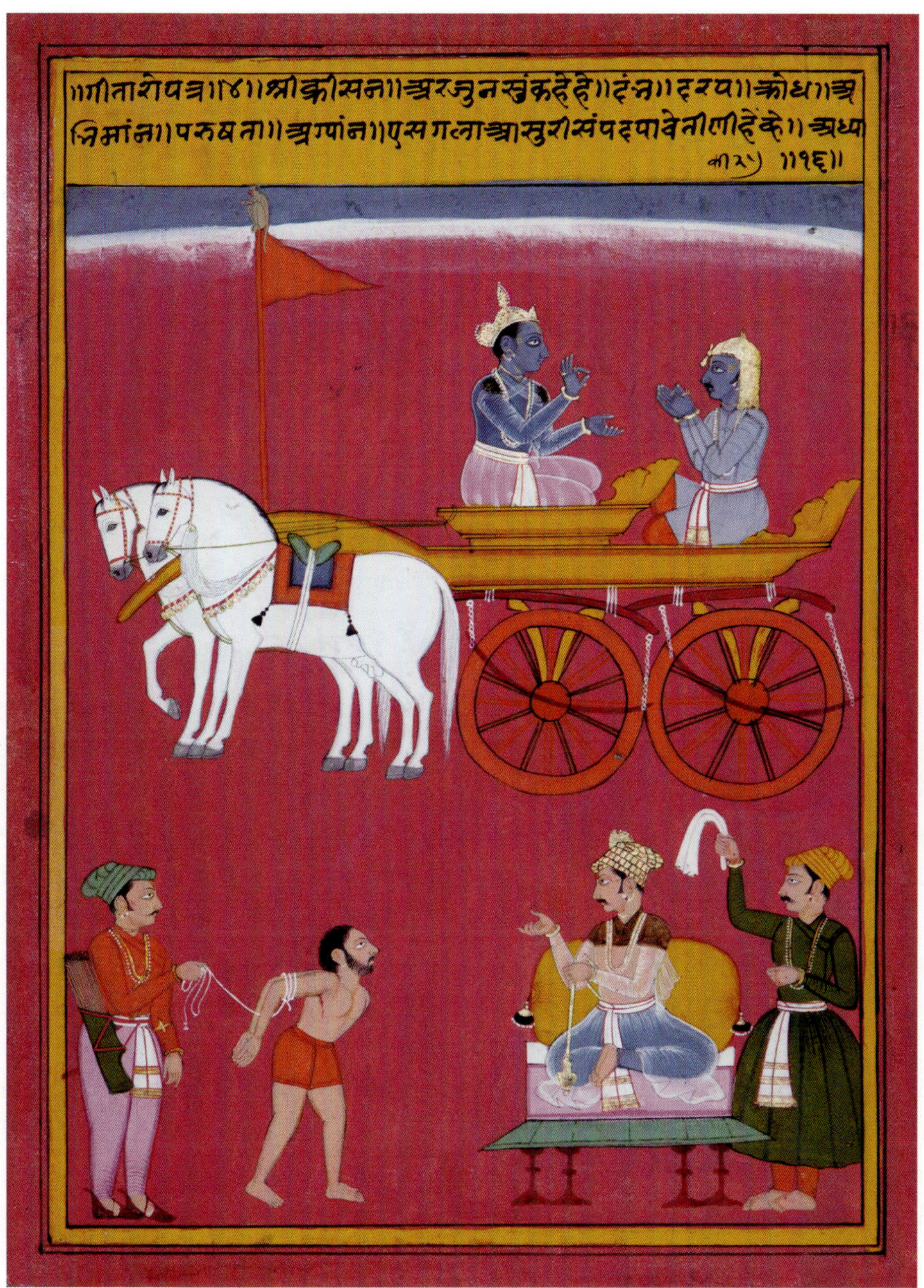

|4| श्री कृष्ण कहने लगे कि हे अर्जुन! पाखंड, अभिमान, दर्प, क्रोध, कठोर वाणी और अज्ञान, ये सभी लक्षण आसुरी संपदा लेकर जन्मे पुरुष के हैं।

|4| Sri Krishna says: Hey Arjuna! Hypocrisy, pride, conceitedness, cruelty, anger, harshness and ignorance are the characteristics of one born under demonic influences.

he lives in accordance with each of the twenty-six qualities, there are three gates which lead to the darkness of hell. All someone has do is to act with insolence or cruelty, out of pride or ignorance, or any other infraction listed by Krishna to be doomed to live in the purgatorial cycle of time and suffering. Thus, the paintings introduce images of common, everyday social violence and punishment. In the painting for verse 4, a half-naked man, trussed in ropes by an officer, is dragged before a ruler sitting on an elevated seat. The entire scene is dramatic and crafted to create a sense of feudal hierarchy. The most attractive figure is that of the prince himself. His bearing is noble; his gesture is restrained. The colour of his clothes is a sober and pale blue. Unlike the yellow and red clothes of the courtier, it does not draw attention to itself. He does not appear to be a figure obsessed with his own rank, but as one who is conscious of his responsibility as the keeper of order. The tableau is not that of a godly state, but of a well-regulated one, even if it is not free from poverty, crime and judicial violence. What is painted is a literal representation of Krishna's assertion in the next verse that godlessness leads to bondage.

The painting for verse 6, in which Krishna unambiguously divides all beings into those who are either divine or demonic, "godly or godless" (Swami 82), is brilliantly painted with sardonic humour. The two men of nobility on the right are painted in pleasingly soft colours. They are elegant men of power and self-control. Their attention is entirely directed towards ensuring an orderly functioning of society. Perhaps, they do not even aspire to walk on the path to redemption. Morally, however, they are far above the two demonic creatures on the left. Like all monsters, both are amorphous, confusing, giant figures—half-man and half-beast. Since the monstrous is a mixture of categories, the two are a collage of different animal heads grafted on human bodies.

The godless claim, as Krishna tells Arjuna, "that the universe is an accident with no purpose and no God;" it has "neither purity nor truth" (Swami 82). The demon with an ash-covered body, hairy chest, donkey's ears, large bewildered eyes and red underwear is a figure of lust. In a sixth-century Sanskrit poem about Ravana by Bhatti, Hanuman tells Rama that a "Demon is a fool" because he is "very full of the madness that disowns shame."[7] The second ungodly figure is puzzling. It is armed and richly adorned with gold necklaces and bracelets. It has the face of a cow but only one horn, making it grotesque. But it is also unthreatening, as it sits calmly debating the stately ruler. Is he articulating, as Krishna says all ungodly creatures do, vain hopes and defending unjust wealth? Or is

7 *Bhatti's Poem: Or the Death of Ravana [Bhattikavya]*, translated by Oliver Fallon (New York: New York University Press, 2009), p. 235.

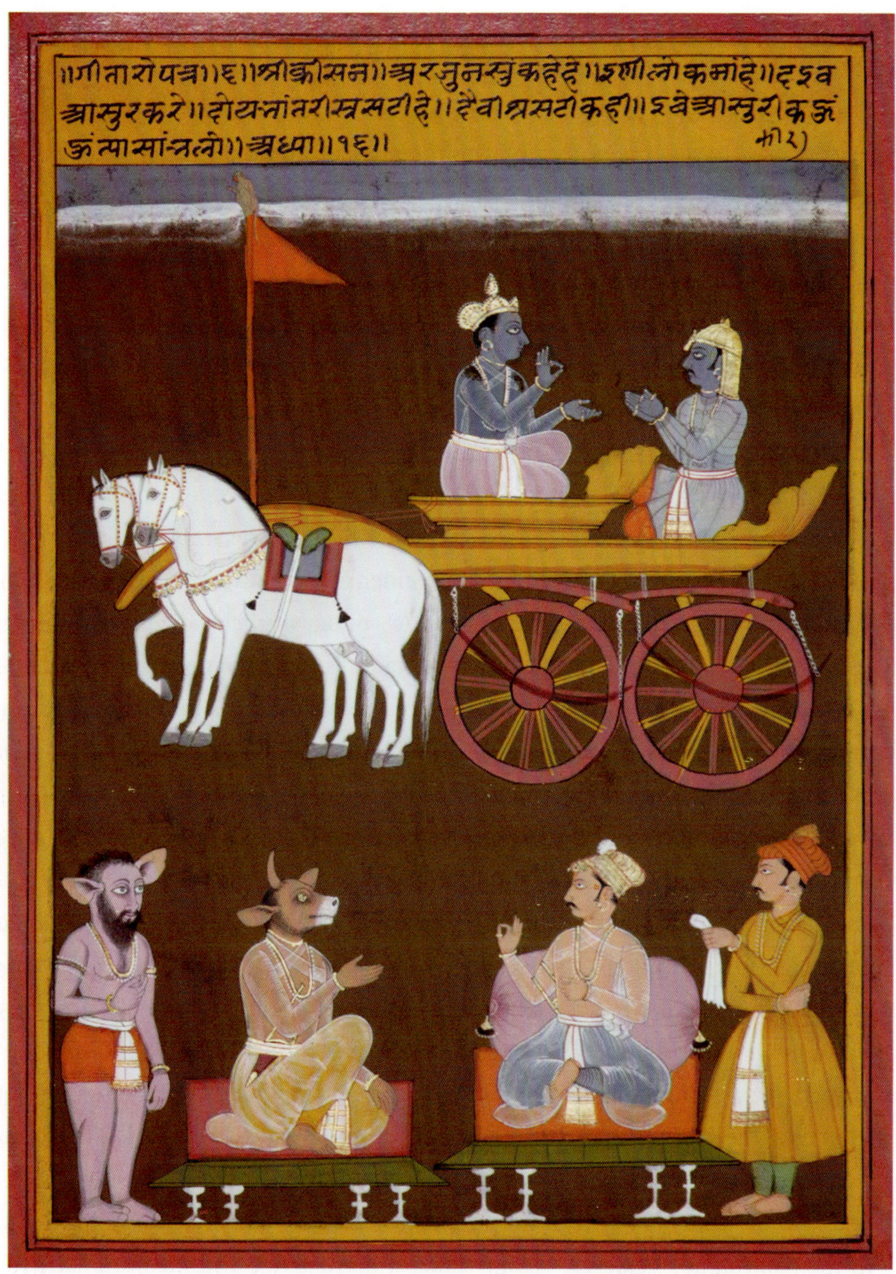

|6| श्री कृष्ण समझाते हुए कहने लगे कि हे अर्जुन! इस लोक में दैवी और आसुरी प्रकृति वाली दो ही प्रकार की सृष्टि है। अब तक मैंने दैवी संपदा के बारे में विस्तार से कहा; अब आसुरी प्रकृति वाले मनुष्यों की बाबत मुझसे सुन!

|6| Explaining further Sri Krishna says: In this world there are two kinds of created beings: the divine and the demonic. Thus far, I have described the characteristics of the blessed; I will now describe those of the demonic.

he differentiating himself from the half-naked creature standing beside him, by seeking from the courtly prince some moral guidance which will help him find a way out of the nightmare in which he is trapped? Further, we are so used to mythic stories in which a hero is supposed to slay the monsters who threaten a traditional social order that this scene of a conversation between the princely figure and the grotesque creature leaves one surprised. But there are ancient tales, as there are modern psychiatric accounts, in which a threatening creature is defeated by reason and imagination or is redeemed. The demonic is the strangeness that haunts the underworld of the mind; it is the troubled vision of humankind which can paralyse the soul; it can transform, like war and its unremitting violence, life and imagination into a source of terrifying deeds.

In the *Mahabharata*, monsters are presentments of the fate that awaits those who either grievously violate social and sexual etiquette or contravene natural and moral law. The scenes painted for verses 7 to 18 depict dramatic examples of the vices of "degraded souls" (Swami 82) which Krishna condemns with unusual vehemence. Thus, the painting for verse 8 shows a game of dice. A woman sits behind a player, watching the game. The reference to Yudhishthira, the Kauravas and Draupadi is obvious. The game of dice was after all one of the causes of the war and a sign of, what Krishna calls, the "unholy purposes" (Swami 83) to which human beings abandon themselves. Insolence and cruelty, lust and wrath, he says, lead societies to the edge of an abyss.

As Krishna's inventory of the endless evil actions that men are capable of grows, his tone acquires a sharper, harder and less forgiving edge. Allah Baksh's imagery too becomes harsh and dark. He begins to paint a social and moral landscape in which action, as in any nightmare, becomes more savage with men ready to steal, inflict gratuitous pain, abduct and rape their victims. In the painting for verse 9, where Krishna speaks of men of limited intelligence who come into the world only to despoil it, a group of four armed men, smoking their hookahs, slouch on the ground and causally plot a crime. Unlike the ascetics and the aristocrats of the previous paintings, their bodies are indolent, their conversation is casual and meandering, and their time is spent, as Krishna says, in "pouring over evil resolutions, which only end in death" (Swami 83).

In the painting for verse 10, villainy takes a more active and melodramatic turn. A man in the lower left corner has waylaid someone and is in the process of beating or robbing him. The headgear of the victim is in disarray pointing to the tawdriness of daily quarrels in contrast with the heroic enterprise in defence of dharma which Arjuna is being urged to undertake. The energy of one and the helplessness of the other are captured in spirited and fluid lines. The green empty space around the two, and

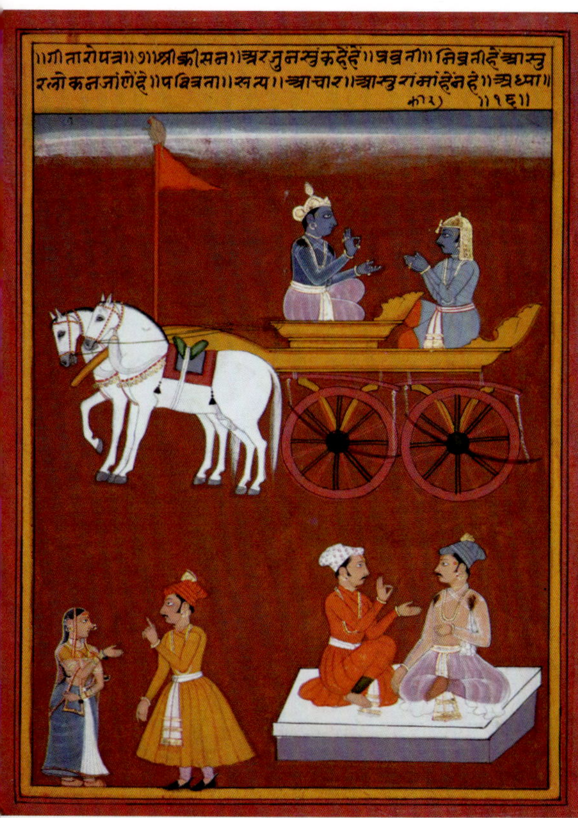

|7| हे अर्जुन! आसुरी स्वभाव वाले प्रवृत्ति और निवृत्ति दोनों को नहीं जानते। उनमें न बाहर-भीतर की शुद्धि होती है, न श्रेष्ठ आचरण होता है, न वे सत्य बोलते हैं।

|7| Hey Arjuna! The demonic do not know the distinction between action and renunciation. They lack inner and outer purity. They do not know what right conduct is, nor do they speak the truth.

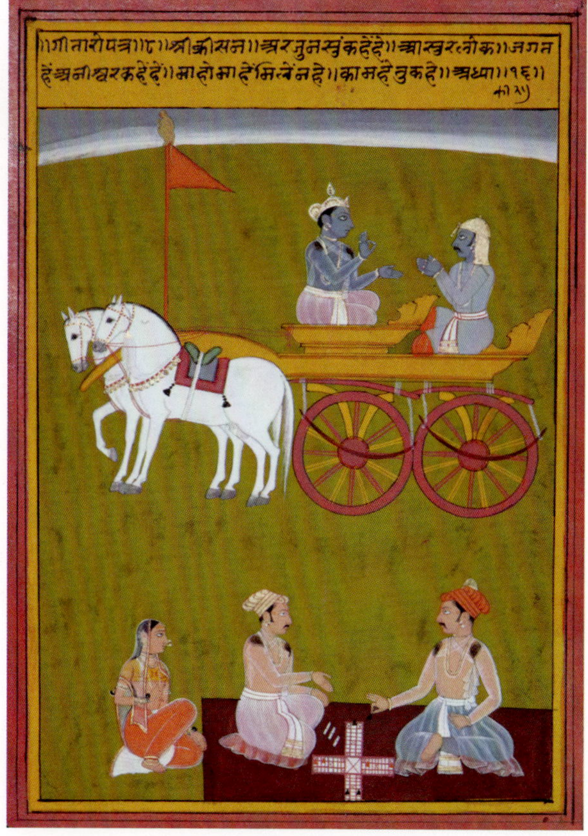

|8| श्री कृष्ण आगे कहने लगे असुरों का मानना है कि यह जगत आश्रयरहित, असत्य और परमात्मा के बिना अपने आप स्त्री-पुरुष के संयोग से जन्मा है केवल काम-भोग ही इस जगत के होने का कारण है।

|8| Sri Krishna further says: The demonic think that this world has no moral basis, and no truth; it has come into being without God through the sexual union of man and woman and only for the fulfilment of desire.

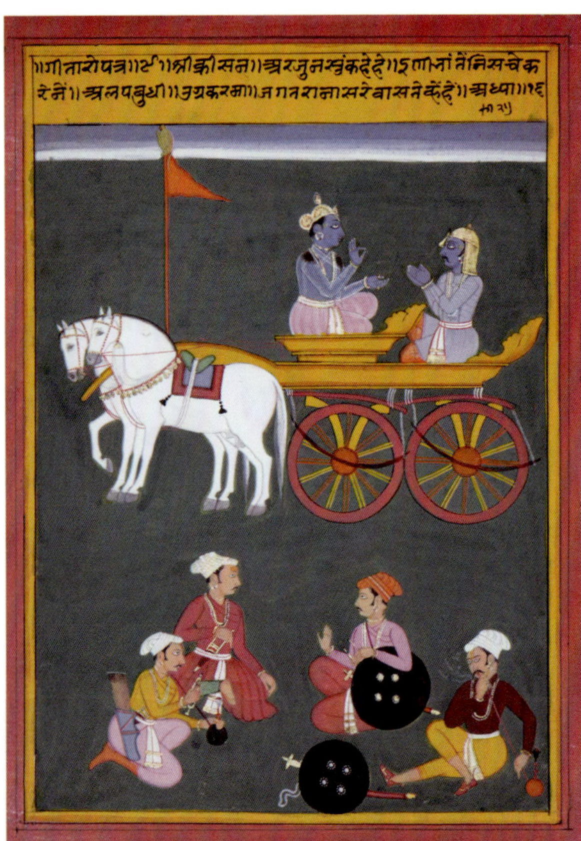

|9| हे अर्जुन! इसी मिथ्याज्ञान के कारण जिनका स्वभाव नष्ट हो गया है। ऐसे अल्पबुद्धि, सभी का अहित करने वाले, क्रूरकर्मी आसुरी मनुष्य केवल जगत के नाश के लिए ही उत्पन्न होते हैं।

|9| Hey Arjuna! That is why such demonic people have little understanding and are deluded. Their acts are fierce and cause damage. They come into the world only to destroy it.

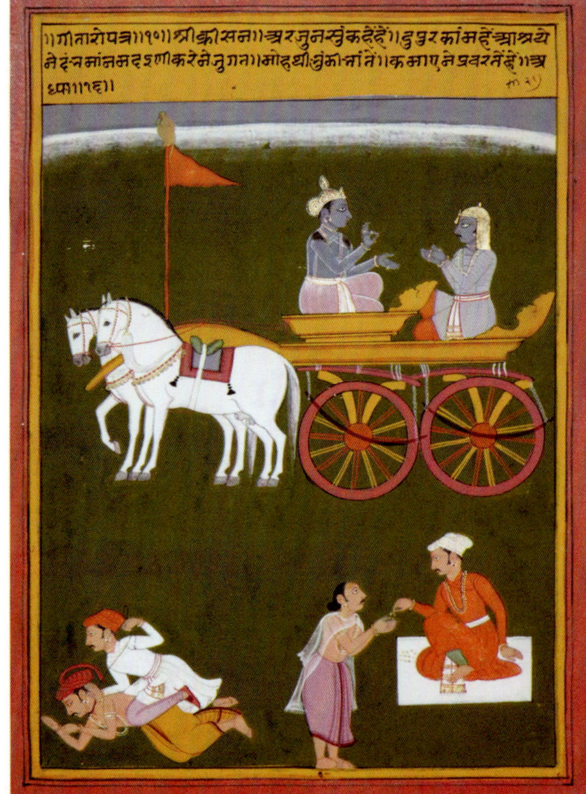

|10| श्री कृष्ण आगे कहने लगे कि दंभ, मान और मद से युक्त मनुष्य कभी पूरी नहीं होने वाली कामनाओं का आश्रय लेकर, अज्ञान से असत्य सिद्धांतों को ग्रहण करके अशुभ आचरण से युक्त हो संसार में रहते हैं।

|10| Sri Krishna further says: Such people who are drunk with pride, hypocrisy and lust, whose desires are insatiable, who are deluded and untruthful, do evil deeds in the world.

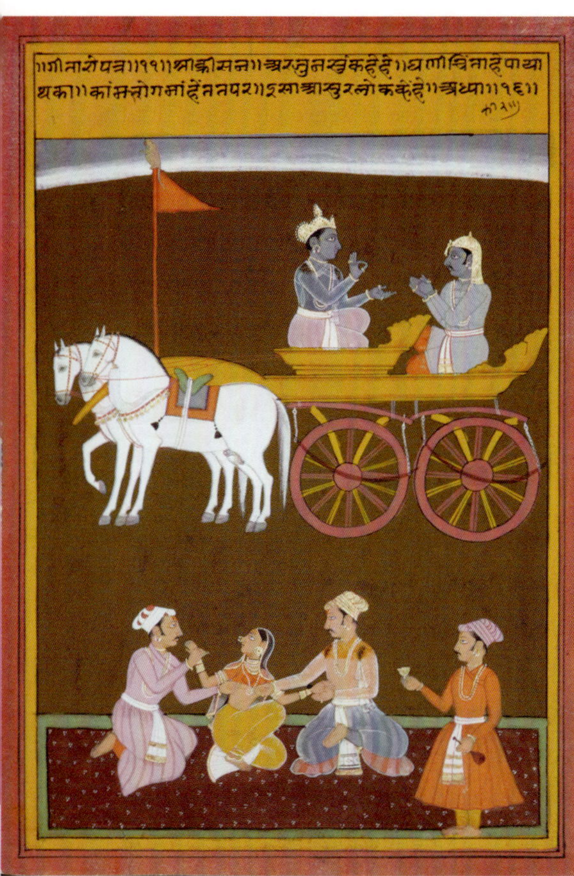

|11| हे अर्जुन! वे मृत्यु तक साथ रहने वाली चिंताओं का आश्रय लेते हैं और विषय भोगों में लगे रहकर 'यही सुख है' इस प्रकार सोचते हैं।

|11| Hey Arjuna! Still anxious at the time of their death, they seek gratification of desire, saying 'this is the only happiness.'

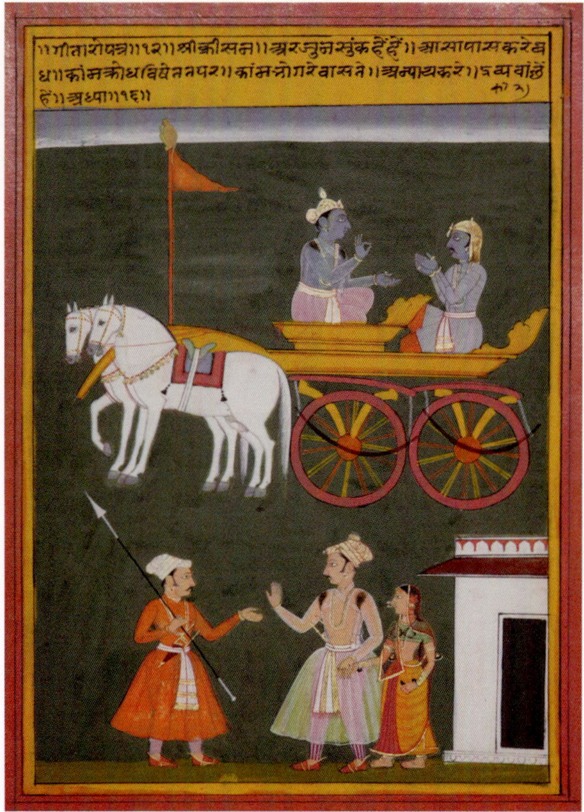

|12| श्री कृष्ण समझाते हुए बोले- वे आशाओं के पाश में फँसे मनुष्य काम-क्रोध के वश में होकर भोगों के लिए अन्यायपूर्वक धनादि पदार्थों का संग्रह करने की चेष्टा करते रहते हैं।

|12| Sri Krishna explains: Caught in the fetters of hope, enslaved by desire-anger, they continue to hoard ill-begotten wealth.

their total disregard for the social and religious authority represented by Krishna and Arjuna, increases our sense of vulnerability. Commenting on verse 9, the *Jnaneshwari* says that men who perform evil deeds are "sunk in the mire of sense pleasures" and "the feeling of respect for heaven and fear of hell have been burnt in them" (2: 188). Looking at these scenes of casual violence, one begins to understand Arjuna's heroic demand that if he must wage war, then it must be on behalf a moral order which will nourish life's worthiness, for only if such a moral order becomes part of the soul can the complex and contradictory call for action at Kurukshetra acquire a tragic dignity.

The contrast between this scene of a common brawl and the quiet certainty of the discourse on the chariot heightens our longing for a society and a time which seriously believes in ahimsa as a moral principle. The scene on the right offers a contrast. It shows charity as a virtue. An aristocrat in his munificence gives alms to a wandering brahmin. Charity, Krishna insists, is a moral quality. It may not be enough to lead to godliness, but it is a step on the path to redemption. Indeed, Krishna never ceases to underscore sacrifice and austerity along with charity. Fearlessness is not the virtue of the warrior alone; it is also that of the renunciant.

The painting for verse 11 is surprisingly dramatic and brutal. The verse is an angry denunciation of those who make the "evil resolution" that in life "the gratification of desire is the highest goal," even if the consequence is death (Swami 83). Painted against a dark brown background, it depicts a criminal scene of abduction and gang rape on a rectangular, crimson carpet with white flowers. The three men are rich, inebriated, and callous. Wealth, they believe, has entitled them to degrade and despoil anyone and anything for their own pleasure. A heavily bejewelled young woman is trying to free herself from the grip of two men who have pushed her down. Her body is twisted as she struggles. Bewildered, she looks around for help and finds the world empty. The men are trying to remove her red choli. What is frightening is the casualness with which they molest her, as if they know they have the time and the leisure. Their unlimited and unchecked power over her is a refutation of our sense that a moral law controls human purposes. The mockery is intensified by the presence of the third man who has just poured a glass of red wine from a flask and is holding it out for others. He is a participant and a witness to the violation. We, as viewers, are offered no relief; Krishna and Arjuna are far removed from the scene. For the artist, it is clear that this act of debasement is an analogue to what was enacted in the Kaurava court when Draupadi was dragged by her hair and dishonoured by the princes in the presence of the learned men of the kingdom; an act which is, to a large measure, responsible for the ferocity of

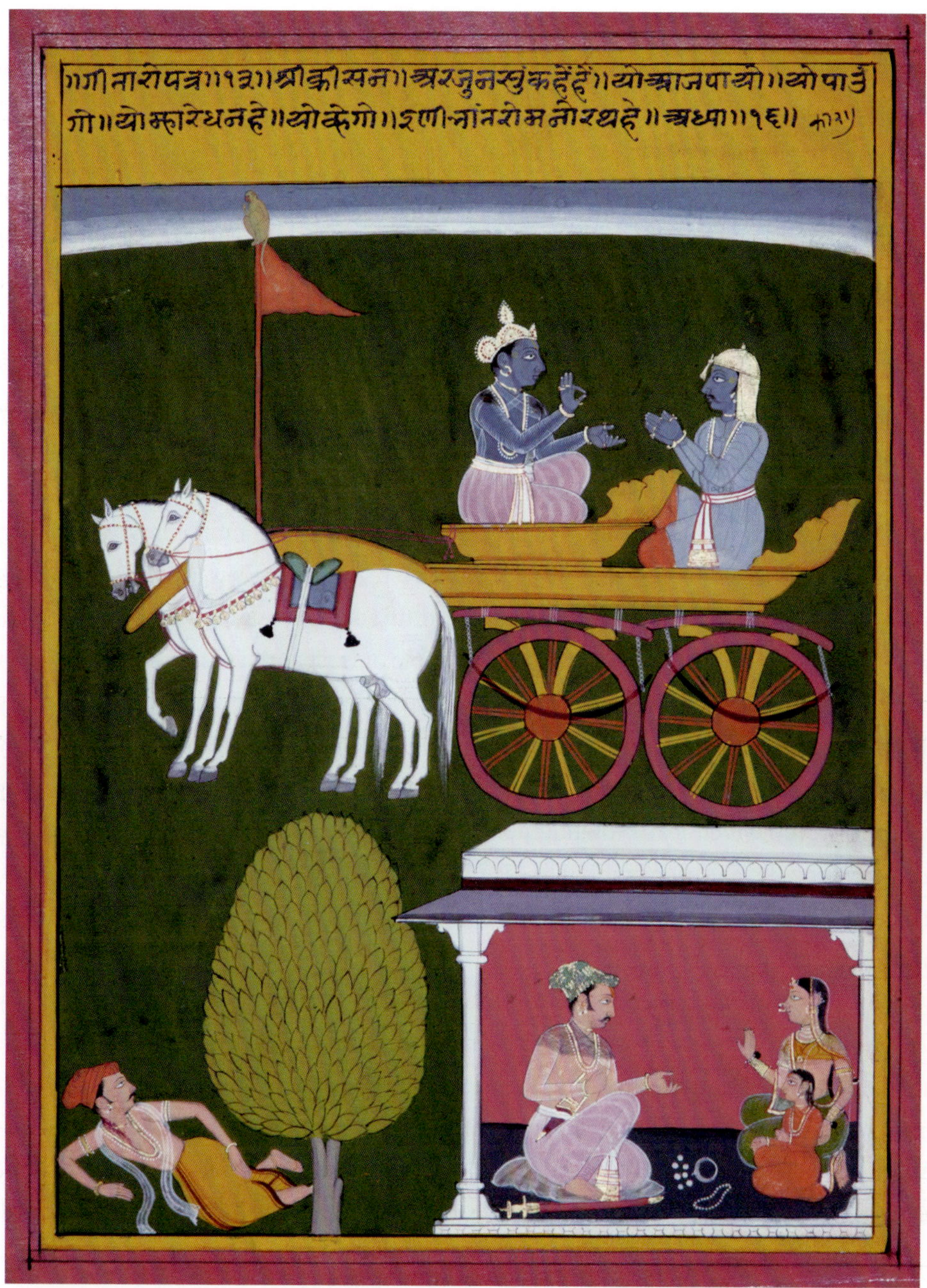

|13| हे अर्जुन! वे सोचा करते हैं कि आज यह पा लिया और शीघ्र ही नए मनोरथ को प्राप्त कर लूँगा। अभी मेरे पास इतना धन है और कल इतना सारा हो जाएगा।

|13| Hey Arjuna! He thinks, I have fulfilled one desire; soon I shall gratify another. Today I have so much wealth; tomorrow I shall have more.

the Kurukshetra war and the relentlessness of Bhima's violence later. Human dignity is fragile. Its preservation requires, this Chapter insists, the courageous working of all the qualities Krishna outlines for the making of a good human being.

Small vignettes of sensual gratification, irresponsible power, theft, pride and self-conceit are the subjects of the paintings for verses 12–18. Each is painted with dramatic verve. Verse 18 begins by condemning power and lust, arrogance and wrath, as wicked, then immediately softens the tone by asserting that divinity dwells in all things, thereby allowing for the possibility of transformative change even in those who are not godly. The visual image for verse 18 which catches one's attention is that of an elegant and ornamentally well-designed axial tree. The blue-bodied god of love, Kama, hides in its rich green leaves and branches. Love, like divinity, has the power of sudden transformation. Kama's presence gives the tree its mythical identity; makes it a place where the sacred and human desires meet for one incandescent moment. We have seen Kama as non-violent, young and mischievous. Here, Kama's arrow, tipped with a pink lotus flower, is tautly drawn and aimed at a youthful couple. His presence is unexpected, and adds to the sexual tension between the couple. It is clear that Allah Baksh does not regard Krishna as a censorious god, but as one who knows how quickly and suddenly desire can be perverted or destroyed. The longing of the couple in this scene is earthly and ordinary. They fulfil some of the qualities Krishna associates with a morally responsible life which leads to enlightenment. A gentle calm and restraint marks the attractive couple. The man is about to eat a rolled beetel leaf for its aphrodisiac qualities. The colours of the woman's clothes are beautifully coordinated: vibrant red, deep-blue and yellow trimmed with gold.

The scene on the other side of the tree is a negation of the eroticism blessed by the god of love. A priest is assaulted by a man with a sword as he kneels to worship a small Shiva lingam under the tree. One of Shiva's attributes is that he brings the world into existence. Therefore, placing a sign representing him under the tree in which Kama resides is understandable. There is, however, no narrative hint in the verse or the painting to explain why the priest is being attacked. He seems harmless and peaceful, simple and regular in his duties—all the qualities, Krishna says, that define a good man. Visually, the assassin's sword duplicates the curve of Kama's bow and occupies the same horizontal space; it is as if one is looking at violence through a dark mirror. One explanation of the scene is that Allah Baksh, reflecting upon his own times, suggests that all acts of violence, especially those against the freedom to love and worship, are arbitrary, casual and meaningless; they dishonour human beings and humiliate the

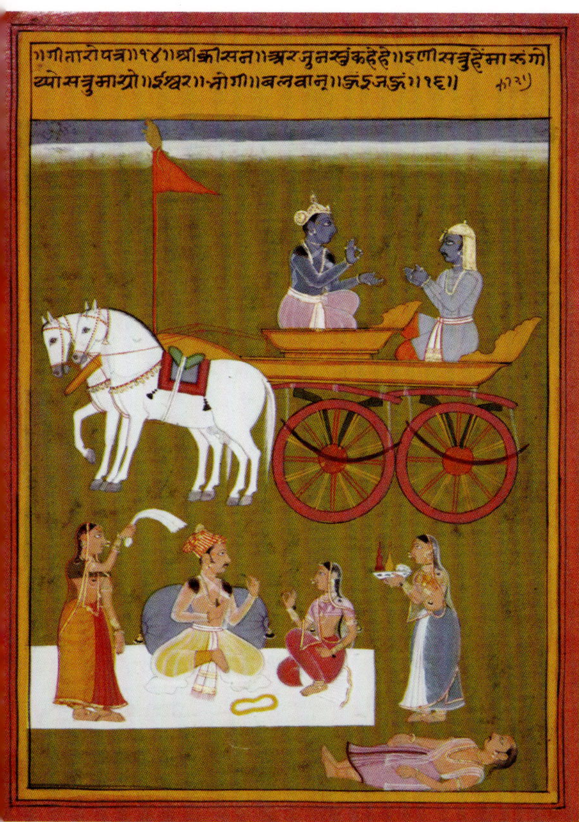

|14| श्री कृष्ण आगे कहने लगे कि वे सोचते हैं कि 'अमुक शत्रु मेरे द्वारा मारा गया। शेष शत्रुओं को भी शीघ्र ही मार गिराऊँगा। मैं ईश्वर हूँ। मैं भोगी हूँ। मैं सिद्ध हूँ, मैं बलवान और सुखी हूँ।'

|14| Sri Krishna further says: They think, 'I have killed one enemy; I shall soon kill other enemies too. I am god. I am happy. I am successful, I am powerful, and at peace.'

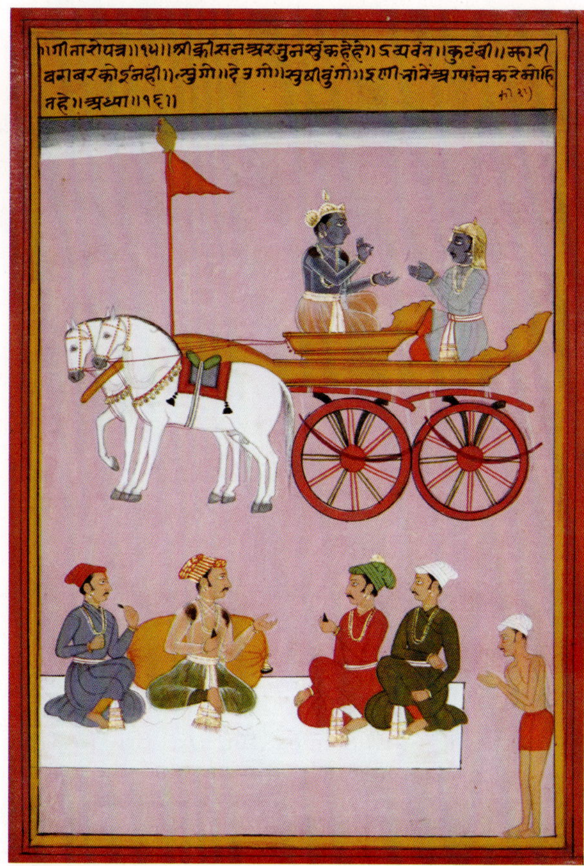

|15| हे अर्जुन! वे सोचते हैं कि 'मैं धनवान और ऊँचे कुल में जन्मा हूँ, मेरे बराबर कौन है? मैं यज्ञ करूँगा, दान करूँगा, आमोद-प्रमोद करूँगा। इस तरह अज्ञान में मोहित हो बातें करते हैं।'

|15| Hey Arjuna! They think, 'I am rich and high-born, who can equal me? I will sacrifice, give in charity, and enjoy myself.' That is how they speak deluded by their ignorance.

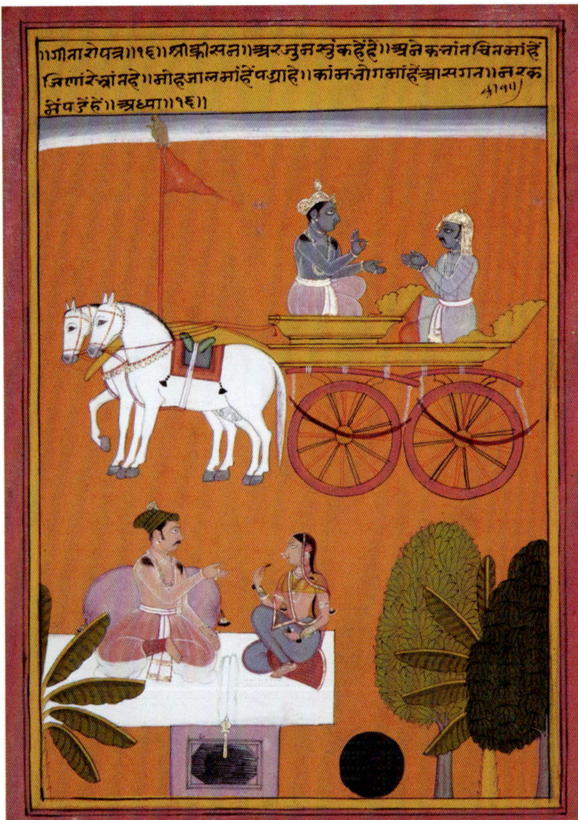

|16| श्री कृष्ण आगे कहने लगे कि जिनके चित्त में अनेक प्रकार के भ्रम हों, वे मोह जाल में फँसकर काम-भोगों में आसक्त हो अपवित्र नरक में जाते हैं।

|16| Sri Krishna further says: Confused by endless thoughts in their minds, caught in the net of delusion, addicted to pleasure, they fall into foul Hell.

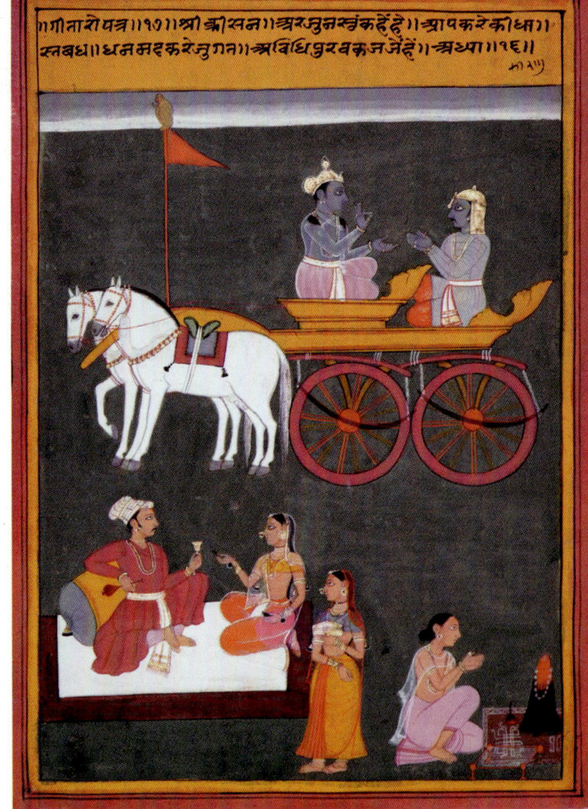

|17| श्री कृष्ण समझाते हुए कहने लगे कि 'वे खुद को श्रेष्ठ मानने वाले दंभी, धन और मान के मद से युक्त हो, पाखंडपूर्वक नाम मात्र के लिए अविधिपूर्वक पूजा करते हैं।'

|17| Explaining further, Sri Krishna says: They are arrogant and think they are the best; drunk with wealth and pride, they offer prayers hypocritically in name only.

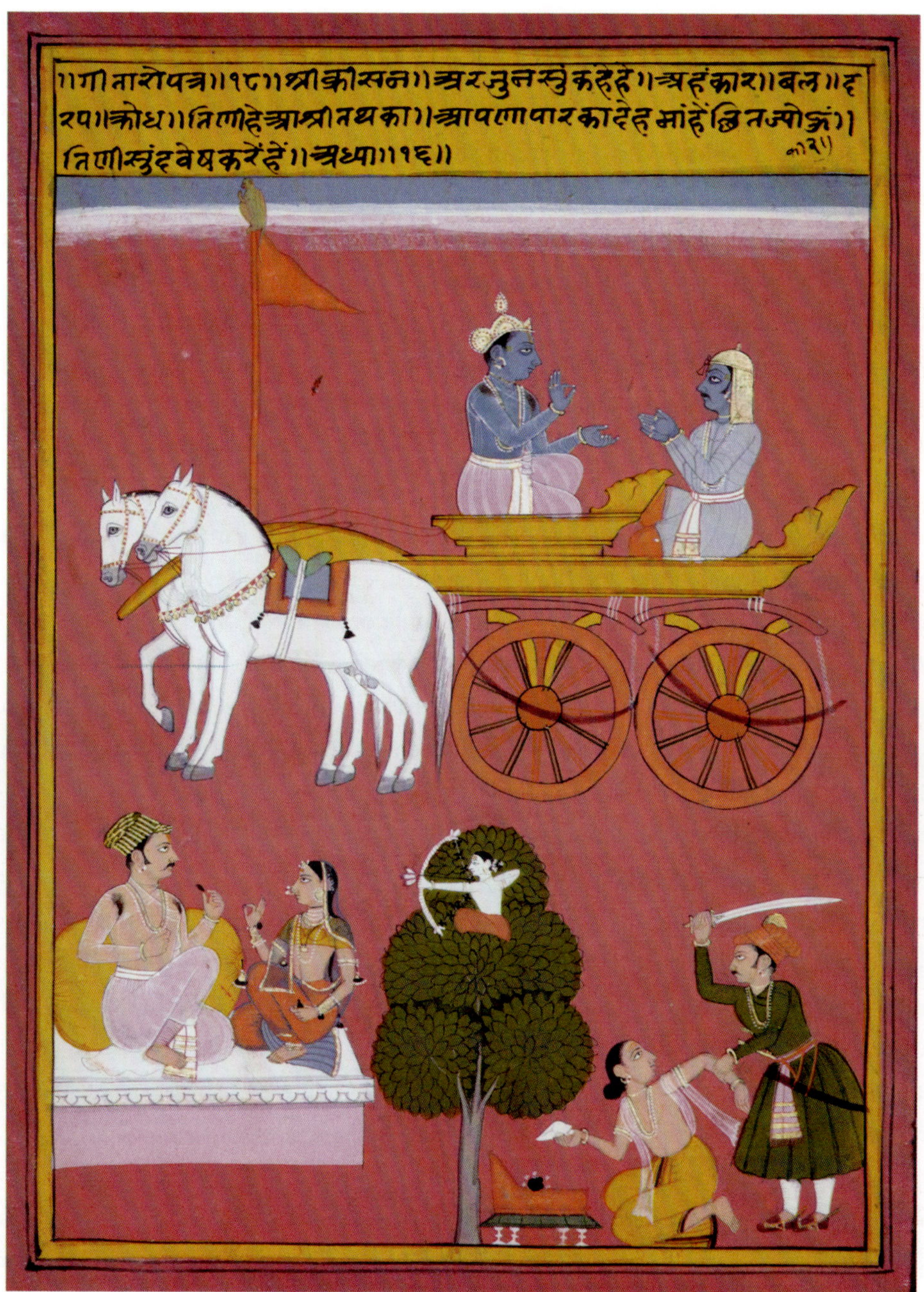

|18| हे अर्जुन! वे अहंकार, बल, दर्प, काम और क्रोध के वश होकर दूसरों की निंदा करने वाले मनुष्य अपनी काया में स्थित परमात्मा से द्वेष करने वाले होते हैं।

|18| Hey Arjuna! These people are arrogant, powerful, full of anger and desire; they they cast aspersions on others, they revile the Supreme Being in their own bodies.

gods. The scene may be an example of what Krishna means when he says that there are many who are so perverted as to want to erase all signs of the divine from the lives of men: “Puffed up by power and inordinate conceit, swayed by lust and wrath, these wicked people hate Me Who am within them, as I am within all” (Swami 83). The emotional effect of the composition is, however, not despondent. Not only does the eye travel back to the lovers and their anticipation, it also transcends the two terrestrial scenes and moves up toward where Krishna and Arjuna are talking in notes of quiet confidence about how to leave behind all that causes sorrow. Thus, viewed under the shadow of the god and the hero, the ordinary happenings on the ground below acquire the character of significant fables of love and war told by great teachers as aids to reflection and action.

In the painting for verse 20, Allah Baksh shows that men who do evil can be metamorphosed into animals. The verse, of course, sanctions such literal transformations into pig-like and donkey-like men—two animals which are archetypes of unrestrained and perverse sexuality in folklore. “Intoxicated with stupidity” (*Jnaneshwari* 2: 193), they are trapped within black circles which are also the entrances to hell described by Krishna. These circles are painted against the background of parched earth—brown and eternally barren. Such darkness should arouse a loathing of sin and fill one with terror at the thought of hell (*Jnaneshwari* 2: 195).

The painting for verses 22 also depicts the three “gates of hell…lust, wrath and avarice” (Swami 84) as black and opaque circles. While in the painting for verse 20, the demonic figures have fallen into the gates of hell, the figures in painting for verse 22 are shown sitting outside the opaque circles as warnings to men to avoid the promptings of passion for their own welfare and liberation (Swami 84). In the painting, Kama, with his arrow of flowers, keeps guard at the edge of one of the circles. The sun lights up the earth in the painting for verse 22 so that, as Krishna says, human beings can consciously follow him and avoid suffering.

Verse 24 ends on a note of profound tranquillity persuading us to turn back to the beginning of the chapter and consider again all the qualities that should guide action. Krishna gives to these virtues a collective name: “the light of the scriptures” (Swami 84). The painting shows two learned men reading the *Ramayana* as they sit on a white platform below the Krishna’s chariot. The two images, read together, take us on a vast intellectual journey, from Valmiki’s question about who is a good man at the turning point of *satya yuga* to Krishna’s *Gita* told just before the world slides away into our age of untruth, ignorance and violence.

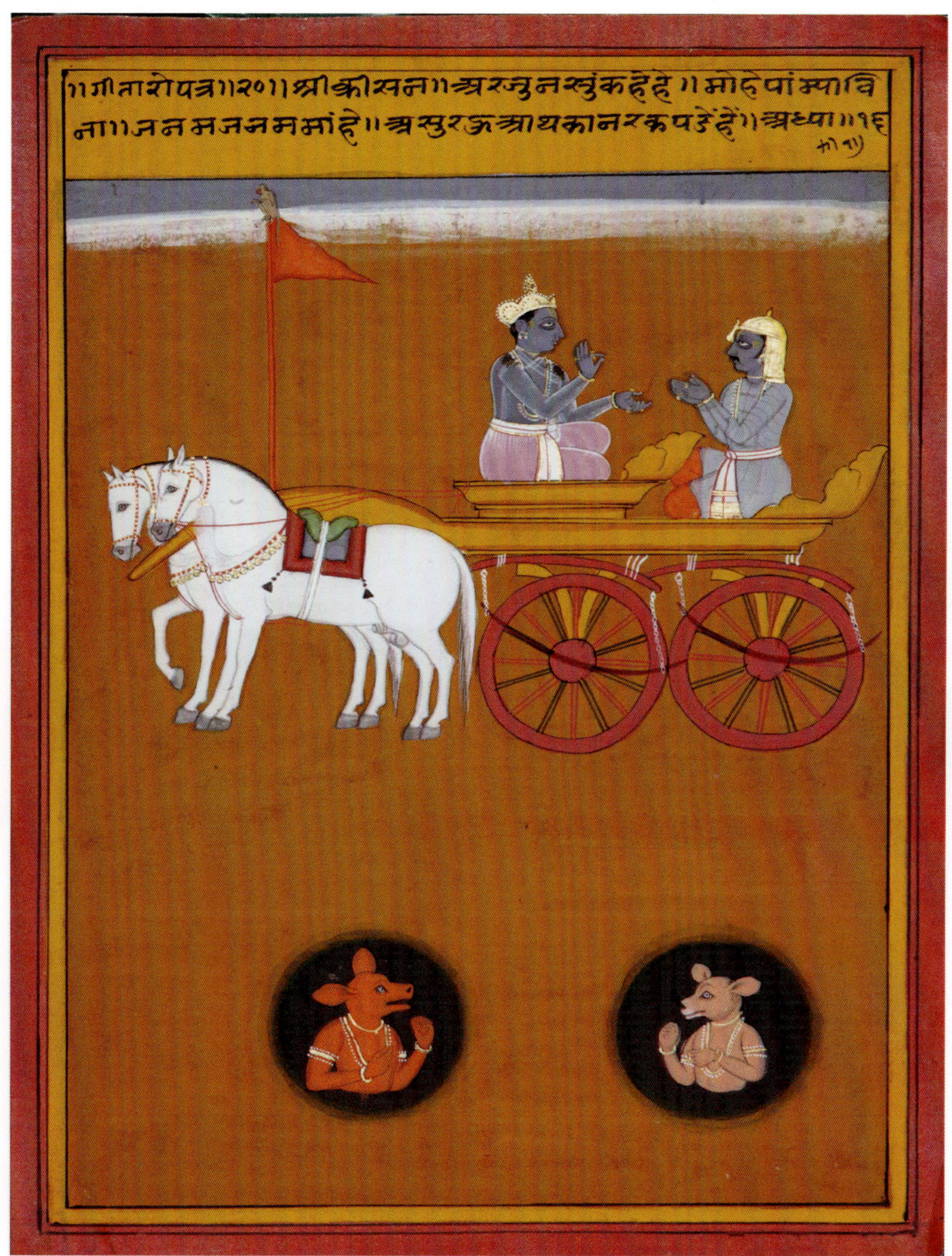

|20| श्री कृष्ण आगे कहने लगे कि- 'वे मूढ़ मुझको न प्राप्त होकर जन्म-जन्मांतरों तक आसुरी योनि को प्राप्त होते हैं और फिर उससे भी नीच गति पाकर नरक में पड़ते हैं।'

|20| Sri Krishna further says: These hateful people, failing to reach me, are born again and again from a demonic womb and descend further into hell.

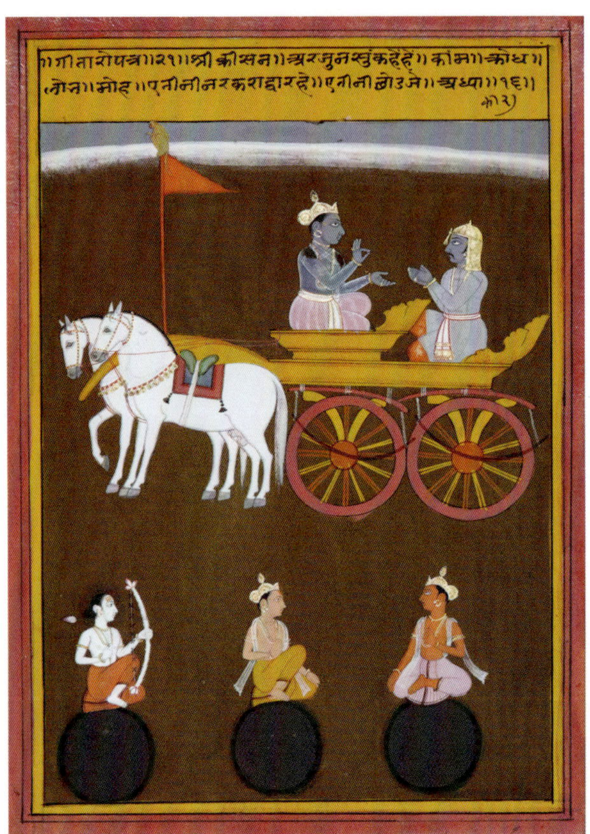

|21| हे अर्जुन! काम, क्रोध और लोभ- ये तीनों आत्मा का नाश करने वाले नरक के द्वार कहे गए हैं। अत: इन तीनों का तू परित्याग कर!

|21| Hey Arjuna! Lust, anger and greed are the three gates of Hell. You must avoid all three.

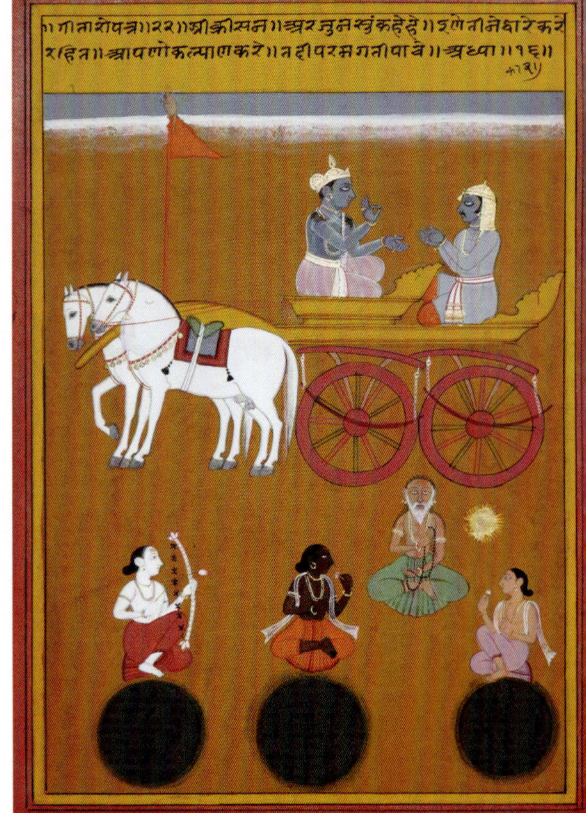

|22| श्री कृष्ण आगे कहने लगे कि यदि नरक के तीनों द्वारों से मुक्त हुआ पुरुष आत्म कल्याण का आचरण करता है तो वह परमगति को प्राप्त होता है!

|22| Sri Krishna further says: The one who avoids all the three gates and practises what is best for him follows the supreme path.

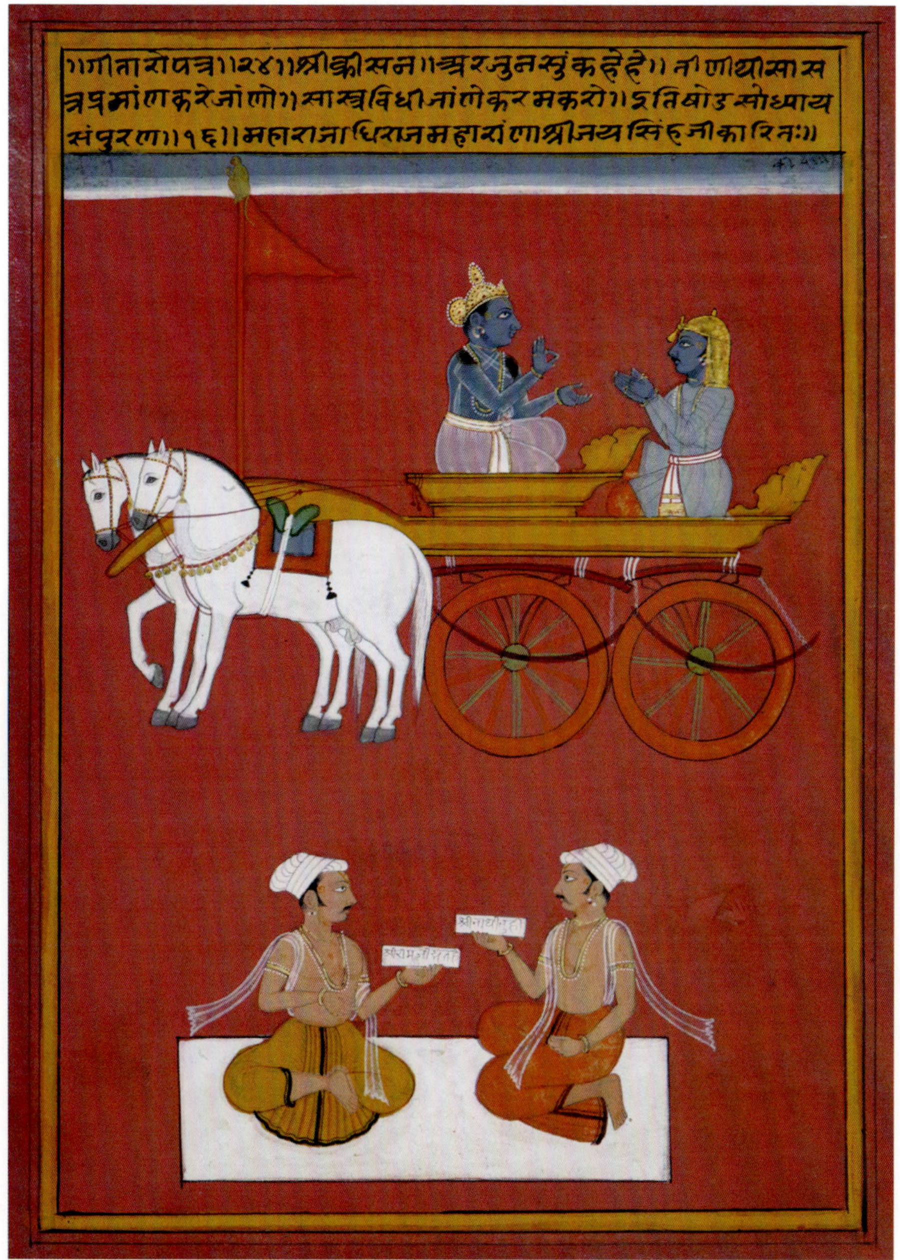

|24| श्री कृष्ण समझाते हुए कहने लगे, हे अर्जुन! कर्तव्य और अकर्तव्य के न्याय के लिए शास्त्र ही प्रमाण है। ऐसा जानकर शास्त्रविधि के अनुसार ही कर्म कर!

|24| Explaining further Sri Krishna says: Hey Arjuna! In judging what to do or not to do, the scriptures are the best guide. Know this and act according to the norms of tradition.

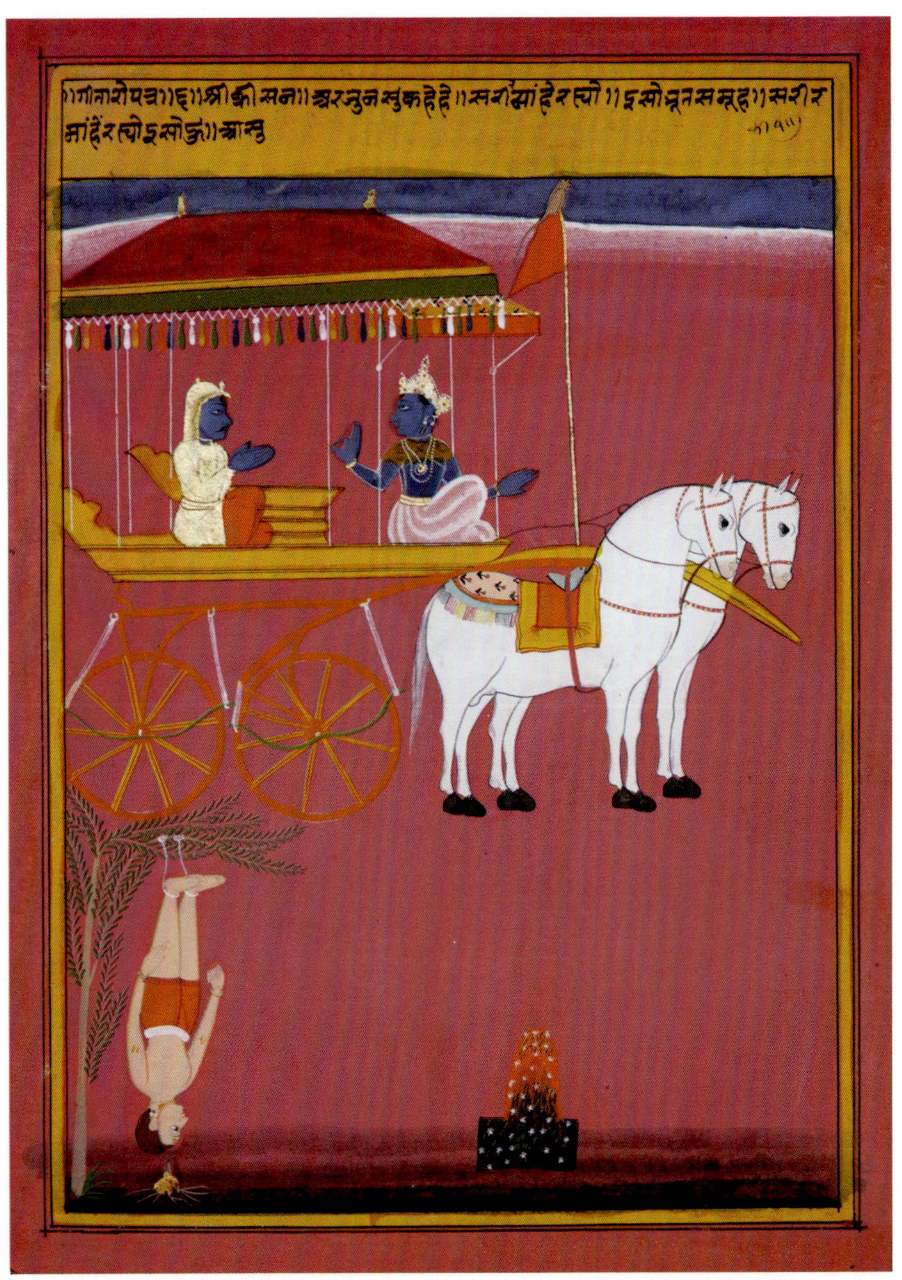

|6| हे अर्जुन! जो अज्ञानी पुरुष शरीर में स्थित भूत-समुदाय को तथा शरीर में स्थित मुझ परमात्मा को भी कष्ट पहुँचाते हैं, उन्हें तू आसुरी स्वभाव वाला जान।

|6| Hey Arjuna! You should know that those who are ignorant, torment their body and hurt even me, the Supreme Being, who lives within. They are demonic in nature.

CHAPTER 17

Allah Baksh must have painted all the twenty-eight verses of this chapter. Unfortunately, we have found only the painting for verse 6. The chapter begins with Arjuna's question about the spiritual status of one who does not know the scriptures but has faith. The question emerges from Krishna's earlier insistence that a man looking for the path to the gate of paradise should follow the authority of the Shastra. According to Gandhi, the Shastra for Krishna is not a set of religious texts or rites, but "the conduct of the worthy" which is marked by "selfless work" on behalf of others and the welfare of the earth (Desai 351). Gandhi interprets the word 'Shastra' in a more inclusive, humane and generous manner than Radhakrishnan who translates it, in conformity with brahmanical orthodoxy, as 'scripture.'[1] Arjuna's question is about those who have ethical merit and intelligence but cannot comprehend the scriptures: "Tell me what the condition of such men will be, whether it will be of goodness, passion or darkness" (*Jnaneshwari* 2:201)? Swami Ramakrishna, when asked about what Shastra he followed, replied, "I follow no particular *Sastra* whatever. I plead with the Deity residing in my heart for directions, and I act and live as I am guided by that Being."[2]

Earlier, Krishna had remarked that people worship according to their faith, nature and desires. How should one regard, Arjuna asks in the first few verses of Chapter 17, those "who do acts of sacrifice" (Swami 85) and are earnestly devoted to their ancestors, but ignore the scriptures or neglect the divine? Krishna responds by repeating the careful discrimination he had made earlier between worship and action undertaken in the purity of spirit without longing for gain, or for what the self desires. The first is the pilgrim-path to paradise, the second to earthly success but not wisdom, and the third to the dark realms of evil. His emphasis is on those acts of selflessness, non-violence, truthfulness and charity which result in the imaginative and productive good of the world. Gandhi gathers all these qualities under the sign *dakshina* (charity and gift-giving), offered to anyone in need and for any cause which will banish the shadows of evil and make space for the light of reason and virtue. He, rightly, disregards the

---

1 Radhakrishnan, *The Bhagavadgita*, p. 403.

2 Quote by Swami Chidbhavananda, *The Bhagavad Gita*, pp. 803-804.

usual interpretation of the word *dakshina* which calls for the giving of alms, gifts or fees to the priests for conducting traditional and orthodox rituals (Desai 351-355). The act of charity, however small, if performed sincerely, according to the capacity of each person, and without any expectation of return, is sufficient. It can spread from person to person, like expanding circles in a lake, till it seeps through the entire society. The *Jnaneshwari* invokes a different metaphor to explain this further: "If with great efforts one man lights a lamp and another lights his lamp [from the first flame], would [the second man's flame] be less effective in giving light" (2: 206)?

In verses 5 and 6, Krishna says that the prayers and rites of proud men in search of profit cause injury and spread darkness. He is harsh on ascetics who torment their bodies in their zeal for sacrifice. Since the body is divine, by tormenting it they torment him. Allah Baksh responds to Krishna's anguish with a bleak painting. The background is an uncomfortable vermillion, a colour that spreads across the sky before sunset as a premonition of violent storms. Krishna's chariot is covered with a festive red canopy festooned with colourful tassels. A fragile tree with sharp needle-like leaves grows in the left corner. A bare-chested ascetic hangs upside down from a thin branch. His feet are tied with ropes, his hands are held close by the side of his body. A small fire burns under his head. The *Jnaneshwari* with scathing distaste says that men perform such austerities only to win praise and become objects of pilgrimage for the ignorant. Sometimes such severe penances cause hallucinations which are mistaken for visions of god. These evil practices, according to Krishna, lead to the desolation of knowledge. An altar fire burns unattended in the middle of the painting and away from the man hanging from the trees. It adds to the sense of bewilderment at the folly of one who regards his body as an enemy (*Jnaneshwari* 2:217). The overwhelming silence of the scene is unnerving. It is not the silence of self-restraint or of the quiet meditation Krishna celebrates in the last resonant verses (from 24 to 28) of the chapter. However morally complex an action is, Krishna insists, summarising his argument, it will lead to spiritual liberation only if it is undertaken in the threefold name of the Supreme Being—*Aum Tat Sat.*

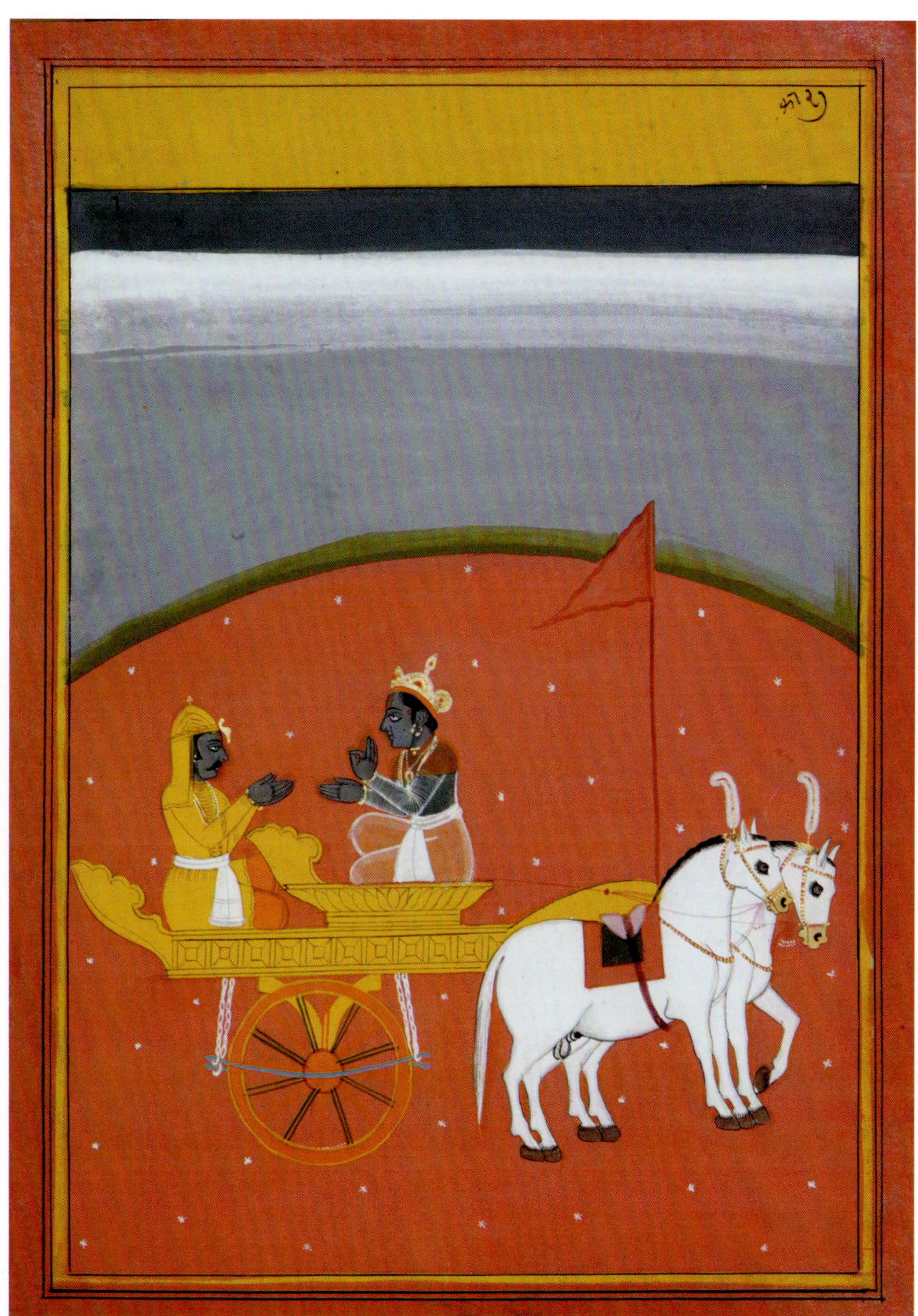

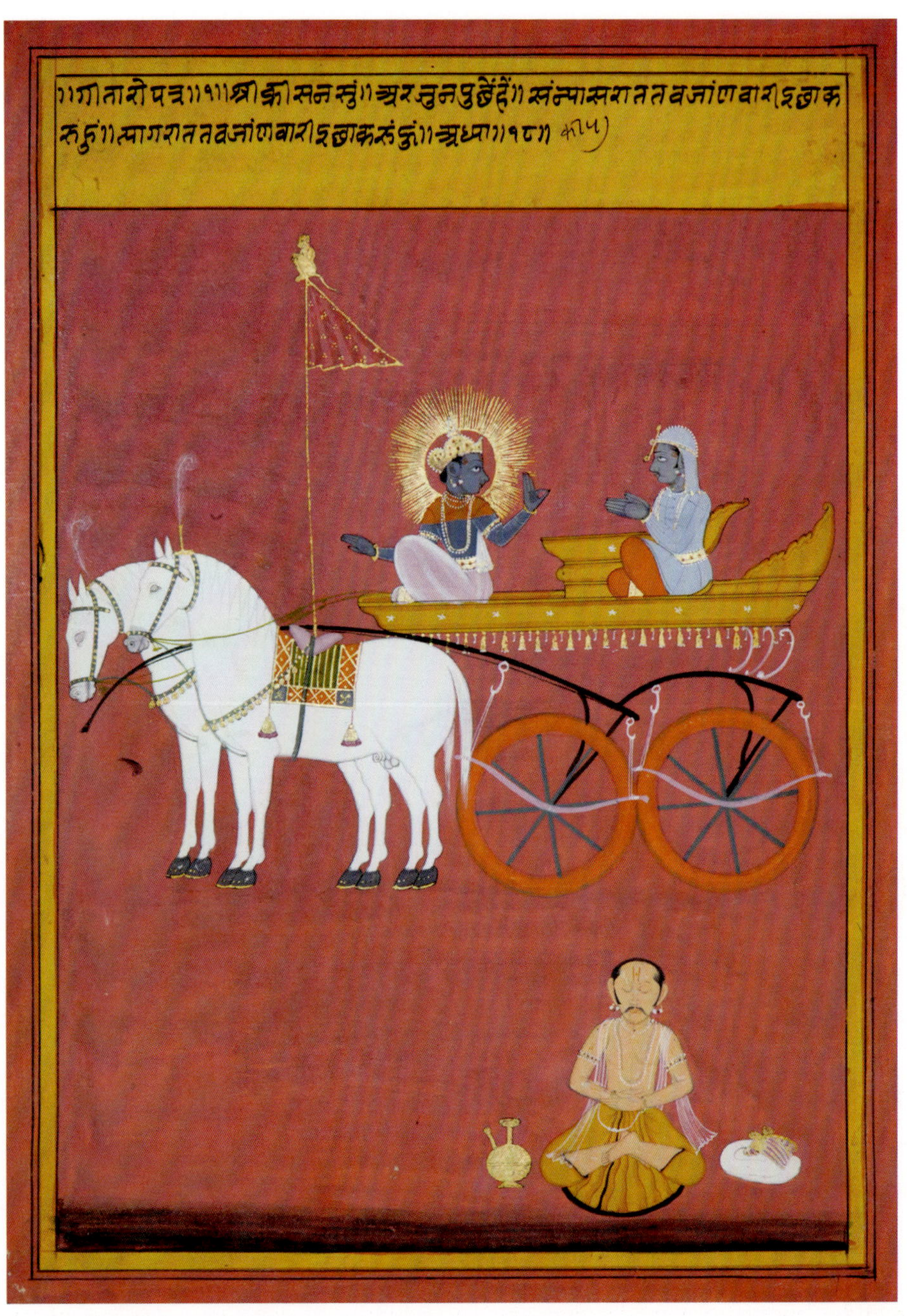

|1| अर्जुन अन्ततः पूछने लगा, हे कृष्ण! मुझे संन्यास के तत्व जानने की इच्छा है और मैं त्याग के तत्व को भी अलग से जानना चाहता हूँ।

|1| Arjuna asks: Hey Krishna! I want to know how to distinguish between relinquishing the world and renouncing it.

CHAPTER 18

The last chapter of the *Gita* is also the longest. Reading the *Gita* as a moral journey, the *Jnaneshwari* says that the final chapter completes the song in the same way as a jewel on the pinnacle of a temple offers a vision of the god within. The chapter is a lyric summation of what Krishna calls a "spiritual discourse" (Swami 94). He now reveals "the Truth, the Mystery of mysteries...the deepest secret of all" to Arjuna (Swami 93). The discussion is about the distinction between renunciation of action and the giving up of the fruit of action. Arjuna asks about the distinction between *sanyasa* and *tyaga* for the last time. His tone is not anguished; he only wants to reassure himself, before taking the momentous decision to act, that he has clearly understood the knowledge that has been revealed to him because it also burdens him with a terrible spiritual and moral responsibility. He knows that he will have to fight; he cannot stop the war. Will Krishna's moral presence, however, ensure that war's spirit of eternal negation does not become part of his being? Having been touched by what is utterly abhorrent, will he ever be healed again? He asks these questions because he is moved by compassion and humility.

Appropriately, the illustrations for verses 1-6 show Arjuna sitting quietly with his hands folded like a devout listener before a resplendent Krishna. Arjuna is wearing his armour, but carries no weapons. He has always known his duty. Does he now feel reassured that when he acts no sin shall accrue to him; that there will, finally, be mercy if he sacrifices the narcissism of power and the conceit of victory? Despite the *Gita*, and like all great books of war, the *Mahabharata* continues to be a text of lamentation; it leaves us wondering if the knowledge of the terrible violence at Kurukshetra will ever be forgotten; if there will ever be any consolation? Once the self has been scarred by the violence of war, it can never be healed; the memory of pain cannot be erased.

Krishna has yet not picked up the reins of the horses (painting for verse 1). An incandescent halo of golden light encircles his head like the persistence of truth, intelligence and goodness even as the forces of the irrational threaten the world. As he turns to Arjuna, he holds up his left hand offering him the solace of his own presence. In spite of the calm poise of the two, there are enough visual indications to show that war is close at hand. Arjuna is wearing his helmet and armour of metal chain. The horses are restless. Hanuman gazes toward the western horizon. Mythically, the path to the west leads to life, time, experience, conflict and suffering; it is a necessary journey. War will have to be fought to save dharma. However, for the moment, there is time and space for quiet and intelligent listening. Arjuna's decision has been deferred for a while.

The painting for verse 1 creates a meditative space where moral teaching can be considered in its complexity without social, political, emotional and ritual distractions. An ascetic sits unperturbed on the same brick-red ground as Krishna. Is he an earthly and historical analogue of Arjuna, a soul-warrior, and as fearless? His eyes are closed. His hands rest on his lap. Two vertical ochre marks on his forehead identify him as a Vaishnavite brahmin. The golden-yellow of his dhoti is in harmony with the colour of Krishna's chariot, the light of the sun and the colophon. These images, together with the verse, create a sense that beauty and divinity interfuses all things in heaven and on earth. Paradoxically, it is the beauty of these images which makes us think again about what is not being painted: the tragedy of war and impossibility of peace; violent action which debases and distorts dharma; and, the refusal to act which will leave the world at the mercy of irresponsible power, devouring ambition and brute ignorance.

As if to democratise knowledge, the painter shows that the ascetic has taken off his turban and placed it on the ground, thereby sacrificing at least a part of his caste and sectarian identity. A man who can do that in a hierarchical society has begun the process of fundamental change in a tradition where so much of power depends upon external symbols of wealth and status; superfluities, Krishna would call them, which veil the eyes with illusions. To see clearly and know the truth, Krishna tells Arjuna, again and again, put aside fabricated ideas and opinions (fabricated, therefore, artificial). Hence, Krishna is also saying, be a maker of your own destiny, your own fable but do that under the sign of heaven or dharma. Reading the *Gita* in the context of the *Mahabharata*, one must remember that there are only a few wise and morally fearless men in the epic, like Vidura and Yuyutsu, who resist the irrationality of power; their social position is ambiguous. They survive the war and suffer, but are honoured.

The ascetic is like Sanjaya, a privileged listener to Krishna's philosophical discussion. Given the silence and the emptiness around him, we realise that he is the imaginative equivalent of Sanjaya. He is an intelligent man who is debating with himself: Should he become an anchorite or seek salvation in the world where ideas and ambitions jostle with each other in perpetual contradiction? He is distinct from Dhritarashtra, who continues to be obtuse even after having heard the entire *Gita* from Sanjaya. The moment Krishna ceases to speak, Dhritarashtra's concern is not with how he should

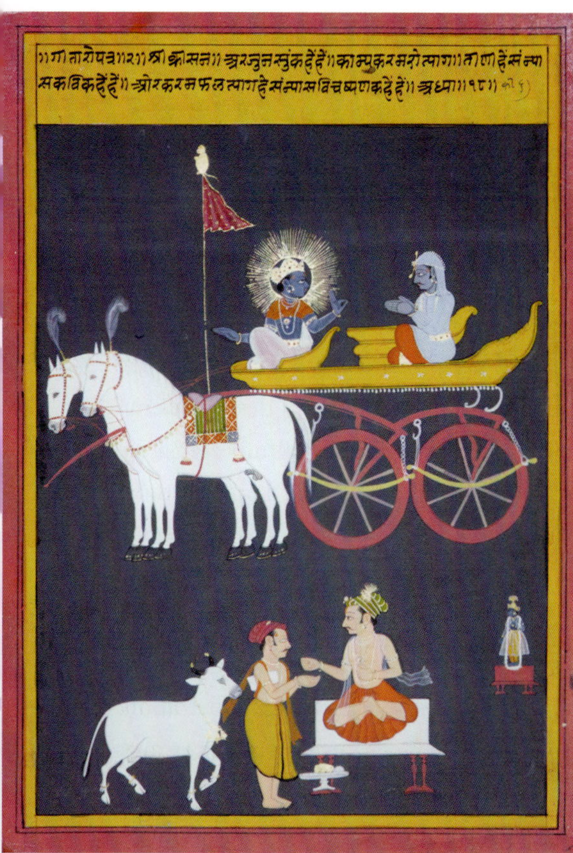

|2| श्री कृष्ण जवाब देते हुए बोले कि हे अर्जुन! कई पंडित काम्य कर्मों के त्याग को संन्यास कहते हैं और कई विद्वान सम्पूर्ण कर्मफलों के त्याग को संन्यास कहते हैं।

|2| Sri Krishna answers: Hey Arjuna! Some sages say that giving up action based on desire is renunciation, while many others say that giving up the fruit of action is renunciation.

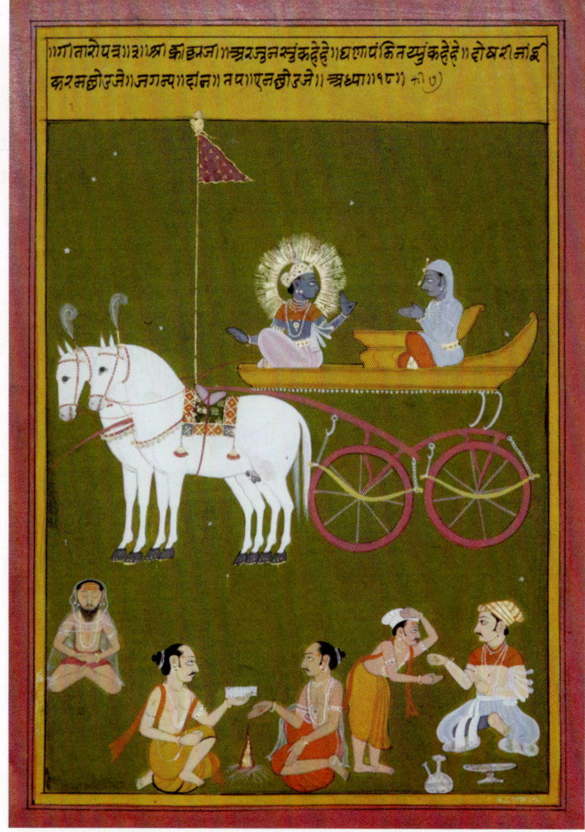

|3| श्री कृष्ण आगे कहने लगे कि कुछ विद्वान कहते हैं कि सभी कर्म दोषयुक्त हैं इसलिए त्याग देने योग्य हैं और कुछ विद्वान कहते हैं कि यज्ञ, दान और तप जैसे कर्म त्यागने योग्य नहीं हैं।

|3| Sri Krishna further says: Some sages say all action is evil and must be given up and others say actions like sacrifice, charity and austerity should not be given up.

act with wisdom, but with the deployment of the armies of the Kauravas and victory. Nothing can renew his spiritual and moral decrepitude, or persuade him to look beyond his obsession with his family and kingdom. In contrast, the *Jnaneshwari* imagines the moment when Arjuna tells Krishna that he is now ready to follow his teachings: "the Lord began to dance with joy. He said, Arjuna has become the fruit of the tree of the universe which is Myself" (2:336).

Writing about this chapter, Mahatma Gandhi says that the knowledge imparted need not be complicated by the subtleties of samkhya (Desai 364). Act, because act one must; act with wisdom; act out of goodwill and benevolence on behalf of all that is good and just. But act without vanity and greed, without passion and desire for any personal reward. Those who are obstinate like Dhritarashtra or who wilfully refuse to understand and recognise the virtue of disinterested action which duty demands only degrade life.

Commenting on verse 2, the *Jnaneshwari* says: all that is required to dispel the night of ignorance is to light a simple lamp (2: 341). Action need not be grand or heroic. In order to clear the path to paradise, action may be as small as giving alms to a wandering scholar or treating an animal with mercy. Appropriately, the illustration for verse 2 shows a noble man sitting with poise on a white platform giving alms to a priest holding a scriptural text under his right arm (see also painting for verse 3). There is humility and courtesy on the faces of both. A delicately painted white cow (a symbol of unselfconscious innocence) stands anxiously behind the priest. With golden bells around its neck and gold-tipped horns, it has walked into the painting's frame from folktales and songs about Krishna. Its presence is neither unexpected nor surprising. Given the discussion about right action, it is significant that the nobleman is not facing the small, pale blue idol of Krishna on the right. What makes the idol visible is the garland of white flowers around its neck. Is the painter suggesting that a karma yogi who practises charity has priority over one who offers ritual worship to idols?

The images of giving, acquiring knowledge and austerity painted for verses 4 and 5 signify acts of sacrifice unblemished by greed. This idea is visually reaffirmed in the painting for verse 10 which shows a priest praying to an idol of Krishna holding a pink lotus flower. Is the painter suggesting that those who venerate Krishna should acquire knowledge and act selflessly instead of assuming that grace will be granted to anyone who sits before his image? For, daily rites before Krishna's idol maybe tainted by lazy routines and selfish desires for earthly gain.

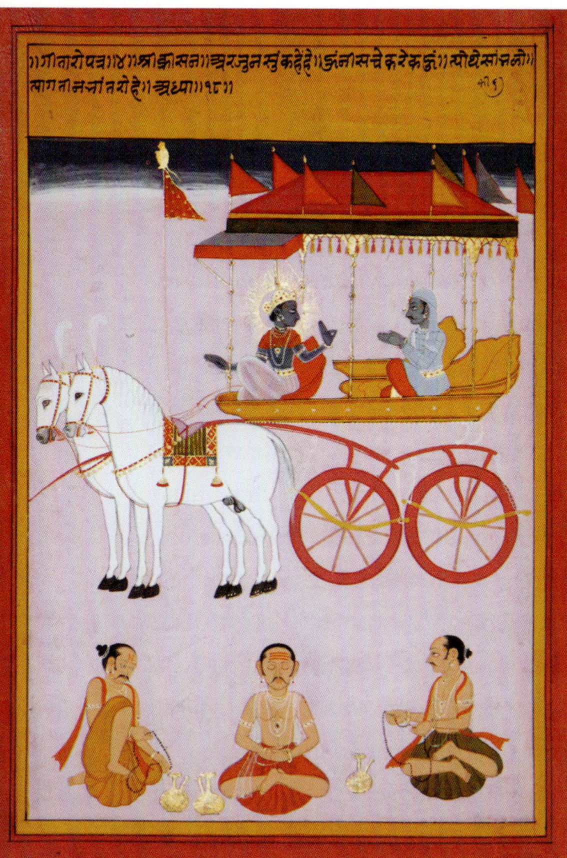

|4| हे अर्जुन! अब त्याग के विषय में मेरा निश्चय सुन। यह त्याग तीन प्रकार का कहा गया है।

|4| Hey Arjuna! Now listen to what I think about relinquishing. There are three kinds of relinquishments.

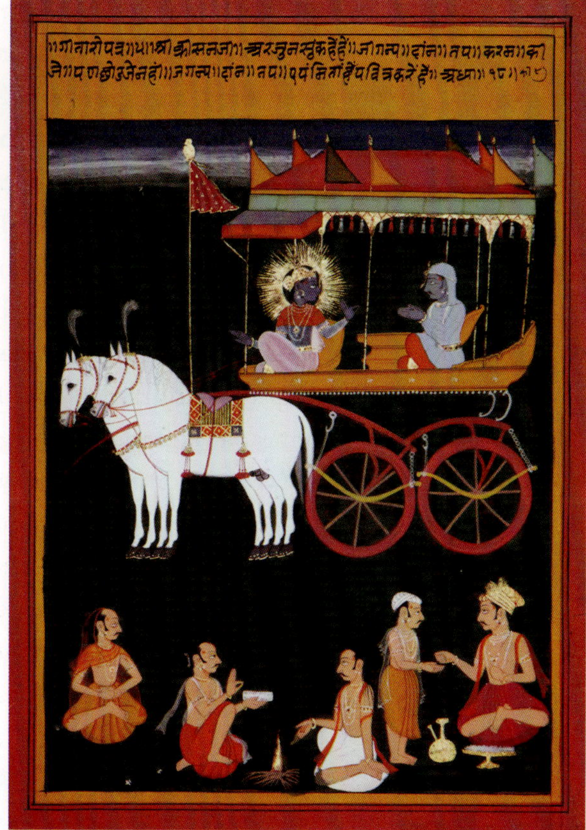

|5| श्री कृष्ण आगे खुलासा करते हुए कहने लगे कि यज्ञ, दान और तप ये त्यागने योग्य नहीं हैं; इन्हें तो करते रहना चाहिए, ये तीनों ही कर्म पवित्र करने वाले हैं।

|5| Explaining further Sri Krishna says: Sacrifice, charity and austerity must not be given up; they must be performed; all three are purifying.

The contrast between the priest's posture and Arjuna's in the painting for verse 11 is striking. While Arjuna sits with humility before Krishna; the priest is arrogant. The painter is careful to depict the priest as physically larger than the idol. Bodily proportions in a work of art, as a text like *Vishnudharmottara* emphasises, carry ethical judgments. When the painter's god is remote, powerful and judgemental, as in Michelangelo's Sistine Chapel, man is reduced in size and gazes up to the heavens for benediction. But, when a painter thinks that god often walks the earth looking for someone who is unselfconsciously good, then his god is as familiar as in Botticelli's drawings for Dante's *Divine Comedy*, the nativity paintings of Fra Della Francesca or Blake's *Songs of Innocence*.

Keeping in mind the painter's idea that the *Gita* is, and ought always to be, accessible to the non-scholarly seeker, the visual spaces in the paintings for verses 6, 7 and 8 are inhabited by a variety of fakirs, pundits and worshippers of fire, water, wind, sun, Shiva and Krishna, thereby expanding the visual lexicon of gods and sects. None of them is painted to suggest that they are more exalted, powerful or knowledgeable than anyone else. They are clad in simple dhotis and are bare-chested. They have no caste marks or necklaces of pearls. One sits on tiger skin, another gazes at a ritual fire, one has matted hair and an ash-smeared body, another gazes at a grove of gorgeous trees. They either live in the simplest of thatch huts as in the painting for verse 6, or in open spaces unmarked by social status in the illustrations for verses 7, 8 and 9, or near a lake's shore waiting to worship the morning sun as in the painting for verse 11, or at the mercy of night winds while offering prayers (in the painting for verses 14). They make no claim to a unique revelation nor ask for any special benediction. Their desires are simple and elemental; their gestures are correspondingly unaggressive and non-threatening. They may not have achieved liberation from the cycle of time and suffering, but they are, as the paintings make sharply clear, not hypnotised by *tamasic* passions.

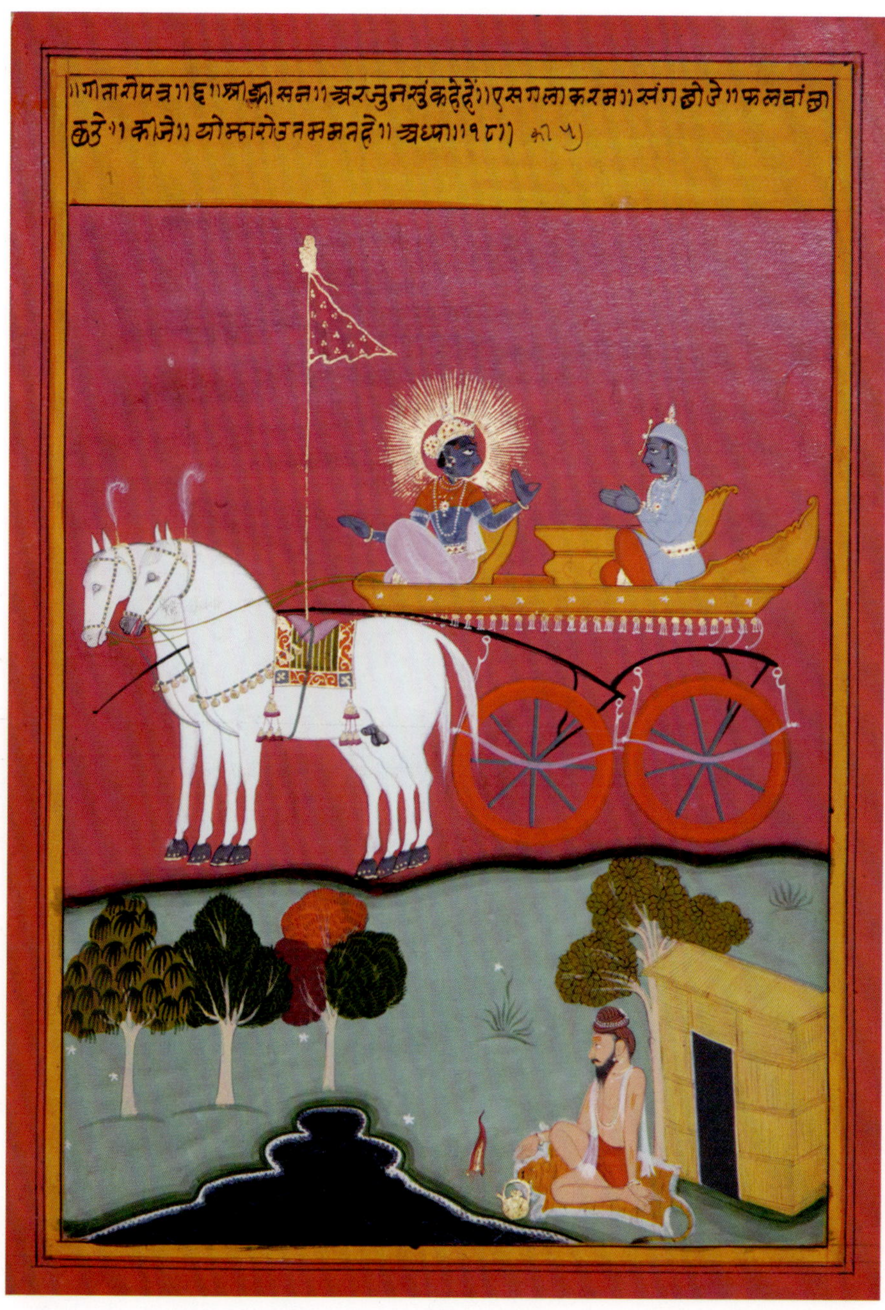

|6| हे अर्जुन! पर इन तीनों कर्मों को तथा अन्य कर्तव्य-कर्मों को आसक्ति और फल का त्याग करके करना चाहिए। यह मेरा मत है।

|6| Hey Arjuna! But these three actions must be performed with detachment; the fruit of such actions must be renounced. That is my firm belief.

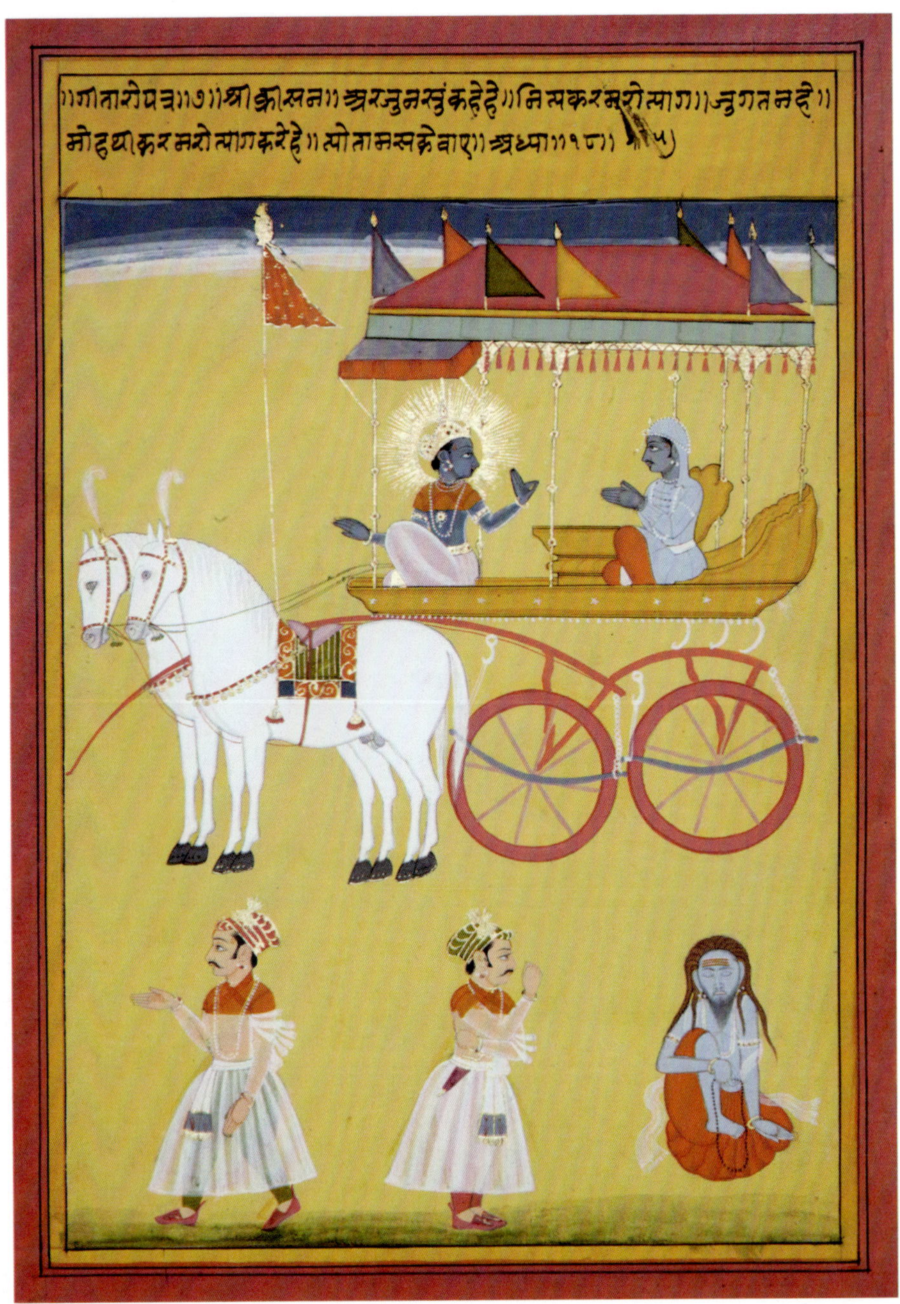

|7| हे अर्जुन ! परन्तु नियत कर्म (शास्त्रोक्त) का त्याग करना उचित नहीं है। इसलिए मोहवश उनका त्याग कर देना तामस त्याग कहा गया है।

|7| Hey Arjuna! It is not right to give up actions which are obligatory. That is why it is said that giving them up is a result of dark inertia.

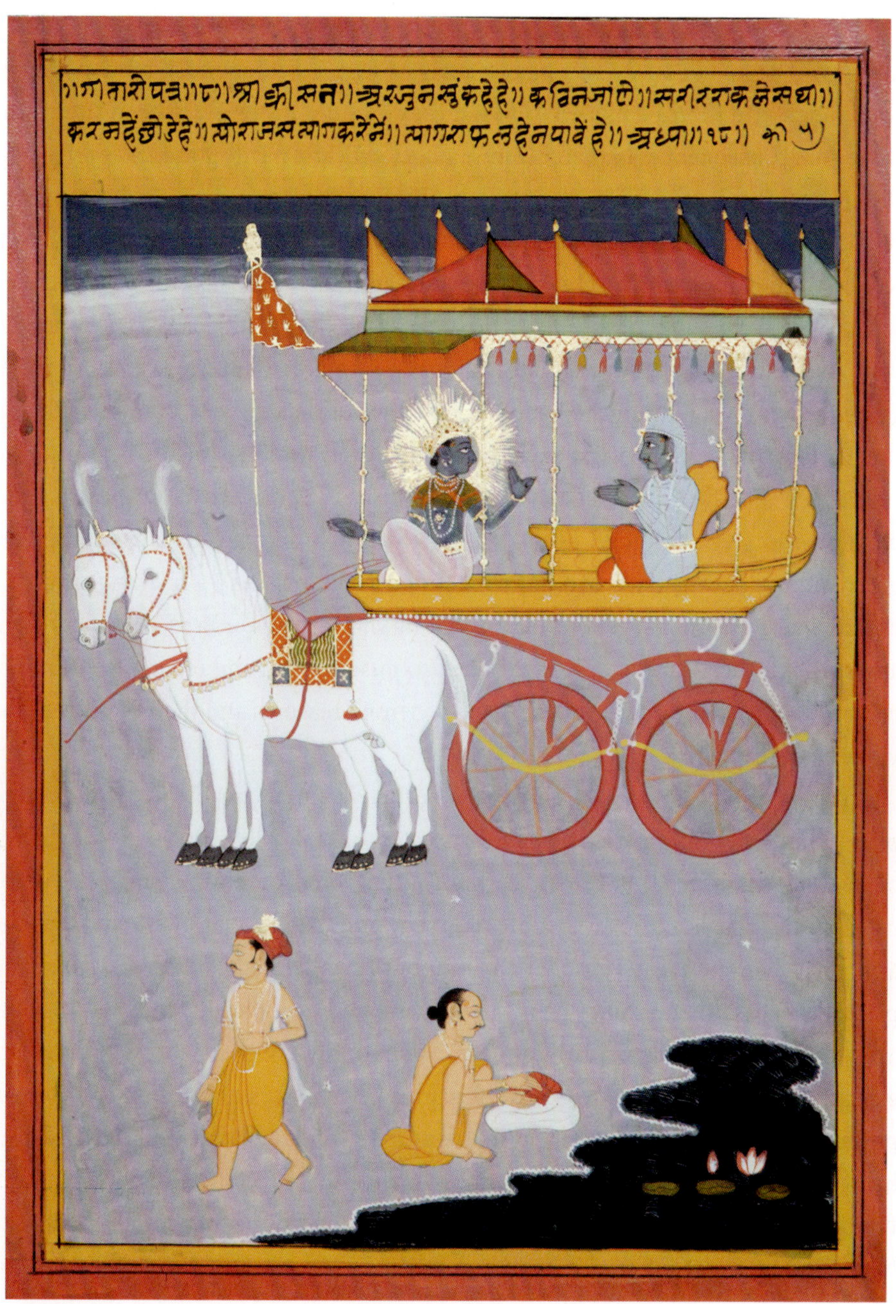

|8| हे अर्जुन! और कर्मों को दुखमय जानकर शारीरिक क्लेश के डर से उनका त्याग करने वाला मनुष्य, राजस त्याग को करके भी त्याग के फल को प्राप्त नहीं होता।

|8| Hey Arjuna! The one who renounces action for fear of physical pain acts out of passion; he will gain nothing from such renunciation.

Krishna, in verse 12, compassionately recognises that most human beings cannot cease to desire completely. What they can do, however, is be aware of the three-fold consequences of their desires: "good, evil, and partly good and partly evil" (Swami 89). The painting for verse 12 stages three scenes from common life to clarify the idea that every action invariably has some moral significance. In keeping with Krishna's quiet tone which acknowledges human frailty, the background is suffused with pale yellow sunlight although the chariot has colourful flags and tassels. A yogi, in a saffron dhoti, sits mediating alone, near a green hill. He is an example of someone who has relinquished action. His sense of detachment from the self and the world may be, as the verse says, 'good.' But, he is not, Krishna insists, amongst the elected few. Those who achieve wisdom, he says, choose to act dispassionately in the world; perform good deeds. An ash-blue demonic creature sits under the green hill. He has the body of a human being. His animal head is a strange mix of a donkey's ears, the small eyes of a pig and a long snout. He wears a red lower garment and carries a stick. An example of evil, he is obtuse and beyond redemption. Even if he defends the scriptures, he does so for the wrong reasons, and thereby adds to the violence of the world.

The painting for verse 12 offers us a second a visual parable. A richly attired prince, under a white parasol, is shown seated on a scarlet throne. His turban is bejewelled, his bearing is proud; he knows that what he desires and achieves is rightfully his. He is addicted to a life of luxury and used to being served. He is not a monster like the creature under the hill, but he is tainted by selfish desires and passionate attachments. Since he is not ignorant and obstinate, he may still become a man of virtue. Sitting across from him is a worldly courtier whose gestures are elegant and tastes are aesthetically pleasing. He knows how to gratify those in power so that his own passions and interests are never jeopardised. In his left hand, he holds a red flower which he offers the prince in expectation of some reward. Like the prince, he is not evil, but his courtesy and art of paying compliments can turn into self-righteous rage if his hopes are thwarted; the forests of affliction,[1] the *Mahabharata* knows, teem with small slights to the ego and can lead to the disasters of war. That is perhaps why the courtier's right hand is on the hilt of a dagger tucked in his cummerbund.

1 The phrase is from Blake's "*Jerusalem*," *Complete Writings*, p. 671.

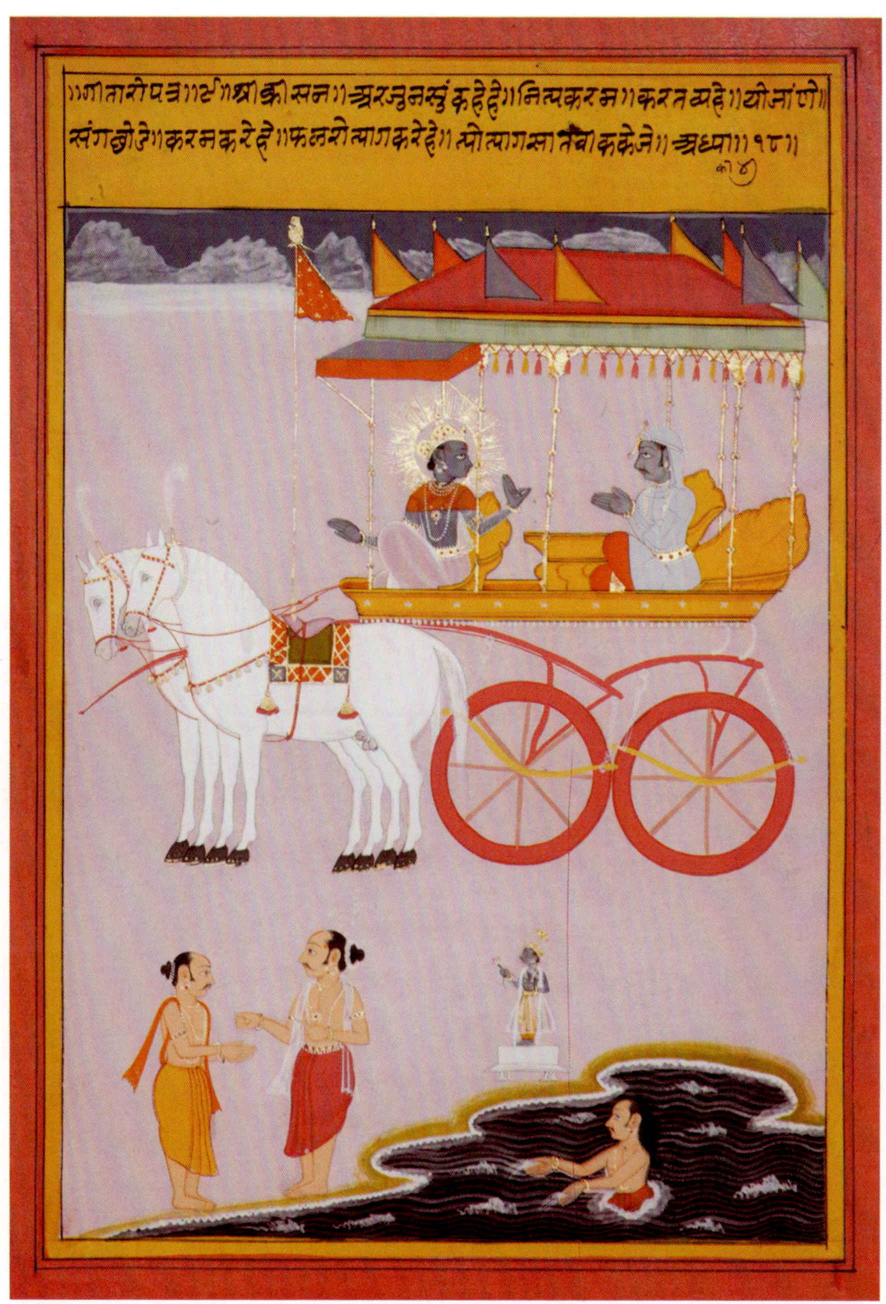

|9| हे अर्जुन! नियत कर्म करना ही कर्तव्य है इस भाव से आसक्ति और फल का त्याग करके जो कर्म किया जाता है, वह सात्विक त्याग कहलाता है।

|9| Hey Arjuna! Action performed out of a sense of duty and without any desire for the fruit of action, is an act of true and pure renunciation.

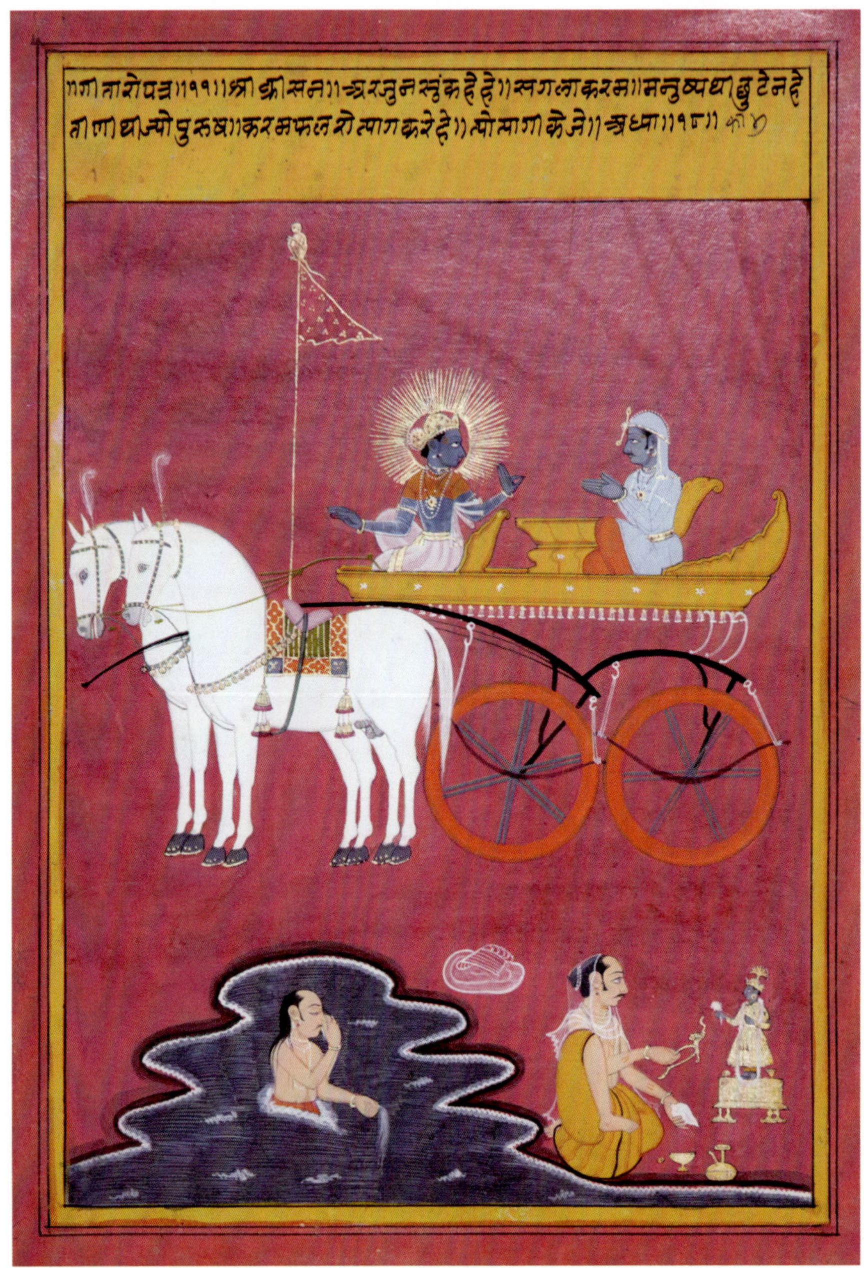

|11| हे अर्जुन! किसी भी देहधारी प्राणी के लिए कर्मों का सम्पूर्ण त्याग असंभव है, इसलिए जो कर्मफल का त्यागी है, वही त्यागी है; ऐसा कहा जाता है।

|11| Hey Arjuna! It is said that since it is impossible for anyone to relinquish all action, the best form of renunciation is to give up the fruit of action.

|12| हे अर्जुन! पर जो कर्मफल के त्यागी नहीं हैं उनको अनिष्ट, इष्ट और अनिष्टानिष्ट तीन प्रकार के कर्मफल होते हैं, जो मरने के बाद मिलते हैं किन्तु कर्मफल के पूर्ण त्यागी को कर्मों का फल किसी भी काल में नहीं मिलता।

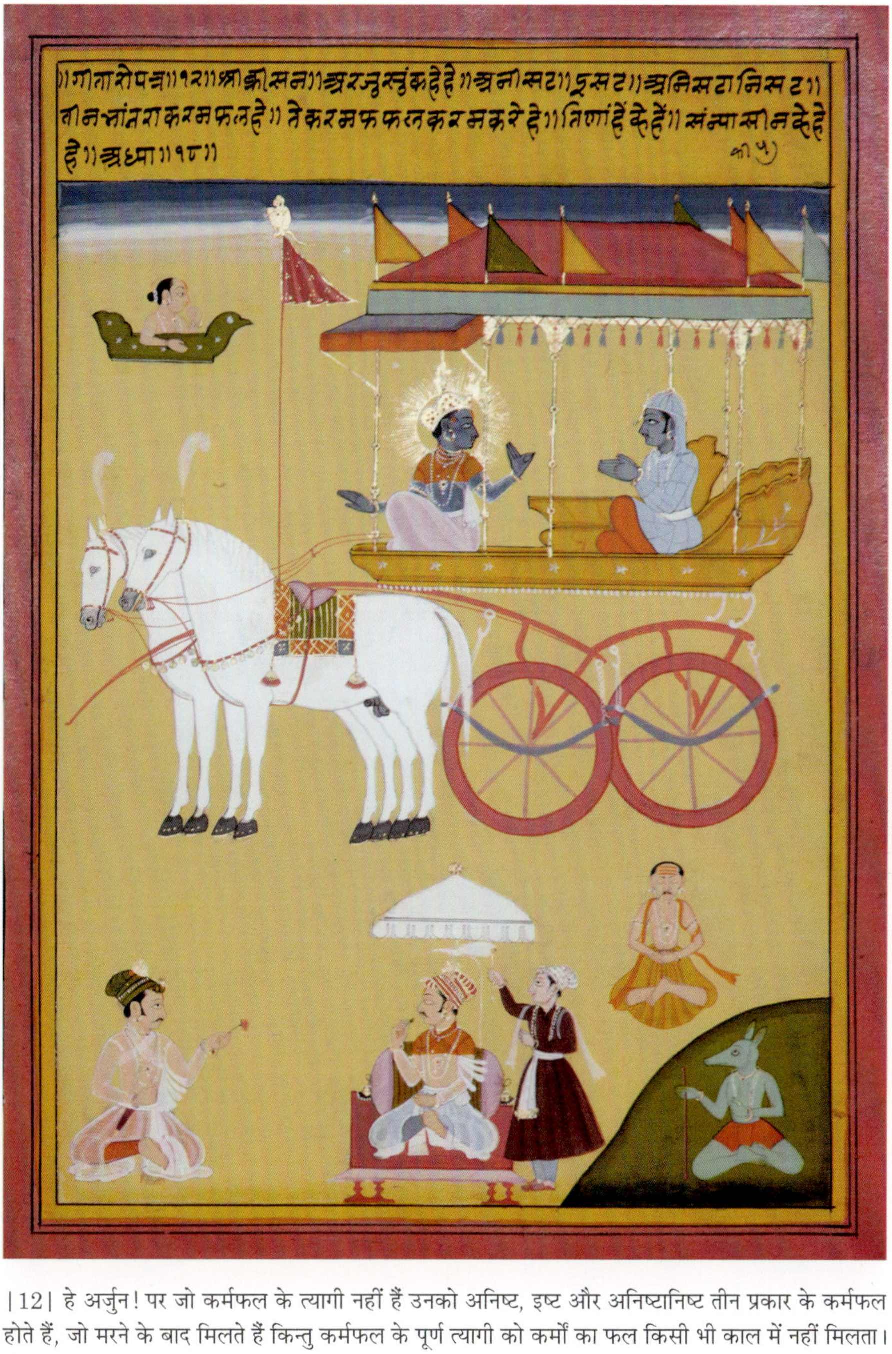

|12| Hey Arjuna! Those who cannot renounce the fruit of action receive three kinds of fruits of action after death: good, evil and good-evil. But the one who renounces the fruit of action is free for all time.

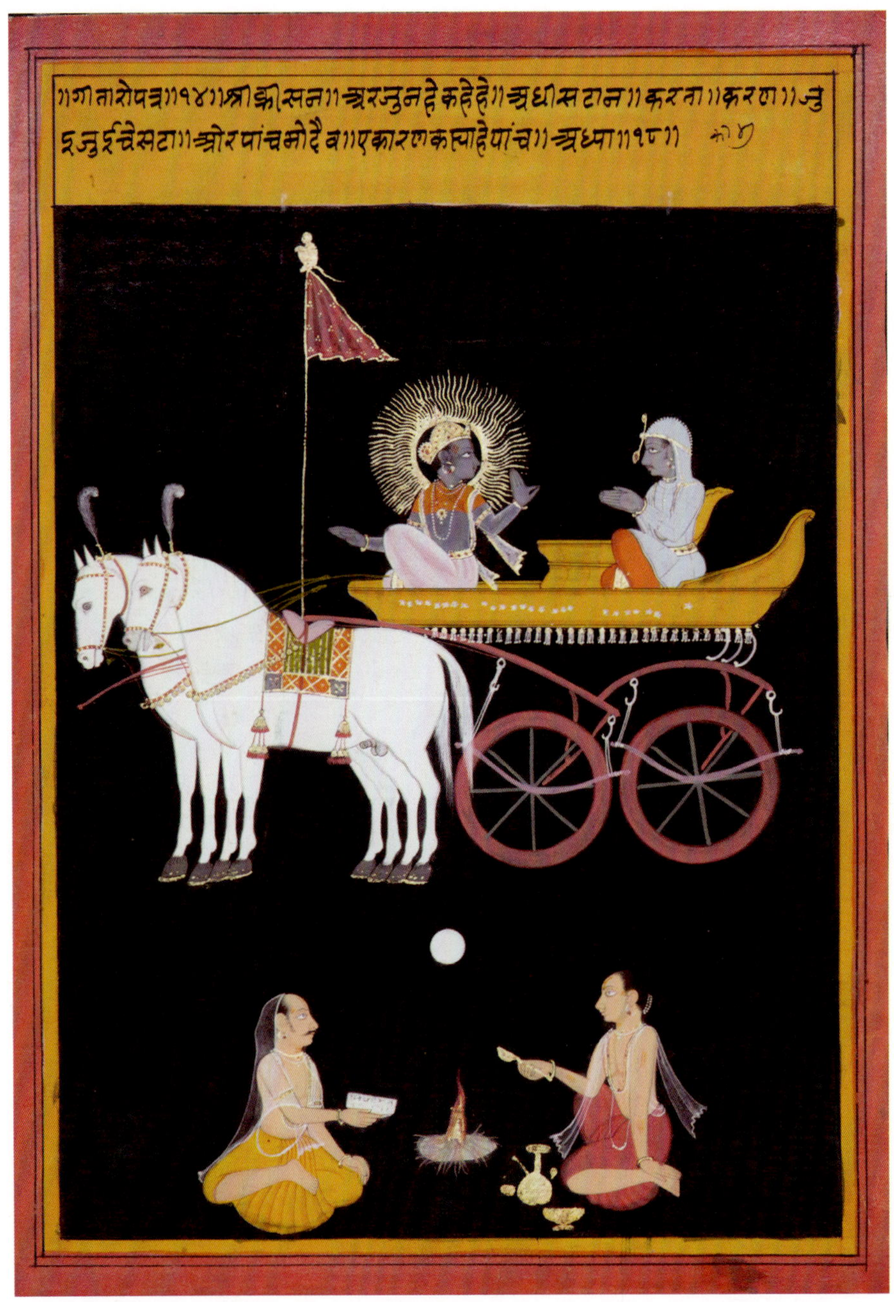

|14| श्री कृष्ण आगे समझाने लगे कि कर्मों की सिद्धि में अधिष्ठान, कर्ता, विभिन्न इन्द्रियाँ, नाना प्रकार की अलग-अलग चेष्टाएँ और पाँचवाँ कारण दैवीय होता है।

|14| Sri Krishna further explains: There are five reasons for any action. They are the body, the person, different physical organs, various desires and fate.

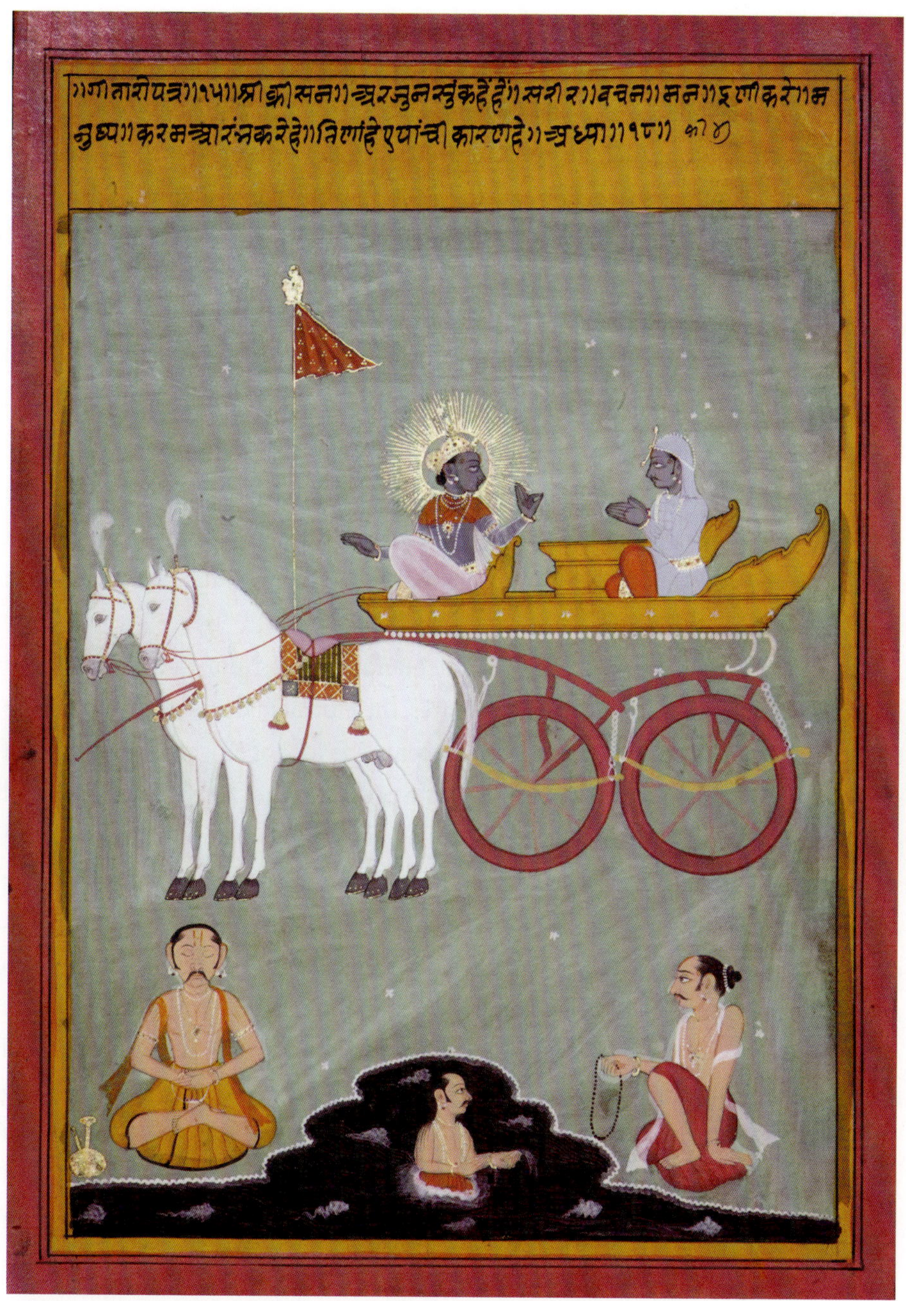

|15| हे अर्जुन! मनुष्य मन, वचन और काया से शास्त्र के अनुसार अथवा विपरीत जो कुछ भी कर्म आरंभ करता है, उसके ये पाँचों ही कारण हैं।

|15| Hey Arjuna! Whether an action is right or wrong, there are only five causes of all physical, mental and verbal action.

The painting for verse 20 is about kinder and gentler interactions between human and non-human life. The background is suffused with the golden light of the sun. The chariot is colourful and lively with fluttering flags. The emotional charge of the painting is in keeping with the spirit of the verse about the idea that a gift is precious only if it is "given without thought of recompense, in the belief that it ought to be made...to a deserving person" (Swami 86). Such a gift should be offered with the purity of heart and in the spirit of renunciation. In the painting, an ordinary man, wearing a red dhoti, offers a red flower to the image of Krishna. He does not seem to ask for anything in return. There is gracefulness in his gesture; humility and dignity in his posture before god. His sense of self-sufficiency, of gentle acceptance of what life has given him, finds symbolic extension in the images of the white cow, the white pigeon and the green tree behind him. Looking at the peaceful cluster, one wonders if eternity is nothing more than being in the presence of this animal, this bird or this tree.

Only the arrogant and the envious demand favours from the gods and the realignment of the stars to satisfy their desires; they torment themselves and debase the gods; of course, the stars remain indifferent. The idol of Krishna standing on a scarlet pedestal is very small. It is painted with precision and care in blue, silver and gold. What is unique is that Krishna holds a small blue flower on a green-leaved stem in his right hand and offers it as a gift to his worshipper. It is a gift of peace; an offering of beauty; a lesson about frailty and temporality; an invitation to think about the essential qualities of non-violence that govern earthly ecology. It is also an assurance of renewal; a sign of cultivation; of culture. It is a reminder of all those countless Indian stories and paintings in which the gods rain down flowers on small acts of virtue which are performed in the most extreme conditions without being mindful of rewards. We may be persuaded to suggest that this painterly gesture of peace and beauty by Krishna on behalf of the earth belongs to less vicious times of myth. The flower that Krishna extends toward the worshipper may be symbolic of the covenant which human beings must make with the earth so that, even when moral reason fails and monstrous passions threaten violence, there will be room for mercy and ground for pity. Is that also not what Krishna's intervention at the end of the war means when he saves one child, the last of the Arjuna's lineage, after Ashwatthama releases his universe-destroying weapon?

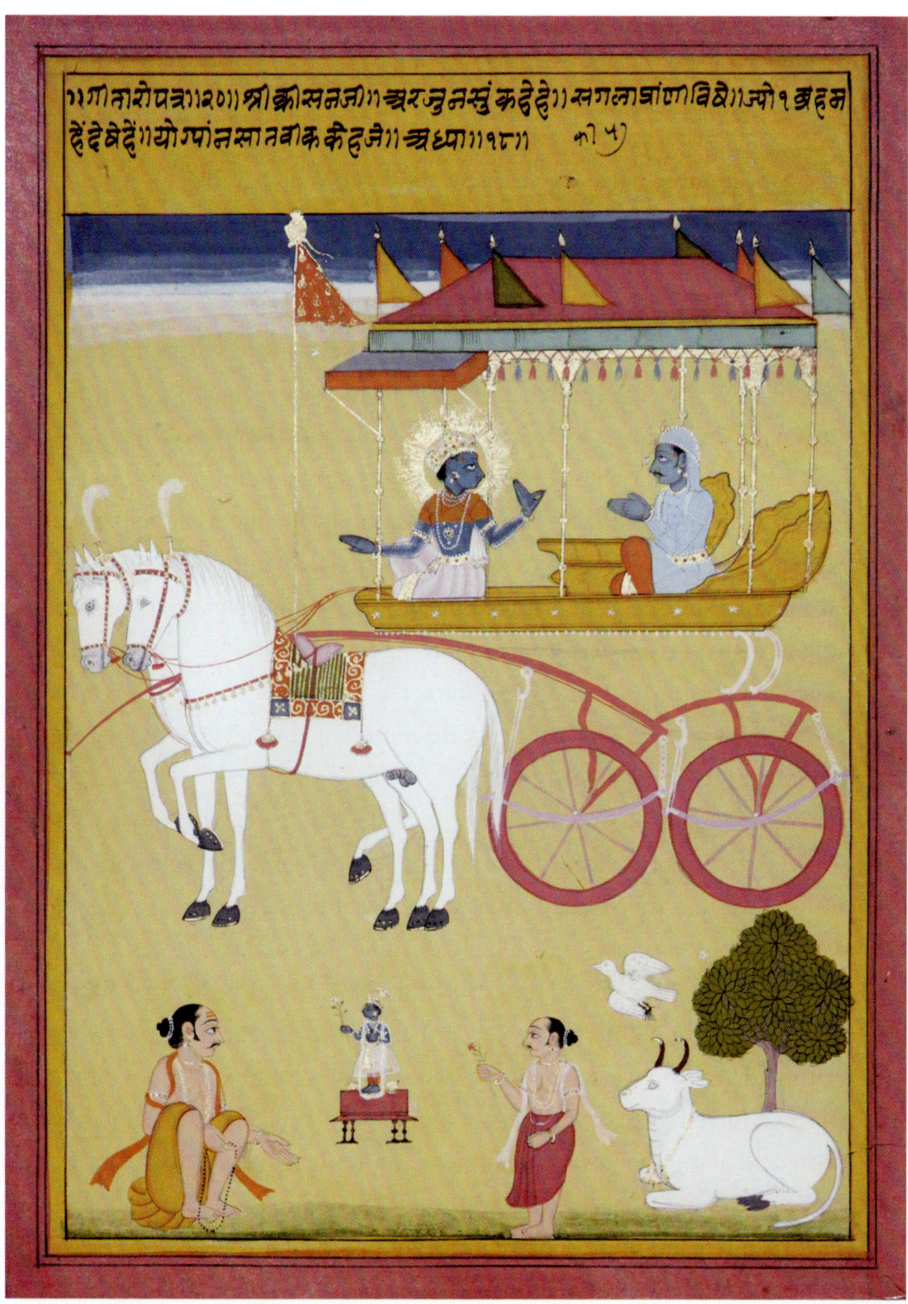

|20| श्री कृष्ण आगे कहने लगे कि हे अर्जुन! जिस ज्ञान से मनुष्य अलग-अलग सब प्राणियों में एक अविनाशी ब्रह्म को देखता है। ऐसे ज्ञान को तू सात्विक जान।

|20| Sri Krishna further says: The knowledge which enables human beings to see the indestructible Brahma in all creatures is called Pure Knowledge.

If one considers the scene in the chariot again, one will notice that Krishna's gestures seem to teach a similar moral parable to Arjuna. Krishna blesses the sunlit ground and the white horses. His right is held up in *mayur mudra* toward Arjuna urging him to be fearless. Hanuman, looking down at the animals and trees below, is witness to the truth that there is enough under the sky and on the earth to ensure a life of self-sufficiency, peace and harmony. One can trace a line of gold from Hanuman's body down to Krishna, the horse and the tips of the cow's horns; it runs like a rich seam of precious ore across nature. One can also imagine a melodious white arc as it is lifted up by the flight of the pigeon from the cow on the ground toward the horses of divinity. What else can the gods offer human beings except the visionary intelligence to consider, without self-regard, what is already available in its infinite variety and which ought to suffice? And yet, as one looks at this painting, one is also saddened at the thought that the world represented in it is threatened by the approaching endgame, by war.

Thinking more about *tamas* in verse 22, Krishna says that those who cling dogmatically to the idea that there is only one god, one truth and one law for everyone are people of *tamasic* vision; their insistence is "without logic, truth or insight," and "has its origin in Darkness" (Swami 90). And, of course, they believe that they themselves are the singular focus of divine attention. The painter's commentary is trenchant. He draws a youthful, handsome and armed prince who has ordered a religious ritual to be conducted by his court's priest for his personal benefit. Krishna has insisted all along that a sustained moral action is required by the self to achieve salvation. Does the prince hope that his priest shall abbreviate the effort required and find a short-cut to paradise for him? The irony, which the beauty of the figures makes sharper, is easier to catch if we note that the princely figure has turned his back on the presence of Shiva who sits cross-legged on the ground near him.

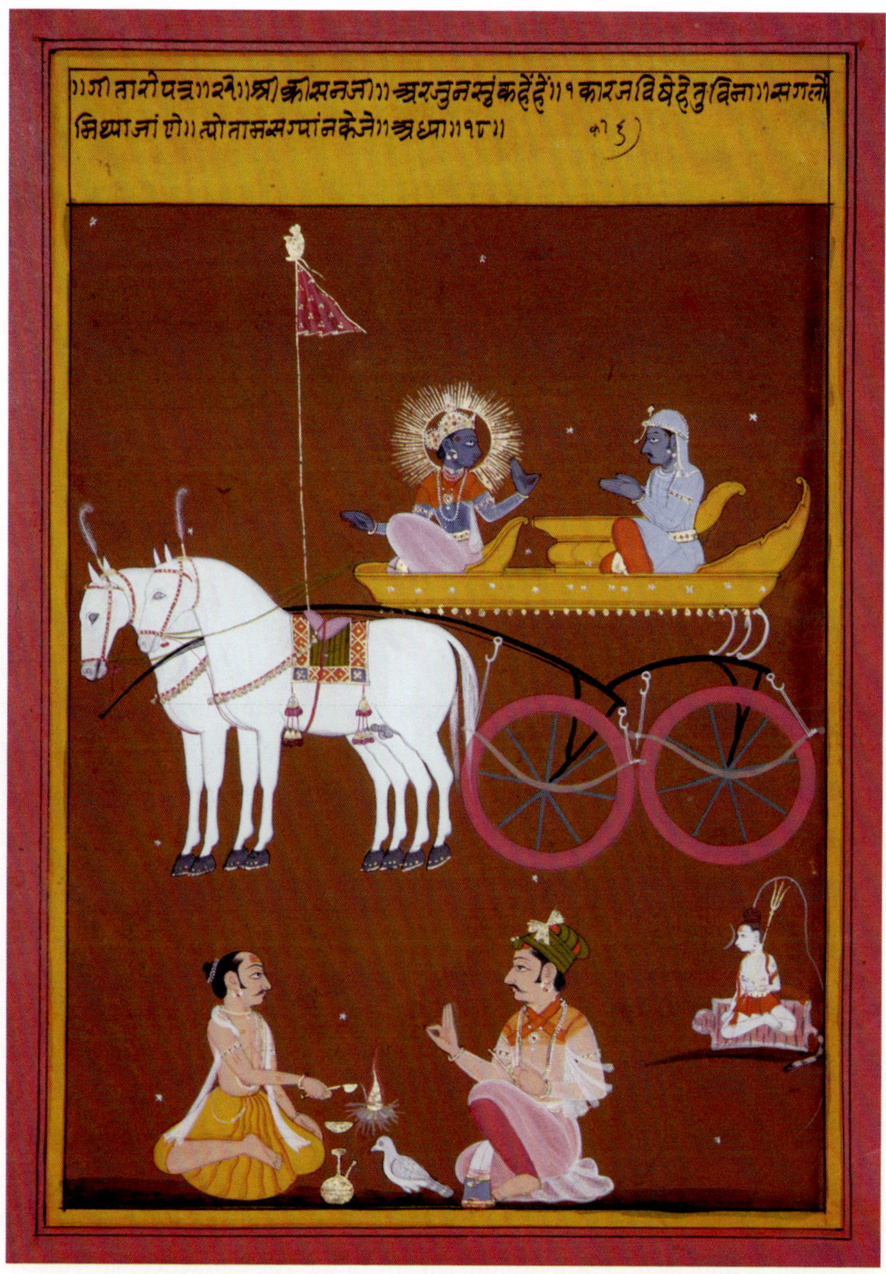

|22| हे अर्जुन! और जिस ज्ञान के द्वारा मनुष्य एक कार्यरूप शरीर को ही सब कुछ मानकर उसी में आसक्त है तथा जो युक्ति रहित, तात्विक अर्थ से रहित और तुच्छ है, वह तामस ज्ञान कहा गया है।

|22| Hey Arjuna! And knowledge that makes human beings firmly believe that the body is the only reality is without logic, truth and insight. Such knowledge arises from dark inertia.

There is another ironic painting directed at those who believe they can arrive at God's door if they practise yogic contortions. The painting for verse 24 is quietly witty; colours enact its ironic play. The background is a radiant vermillion, a colour which Kandinsky says, carries "spiritual vibrations."[2] The painting's small parable of failure in everyday life is set against a colour which has emotional significance. The water in the lake is so blue that it almost appears black. The colour is disturbing; the water is motionless. It leaves the eye feeling burdened; the mind deadened. The more one looks upon the dark, small lake against the fiery vermillion, the more it seems like a negation of the analogies between the ceaseless motion of water and human life; it is symbolic of the inertia that, as Krishna tells Arjuna, seeps into the soul when the active intellectual quest for knowledge is replaced by custom and dead habit. The conversation between Krishna and Arjuna is an example of that redeeming spirit which refuses to yield its right to know the truth on its own terms.

Ritual characterises the priestly man bathing in the lake. He faces east and, with water cupped in his hands, piously invokes the morning sun to illuminate his intellect and life. A white skittering line separates the lake from the land. It leaves one feeling uneasy because it encloses the sun worshipper, as if indicating how bounded the soul becomes when it is governed by routine. Traditionally performed action, it suggests, is a sign of one who is not open to a conversation, a new thought, an unexpected idea or a chance happening which may radically change all that one knows. The fascination of Allah Baksh's paintings lies in his profound understanding that the *Gita* is part of this continuous struggle for clarification.

Near the lake, another seeker of grace hangs upside down from the thin branch of a dry and very frail tree. Allah Baksh has drawn similar figures earlier, but here the critique is sharper and directly linked with the *Gita*'s final and firm rejection of all forms of asceticism. This yogi is an unambiguous caricature of religiosity. He does not act, but pleads for god's special regard. Every morning, the sun finds him hanging upside down. Day by day he shall wither till he becomes frail and dry like the tree he hangs from. The whimsicality of his action is depicted by the whimsicality of the visual image. It underscores how arbitrary many of the yogic practices are since they are not guided by any rationally argued system of ethicality. In fact, verse 24 explicitly says that many of these extreme practices of self-torment are nightmares: "But even though an action involves the most strenuous endeavour, yet if the doer is seeking to

2 Kandinsky, *Concerning the Spiritual in Art*, n.p.

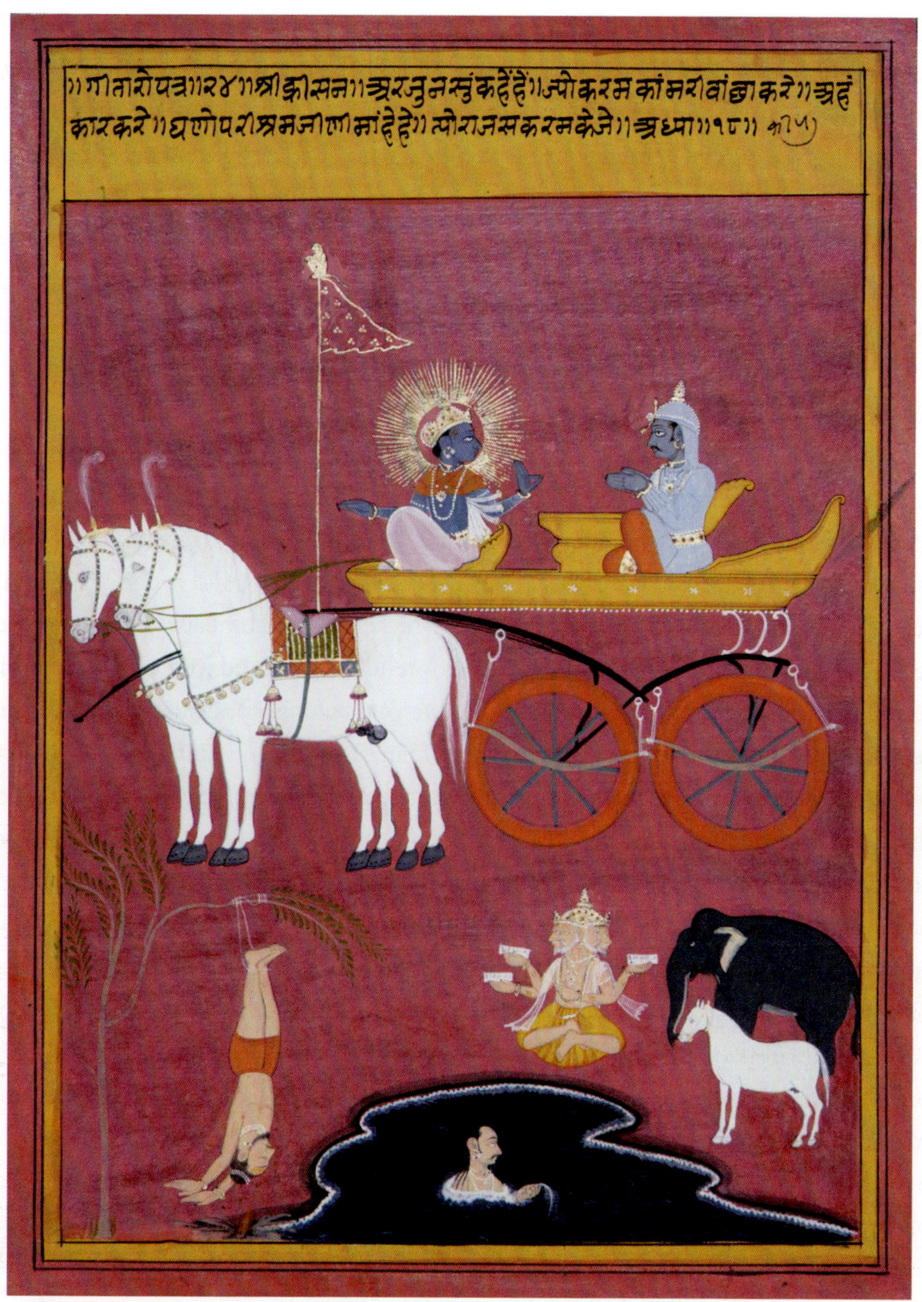

|24| श्री कृष्ण आगे कहने लगे कि जो कर्म भोगों को चाहने वाले पुरुष द्वारा अहंकार से और कठिन परिश्रमपूर्वक किया जाता है, वह कर्म राजस कहा जाता है।

|24| Sri Krishna further says: But the action which is performed with great effort out of vanity and for rewards is called passionate action.

gratify his desires, and is filled with personal vanity, it may be assumed to originate in passion" (Swami 90). If yogic contortions dishonour the mind and the body which are potentially incarnations of the divine, then physical and intellectual self-indulgence or apathy disgrace all that is human as the verses 27 and 28 assert. Indolence, they say, is mean-minded, dishonest, vulgar and malicious because it transfers the burdens of the self to someone else. The one who does that, Krishna says, lives in "darkness" (Swami 90). The lower half of the paintings for the two verses is green. Kandinsky associates the colour with sanity and gratitude, useful action and new beginnings, and Goethe with the restful satisfaction a soul feels after honest effort.[3] These are also the moral norms Krishna evokes in the verses.

The critique of power and the assumption that it has the sanction of the gods is sharpened in the painting for verse 25. The two noble princes not only turn their backs on a diminutive Shiva, but pay grovelling attention to a naked fakir whose body is smeared with blue ash as a sort of ersatz Shiva. The background is dark. The night scene is illuminated by five earthen lamps which encircle the fakir who sits cross-legged with his eyes closed in meditation. His forehead is smeared with yellow turmeric paste. The five lamps, perhaps, indicate that the yogi belongs to the nathpanthi tantric sect. He looks more like ghoul than a holy man. The image painted is inspired by what the verse says about the evil that ignorant action causes: "An action undertaken through delusion, and with no regard to the spiritual issues involved, or to the real capacity of the doer, or to the injury which may follow, such an act may be assumed to be the product of Ignorance" (Swami 90). But the two princes may believe, like all superstitious people, that the fakir would be easier to delude with some offerings than Shiva who, myths say, is notoriously difficult to appease. Indeed, we recall how it took Arjuna years of arduous penance before Shiva agreed to give him a gift of sacred arms to fight the Kauravas. He had to prove his moral worth, his commitment to the cause of justice, before Shiva acquiesced.

The painting for verse 27 depicts three men of leisure, dressed with the elegant care of the leisure class who are not required to work. Their turbans are elaborately styled, their jamas are transparent, and they carry daggers tucked into the sashes around their waists. The daggers are affectations, not signs of courage. They are engaged in an aggressive argument. Their eyes are wide with anger; their gestures are full of challenge. A quiet and docile looking priest sits in a corner tending to his ritual fire. The men

3 Goethe, "Theory of Colour," *Essential Goethe*, p. 964.

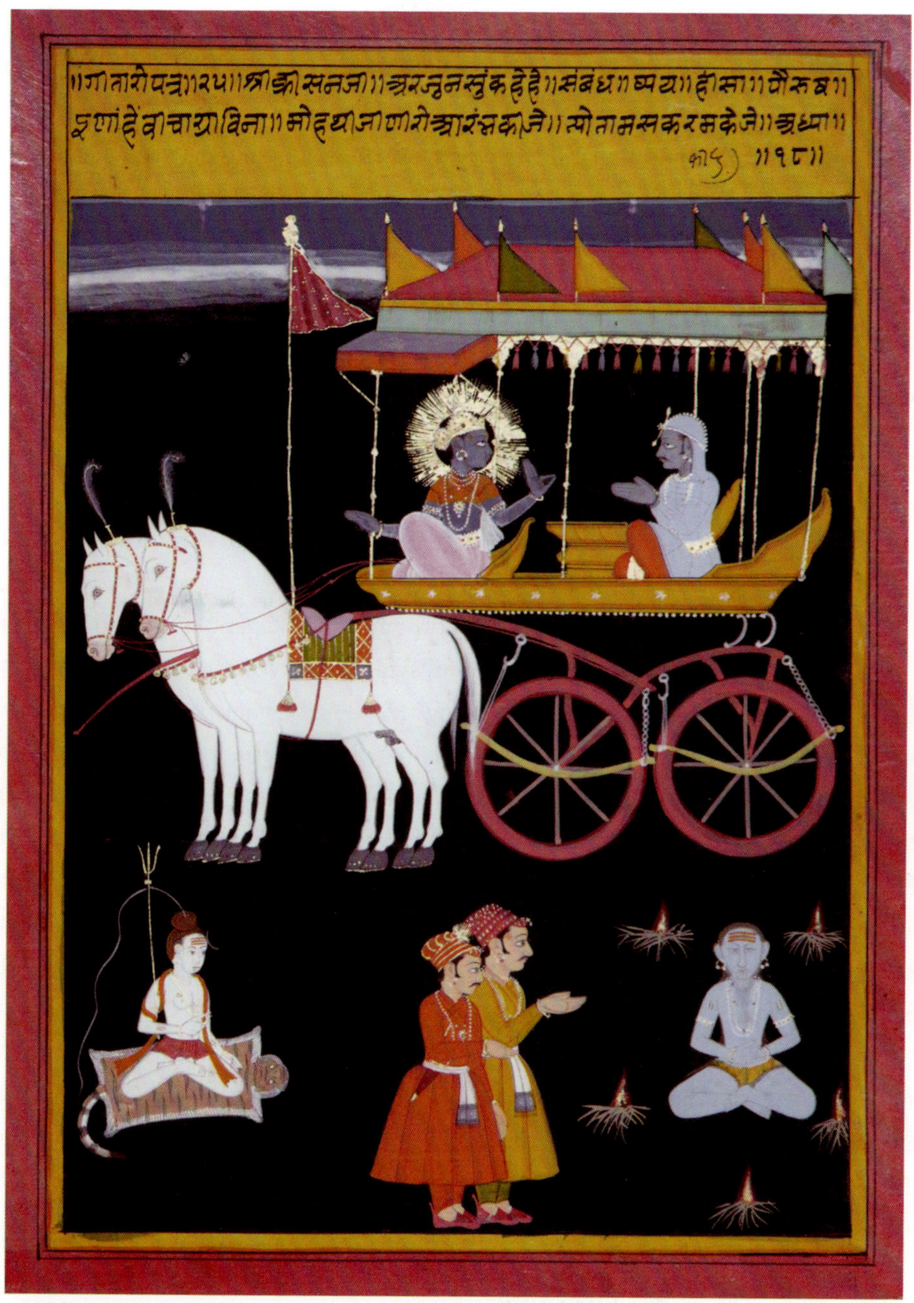

|25| श्री कृष्ण आगे कहने लगे, हे अर्जुन! जो कर्म परिणाम, हानि, हिंसा और सामर्थ्य को न विचारकर केवल अज्ञान से आरंभ किया जाता है, वह तामस (कर्म) कहा जाता है।

|25| Sri Krishna says: Hey Arjuna! That action which is undertaken for gain or is performed out of ignorance is violent and causes harm is called passionate action.

are oblivious to the religious hymns he is chanting and the rite he is performing. So absorbed are they in their own animosities that they do not notice that the green field around them has beautiful white and red flowers. Satire, as we know, is close to the comic for it depends upon the absurd incongruity in human life between what moral words profess and the action performed; however, it is also close to sorrow, because it knows that its capacity to bring about change is limited.[4]

The painting for verse 28 shows a youthful prince in his palace chamber, lying on a couch covered by an elaborately embellished sheet. His eyes are wide open. His face reflects slothfulness. Two attendants hover near him. A young woman massages his legs, while a dark-bodied man presses his feet. The prince is the very image of apathy and arrogant disregard. A fire burns uselessly in the ground outside. The entire scene encodes, through a few deft images and gestures, what Krishna means when he declares that an intellect in quest of truth learns to discriminate between actions which either lead to bondage or to deliverance.

An alert mind and an active being shall become a participant listener to Krishna's discourse; a man seeking a vision of the good shall sit and converse with the goddess when she appears on earth, as in the paintings for verses 29 and 30. One could, with Emerson, characterise this meeting between a man and the goddess as a prayer which asks for nothing; a prayer which is "the contemplation of the facts of life from the highest point of view. It is the soliloquy of a beholding and jubilant soul. It is the spirit of God pronouncing his works good."[5] These encounters between human beings and gods and goddesses may not result in an apocalyptic revelation, as in the case of Arjuna and Krishna, but they relocate the possibility of an ethical ideal in the self, society and historical time.

Thus, for verse 29, in which Krishna simply declares that, he will teach Arjuna the threefold distinction between wisdom and a steadfast mind, Allah Baksh paints two gently luminous vignettes as dramatic examples for us to think about. In the chariot, which glows with sunlight against a rich brown earth, Krishna and Arjuna sit face to face, each reflecting the other as in a mirror of glory.[6] Below them, on a pale blue-green earth strewn with flowers, Allah Baksh quietly paints an encounter between a learned priest and a goddess, who sits in a mudra of peaceful repose on a white sheet

4 Frye, *Anatomy of Criticism*, p. 224.

5 "Self-Reliance," in *Selections from Ralph Waldo Emerson*, p. 162.

6 The Bible, 2 Corinthians, 3:18.

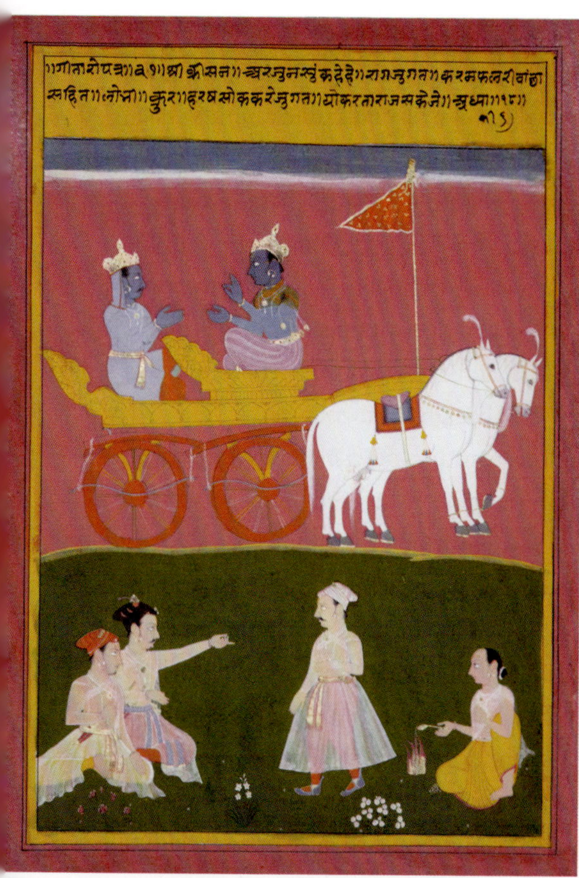

|27| श्री कृष्ण आगे कहने लगे कि जो कर्ता आसक्तियुक्त, कर्मफल की कामना रखने वाला, लोभी, हिंसक, अपवित्र तथा हर्ष-शोक में विचलित होता है, वह राजस कहा जाता है।

|27| Sri Krishna says: The man who longs for rewards, who is distracted, is greedy, violent and is torn between joy-sorrow is a man of passion.

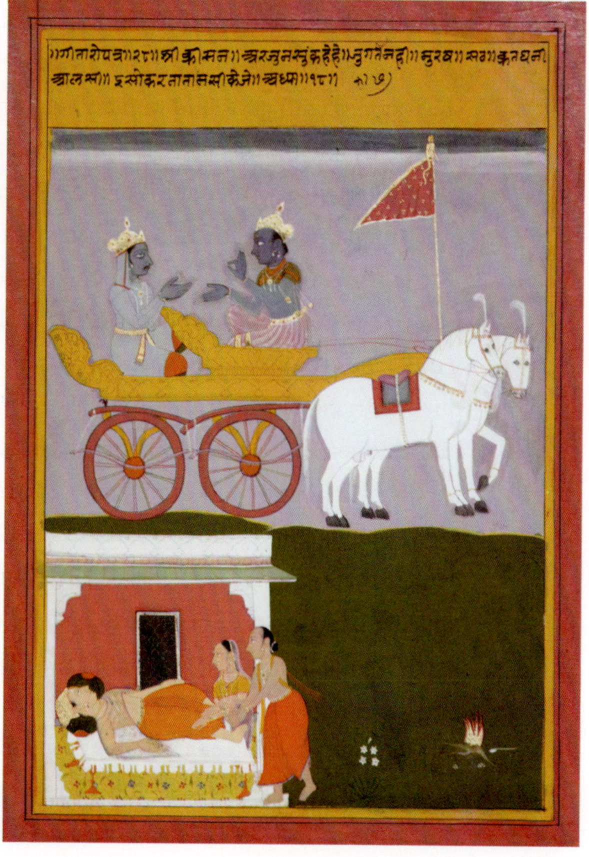

|28| श्री कृष्ण समझाते हुए आगे कहने लगे कि जो कर्ता अयुक्त, असभ्य, घमंडी, कपटी, दूसरों के कार्यों में विघ्न डालने वाला, आलसी, दुखी और कार्य को कल पर टालने वाला हो, वह तामस कहा जाता है।

|28| Sri Krishna explains further: The one who is infirm, vulgar, arrogant, and dishonest; interferes in the business of others; is lazy, depressed and procrastinates is a man of inertia.

decorated with multi-coloured flowers. Her beauty does not inspire awe, but invites a conversation which is an analogue of the Krishna-Arjuna dialogue above. The two scenes are symbolic of the ever-present possibility that eternity and time can meet even in the darkest of yugas. The learned man, who is perfectly at ease, is reading the Vedas to her. However, even as we admire the images, we should not forget that the *Gita* is a song in the middle of a battlefield. Both the scenes of knowledge-making in the painting suggest that intelligent peace is possible only when we learn how to "allow each other to grow great, because diminishing/comes easily to us and does not need to be learned."[7]

The quiet peacefulness that radiates from this painting is transformed, in the next painting for verse 30, into a sacred song of joy. The background colours are now self-consciously reversed from the ones in the previous painting—Krishna's chariot stands against a blue-green sky. In the scene below, four gorgeously painted men and women and two divine beings sit on a fertile, dark brown earth on which flowers bloom in abundance. A mendicant, with a shaven head, a garland of white flowers around his neck and wearing a pale yellow dhoti, is being blessed by the goddess. In the previous painting, she was the hierophantic centre, her singular physical presence radiating light and energy. In this painting, there are other divine presences too and other incarnations; she mingles with gods and human beings in a celebratory circle. The entire scene is in consonance with the basic and profound metaphysical assumption which informs all non-sectarian ways of looking at the world; every phenomenon can also be a revelation; every temporal act can also be a little ritual commemorating eternity.

There is humility and gratitude in the mendicant's gestures; the alms offered to him by the goddess are sufficient. The goddess carries no emblems of plenitude in her hands; she promises nothing more than fearless self-sufficiency, and a few of the primal qualities (*gunas*) which are essential for the attainment of a peaceful and a harmonious life. This peaceful scene in which the Devi and the mendicant sit talking to each other is supplemented and replicated by the adjacent image cluster of the simple and ordinary men, women and children thankful for the darshan of Krishna. Their clothes are not ornate; their gestures are gentle, charming, and non-aggressive; their postures are self-effacing. They are confident participants in the revelatory moment Krishna describes in verse 30; the moment when all distinction between creation and dissolution, bondage and deliverance, ceases to be part of consciousness. As the eye travels across the images, moves up toward the chariot and then circles back, it traces a fine harmony of colours

7 Rainer Maria Rilke, "Requiem for a Friend," in William Gass, *Reading Rilke: Reflections on the Problem of Translation* (New York: Alfred A. Knopf, 1999), p. 132.

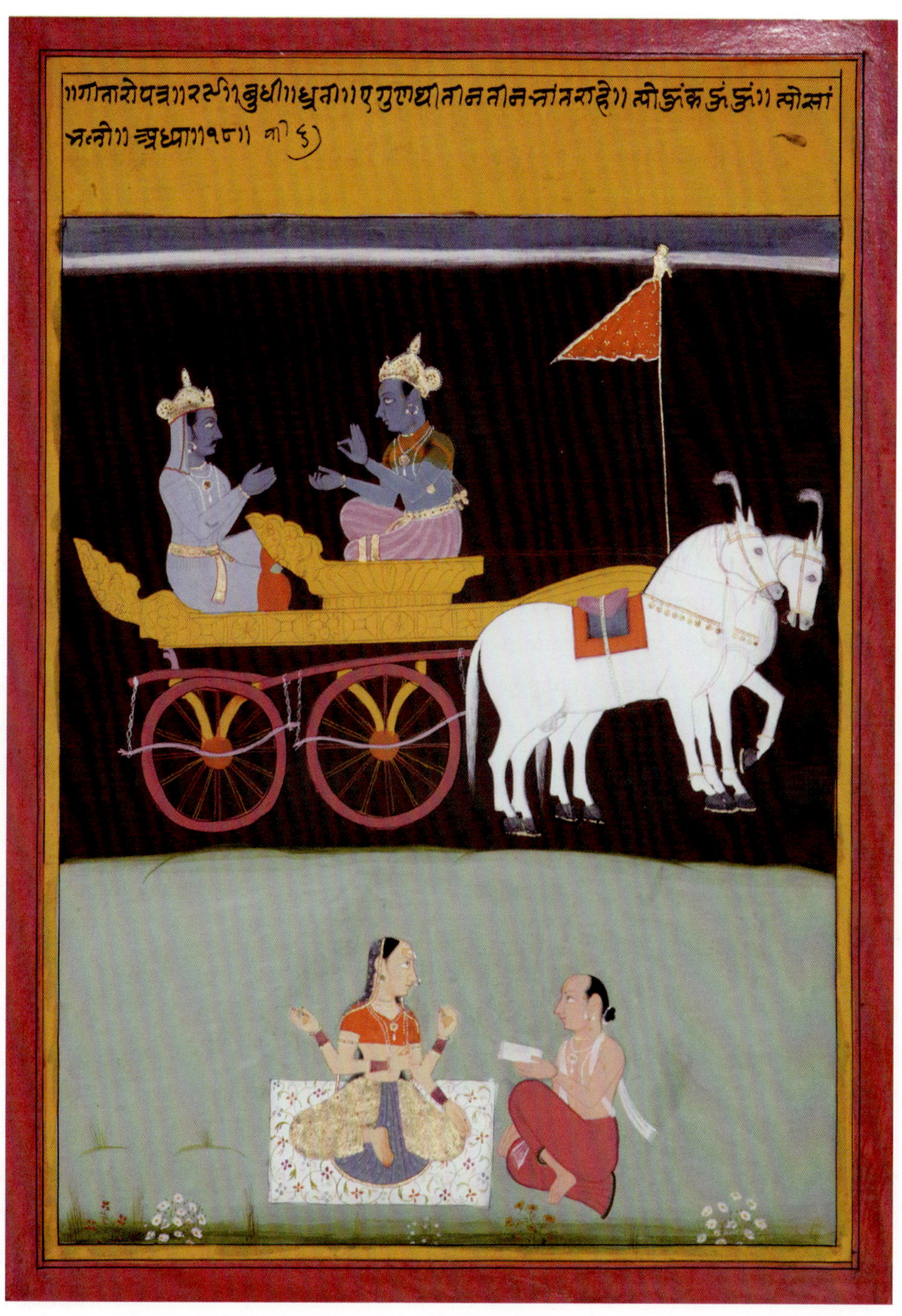

|29| हे अर्जुन! अब तू बुद्धि और धारणशक्ति का भी गुणों के कारण तीन प्रकार का भेद अलग-अलग मुझसे सुन।

|29| Hey Arjuna! Now listen to the three distinct aspects of Intellect and Resolve.

so as to suggest that there really is no rupture, or ought not to ever be, between the sacred and the profane worlds.

The woman in the middle carries a child in her arms as if to ensure that the future of mankind will not be erased. We are reminded of the horrific act of Ashwatthama who killed all the children in their mother's wombs. The sublimely gentle and beautiful images of the Devi beside the mother and child in the last of the paintings of this *Gita* folio are neither unselfconscious nor naive. They must be considered attentively, for they are surely deliberate. Allah Baksh painted similar images for verses in the previous chapters. They are a counter plea for ahimsa as the only guarantee for the ongoingness of life; and, at the same time, a prophecy that in the approaching disaster of war, women and children shall be its most tragic victims. In the *Stree Parva*, the wives of the slain stumble over mutilated corpses looking for what remains of their men. No words can describe their disillusion and despair. Neither Draupadi nor Gandhari can offer consolation. The *Stree Parva* is the shortest chapter in the *Mahabharata*. The sorrow it describes is not unique in human history, but typical and repetitive. However, Allah Baksh's images of beauty in this painting offer a counter-narrative to help us think about another possible reality, a different promise of life, a fearless heroism which is willing to lay a wager on peace. Allah Baksh is responding to Krishna's call to the "intellect which understands the creation and dissolution of life, what actions should be done and what not..." (Swami 90).

None of the ordinary men and women painted in the folio is a hero or has heroic ambitions. Only sad times need heroes. If the stories of the human beings represented in these last paintings ever get told, they would be satisfying parables of lives where some space was always left for the *numen* to enter. Indeed, as one realises how charming and innocent the figures Allah Baksh paints are (see paintings for verses 56, 57, 62, 64, 66, 68, 69, 71 and 73), one begins to sense the presence of myths. After all, it is only in myths when human beings, nature and the gods meet that uncanny stories take shape and one understands that there is a divinity in the survival or fall of a sparrow. Krishna tells Arjuna: the wise know what is to be done; they know how to keep in focus some clear ethical sign-posts to guide their actions; how to find a way through the endlessly changing shadows of fearful passions in which human beings get lost. They also know that instead of being transfixed by a single idea, one should accept that there are multiple ways of seeing the real. If one can understand that, one can see the world in its plenitude and give up the predatory impulse to war.

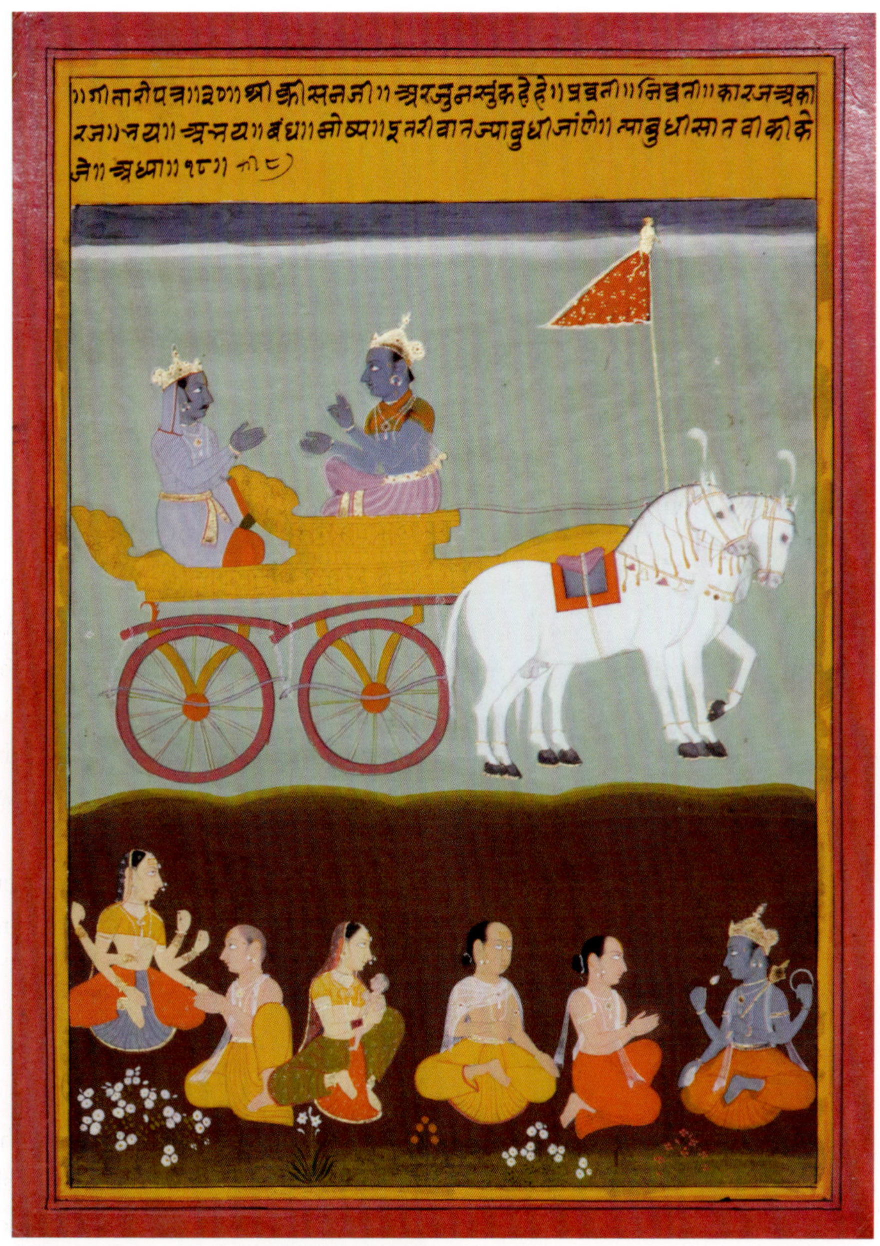

|30| श्री कृष्ण आगे कहने लगे कि जो बुद्धि- प्रवृत्ति और निवृत्ति को कर्तव्य और अकर्तव्य को, भय और अभय को तथा बंधन एवं मोक्ष को यथार्थ जानती है- वह बुद्धि सात्विक है।

|30| Sri Krishna says: The Intellect which discriminates between creation and dissolution, knows which action should be performed as duty and which must not be performed, knows fear and fearlessness, bondage and freedom, is called Pure Reason.

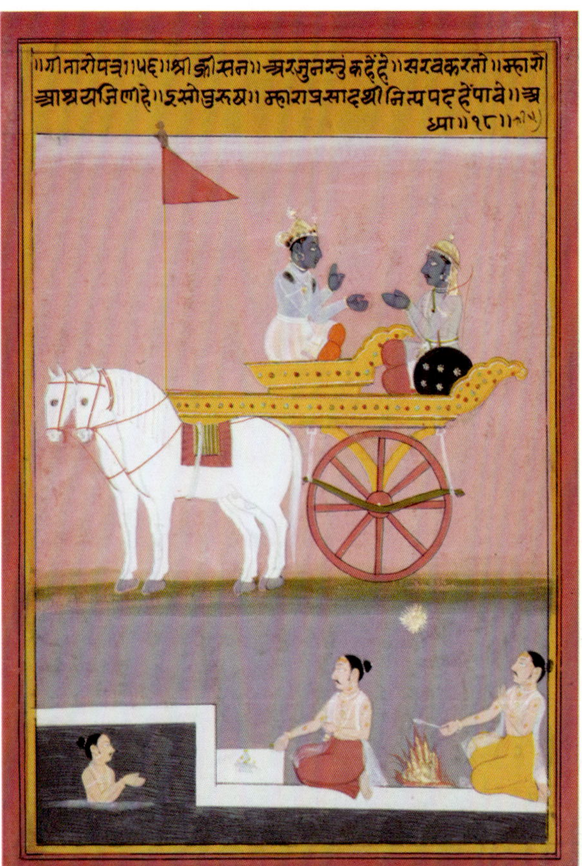

|56| हे अर्जुन! मुझ पर आश्रित वह कर्मयोगी निरंतर सारे कर्मों को करता हुआ मेरी कृपा से अविनाशी परमपद को प्राप्त हो जाता है।

|56| Hey Arjuna! The one who takes refuge in me and continues to act with discipline, reaches an eternal, immutable place with my grace.

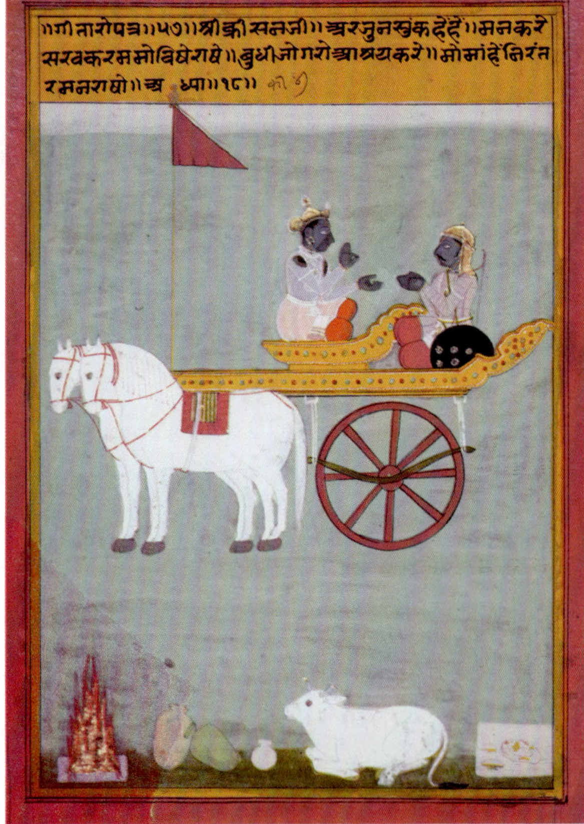

|57| श्री कृष्ण आगे कहने लगे, हे अर्जुन! सभी कर्मों को मन से मुझे समर्पित करके तथा बुद्धियोग का आश्रय लेकर निरंतर चित्त मुझमें लगा।

|57| Sri Krishna further says: Hey Arjuna! Surrender all your actions to me and with your intellect, concentrate on me alone.

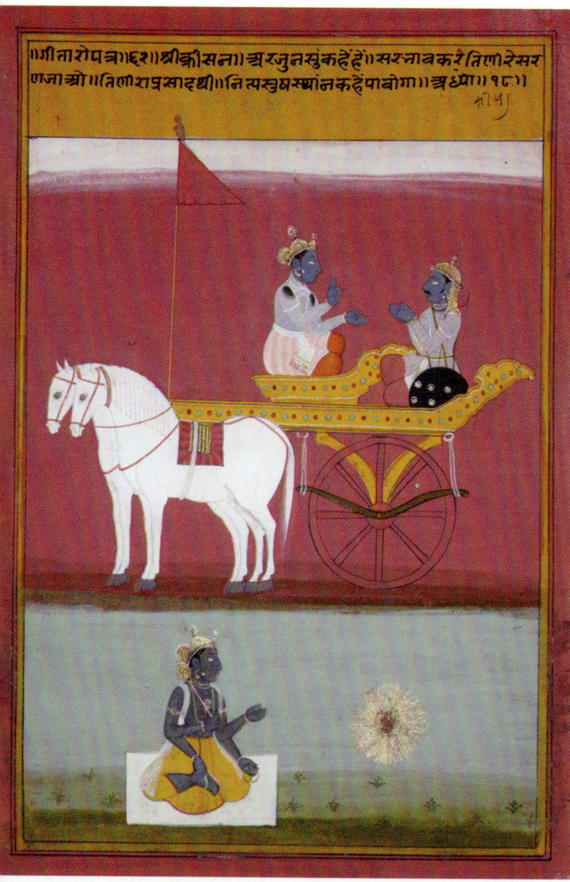

|62| श्री कृष्ण आगे कहने लगे कि सम्पूर्ण भाव से उस ईश्वर की शरण में जा। उसकी कृपा से ही परम शांति और शाश्वत परमधाम को प्राप्त होगा।

|62| Sri Krishna further says: Seek the shelter of the Supreme Being with all your strength. Only with His grace will you attain eternal peace and an eternal home.

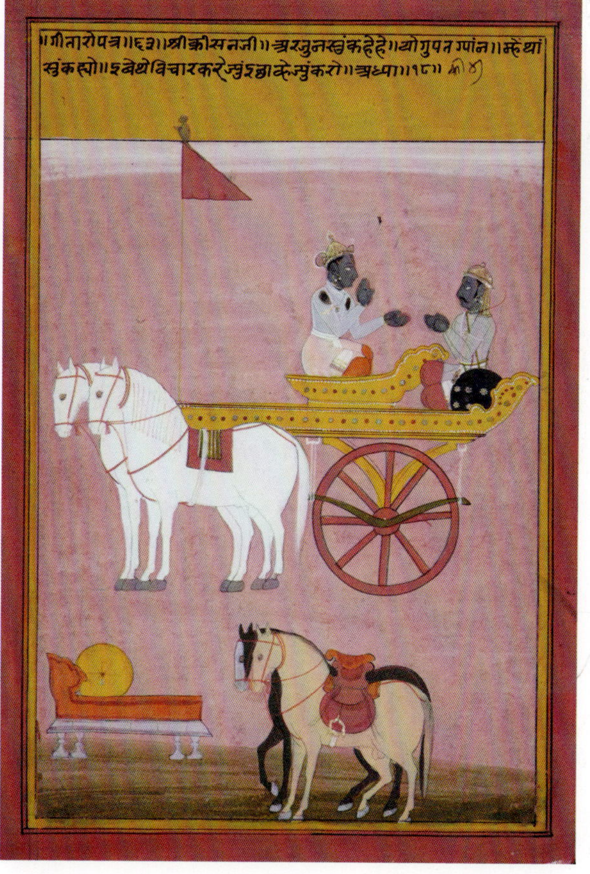

|63| हे अर्जुन! इस प्रकार यह गोपनीय से भी गोपनीय ज्ञान मैंने तुझसे कह दिया है। इस ज्ञान पर अच्छी तरह विचार करने के बाद फिर जैसी तेरी इच्छा हो, वैसा कर।

|63| Hey Arjuna! I have revealed to you knowledge which is the mystery of mysteries. Think carefully about this knowledge and then act as you wish.

The secular spaces in Allah Baksh's paintings are so rich in their diversity that it would be an illusion to regard the human and the divine, Arjuna and Krishna, man and God, as two distinct levels of existence. Instead, these paintings are illustrations of the idea that the holy and the secular worlds conduct an unending conversation with each other. If the upper, the sacred half of the pictorial space, carries the *Gita* forward verse after verse, the lower half, records stories of elegant princes, wandering singers, ascetics, writers of scriptures, women and children, ritual priests, enlightened travellers in sky-boats and tillers of fields whose labour turns the earth into a place of beauty. It is important to note that throughout the series, the earth is painted as generous, the sky as graceful, and the animal and trees as patient. The paintings acknowledge the war; they express gratitude for the earth's survival.

Allah Baksh's painting for verse 73 is in response to Arjuna's final words: "My delusion has fled. By thy Grace, O Changeless One, the light has dawned. My doubts are gone, and I stand before Thee ready to do Thy will" (Swami 92). Then, there is silence; rather one can hear the harmony that silence carries like a pause in a musical composition. Krishna and Arjuna are still sitting face to face. There are no other human figures. The horses are quiet and motionless. The chariot is standing in sunlight. Astonishingly, the earth is covered with new grass. For this one moment at least, we must believe that the ground shall always be green.

For Allah Baksh, the *Gita* is not merely an addition to an esoteric philosophic library; neither is it an advocate of man's fearful surrender to an overpowering divinity; nor is it an endorsement of a warrior's ethic. It is, instead, a call to a life wisely lived.

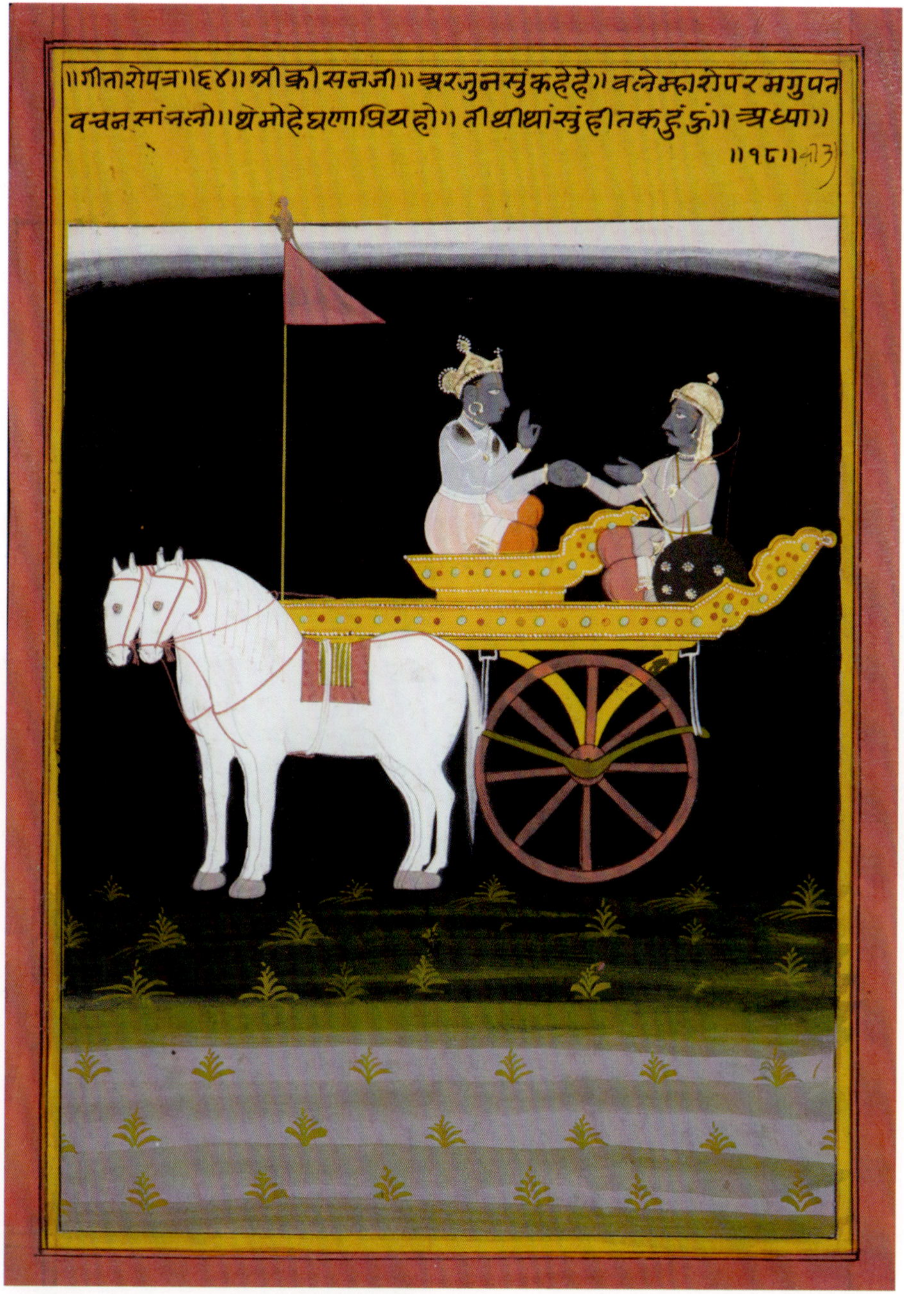

|64| श्री कृष्ण कहने लगे कि मेरे अति गोपनीय परम वचन को तू मुझसे फिर सुन! क्योंकि तू मुझे अत्यन्त प्रिय है, इसी कारण यह कल्याणकारी वचन तुझसे कहूँगा।

|64| Sri Krishna says: Listen to the most secret of words once more from me! Because I love you dearly, I shall tell you these words for your welfare.

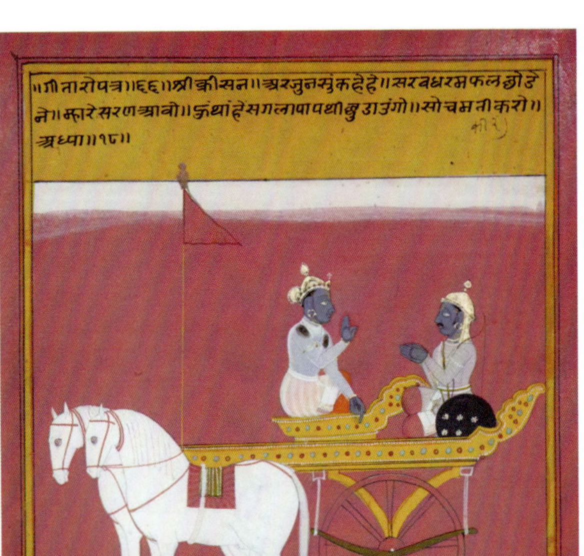

|66| श्री कृष्ण आगे कहने लगे कि सभी धर्मों को त्याग कर तू केवल एक मेरी शरण में आ जा। मैं तुझे सारे पापों से मुक्त कर दूँगा, तू शोक मत कर।

|66| Sri Krishna further says: Sacrifice all other sacred duties, take refuge only in me, and I shall absolve you of all your sins; do not grieve.

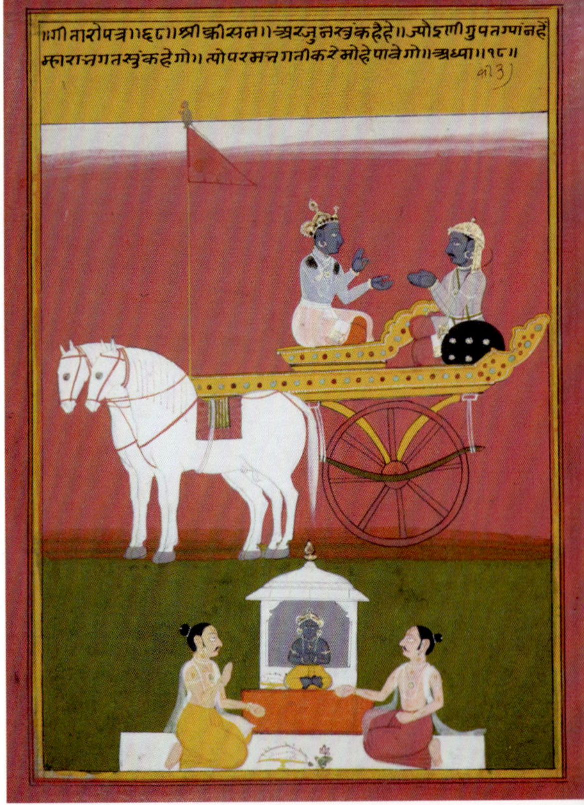

|68| श्री कृष्ण आगे कहने लगे कि जो प्राणी मुझमें परमभक्ति रख कर इस परम गोपनीय ज्ञान को मेरे भक्त को कहेगा, वह मुझे ही प्राप्त होगा, इसमें कोई संशय नहीं।

|68| Sri Krishna further says: But the one who is devoted to me and teaches this deepest mystery to another devotee of mine shall, without doubt, come to me.

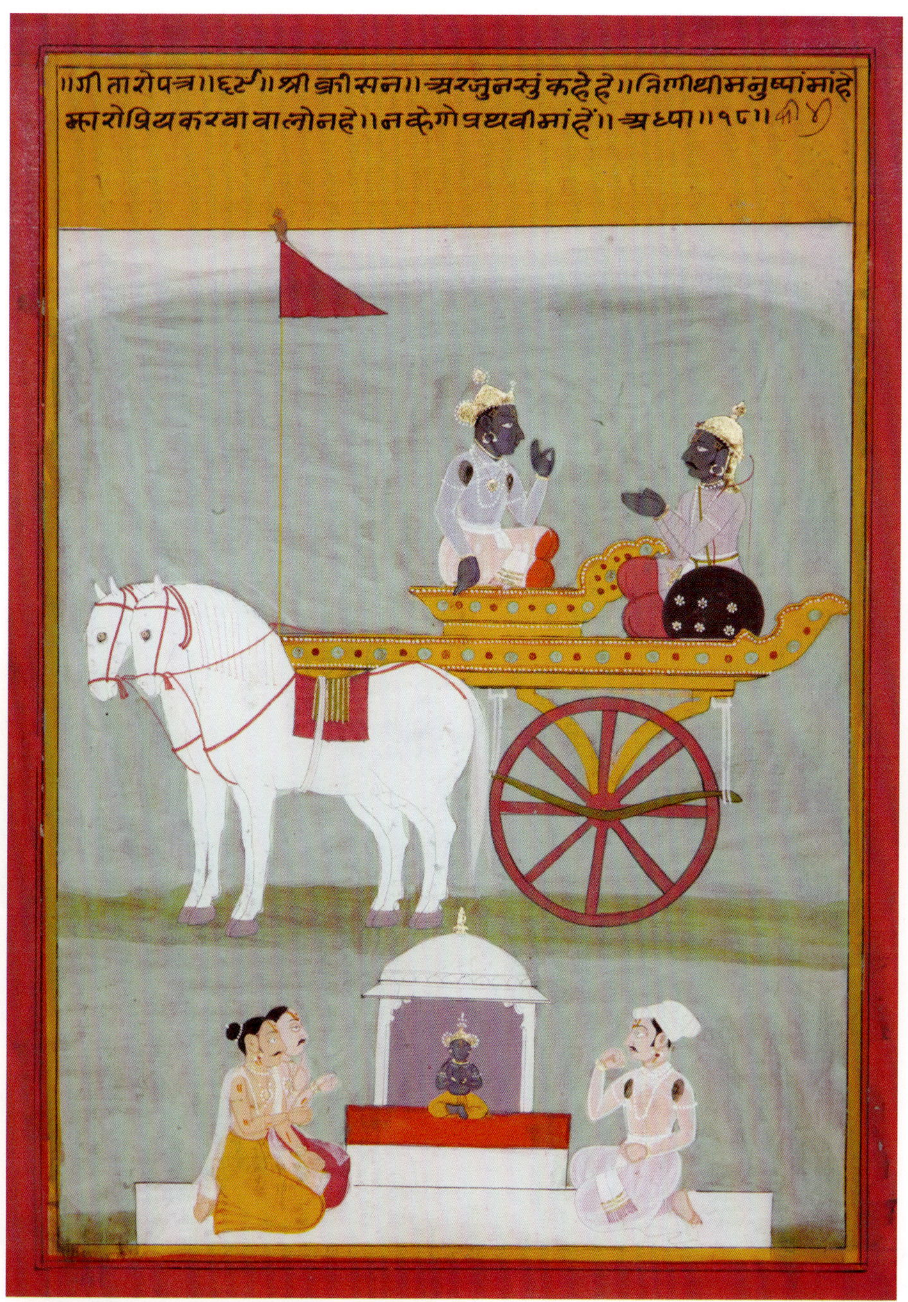

|69| श्री कृष्ण कहने लगे कि ऐसे भक्त से बढ़कर मेरा प्रिय कार्य करने वाला मनुष्यों में कोई भी नहीं और इस पृथ्वी पर उससे बढ़कर मुझे अन्य कोई प्रिय भी नहीं होगा।

|69| Sri Krishna says: There is no other devotee on earth who is dearer to me than the one who performs a valuable service to me.

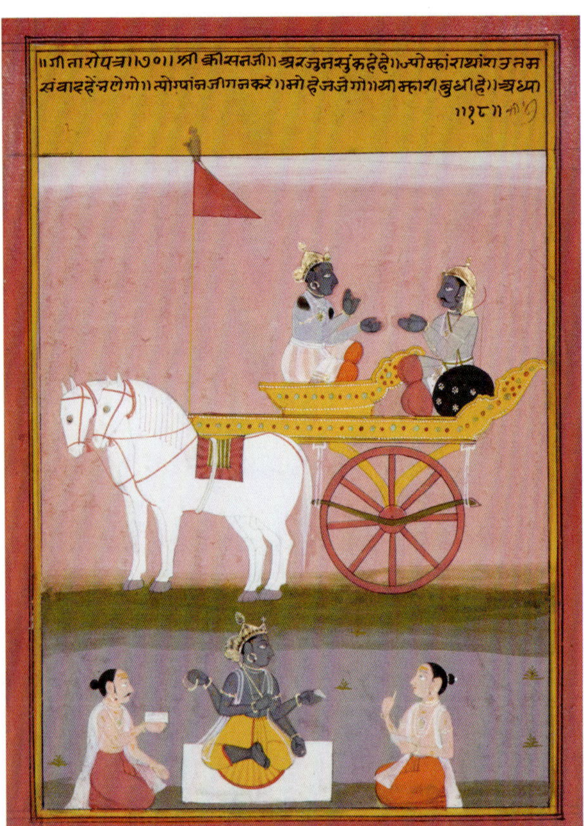

|70| हे अर्जुन! जो मनुष्य हम दोनों के इस धर्ममय संवाद का अध्ययन करेगा, वह ज्ञानयज्ञ से मेरी ही पूजा करेगा। ऐसा मेरा मत है।

|70| Hey Arjuna! The one who will study this sacred discourse of ours will worship me in the world of knowledge.

|71| और हे अर्जुन! जो मनुष्य श्रद्धायुक्त और दोषदृष्टि रहित होकर इस संवाद को सुनेगा, वह भी पापों से मुक्त होकर पुण्य कर्म करने वालों के शुभ लोक को प्राप्त होगा।

|71| And hey Arjuna! Even the one who listens to this discourse, with faith and without finding fault, shall be absolved of all sins and find a place in the purest of realms.

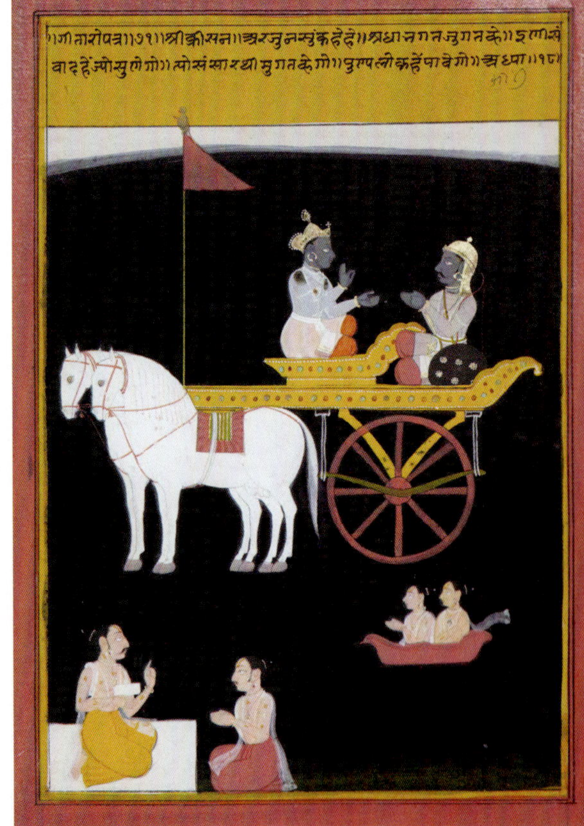

|73| This is the last painting in this *Gita* folio. In verse 73, Arjuna finally surrenders to the will of Sri Krishna and says: My Lord! I no longer doubt. I stand before you in complete faith. I am ready to do your will.

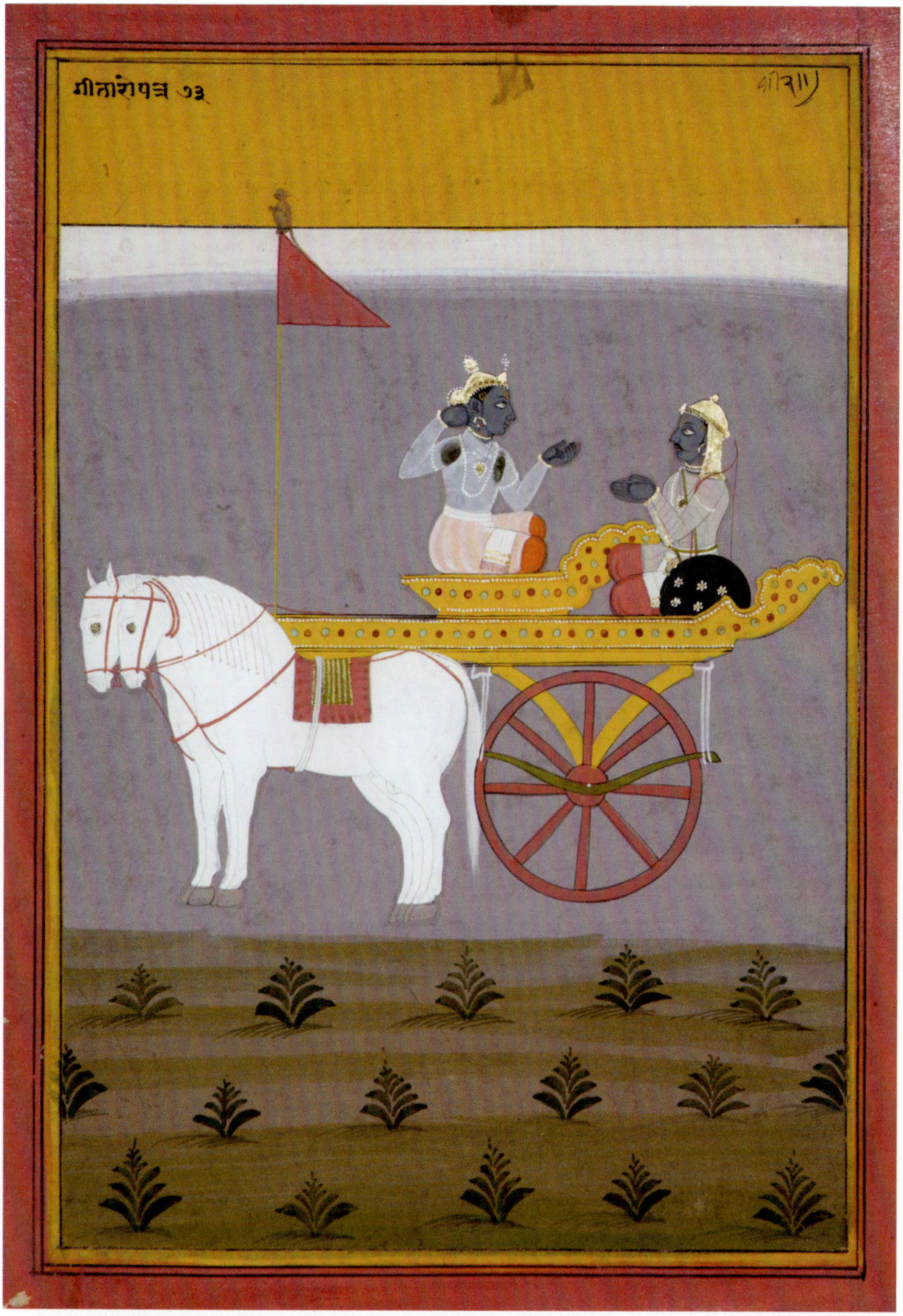

BIBLIOGRAPHY

Abhinavagupta. *Commentary on the Bhagavad Gita*. Translated by Boris Marjanovic. Varanasi: Indica, 2002.

Abrams, M. H. *Natural Supernaturalism: Tradition and Revolution in Romantic Literature*. New York: Norton, 1971.

Adorno, Theodor. *Minima Moralia: Reflections from Damaged Life* .Translated by E.F.N. Jephcott. London: New Left Books, 1974.

Alain. *The Gods*. Translated by Richard Pevear. London: Quartet Books, 1973.

Anhalt, Emily Katz, *Enraged: Why Violent Times Need Ancient Greek Myths*. New Haven: Yale University Press, 2017.

Annamayya. *God on the Hill: Temple Poems from Tirupati*. Translated by Velcheru Narayan Rao and David Shulman. New Delhi: Oxford University Press, 2005.

Asvaghosa. *Buddhacharitra: Or Life of the Buddha*. Translated by Patrick Olivelle. New York: New York University Press, 2008.

Aurelius, Marcus. *Meditations*, translated by Martin Hammond. London: Penguin, 2006.

Aurobindo, Sri. *On the Mahabharata*. Pondicherry: Sri Aurobindo Ashram, 1991.

Bandyopadhyay, Sibaji. *Three Essays of the Mahabharata: Exercises in Literary Hermeneutics*. New Delhi: Orient Black Swan, 2016.

Benjamin, Walter. *Illuminations*. Translated by Harry Zohn. New York: Schoken, 1969.

Bhatti. *Bhatti's Poem: Or the Death of Ravana [Bhattikavya]*. Translated by Oliver Fallon. New York: New York University Press, 2009.

Binyon, Lawrence. *The Spirit of Man in Asian Art* (1936). New York: Dover, 1965.

Blake, William. *Complete Works*, edited by Geoffrey Keynes. London: Oxford University Press, 1966.

Borges, Jorge Luis. *Selected Non-Fictions*, edited by Eliot Weinberger. New York: Penguin, 1999.

Buitenen, J. A. B. van. Translator. *The Bhagavadgita in the Mahabharata*. Chicago: University of Chicago Press, 1981.

Cavell, Stanley. *The Senses of* Walden. Chicago: Chicago University Press, 1981.

Cavell, Stanley. *Conditions Handsome and Unhandsome: The Constitution of Emersonian Perfectionism*. Chicago: University of Chicago Press, 1990.

Cavell, Stanley and Cora Diamond. Editors. *Philosophy and Animal Life*. New York: Columbia University Press, 2008.

Clark, Kenneth. *The Art of Humanism*. London: John Murray, 1983.

Chidbhavananda, Swami. *The Bhagavad Gita*. Tirupparaitturai: Sri Ramakrsihna Tapovanam, 1979.

Chakrabarti, Arindam and Sibaji Bandyopadhyay. Editors. *Mahabharata Now: Narration, Aesthetics, Ethics*. New Delhi: Routledge 2014.

Ethics. New Delhi: Routledge 2014.

Coomaraswamy, Ananada K. "Ornament," *The Art Bulletin*, 21:3 (1939), 377 – 381.

Cummins, Joan. *Vishnu: Hinduism's Blue-Skinned Savior.* Ahmedabad: Mapin, 2011.

Davis, Richard H. *The Bhagavad Gita: A Biography*. Princeton: Princeton University Press, 2015.

Desai, Mahadev. *The Gospel of Selfless Action: Or The Gita According to Gandhi*. Ahmedabad: Navjivan, 1946.

Dumezil, Georges. *The Destiny of the Warrior*. Translated by Alf Hiltebeitel. Chicago: University of Chicago Press, 1969.

Eck, Diana L. *Darsan: Seeing the Divine Image in India*. Pennsylvania: Anima Books, 1985.

Eliade, Mircea. *Cosmos and History: The Myth of the Eternal Return*. Translated by Willard R. Trask. New York: Harper and Row, 1959.

Eliade, Mircea. *The Sacred and the Profane: The Nature of Religion*. Translated by Willard R. Trask. New York: Harcourt, Brace and World, 1959.

Eliot, T. S. *Four Quartets*. London: Faber and Faber, 1944.

Emerson, Ralph Waldo. *Selections from Ralph Waldo Emerson*. Edited by Stephen E. Whicher. Boston: Houghton Mifflin, 1960.

Friedrich, Paul. *The* Gita *within Walden*. New York: State University of New York Press, 2008.

Frye, Northrop. *Fearful Symmetry: A Study of William Blake.* Boston: Beacon Press, 1967.

Frye, Northrop. *Anatomy of Criticism: Four Essays*. New York: Atheneum, 1969.

Fry, Northrop. *Words with Power: Bible and Literature*. San Diego: Haracourt, Brace Jovanovich, 1990.

Gandhi, Ramchandra. *Sita's Kitchen: A Testimony of Faith and Inquiry.* New Delhi: Penguin, 1992.

Gass, William. *Reading Rilke: Reflections on the Problem of Translation*. New York: Alfred A. Knopf, 1999.

Goethe, Johan Wolfgang von. *The Essential Goethe*. Edited by Matthew Bell. Princeton: Princeton University Press, 2016.

Gombrich, E. H. *Art and Illusion: A Study in the Psychology of Pictorial Representation*. Oxford: Phaidon, 1960.

Gombrich, E. H. *The Sense of Order: A Study in the Psychology of Decorative Art.* Oxford: Phaidon, 1979.

Gombrich, E. H. *The Image and the Eye: Further Studies in the Psychology of Pictorial Representation.* Oxford: Phaidon, 1982.

Goswamy, B.N. *Oxford Readings in Indian Art.* New Delhi: Oxford University Press, 2018.

Goswamy, B.N. *The Spirit of Indian Painting.* Gurgaon: Penguin, 2014.

Hawley, John Starton and Mark Jurgensmeyer. *Songs of the Saints of India*. Oxford: Oxford University Press, 1988, p.167.

Hitelbeitel, Alf. *Rethinking the Mahabharata: A Reader's Guide to the Education of the Dharma King.* Oxford: Oxford University Press, 2002.

Hitelbeitel, Alf. *Dharma: It's Early History in Law, Religion and Narrative*. Oxford: Oxford University Press, 2011.

Hofmeyr, Isabel. *Gandhi's Printing Press: Experiments in Slow Reading*. Cambridge, Mass.: Harvard University Press, 2013.

Holmes, Richard. *Coleridge: Dark Reflections, 1804-1834*. London: Harper Collins, 1998.

Hudson, D. Dennis. *Krishna's Mandala: Bhagavata, Religion and Beyond*. New Delhi: Oxford University Press, 2010.

Hume, Robert Earnest. *The Thirteen Principal Upanishads*. London: Oxford University Press, 1877.

Jnaneshwari. 2 volumes. Translated by V. G. Pradhan. London: George Allen and Unwin, 1967.

Kandinsky, Wassily. *Concerning the Spiritual in Art*. Translated by Michael T. H. Sadler. New York: Dover, 1977.

Kapila, Shruti and Faisal Bevji. Editors. *Political Thought in Action: The Bhagavad Gita and Modern India*. Cambridge: Cambridge University Press, 2013.

Katz, Ruth Cecily. *Arjuna in the Mahabharata: Where Krishna is, There is Victory* (Delhi: Motilal Banarasidass, 1990.

Khannna, Madhu. "Nature as Feminine: Ancient Vision of Geopiety and Goddess Ecology," in *Prakriti: The Integral Vision*. Edited by Baidyanath Sarasvati. New Delhi: Indira Gandhi National Centre for the Arts, 1995.

Kinsley. David R. *The Sword and the Flute: Kali and Krishna, Dark Visions of the Terrible and the Sublime in Hindu Mythology*. Berkeley: University of California Press, 1975.

Kramrisch, Stella. *Exploring India's Sacred Art: Selected Writings*. Edited by Barbara Stoler Miller. New Delhi: Indira Gandhi Centre for the Arts, 1994.

Kristeva, Julia. *The Incredible Need to Believe*. Translated by Beverley BieBrahic. New York: Columbia University Press, 2009.

Lear, Jonathan. *A Case for Irony*. Cambridge, Mass.: Harvard University Press, 2011.

Levi-Strauss, Claude. *Myth and Meaning: Cracking the Code of Culture*. New York: Schoken, 1995.

Male, Emile. *The Gothic Image: Religious Art in France of the Thirteenth Century*. Translated by Dora Nussy. New York: Harper and Row, 1958.

Mehta, J. L. "Krishna Dvaipayana: Poet of Being and Becoming," in *Philosophy and Religion: Essays in Interpretation*. New Delhi: Munshiram Manoharlal, 1990.

Miller, Barbara Stoler. *Phantasies of a Love-Thief: The Caurapancasika attributed to Bilhana*. New York: Columbia University Press, 1971.

Montaigne, Michel De. *The Complete Works*. Translated by Donald M. Frame. New York: Everyman's Library, 1948.

Murdoch, Iris. *The Fire and the Sun*. Oxford: Oxford University Press, 1977.

Palishkar, Sanjay. *Evil and the Philosophy of Retribution: Modern Commentaries on the Bhagavad Gita*. New Delhi: Routledge, 2014.

Panosfsky, Erwin. *Meaning in the Visual Arts*. Harmondsworth: Penguin, 1955.

Paz, Octavio. *The Bow and the Lyre: The Poem, the Poetic Revelation, Poetry and History*. Translated by Ruth L.C. Simms. Austin: University of Texas Press, 1973.

Plato, *Collected Dialogues of Plato*. Edited by Edith Hamilton and Huntington Cairns. Princeton: Princeton University Press, 1973.

Radhakrishnan, S. *The Bhagavadgita*. New Delhi: HarperCollins, 2014.

Radhakrishnan, S. *The Principal Upanishads*. London: George Allen and Unwin, 1953.

Rao, D. Venkat. *Cultures of Memory in South Asia: Orality, Literacy and the Problem of Inheritance*. Heidelberg: Springer, 2014.

Richardson Jr., Robert D. *Thoreau: A Life of the Mind*. Berkeley: University of Californian Press, 1986.

Santideva. *The Bodhicaryavatara of: Entering the Path of Enlightenment*. Translated by Marion L. Matics. Delhi: Motilal Banarsidas, 2007.

Sawhney, Simona. *Modernity of Sanskrit*. Ranikhet: Permanent Black, 2009.

Schelling, Andrew. Editor. *Bright as an Autumn Moon: Fifty Poems from the Sanskrit. Manoa*, 25:2 !1913.

Spinoza, Benedict de. *A Theologico-Political Treatise and a Political Treatise*. Translated by R. H. M. Elwes. New York: Dover, 1951.

Staal, Frits. *Discovering the Vedas: Origins, Manners, Rituals, Insights*. Gurgaon: Penguin Random House, 2008.

Suhrud, Tridip and Peter Ronald DeSouza. Editors. *Speaking of Gandhi's Death*. Hyderabad: Orient Black Swan, 2010.

Suhrud, Tridip and Thomas Weber. Editors. *Beloved Bapu: The Gandhi-Mirabehn Correspondence*. Hyderabad: Orient Black Swan, 2014.

Swami, Sri Purohit. *The Geeta: The Gospel of the Lord Sri Krishna*. London: Faber and Faber, 1965.

Thacker. Eugene, "Black on Black," in *The Public Domain Review*.https://publicdomainreview.org/2015/04/09/black-on-black.

Thoreau, Henry David, *Walden: Civil Disobedience*. Edited by Owen Thomas. New York: W. W. Norton, 1966.

Turner, Victor. *Dramas, Fields and Metaphors: Symbolic Action in Human Society*. Ithaca: Cornell University Press, 1974.

Vatsyayan, Kapila. "Indian Arts, Their Ideational Background and Principles of Form," in *Paroksha: Coomaraswamy Centenary Seminar Papers*. Edited by Gulam Mohammad Sheikh, K. G. Subramanyan and Kapila Vatsyayan. New Delhi: Lalit Kala Akademi, 1984.

Vishnudhamottra: A Treatise on Indian Painting and Image Making. Translated by Stella Kramrisch. Patliputra: Eastern Book House, 1993.

Vlastos, Gregory. *Socrates: Ironist and Moral Philosopher*. Cambridge: Cambridge University Press, 1991.

Weil, Simone. *The Notebooks of Simone Weil*. Translated by Arthur Wills. London: Routledge, 2004.

Zimmer, Heinrich. *Myths and Symbols in Indian Art and Civilization*. Edited by Joseph Campbell. New York: Harper and Row, 1962.

Zimmer, Heinrich. *Artistic Form and Yoga in the Sacred Images of India*. Translated by Gerald Chapple and James B. Lawson. Princeton: Princeton University Press, 1984.

INDEX